Lecture Notes in Computer Scie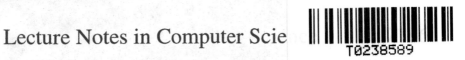

T0238589

Commenced Publication in 1973
Founding and Former Series Editors:
Gerhard Goos, Juris Hartmanis, and Jan van Leeuwen

Sarfraz Khurshid   Koushik Sen (Eds.)

Runtime Verification

Second International Conference, RV 2011
San Francisco, CA, USA, September 27-30, 2011
Revised Selected Papers

Springer

Volume Editors

Sarfraz Khurshid
The University of Texas at Austin
Electrical and Computer Engineering
1 University Station C5000
Austin, TX 78712-0240, USA
E-mail: khurshid@ece.utexas.edu

Koushik Sen
University of California
Department of Electrical Engineering
and Computer Sciences
581 Soda Hall #1776
Berkeley, CA 94720-1776, USA
E-mail: ksen@cs.berkeley.edu

ISSN 0302-9743   e-ISSN 1611-3349
ISBN 978-3-642-29859-2   e-ISBN 978-3-642-29860-8
DOI 10.1007/978-3-642-29860-8
Springer Heidelberg Dordrecht London New York

Library of Congress Control Number: 2012937468

CR Subject Classification (1998): D.2, F.2, D.2.4, D.1, F.3, D.3, C.2

LNCS Sublibrary: SL 2 – Programming and Software Engineering

Typesetting: Camera-ready by author, data conversion by Scientific Publishing Services, Chennai, India

Printed on acid-free paper

Springer is part of Springer Science+Business Media (www.springer.com)

Preface

The Second International Conference on Runtime Verification (RV 2011) was held in the historic Fairmont Hotel in San Francisco, California, USA, during September 27–30, 2011. The conference program included invited talks, peer-reviewed presentations and tool demonstrations, as well as tutorials.

RV 2011 was attended by researchers and industrial practitioners from all over the world. It provided a forum to present foundational theories and practical tools for monitoring and analysis of software or hardware system executions, as well as a forum for presenting applications of such tools to real-world problems. The field of runtime verification is often referred to under different names, such as runtime verification, runtime monitoring, runtime checking, runtime reflection, runtime analysis, dynamic analysis, runtime symbolic analysis, trace analysis, log file analysis, etc. Runtime verification can be used for many purposes, such as security or safety policy monitoring, debugging, testing, verification, validation, profiling, fault protection, behavior modification (e.g., recovery), etc. A running system can be abstractly regarded as a generator of execution traces, i.e., sequences of relevant states or events. Traces can be processed in various ways, e.g., checked against formal specifications, analyzed with special algorithms, visualized, etc. Runtime verification now has a number of sub-fields, for example, program instrumentation, specification languages for writing monitors, dynamic concurrency analysis, intrusion detection, dynamic specification mining, and program execution visualization. Additionally, techniques for runtime verification have strong connections to techniques in other related fields such as combined static and dynamic analysis, aspect-oriented programming, and model-based testing. This year's conference included, in addition to papers that advance analyses commonly used for runtime verification, papers on symbolic execution, a well-known program analysis technique, which so far has not seen much use in this field but holds promise in enabling novel approaches to runtime verification.

The Runtime Verification series of events started in 2001, as an annual workshop. The workshop series continued through 2009. Each workshop was organized as a satellite event to an established forum, including CAV (2001–2003, 2005–2006, and 2009), ETAPS (2004 and 2008), and AoSD (2007). The RV 2006 workshop was organized jointly with the Formal Aspects of Testing workshop. The proceedings for RV from 2001 to 2005 were published in *Electronic Notes in Theoretical Computer Science*. Since 2006, the RV proceedings have been published in *Lecture Notes in Computer Science*.

Starting with the year 2010, RV became an international conference to recognize the sense of community that had emerged and the maturity the field had reached over the decade since the inception of the series. Broadening the scope of the event to a conference allowed further enlarging of the community and increasing the visibility of RV events as well as making submission and participation more attractive to researchers. This was evident in the record number of submissions at RV 2010, which received a total of 74 submissions of which 15 were tutorials and tool demonstrations.

RV 2011 received a slightly smaller number of submissions – a total of 71 submissions of which 10 were tutorial and tool demonstrations. Thus, there was an increase of two research paper (full/short) submissions and a decrease of five tutorial or tool demonstration submissions over the previous year. All research paper and tool demonstration submissions to RV 2011 were reviewed by the Program Committee, with each paper receiving at least three reviews. The Program Committee selected 22 full papers (of 52 submissions), 2 short papers (of 9 submissions), and 4 tool demonstrations (of 5 submissions) for presentation at the conference. Four tutorials (of five submissions) were selected for presentation by the Chairs. Invited talks at RV 2011 were given by Dawson Engler (Stanford University), Cormac Flanagan (UC Santa Cruz), Wolfgang Grieskamp (Google), Sharad Malik (Princeton University), and Steven P. Reiss (Brown University).

RV 2011 gave two awards to peer-reviewed submissions. The "Best Paper Award" was given to "Runtime Verification with State Estimation" by Scott Stoller, Ezio Bartocci, Justin Seyster, Radu Grosu, Klaus Havelund, Scott Smolka and Erez Zadok. The "Best Tool Paper Award" was given to "MONPOLY: Monitoring Usage-Control Policies" by David Basin, Matus Harvan, Felix Klaedtke and Eugen Zalinescu.

The Chairs would like to thank the Program Committee for their high-quality reviews and hard work in making RV 2011 a successful event. Financial support for the conference was provided by Microsoft Research, the ARTIST Network of Excellence on Embedded Systems Design, Intel Corporation, Google Inc., the PRECISE Research Center of University of Pennsylvania, Laboratory for Reliable Software (LaRS) at NASA's Jet Propulsion Laboratory, and the University of California, Berkeley. We would like to particularly thank the local Organizing Chairs Jacob Burnim and Nicholas Jalbert, and Klaus Havelund for extensive help in making arrangements and organizing the event, and Oleg Sokolsky for handling the finances and accounting. Submission and evaluation of papers, as well as the preparation of this proceedings volume, was handled by the Easy-Chair conference management service.

We hope that the strength of programs at RV conferences will continue to provide a flagship venue for the RV community and to foster new collaborations with researchers in related fields.

November 2011

Sarfraz Khurshid
Koushik Sen

Organization

Program Committee

Howard Barringer	University of Manchester, UK
Eric Bodden	Technical University Darmstadt, Germany
Rance Cleaveland	University of Maryland, USA
Mads Dam	Kungliga Tekniska högskolan, Sweden
Wim De Pauw	IBM T.J. Watson Research Center, USA
Brian Demsky	University of California at Irvine, USA
Bernd Finkbeiner	Saarland University, Germany
Cormac Flanagan	University of California at Santa Cruz, USA
Patrice Godefroid	Microsoft Research Redmond, USA
Jean Goubault-Larrecq	ENS Cachan, France
Susanne Graf	Verimag, France
Radu Grosu	State University of New York at Stony Brook, USA
Lars Grunske	University of Kaiserslautern, Germany
Aarti Gupta	NEC Laboratories America, USA
Rajiv Gupta	University of California at Riverside, USA
Klaus Havelund	NASA/JPL, USA
Mats Heimdahl	University of Minnesota, USA
Gerard Holzmann	NASA/JPL, USA
Sarfraz Khurshid	University of Texas at Austin, USA
Viktor Kuncak	École Polytechnique Fédérale De Lausanne, Switzerland
Kim Larsen	Aalborg University, Denmark
Martin Leucker	University of Lübeck, Germany
Rupak Majumdar	Max Planck Institute, Germany, and University of California at Los Angeles USA
Greg Morrisett	Harvard University, USA
Mayur Naik	Intel Berkeley Labs, USA
Brian Nielsen	Aalborg University, Denmark
Klaus Ostermann	University of Marburg, Germany
Corina Pasareanu	NASA Ames, USA
Doron Peled	Bar Ilan University, Israel
Suzette Person	NASA Langley, USA
Gilles Pokam	Intel, Santa Clara, USA
Shaz Qadeer	Microsoft Research Redmond, USA
Derek Rayside	University of Waterloo, Canada
Grigore Rosu	University of Illinois at Urbana-Champaign, USA
Wolfram Schulte	Microsoft Research Redmond, USA
Koushik Sen	University of California, Berkeley, USA

Peter Sestoft   IT University of Copenhagen, Denmark
Scott Smolka   State University of New York at Stony Brook, USA
Oleg Sokolsky   University of Pennsylvania, USA
Manu Sridharan   IBM T.J. Watson Research Center, USA
Mana Taghdiri   Karlsruhe Institute of Technology, Germany
Serdar Tasiran   Koc University, Turkey
Nikolai Tillmann   Microsoft Research Redmond, USA
Shmuel Ur   Shmuel Ur Innovation, Israel
Willem Visser   University of Stellenbosch, South Africa
Mahesh Viswanathan   University of Illinois at Urbana-Champaign, USA
Xiangyu Zhang   Purdue University, USA

Additional Reviewers

Akhin, Marat   Le Guernic, Gurvan
Ayoub, Anaheed   Lin, Changhui
Bartocci, Ezio   Lundblad, Andreas
Bekar, Can   Meredith, Patrick
Benzina, Hedi   Mikučionis, Marius
Bollig, Benedikt   Pohlmann, Christian
Bulychev, Peter   Reger, Giles
Charan K., Sai   Seyster, Justin
Decker, Normann   Stümpel, Annette
Dimitrova, Rayna   Tan, Li
Ehlers, Rüdiger   Thoma, Daniel
Elmas, Tayfun   Tkachuk, Oksana
Eom, Yong Hun   Wang, Shaohui
Faymonville, Peter   Wang, Yan
Feng, Min   Wies, Thomas
Gerke, Michael   Xiao, Xusheng
Gottschlich, Justin   Zhang, Pengcheng
Jobstmann, Barbara   Zorn, Benjamin
Komuravelli, Anvesh

Table of Contents

H: Foundational Techniques and Multi-valued Approaches I

I: Foundational Techniques and Multi-valued Approaches II

Internal versus External DSLs for Trace Analysis*
(Extended Abstract)

Howard Barringer[1] and Klaus Havelund[2]

[1] School of Computer Science, University of Manchester, UK
Howard.Barringer@manchester.ac.uk
[2] Jet Propulsion Laboratory, California Institute of Technology, USA
Klaus.Havelund@jpl.nasa.gov

Abstract. This tutorial explores the design and implementation issues arising in the development of domain-specific languages for trace analysis. It introduces the audience to the general concepts underlying such special-purpose languages building upon the authors' own experiences in developing both external domain-specific languages and systems, such as EAGLE, HAWK, RULER and LOGSCOPE, and the more recent internal domain-specific language and system TRACECONTRACT within the SCALA language.

Keywords: run-time verification, trace analysis, domain-specific language (DSL), external DSL, internal DSL, TRACECONTRACT, SCALA.

Domain-specific languages (DSLs) are simply special-purpose programming languages and, as such, are far from being a new concept; for example in the field of text processing one can find COMIT [16] in the 1950s, which led to SNOBOL [8] in the 1960s, then on to the likes of AWK [1], Perl [15], etc. The naming of such special-purpose programming languages as DSLs is a more recent development that has come about through the field of domain-specific modelling. Fowler [9] presents a rather comprehensive volume on DSLs and their application.

Within the field of run-time verification, as in formal methods in general, specification languages and logics have usually been created as separate, standalone, languages, with their own parsers; these are usually referred to as *external DSLs*. We have ourselves developed several external DSLs for trace analysis, e.g. EAGLE [2], HAWK [7], RULER [6], LOGSCOPE [3], and observe two key points: (i) once a DSL is defined, it is labourious to change or extend it later; and (ii) users often ask for additional features, some of which are best handled by a general purpose programming language. An alternative approach is to try to use a high level programming language that can be augmented with support for temporal specification. These are usually referred to as *internal DSLs*. An internal DSL is really just an API in the host language, formulated using the language's own primitives. Recently, we chose to develop an internal DSL, TRACE-CONTRACT [4], for trace analysis in SCALA [12]. Indeed, SCALA is particularly well

---

* Part of the work to be covered in this tutorial was carried out at Jet Propulsion Laboratory, California Institute of Technology, under a contract with the National Aeronautics and Space Administration.

S. Khurshid and K. Sen (Eds.): RV 2011, LNCS 7186, pp. 1–3, 2012.

suited for this because of (i) the language's in-built support for defining internal DSLs, and (ii) the fact that it supports functional as well as object oriented programming. A functional programming language seems well suited for defining an internal DSL for monitoring, as also advocated in [13] in the case of HASKELL [14]. An embedding of an internal DSL may be termed as *shallow*, meaning that one makes the host language's constructs part of the DSL, or it may be termed as *deep*, meaning that a separate internal representation is made of the DSL (an abstract syntax), which is then interpreted or compiled as in the case of an external DSL. A shallow embedding has disadvantages, for example not being easily analyzable. In [10] it is argued that the advantage of a deep embedding is that *"We 'know' the code of the term, for instance we can print it, compute its length, etc"*, whereas the advantage of a shallow embedding is that *"we do not know the code, but we can run it"*. Generally, the arguments *for* an internal DSL are: limited implementation effort due to direct executability of DSL constructs, feature richness through inheriting the host language's constructs, and tool inheritance, i.e. it becomes possible to directly use all the tool support available for the host language, such as IDEs, editors, debuggers, static analyzers, and testing tools. In summary, the arguments *against* an internal DSL are: (i) lack of analyzability, i.e. one cannot analyze internal DSLs without working with the usually complex host language compiler, which can then have consequences for performance and reporting to users, and (ii) high complexity of language, i.e. one now has to learn and use the bigger host programming language, which may exclude non-programmers from using the language, and which may lead to more errors. Our main observation is, however, that feature richness and adaptability are both very attractive attributes. To some extent, adaptability "solves" the problem of what is the right logic for runtime monitoring. An additional argument is that often one wants to write advanced properties for which a simple logic does not suffice, including counting and collecting statistics. In a programming language this all becomes straightforward. The use of SCALA, whose functional features can be considered as a specification language in its own right, provides further advantage.

In this tutorial, we will introduce the audience to the above issues in the design of DSLs, both external and internal, in the context of run-time verification. In particular, we will use our own experience with the development of RULER, as an external DSL, and TRACECONTRACT, an internal DSL, to show advantages and disadvantages of these approaches. The tutorial will be presented through a series of examples, it will show how an internal DSL can be quickly implemented in SCALA (within the tutorial session), and it will demonstrate why TRACECONTRACT is being used for undertaking flight rule checking in NASA's LADEE mission [11,5].

References

1. Aho, A.V., Kernighan, B.W., Weinberger, P.J.: The AWK programming language. Addison-Wesley (1988)
2. Barringer, H., Goldberg, A., Havelund, K., Sen, K.: Rule-Based Runtime Verification. In: Steffen, B., Levi, G. (eds.) VMCAI 2004. LNCS, vol. 2937, pp. 44–57. Springer, Heidelberg (2004)
3. Barringer, H., Groce, A., Havelund, K., Smith, M.: Formal analysis of log files. Journal of Aerospace Computing, Information, and Communication 7(11), 365–390 (2010)

4. Barringer, H., Havelund, K.: TRACECONTRACT: A Scala DSL for Trace Analysis. In: Butler, M., Schulte, W. (eds.) FM 2011. LNCS, vol. 6664, pp. 57–72. Springer, Heidelberg (2011)

5. Barringer, H., Havelund, K., Kurklu, E., Morris, R.: Checking flight rules with TraceContract: Application of a Scala DSL for trace analysis. In: Scala Days 2011. Stanford University, California (2011)

6. Barringer, H., Rydeheard, D.E., Havelund, K.: Rule systems for run-time monitoring: from Eagle to RuleR. J. Log. Comput. 20(3), 675–706 (2010)

7. d'Amorim, M., Havelund, K.: Event-based runtime verification of Java programs. ACM SIG-SOFT Software Engineering Notes 30(4), 1–7 (2005)

8. Farber, D., Griswold, R., Polonsky, I.: SNOBOL, A string manipulation language. Jounral of the ACM 11(1), 21–30 (1964)

9. Fowler, M., Parsons, R.: Domain-Specific Languages. Addison-Wesley (2010)

10. Garillot, F., Werner, B.: Simple Types in Type Theory: Deep and Shallow Encodings. In: Schneider, K., Brandt, J. (eds.) TPHOLs 2007. LNCS, vol. 4732, pp. 368–382. Springer, Heidelberg (2007)

11. Lunar Atmosphere Dust Environment Explorer, http://www.nasa.gov/mission_pages/LADEE/main

12. Scala, http://www.scala-lang.org

13. Stolz, V., Huch, F.: Runtime verification of concurrent Haskell programs. In: Proc. of the 4th Int. Workshop on Runtime Verification (RV 2004). ENTCS, vol. 113, pp. 201–216. Elsevier (2005)

14. The Haskell Programming Language, http://www.haskell.org/haskellwiki/Haskell

15. The Perl Programming Language, http://www.perl.org

16. Yngve, V.H.: A programming language for mechanical translation. Mechanical Translation 5(1), 25–41 (1958)

Predicting Concurrency Failures in the Generalized Execution Traces of x86 Executables

Chao Wang[1] and Malay Ganai[2]

[1] Virginia Tech, Blacksburg, VA 24061, USA
[2] NEC Laboratories America, Princeton, NJ 08540, USA

Abstract. In this tutorial, we first provide a brief overview of the latest development in SMT based symbolic predictive analysis techniques and their applications to runtime verification. We then present a unified runtime analysis platform for detecting concurrency related program failures in the x86 executables of shared-memory multithreaded applications. Our platform supports efficient monitoring and easy customization of a wide range of *execution trace generalization* techniques. Many of these techniques have been successfully incorporated into our in-house verification tools, including BEST (Binary instrumentation based Error-directed Symbolic Testing), which can detect concurrency related errors such as deadlocks and race conditions, generate failure-triggering thread schedules, and provide the visual mapping between runtime events and their program code to help debugging.

1 Introduction

Parallel and concurrent programming is rapidly becoming a mainstream topic in today's corporate world, propelled primarily by the use of multicore processors in all application domains. As the CPU clock speed remains largely constant, developers increasingly need to write concurrent software to harness the computing power of what soon will be the tens, hundreds, and thousands of cores [1]. However, manually analyzing the behavior of a concurrent program is often difficult. Due to the scheduling nondeterminism, multiple runs of the same program may exhibit different behaviors, even for the same program input. Furthermore, the number of possible interleavings in a realistic application is often astronomically large. Even after a failure is detected, deterministically replaying the erroneous behavior remains difficult. Therefore, developers need more powerful analysis and verification tools than what they currently have, in order to deal with concurrency problems such as deadlocks and race conditions.

Although static and dynamic methods for detecting concurrency bugs have made remarkable progress over the years, in practice they can still report too many false alarms or miss too many real bugs. Furthermore, most of the existing bug detection tools target *application-level* software written in languages such as Java or C#. Tools that can directly check the x86 executables of the *system-level* software are lagging behind. Software in the latter category are often more critical to the reliability of the entire system. They may be developed using a wide range of programming languages, including C/C++, and may use external libraries whose source code are not available. This is one reason why we need tools to directly verify x86 executables. Another reason is that x86 executables more accurately reflect the instructions that are executed by the multicore

S. Khurshid and K. Sen (Eds.): RV 2011, LNCS 7186, pp. 4–18, 2012.

hardware. Almost all microprocessors today are based on the multicore architecture and employ some form of relaxed memory model. Programming languages such as Java and C++ are also in the process of incorporating language-level relaxed memory models [2, 3]. In this case, the behavior of the x86 executable may be drastically different from the source code due to compiler optimizations, especially when the program has concurrency bugs. Therefore, analyzing only the source code is no longer adequate.

We present a runtime analysis and verification platform that can work directly on the x86 executables of Linux applications. We use PIN [4] to instrument both the executables and all the dynamically linked libraries upon which the applications depend. The additional code injected during this instrumentation process are used to monitor and control the synchronization operations such as lock/unlock, wait/notify, thread create/join, as well as the shared memory accesses. We then use a logical constraint based symbolic predictive analysis [5–8] to detect runtime failures by generalizing the recorded execution trace. Our trace generalization model is capable of capturing all the possible interleavings of events of the given trace. We check whether any of the interleaving can fail, by first encoding these interleavings and the error condition as a set of quantifier-free first-order logic formulas, and then deciding the formulas with an off-the-self SMT solver.

Our trace generalization model can be viewed as a kind of lean program slice, capturing a subset of the behaviors of the original program. By focusing on this trace generalization model rather than the whole program, many rigorous but previously expensive techniques, such as symbolic execution [9, 10], become scalable for practical uses.

The remainder of this paper is organized as follows. We give a brief overview of the existing predictive analysis methods in Section 2. We introduce our symbolic predictive analysis in Section 3. The major analysis steps of our BEST tool are presented in Section 4, followed by a discussion of the implementation and evaluation. We review related work in Section 6, and give our conclusions in Section 7.

2   A Brief Overview of Predictive Analysis Methods

Concurrency control related programming errors are due to incorrectly constrained interactions of the concurrent threads or processes. Despite their wide range of symptoms, these bugs can all be classified into two categories. Bugs in the first category are due to *under-constraining*, where the threads have more freedom in interacting with other threads than they should have, leading to *race conditions*, which broadly refer to data races, atomicity violations, and order violations. Bugs in the second category are due to *over-constraining*, where the threads are more restricted than they should be, leading to either deadlocks or performance bugs. Since these bugs are scheduling sensitive, and the number of possible thread interleavings is often astronomically large, they are often rare events during the program execution. Furthermore, in a runtime environment where the scheduling is controlled by the underlying operating system, merely running the same test again and again does not necessarily increase the chance of detecting the bug.

Fig. 1 shows an example of two concurrent threads sharing a pointer p. Due to under-constraining, an atomicity violation may be triggered in some interleaved executions. More specifically, the statements e_2-e_5 in Thread T_1 are meant to be executed atomically. Note that such *atomicity* property (between the check e_2e_3 and the use e_4e_5)

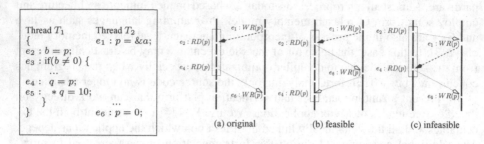

Fig. 1. The given trace $e_1 e_2 \ldots e_6$ in (a) is not buggy, but the alternative interleaving in (b) has an atomicity violation, leading to the null pointer dereference failure at e_5. Assuming that $p=0$ initially, the interleaving in (c) is bogus since e_4 cannot be executed when $b = 0$.

always holds in sequential programs, but may be broken in a concurrent program unless it is enforced explicitly using synchronizations such as locks. For example, assume that $p = 0$ initially in Fig. 1, then executing e_6 in between e_2, e_4 would lead to a null pointer dereference at e_5. Atomicity violations are different from data races, i.e. a situation where two threads can access the same memory location without synchronization. In Fig. 1, for example, even if we add a lock-unlock pair to protect each access to p (in e_1, e_2, e_4, e_6), the failure at e_5 due to atomicity violation will remain.

Runtime concurrency bug detection and prediction have become an active research topic in recent years [11–18]. Broadly speaking, these existing techniques come in two flavors. When the goal is to detect runtime errors exposed by the given execution, it is called the *monitoring* problem (e.g. [12, 13, 18]). When the goal is to detect errors not only in the given execution, but also in other possible interleavings of the events of that execution, it is called the *prediction* problem. For example, in Fig. 1, the given trace in (a) does not fail. However, from this trace we can infer the two alternative interleavings in (b) and (c). Both interleavings, if feasible, would lead to a runtime failure at e_5. A more careful analysis shows that the trace in (b) is feasible, meaning that it can happen during the actual program execution, whereas the trace in (c) is infeasible, i.e. it is a false alarm.

Depending on how they infer new interleavings from the given trace, predictive analysis methods in the literature can be classified into two groups. Methods in the first group (e.g. [11, 15, 19–22]) detect must-violations, i.e. the reported violation must be a real violation. Methods in the second group (e.g. [14, 16, 23–26]) detect may-violations, i.e. the reported violation may be a real violation. Conceptually, methods in the first group start by regarding the given trace ρ as a totally ordered set of events (ordered by the execution sequence in ρ), and then removing the ordering constraints imposed solely by the nondeterministic scheduling. However, since the type of inferred interleavings are limited, these methods often miss many real bugs. In contrast, methods in the second category start by regarding the given trace ρ as an unordered set of events, meaning that any permutation of ρ is initially allowed, and then filtering out the obviously bogus ones using the semantics of the synchronization primitives. For example, if two consecutive events $e_1 e_2$ in one thread and e_3 in another thread are both protected by lock-unlock pair over the same lock, then the permutation $e_1 e_3 e_2$ is forbidden based on the mutual exclusion semantics of locks.

The entire spectrum of predictive analysis methods is illustrated in Fig. 2. Given an execution trace ρ, the left-most point represents the singleton set containing trace ρ itself, whereas the right-most point represents the set of all possible permutations of trace ρ, regardless of whether the permutations are feasible or not. Therefore, the left-most point denotes the coarsest under-approximated predictive model, whereas the right-most point denotes the coarsest over-approximated predictive model. The left-to-middle horizontal line represents the evolution of the under-approximated analysis methods in the first group – they all report must-violations, and they have been able to cover more and more real bugs over the years. This line of research originated from the happens-before causality relationship introduced by Lamport [19]. The right-to-middle horizontal line represents the evolution of the over-approximated analysis methods in the second group – they all report may-violations, and they have been able to steadily reduce the number of false alarms over the years. Some early developments of this line of research include the Eraser-style lockset analysis [23] and the lock acquisition history analysis [27]. Although significant progress has been made over the years, it is still the case that these existing methods may either miss many real bugs or generate many false alarms. For example, if an over-approximated method relies solely on the control flow analysis while ignoring data, it may report Fig. 1 (c) as a violation although the interleaving is actually infeasible. If an under-approximated method strives to avoid false alarms, but in the process significantly restricts the type of inferred traces, it may miss the real violation in Fig. 1 (b).

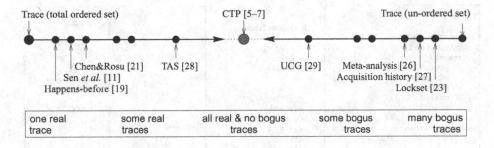

Fig. 2. The landscape of predictive analysis methods

In our recent work [5–7], we introduced a precise trace generalization model together with an efficient logical constraint based symbolic analysis. Our model, called the Concurrent Trace Program (CTP), captures all the interleavings that can possibly be inferred from a given trace, without introducing any bogus interleavings. As illustrated in Fig. 2, CTP represents the theoretically optimal point, where the two long lines of research on predictive methods converge. However, the practical use of CTP as a predictive model depends on how efficient its error detection algorithm is. We believe that the key to its widespread use will be the judicious application of *symbolic analysis* techniques and *interference abstractions*. SMT based symbolic analysis will help combat *interleaving explosion*, the main bottleneck in analysis algorithms based on explicitly enumerating the interleavings. Explicit enumeration is avoided entirely in our SMT-based symbolic analysis. Interference abstraction refers to the over- or under-approximated modeling of the thread interactions with a varying degree of precision. The main idea is that, for the purpose of deciding a property at hand, we often do not need to precisely model all the details of the thread interactions. Our SMT based symbolic analysis provides a flexible and unified framework for soundly performing such over- or under-approximations, without forcing us to worry about the validity of the analysis results.

3   SMT-Based Symbolic Predictive Analysis

Recall that the Concurrent Trace Program (CTP) is the optimal predictive model because it can catch all real bugs that can possibly be predicted from a given trace, without introducing any bogus bug. Fig. 3 shows how the CTP is derived from a concrete execution trace. Here the main thread T_0 creates threads T_1 and T_2, waits for their termination, and asserts $(x \neq y)$. This given execution does not violate the assertion. From this trace, however, we can derive the model on the right-hand side, which is a parallel composition of the three bounded straight-line threads. In this model, we remove all the execution ordering constraints (of the given trace) imposed solely by the nondeterministic scheduling. For example, e_{15} can execute after e_{21} although it was executed before e_{21} in the given trace. However, not all interleavings are allowed: interleaving $e_1 e_2 e_{21} e_{26} e_{27} e_{28} e_{11} \ldots e_{15} e_{18} e_3 \ldots e_5$ is not allowed, because the assume condition in e_{26} is invalid, and as a result, we cannot guarantee the feasibility of this interleaving. In other words, this interleaving may be bogus.

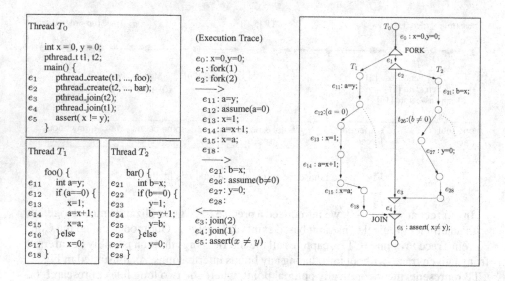

Fig. 3. A multithreaded C program, an execution trace, and the concurrent trace program (CTP)

CTP is ideally suited for detecting concurrency bugs since it is a concurrency control *skeleton*, with most of the complications of typical sequential code removed. For example, pointers have been dereferenced, loops have been unrolled, and recursion has been applied during the concrete execution. Assignment such as $(*p) := 10$ is modeled as assume($p{=}\&a$); $a{:=}10$ if p points to variable a in the given execution. As a result, the interleavings in which p does not match the memory address $\&a$ are excluded from the model. In other words, pointer p has been replaced by one of its constant value $\&a$. The variables and expressions whose valuations are insensitive to thread scheduling can be replaced by their concrete values in the given trace. The only source of nondeterminism in a CTP comes from the thread interleaving.

3.1 SMT-Based Symbolic Encoding

We check for property violation by formulating this verification problem as a constraint solving problem. That is, we build a quantifier-free first-order logic formula Φ such that Φ is satisfiable if and only if there is an erroneous interleaving in the CTP. Conceptually, $\Phi := \Phi_{TM} \wedge \Phi_{SC} \wedge \Phi_{PRP}$, where Φ_{TM} is the thread model encoding the individual behaviors of all threads, Φ_{SC} is the sequential consistency model encoding all the valid thread interactions, and Φ_{PRP} is the property constraint encoding the failure condition. Central to the analysis is Φ_{SC}, which specifies, in a valid interleaving, which shared memory read should be mapped to which shared memory write and under what condition. For example, each shared memory read r_x must match a preceding shared memory write w_x for the same memory location x; and if r_x matches w_x, then any other write w'_x to the same location must happen either before w_x or after r_x. Synchronization operations such as lock-unlock and wait-notify are modeled similarly. The logic formula Φ is then decided by an off-the-shelf SMT solver.

Compared to existing methods, our constraint-based approach provides a unified analysis framework with the following advantages. First, it is flexible in checking a diverse set of concurrency related properties; there is no longer a need to develop separate algorithms for detecting deadlocks, data races, atomicity violations, etc. All these properties can be modeled in our framework as a set of logical constraints. Second, it is efficient since the program behaviors are captured *implicitly* as a set of mathematical relations among all synchronization operations and shared-memory accesses, therefore avoiding the interleaving explosion. Third, our analysis is more precise and covers more interleavings. It also allows easy exploitation of the various trade-offs between the analysis precision and the computation overhead, simply by adding or removing some logic constraints. This is crucially importantly because, as we have mentioned earlier, not all the inference constraints (in Φ_{SC}) may be needed for deciding the property at hand. Forth, our symbolic encoding is compositional in that the behaviors of the individual threads are modeled as one set of logical constraints (in Φ_{TM}), while the thread interference is modeled as another set of logical constraints (in Φ_{SC}). The parallel composition is accomplished by conjoining these two sets of constraints together. Finally, symbolic partial order reduction techniques such as [30] can be applied to reduce both the logical formula and the search space.

3.2 Interference Abstractions

While the CTP model and the associated symbolic predictive analysis provide a solid theoretical foundation, their practical use will hinge upon the judicious application of proper interference abstractions. Interference abstraction refers to the over- or underapproximated modeling of the thread interactions with a varying degree of precision. In our symbolic analysis framework, interference abstractions are manifested as the over- or under-approximations of formula Φ_{SC}. Since modeling the thread interactions is the most expensive part of the concurrent program analysis, without abstraction, symbolic analysis will not be able to scale to large applications. Our main hypothesis is that, since concurrency bugs typically involve a small number of unexpected thread interferences, they can often be captured by succinct interference abstractions.

In a previous work [29], we proposed an over-approximated interference abstraction, called the *Universal Causality Graph (UCG)*, where the shared-memory accesses are abstracted away while the control flow and the synchronization primitives are retained. We represent the happens-before causality relationship among trace events as a graph, where the nodes are the events and the edges are must-happen-before relations between the events, as imposed by the thread-local program order, the synchronization primitives, and the property. Checking whether a property holds can be reduced to the problem of checking whether these causality edges can form a cycle. The existence of a cycle means that none of the interleavings of the CTP can satisfies the property. However, due to over-approximations, this analysis is conservative in that it guarantees to catch all violations that can possibly be predicted from a given trace, but may report some false alarms. Our UCG based analysis is provably more accurate than the existing methods in the same category, e.g. the widely used lockset based methods [14, 16, 23–26]. The reason is that lockset analysis typically models locks precisely, but cannot robustly handle synchronization primitives other than locks, such as wait-notify and fork-join. In contrast, our UCG based method precisely model the semantics of all common synchronization primitives, as well as the synergy between the different types of primitives.

In another work [28], we proposed an under-approximated interference abstraction called the *Trace Atomicity Segmentation (TAS)*, which can soundly restrict the search space that needs to be considered to detect the most general form of atomicity violations. More specifically, the TAS is a trace segment consisting of all the events in the surrounding areas of an atomic block, such that these events are sufficient for checking whether this atomicity property can be violated. Different from most existing work, our method can detect violations that involve an arbitrary number of variables and threads, rather than the simplest atomicity violations involving a single variable and three memory accesses. As illustrated in Fig. 2, TAS is regarded as an under-approximation. The case for using TAS in practice is when the runtime analysis does not have access to the program code, or cannot afford to monitor every instruction, but is still required to guarantee no false alarms. Our preliminary experiments in [28] show that the TAS is typically small even in an otherwise long execution trace.

We also proposed an algorithm to automatically find the interference abstraction that is optimal to the property at hand. Unlike the ones with a prescribed precision, a property specific interference abstraction can be more efficient since it only needs a minimal set of interference constraints. The rationale behind is that sometimes we can prove a property using an over-approximated abstraction, e.g. the control-state reachability analysis [26, 29]. Sometimes we can detect real bugs with an under-approximated abstraction, e.g. by artificially bounding the number of context switches, since the bugs may be scheduling-insensitive, and therefore may show up even in serial executions or when threads interleave only sporadically [31, 32]. However, it is generally difficult to decide *a priori* which abstraction is more appropriate. To solve this problem, we proposed an iterative refinement algorithm [33]. We will start with a coarse initial abstraction which is either over- or under-approximated, based on whether the property likely holds or not. Depending on the initial abstraction, this refinement process may be either under-approximation widening or over-approximation refinement. It is interesting to point out that, *optimal* interference abstraction, defined as the most succinct abstraction that is sufficient to decide the property, may not be a purely over-approximated model or a purely under-approximated model, but a hybrid model as represented by the dots in the middle of Fig. 4. In this figure, we have bent over the right-to-middle horizontal line in Fig. 2 to make it the bottom-to-top vertical line. Most of the points in this two-dimensional plane correspond to the hybrid models. As we have shown in [33], with a careful analysis, such hybrid models can still be used to accurately decide the property at hand, despite the fact that they are considered as neither sound nor complete in the traditional sense. Fig. 5 shows that small interference abstractions are often sufficient for checking properties in realistic applications, and that their use can drastically improve the scalability of our symbolic analysis.

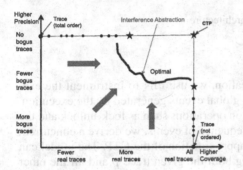

Fig. 4. Finding the optimal interference abstraction: identifying the smallest set of interference constraints that are sufficient for deciding the property

Fig. 5. Experimental results from [33]: using interference abstraction can lead to faster property checking than using the full-blown interference constraints

4   The BEST Platform

Our *Binary instrumentation-based Error-directed Symbolic Testing (BEST)* tool implements some of the symbolic predictive analysis techniques introduced in the previous sections, and is capable of detecting concurrency errors by directly monitoring an unmodified x86 executable at runtime. In the remainder of this paper, we shall use atomicity violations as an example to illustrate the features of our framework. As shown in Fig. 6, the predictive analysis in BEST consists of the following stages:

– Stage I, recording the execution trace and building the predictive model;
– Stage II, simplifying the model using sound program transformations;
– Stage III, inferring and then statically pruning the atomicity properties;
– Stage IV, predicting the violations of the atomicity properties;
– Stage V, replaying the erroneous interleaving, to see if it can cause runtime failures.
– Go back to Stage I.

Before using this tool, the developer needs to provide an execution environment for the program under test, i.e. a test harness. Details of the stages are illustrated as follows.

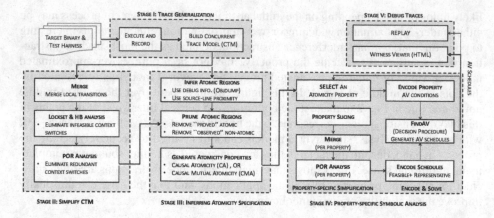

Fig. 6. BEST architecture

4.1 The Staged Analysis

Stage I. While testing the concurrent application, we use PIN to instrument the executable at run time to record the sequence of global events generated by the execution. The global events include both synchronization operations such as lock-unlock and the shared memory reads and writes. From this sequence of events, we derive a concurrent trace model (CTM), which may be an over-approximation of the CTP. The model can be viewed as a *generator* of traces, including both the given trace ρ and all the other interleavings that can be obtained by relaxing the ordering constraints (in ρ) imposed by the non-deterministic scheduling. Even if the given execution trace ρ does not fail, a runtime failure may still occur in some of the alternative interleavings.

Stage II. Given the initial model, we perform the following simplifications. First, we identify the operations over only thread-local variables, where the thread-local variables are identified by checking whether their memory locations are accessed by more than one concurrent threads. Then, we merge consecutive thread-local operations into a single operation. Next, we perform constant value propagation to simplify all the expressions that are scheduling-insensitive. These simplifications can lead to orders-of-magnitude reduction in the model size, measured in terms of the number of trace events. Finally, we use sound static analysis techniques such as lockset analysis and simple happen-before (HB) analysis to quickly identify the ordering constraints imposed by synchronizations (which must be satisfied by all valid interleavings) and then eliminate the obviously infeasible interleavings.

Stage III. On the simplified model, we infer the likely atomic regions based on the structure of the program code. Note that these atomic regions may involve multiple shared variable accesses. We also assume that the given trace is good (unless it fails) and therefore remove any region that is not atomic in the given execution. The remaining regions are treated as atomic. We use the notion of *causal atomicity* as in [34] as well as the notion of *causal mutual atomicity* (CMA) as in [35]. In the latter case, we check the violation of two pair-wise atomic regions from different threads with at least two conflicting transitions.

Stage IV. For each atomicity property, we perform a property specific program slicing, followed by another pass of simplifications and merging of the consecutive thread-local events. We check for violations of the atomicity properties by formulating the problem as a constraint solving problem. That is, we build a quantifier-free first-order logic formula Φ such that Φ is satisfiable if and only if there is an erroneous interleaving. The logic formula Φ is then decided by an off-the-shelf SMT solver.

Stage V. Once our SMT based analysis detects a violation, it will generate an erroneous thread schedule. To replay it, we use PIN to instrument the executables at runtime, and apply the externally provided schedule. After Stage V, we go back to Stage I again. The entire procedure stops either when a runtime failure (e.g. crash) is found, or when the time limit is reached.

Our BEST tool can provide the visualization of the failure-triggering execution. If the executable contains the compiler generated debugging information, BEST can also provide a mapping from the trace events to the corresponding program statements. On the Linux platform, for example, we use a gnu utility called `objdump` to obtain the mapping between processor instructions and the corresponding source file and line information.

4.2   Inferring Atomicity Properties

Programmers often make some implicit assumptions regarding the concurrency control of the program, e.g. certain blocks are intended to be mutually exclusive, certain blocks are intended to be atomic, and certain instructions are intended to be executed in a specific order. However, sometimes these implicit assumptions are not enforced using synchronization primitives such as locks and wait-notify. Concurrency related program failures are often the result of these implicit assumptions being broken, e.g. data races, atomicity violations, and order violations. There are existing methods (e.g. [12]) for statically mining execution order invariants form the program source code. There are also dynamic methods (e.g. [13]) for inferring invariants at runtime. For example, if no program failure occurs during testing, then the already tested executions often can be assumed to satisfy the programmer's intent.

Our BEST tool heuristically infers such likely atomicity properties from the x86 executables. Our approach is an application of the existing methods in [12, 13] together with the following extensions. Let a global access denote either a synchronization operation or a shared memory accesses. When inferring the likely atomic regions, we require each region to satisfy the following conditions:

- the region must contain at least one shared memory read/write;
- the first and/or last global access must be a shared memory read/write;
- the global accesses must be within a procedure boundary;
- the global accesses must be close to each other in the program code;

In additional, the region should not be divided by blocking synchronization operations such as thread creation/join or the wait/notify, which will make the region non-atomic.

Fig. 7 shows an example of inferring the likely atomic regions from the program code, by following the above guidelines. This figure contains the output of *objectdump* for a small C program called *atom.c* at Lines 59, 61, 63, and 65. The entire execution trace,

```
       .......
       ./atom.c:59
        pthread_mutex_lock(12);
       .......
        8048776:        e8 c1 fd ff ff        call    804853c
       ./atom.c:61
  ┌──   ++Z;
  │     804877b:        a1 28 9a 04 08        mov     0x8049a28,%eax
intended 8048780:      83 c0 01              add     $0x1,%eax
  │     8048783:        a3 28 9a 04 08        mov     %eax,0x8049a28
  │    ./atom.c:63
  │     X = (char *)malloc(Z);
  │     8048788:        a1 28 9a 04 08        mov     0x8049a28,%eax
  │     804878d:        89 04 24              mov     %eax,(%esp)
  │     8048790:        e8 97 fd ff ff        call    804852c
  └──   8048795:        a3 2c 9a 04 08        mov     %eax,0x8049a2c
       ./atom.c:65
        pthread_mutex_lock(11);
        80487a1:        e8 96 fd ff ff        call    804853c
       .......
```

Fig. 7. Inferring atomicity with objdump using code structure

together with its CTM and interleaving lattice, can be found in [36]. The transition corresponding to pthread_mutex_lock(12) is assigned a tag $\langle atom.c, 59 \rangle$. Similarly, the transitions corresponding ++Z is assigned a tag $\langle atom.c, 61 \rangle$. Using the rules for inferring atomic regions, we mark the transitions corresponding to statements ++Z and X=(char*)malloc(Z) as the likely atomic region. In other words, if we can find an interleaved execution which breaks this atomicity assumption, the execution will be regarded as risky – it is more likely to lead to a program failure. In Stage V of our BEST tool, we will replay such interleavings in order to maximize the exposure of the real failures.

5 Implementation and Evaluation

Our tool has been implemented for x86 executables on the Linux platform. We use PIN [4] for dynamic code instrumentation and the YICES [37] solver for symbolic predictive analysis. Our BEST tool can directly check for concurrency failures in executables that use the POSIX threads. Whenever the program source code are available, for example, in C/C++/Java, we use *gcc/g++/gcj* to compile the source code into x86 executables before checking them. With the help of dynamic instrumentation form PIN, we can model the instructions that come from both the application and the dynamically linked libraries. Specifically, we are able to record all the POSIX thread synchronizations such as wait/notify, lock/unlock, and fork/join, as well as the shared memory accesses.

For efficiency reasons, BEST may choose to turn off the recording of the thread-local operations such as stack reads/writes. This option in principle may lead to a further over-approximation of the trace generalization model, meaning that some of the violations reported by our analysis may be spurious. As a result, replay in Stage V may fail (our bailout strategy is to start a free run as soon as the replay fails). However, such cases turn out to be rare in our experiments.

We have experimented with some public domain multi-threaded applications from the sourceforge and freshmeat websites. The size of these benchmarks are in the range of 1K-33K lines of C/C++ or Java code. They include *aget* (1.2K LOC, C), *fastspy* (1.5K LOC, C), *finalsolution* (2K LOC, C++), *prozilla* (2.7K LOC, C++), *axel* (3.1K LOC, C), *bzip2smp* (6.4K LOC, C), *alsaplayer* (33K LOC, C++), and *tsp* (713, Java). The length of the execution trace ranges from a few hundreds to 34K events, with 4 to 67 threads. Most of the inferred atomic regions involve more than one variable accesses. Due to the use of interference abstractions and the various model simplification and search space reduction techniques, the CPU time per check by our analysis is a few seconds on average.

Our BEST tool found several previously known/unknown atomicity violations. The bug list can be found in http://www.nec-labs.com/~malay/notes.html.

6   Related Work

We have reviewed the existing methods for runtime monitoring and prediction of concurrency failures in Section 2. It should be clear that for such analysis to detect a failure, a *failure-inducing* execution trace should be provided as input, which contains all the events that are needed to form a *failure-triggering* interleaving. While we have assumed that this failure-inducing execution trace is available, generating such trace can be a difficult task in practice, since it requires both the *right* thread schedule and the *right* program input.

When the thread scheduling is controlled by the operating system, it is difficult to generate a failure-inducing thread schedule – repeating the same test does not necessarily increase the coverage. Standard techniques such as load/stress tests and randomization [38] are not effective, since they are highly dependent on the runtime environment, and even if a failure-inducing schedule is found, replaying the schedule remains difficult. CHESS-like tools [32, 39, 40] based on stateless model checking [41] are more promising, but too expensive due to interleaving explosion, even with partial order reduction [42] and context bounding [43, 44]. A more practical approach is to systematically, but also selectively, test a subset of thread schedules while still cover the common bug patterns. Similar approaches have been used in CalFuzzer [45], PENELOPE [46], and our recent work in [47].

Generating the failure-inducing execution trace also requires the right data input. In practice, test inputs are often hand crafted, e.g. as part of the testing harness. Although DART-like automated test generation techniques [48–55] have made remarkable progress for sequential programs, extending them to concurrent programs has been difficult. For example, ESD [56] extended the test generation algorithm in KLEE [53] to multithreaded programs; Sen and Agha [20] also outlined a concolic testing algorithm for multithreaded Java. However, these existing methods were severely limited by interleaving explosion – it is difficult to systematically achieve a decent code and interleaving coverage within a reasonable period of time. In ESD, for example, heuristics are used to artificially reduce the number of interleavings; however, the problem is that the reduction is arbitrary and often does not match the common concurrency bug patterns. This leads to missed bugs, and also makes it difficult to identify which part of the search space is covered and which part is not. Therefore, we consider efficient test generation for concurrent programs as an interesting problem for a future work.

7   Conclusions

In this paper, we have provided a brief overview of the latest development in SMT-based symbolic predictive analysis. We have also presented our BEST tool for detecting runtime failures in unmodified x86 executables on the Linux platform using POSIX threads. BEST uses a staged analysis with various simplifications and model reduction techniques to improve the scalability of the symbolic analysis. It infers likely atomicity properties and then checks them using the symbolic analysis. Thread schedules that violate some of these likely atomicity properties are used to re-direct the testing toward the search subspaces with a higher risk. BEST also provides the visualization of trace events by mapping them to the program statements to help debugging. We believe that these SMT-based symbolic predictive analysis techniques hold great promise in significantly improving concurrent program verification.

References

1. Ross, P.E.: Top 11 technologies of the decade. IEEE Spectrum 48(1), 27–63 (2011)
2. Manson, J., Pugh, W., Adve, S.V.: The java memory model. In: ACM SIGACT-SIGPLAN Symposium on Principles of Programming Languages, pp. 378–391 (2005)
3. Boehm, H.J., Adve, S.V.: Foundations of the c++ concurrency memory model. In: ACM SIGPLAN Conference on Programming Language Design and Implementation, pp. 68–78 (2008)
4. Luk, C.K., Cohn, R., Muth, R., Patil, H., Klauser, A., Lowney, G., Wallace, S., Reddi, V.J., Hazelwood, K.: PIN: Building customized program analysis tools with dynamic instrumentation. In: ACM SIGPLAN Conference on Programming Language Design and Implementation, pp. 190–200. ACM, New York (2005)
5. Wang, C., Kundu, S., Ganai, M., Gupta, A.: Symbolic Predictive Analysis for Concurrent Programs. In: Cavalcanti, A., Dams, D.R. (eds.) FM 2009. LNCS, vol. 5850, pp. 256–272. Springer, Heidelberg (2009)
6. Wang, C., Chaudhuri, S., Gupta, A., Yang, Y.: Symbolic pruning of concurrent program executions. In: ACM SIGSOFT Symposium on Foundations of Software Engineering, pp. 23–32 (2009)
7. Wang, C., Limaye, R., Ganai, M., Gupta, A.: Trace-Based Symbolic Analysis for Atomicity Violations. In: Esparza, J., Majumdar, R. (eds.) TACAS 2010. LNCS, vol. 6015, pp. 328–342. Springer, Heidelberg (2010)
8. Kundu, S., Ganai, M.K., Wang, C.: CONTESSA: Concurrency Testing Augmented with Symbolic Analysis. In: Touili, T., Cook, B., Jackson, P. (eds.) CAV 2010. LNCS, vol. 6174, pp. 127–131. Springer, Heidelberg (2010)
9. King, J.C.: Symbolic execution and program testing. Commun. ACM 19(7), 385–394 (1976)
10. Clarke, L.A.: A system to generate test data and symbolically execute programs. IEEE Trans. Software Eng. 2(3), 215–222 (1976)
11. Sen, K., Rosu, G., Agha, G.: Runtime safety analysis of multithreaded programs. In: ACM SIGSOFT Symposium on Foundations of Software Engineering, pp. 337–346 (2003)
12. Xu, M., Bodík, R., Hill, M.D.: A serializability violation detector for shared-memory server programs. In: ACM SIGPLAN Conference on Programming Language Design and Implementation, pp. 1–14 (2005)
13. Lu, S., Tucek, J., Qin, F., Zhou, Y.: AVIO: detecting atomicity violations via access interleaving invariants. In: Architectural Support for Programming Languages and Operating Systems, pp. 37–48 (2006)
14. Wang, L., Stoller, S.D.: Runtime analysis of atomicity for multithreaded programs. IEEE Trans. Software Eng. 32(2), 93–110 (2006)
15. Chen, F., Serbanuta, T., Rosu, G.: jPredictor: a predictive runtime analysis tool for java. In: International Conference on Software Engineering, pp. 221–230 (2008)
16. Flanagan, C., Freund, S.N.: Atomizer: A dynamic atomicity checker for multithreaded programs. In: Parallel and Distributed Processing Symposium (2004)

17. Flanagan, C., Freund, S.N., Yi, J.: Velodrome: a sound and complete dynamic atomicity checker for multithreaded programs. In: ACM SIGPLAN Conference on Programming Language Design and Implementation, pp. 293–303 (2008)
18. Farzan, A., Madhusudan, P.: Monitoring Atomicity in Concurrent Programs. In: Gupta, A., Malik, S. (eds.) CAV 2008. LNCS, vol. 5123, pp. 52–65. Springer, Heidelberg (2008)
19. Lamport, L.: Time, clocks, and the ordering of events in a distributed system. Commun. ACM 21(7), 558–565 (1978)
20. Sen, K., Roşu, G., Agha, G.: Detecting Errors in Multithreaded Programs by Generalized Predictive Analysis of Executions. In: Steffen, M., Tennenholtz, M. (eds.) FMOODS 2005. LNCS, vol. 3535, pp. 211–226. Springer, Heidelberg (2005)
21. Chen, F., Roşu, G.: Parametric and Sliced Causality. In: Damm, W., Hermanns, H. (eds.) CAV 2007. LNCS, vol. 4590, pp. 240–253. Springer, Heidelberg (2007)
22. Sadowski, C., Freund, S.N., Flanagan, C.: SingleTrack: A Dynamic Determinism Checker for Multithreaded Programs. In: Castagna, G. (ed.) ESOP 2009. LNCS, vol. 5502, pp. 394–409. Springer, Heidelberg (2009)
23. Savage, S., Burrows, M., Nelson, G., Sobalvarro, P., Anderson, T.: Eraser: A dynamic data race detector for multithreaded programs. ACM Trans. Comput. Syst. 15(4), 391–411 (1997)
24. von Praun, C., Gross, T.R.: Object race detection. In: ACM SIGPLAN Conference on Object Oriented Programming, Systems, Languages, and Applications, pp. 70–82 (2001)
25. Farzan, A., Madhusudan, P.: The Complexity of Predicting Atomicity Violations. In: Kowalewski, S., Philippou, A. (eds.) TACAS 2009. LNCS, vol. 5505, pp. 155–169. Springer, Heidelberg (2009)
26. Farzan, A., Madhusudan, P., Sorrentino, F.: Meta-analysis for Atomicity Violations under Nested Locking. In: Bouajjani, A., Maler, O. (eds.) CAV 2009. LNCS, vol. 5643, pp. 248–262. Springer, Heidelberg (2009)
27. Kahlon, V., Ivančić, F., Gupta, A.: Reasoning About Threads Communicating via Locks. In: Etessami, K., Rajamani, S.K. (eds.) CAV 2005. LNCS, vol. 3576, pp. 505–518. Springer, Heidelberg (2005)
28. Sinha, A., Malik, S., Wang, C., Gupta, A.: Predictive analysis for detecting serializability violations through trace segmentation. In: International Conference on Formal Methods and Models for Codesign (2011)
29. Kahlon, V., Wang, C.: Universal Causality Graphs: A Precise Happens-Before Model for Detecting Bugs in Concurrent Programs. In: Touili, T., Cook, B., Jackson, P. (eds.) CAV 2010. LNCS, vol. 6174, pp. 434–449. Springer, Heidelberg (2010)
30. Ganai, M.K., Kundu, S.: Reduction of Verification Conditions for Concurrent System Using Mutually Atomic Transactions. In: Păsăreanu, C.S. (ed.) SPIN 2009. LNCS, vol. 5578, pp. 68–87. Springer, Heidelberg (2009)
31. Qadeer, S., Rehof, J.: Context-Bounded Model Checking of Concurrent Software. In: Halbwachs, N., Zuck, L.D. (eds.) TACAS 2005. LNCS, vol. 3440, pp. 93–107. Springer, Heidelberg (2005)
32. Musuvathi, M., Qadeer, S., Ball, T., Basler, G., Nainar, P.A., Neamtiu, I.: Finding and reproducing heisenbugs in concurrent programs. In: OSDI, pp. 267–280 (2008)
33. Sinha, N., Wang, C.: On interference abstractions. In: ACM SIGACT-SIGPLAN Symposium on Principles of Programming Languages, pp. 423–434 (2011)
34. Farzan, A., Madhusudan, P.: Causal Atomicity. In: Ball, T., Jones, R.B. (eds.) CAV 2006. LNCS, vol. 4144, pp. 315–328. Springer, Heidelberg (2006)
35. Ganai, M.K.: Scalable and precise symbolic analysis for atomicity violations. In: IEEE/ACM International Conference on Automated Software Engineering (2011)
36. Ganai, M.K., Arora, N., Wang, C., Gupta, A., Balakrishnan, G.: BEST: A symbolic testing tool for predicting multi-threaded program failures. In: IEEE/ACM International Conference on Automated Software Engineering (2011)
37. Dutertre, B., de Moura, L.: A Fast Linear-Arithmetic Solver for DPLL(T). In: Ball, T., Jones, R.B. (eds.) CAV 2006. LNCS, vol. 4144, pp. 81–94. Springer, Heidelberg (2006)

38. Farchi, E., Nir, Y., Ur, S.: Concurrent bug patterns and how to test them. In: Parallel and Distributed Processing Symposium, p. 286 (2003)
39. Godefroid, P.: Software model checking: The VeriSoft approach. Formal Methods in System Design 26(2), 77–101 (2005)
40. Yang, Y., Chen, X., Gopalakrishnan, G.: Inspect: A runtime model checker for multithreaded C programs. Technical Report UUCS-08-004, University of Utah (2008)
41. Godefroid, P.: VeriSoft: A Tool for the Automatic Analysis of Concurrent Reactive Software. In: Grumberg, O. (ed.) CAV 1997. LNCS, vol. 1254, pp. 476–479. Springer, Heidelberg (1997)
42. Flanagan, C., Godefroid, P.: Dynamic partial-order reduction for model checking software. In: ACM SIGACT-SIGPLAN Symposium on Principles of Programming Languages, pp. 110–121 (2005)
43. Qadeer, S., Wu, D.: KISS: keep it simple and sequential. In: ACM SIGPLAN Conference on Programming Language Design and Implementation, pp. 14–24 (2004)
44. Musuvathi, M., Qadeer, S.: Partial-order reduction for context-bounded state exploration. Technical Report MSR-TR-2007-12, Microsoft Research (December 2007)
45. Joshi, P., Naik, M., Park, C.-S., Sen, K.: CALFUZZER: An Extensible Active Testing Framework for Concurrent Programs. In: Bouajjani, A., Maler, O. (eds.) CAV 2009. LNCS, vol. 5643, pp. 675–681. Springer, Heidelberg (2009)
46. Sorrentino, F., Farzan, A., Madhusudan, P.: PENELOPE: weaving threads to expose atomicity violations. In: ACM SIGSOFT Symposium on Foundations of Software Engineering, pp. 37–46 (2010)
47. Wang, C., Said, M., Gupta, A.: Coverage guided systematic concurrency testing. In: International Conference on Software Engineering, pp. 221–230 (2011)
48. Khurshid, S., Păsăreanu, C.S., Visser, W.: Generalized Symbolic Execution for Model Checking and Testing. In: Garavel, H., Hatcliff, J. (eds.) TACAS 2003. LNCS, vol. 2619, pp. 553–568. Springer, Heidelberg (2003)
49. Godefroid, P., Klarlund, N., Sen, K.: DART: directed automated random testing. In: Programming Language Design and Implementation, pp. 213–223 (June 2005)
50. Godefroid, P., Levin, M.Y., Molnar, D.A.: Automated whitebox fuzz testing. In: Network and Distributed System Security Symposium (2008)
51. Sen, K., Marinov, D., Agha, G.: CUTE: a concolic unit testing engine for C. In: ACM SIGSOFT Symposium on Foundations of Software Engineering, pp. 263–272 (2005)
52. Burnim, J., Sen, K.: Heuristics for scalable dynamic test generation. In: ASE, pp. 443–446 (2008)
53. Cadar, C., Dunbar, D., Engler, D.R.: KLEE: Unassisted and automatic generation of high-coverage tests for complex systems programs. In: OSDI, pp. 209–224 (2008)
54. Lewandowski, G., Bouvier, D.J., Chen, T.Y., McCartney, R., Sanders, K., Simon, B., VanDeGrift, T.: Commonsense understanding of concurrency: computing students and concert tickets. Commun. ACM 53, 60–70 (2010)
55. Cadar, C., Godefroid, P., Khurshid, S., Pasareanu, C.S., Sen, K., Tillmann, N., Visser, W.: Symbolic execution for software testing in practice: preliminary assessment. In: International Conference on Software Engineering, pp. 1066–1071 (2011)
56. Zamfir, C., Candea, G.: Execution synthesis: a technique for automated software debugging. In: EuroSys, pp. 321–334 (2010)

Runtime Monitoring of Time-Sensitive Systems
[Tutorial Supplement]

Borzoo Bonakdarpour and Sebastian Fischmeister

University of Waterloo
200 University Avenue West
Waterloo, Ontario, Canada, N2L 3G1
borzoo@cs.uwaterloo.ca, sfischme@uwaterloo.ca

Abstract. This tutorial focuses on issues involved in runtime monitoring of time-sensitive systems, where violation of timing constraints are undesired. Our goal is to describe the challenges in instrumenting, measuring, and monitoring such systems and present our solutions developed in the past few years to deal with these challenges. The tutorial consists of two parts. First, we present challenge problems and corresponding solutions on instrumenting real-time systems so that timing constraints of the system are respected. The second part of the tutorial will focus on *time-triggered* runtime monitoring, where a monitor is invoked at equal time intervals, allowing designers to schedule regular and monitoring tasks hand-in-hand.

1   Overview of Tutorial

In computing systems, *correctness* refers to the assertion that a system satisfies its specification. *Verification* is a technique for checking such an assertion and *runtime verification* refers to a lightweight technique where a *monitor* checks at run time whether the execution of a system under inspection satisfies or violates a given correctness property. Deploying runtime verification involves instrumenting the program under inspection, so that upon occurrence of events (e.g., value changes of a variable) that may change the truthfulness of a property, the monitor will be called to re-evaluate the property. We call this method *event-triggered* runtime verification, because each change prompts a re-evaluation. Event-triggered runtime verification suffers from two drawbacks: (1) *unpredictable* overhead, and (2) possible *bursts* of events at run time.

The above defects are undesired in the context of real-time embedded systems, where predictability and timing constraints play a central role. This tutorial focuses on describing our solutions to two challenge problems:

- **Time-aware instrumentation.** Instrumentation is a technique to extract information or trigger events in programs under inspection. Instrumentation is a vital step for enabling system monitoring; i.e. the system is augmented with instructions that invokes a monitor when certain events occur. Instrumentation of software programs while preserving logical correctness is an

S. Khurshid and K. Sen (Eds.): RV 2011, LNCS 7186, pp. 19–33, 2012.

established field. However, current approaches are inadequate for real-time embedded applications. The key idea behind the *time-aware instrumentation* of a system is to transform the execution-time distribution of the system so as to maximize the coverage of the trace while always staying within the time budget.

– **Time-triggered monitoring.** In *time-triggered* runtime verification, a monitor runs in parallel with the program and samples the program state periodically to evaluate a set of system properties. The main challenge in time-triggered runtime verification is to guarantee accurate program state reconstruction at sampling time. Providing such guarantee results in solving an an optimization problem where the objective is to find the minimum number of critical events that need to be buffered for a given sampling period. Consequently, the time-triggered monitor can successfully reconstruct the state of the program between two successive samples.

This tutorial will discuss in detail our techniques developed in the past few years while exploring time-aware instrumentation and time-triggered monitoring. In Section 2, we introduce the problem of timing in real-time embedded systems. Section 3 is dedicated to our techniques on time-aware instrumentation. Time-triggered runtime monitoring is discussed in Section 4. Finally, we present a set of future research directions in Section 5.

2   Real-Time Embedded Software Primer

Embedded software is the essence of our modern computerized standard of living. It is omnipresent and controls everything from everyday consumer products such as microwaves and digital cameras to large systems for factory automation, aircraft, and automotive applications. Software enables devices that make life more pleasant (i.e., adaptive cruise control in cars), more acceptable (i.e., implanted insulin infusion pumps), or even possible (i.e., implanted pacemakers and defibrillators). Many companies define innovation in their products through adding new features implemented in software, thus future systems will contain more complex and larger portions of software. For example, the next generation automobile is a highly distributed system expected to run several million lines of code [3].

A special class of embedded software is real-time embedded software. A real-time application is time sensitive and this generally means that delivering a correct value at the wrong point in time—especially too late—can still cause service failures. Thus a real-time system must work correctly in the logic and timing domain. Examples of such system span almost all domains of embedded software including consumer devices (e.g., video decoders), avionics platforms (e.g., flight control in autopilots), automotive (e.g., distance measurement in adaptive cruise control), medical devices (e.g., pacemakers), finance (e.g., high-frequency trading), communications (e.g., software-defined radio), and space (e.g., thrust control).

Table 1 shows the relationship between timing, logic, and correctness of a real-time application for two basic classes. Naturally, more classes have been defined over time. These additional classes refine and extend some of the properties such as firm real-time constraints [13] and imprecise computation [14]. Soft real-time applications have soft timing constraints. This means that if the application sometimes misses deadlines, the application will still function. A typical example of such an application is video decoding; dropping a frame sometimes will remain unnoticed by the viewer, however, frequent drops in frames will degrade the experience. The threshold for an acceptable number of missed deadlines depends on the application. Hard real-time applications have hard timing constraints. Missing a single deadline can result in an error in the system. Typical applications for this domain are safety-critical systems like a shutdown routine in a nuclear power station, flight surface control while piloting airplanes, and pacing control in a heart pacemaker. Obviously, such hard real-time systems require meticulous control of system resources and execution to guarantee proper system functioning and ultimately system safety. Hence, such control is also the main focus of research on real-time systems.

Table 1. Real-time system classification

	Soft RT		Hard RT	
	On time	Too late	On Time	Too late
Wrong value	Error	Error	Error	Error
Right value	Ok	Maybe ok	Ok	Error

Reduction in complexity through limiting the programming languages is one approach to provide better control of resources, execution, and timing. With this goal in mind, several standards on developing safety-critical and real-time embedded systems have emerged over the years. They find use in different domains. For example MISRA C [12] provides coding guidelines and reduces the complexity of C code by forbidding, for instance, recursion, unbounded loops, and dynamic memory allocation. The automotive and other industries use MISRA C. Ravenscar [5] and SPARK [2] address similar issues for the Ada programming language. The RTCA/DO 178B [16] specifies guidelines for developing safety-critical software systems for the avionics domain. The standard touches major topics of the software development cycle and specifies required documentation for different activities. Other domains, like the nuclear domain, have similar standards. Such standards are relevant as they define classes of systems to which solutions can be tailored to. For example, while static analysis is impractical in the general case, the limited use of pointers in MISRA C compliant code permits subjecting such programs to static analysis.

Another popular approach to handling resources, execution, and timing is to follow a time-triggered approach. In these approaches, time is split into small slices. The system scheduler assigns resource users mutually exclusive access to the resource based on these slices. For example, the time-triggered approach for task scheduling is round robin scheduling. The scheduler assigns one slice of processor time to one process at a time. In communication, Time Division Multiple Access (TDMA) implements a time-triggered approach to limit concurrent access to the shared communication medium. In safety-critical applications, sometimes the developer creates the time-triggered schedule by laying out the time line and determining when which process gets to compute and communicate, so all operations meet their timing deadlines. One advantage of the time-triggered approach is its determinism and thus predictable operation. Time-triggered approaches make operational decisions solely based on a clock. Controlling the clock means controlling all aspects in the system that get derived from that clock. This single source for controlling operations is attractive, because it reduces operational dependencies and thus reduces complexity. Naturally, event-triggered approaches also offer benefits and picking one over the other is a complicated matter and a lasting debate [10].

3   Time-Aware Instrumentation

Instrumentation of software programs while preserving logical correctness is an established field. Developers instrument programs for tasks including profiling, testing, debugging, tracing, and monitoring the software systems (e.g., for runtime verification). Today several approaches to instrument software while preserving logical correctness exist and in the tutorial, we will briefly discuss the most relevant works including manual instrumentation, static instrumentation frameworks, dynamic instrumentation with binary rewriting, and hardware-based approaches. However, current approaches are inadequate for real-time embedded applications.

The key idea behind the *time-aware instrumentation* of a system is to transform the execution-time distribution of the system so as to maximize the coverage of the trace while always staying within the time budget. Our notion of coverage implies that the instrumentation will provide useful data over longer periods of tracing. A time-aware instrumentation injects code, potentially extending the execution time on all paths, while ensuring that no path takes longer than the specified time budget.

The time budget is the worst-case execution time of a function without violating a specification. In hard real-time systems, the time budget can be the longest execution time without missing any deadline, and depending on the longest execution time of the non-instrumented version, more or less time will be available for the instrumentation. In systems without deadlines, the time budget can be the current maximum execution time plus a specified non-zero maximum overhead for tracing to the current maximum execution time.

Figure 1 shows the expected consequences of time-aware instrumentation in a hard real-time application on the execution time profile (i.e., the probability density function on the execution time). The x-axis specifies the execution time of the function, while the y-axis indicates the frequency of the particular execution time. The original uninstrumented code has some arbitrary density function. We have chosen the Gaussian distribution for this example for illustrative purposes; Li et al. provide details from empirical observations of distribution functions [11]. The distribution for the instrumented version differs from the original one. It is shifted towards the right, but still never passes the deadline. This shift occurs because time-aware instrumentation adds to paths, increasing their running times, but ensures that execution times never exceed the deadline.

Note that our execution-time model concentrates on the overhead involved in acquiring data. A related problem is to transport the collected data from the embedded system to an external analysis unit. While that problem admits many solutions, one common solution is to piggyback the buffer information onto serial or network communication.

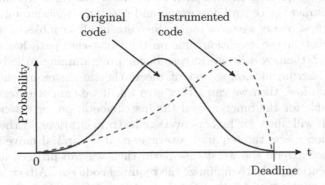

Fig. 1. Execution-time distribution for a code block before and after time-aware instrumentation showing the shift in the expected execution time

The implementation challenge is to efficiently realize this right shift in the execution time profile without exceeding the deadline. This requires answers to several questions: where to instrument, what to instrument, and how to instrument? We worked on both, a software- and a hardware-based solution.

3.1 Basic Overview [7, 8]

We propose the following instrumentation stages:

- **Source analysis:** The source-code analyzer breaks the functions into basic blocks and generates a call graph. The analyzer also presents a list of variables which are assigned in these basic blocks and the developer can choose a subset of these variables to trace. For hard real-time applications, the analyzer annotates the call graph using execution time information obtained through static analysis or measurements [17].

- **Naive instrumentation:** Using the control-flow graph, the execution times of the basic blocks, and the input variables for the trace, we inject code into the selected function at all instrumentation points.
- **Enforce time budget:** If the naive instrumentation exceeds the time budget, we use an optimization technique to compute an instrumentation which does respect the time budget while maximizing the coverage of the instrumentation.
- **Minimize code size:** If the instrumentation is reliable enough, then we apply semantics-preserving, decreasing transformations to reduce the size of the instrumented code.
- **Collect traces:** The developer finally recompiles and executes the instrumented program.

Figure 2 shows the workflow that results from the steps. To instrument a function, we start by picking the function of interest. We then use the assembly analyzer to extract the control flow graph and break the function into execution paths. In the first phase, we use a tool to instrument all variables of interest and then check whether the execution time on the worst-case path has changed. If it has changed, then we will use integer linear programming to lower the coverage of the instrumentation so that it meets the timing requirements. If the coverage is too low, then we can either give up, if we cannot extend the time budget available for the function and the instrumentation; or extend the time budget, which will allow for higher-coverage instrumentations. If the optimized instrumentation meets the required coverage, or if the initial naive instrumentation does not extend the worst-case path, then we will proceed and use the identified execution paths to minimize the required code size. Afterwards, we can recompile the program and collect the desired traces from the instrumentation.

3.2   Case Study: Flash File System

We investigated an implementation of a wear-levelling FAT-like filesystem for flash devices [4]. The code was originally written by Hein de Kock for 8051 processors. We slightly modified the original implementation so that it would compile with sdcc; in particular, we needed to modify the header files to get the code to compile. The implementation consists of about 3000 non-blank, non-comment lines of C code. We ran our tool on 30 functions from the fs.c file, dropping some uninteresting functions with mostly straight-line control-flow. Of the 30 functions, 4 functions had more than 100 basic blocks, and fclose had 200 basic blocks. For this case study, we also assume that the time budget is the execution time of the longest running path in the function and no interrupts.

Measurements. Figure 3 compares density functions for four procedures in the filesystem implementation, both before and after instrumentation. The solid blue line represents the density function of the original procedures, while the dashed red line represents the density function for the instrumented versions. Each of

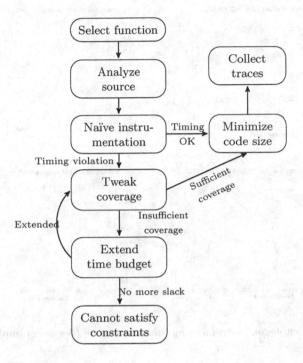

Fig. 2. Workflow of applying time-aware instrumentation

this figures clearly shows that the original idea underlying our method of time-aware instrumentation, as outlined in Figure 1, works well.

The procedure *fsetpos* shown in Figure 3(b) exhibits the biggest difference between instrumented and non-instrumented versions. The reason is that although this procedure contains many assignments spread across different paths, most assignments do not lie on the worst-case path. The instrumentation engine can therefore capture assignments along these non-critical paths, raising their execution time and putting them closer to the execution time of the worst-case path. Since the engine can capture assignments on many paths, the density function of the execution time for the instrumented version shows a large increase on the right part of the figure, along with a steep decrease on the left part of the figure.

The procedure *rename* shown in Figure 3(d) demonstrates that sometimes the developer might want to add time to the budget for instrumenting to enable the instrumentation of the worst-case path. Figure 4 shows that even with a small increase in the time budget, the coverage can increase significantly. Figure 3 shows the function *fputs* without any additional increase in the time budget, Figure 4(a) shows the function with an extra budget of three assignments, and Figure 4(c) shows the function with an extra budget of 15 assignments. Figure 4(d) summarizes how instrumenting *fputs* improves as we add more time to the time budget for the instrumentation.

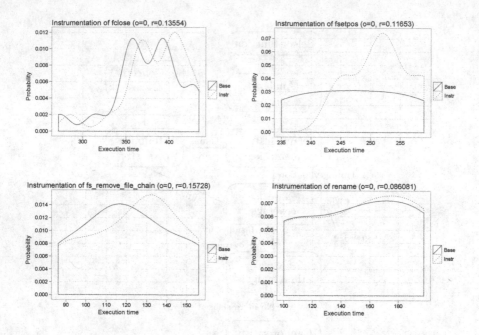

Fig. 3. Examples in instrumenting functions in the filesystem implementation

4   Time-Triggered Runtime Monitoring

Most monitoring approaches in runtime verification are *event-triggered*, where
the occurrence of every new event (e.g., change of value of a variable) invokes the
monitor. This constant invocation of the monitor leads to *unpredictable overhead*
and *bursts* of new events at run time. These defects can cause serious issues at
run time especially in embedded safety/mission-critical systems. *Time-triggered*
monitoring aims at tackling these drawbacks. Specifically, a time-triggered monitor runs in parallel with the program and samples the program state periodically
to evaluate a set of properties.

The second part of the tutorial will focus on two methods: time-triggered
path monitoring [6] and time-triggered runtime verification [1]. In both methods,
the monitor has to execute at the speed of shortest best-case execution time
of branching statements. This ensures that the monitor does not overlook any
property violations and can reconstruct the execution path at each sampling
point. However, executing the monitor at the speed of best-case execution time
results in high involvement of the monitor in execution of the system under
inspection.

In this section, we review two techniques for sampling-based execution monitoring [6] and runtime verification [1] in Subsections 4.1 and 4.2, respectively.
Both methods employ the notion of *control-flow graphs* (CFG) in order to reason
about program execution and its timing characteristics.

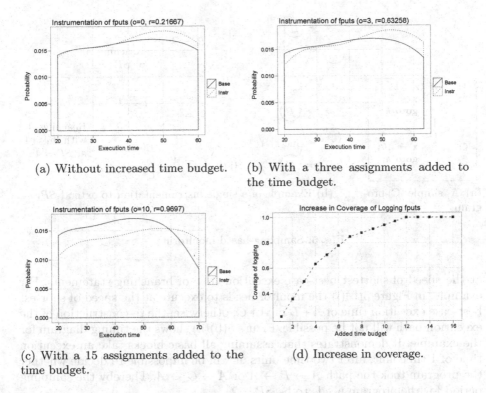

(a) Without increased time budget.

(b) With a three assignments added to the time budget.

(c) With a 15 assignments added to the time budget.

(d) Increase in coverage.

Fig. 4. Examples of increasing the coverage by increasing the time budget

Definition 1. *The* control-flow graph *of a program P is a weighted directed simple graph $CFG_P = \langle V, v^0, A, w \rangle$, where:*

- *V: is a set of vertices, each representing a basic block of P. Each basic block consists of a sequence of instructions in P.*
- *v^0: is the initial vertex with indegree 0, which represents the initial basic block of P.*
- *A: is a set of arcs (u, v), where $u, v \in V$. An arc (u, v) exists in A, if and only if the execution of basic block u can immediately lead to the execution of basic block v.*
- *w: is a function $w : A \to \mathbb{N}$, which defines a weight for each arc in A. The weight of an arc is the best-case execution time (BCET) of the source basic block.* □

For example, Figure 5(a) shows a simple C program with three basic blocks labeled *A*, *B*, and *C* and Figure 5(b)(i) shows the resulting control-flow graph.

4.1 Sampling-Based Execution Monitoring [6]

In execution monitoring, the objective is to take periodic samples such that the monitor can re-construct execution paths. To this end, the monitor has to execute

```
A:    if (x < 5) {
B:        x++;
          goto A
      }
      else {
C:        x -= 10;
          goto A;
      }
```

(a) A simple C program.

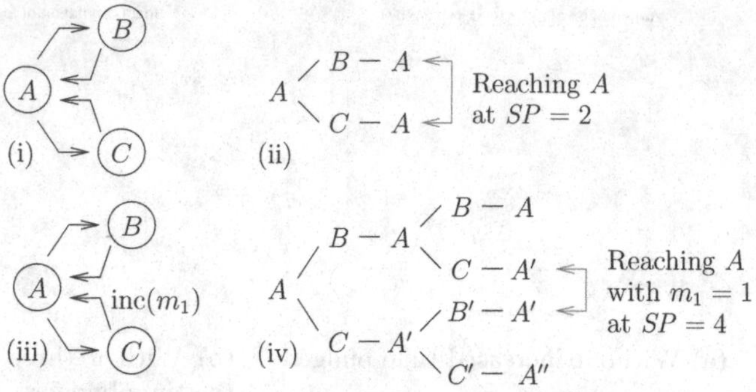

(i) A → B, A → C (cycle)

(ii) A — $B - A$, $C - A$ Reaching A at $SP = 2$

(iii) A → B, A ← inc(m_1), A → C

(iv) A — $B - A$ (with branches $B - A$, $C - A'$, $B' - A'$, $C - A'$, $C' - A''$)   Reaching A with $m_1 = 1$ at $SP = 4$

(b) Example of a single instrumentation to extend SP.

Fig. 5. Sampling-based monitoring

at the speed of shortest best-case execution time of branching statements. For example, in Figure 5(b)(i) the monitor needs to execute at the speed of shortest best-case execution time of $A+B$ or $A+C$; otherwise, the re-construction of the execution path will not be possible. Figure 5(b)(ii) shows the timing diagram for the example. It demonstrates that, assuming all basic blocks take an execution time of 1 time unit, after two time units, it will be impossible to decide whether the program took the path $A \to B \to A$ or $A \to C \to A$. Thereby the sampling period for the program needs to be $SP = 2$.

To increase the sampling period and, hence, decrease the involvement of the monitor, we introduce *markers* to the program. A marker is a simple variable that can be manipulated in basic blocks to distinguish different paths and, hence, resulting in a larger sampling period. In our example, we introduce marker m_1 and instrument vertex C (see Figure 5(b)(iii)). Vertex C manipulates the value of marker m_1 by incrementing it. Thus, the monitor can re-store the basic block *id* (vertex A, B, or C), the current value of m_1, and a time stamp. The timing diagram in Figure 5(b)(iv) shows that introducing the marker increases the sampling period to $SP = 4$, because only after five time units will the program have two or more paths with the same number of increments of m_1 and the same basic block *id*s.

4.2 Sampling-Based Runtime Verification [1]

Let P be a program and Π be a logical property (e.g., in LTL), where P is expected to satisfy Π. Let $\mathcal{V}_\Pi$ denote the set of variables that participate in Π. In our idea of sampling-based runtime verification, the monitor reads the value of variables in $\mathcal{V}_\Pi$ and evaluates Π. The main challenge in this mechanism is accurate re-construction of the state of P between two samples; i.e., if the value of a variable in $\mathcal{V}_\Pi$ changes more than once between two samples, the monitor may fail to detect violations of Π. For instance, in the program of

Figure 5(a), if we are to verify the property $\Pi \equiv -5 \leq x \leq 5$, then the monitor requires a fresh value of variable x without overlooking any changes. Thus the sampling period for the program needs to be $SP = 2$. Notice that although there are similarities, execution monitoring and runtime verification focus on different issues: the former concentrates on execution paths and the latter on state variable changes.

To increase the sampling period, we introduce *history variables* to the program. For example, in Figure 5(a), we introduce history variables x1 and x2 and add instrumentation instructions x1 := x and x2 := x to basic blocks B and C, respectively. Thus, if the execution of each instrumentation instruction takes 1 time unit, then we can increase the sampling period to $SP = 5$. This is due to the fact that only after six time units the value of x1 or x2 will be over written. Thus, sampling period $SP = 5$ allows the monitor to fully re-construct the state of the program using history variables when it takes a sample.

The above example shows how one can take advantage of memory to increase the sampling period of a time-triggered monitor and, hence, impose less overheard on the system. However, there is a tradeoff between the amount of auxiliary memory the system uses at run time and the sampling period. Ideally, we want to maximize the sampling period and minimize the number of history variables. In [1], we showed that this optimization problem is NP-complete.

There are two general approaches to tackle the exponential complexity: (1) mapping our problem to an existing NP-complete problem for which powerful solvers exist (e.g., the Boolean satisfiability problem and integer linear programming), and (2) devising efficient heuristics. The first approach (explored in [1]) involves transforming our optimization problem to integer linear programming (ILP). We now discuss the results of our experiments using this approach. Consider the Blowfish benchmark from the MiBench [9] benchmark suite. This program has 745 lines of code, which results in a CFG of 169 vertices and 213 arcs. We take 20 variables for monitoring. We consider the following different settings for our experiments:

- **Event-based:** gdb extracts the new value of variables of interest whenever they get changed throughout the program execution.
- **Time-triggered with no history:** gdb is invoked every MSP time units to extract the value of all the variables of interest.
- **Sampling-based with history:** This setting incorporates our ILP optimization. Thus, whenever gdb is invoked, it extracts the value of variables of interest as well as the history.

In the event-based setting (see Figure 6), since the monitor interrupts the program execution irregularly, unequal bursts in the overhead can be seen. Moreover, the overhead caused by each data extraction is proportional to the data type. Hence, the data extraction overhead varies considerably from one interruption to another. Thus, the monitor introduces probe-effects, which in turn may create unpredictable and even incorrect behaviour. This anomaly is, in particular, unacceptable for real-time embedded and mission-critical systems.

On the contrary, since the time-triggered monitor interrupts the program execution on a regular basis, the overhead introduced by data extraction is not subject to any bursts and, hence, remains consistent and bounded (see Figure 6). Consequently, the monitored program exhibits a predictable behaviour. Obviously, the time-triggered monitor may potentially increase the overhead, which extends the overall execution time. Nonetheless, in many commonly considered applications, designers prefer predictability at the cost of larger overhead.

Figure 6 show the results of our experiments for sampling period of $50 * MSP$. As can be seen, increasing the sampling period results in larger overhead. This is because the monitor needs to read a larger amount of data formed by the history. However, the increase in overhead is considerably small (less than twice the original overhead). Having said that, the other side of the coin is that by increasing the sampling period, the program is subject to less monitoring interrupts. This results in significant decrease in the overall execution time of the programs. This is indeed advantageous for monitoring hard real-time programs. Although adding history causes variability in data extraction overhead, the system behavior is still highly predictable as compared to the event-based setting. The above observations are valid for the case, where we increase the sampling period by $100 * MSP$ as well (see Figures 7).

The tradeoff between execution time and the added memory consumption when the sampling period is increased is shown in Figure 8. As can be seen, as we increase the sampling period, the system requires negligible extra memory. Also, one can clearly observe the proportion of increase in memory usage versus the reduction in the execution time. In other words, by employing small amount of auxiliary memory, one can achieve considerable speedups.

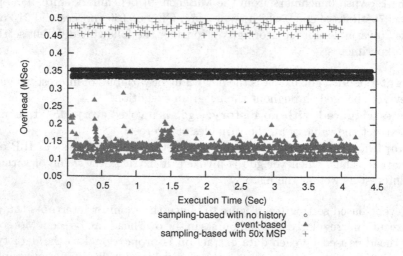

Fig. 6. Experimental results for Blowfish ($50 * MSP$ sampling period)

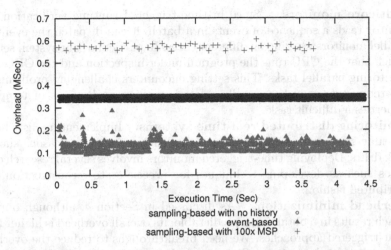

Fig. 7. Experimental results for Blowfish $(100 * MSP$ sampling period)

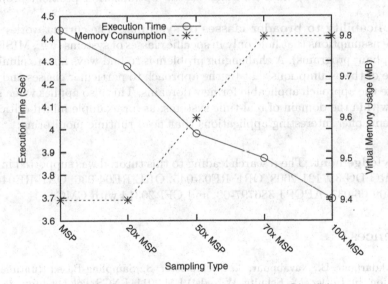

Fig. 8. Memory usage vs. execution time Blowfish

Although the ILP-based approach always finds the optimal solution to our problem and one can use state-of-the-art ILP-solvers, it cannot deal with huge programs due to the worst-case exponential complexity. For such cases alternative approaches that find near-optimal solutions are proposed in [15].

5   Open Problems

We believe our work on instrumentation and runtime verification of real-time systems has paved the way for numerous future research directions. Interesting open problems include the following:

- **Multicore monitors.** Since in time-triggered runtime verification, the monitor reads a sequence of events in a batch, it can dispatch the events to parallel monitors working on different cores. In particular, our system setting is such that the CPU runs the program under inspection and the GPU runs monitoring parallel tasks. This setting encounters challenging problems, as buffered events may be causally related, making evaluations of temporal properties a difficult task.
- **Monitoring distributed real-time systems.** Implementing distributed real-time systems has always been a challenge for obvious reasons such as clock drifts. Deploying time-triggered monitors involves several research challenges such as developing techniques for precise state reconstruction in a distributed fashion.
- **Overhead minimization.** As discussed in Section 4, although our approach results in a obtaining a predictable, its overall overhead is higher than event-triggered approaches. We need breakthroughs to reduce the overhead of time-triggered monitors. One approach is to develop efficient heuristics that find nearly optimal solutions to the optimization problem proposed in [1].
- **Applicability to broader classes of systems.** The current work makes some assumptions that hold only in specific classes of systems (e.g., MISRA C compliant programs). A challenging problem is to find ways how to eliminate some of the assumptions that tie the approach to particular classes and thus make the approach applicable for new domains. This also applies when staying within the domain of real-time systems, as for example mixed-criticality systems offer interesting applications that need runtime monitoring.

Acknowledgement. The research leading to this tutorial was supported in part by NSERC DG 357121-2008, ORF RE03-045, ORE RE04-036, ORF-RE04-039, ISOP IS09-06-037, APCPJ 386797-09, and CFI 20314 with CMC.

References

1. Bonakdarpour, B., Navabpour, S., Fischmeister, S.: Sampling-Based Runtime Verification. In: Butler, M., Schulte, W. (eds.) FM 2011. LNCS, vol. 6664, pp. 88–102. Springer, Heidelberg (2011)
2. Carré, B., Garnsworthy, J.: SPARK—an annotated Ada subset for safety-critical programming. In: Proceedings of the Conference on TRI-ADA, pp. 392–402. ACM, New York (1990)
3. Charette, R.N.: This Car Runs on Code. IEEE Spectrum (2009)
4. de Kock, H.: small-ffs (September 2009), http://code.google.com/p/small-ffs
5. Dobbing, B., Burns, A.: The Ravenscar Tasking Profile for High Integrity Real-time Programs. In: Proceedings of the 1998 Annual ACM SIGAda International Conference on Ada (SIGAda), pp. 1–6. ACM, New York (1998)
6. Fischmeister, S., Ba, Y.: Sampling-based Program Execution Monitoring. In: ACM International Conference on Languages, Compilers, and Tools for Embedded Systems (LCTES), pp. 133–142 (2010)

7. Fischmeister, S., Lam, P.: On Time-Aware Instrumentation of Programs. In: Proceedings of the 15th IEEE Real-Time and Embedded Technology and Applications Symposium (RTAS), San Fransisco, United States, pp. 305–314 (April 2009)
8. Fischmeister, S., Lam, P.: Time-aware Instrumentation of Embedded Software. IEEE Transactions on Industrial Informatics (2010)
9. Guthaus, M.R., Ringenberg, J.S., Ernst, D., Austin, T.M., Mudge, T., Brown, R.B.: MiBench: A free, commercially representative embedded benchmark suite. In: IEEE International Workshop on In Workload Characterization (WWC), pp. 3–14 (2001)
10. Kopetz, H.: Event-Triggered Versus Time-Triggered Real-Time Systems. In: Karshmer, A.I., Nehmer, J. (eds.) Dagstuhl Seminar 1991. LNCS, vol. 563, pp. 87–101. Springer, Heidelberg (1991)
11. Li, M., Achteren, T.V., Brockmeyer, E., Catthoor, F.: Statistical Performance Analysis and Estimation of Coarse Grain Parallel Multimedia Processing System. In: Proc. of the 12th IEEE Real-Time and Embedded Technology and Applications Symposium (RTAS), pp. 277–288. IEEE Computer Society, Washington, DC (2006)
12. McCall, G.: Misra-C: 2004. MIRA Limited, Warwickshire (2004)
13. Mok, A.: Firm Real-time Systems. ACM Comput. Surv. 28 (December 1996)
14. Natarajan, S.: Imprecise and Approximate Computation. Kluwer Academic Publishers, Norwell (1995)
15. Navabpour, S., Wu, C.W.W., Bonakdarpour, B., Fischmeister, S.: Efficient Techniques for Near-Optimal Instrumentation in Time-Triggered Runtime Verification. In: Khurshid, S., Sen, K. (eds.) RV 2011. LNCS, vol. 7186, pp. 208–222. Springer, Heidelberg (2012)
16. Radio Technical Commission for Aeronautics (RTCA). Software Considerations in Airborne Systems and Equipment Certification (December 1992)
17. Wilhelm, R., Engblom, J., Ermedahl, A., Holsti, N., Thesing, S., Whalley, D., Bernat, G., Ferdinand, C., Heckmann, R., Mitra, T., Mueller, F., Puaut, I., Puschner, P., Staschulat, J., Stenström, P.: The Worst-case Execution-time Problem—Overview of Methods and Survey of Tools. Trans. on Embedded Computing Sys. 7(3), 1–53 (2008)

Teaching Runtime Verification

Martin Leucker

Universtität zu Lübeck
Institut für Softwaretechnik und Programmiersprachen

Abstract. In this paper and its accompanying tutorial, we discuss the topic of teaching runtime verification. The aim of the tutorial is twofold. On the one hand, a condensed version of a course currently given by the author will be given within the available tutorial time, giving an idea about the topics of the course. On the other hand, the experience gained by giving the course should also be presented and discussed with the audience. The overall goal is to simplify the work of colleagues developing standard and well accepted courses in the field of runtime verification.

1 Introduction

Runtime Verification (RV) has become a mature field within the last decades. It aims at checking correctness properties based on the actual execution of a software or hardware system.

Research on runtime verification is traditionally presented at formal methods conferences like CAV (computer aided verification) or TACAS (tools and algorithms for the analysis of systems), or, software engineering conferences like ICSE or ASE. Starting in 2001, the RV community has formed its own scientific event, the runtime verification workshop, which has in the meantime been upgraded to the runtime verification conference. There is a community forming webpage that is available under the address www.runtime-verification.org and first definitions and explanations entered their way into the online dictionary wikipedia. Last but not least, several courses on runtime verification are given to PhD, master, or even bachelor students at several universities.

So far, however, no dedicated text book on the topic of runtime verification is available and actual courses on runtime verification are still to be considered preliminary as the field of runtime verification is still undergoing rapid changes and no kernel material of the field has been identified, or, at least has not been fixed by the community.

In this paper and its accompanying tutorial, we discuss the topic of *teaching runtime verification*. It is based on the author's course given at the University of Lübeck. The course took place once a week, each time 1.5 hours, and in total about 14 times. The aim of this paper and its accompanying tutorial is twofold. On the one hand, a condensed version of the course should be shown, giving an idea about the outline and topics of the course. On the other hand, the experience gained by giving the course are also presented and discussed with the audience. The overall goal of the tutorial is to simplify the work of colleagues developing standard and well accepted courses in the field of runtime verification.

S. Khurshid and K. Sen (Eds.): RV 2011, LNCS 7186, pp. 34–48, 2012.

Content of the RV course

1. The tutorial/course starts with a short discussion on typical areas that are preferably addressed at runtime. It is motivated why static verification techniques must often be encompassed by runtime verification techniques.
2. Runtime verification is defined and a taxonomy for runtime verification is developed. The taxonomy will be the basis for getting a systematic picture on the field of runtime verification and may also be used to organize the different contributions by the runtime verification community. Runtime verification is identified as a research discipline aiming at synthesizing monitors from high level specifications, integrating them into existing execution frameworks, and using the results of monitors for steering or guiding a program. It may work on finite, finite but continuously expanding, or on prefixes of infinite traces.
3. In the subsequent part of the tutorial/course synthesis techniques for Linear Temporal Logic (LTL) will be presented. Both, approaches based on rewriting the formula to check and approaches based on translating the formula at hand into an automaton will be briefly described. Moreover the conceptual difference between these two fundamental approaches will be explained.
4. The second part of the tutorial deals with integrating monitors into running systems and with techniques for steering the executing system based on the results of monitors.
5. In the third part we will list existing runtime verification frame works, which will eventually be classified with respect to the initially developed taxonomy.

Intended Audience. The tutorial is especially intended for current or future lecturers in the field of runtime verification. At the same time, as the main ideas of the underlying course are taught, it is of interest to advanced master students and PhD students for getting an introduction to the field of runtime verification. Finally, researchers active in formal methods who want to get comprehensive picture on the field of runtime verification may benefit from the tutorial as well.

2   The Virtue of Runtime Verification

The course starts with a short discussion on typical areas that are preferably addressed at runtime. It is motivated why static verification must often be encompassed by runtime verification techniques. We do so by listing certain application domains, highlighting the distinguishing features of runtime verification:

– The verification verdict, as obtained by model checking or theorem proving, is often referring to a model of the real system under analysis, since applying these techniques directly to the real implementation would be intractable. The model typically reflects most important aspects of the corresponding implementation, and checking the model for correctness gives useful insights to the implementation. Nevertheless, the implementation might behave slightly different than predicted by the model. Runtime verification may then be used to easily check the actual execution of the system, to make sure that the implementation really meets its correctness properties. Thus, runtime verification may act as a partner to theorem proving and model checking.

- Often, some information is available only at runtime or is conveniently checked at runtime. For example, whenever library code with no accompanying source code is part of the system to build, only a vague description of the behavior of the code might be available. In such cases, runtime verification is an alternative to theorem proving and model checking.
- The behavior of an application may depend heavily on the environment of the target system, but a precise description of this environment might not exist. Then it is not possible to only test the system in an adequate manner. Moreover, formal correctness proofs by model checking or theorem proving may only be achievable by taking certain assumptions on the behavior of the environment—which should be checked at runtime. In this scenario, runtime verification outperforms classical testing and adds on formal correctness proofs by model checking and theorem proving.
- In the case of systems where security is important or in the case of safety-critical systems, it is useful also to monitor behavior or properties that have been statically proved or tested, mainly to have a double check that everything goes well: Here, runtime verification acts as a partner of theorem proving, model checking, and testing.

3   Runtime Verification—Definition and Taxonomy

3.1   Towards a Definition

A *software failure* is the deviation between the *observed* behavior and the *required* behavior of the software system. A *fault* is defined as the deviation between the current behavior and the expected behavior, which is typically identified by a deviation of the current and the expected state of the system. A fault might lead to a failure, but not necessarily. An error, on the other hand, is a mistake made by a human that results in a fault and possibly in a failure [1].

According to IEEE [2], *verification* comprises all techniques suitable for showing that a system satisfies its specification. Traditional verification techniques comprise theorem proving [3], model checking [4], and testing [5,6]. A relatively new direction of verification is *runtime verification*,[1] which manifested itself within the previous years as a *lightweight* verification technique:

Definition 1 (Runtime Verification). Runtime verification *is the discipline of computer science that deals with the study, development, and application of those verification techniques that allow checking whether a run of a system under scrutiny (SUS) satisfies or violates a given correctness property. Its distinguishing research effort lies in* synthesizing monitors from high level specifications.

---

[1] http://www.runtime-verification.org

Monitors. A run of a system is understood as a possibly infinite sequence of the system's states, which are formed by current variable assignments, or as the sequence of (input/output) actions a system is emitting or performing. Formally, a run may be considered as a possibly infinite *word* or *trace*. An *execution* of a system is a *finite prefix* of a run and, formally, it is a finite trace. When running a program, we can only observe executions, which, however, restrict the corresponding evolving run as being their prefix. While, in verification, we are interested in the question whether a run, and more generally, all runs of a system adhere to given correctness properties, executions are the primary object analyzed in the setting of RV.

Checking whether an execution meets a correctness property is typically performed using a *monitor*. In its simplest form, a monitor decides whether the current execution satisfies a given correctness property by outputting either *yes/true* or *no/false*. Formally, when $[\![\varphi]\!]$ denotes the set of valid executions given by property φ, runtime verification boils down to checking whether the execution w is an element of $[\![\varphi]\!]$. Thus, in its mathematical essence, runtime verification answers the *word problem*, i. e. the problem whether a given word is included in some language. However, to cover richer approaches to RV, we define the notion of monitors in a slightly more general form:

Definition 2 (Monitor). *A* monitor *is a device that reads a finite trace and yields a certain* verdict.

Here, a verdict is typically a truth value from some truth domain. A truth domain is a lattice with a unique top element *true* and a unique bottom element *false*. This definition covers the standard two-valued truth domain $\mathbb{B} = \{true, false\}$ but also fits for monitors yielding a probability in $[0, 1]$ with which a given correctness property is satisfied (see Section 4.1 for a precise definition). Sometimes, one might be even more liberal and consider also verdicts that are not elements of a truth domain.

3.2 Taxonomy

A taxonomy may be used to get a systematic account to the field of runtime verification and to organize the different contributions by the RV community into a global picture. Figure 1 shows a taxonomy that is briefly described in the following.

First, runtime verification may work on (i) finite (terminated), (ii) finite but continuously expanding, or (iii) on prefixes of infinite traces. For the two latter cases, a monitor should adhere to the two maxims *impartiality* and *anticipation*. *Impartiality* requires that a finite trace is not evaluated to *true* or, respectively *false*, if there still exists an (infinite) continuation leading to another verdict. *Anticipation* requires that once every (infinite) continuation of a finite trace leads to the same verdict, then the finite trace evaluates to this very same verdict. Intuitively, the first maxim postulates that a monitor only decides for *false*—meaning that a misbehavior has been observed—or *true*—meaning that the current behavior fulfills the correctness property, regardless of how it continues—only if this

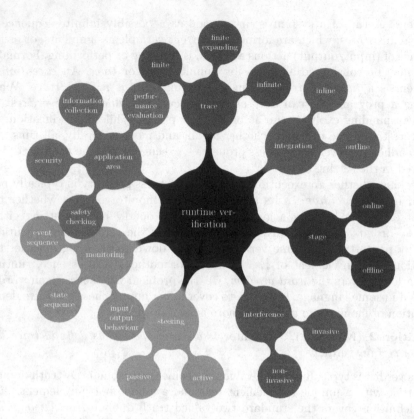

Fig. 1. Taxonomy of runtime verification

is indeed the case. Clearly, this maxim requires to have at least three different truth values: *true*, *false*, and *inconclusive*, but of course more than three truth values might give a more precise assessment of correctness. The second maxim requires a monitor to indeed report *true* or *false*, if the correctness property is indeed violated or satisfied. In simple words, *impartiality* and *anticipation*, guarantee that the semantics is neither premature nor overcautious in its evaluations.

RV approaches may differ in what part of a run is actually monitored. For example, a system may be analyzed with respect to its *input/output behavior*, one of its *state sequences*, or wrt. a sequence of *events* related to the system's execution.

A monitor may on one hand be used to check the *current* execution of a system. In this setting, which is termed *online monitoring*, the monitor should be designed to consider executions in an *incremental fashion*. On the other hand, a monitor may work on a (finite set of) *recorded* execution(s), in which case we speak of *offline monitoring*.

Synthesized monitoring code may be interweaved with the program to check, i.e. it may be *inlined*, or, it may be used to externally synthesize a monitoring device, i.e., it may be *outlined*. Clearly, inlined monitors act online.

The monitor typically interferes with the system to observe, as it runs, for example, on the same CPU as the SUS. However, using additional computation resources, monitoring might not change the behavior of the SUS. We distinguish these two cases using the terms *invasive* and *non-invasive* monitoring.

While, to our understanding, runtime verification is mainly concerned with the synthesis of efficiently operating monitors, RV frameworks may be distinguished by whether the resulting monitor is just observing the program's execution and reporting failures, i.e., it is *passive*, or, whether the monitor's verdict may be used to actually steer or heal the system's execution, i.e., it is *active*.

Runtime verification may be used for different applications. Most often, it is used to check *safety conditions*. Similarly, it may be used to ensure *security conditions*. However, it is equally suited to simply *collect information* of the system's execution, or, for *performance evaluation* purposes.

4   Runtime Verification for LTL

As considered the heart of runtime verification, the main focus of an RV course lies on synthesis procedures yielding monitors from high-level specifications. We outline several monitor synthesis procedures for Linear-time Temporal Logic (LTL, [7]). In general, two main approaches can be found for synthesizing monitoring code: Monitors may either be given in terms of an automaton, which is precomputed from a given correctness specification. Alternatively, the correctness specification may be taken directly and *rewritten* in a tableau-like fashion when monitoring the SUS. We give examples for both approaches.

4.1   Truth Domains

We consider the traditional two-valued semantics with truth values *true*, denoted with $\top$, and *false*, denoted with $\bot$, next to truth values giving more information to which degree a formula is satisfied or not. Since truth values should be combinable in terms of Boolean operations expressed by the connectives of the underlying logic, these truth values should form a certain lattice.

A *lattice* is a partially ordered set $(\mathcal{L}, \sqsubseteq)$ where for each $x, y \in \mathcal{L}$, there exists (i) a unique *greatest lower bound* (glb), which is called the *meet* of x and y, and is denoted with $x \sqcap y$, and (ii) a unique *least upper bound* (lub), which is called the *join* of x and y, and is denoted with $x \sqcup y$. A lattice is called *finite* iff $\mathcal{L}$ is finite. Every finite lattice has a well-defined unique least element, called *bottom*, denoted with $\bot$, and analogously a greatest element, called *top*, denoted with $\top$. A lattice is *distributive*, iff $x \sqcap (y \sqcup z) = (x \sqcap y) \sqcup (x \sqcap z)$, and, dually, $x \sqcup (y \sqcap z) = (x \sqcup y) \sqcap (x \sqcup z)$. In a *de Morgan* lattice, every element x has a unique *dual* element $\overline{x}$, such that $\overline{\overline{x}} = x$ and $x \sqsubseteq y$ implies $\overline{y} \sqsubseteq \overline{x}$. As the common denominator of the semantics for the subsequently defined logics is a finite de Morgan lattice, we define:

Definition 3 (Truth domain). *We call $\mathcal{L}$ a* truth domain, *if it is a finite de Morgan lattice.*

4.2   LTL—Syntax and Common Semantics

As a starting point for all subsequently defined logics, we first recall linear temporal logic (LTL).

For the remainder of this paper, let AP be a finite and non-empty set of *atomic propositions* and $\Sigma = 2^{AP}$ a finite *alphabet*. We write a_i for any single element of Σ, i.e., a_i is a possibly empty subset of propositions taken from AP.

Finite traces (which we call interchangeably words) over Σ are elements of Σ^*, usually denoted with $u, u', u_1, u_2, \ldots$ The empty trace is denoted with ϵ. Infinite traces are elements of Σ^ω, usually denoted with $w, w', w_1, w_2, \ldots$ For some infinite trace $w = a_0 a_1 \ldots$, we denote with w^i the suffix $a_i a_{i+1} \ldots$ In case of a finite trace $u = a_0 a_1 \ldots a_{n-1}$, u^i denotes the suffix $a_i a_{i+1} \ldots a_{n-1}$ for $0 \leq i < n$ and the empty string ϵ for $n \leq i$.

The set of LTL formulae is defined using *true*, the atomic propositions $p \in$ AP, *disjunction*, *next* X, and *until* U, as positive operators, together with *negation* $\neg$. We moreover add dual operators, namely *false*, $\neg p$, *weak next* $\bar{X}$, and *release* R, respectively:

Definition 4 (Syntax of LTL formulae). *Let p be an atomic proposition from a finite set of atomic propositions* AP. *The set of LTL formulae, denoted with LTL, is inductively defined by the following grammar:*

$$\varphi ::= true \mid p \mid \varphi \vee \varphi \mid \varphi\, U\, \varphi \mid X\varphi$$
$$\varphi ::= false \mid \neg p \mid \varphi \wedge \varphi \mid \varphi\, R\, \varphi \mid \bar{X}\varphi$$
$$\varphi ::= \neg\varphi$$

In a corresponding course, typically further operators are introduced as abbreviations like *finally* F and *globally* G etc.

In the sequel, we introduce several semantic functions, both classical versions for finite and infinite traces and versions adapted to suit the needs in runtime verification. To this end, we consider linear temporal logics $\mathcal{L}$ with a syntax as in Definition 4, together with a semantic function $[\_\models\_]_\mathcal{L} : \Sigma^{\omega/*} \times \text{LTL} \to \mathbb{B}_\mathcal{L}$ that yields an element of the truth domain $\mathbb{B}_\mathcal{L}$, given an infinite or finite trace and an LTL formula. The logics considered in the following have a common part, but differ in certain aspects. The common part of the semantics is shown in Figure 2.

For two formulae $\varphi, \psi \in \text{LTL}$, we say that φ is equivalent to ψ, denoted with $\varphi \equiv_\mathcal{L} \psi$, iff for all $w \in \Sigma^{\omega/*}$, we have $[w \models \varphi]_\mathcal{L} = [w \models \psi]_\mathcal{L}$.

4.3   LTL on Finite Traces

Let us first turn our attention to linear temporal logics over finite traces. We start by recalling a finite version of LTL on finite traces described by Manna and Pnueli [8], here called FLTL.

When interpreting LTL formulae over finite traces, the question arises, how to understand $X\varphi$ when a word consists of a single letter, since then, no next position exists on which one is supposed to consider φ. The classical way to deal with this situation, as apparent for example in Kamp's work [9] is to understand

Boolean constants

$$[w \models true]_{\mathcal{L}} = \top$$
$$[w \models false]_{\mathcal{L}} = \bot$$

Boolean combinations

$$[w \models \neg\varphi]_{\mathcal{L}} = \overline{[w \models \varphi]_{\mathcal{L}}}$$
$$[w \models \varphi \vee \psi]_{\mathcal{L}} = [w \models \varphi]_{\mathcal{L}} \sqcup [w \models \psi]_{\mathcal{L}}$$
$$[w \models \varphi \wedge \psi]_{\mathcal{L}} = [w \models \varphi]_{\mathcal{L}} \sqcap [w \models \psi]_{\mathcal{L}}$$

atomic propositions

$$[w \models p]_{\omega} = \begin{cases} \top & \text{if } p \in a_0 \\ \bot & \text{if } p \notin a_0 \end{cases} \qquad [w \models \neg p]_{\omega} = \begin{cases} \top & \text{if } p \notin a_0 \\ \bot & \text{if } p \in a_0 \end{cases}$$

until/release

$$[w \models \varphi\ U\ \psi]_{\mathcal{L}} = \begin{cases} \top & \text{there is a } k, 0 \leq k < |w| : [w^k \models \psi]_{\mathcal{L}} = \top \text{ and} \\ & \text{for all } l \text{ with } 0 \leq l < k : [w^l \models \varphi] = \top \\ \bot & \text{else} \end{cases}$$

$$[w \models \varphi\ R\ \psi]_{\mathcal{L}} = \begin{cases} \top & \text{for all } k, 0 \leq k < |w| : [w^k \models \psi]_{\mathcal{L}} = \top \text{ or} \\ & \text{there is a } k, 0 \leq k < |w| : [w^k \models \varphi]_{\mathcal{L}} = \top \text{ and} \\ & \text{for all } l \text{ with } 0 \leq l \leq k : [w^l \models \psi] = \top \\ \bot & \text{else} \end{cases}$$

Fig. 2. Semantics of LTL formulae over a finite or infinite trace $w = a_0 a_1 \ldots \in \Sigma^{*/\omega}$

X as a *strong* next operator, which is false if no further position exists. Manna and Pnueli suggest in [8] to enrich the standard framework by adding a dual operator, the weak next $\bar{X}$, which allows to smoothly translate formulae into negation normal form. In other words, the *strong* X operator is used to express with $X\varphi$ that a next state must exist and that this next state has to satisfy property φ. In contrast, the *weak* $\bar{X}$ operator in $\bar{X}\varphi$ says that if there is a next state, then this next state has to satisfy the property φ. We call the resulting logic FLTL defined over the set of LTL formulae (Definition 4) FLTL.

Definition 5 (Semantics of FLTL [8]). *Let $u = a_0 \ldots a_{n-1} \in \Sigma^*$ denote a finite trace of length n, with $u \neq \epsilon$. The truth value of an FLTL formula φ wrt. u, denoted with $[u \models \varphi]_F$, is an element of $\mathbb{B}_2$ and is inductively defined as follows: Boolean constants, Boolean combinations, and atomic propositions are defined as for LTL (see Figure 2, taking u instead of w). (Weak) next are defined as shown in Figure 3.*

Let us first record that the semantics of FLTL is *not* given for the empty word. Moreover, note that a single letter does satisfy *true* but does not satisfy $X\ true$. Also, $[u \models \neg X\varphi]_F = [u \models \bar{X}\neg\varphi]_F$ follows from LTL whenever $|u| > 1$

(weak) next

$$[u \models X\varphi]_F = \begin{cases} [u^1 \models \varphi]_F & \text{if } u^1 \neq \epsilon \\ \bot & \text{otherwise} \end{cases} \qquad [u \models \bar{X}\varphi]_F = \begin{cases} [u^1 \models \varphi]_F & \text{if } u^1 \neq \epsilon \\ \top & \text{otherwise} \end{cases}$$

Fig. 3. Semantics of FLTL formulae over a trace $u = a_0 \ldots a_{n-1} \in \Sigma^*$

and from inspecting the semantics in Figure 3 when $|u| = 1$. Thus, every FLTL formula can be transformed into an equivalent formula in negation normal form.

Monitors for LTL on finite traces The simple answer here is to say that for a finite word, the semantics of an LTL formula can immediately be computed from the semantics definition. However, a slightly more clever way is presented in the next subsection.

4.4   LTL on Finite But Expanding Traces

Let us now consider an LTL semantics adapted towards monitoring finite but expanding traces. Especially when monitoring online, a run of SUS may be given letter-by-letter, say, state-by-state, event-by-event etc. A corresponding monitoring procedure should ideally be able to process such an input string letter-by-letter and should be impartial wrt. the forthcoming letters to receive.

The idea, which is already used in [10], is to use a four-valued semantics, consisting of the truth values *true* ($\top$), *false* ($\bot$), *possibly true* ($\top^p$), and *possibly false* ($\bot^p$). The latter two values are used to signal the truth value of the input word wrt. the two valued semantics *provided the word will terminate now*. More specifically, the four-valued semantics differs from the two-valued semantics shown in the previous subsection only be yielding *possibly false* rather than *false* at the end of a word for the strong next operator and *possibly true* rather than *true* for the weak next operator. We sometimes call the resulting logic FLTL$_4$.

Definition 6 (Semantics of FLTL$_4$). *Let $u = a_0 \ldots a_{n-1} \in \Sigma^*$ denote a finite trace of length n, with $u \neq \epsilon$. The truth value of an FLTL$_4$ formula φ wrt. u, denoted with $[u \models \varphi]_4$, is an element of $\mathbb{B}_4$ and is inductively defined as follows: Boolean constants, Boolean combinations, and atomic propositions are defined as for LTL (see Figure 2, taking u instead of w). (Weak) next are defined as shown in Figure 4.*

Monitoring expanding traces. While for a given finite trace, the semantics of an LTL formula could be computed according to the semantics definition, it is important for practical applications, especially in online verification, to compute the semantics in an incremental, more precisely, in a left-to-right fashion for the given trace.

(weak) next

$$[u \models X\varphi]_4 = \begin{cases} [u^1 \models \varphi]_4 & \text{if } u^1 \neq \epsilon \\ \bot^p & \text{otherwise} \end{cases} \qquad [u \models \bar{X}\varphi]_4 = \begin{cases} [u^1 \models \varphi]_4 & \text{if } u^1 \neq \epsilon \\ \top^p & \text{otherwise} \end{cases}$$

Fig. 4. Semantics of FLTL_4 formulae over a trace $u = a_0 \ldots a_{n-1} \in \Sigma^*$

To do so, we provide a *rewriting* based approach (see also [11]). Thanks to the equivalences $\varphi\ U\ \psi \equiv \psi \vee (\varphi \wedge X(\varphi\ U\ \psi))$ and $\varphi\ R\ \psi \equiv \psi \wedge (\varphi \vee \bar{X}(\varphi\ R\ \psi))$ for until and release, we may always assume that the given formula is a boolean combination of atomic propositions and next-state formulas. Now, given a single, presumably final letter of a trace, the atomic propositions may be evaluated as to whether the letter satisfies the proposition. Each (strong) next-formula, i.e., a formula starting with a strong next, evaluates to *possibly false*, while each weak-next formula evaluates to *possibly true*. The truth value of the formula is then the boolean combination of the respective truth values, reading $\wedge$ as $\sqcap$, $\vee$ as $\sqcup$, and $\neg$ as $\bar{\ }$. Likewise, the formula to check may be rewritten towards a formula to be checked when the next letter is available. An atomic proposition is evaluated as before yielding the formulas *true* or *false*. A formula of the form $X\varphi$ or $\bar{X}\varphi$ is rewritten to φ. In Algorithm 1, a corresponding function is described in pseudo code, yielding for the formula to check and a single letter a tuple consisting of the current truth value in the first component and the formula to check with the next letter in the second component.

The same algorithm may also be used for evaluating the (two-valued) semantics of an FLTL formula in a left-to-right fashion, by mapping *possibly true* to *true* and *possibly false* to *false*, when reaching the end of the word.

4.5   LTL on Infinitive Traces

LTL formulae over infinite traces are interpreted as usual over the two valued truth domain $\mathbb{B}_2$.

Definition 7 (Semantics of LTL [7]). *The semantics of LTL formulae over infinite traces $w = a_0 a_1 \ldots \in \Sigma^\omega$ is given by the function $[\_ \models \_]_\omega : \Sigma^\omega \times LTL \to \mathbb{B}_2$, which is defined inductively as shown in Figures 2,5.*

Inspecting the semantics, we observe that there is no difference of X and $\bar{X}$ in LTL over infinite traces. Recall that $\bar{X}$ acts differently when finite words are considered.

We call $w \in \Sigma^\omega$ a *model* of φ iff $[w \models \varphi] = \top$. For every LTL formula φ, its set of models, denoted with $\mathcal{L}(\varphi)$, is a regular set of infinite traces which is accepted by a corresponding Büchi automaton [12,13].

Algorithm 1. Evaluating FLTL4 for each subsequent letter

```
evalFLTL4 true    a = (⊤,⊤)
evalFLTL4 false   a = (⊥,⊥)
evalFLTL4 p       a = ((p in a),(p in a))
evalFLTL4 ¬φ      a = let (valPhi,phiRew) = evalFLTL4 φ a
                      in (valPhi,¬phiRew)
evalFLTL4 φ∨ψ     a = let
                          (valPhi,phiRew) = evalFLTL4 φ a
                          (valPsi,psiRew) = evalFLTL4 ψ a
                      in (valPhi ⊔ valPsi,phiRew ∨ psiRew)
evalFLTL4 φ∧ψ     a = let
                          (valPhi,phiRew) = evalFLTL4 φ a
                          (valPsi,psiRew) = evalFLTL4 ψ a
                      in (valPhi ⊓ valPsi,phiRew ∧ psiRew)
evalFLTL4 φ U ψ   a = evalFLTL4 ψ∨(φ∧X(φ U ψ)) a
evalFLTL4 φ R ψ   a = evalFLTL4 ψ∧(φ∨X̄(φ R ψ)) a
evalFLTL4 Xφ      a = (⊥^p,φ)
evalFLTL4 X̄φ      a = (⊤^p,φ)
```

(weak) next

$$[w \models X\varphi]_\omega = [w^1 \models \varphi]_\omega$$
$$[w \models \bar{X}\varphi]_\omega = [w^1 \models \varphi]_\omega$$

Fig. 5. Semantics of LTL formulae over an infinite traces $w = a_0 a_1 \ldots \in \Sigma^\omega$

LTL₃ In[14], we proposed LTL_3 as an LTL logic with a semantics for finite traces, which follows the idea that a finite trace is a prefix of a so-far unknown infinite trace. More specifically, LTL_3 uses the standard syntax of LTL as defined in Definition 4 but employs a semantics function $[u \models \varphi]_3$ which evaluates each formula φ and each finite trace u of length n to one of the truth values in $\mathbb{B}_3 = \{\top, \bot, ?\}$. $\mathbb{B}_3 = \{\top, \bot, ?\}$ is defined as a de Morgan lattice with $\bot \sqsubset ? \sqsubset \top$, and with $\bot$ and $\top$ being complementary to each other while $?$ being complementary to itself.

The idea of the semantics for LTL_3 is as follows: If every infinite trace with prefix u evaluates to the same truth value $\top$ or $\bot$, then $[u \models \varphi]_3$ also evaluates to this truth value. Otherwise $[u \models \varphi]_3$ evaluates to $?$, i.e., we have $[u \models \varphi]_3 =?$ if different continuations of u yield different truth values. This leads to the following definition:

Definition 8 (Semantics of LTL₃). *Let $u = a_0 \ldots a_{n-1} \in \Sigma^*$ denote a finite trace of length n. The truth value of a LTL_3 formula φ wrt. u, denoted with $[u \models \varphi]_3$, is an element of $\mathbb{B}_3$ and defined as follows:*

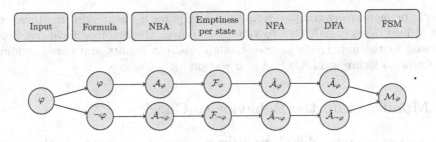

Fig. 6. The procedure for getting $[u \models \varphi]$ for a given φ

$$[u \models \varphi]_3 = \begin{cases} \top & \textit{if } \forall w \in \Sigma^\omega : [uw \models \varphi]_\omega = \top \\ \bot & \textit{if } \forall w \in \Sigma^\omega : [uw \models \varphi]_\omega = \bot \\ ? & \textit{otherwise.} \end{cases}$$

Monitoring of LTL₃. We briefly sketch the monitor synthesis procedure developed in [15]. The synthesis procedure follows the automata-based approach in synthesizing a Moore machine as a monitor for a given correctness property. While, in general, also a Moore machine could have been generated for FLTL as well, we refrained to do so for two reasons: First, the presented procedure for FLTL works *on-the-fly* and thus might be more efficient in practice. Second, both a rewriting approach and an automaton-based approach should be presented in the underlying course.

For LTL₃, an automaton approach is more adequate due to the fact that LTL₃ is *anticipatory*. Anticipation typically requires rewrite steps followed by a further analysis easily done using automata theory. See [16] for a more elaborate discussion of these issues in the context of linear temporal logic.

The synthesis procedure for LTL₃ first translates a given formula into the Büchi automaton accepting all its models. Reading a finite prefix of a run, using the corresponding automaton, *false* can be derived for the given formula, whenever there is no accepting continuation in the respective Büchi automaton. Likewise, *true* can be derived, when, for a given finite word, the automaton accepting all counter examples reaches only states the have no accepting continuation anymore. Using this idea, the corresponding Büchi automata can be translated into NFA, then DFA, and, finally into a (minimal) FSM (Moore machine) as *the* (unique) monitor for a given LTL₃ formula (see Figure 6).

While the sketched procedure should be improved in practical implementations, the chosen approach manifests itself beneficial for teaching, as a simple, clear, roadmap is followed.

4.6   Extensions

The studied versions of LTL were chosen to show certain aspects of monitoring executions. For practical applications, several extensions such as real-time aspects or monitoring computations, which requires a meaningful treatment of data values, is essential. Due to time constraints, these topics have not been adressed in the underlying course, though research results and corresponding RV frameworks are available (see also Section 6).

5   Monitors and the Behavior to Check

This part of the tutorial deals with the problem of integrating monitors into SUS and with techniques to steer the executing system by means of the results of monitors. This aspect of runtime verification was discussed only briefly in the corresponding runtime verification course. The main goal was to give a general overview of approaches for connecting monitors to existing systems.

Monitoring systems. Generally, we distinguish using *instrumentation*, using *logging APIs*, using *trace tools*, or dedicated *tracing hardware*. Popular in runtime verification is the use of code instrumentation, for which either the *source code*, the (virtual) *byte code*, or the *binary code* of an application is enriched by the synthesized monitoring code. Code instrumentation allows a tight integration with the running system and is especially useful when monitoring online. However, code instrumentation affects the runtime of the original system. It is thus not recommend whenever the underlying systems has been verified to meet certain safety critical timing behavior. Using standard logging frameworks, like *log4j*, allows to decompose the issue of logging information of the running system from the issue of analyzing the logged information with respect to failures. In principal, the logged information may be stored and analyzed later, or, using additional computing ressources online, thus not affecting system's execution. Logging APIs, however, require the source code of the SUS. Tracing tools like Unix' *strace* run the system under scrutiny in a dedicated fashion an provide logging information. Again, the timing behavior of the system may be influenced. The advantage of such tracing tools lies in their general applicability, the disadvantage in their restricted logging information. Finally, dedicated tracing hardware may be used to monitor a system *non-invasively* [17].

Steering systems. Whenever a monitor reports a failure, one might be interested in responding to the failure, perhaps even healing the failure. Clearly, this goal is only meaningful in an online monitoring approach. We distinguish the following forms of responding to failures: *informing*, where only further information is presented to a tester or user of a system, *throwing exceptions* for systems that can deal with exceptions, or *executing code*, which may be user provided or synthesized automatically. The latter approach is well supported by frameworks using code instrumentation as healing code may easily be provided together with the monitoring property.

Runtime verification frameworks may differ in their understanding of failures. Most frameworks identify failure and fault. Then, whenever a monitor reports a failure and thus a fault, healing code may be executed to deal with the fault.

When distinguishing between failures and faults, it may be beneficial to start a *diagnosis* identifying a fault, whenever a monitor reports a failure (see [18]).

6   Existing Frameworks

In the third part we will visit existing runtime verification frame works and map the approaches to the initially developed taxonomy. Due to the limited space of the proceedings, we only list the considered frameworks in an alphabetical order: (i) Eagle [19] (ii) J-LO [20] (iii) Larva [21] (iv) LogScope [22] (v) LoLa [23] (vi) MAC [24] (vii) MOP [25] (viii) RulerR [26] (ix) Temporal Rover [10] (x) TraceContract [27] (xi) Tracesmatches [28] .

Acknowledgement. We thank Klaus Havelund for many fruitful discussions on the topic of this paper.

References

1. Delgado, N., Gates, A.Q., Roach, S.: A taxonomy and catalog of runtime software-fault monitoring tools. IEEE Transactions on Software Engineering (TSE) 30(12), 859–872 (2004)
2. IEEE Std 1012 - 2004 IEEE standard for software verificiation and validation. IEEE Std 1012-2004 (Revision of IEEE Std 1012-1998), 1–110 (2005)
3. Bertot, Y., Castéran, P.: Interactive Theorem Proving and Program Development Coq'Art: The Calculus of Inductive Constructions. An EATCS Series. Springer, Heidelberg (2004)
4. Clarke, E.M., Grumberg, O., Peled, D.A.: Model Checking. The MIT Press, Cambridge (1999)
5. Myers, G.J., Badgett, T., Thomas, T.M., Sandler, C.: The Art of Software Testing, 2nd edn. John Wiley and Sons (2004)
6. Broy, M., Jonsson, B., Katoen, J.P., Leucker, M., Pretschner, A. (eds.): Model-Based Testing of Reactive Systems. LNCS, vol. 3472, pp. 391–438. Springer, Heidelberg (2005)
7. Pnueli, A.: The temporal logic of programs. In: Proceedings of the 18th IEEE Symposium on the Foundations of Computer Science (FOCS-77), October 31-November 2, pp. 46–57. IEEE Computer Society Press, Providence (1977)
8. Manna, Z., Pnueli, A.: Temporal Verification of Reactive Systems: Safety. Springer, New York (1995)
9. Kamp, H.W.: Tense Logic and the Theory of Linear Order. PhD thesis, University of California, Los Angeles (1968)
10. Drusinsky, D.: The Temporal Rover and the Atg Rover. In: Havelund, K., Penix, J., Visser, W. (eds.) SPIN 2000. LNCS, vol. 1885, pp. 323–330. Springer, Heidelberg (2000)
11. Geilen, M.: On the construction of monitors for temporal logic properties. Electronic Notes on Theoretical Computer Science (ENTCS) 55(2) (2001)
12. Vardi, M.Y., Wolper, P.: An automata-theoretic approach to automatic program verification. In: Symposium on Logic in Computer Science (LICS 1986), pp. 332–345. IEEE Computer Society Press, Washington, D.C (1986)

13. Vardi, M.Y.: An Automata-Theoretic Approach to Linear Temporal Logic. In: Moller, F., Birtwistle, G. (eds.) Logics for Concurrency. LNCS, vol. 1043, pp. 238–266. Springer, Heidelberg (1996)
14. Bauer, A., Leucker, M., Schallhart, C.: Monitoring of Real-Time Properties. In: Arun-Kumar, S., Garg, N. (eds.) FSTTCS 2006. LNCS, vol. 4337, pp. 260–272. Springer, Heidelberg (2006)
15. Bauer, A., Leucker, M., Schallhart, C.: Runtime verification for LTL and TLTL. ACM Transactions on Software Engineering and Methodology (TOSEM) 20(4) (July 2011) (in press)
16. Bauer, A., Leucker, M., Schallhart, C.: Comparing LTL semantics for runtime verification. Journal of Logic and Computation 20(3), 651–674 (2010)
17. Hochberger, C., Leucker, M., Weiss, A., Backasch, R.: A generic hardware architecture for runtime verification. In: ECSI (ed.) Proceedings of the 2010 Conference on System, Software, SoC and Silicon Debug, pp. 79–84 (2010)
18. Bauer, A., Leucker, M., Schallhart, C.: Model-based runtime analysis of distributed reactive systems. In: Proceedings of the Australian Software Engineering Conference (ASWEC 2006), pp. 243–252. IEEE (2006)
19. Barringer, H., Goldberg, A., Havelund, K., Sen, K.: Rule-Based Runtime Verification. In: Steffen, B., Levi, G. (eds.) VMCAI 2004. LNCS, vol. 2937, pp. 44–57. Springer, Heidelberg (2004)
20. Stolz, V., Bodden, E.: Temporal Assertions using AspectJ. In: Fifth Workshop on Runtime Verification (RV 2005). ENTCS, Elsevier (2005)
21. Colombo, C., Pace, G.J., Schneider, G.: Larva — safer monitoring of real-time java programs (tool paper). In: Hung, D.V., Krishnan, P. (eds.) SEFM, pp. 33–37. IEEE Computer Society (2009)
22. Barringer, H., Groce, A., Havelund, K., Smith, M.H.: An entry point for formal methods: Specification and analysis of event logs. In: Bujorianu, M.L., Fisher, M. (eds.) FMA. EPTCS, vol. 20, pp. 16–21 (2009)
23. D'Angelo, B., Sankaranarayanan, S., Sánchez, C., Robinson, W., Finkbeiner, B., Sipma, H.B., Mehrotra, S., Manna, Z.: LOLA: runtime monitoring of synchronous systems. In: Proceedings of the 12th International Symposium on Temporal Representation and Reasoning (TIME 2005), pp. 166–174 (2005)
24. Kim, M., Viswanathan, M., Kannan, S., Lee, I., Sokolsky, O.: Java-mac: A run-time assurance approach for java programs. Formal Methods in System Design 24(2), 129–155 (2004)
25. Chen, F., Roşu, G.: MOP: An Efficient and Generic Runtime Verification Framework. In: Object-Oriented Programming, Systems, Languages and Applications, OOPSLA 2007 (2007)
26. Barringer, H., Rydeheard, D.E., Havelund, K.: Rule systems for run-time monitoring: from eagle to ruler. J. Log. Comput. 20(3), 675–706 (2010)
27. Barringer, H., Havelund, K.: TraceContract: A Scala DSL for Trace Analysis. In: Butler, M., Schulte, W. (eds.) FM 2011. LNCS, vol. 6664, pp. 57–72. Springer, Heidelberg (2011)
28. Avgustinov, P., Tibble, J., Bodden, E., Hendren, L.J., Lhoták, O., de Moor, O., Ongkingco, N., Sittampalam, G.: Efficient trace monitoring. In: Tarr, P.L., Cook, W.R. (eds.) OOPSLA Companion, pp. 685–686. ACM (2006)

Runtime Verification:
A Computer Architecture Perspective

Sharad Malik

Princeton University
sharad@princeton.edu

Abstract. A major challenge in hardware verification is managing the
state explosion problem in pre-silicon verification. This is seen in the high
cost and low coverage of simulation, and capacity limitations of formal
verification. Runtime verification, through on-the-fly property checking
of the current trace and a low-cost error recovery mechanism, provides
us an alternative attack in dealing with this problem. There are several
interesting examples of runtime verification that have been proposed in
recent years in the computer architecture community. These have also
been motivated by the resiliency needs of future technology generations
in the face of dynamic errors due to device failures. I will first highlight
the key ideas in hardware runtime verification through specific examples
from the uni-processor and multi-processor contexts. Next, I will discuss
the challenges in implementing some of these solutions. Finally I will
discuss how the strengths of runtime verification and model checking
can be used in a complementary fashion for hardware.

1 Runtime Verification in the Hardware Context

1.1 Increasing Hardware Verification Costs

Traditionally, the design of hardware has had stronger requirements for correctness than typical software. This has largely to do with the cost of fixing errors –
hardware errors detected in the field generally cannot be fixed by downloading
a patch. Serious errors may even lead to a product recall which can be very
expensive. The notorious Intel FDIV bug is reported to have cost about USD
450M in recall costs. However, not all errors lead to a recall; processor companies
regularly publish bug errata lists informing the users of known bugs. Generally
these errors do not result in incorrect computation results. They tend to be
performance bugs that lead to slower than expected speed for certain scenarios,
but deliver the correct results, or bugs that result in a system crash/hang in
extremely rare scenarios. In either case, there is no silent corruption of the expected results, and the user is expected to live with these bugs in the product.
This is tolerated as these bugs are expected to be extremely rare and not noticeable by the typical user. Thus, overall the obligation to deliver correct working
hardware is very high, leading to high hardware verification costs. This covers
pre-silicon verification using both simulation and formal verification techniques,

S. Khurshid and K. Sen (Eds.): RV 2011, LNCS 7186, pp. 49–62, 2012.

as well as post-silicon validation which continues verification through the initial silicon prototypes which can be debugged at speed, thus enabling the use of long complex traces which cannot be run in reasonable time on the design models (built in software) that are used in pre-silicon simulation (e.g. Verilog models) or formal verification (e.g. SMV models used in model checking). However, with increasing hardware complexity, these verification costs are becoming prohibitive, and even limiting our ability to provide greater design functionality. It is not uncommon now for certain hardware blocks to be not turned on in the final product due to insufficient confidence in their correct functioning.

1.2   The Design Complexity Gap

Intuitively, this gap between what we can design and what we can verify can be understood in terms of the growth in design complexity. While Moores Law provides us with an exponential growth rate in the number of circuit components; the state space, which serves as a proxy for design complexity, grows doubly exponentially. Moores Law also comes to our help by exponentially increasing the computing power available for verification; however, this is insufficient to keep pace with the growth in design complexity. This intuitive argument is also consistent with chip design data released by the Electronic Design Automation Consortium (EDAC). The fraction of designs that work correctly on first silicon has been dropping over the years, and since 2007 there has been a small fraction of designs that has required more than three silicon spins. A large fraction of the failures are attributed to logical errors (>80%) and this fraction has been increasing over the years. While significant breakthroughs have happened in formal verification techniques over the years, these have not been able to keep pace with increasing hardware complexity. Formal verification has dealt with this increasing complexity through significant design abstraction, but this has not seen significant adoption due to limited automation. Dynamic (simulation based) verification continues to be the workhorse, but is challenged by limited and difficult to characterize design coverage.

In the context of the growing complexity gap, runtime verification of hardware offers a useful value proposition. At any time, the verification obligation is limited to the current trace, and not all possible traces/the entire state space. This makes the verification much more tractable, and if all the verification tasks can be covered through runtime verification – it is potentially complete.

1.3   Technology Driven Dynamic Errors

Besides the complexity gap, there is a further technology push for considering runtime verification for hardware. This has to do with the smaller device sizes in future technology generations. Smaller devices are much more vulnerable to failures in the field due to a variety of causes [1]. The first of these deals with soft-errors that are transient faults that may result from cosmic rays and alpha particle hits. The second deals with increasing parametric variability where small absolute variations in manufacturing create large relative variations in device parameters and consequently device behavior. This can get amplified with environment (e.g. temperature) changes. These failures are dynamic, and thus require runtime support. *Runtime verification has the potential to address both logical faults as well as device failures through a unified approach that recognizes the consequent error of the fault through a checking mechanism and then provides an appropriate recovery mechanism to recover from this error.*

1.4   Computer Architecture Solutions for Runtime Verification

In response to both the design complexity and technology pushes, the last decade or so has seen several interesting projects that offer computer architectures that integrate runtime verification as an essential architectural component. This covers both uni-processor as well as multi-processor issues. This paper reviews the major contributions in this area, and draws out the key issues illustrated by these case studies as well as the challenges still faced in the widespread adoption of these solutions. The primary issues that each of these case studies deals with are:

- What to check.
- How to recover in case of error.
- How to keep the checking and recovery overhead low.

The last of these is especially important, as hardware is very cost-sensitive and any additional checking and recovery logic may be unacceptable if the cost overhead is too high. Most of the research efforts described in this paper strive to keep the logic, power and performance overhead to under 5%. There is added rationale for this low cost imperative. With Moores Law the cost per transistor decreases with each generation. Conversely runtime verification support has an amortized cost per transistor. This latter addition cannot outweigh the reduction in transistor cost, or the benefits of scaling under Moores Law will be lost. Keeping overheads low demands innovative solutions, since simple replication is unacceptable under these stringent budgets. Thus, the architectural solutions described here have a system-level, rather than a component-level, approach.

This paper is organized as follows. Sections 2 and 3 focus on case studies that deal with the checker and recovery logic for the uni-processor and multi-processor case respectively. Section 4 focuses solutions that are primary concerned with backward recovery through check-pointing and rollback. Section 5 considers solutions for forward recovery through bug-patching. Section 6 makes the connections with formal verification and presents some insights on the complementary roles of runtime checking and formal verification for hardware. Finally Section 7 provides some summary observations.

2   Checkers and Recovery in Uni-processors

2.1   The DIVA Processor

The DIVA processor architecture [2] was pioneering in its use of runtime verification integrated as a critical component of the architecture. In this architecture, the main or core processor is augmented with a checker processor. This checker processor is responsible for checking the computation being done by the core processor, and in case of an error being detected for forward recovery by providing the correct results and restarting the core processor. In contrast to the complex core processor, the checker processor is a simple in-order processor. Thus, its overhead is a small fraction (<6%) of the size of the complex core. *The key innovation in this design is making sure that a simple checker can keep pace with a complex core processor.* This is done by letting the complex core do all the heavy lifting in terms of the performance optimizations and letting the checker just confirm that the results of these are indeed correct. This is done as follows: the core processor provides the checker with the speculative instruction stream that includes the program counter (PC), the instruction, as well as instruction register and memory operands. The checker ensures that the instruction being executed in the core is indeed the instruction pointed to by the program counter, that the arguments for this instruction are indeed those pointed to by the core processor, and finally that the result of the computation on these arguments is indeed as computed by the core processor. In these tasks the checker never suffers from the performance hits such as cache misses, branch mis-predictions and pipeline stalls that the core has overcome. This enables it to process the instruction stream being generated by the core processor in real time. If the results of the checking are correct, the core is allowed to commit this instruction. If not, then the checker executes the instruction directly. This result is considered to be correct as the checker processor has been formally verified and is made electrically more resilient through larger devices. Both of these are made possible by the relatively small size of the checker. As the checker processor is slower, there is an overhead in recovery mode. However, even with reasonable error rates, the performance overhead is <5%.

This design illustrates an important principle that recurs in other designs. *Computer architecture has long provided performance at the cost of complexity.* Processor architectures optimize for the typical case by providing complex microarchitectural components such as branch-predicators and support for speculative execution. While these provide significant performance enhancement, it comes at the cost of design complexity and the consequent verification burden. *The recovery architecture makes this tradeoff in the opposite direction. The checker processor is made intentionally simple even though this makes it slow. Overall, this approach works as errors are relatively infrequent, and thus the amortized performance overhead of recovery tends to be low.*

2.2   Semantic Guardians

The Semantic Guardians project [3] exploits the difference between the static and dynamic views of the state space. The static view considers all possible reachable states and thus verification attempts to cover all these reachable states. Typically, only a small fraction of the complete state space ends up being covered. Nonetheless, most designs tend to work correctly almost all the time. This can be easily explained through a dynamic view of the state space. Most of the actual execution time is spent in a small fraction of the states, and these are easily verified during verification as they are not the so called corner cases. The main idea behind semantic guardians is to maintain predicates for parts of the state space that have not been completely verified during verification. From a dynamic point of view, these predicates will rarely evaluate to true. The semantic guardian is the checking logic which continuously evaluates these predicates to see if the design is entering the unverified part of the state space. When this is detected, control is passed to a reliable design component, referred to as the inner core, which has the same functionality as the main design, but is known to be correct. At the end of a prescribed unit of computation, for example, an instruction in a processor, control is passed back to the main design. This, of course, begs the question: why not use the inner core all the time? The reason why this is not a viable option is that the inner core, like the checker processor in DIVA, makes the tradeoff of simplicity for performance, and thus is slow. As in the DIVA case, this is acceptable in the current context, since it is brought into action only rarely, and thus the amortized performance overhead is low.

The Semantic Guardian project is done in the context of uni-processors, where the main design is a complex processor, and the inner core is a simple fully verified processor. The predicates checked by the semantic guardian are the states of the complex pipeline that have not been completely verified. A key question that this raises is: how well does this intuitive and appealing runtime verification methodology scale to other kinds of designs. *Specifically, it is typically difficult to characterize the non-verified part of the state space through simple predicates. And even when this characterization may be possible, the state may be highly distributed in space, and thus not easy to check.* This is a general issue with runtime verification in hardware and will be revisited later in the paper.

3   Checkers and Recovery in Multi-processors

As we saw in the DIVA and Semantic Guardians case studies, the uni-processor case offers some advantages in terms of runtime verification. The first is that the instruction is a well-defined unit of computation that needs to be checked, and possibly recomputed. The second is that the checkers need to examine relatively local information – predicates on the control state, or instruction and operand bits. This enables the checkers to be relatively simple. In contrast, the multi-processor case is much more complex. The correctness criteria are not as easily defined as the processing of an instruction. Further, they will likely depend on state that is distributed across processors – this complicates the design of checkers as they will need to monitor distributed state. These issues are addressed head-on by a couple of projects dealing with runtime verification of an important multi-processor correctness property, viz. memory consistency.

As part of the performance optimization of modern processors, instructions are allowed to execute out of order in order to overcome the performance penalty of resource based stalls. For example, if an instruction suffers a cache miss, then the following instructions can continue to execute while this cache miss is being serviced. Of course, bookkeeping logic is needed to ensure that the instruction operands continue to receive the correct values as required by a pure in-order execution. This book-keeping logic monitors the current instruction trace on the processor to ensure this. However, it is entirely possible that a reordering that is legal for one thread may lead to an inconsistent ordering of variable values for a parallel thread running on a different processor. To avoid this, multi-processors define memory consistency rules for specifying which re-orderings are allowed. Different processors have accepted different consistency rules such as sequential consistency, total store order, various forms of relaxed consistency etc. The memory consistency model serves as a hardware-software interface contract for multi-processors, much in the same way as the instruction set architecture serves as the hardware-software contract for uni-processors [4]. The architectural memory consistency verification problem is to ensure that the hardware implementation obeys the memory consistency model. What makes this difficult to check, is that unlike the instruction in the uni-processor case, single units of computation are insufficient to check the memory consistency property. Each individual reordering may be correct by itself, but it is combinations of re-orderings across processors that could violate memory consistency. This also implies that, unlike the uni-processor case, the checking logic needs to monitor state that will be spatially distributed across processors. Both these issues pose key challenges for runtime verification. The following two projects provide two different approaches to dealing with this challenge.

3.1   Runtime Constraint Graph Checking

The constraint graph model [5] provides a uniform way to express various memory consistency models using a graphical representation. The vertices in this graph represent individual memory accesses. The edges represent ordering relationships between these memory accesses. The edges can be partitioned into two sets, intra-thread edges that exist between vertices corresponding to memory accesses in the same thread, and inter-thread edges that exist between vertices corresponding to memory accesses in different threads. An intra-thread edge (u, v) indicates that the memory consistency model requires memory access u to appear to be before memory access v. For example, in sequential consistency, all loads and stores must appear to be in the program order. In contrast, in the Total Store Order (TSO) model the edge from a store to a load of a different address is relaxed, i.e. dropped from the program order edges. An inter-thread edge (u, v) captures the dependent ordering relationships (read-after-write, write-after-write, write-after-read) between vertices across threads that access the same memory location. These edges are based on the actual time ordering of these memory operations. In the constraint graph model, there is a memory consistency violation if and only if there is a cycle in the constraint graph. This result is helpful as it provides a specific graph condition to check for. Further, checking for cycles in a directed graph is computationally easy in the size of the graph.

However, runtime checking this graph poses several challenges. There is no bound on the size of the cycle, thus the complete graph may need to be stored. This is obviously impractical since modern processors execute billions of memory instructions per second, and storing (and checking) a multi-billion vertex graph is impractical. This project [6] provides two key innovations that help manage the size of the graph that needs to be stored and checked. The first is graph compression – the intra-thread edges are compressed using on-the-fly transitive closure – only those vertices need to be stored that participate in inter-thread edges. Since these correspond to shared variable accesses, this number is a small fraction of the total number of memory accesses. The second is graph slicing – by periodically pausing the execution, a graph slice is identified that is sufficient for detecting cycles in the complete graph, i.e. a cycle exists in the complete graph if and only if it exists in the graph slice for some time epoch. While theoretically this slice could comprise the entire graph, in practice pausing execution every ten thousand cycles results in a graph slice of about a hundred vertices. This is very manageable in terms of both graph storage, as well as the dedicated checking logic that works on this graph.

While the above innovations help in bounding an unbounded problem, the practical issue of building and checking such a graph remains. This highlights the major challenge in runtime verification of hardware – observing and managing distributed state. This project addresses this by judicious use of existing architectural components and new dedicated components specifically designed for this purpose. The inter-thread edges are inferred by monitoring cache protocol activity. Since each inter-thread edge corresponds to accesses to the same memory location in two different processors, this results in corresponding cache protocol activity depending on the access. These inferred edges are then communicated on the existing connection network (bus or on-chip network) to the dedicated graph checker. The checker gathers the edges, builds the graph and at the end of each time epoch checks the graph for cycles. This is done in a pipelined fashion so as not to stall the main computation in the processors. Finally, if the checker detects a violation, then it reverts to a simple mode for this epoch where memory operations complete sequentially instead of in parallel. This trading-off of performance for simplicity is similar to what we saw earlier with DIVA and Semantic Guardians.

While the experimental results show relatively low overhead for both the area and runtime required for checking, the distributed architecture for gathering and communicating the graph edges is of non-trivial complexity and illustrates *the challenge in observing and checking distributed state in hardware. The other issue this case study raises is that of the size of the checker state.* While runtime verification does offer the advantage of focusing on the current trace rather than the entire state space, it may still need to deal with large, potentially unbounded, checker state. This case study shows one specific design to address this issue, and illustrates the difficulty in generalizing this solution.

In a follow-up project [7] the authors show how the same basic idea of constraint graph checking can be applied to runtime verification of transactional memory systems. The main additional insight is that each transaction is modeled as a meta-vertex in the constraint graph. The rest of the architecture is very similar.

3.2   Proofs through Lemmas

The runtime constraint graph checking project focused on checking for end to end correctness, i.e. it directly checked for the memory consistency property. An alternate attack on runtime verification for memory consistency works by breaking the consistency check into three checks that are sufficient to guarantee memory consistency [8].

- **Uni-processor Ordering:** This check verifies that for each thread the values propagated within the thread are correct. This is local to each thread.
- **Legal Reordering:** This check verifies that the operation order at the cache is legal. This is dependent on the specific memory consistency model.
- **Single-Writer Multiple-Reader Cache Coherence:** This check at the memory verifies inter-processor data propagation and global ordering.

These three checks have the nice property that they can be done locally at different levels in the memory hierarchy – at the processor, cache and main memory level respectively. This allows for observing only local state and overcomes the problem of observing distributed state that the constraint graph checking solution has to deal with. However, this simplicity comes at a cost. These lemmas are sufficient, but not necessary for checking memory consistency. Thus, this method can result in false positives, where a consistency violation may be reported when none exists, and this will lead to additional recovery overhead. Nonetheless, this case study is useful in illustrating the tradeoff between precision and design complexity.

4   Backward Recovery in Multi-processors

4.1   Safety Net

The ReVive [9] and Safety Net [10] projects focus on developing architectures for backward recovery (check-pointing and rollback) in multi-processor architectures. There are multiple motivations for this. In addition to providing support for error recovery, this also provides support for aggressive speculative execution, where processors may optimize for the typical case by speculatively executing along some instruction sequence, but may need to recover in case of mis-speculation. These projects have many similarities, so I will focus on one of these - Safety Net. The primary check-pointing mechanism is a checkpoint log buffer (CLB) at each cache and also main memory. This saves a log of all block writes and transfers. In addition to this, the architectural state at each processor is also check-pointed. Time is broken up into epochs and there is a checkpoint for each epoch. One important issue in this case is the size of the CLBs, since this will grow with the length of the epoch. Further, as seen before, an important issue in distributed systems is observing/recording distributed state. While each CLB records the writes/transfers in an epoch, there may be messages in flight that need to be accounted for. Thus, to determine a consistent system state, the check-pointed state of all CLBs at the end of an epoch has to be validated. This is done in the background and may lag by several epochs. At any point though, there is always one consistent checkpoint that has been validated. This serves as the recovery point in case of error.

5   Forward Recovery through Bug-Patching

As mentioned earlier, it is not uncommon for modern processors to have bugs in released products. Typically these bugs will not result in erroneous results, but rather system crashes (or hangs) – thus there is no possibility of silent data corruption. These bugs are reported on bug errata sheets which are publicly available. The two projects described in this section provide forward error recovery for these reported bugs through error detection and bug-patching.

5.1   The Phoenix Project

In the Phoenix project [11], the authors did a study of uni-processor bugs reported in errata documents. These bugs were then classified into critical and non-critical bugs. The non-critical bugs were typically associated with various book-keeping logic such as performance counters, error reporting registers, break-point support etc. These could lead to performance degradation, but no catastrophic behavior such as a system crash or hang. In contrast, the critical bugs were associated with faults in memory, IO etc. which could lead to a system crash or hang. The critical bugs were further divided on the basis of how they are to be detected. A bug was classified as being concurrent if its condition could be described as a propositional logic formula on the system signals. It was classified as being complex if its condition was described in terms of a temporal formula on sequences of system signals. Roughly two-thirds of the critical bugs were classified as concurrent and the rest as complex. The project focuses on concurrent bugs and detects and patches them using method similar to the FRCLe project described next.

5.2   The FRCLe Project

This project [12] focuses on errors in microprocessor pipelines. Like the Phoenix project, the focus is on errors which can be captured using predicates that are combinations of system signals. These system signals are monitored at runtime, with the offending combinations stored in a content addressable memory (CAM). A match to one of the entries in the CAM indicates an error. This triggers the recovery circuit, which in this case passes control to the trusted inner-core (similar to the Semantic Guardian Project). The main issue in this design is the size of the CAM. This can be viewed as the checker state. As in the case of constraint graph checking, even though the checker is focusing on a single trace, the checker state may end up having a significant overhead.

6   Connections with Formal Verification

6.1   Specific Properties vs. End-to-End Correctness

The range of solutions outlined above have a common characteristic. In each case the focus is on checking end-to-end-correctness. For the uni-processor case, this specification is easy, it is ensuring that each instruction executes correctly. For the multi-processor case, it was ensuring that the rules of memory consistency or transactional memory were correctly followed. This is in contrast to the formal verification of complex hardware designs, where often there is no complete design specification, but rather an incomplete specification in terms of a set of properties specified in some logic – typically temporal logic. While there has been work done in synthesizing automata for temporal logic assertions (specified in the PSL language) (e.g. [13]), and this has been used for synthesizing monitors during logic simulation, this is not particularly suitable for runtime verification for hardware. There are a couple of reasons for this. The first is that this form of partial specification may require a very large number of properties, and thus the synthesized logic may have a large overhead. The second is that, while these checkers may be useful for error detection, it is unclear how the system would recover from these. Thus, the end-to-end correctness checks are very attractive for runtime verification as they provide for a direct check of the specification, and also easily implementable recovery logic.

6.2   Offline vs. Runtime Verification

The case studies discussed above provide some key insights into the relative strengths of offline vs. runtime verification. The term offline verification here includes both formal verification as well as simulation based verification. These have been discussed at several points along the paper, but are summarized here for completeness.

– **Trace Coverage:** Offline verification strives to cover the entire state space. This leads to the so-called state explosion problem, which limits the coverage we can obtain through offline verification. In contrast runtime verification focuses on a single trace at a time and thus does not directly have to deal with the state explosion problem. However, as observed in a couple of the case studies, the checker state may still be quite large, and even potentially unbounded. However, at least for the case studies in this paper, this issue is practically addressed through innovative solutions.
– **Design Overhead:** Runtime verification comes with a design overhead – this includes the area for the checking and recovery logic as well as the power and performance overhead for its operation. As discussed in the paper, there

is a strong imperative to keep this overhead low, with 5% as the self-imposed threshold. Any significant overhead will be unacceptable in hardware design and reduce the benefits of scaling provided by Moore's Law. In contrast, offline checking has no hardware design overhead, as it operates only on a software design model.

– **Managing Distributed State:** As illustrated by the Constraint Graph Checking and the Safety Net case studies, managing distributed state poses major challenges in hardware runtime verification. There are two distinct issues here. The first deals with ensuring that the distributed state is consistent. Since the values of the distributed state components may not all refer to the exact same time instant, additional steps may be needed to ensure consistency. The second issue deals with computing using distributed state. This requires some distributed computation where either the state components or partial computation results need to be communicated across the design. This adds to design complexity and overhead. In contrast, this is never a problem in offline verification. All state variables are just variables in the software model, and can be equally accessed regardless of physical separation.

6.3   Runtime Verification and Model Checking

The relative strengths of offline vs. runtime verification have led to some exploration of verification techniques that use model checking and runtime verification in a complementary way [14]. Specifically this work explores how model checking can be used to deal with distributed state, while runtime verification helps with the state explosion problem by focusing on a specific trace.

One such complementary attack deals with verifying the composition of interacting modules. Model checking using the assume guarantee reasoning technique would check the property for each model with some assumptions about the environment of this model. This environment would contain variables from the other modules, i.e. would have distributed state. However, these assumptions need to be verified, which often faces the state explosion problem. Since these assumptions relate to behavior at the boundary of the module, these could be locally checked at runtime, and recovery logic triggered on failure.

7   Summary Observations

Runtime verification for hardware offers some key advantages. It helps with the growing complexity gap by offering a mechanism to deal with the inevitable bug escapes. This decreases product costs by eliminating expensive silicon respins. Further, this mechanism allows for predictable verification schedules. The burden on pre-silicon verification can now be reduced since runtime verification can deal with bug-escapes. Chips no longer need to be verified to death, they just need to be verified to life. However, it is important to note that even with end-to-end correctness checks runtime verification cannot replace pre-silicon verification.

For runtime verification to be viable the power and performance overhead needs to be low. This implies very low error rates, which in turn implies significant pre-silicon verification to eliminate all but the rarest of corner case errors.

Another key advantage of runtime verification is its ability to deal with a variety of failure modes. In addition to logical faults, it is being used to address the resiliency needs of future computing fabrics. These fabrics are showing increased fragility due to increasing susceptibility to soft errors, as well as devices failing due to increasing parametric variability. This ability to deal with various failure modes is enabled by the checkers focusing on the symptoms, rather than the cause of failure. However, recovery solutions do need to consider the source of failure – while transient errors can be dealt with temporal redundancy, errors due to device failure or logical bugs will need some form of spatial redundancy for recovery.

A common theme in several of the solutions discussed in this paper is how performance-complexity tradeoffs are handled. Modern processor architectures focus on the typical case to enhance the average case performance, and this results in microarchitectures with significant complexity. Interestingly the recovery solutions in runtime verification make this tradeoff in the opposite direction – using solutions that are slow but very reliable. The low performance in this case is easily amortized due to the low error rate.

One trend that supports architectural solutions for runtime verification is the increasing use of speculative execution for improving processor performance. With speculative execution, entire program paths may be executed with the expectation that these may be taken in the future. This enables the processor to run ahead and explore multiple possible program paths in advance. This, in turn, requires some recovery support, either forward or backward. In forward recovery, a speculative thread may commit only after its guard evaluates to true. In backward recovery, any state updates by an aborted speculative thread need to be undone through rolling back to a valid checkpoint. The existence of these mechanisms for performance enhancement makes it convenient to repurpose them for runtime verification.

The complementary strengths of offline vs. runtime verification are how they need to deal with the state space and state variables. Offline verification has the disadvantage that it needs to deal with the entire state space and thus faces the state explosion problem. This is not an issue with runtime verification, since it deals with only the current trace at a time. However, the state that the checker may need to maintain may still be prohibitive. Conversely runtime verification has the challenge of processing distributed state. Distributed state needs to be consistent in that it reflects a specific point in time. Further, it may need communication of values across the chip to allow for its processing, further adding to design complexity.

While this paper discusses over a decade of research in architectural solutions for runtime verification, this entire direction still faces major challenges before these solutions see practical adoption. Hardware is very cost sensitive, thus there is strong resistance to adding additional hardware to an existing design. Perhaps even greater verification pain will tilt the scale on this. A somewhat related issue is the added design complexity due to the checking and recovery circuits. While these are generally designed to be simple and easily verifiable, the overall system complexity does increase and reasoning about the error and error free modes needs to be added to the verification tasks. Finally, while the solutions reviewed in this paper demonstrate significant innovation in what they accomplish, and have several common themes, they are far from delivering on a general methodology for runtime verification for hardware.

Acknowledgements. Several projects described in this paper (DIVA, Semantic Guardians, FRCLe, Runtime Constraint Graph Checking) were funded by the Gigascale Systems Research Center, which is one of six research centers funded under the Focus Center Research Program, a Semiconductor Research Corporation program. The author also acknowledges helpful discussions with, and useful material from, Todd Austin, Valeria Bertacco, Daniel Sorin and Josep Torrellas.

References

1. Austin, T.M., Bertacco, V., Blaauw, D., Mudge, T.N.: Opportunities and challenges for better than worst-case design. In: Asia and South Pacific Design Automation Conference (ASP-DAC), pp. 2–7. ACM (2005)
2. Austin, T.M.: DIVA: a reliable substrate for deep submicron microarchitecture design. In: ACM/IEEE International Symposium on Microarchitecture (MICRO), pp. 196–207. IEEE Computer Society (1999)
3. Wagner, I., Bertacco, V.: Engineering trust with semantic guardians. In: Design Automation and Test in Europe (DATE), EDA Consortium, pp. 743–748 (2007)
4. Adve, S.V., Gharachorloo, K.: Shared memory consistency models: A tutorial. IEEE Computer 29, 66–76 (1996)
5. Cain, H.W., Lipasti, M.H., Nair, R.: Constraint graph analysis of multithreaded programs. Journal of Instruction-Level Parallelism 6 (2004)
6. Chen, K., Malik, S., Patra, P.: Runtime validation of memory ordering using constraint graph checking. In: International Conference on High-Performance Computer Architecture (HPCA), pp. 415–426. IEEE Computer Society (2008)
7. Chen, K., Malik, S., Patra, P.: Runtime validation of transactional memory systems. In: International Symposium on Quality of Electronic Design (ISQED), pp. 750–756. IEEE Computer Society (2008)
8. Meixner, A., Sorin, D.J.: Dynamic verification of memory consistency in cache-coherent multithreaded computer architectures. IEEE Transactions on Dependable Secure Computing 6, 18–31 (2009)
9. Prvulovic, M., Torrellas, J., Zhang, Z.: ReVive: Cost-effective architectural support for rollback recovery in shared-memory multiprocessors. In: International Symposium on Computer Architecture (ISCA), pp. 111–122. IEEE Computer Society (2002)
10. Sorin, D.J., Martin, M.M.K., Hill, M.D., Wood, D.A.: SafetyNet: Improving the availability of shared memory multiprocessors with global checkpoint/recovery. In: International Symposium on Computer Architecture (ISCA), pp. 123–134. IEEE Computer Society (2002)

11. Sarangi, S.R., Tiwari, A., Torrellas, J.: Phoenix: Detecting and recovering from permanent processor design bugs with programmable hardware. In: ACM/IEEE International Symposium on Microarchitecture (MICRO), pp. 26–37. IEEE Computer Society (2006)
12. Wagner, I., Bertacco, V., Austin, T.M.: Shielding against design flaws with field repairable control logic. In: Design Automation Conference (DAC), pp. 344–347. ACM (2006)
13. Abarbanel, Y., Beer, I., Gluhovsky, L., Keidar, S., Wolfsthal, Y.: FoCs: Automatic Generation of Simulation Checkers from Formal Specifications. In: Emerson, E.A., Sistla, A.P. (eds.) CAV 2000. LNCS, vol. 1855, pp. 538–542. Springer, Heidelberg (2000)
14. Bayazit, A.A., Malik, S.: Complementary use of runtime validation and model checking. In: International Conference on Computer-Aided Design (ICCAD), pp. 1052–1059. IEEE Computer Society (2005)

Isolating Determinism in Multi-threaded Programs

Lukasz Ziarek, Siddharth Tiwary, and Suresh Jagannathan

Purdue University
{lziarek,stiwary,suresh}@cs.purdue.edu

Abstract. Futures are a program abstraction that express a simple form of fork-join parallelism. The expression future (e) declares that e can be evaluated concurrently with the future's continuation. *Safe*-futures provide additional deterministic guarantees, ensuring that all data dependencies found in the original (non-future annotated) version are respected. In this paper, we present a dynamic analysis for enforcing determinism of safe-futures in an ML-like language with dynamic thread creation and first-class references. Our analysis tracks the interaction between futures (and their continuations) with other explicitly defined threads of control, and enforces an *isolation* property that prevents the effects of a continuation from being witnessed by its future, indirectly through their interactions with other threads. Our analysis is defined via a lightweight capability-based dependence tracking mechanism that serves as a compact representation of an effect history. Implementation results support our premise that futures and threads can extract additional parallelism compared to traditional approaches for safe-futures.

1 Introduction

A *future* is a program construct used to introduce parallelism into sequential programs. The expression future(*e*) returns a future object F that evaluates e in a separate thread of control that executes concurrently with its continuation. The expression touch(*F*) blocks execution until F completes. A *safe-future* imposes additional constraints on the execution of a future and its continuation to preserve sequential semantics. By doing so, it provides a simple-to-understand mechanism that provides *deterministic parallelism*, transforming a sequential program into a safe concurrent one, without requiring any code restructuring. The definition of these constraints ensures that (a) the effects of a continuation are never witnessed by its future, and (b) a read of a reference r performed by a continuation is obligated to witness the last write to r made by the future.

In the absence of side-effects, a program decorated with safe-futures behaves identically to a program in which all such annotations are erased, assuming all future-encapsulated expressions terminate. In the presence of side-effects, however, unconstrained interleaving between a future and its continuation can lead to undesirable racy behavior. The conditions described above which prevent such behavior can be implemented either statically through the insertion of synchronization barriers [1,2], or dynamically by tracking dependencies [3], treating

S. Khurshid and K. Sen (Eds.): RV 2011, LNCS 7186, pp. 63–77, 2012.

continuations as potentially speculative computations, aborting and rolling them back when a dependence violation is detected.

Earlier work on safe-futures considered their integration into sequential programs. In this context, the necessary dependence analysis has only to ensure that the effects of concurrent execution adhere to the original sequential semantics. As programs and libraries migrate to multicore environments, it is likely that computations from which we can extract deterministic parallelism are already part of multi-threaded computations, or interact with libraries and/or other program components that are themselves explicitly multi-threaded.

When safe-futures are integrated within an explicitly concurrent program (e.g., to extract additional concurrency from within a sequential *thread* of control), the necessary safety conditions are substantially more complex than those used to guarantee determinacy in the context of otherwise sequential code. This is because the interaction of explicitly concurrent threads among one another may indirectly induce behavior that violates a safe-future's safety guarantees. For example, a continuation of a future F created within the context of one thread may perform an effectful action that is witnessed by another thread whose resulting behavior affects F's execution, as depicted in the following program fragment:

```
let val x = ref 0
    val y = ref 0
in spawn( ...  future (... !y ...); x := 1);
   if !x = 1
   then y := 1
end
```

In the absence of the future annotation, the dereference of y (given as !y) would always yield 0, regardless of the interaction between the future's continuation (here, the assignment x := 1) and the second thread[1]. (The expression spawn(e) creates a new thread of control to evaluate e with no deterministic guarantees.)

In this paper, we present a dynamic program analysis that tracks interactions between threads, futures, and their continuations that prevents the effects of continuations from being witnessed by their futures through cross-thread dataflow, as described in the example above. Our technique allows seamless integration of safe-futures into multi-threaded programs, and provides a mechanism that enables extraction of additional parallelism from multi-threaded code without requiring any further code restructuring, or programmer-specified synchronization. To the best of our knowledge, ours is the first analysis to provide lightweight thread-aware dynamic dependence tracking for effect isolation in the context of a language equipped with dynamic thread creation, first-class references, to support deterministic parallelism.

---

[1] For the purposes of the example, we assume no compiler optimizations that reorders statements.

Our contributions are as follows:

1. We present a dynamic analysis that *isolates* the effects of a continuation C from its future F even in the presence of multiple explicit threads of control. The isolation property is selective, allowing C to interact freely with other threads provided that the effects of such interactions do not leak back to F.
2. We introduce *future capabilities*, a new dependence analysis structure, that enables lightweight dynamic tracking of effects, suitable for identifying dependence violations between futures and their continuations.
3. We describe an implementation of futures and threads in MultiMLton, an optimizing compiler for Standard ML, and show benefits compared to traditional safe-futures.

2 Safe Futures and Threads

Safe futures are intended to ensure deterministic parallelism; they do so by guaranteeing the following two safety properties: (1) a future will never witness its continuation's effects and (2) a continuation will never witness the future's intermediate effects. In a sequential setting, the second condition implies a continuation *must* witness the *logically last* effects of a future.

To illustrate these properties, consider the two example programs given in Fig. 1. The code that is executed by the future is highlighted in gray. When a future is created it immediately returns a placeholder, which when touched will produce the return value of the future. A touch defines a synchronization point between a future and its continuation; execution following the touch are guaranteed that the future has completed.

Initially: x=0, y=0

Program 1	Program 2

```let fun f() = x := 1```
```   val tag = future (f)```
```in !x ; touch (tag)```
```end```
	```let fun f() = !y```
	``` val tag = future (f)```
	```in y := 1 ; touch (tag)```
	```end```

Fig. 1. Two programs depicting the safety properties that must be enforced to achieve deterministic parallelism for sequential programs annotated with futures

In the program on the left, the future writes 1 to the shared variable x. The continuation (the code following in) reads from x. To ensure that the behavior of this program is consistent with a sequential execution, the continuation is only allowed to read 1. In the program on the right, the future reads from the shared variable y while the continuation writes to y. The future cannot witness any effects from the continuation, and therefore can only read 0 for y. To correctly execute the futures in programs 1 and 2 concurrently with their continuations we must ensure that the future is isolated from the effects of the continuation and that the future's final effects are propagated to the continuation.

2.1 Interaction with Threads

The creation of new threads by either the future or the continuation requires reasoning about the created threads' actions. If a future internally creates a thread of control T, T's shared reads and writes *may* need to be isolated from the continuation's effects. We need to ensure that if a future witnesses a write performed by the thread it created, the future's continuation cannot witness any prior writes. On the other hand, a future *must* be isolated from the effects of any threads that a continuation creates. These threads are created *logically after* the future completes and therefore the future cannot witness any of their effects. To illustrate, consider the two examples programs given in Fig. 2.

```
                   Initially: x=0, y=0, z=0
          Program 1                              Program 2
let fun g() = x := 1          let fun h() = z := 2
    fun f() = spawn (g)           fun f() = !z
             if !x = 1            val tag = future (f)
             then y := 2      in z := 1; spawn(h);
      val tag = future (f)       touch (tag)
in !x ; !y; touch (tag)       end
end
```

Fig. 2. Two programs depicting the safety properties that must be enforced to achieve deterministic parallelism for futures and continuations which spawn threads

In the program on the left, the future creates a thread which writes to the shared variable x. The future then branches on the contents of x, and if x contains the value 1 it writes 2 to y. The continuation reads from both x and y. There are two valid outcomes: (1) if the body of the future executes before the assignment of x to 1 by the internally created thread, the continuation could read 0 for x and 0 for y; or (2), if the body of the future executes after the assignment by the internally created thread, the continuation would read 1 for x and 2 for y. An invalid result would be for the continuation to read 0 for x and 2 for y - this would imply that the continuation witnessed an intermediate value for x (here 0) that was not the last value witnessed by its future (which observed x to be 1). In the program on the right, the continuation creates a thread which writes to the shared variable z. Since the thread that the continuation creates should logically execute *after* the completion of the future, the future should only see the value 0 for z.

2.2 Transitive Effects

In the presence of multiple threads of control a future may incorrectly witness a continuation's effects transitively. Consider the sample program given in Fig. 3 that consists of two threads of control and one future denoted by the gray box. Notice that the future and its continuation do not access the same memory locations. The future simply reads from y and the continuation writes to x. Can the future read the value 2 from the shared variable y? Reading the value 2 for y would be erroneous because Thread 2 writes the value 2 to y only if x contains the value 1, implying the continuation's effects were visible to its future.

```
                   Initially: x=0, y=0, z=0
```

Thread 1	Thread 2

`let fun f() = !y`
`    val tag = future (f)`
`in x := 1; touch (tag)`
`end`
	`if x = 1`
	`then y := 2`
	`else y := 3`

```
            Can the future see y = 2?
```

Fig. 3. Although the future and continuation do not conflict in the variables they access, the future, by witnessing the effects of Thread 2, transitively witnesses the effects of the continuation

Similarly, a continuation may incorrectly witness a future's intermediate effects transitively (see Fig. 4). Here, functions g, h, and i *force* a particular interleaving between the future and Thread 2. It is incorrect for the continuation to witness the write of 1 to z by Thread 2 because Thread 2 subsequently overwrites z and synchronizes with the future by writing to y and then waiting until the future writes 2 to x. Thus, the continuation should only witness the value 2 for z.

```
                   Initially: x=0, y=0, z=0
```

Thread 1	Thread 2

`let fun g() = if !y = 2`
`              then ()`
`              else g()`
`    fun f() = x := 1;g();`
`             x := 2`
`    val tag = future (f)`
`in !z; touch (tag)`
`end`
	`let fun h() = if !x = 1`
	`              then z := 1`
	`              else h()`
	`    fun i() = if !x = 2`
	`             then ()`
	`             else i()`
	`in h(); z:= 2; y := 2; i()`
	`end`

```
            Can the continuation see z = 1?
```

Fig. 4. Although the future and continuation do not conflict in the variables they access, the continuation may incorrectly witness the future's intermediate effects through updates performed by Thread 2

As another example, consider the program given in Fig. 5 consisting of two explicitly created threads and one future denoted by the gray box. The functions g() and h() encode simple barriers that ensure synchronization between the future and Thread 2 - the future computation completes only after Thread 2 finishes. Is it possible for the continuation to read the value 1 for the shared variable z? Notice that the future does perform a write of 1 to z and in fact this is the last write the future performs to that shared variable. However, Thread 2 assigns 2 to z prior to assigning 2 to y. The future in Thread 1 *waits*, by executing the function g, until Thread 2 writes 2 to y. Therefore, the continuation *must* witness the write of 2 to z as this shared update logically occurs *prior* to the completion of the future. The future's write of 1 to z is guaranteed to occur prior to the write of 2 to z in Thread 2, since Thread 2 waits until the write to x to perform its update to z.

```
              Initially: x=0, y=0, z=0

Thread 1                          Thread 2
let fun g() = if !y = 2           let fun h() = if !x = 1
                then ()                           then ()
                else g()                          else h()
        fun f() = z := 1;         in h(); z := 2; y := !z
                  x := 1; g()     end
        val tag = future (f)
in !z; touch (tag)
end
```

Can the continuation see z = 1?

Fig. 5. The continuation cannot witness the future's write to z as this is an intermediate effect. The write to z in Thread 2 is transitively made visible to the continuation since the future synchronizes with Thread 2.

2.3   Future and Future Interaction

Similar issues arise when two futures witness each other's effects (see Fig. 6). Here, each thread creates a future; there are no dependencies between the future and its continuation. Assuming no compiler reorderings, the continuation of the future created by Thread 1 writes to x and the continuation of the future created by Thread 2 writes to y. The futures created by Thread 1 and 2 read from y and x respectively. It should be impossible for Thread 1 to read 1 from y and Thread 2 to read 1 from x. However, executing the futures arbitrarily allows for such an ordering to occur if the continuation of the future created by Thread 2 executes prior to the future in Thread 1 and the continuation of that future executes prior to the future created by Thread 2. In such an execution the futures witness values that logically should occur *after* their executions.

3   High Level Semantics

In this section, we define an operational semantics to formalize the intuition highlighted by the examples presented above; the semantics is given in terms of a core call-by-value functional language with first-class threads and references. The safety conditions are defined with respect to traces ($\bar{\tau}$). The language includes primitives for creating threads (spawn), creating shared references (ref), reading

```
                      Initially: x=0, y=0, z=0
```

Thread 1	Thread 2

let fun f() = !y;
    val tag = future (f)
in x := 1; touch (tag)
end
	let fun g() = !x;
	    val tag = future (g)
	in y := 1; touch (tag)
	end

```
Can the future in Thread 1 see y = 1 and the future
in Thread 2 x = 1?
```

Fig. 6. Two futures created by separate threads of control may interact in a way that violates sequential consistency even though each future has no violations

from a shared reference (!), and assigning to a shared reference (:=). We extend this core language with primitives to construct futures (**future**) and to wait on their completion (**touch**) (see Fig. 7).

Our language omits locking primitives; locks ensure that multiple updates to shared locations occur without interleavings from other threads. For our purposes, it is sufficient to track reads and updates to shared locations to characterize the safety conditions underlying the examples given in the previous section. As such, locks do not add any interesting semantic issues and are omitted for brevity.

In our syntax, v ranges over values, l over locations, e over expressions, x over variables, ℓ_f over future identifiers, ℓ_c to label computations associated with the continuation of a future, and t over thread identifiers. A program state is defined as a store (σ), a set of threads ($\overline{T}$), and a trace ($\overline{\tau}$). We decorate thread identifiers that are associated with futures with the identifier of the future, its continuation, or ϕ if the thread was created via a **spawn** operation. We assume future identifiers embed sufficient information about ancestry (i.e. futures created by another future or continuation) so that we can create fresh identifiers based on the parent's identifier ($fresh^I$) [2].

A trace ($\overline{\tau}$) is a sequence of actions represented by four types of trace elements: (1) $R(id, l)$ to capture the identifier id of the thread or future performing the read as well as the location (l) being read, (2), $W(id, l)$ defined similarly for writes, $S(id, id')$ to record spawn actions for a newly created thread with identifier id' created by thread id, and (4) $F(id, id')$ to record the parent/child relation for newly created futures either from other futures or threads.

There are two safety rules that capture the notion of a well-behaved execution defined in terms of traces. The first rule states that an execution is safe if its trace enforces serial execution between all futures and their continuations. Serializability holds if the last action of a future precedes the first action of its continuation. The auxiliary relations min and max are defined in the obvious manner and return the first trace element and last trace element for a given identifier respectively. We use the notation $<_{\overline{\tau}}$ to order two trace elements in the trace $\overline{\tau}$.

The second rule defines an equivalence relation over safe traces in terms of a *dependency preserving permutation*: given an execution having a safe trace, any

$$v \in Value$$
$$\ell_f, \ell_c \in Id$$
$$\mathbf{t} \in TID$$
$$l \in Location$$
$$T \in Thread := (\mathbf{t}^{Id}, e)$$

$$id \in ID := \mathbf{t}^{\phi} + \mathbf{t}^{\ell_f} + \mathbf{t}^{\ell_c}$$
$$\sigma \in Store := Location \xrightarrow{fin} Value$$
$$\tau \in TraceElement := R(id, l) + W(id, l) +$$
$$\qquad\qquad S(id, id) + F(id, id) + A(id, \_)$$
$$\overline{T} := T \mid T \parallel \overline{T}$$

$$e := \mathbf{unit} \mid x \mid v \mid \lambda x.e \mid e\, e$$
$$\quad \mid \mathbf{spawn}\ e \mid \mathbf{ref}\ e \mid \mathbf{touch}\ e$$
$$\quad \mid e := e \mid !e \mid \mathbf{future}\ e$$

$$v := \mathbf{unit} \mid l \mid \ell \mid \lambda x.e$$
$$E := \cdot \mid E\, e \mid v\, E \mid \mathbf{touch}\ E$$
$$\quad \mid E := e \mid l := E \mid \mathbf{ref}\ E \mid !E$$

SAFETY

$$\frac{\bar{\tau} \rightsquigarrow \bar{\tau}' \quad safe(\bar{\tau}')}{safe(\bar{\tau})}$$

$$\frac{\forall \mathbf{t}^{\ell_f} \in \bar{\tau} \mid max(\bar{\tau}, \mathbf{t}^{\ell_f}) <_{\bar{\tau}} min(\bar{\tau}, \mathbf{t}^{\ell_c})}{safe(\bar{\tau})}$$

DEPENDENCY PRESERVING PERMUTATION

$$\frac{\begin{array}{c} \tau_3 = A(id, \_) \quad A(id, \_) \notin \bar{\tau}_2 \\ \bar{\tau} = \bar{\tau}_1 : \bar{\tau}_2 : \tau_3 : \bar{\tau}_4 \\ \bar{\tau}' = \bar{\tau}_1 : \tau_3 : \bar{\tau}_2 : \bar{\tau}_4 \\ dep(\bar{\tau}, \bar{\tau}') \end{array}}{\bar{\tau} \rightsquigarrow \bar{\tau}'}$$

INTER-THREAD DEPENDENCIES

$$\frac{\bar{\tau} = \bar{\tau}_1 : \bar{\tau}_2 : R(id, l) : \bar{\tau}_3 \quad \bar{\tau}' = \bar{\tau}_1 : R(id, l) : \bar{\tau}_2 : \bar{\tau}_3 \\ W(id', l) \notin \bar{\tau}_2 \quad S(id', id) \notin \bar{\tau}_2 \quad F(id', id) \notin \bar{\tau}_2 \quad id' \neq id}{dep(\bar{\tau}, \bar{\tau}')}$$

$$\frac{\bar{\tau} = \bar{\tau}_1 : \bar{\tau}_2 : W(id, l) : \bar{\tau}_3 \quad \bar{\tau}' = \bar{\tau}_1 : W(id, l) : \bar{\tau}_2 : \bar{\tau}_3 \\ R(id', l) \notin \bar{\tau}_2 \quad S(id', id) \notin \bar{\tau}_2 \quad F(id', id) \notin \bar{\tau}_2 \quad id' \neq id}{dep(\bar{\tau}, \bar{\tau}')}$$

Fig. 7. Language Syntax and Grammar

safe permutation of that trace (as defined by this relation) is also safe, and thus any execution that yields such a trace is well-behaved. The permutation rules preserve two types of dependencies: (1) intra-thread dependencies that ensure logical consistency of a given thread of control and (2) inter-thread dependencies that define a *happens-before* relationship among threads. The wild card trace element ($A(id, \_)$) matches any action performed by a future, continuation, or thread with the identifier id. A trace element can be permuted to the left of a series of actions $\bar{\tau}_2$ as long as that sub-trace does not contain any trace elements with the same identifier.

Inter-thread dependencies are defined by the relation *dep* that compares the permuted trace to the original trace. There are two rules that assert that inter-thread dependencies are preserved, one for reads and one for writes. The two

APP

$$\frac{}{\begin{array}{c}\sigma,\bar{\tau},(\mathbf{t}^I,E[(\lambda x.e)\ v])\ \|\ \overline{T}\ \rightarrow\\ \sigma,\bar{\tau},(\mathbf{t}^I,E[e[v/x]])\ \|\ \overline{T}\end{array}}$$

REF

$$\frac{l\ fresh\quad \tau = W(\mathbf{t}^I,l)}{\begin{array}{c}\sigma,\bar{\tau},(\mathbf{t}^I,E[\mathbf{ref}\ v])\ \|\ \overline{T}\ \rightarrow\\ \sigma[l\mapsto v],\bar{\tau}.\tau,(\mathbf{t}^I,E[l])\ \|\ \overline{T}\end{array}}$$

TOUCH

$$\frac{\overline{T}=(\mathbf{t}^{\ell_f},v)\ \|\ \overline{T}'}{\sigma,\bar{\tau},(\mathbf{t}^I,E[\mathbf{touch}\ \ell_f])\ \|\ \overline{T}\ \rightarrow\ \sigma,\bar{\tau},(\mathbf{t}^I,E[v])\ \|\ \overline{T}}$$

SPAWN

$$\frac{t'\ fresh\quad \tau = S(\mathbf{t}^I,\mathbf{t}'^{\phi})}{\sigma,\bar{\tau},(\mathbf{t}^I,E[\mathbf{spawn}\ e])\ \|\ \overline{T}\ \rightarrow\ \sigma,\bar{\tau}.\tau,(\mathbf{t}'^{\phi},e)\ \|\ (\mathbf{t}^I,E[\mathbf{unit}])\ \|\ \overline{T}}$$

FUTURE

$$\frac{t'\ fresh\quad \ell_f,\ell_c\ fresh^I\quad \tau=F(\mathbf{t}^I,\mathbf{t}^{\ell_f})}{\sigma,\bar{\tau},(\mathbf{t}^I,E[\mathbf{future}\ e])\ \|\ \overline{T}\ \rightarrow\ \sigma,\bar{\tau}.\tau,(\mathbf{t}^{\ell_c},e)\ \|\ (\mathbf{t}'^{\ell_f},E[\ell])\ \|\ \overline{T}}$$

READ

$$\frac{\tau = R(\mathbf{t}^I,l)}{\begin{array}{c}\sigma,\bar{\tau},(\mathbf{t}^I,E[!\ l])\ \|\ \overline{T}\ \rightarrow\\ \sigma,\bar{\tau}.\tau(\mathbf{t}^I,E[v])\ \|\ \overline{T}\end{array}}$$

WRITE

$$\frac{\tau = W(\mathbf{t}^I,l)}{\begin{array}{c}\sigma,\bar{\tau},(\mathbf{t}^I,E[l:=v])\ \|\ \overline{T}\ \rightarrow\\ \sigma[l\mapsto v],\bar{\tau}.\tau(\mathbf{t}^I,E[\mathbf{unit}])\ \|\ \overline{T}\end{array}}$$

Fig. 8. Evaluation rules

relations mirror one another. A trace element $R(id,l)$ commutes to the left of a trace subsequence $\bar{\tau}_2$ if $\bar{\tau}_2$ does not contain an action performed by another that either writes to l (which would result in a read-after-write dependence), or does not spawn a thread or a future with identifier id. A similar right-mover [4] construction applies to writes.

The evaluation rules used to generate traces are given in Fig. 8, and are standard. To illustrate the rules, consider the unsafe execution of the program shown Fig. 6. Let the trace be $F(1,3_f)\ F(2,4_f)\ W(4_c,y)\ W(3_c,x)\ R(3_f,y)$ $R(4_c,x)$. Here, $F(1,3_f)$ denotes the creation of the future by thread 1 with label 3_f, $F(2,4_f)$ denotes the creation of the future in thread 2 with label 4_f, $W(4_f,y)$ denotes the write of variable y by this future's continuation, $W(3_c,x)$ denotes the write of variable x by future 3_f's continuation, $R(3_f,y)$ denotes the read of y by the first future, and $R(4_c,x)$ captures the read of x by the second future.

In the above trace, not all continuation actions occur after their future's. Because it is not a trivially serial trace, we need to consider whether it can be safely permuted. We can permute this trace to $F(1,3_f)\ F(2,4_f)\ W(4_c,y)\ R(3_f,y)$ $W(3_c,x)\ R(4_f,x)$; such a permutation preserves all inter-thread dependencies found in the original. But, no further permutations are possible; in particular, commuting $R(4_f, x)$ to the left of $W(4_c y)$ would break the dependency between $W(3_c, x)$ and $R(4_f, x)$. Similar reasoning applies if we permuted the actions of the second future with its continuation. Hence, we conclude the trace is unsafe.

4 Implementation

To enable scalable construction of safe futures, we formulate a strategy that associates *capabilities* with threads, futures, as well as the locations they modify and read. Abstractly, capabilities are used to indicate which effects have been witnessed by a future and its continuation, either directly or indirectly, as well as to constrain which locations a future and its continuation may read or modify. Capabilities ensure that *happens-before* dependencies are not established that would violate sequential consistency for a given thread of control. Thus, capabilities guarantee that an execution is equivalent to an execution where the future completes prior to its continuation's start in much the same way that the depedency preserving permutation asserts equivalence between traces.

A capability is defined as a binding between a label ℓ, denoting the dynamic instances of a future, and a *tag*. There are three tags of interest: F to denote that a thread or location has been influenced by a future, C to denote hat a thread or location has been influenced by a continuation, and FC to denote that a thread or location that first was influenced by a future and later by its continuation. It is illegal for a computation to witness the effects of a continuation and then the continuation's future (i.e., there is no CF tag). Tracking multiple labels allows us to differentiate between effects of different futures.

When a future with label ℓ is created, a constraint is established that relates the execution of the thread executing this future with its continuation. Namely, we add a mapping from ℓ to F for the thread executing the future and a mapping from ℓ to C for the thread executing the continuation. When the future or continuation reads or writes from a given location, we propagate its constraints to that location. Therefore, capabilities provide a *tainting* property that succinctly records the history of actions performed by a thread, and which threads as well as locations those actions have influenced.

To ensure a thread T's read or write is correct, it must be the case that either (a) T has thus far only read values written by the future ℓ; (b) T has thus far only witnessed values written by the continuation of future ℓ; or (c) T had previously read values written by the future, but now only reads values written by the future's continuation. If T has previously read values written by the future ℓ, and then subsequently read values written by its continuation; allowing T to read further values written by the future would break correctness guarantees on the future's execution. Thus, prior to a read or a write to a location, if that location has capabilities associated with it, we must ensure that the thread which is trying to read or write from that location also has the same capabilities.

4.1   Capability Lifting

Capabilities can be lifted in the obvious manner. A capability can be lifted to a new capability that is more constrained. A thread or location with no capability for a given label ℓ can lift to either C or F. A thread which has a capability of F can lift the capability to FC and similarly a thread with a capability C can lift the capability to FC. A future and its continuation can never lift their capabilities for their own label. We allow a given thread to read or write to a location if its capabilities are equal to those for the given location. When a future completes, it is safe to discard all capabilities related to the future.

Based on capability mappings, we can distinguish between *speculative* and non-speculative computations. A continuation of a future is a speculative computation until the future completes. Similarly, any thread which communicates with a continuation of a future, becomes speculative at the communication point. On the other hand, any thread which has only F capabilities or an empty capability map is *non-speculative*. A future may in turn be speculative. As an example, consider the following program fragment which creates nested futures:

```
let fun g() = ...
    fun h() = ... future(g) ...
    fun i() = ... future(h) ...
in i()
end
```

At the point of the creation of the future to evaluate g, the remainder of the function h (the future evaluating g's continuation) is speculative. The thread evaluating g as a future would have capabilities $\ell_g \mapsto F$ and $\ell_h \mapsto F$ and the thread evaluating the continuation would have capabilities $\ell_g \mapsto C$ and $\ell_h \mapsto F$.

Using our notion of capabilities, we can handle future to future interactions by ensuring that the future and its continuation have consistent capabilities upon the futures completion. Since multiple threads of control can create futures (as in our example in Fig. 6) it is possible for a continuation of a future f to witness the effects of some other future g while the future f witnesses the effects of g's continuation. This would violate the dependencies imposed by sequential evaluation of both threads of control. To account for this, we check that a future and its continuation have consistent capabilities when a future completes. In addition, when a location or thread that has a *speculative* capability (i.e. C, FC) acquires a capability for a future ℓ (i.e. $\ell \mapsto F$) we impose an *ordering* constraint between the future of the speculative capability and the future ℓ. Namely, the future ℓ logically *must* occur *after* the future of the continuation whose effect was witnessed. The manifestation of these checks directly mirrors the dependency preserving permutation rules described earlier.

4.2   Evaluation

To illustrate the benefits of our capability mechanism to provide safety in presence of *both* futures and threads, we tested our prototype implementation, comparing traditional safe-futures to threads and futures. All experiments were executed on a 16-way 3.2 Ghz AMD Opteron with 32 GB main memory. We executed the benchmark in two configurations. The first was a traditional safe-future implementation that leveraged capabilities for commit checks. This configuration did not include any mechanisms to track future to thread dependencies nor the rollback mechanism to revert multiple threads. The second configuration was our futures and threads implementation described above.

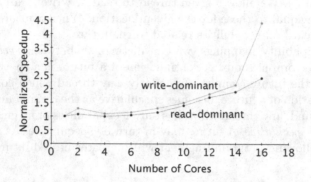

Fig. 9. Comparison of safe futures to futures and threads on all-pairs shortest path

We tested both implementations on an all-pairs shortest path algorithm (Floyd-Warshall). The algorithm operates over a matrix representation of a graph of 16 million nodes. It executes a phase to calculate the shortest path through a given node in the graph, making the total number of phases proportional to the number of nodes in the graph. The algorithm takes as input the edge-weight matrix of a weighted directed graph and returns the matrix of shortest-length paths between all pairs of nodes in the graph. The algorithm works by first computing the shortest path between two given nodes of length one. It then computes the shortest path between the two nodes by increasing length.

Safe futures are able to extract parallelism between separate phases, allowing the computation of distinct phases in parallel. Although each phase depends on the phase prior, it is possible to execute multiple phases in parallel by staggering their executions. The amount of parallelism is limited by the dependencies between phases. The futures and threads implementation can not only extract parallelism between separate phases of the algorithm, but also parallelism within a phase. This is accomplished using fork-join parallelism, and is not easily expressible using only safe futures without significant modifications to the program structure. We observe that threads can be allocated to compute over different parts of the matrix within a given phase by splitting the matrix into conceptual chunks. Although this is easily expressed using threads, safe-futures require the programmer to express the splitting of the matrix via control flow within each phase. This occurs because there does not exists a mechanism to constrain the execution of a future over a part of a data structure.

In addition, a safe futures-only strategy would enforce serializability between each chunk, even though this is not necessary. Results are summarized in Fig. 9. Notice that after executing 6 phases in parallel, the benefits of using only safe futures decreases. This occurs due to the higher rate of aborts from the dependencies between phases. In this workload, one future is created for each available processor meaning that on four cores four phases are executed in parallel at any given moment. In all cases roughly 16 million futures are created (one per phase), but the number of phases executed in parallel depends on the availability of processors. In the futures and threads implementation, we create one thread for every two available processors per each phase. Each thread is split into a future and continuation, allowing the computation of two phases in parallel. The total number of threads (and futures) is therefore 16 million times the number of cores/2. In both implementations, it is not beneficial to create more speculative work than the amount of processors available.

Fig. 9 shows the benefits of using futures with threads on two different types of workloads for the all-pair shortest path problem, one containing 5% writes (read-dominant) and the other 75% writes (write-dominant). The workloads are generated using the observation that paths through nodes which are ranked higher in the matrix are utilized in later phases. If the weights of edges between higher ranked nodes are smaller more writes occur since new smaller paths are found in successive phases. The read-dominant workload, on the other hand, is generated by making the edge-wights between lower ranked nodes smaller than the those between high ranked nodes. We see that futures with threads outperform using only safe futures in both styles of workload. In the read-dominant workload, the number of aborts for having futures-only is roughly 2 times higher (5432 aborts total). In comparison, in the write-dominant workload, the number of aborts for having just safe futures goes as high as 5 times (around 25255 aborts total) more than having both futures and threads. In both the workloads, we see more aborts due to the large number of cross phase data dependencies. This is especially true when speculating across more than four phases of the algorithm as the benefits of staggering executions becomes muted. The write-dominant workload results in more aborts as the number of data dependencies between any two phases increases. The above experiment illustrates the benefits of using futures with threads over just safe futures for a benchmark which is more write-dominant. This occurs because the futures with threads scheme can extract parallelism from within each phase, thereby limiting the number of parallel speculative phases necessary to keep all processors busy.

5   Related Work and Conclusion

Futures are a well known programming construct found in languages from Multilisp [5] to Java [6]. Many recent language proposals [7,8,9] incorporate future-like constructs. Futures typically require that they are manually claimed by explicitly calling touch. Pratikakis et. al [10] simplify programming with futures by providing an analysis to track the flow of future through a program and automating the injection of claim operations on the future at points where the value yielded by the future is required, although the burden of ensuring safety still rests with the programmer.

There has been a number of recent proposals dealing with *safe-futures*. Welc et. al [3] provide a dynamic analysis that enforces deterministic execution of sequential Java programs. In sequential programs, static analysis coupled with simple program transformations [1] can ensure deterministic parallelism by providing coordination between futures and their continuations in the presence of mutable state. Unfortunately neither approach provided safety in the presences of exceptions. This was remedied in [11,2] which presented an implementation for exception-handling in the presence of *safe futures*.

Flanagan and Felleisen [12] presented a formal semantics for futures, but did not consider how to enforce safety (i.e. determinism) in the presence of mutable state. Navabi and Jagannathan [13] presented a formulation of safe-futures for a higher-order language with first-class exceptions and first-class references. Neither formulation consider the interaction of futures with explicit threads of control. Futures have been extend with support for asynchronous method calls and active objects [14]. Although not described in the context of safe-futures, [15] proposed a type and effect system that simplifies parallel programming by enforcing deterministic semantics. Grace [16] is a highly scalable runtime system that eliminates concurrency errors for programs with fork-join parallelism by enforcing a sequential commit protocol on threads which run as processes. Boudol and Petri [17] provide a definition for valid speculative computations independent of any implementation technique. Velodrome [18] is a sound and complete atomicity checker for multi-threaded programs that analyzes traces of programs for atomicity violations.

This paper presents a dynamic analysis for enforcing determinism in an explicitly concurrent program for a higher-order language with references. Safety is ensured dynamically through the use of a light weight capability tracking mechanism. Our initial prototype indicates that futures and threads are able to extract additional parallelism over a traditional safe-future approach.

Acknowledgements. This work is supported by the National Science Foundation under grants CCF-0701832 and CCF-0811631.

References

1. Navabi, A., Zhang, X., Jagannathan, S.: Quasi-static Scheduling for Safe Futures. In: PPoPP, pp. 23–32. ACM (2008)
2. Navabi, A., Zhang, X., Jagannathan, S.: Dependence Analysis for Safe Futures. Science of Computer Programming (2011)
3. Welc, A., Jagannathan, S., Hosking, A.: Safe Futures for Java. In: OOPSLA, pp. 439–435. ACM (2005)
4. Flanagan, C., Qadeer, S.: A Type and Effect System for Atomicity. In: PLDI, pp. 338–349 (2003)

5. Halstead, R.: Multilisp: A Language for Concurrent Symbolic Computation. ACM Trans. Program. Lang. Syst. 7, 501–538 (1985)
6. http://java.sun.com/j2se/1.5.0/docs/guide/concurrency
7. Allan, E., Chase, D., Hallett, J., Luchangco, V., Maessen, J., Ryu, S., Steele, G., Tobin-Hochstadt, S.: The Fortress Language Specification Version 1.0. Technical report, Sun Microsystems, Inc. (2008)
8. Charles, P., Grothoff, C., Saraswat, V., Donawa, C., Kielstra, A., Ebcioglu, K., von Praun, C., Sarkar, V.: X10: an object-oriented approach to non-uniform cluster computing. In: OOPSLA, pp. 519–538. ACM (2005)
9. Liskov, B., Shrira, L.: Promises: Linguistic Support for Efficient Asynchronous Procedure Calls in Distributed Systems. In: PLDI, pp. 260–267. ACM (1988)
10. Pratikakis, P., Spacco, J., Hicks, M.: Transparent Proxies for Java Futures. In: OOPSLA, pp. 206–223. ACM (2004)
11. Zhang, L., Krintz, C., Nagpurkar, P.: Supporting Exception Handling for Futures in Java. In: PPPJ, pp. 175–184. ACM (2007)
12. Flanagan, C., Felleisen, M.: The semantics of future and an application. Journal of Functional Programming 9, 1–31 (1999)
13. Navabi, A., Jagannathan, S.: Exceptionally Safe Futures. In: Field, J., Vasconcelos, V.T. (eds.) COORDINATION 2009. LNCS, vol. 5521, pp. 47–65. Springer, Heidelberg (2009)
14. de Boer, F.S., Clarke, D., Johnsen, E.B.: A Complete Guide to the Future. In: De Nicola, R. (ed.) ESOP 2007. LNCS, vol. 4421, pp. 316–330. Springer, Heidelberg (2007)
15. Adve, S.V., Heumann, S., Komuravelli, R., Overbey, J., Simmons, P., Sung, H., Vakilian, M.: A type and effect system for deterministic parallel java. In: OOPSLA (2009)
16. Berger, E.D., Yang, T., Liu, T., Novark, G.: Grace: safe multithreaded programming for c/c++. In: OOPSLA, pp. 81–96. ACM, New York (2009)
17. Boudol, G., Petri, G.: A Theory of Speculative Computation. In: Gordon, A.D. (ed.) ESOP 2010. LNCS, vol. 6012, pp. 165–184. Springer, Heidelberg (2010)
18. Flanagan, C., Freund, S.N., Yi, J.: Velodrome: a sound and complete dynamic atomicity checker for multithreaded programs. In: PLDI, pp. 293–303 (2008)

Efficiency Optimizations for Implementations of Deadlock Immunity

Horatiu Jula, Silviu Andrica, and George Candea

School of Computer and Communication Science
École Polytechnique Fédérale de Lausanne (EPFL), Switzerland

Abstract. Deadlock immunity is a property by which programs, once afflicted by a deadlock, develop resistance against future occurrences of that deadlock. Our deadlock immunity system, called Dimmunix, provides transparent immunization against deadlocks involving mutex locks.

In this paper, we focus on efficiently protecting systems against deadlocks regardless of the rate of synchronization operations performed. We describe five optimizations that reduce the runtime overhead imposed by Dimmunix on the host system: (1) offline deadlock detection and signature extraction, which avoids runtime tracking of lock-to-thread allocations; (2) selective program instrumentation, whereby only vulnerable synchronization statements are monitored; (3) inline matching of deadlock signatures, which avoids expensive call stack retrieval; (4) false positive reduction, which avoids unnecessary thread serialization; and (5) safe early resumption of threads, allowing suspended threads to resume their execution more quickly than in the original Dimmunix. Our optimizations enable Dimmunix to achieve a reduction of 2.8x-5.2x in the runtime overhead it introduces for real-world systems like Eclipse, Vuze, and MySQL JDBC.

1 Introduction

When threads do not coordinate correctly in their use of locks, a deadlock can occur—a situation whereby a group of threads cannot make progress (i.e., they hang), because each thread is waiting for another thread to release a lock. Although deadlocks involving other types of synchronization mechanisms exist (e.g., deadlocks caused by condition variables) deadlocks involving locks are prevalent [4,2,7].

Deadlocks are an important cause of system failures, as revealed by multiple surveys [4,2,7], yet avoiding their introduction during development is challenging. Large software systems are developed by many programmers, which makes it hard to maintain the coding discipline needed to avoid deadlocks. Exercising all possible execution paths and thread interleavings during testing is infeasible in practice for large programs, and even deadlock-free code is not guaranteed to execute free of deadlocks once deployed in the field, due to dependencies on deadlock-prone third party libraries and plugins.

Debugging deadlocks is hard—merely seeing a deadlock happen does not mean the bug is easy to fix. Deadlocks often require complex sequences of low-probability events to manifest (e.g., timing or workload dependencies, presence or absence of debug code, compiler optimization options), making them hard to reproduce and diagnose. Sometimes deadlocks are too costly to fix, because a fix would entail drastic redesign.

S. Khurshid and K. Sen (Eds.): RV 2011, LNCS 7186, pp. 78–93, 2012.

Patches, too, are error-prone: many concurrency bug fixes either introduce new bugs or, instead of fixing the underlying bug, merely decrease the probability of occurrence [4].

To address these problems, we developed a technique called deadlock immunity [3]. It helps applications defend against deadlocks by enabling them, once afflicted by a given deadlock, to automatically develop resistance against future occurrences of that deadlock. We implemented this technique in a system called Dimmunix, which has two modules running simultaneously: (1) a detector that dynamically detects deadlocks and extracts their signatures, and (2) an avoidance module that uses the signatures as antibodies to avoid future occurrences of these deadlocks. A signature is an approximation of the execution flow that led to a deadlock. To avoid a previously encountered deadlock, Dimmunix temporarily suspends the threads whose executions are about to match the signature of that deadlock.

The challenge of efficiently scaling Dimmunix to synchronization-intensive systems resides in its necessity to process *every* lock operation. A high synchronization rate creates a large amount of work for Dimmunix, causing it to induce a high runtime overhead. In this paper, we describe optimizations that are generally applicable to all runtimes implementing deadlock immunity. These optimizations enable the runtimes to protect systems against deadlocks regardless of the rate of synchronization operations.

We present five main optimizations for runtimes implementing deadlock immunity: (1) offline deadlock detection, i.e., deadlocks are detected and their signatures extracted only when the program terminates, instead of performing these tasks whenever a thread requests a lock; (2) selective program instrumentation, whereby only vulnerable synchronization statements are monitored; (3) inline matching of deadlock signatures, which avoids expensive call stack retrieval; (4) false positive reduction, which avoids unnecessary thread serialization; and (5) safe early resumption of threads, allowing suspended threads to resume their execution more quickly than in the original Dimmunix.

We implemented these optimizations in Dimmunix and achieved a reduction of 2.8x-5.2x in the runtime overhead Dimmunix introduces for real world systems like Eclipse, Vuze, and MySQL JDBC.

In the rest of the paper we present background information about Dimmunix (§2), then describe the optimizations (§3), and assess their effectiveness (§4). We then review related work (§5) and conclude (§6).

2   Background

Deadlock immunity is a property by which programs, once afflicted by a deadlock, develop resistance against future occurrences of that deadlock. Dimmunix [3] provides immunization against deadlocks involving mutex locks, with no assistance from programmers or users. Dimmunix can be used by customers to defend themselves against deadlocks while waiting for a fix, and by software vendors as a safety net. Its architecture consists of two parts: (1) a module that detects deadlocks and adds their signatures to a persistent deadlock history, and (2) an avoidance module that prevents occurrences of previously encountered deadlocks, by avoiding execution flows matching signatures from history: whenever the execution of a thread may lead to a previously encountered deadlock, Dimmunix suspends that thread until the deadlock danger passes.

Dimmunix detects and avoids deadlocks by taking control of the program whenever a thread requests a lock, after it acquires that lock, and before it releases that lock. Dimmunix uses these events to update the synchronization state of the program, represented as a resource allocation graph (RAG) whose nodes are threads and locks. The RAG edges are of three types: an edge from a thread t to a lock l denotes that t is waiting to acquire l; an edge from l to t denotes that t is holding l; an edge from a thread t_1 to a thread t_2 means that Dimmunix suspended t_1 because of t_2, in order to avoid a deadlock. Edges are annotated with the call stack a thread had when the edge was created.

Dimmunix detects deadlocks by looking for cycles in the RAG every time a thread requests a lock, and if a cycle is found, it saves the deadlock's signature to a persistent history, to prevent future occurrences of this deadlock. A signature characterizes the deadlocking execution via the program positions of the nested synchronization statements it involves. A program position represents a location in the source code or an offset in the program binary; for Java programs, Dimmunix uses source code locations. We call the nested synchronization statements involved in the deadlock "outer" and "inner" lock statements. The outer lock statements correspond to the acquisitions of the locks involved in the deadlock. The inner lock statements correspond to the places where the threads deadlocked. Since these statements can be reached by a multitude of program executions, of which only a few deadlock, Dimmunix additionally saves in the deadlock signature the call stacks the deadlocked threads had when they acquired the locks involved in the deadlock (called "outer call stacks") and the call stacks the deadlocked threads had at the time of the deadlock (called "inner call stacks"). Each frame of an outer/inner call stack is a program position; the top frame points to a synchronization statement. The top frame of an outer (inner) call stack points to an outer (respectively inner) lock statement.

Imagine a deadlock involving threads t_1 and t_2 that have acquired locks l_1 and l_2, respectively, and now wait to acquire the other lock. This deadlock appears in the RAG as the cycle $l_1 \xrightarrow{CS_1^{out}} t_1 \xrightarrow{CS_1^{in}} l_2 \xrightarrow{CS_2^{out}} t_2 \xrightarrow{CS_2^{in}} l_1$, and the signature of the deadlock consists of the pairs of outer and inner call stacks, i.e., $\{(CS_1^{out}, CS_1^{in}), (CS_2^{out}, CS_2^{in})\}$. The signature is saved to a history file that persists across multiple executions of the program.

An instantiation of a signature S with outer call stacks $CS_1^{out}, ..., CS_n^{out}$ is a situation where threads $t_1, ..., t_n$ hold (or are allowed to acquire) locks $l_1, ..., l_n$ while having call stacks $CS_1^{out}, ..., CS_n^{out}$. Each outer call stack CS_i^{out} is matched up to a predefined depth, called matching depth, defined as the number of consecutive frames in CS_i^{out} to be matched against a thread's call stack, starting from the top frame. We formally represent the instantiation as the set $I = \{(t_1, l_1, CS_1^{out}), ..., (t_n, l_n, CS_n^{out})\}$.

Avoiding previously seen deadlocks consists of avoiding instantiations of signatures from the deadlock history. Consider that thread t_1 requests lock l_1 while having call stack CS_1^{out}. To avoid instantiations of signature S, Dimmunix first "pretends" to allow t_1 to acquire l_1, i.e., it does not allow t_1 to proceed, but it updates the RAG as if it did. Then, Dimmunix checks if instantiations of S are possible; if yes, Dimmunix suspends t_1 until no instantiations of S are possible. When Dimmunix suspends a thread, we say that the thread "yields."

Dimmunix automatically handles avoidance-induced deadlocks: when one occurs, Dimmunix saves its signature (so it will avoid its reoccurrence, just like for a normal deadlock) and resumes the suspended threads. More details appear in [3].

3 Optimizations

In this section, we present the optimizations we performed to Dimmunix to achieve low runtime overhead for Java programs regardless of the synchronization operation throughput. There are three improvements that we achieve: first, we reduce the number of synchronization operations that are intercepted by Dimmunix. Second, we optimize Dimmunix's performance-critical computations. Third, we reduce the amount of time Dimmunix suspends threads to avoid deadlocks.

For Dimmunix to intercept fewer synchronization operations, we needed to implement two optimizations: first, Dimmunix detects deadlocks and extracts their signatures offline, when the program is forcefully terminated. To detect deadlocks, Dimmunix invokes the JVM's deadlock detection method. Previously, Dimmunix used online deadlock detection, i.e., the RAG was updated upon each synchronization operation and the deadlock detection was performed periodically [3]; therefore, Dimmunix needed to intercept every synchronization operation.

We implemented the offline signature extraction for deadlocks involving synchronized blocks/methods. Upon a deadlock, Dimmunix automatically infers the outer call stacks of a deadlock signature from the inner call stacks, which are available at the time of the deadlock. Previously, Dimmunix retrieved and stored upon each lock acquisition the call stack of the thread that requested the lock [3]. Section 3.1 presents details about the inference of outer call stacks.

Second, Dimmunix instruments only the synchronized blocks/methods previously involved in deadlocks. This optimization is effective because most of the mutex synchronization statements (i.e., lock/unlock statements) are synchronized blocks/methods (e.g., more than 96% in Vuze, ActiveMQ, Limewire, and JBoss, and 58.3% in Eclipse) and only the ones previously involved in deadlocks are instrumented. Section 3.2 describes the selective program instrumentation.

We identified one performance-critical computation in Dimmunix: the matching of deadlock signatures' call stacks. Most of the computations are involved in checking whether a previously encountered deadlock is about to reoccur. Previously, Dimmunix used standard call stack retrieval methods (e.g., Java's *Thread.getStackTrace()* method) to obtain the call stack of a thread upon a lock acquisition and compared it to the call stacks of the signatures in the history [3]. Dimmunix spent most of the execution time in the call stack retrieval. We optimized it by inlining the call stack matching (§3.3).

Finally, we reduce the amount of time Dimmunix suspends threads to avoid deadlocks (i.e., the thread serialization), by performing two optimizations: first, Dimmunix automatically detects a posteriori if the decisions to suspend threads to avoid deadlocks were false positives (FPs), and increases the signature matching accuracy whenever an FP is encountered (§3.4). Increasing the matching depth for a signature reduces the probability of matching the signature at runtime, which means that thread yields are less frequent; therefore, the amount of thread serialization decreases. We already introduced in [3] the FP detection mechanism; however, this paper is the first one explaining it in depth. Second, Dimmunix resumes the threads suspended to avoid deadlocks as soon as the program execution reaches a point from which the deadlock situation becomes unreachable, i.e., the inner lock statements involved in the deadlock become unreachable (§3.5). Resuming threads earlier reduces the duration of the yields, which means less thread serialization. Previously, Dimmunix resumed the suspended threads only when at least one lock involved in an avoided signature instantiation was released [3].

3.1   Inferring the Outer Call Stacks of a Signature

To be able to selectively instrument only the synchronized blocks/methods previously involved in deadlocks, Dimmunix needs to automatically infer the outer call stacks of a deadlock signature from the inner call stacks, which are available at the time of the deadlock. Otherwise, Dimmunix would have to retrieve and store the call stack of the caller thread upon each lock acquisition.

To deterministically infer the outer call stack of a signature, we require usage of properly nested synchronization statements, i.e., locks are released in the reverse order of their acquisitions. For example, this is the case for Java's synchronized blocks/methods, but the technique is not limited to these only. Properly nested synchronization statements enable us to deterministically obtain the outer call stacks of a signature from inner call stacks by removing frames from the top of the latter, because the outer call stacks are prefixes of the inner call stacks.

Inferring outer call stacks works as follows: first, Dimmunix finds the threads that acquired the locks involved in a deadlock, as described in Algorithm 1. This requires access to each thread's lock stack, which contains the locks that thread acquired (and still holds) and the requested one on top. For Java programs, these stacks are obtained from the JVM. For each lock l_i involved in the deadlock, Dimmunix finds the program position where lock l_i was acquired. It is not possible to infer this program position based solely on the information provided by the CFG, because the CFG does not contain lock identities. Therefore, Dimmunix needs to find the index k_j of lock l_i in the lock stack LS_j of thread t_j owning l_i (lines 1–4). Next, Dimmunix finds where thread t_j acquired l_i (i.e., its k_j-th lock), by exploring backward the CFG the application and popping call frames from the inner call stack, as shown in Algorithm 2 (lines 8–12). Every time a lock (respectively unlock) statement is encountered, the counter $k_{nesting}$ storing the nesting level is incremented (respectively decremented); initially, $k_{nesting} = 0$ (lines 1–7). The outer lock statement is reached when $k_{nesting} = k_j$, and the algorithm returns the current call stack with the top frame replaced by the current lock statement (lines 4–5). The algorithm is deterministic because exploring backward any execution path leads to the same outer lock statement.

3.2   Selective Program Instrumentation

Dimmunix instruments only the synchronized blocks/methods previously involved in deadlocks. To avoid previously encountered deadlocks, it is sufficient for Dimmunix to instrument only these statements.

Input: Deadlocked threads $t_1, ..., t_n$ with call stacks $CS_1^{inner}, ..., CS_n^{inner}$, lock stacks
$LS_1, ..., LS_n$, and requested locks $l_1, ..., l_n$.
Output: Signature $S = \{(CS_1^{outer}, CS_1^{inner}), ..., (CS_n^{outer}, CS_n^{inner})\}$, where CS_i^{outer} are the
inferred outer call stacks.

1 **foreach** $i \in [1, n]$ **do**
2   Let t_j be the thread holding l_i
3   Find the index k_j of l_i in LS_j, corresponding to l_i's acquisition
4 **foreach** $i \in [1, n]$ **do**
5      $CS_i^{outer} := getOuterCallStack(CS_i^{inner}, k_i, CS_i^{inner}.top, 0)$
6 **return** $\{(CS_1^{outer}, CS_1^{inner}), ..., (CS_n^{outer}, CS_n^{inner})\}$

Algorithm 1. *getSignature*: building the signature of a deadlock

Input: Inner call stack CS^{inner}; Lock stack index k; Current statement s, initially the
statement corresponding to CS^{inner}'s top frame; Current nesting level $k_{nesting}$,
initially 0.
Data: Control flow graph (CFG) of the method containing s.
Output: Inferred outer call stack CS^{outer}.

1 **if** there exists an unexplored predecessor s' of s in the CFG **then**
2   **if** s' is *lock acquisition* **then**
3         $k_{nesting} := k_{nesting} + 1$
4   **if** $k_{nesting} = k$ **then**
5   **return** $CS^{inner}.pop().push(s')$ // replace the top frame with s'
6   **if** s' is *lock release* **then**
7         $k_{nesting} := k_{nesting} - 1$
8   **return** $getOuterCallStack(CS^{inner}, k, s', k_{nesting})$
9 **else**
10      $CS^{inner} := CS^{inner}.pop()$ // remove the top frame
11   **return** $getOuterCallStack(CS^{inner}, k, CS^{inner}.top, k_{nesting})$

Algorithm 2. *getOuterCallStack($CS^{inner}, k, s, k_{nesting}$)*: recursively computes the outer
call stack corresponding to an inner call stack CS^{inner} and a lock stack index k

Dimmunix instruments the outer and inner lock statements involved in a deadlock
(i.e., the program positions referenced by the top frames of the deadlock's signature),
and the corresponding unlock statements. Since synchronized blocks are properly nested,
the unlock statements corresponding to a lock statement s_l are easily found by exploring forward the CFG and keeping track of the nesting level. Matching lock and unlock
statements have the same nesting level.

The outer call stacks of a deadlock signature cannot be inferred deterministically
(in the general case) for explicit lock acquisition statements, like Java's *Reentrant-
Lock.lock()* Therefore, Dimmunix needs to intercept each explicit lock acquisition and
store the call stack of the caller thread, in order to obtain the outer call stacks. However, since Java programs mostly use synchronized blocks/methods to acquire locks,
the amount of instrumentation is substantially reduced for Java programs.

Input: Outer call stack CS; Depth d. The call frame at depth d in CS is currently matched
    by thread t's execution.
Data: Counter $matches[CS, t]$, initialized to $CS.depth$.
Output: True if CS is matched up to its matching depth $CS.depth$, False otherwise.
1 **if** $d > CS.depth$ **then**
2   **return** False
3 **if** $d = CS.depth$ **then**
4     $matches[CS, t] := d - 1$
5 **else**
6   **if** $d = matches[CS, t]$ **then**
7         $matches[CS, t] := matches[CS, t] - 1$
8 **return** $matches[CS, t] = 0$

Algorithm 3. *inlineMatch(CS, d, t)*: checks whether thread t's execution, currently
matching the frame at depth d in call stack CS, matches CS up to its matching depth
$CS.depth$, i.e., matches the top $CS.depth$ frames of CS

3.3   Inline Call Stack Matching

A straightforward way to match a signature S is to retrieve the current call stack of
a thread upon a lock request and compare it to the outer call stacks of S up to their
matching depth. If the outer call stacks end in lock statements that execute often, this
matching mechanism becomes a bottleneck, because retrieving call stacks is expensive
for platforms like the JVM. Inlining the call stack matching considerably reduces the
performance overhead incurred by Dimmunix, as we show in §4.

In inline matching, the outer call stacks of a signature are incrementally matched,
as the program executes; we present this mechanism in detail in Algorithm 3. For each
outer call stack CS of a signature in the deadlock history, Dimmunix automatically
instruments the program bytecode before the statements referenced by the frames in
CS with code that works as follows: before a thread t executes such a statement, the
matching code decrements the counter $matches[CS, t]$ (lines 3–7). The counter represents the number of frames in CS that are yet unmatched by thread t, starting from
CS's matching depth, i.e., $CS.depth$; the counter is initialized to $CS.depth$. The matching
depth $CS.depth$ is initialized and updated by Dimmunix, as shown in §3.4. The matching is successful only if the depth d of the currently matched frame in CS is equal to
$matches[CS, t]$ (line 6). If $d = CS.depth$, the matching restarts, i.e., the counter is reset to $d - 1$ (lines 3–4). Thread t's execution matches CS up to $CS.depth$ if and only if
$matches[CS, t] = 0$ (line 9).

Inline matching means accepting non-contiguous matches, i.e., extraneous frames in
a thread's call stack are allowed, as long as the frames referenced by a signature are
in the correct order. Dimmunix is oblivious to method calls outside an outer call stack,
because they are not instrumented for matching. Since this matching mechanism is less
accurate than the straightforward one, the number of false positives may increase; however, the inline matching may protect the application against deadlock manifestations
that are not yet captured by the signature.

3.4   Reducing the Number of False Positives

Approaches that try to predict the future with the purpose of avoiding bad outcomes may suffer from false positives (FP), i.e., wrongly predict that the bad outcome will occur. In Dimmunix, FPs can arise when the outer call stacks of a signature are matched too shallowly, or when the lock order depends on inputs, program state, etc.

When an FP occurs, Dimmunix serializes threads in order to avoid an apparent impending deadlock that would actually not have occurred; this can have negative effects on performance, due to a loss in parallelism. Dimmunix "needlessly" serializes a portion of the program execution, causing the program to run slower.

Dimmunix reduces the number of FPs as follows: whenever a deadlock signature S is avoided, Dimmunix checks if the avoidance of S's instantiation was an FP. If it was, then Dimmunix recalibrates the matching accuracy for S.

Detecting False Positives.   Dimmunix determines whether forcing a thread to yield indeed avoided a deadlock or not, by looking for lock inversions after the yield. A false positive (FP) is a situation where the deadlock could not have happened, under any thread interleaving, for the current program inputs, even if Dimmunix had not avoided the deadlock. Since a yield represents the avoidance of a signature instantiation, Dimmunix associates the notion of false positive with a signature instantiation. Dimmunix classifies an instantiation I as an FP when no lock inversion occurred after avoiding I.

The following data structures are used for FP detection: in a signature instantiation $I = \{(t_1, l_1, CS_1), ..., (t_n, l_n, CS_n)\}$, Dimmunix keeps for each lock l_i the set $I.locksAcq[l_i]$ of locks acquired while holding l_i; for each thread t and lock l, Dimmunix stores the set $instances[t, l]$ of signature instantiations involving t and l that Dimmunix avoided since t acquired l last time. Dimmunix initializes with *null* each set $I.locksAcq[l_i]$ when I is constructed, and updates the set only when l_i is released. If a lock l_i is reacquired before I is analyzed, Dimmunix does not change the set $I.locksAcq[l_i]$, i.e., it freezes the set as soon as l_i is released. We denote by $I.sig$ the signature instantiated by I.

When a thread t is about to release a lock l, Dimmunix analyzes every signature instantiation $I = \{(t_1, l_1, CS_1), ..., (t_n, l_n, CS_n)\}$ from the $instances[t, l]$ set to determine whether it was a false positive (FP), as illustrated in Algorithm 4. When all the sets $I.locksAcq[l_i]$ are non-null, it means that all the locks l_i have been released, and Dimmunix analyzes I (line 4). Dimmunix classifies I as an FP if and only if there is no lock inversion in I, i.e., $l_1 \notin I.locksAcq[l_2], ...,$ or $l_n \notin I.locksAcq[l_1]$ (lines 5–6).

Classifying an instantiation I as an FP if no lock inversion occurred is sound, under the assumption that the thread scheduling does not affect lock identities and expressions controlling the inner lock statements (e.g., through data races).

Calibrating the Signature Matching Accuracy.   A signature S captures all the possible manifestations of a deadlock bug if and only if all the possible signatures of the same deadlock match S up to the matching depths of its outer call stacks. Choosing too large matching depths can cause Dimmunix to miss manifestations of the deadlock, while choosing too shallow ones can lead to mispredicting a runtime call flow as being headed for deadlock (i.e., an FP).

Input: Thread t releasing l; Set *instances[t, l]*; Sets $I.locksAcq[l_i]$ for each instantiation
   $I = \{(t_1, l_1, CS_1), ..., (t_n, l_n, CS_n)\}$ in *instances[t, l]*.
Output: Number of FPs *numFPs[S]* corresponding to each signature S.
1 // before releasing l, check if the instantiations avoided by t before l's acquisition were FPs
2 **foreach** $I = \{(t_1, l_1, CS_1), ..., (t_n, l_n, CS_n)\} \in$ *instances[t, l]* **do**
3   // if all the locks involved in I were released
4   **if** $\forall i \in [1, n]\ :\ I.locksAcq[l_i] \neq null$ **then**
5   **if** $\exists i \in [1, n]$ s.t. $l_i \notin I.locksAcq[l_{(i+1)\%n}]$ **then**
6           $numFPs[I.sig] := numFPs[I.sig] + 1$
7 **unlock(l)**

Algorithm 4. *detectFPs(t, l)*: checks if the signature instantiations that t avoided last time it requested l were FPs

We now describe how Dimmunix calibrates the matching depths at runtime to reduce FPs while maintaining effectiveness. When a signature S is created, the matching depths of its outer call stacks are set to 1. Hence, S initially captures all the possible manifestations of the deadlock bug. Every time an FP is encountered when avoiding an instantiation of S, the matching depths of S's outer call stacks are incremented.

A scenario where dynamically increasing the matching precision helps is one when an application uses synchronization wrappers, and the lock acquisitions always execute at the same program position. Keeping the matching depth at 1 serializes all the critical sections, which is not desirable. Increasing the matching depth dynamically when FPs are encountered solves this problem.

When the matching depth becomes too large, a signature may not capture all the possible manifestations of the deadlock bug, because there may exist other signatures of the same deadlock bug ending in call stack suffixes that no longer match S. To prevent this situation, Dimmunix merges signatures.

Dimmunix merges the signature S' of a new manifestation of a deadlock bug with the existing signature S of the same deadlock as follows: first, it finds the common suffix of maximum length of the outer call stacks of S and S'. Then, Dimmunix decrements the matching depths for S's outer call stacks to this length, and freezes them. Finally, Dimmunix discards signature S', to keep the deadlock history at a minimal size. If the deadlock reoccurs, with another signature S'', Dimmunix merges S and S'', and so on. This way, Dimmunix finds the deepest matching depth for S, while preserving the ability to avoid all the possible manifestations of the deadlock bug.

From our experience, the number of signatures corresponding to a deadlock bug is low, the maximum being two. If a deadlock bug has few signatures, it takes few occurrences of the deadlock to converge to an optimal matching precision. However, if a deadlock bug has many manifestations with different outer call stack suffixes, Dimmunix will most likely need to encounter only a couple of them to fully protect the application against the deadlock bug, because with each newly discovered signature the calibration algorithm decreases the matching depth of the original signature.

Input: Signature S, with outer lock statements $s_1^{out}, ..., s_n^{out}$ and inner lock statements $s_1^{in}, ..., s_n^{in}$.

Data: Control flow graph (CFG).

Output: The set of escape branches.

1 $escape := \emptyset$
2 **foreach** $i \in [1, n]$ **do**
3   **foreach** branch statement $s \in CFG$ s.t. $s_i^{out} \leadsto s$ **do**
4   Let B be the set of branches of s
5   **if** $\exists b \in B$ s.t. $b \leadsto s_i^{in}$ **then**
6              $escape := escape \cup \{b' \in B \mid \neg b' \leadsto s_i^{in}\}$
7 **return** $escape$

Algorithm 5. *findEscapeBranches(S)*: finds the escape branches for a signature S

3.5 Reducing the Yielding Time

To reduce the duration of a yield, Dimmunix exploits the branches that escape the deadlock, i.e., branches that lead the program away from acquiring the inner lock that triggers the deadlock. When such a branch is taken, Dimmunix stops the avoidance process by canceling the active yields and preventing future ones, until the lock whose acquisition triggered the avoidance is released.

Given the outer and inner call stacks of a deadlock signature, Dimmunix statically detects in the CFG of the application bytecode the "escape branches" that bypass the deadlock; we illustrate this mechanism in detail in Figure 5. To determine these branches, Dimmunix first finds the "critical branches" that need to be taken in order to reach the inner lock statements from the outer lock statements (lines 3–5). If a conditional statement has one or more critical branches (line 5), the remaining branches (if any) are escape branches (line 6). We use the notation $x \leadsto y$ to denote the fact that statement y is reachable from statement x in the CFG.

Dimmunix inserts code to stop the avoidance process at the escape branches and right after the inner lock statement, if that statement is not in a loop. Since the deadlock situation cannot be reached from these positions, the yielding threads can be safely resumed. If a deadlock occurs due to stopping the avoidance, that deadlock will have different inner lock statements, and therefore it is a new deadlock bug. A new signature is constructed for this deadlock.

4 Evaluation

The goal of this section is to assess the performance improvements that result from employing the five optimizations described above.

First, we evaluate the benefits brought by the optimizations in synchronization -intensive scenarios on three real-world applications: Eclipse IDE, Vuze BitTorrent client, and MySQL JDBC. We found that Eclipse and Vuze are synchronization-intensive at startup: they perform 78,536 and respectively 28,872 synchronization operations per second. For MySQL JDBC, we used the JDBCBench benchmark, which performs 100,855 synchronization operations per second.

The measurements for the three applications are end-to-end: for Eclipse and Vuze, we compute the runtime overheads introduced by various Dimmunix configurations by comparing the time it takes for the application to start and immediately shut down when Dimmunix is running to the time it takes without Dimmunix; for MySQL JDBC, we compare the number of transactions performed when Dimmunix is running to the number of transactions when Dimmunix is not running.

Our experiments explore Dimmunix's behavior in worst-case scenarios, even though they are unlikely to manifest during steady state operation. In the original article [3] we focus instead on realistic steady state scenarios. A worst-case scenario is one with a high rate of synchronization operations and with deadlock signatures that cover frequently executed nested synchronization statements. For our experiments, we manually generate 20 such signatures for deadlocks involving two threads. By default, Dimmunix is configured to use selective instrumentation, FP detection and matching depth calibration, inline call stack matching, and an initial matching depth of 5.

To measure the benefit of selective instrumentation, we compare the overhead introduced by Dimmunix with and without selective instrumentation. Figure 1a shows that this optimization reduces the overhead caused by Dimmunix by a factor of 1.3x–1.9x.

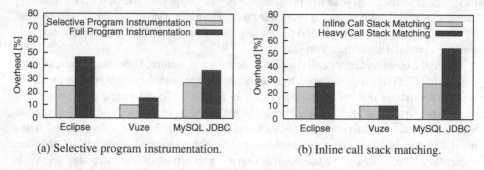

(a) Selective program instrumentation.   (b) Inline call stack matching.

Fig. 1. Benefit of selective instrumentation and inline call stack matching

To measure the benefit of the inline call stack matching, we compare the use of Java's *getStackTrace()* method for call stack matching against the default configuration. As Figure 1b shows, this optimization reduces the runtime overhead by up to 2x.

To measure the usefulness of a high signature matching accuracy, we change the initial matching depth to 1 in the default configuration. As Figure 2a shows, increasing the matching depth from 1 to 5 reduces the overhead by a factor of up to 2.6x.

We evaluate the benefit of enabling selective instrumentation and inline call stack matching together, by comparing the runtime overhead introduced by Dimmunix when both optimizations are missing against the default configuration. Figure 2b shows that the effects of the two optimizations compound: together, they reduce Dimmunix's overhead by a factor of 2.8x–5.2x. The performance improvement is higher compared to the sum of the improvements brought by the individual optimizations. The explanation is that using heavy call stack matching for all the synchronization statements is worse than using it for only several synchronization statements.

Although the signatures we generated end in program positions where most synchronization operations execute, they are not instantiated often because the applications'

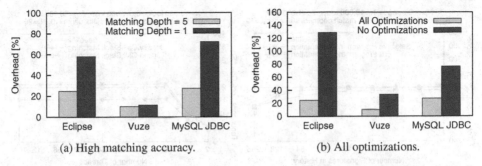

(a) High matching accuracy.   (b) All optimizations.

Fig. 2. Benefit of high matching accuracy and enabling all the optimizations at once

threads seldom synchronize as described in our signatures. Therefore, the benefit of automatically detecting FPs and increasing the matching accuracy, and exploiting the escape branches is marginal. We evaluate the effectiveness of these two optimizations on a separate microbenchmark in which signatures are instantiated often.

To dissect Dimmunix's performance behavior and understand how it varies with various parameters, we wrote a synchronization-intensive microbenchmark that creates N_t threads that synchronize on locks from a total of N_l shared locks. A thread acquires a lock by executing one of N_p lock acquisition statements, then executes δ_{in} statements, then releases the lock, then executes δ_{out} statements, then acquires another lock. The δ_{in} and δ_{out} delays are implemented as busy loops that execute incrementation statements, to simulate computation. The threads call multiple functions within the microbenchmark so as to build up different call stacks; which function is called is chosen randomly, generating a uniformly distributed selection of call stacks.

We also wrote a tool that generates synthetic deadlock history files containing H signatures of size 2 (the usual number of threads involved in a deadlock [4]). The H signatures cover H lock acquisition statements. If $H = N_p$, then all the lock acquisition statements in the microbenchmark are instrumented. Each signature has two identical call stacks that consist of combinations of the microbenchmark's methods—not signatures of real deadlocks, but avoided as if they were.

Figure 3a shows that the selective program instrumentation is effective for up to 64 signatures. The overhead of Dimmunix with selective instrumentation is 0–6.1% compared to 5.2–16.4% for full instrumentation. With an empty history, there is no overhead if Dimmunix uses selective instrumentation, while with full instrumentation, the overhead is already 5.2%, comparable to selective instrumentation with 64 signatures, because with full instrumentation Dimmunix performs signature matching at program positions where it is not needed. For more signatures, the overhead increases rapidly.

Figure 3b shows that inline call stack matching considerably reduces performance overhead: if Dimmunix uses the JVM's call stack retrieval, the overhead is 26–27%; if the call stack matching is inlined, the overhead goes down to 4–5%.

To measure the effect of detecting false positives and calibrating the signature matching precision, we first show the effect of false positives (FPs) on performance. A FP causes a thread to needlessly yield, decreasing the rate of synchronization operations. Since our microbenchmark has no real deadlocks, all yields are unnecessary. We compute the overhead caused by FPs by comparing the rate of synchronization operations

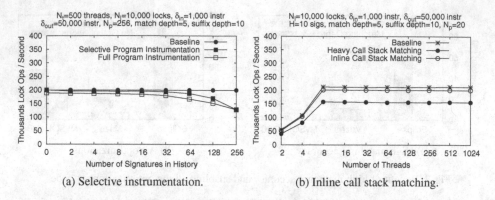

(a) Selective instrumentation.   (b) Inline call stack matching.

Fig. 3. Results for selective instrumentation and inline call stack matching

performed when Dimmunix detects that a deadlock will manifest, but takes no avoidance actions, to the same rate when Dimmunix suspends threads to avoid deadlocks.

Figure 4a shows the results: as the matching depth increases, the overhead induced by FPs decreases. For a matching depth of 1, the overhead due to FP yields is 121%. For a matching depth of 4, the overhead due to FP yields drops by 14x, to 8.56%.

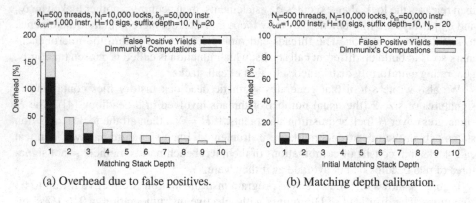

(a) Overhead due to false positives.   (b) Matching depth calibration.

Fig. 4. Detecting false positives and calibrating the signature matching precision

Figure 4b shows the benefit of increasing the matching accuracy as FPs are encountered. Compared to the configuration used for Figure 4a, here Dimmunix is configured to dynamically calibrate the matching depths. If we compare the two figures, the benefit of dynamically increasing the matching accuracy is evident: the overhead becomes acceptable even for an initial matching depth of 1 (i.e., 5.7%).

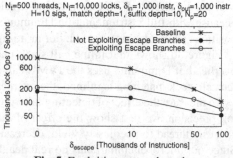

Fig. 5. Exploiting escape branches

Figure 5 shows the benefit of exploiting escape branches to reduce yielding time. The benefit is substantial if (a) the number of instructions on the escape paths that bypass the deadlock (δ_{escape}) is substantially larger than the number of instructions in the critical section preceding the escape branches, i.e., δ_{in}; (b) signatures are instantiated very often, i.e., the matching depth is low and δ_{out} is small; and (c) there are no FPs, even for shallow matching depths. We disable the matching depth calibration, in order to simulate the scenario in which there are no FPs. For $\delta_{escape} = 0$, there is no benefit in exploiting escape branches. For $\delta_{escape} = 10,000$ (respectively 50,000 and 100,000), the overhead is 77% (respectively 67% and 50%) when escape branches are not exploited, compared to 63% (respectively 40% and 32%) when exploiting escape branches.

5 Related Work

There is a spectrum of runtime techniques for avoiding or preventing deadlocks, i.e., techniques that (1) statically detect potential deadlocks and avoid them at runtime; (2) dynamically prevent deadlocks; (3) transparently recover from deadlocks; and (4) techniques that provide deadlock immunity.

Approaches like [1] and Gadara [8] detect potential deadlocks statically and avoid them at runtime. In [1], authors propose to use new locks, while Gadara uses Petri nets. If the static analysis has false positives, these approaches make the applications avoid false deadlock bugs. This is not the case for Dimmunix, because it avoids only previously detected at runtime. Unlike the two approaches, Dimmunix requires no source code. Unlike Dimmunix, Gadara needs source code annotations from the developers to filter out the false positives, yet this is difficult.

A dynamic deadlock prevention technique is [10], which modifies the JVM to serialize threads' accesses to sets of locks acquired in a nested fashion. There are a couple of shortcomings of this approach: First, the lock acquired at a particular program location can change during the same execution; if it changes often (e.g., it may correspond to an array element), then [10] is not effective. Every time new locks are used, [10] has to update the lock sets. Whenever the lock sets are not up to date, the program is vulnerable to deadlocks. Second, the lock sets are not reusable in future runs: in each run, [10] will have to restart the learning process from scratch. Dimmunix eliminates these shortcomings by abstracting the locks involved in a deadlock to call stacks.

Sammati [6] dynamically detects deadlocks and transparently recovers the applications from deadlocks by executing critical sections in isolation from other threads. If a deadlock happens during the execution of a critical section, the updates performed within the scope of that section up to the deadlock are discarded, in effect rolling back the critical section. Since Sammati is essentially a TM customized for deadlock recovery, the TM challenges (e.g., large critical sections, I/O) apply to Sammati as well.

Deadlock immunity approaches include [5,9]. These approaches dynamically detect deadlocks, then avoid future occurrences of the same deadlocks. If a deadlock involving threads t_1 and t_2 and locks l_1 and l_2 occurs, the two approaches save into the signature of the deadlock the program positions p_1 and p_2 where l_1 and l_2 were acquired; [9]

saves, in addition, the positions p_1' and p_2' where t_1 and t_2 deadlocked. In future runs, [5,9] prevent the deadlock from reoccurring by acquiring a "gate lock" every time the lock statement at p_1 or p_2 is about to execute. If the lock at p_1' (or p_2') can be soundly inferred at runtime from p_1 (respectively p_2), [9] swaps the lock acquisitions at p_1 and p_1' (respectively p_2 and p_2'), instead of acquiring a gate lock. The latter avoidance mechanism is difficult in the general case, because predicting which lock objects will be used is undecidable. Therefore, speculatively acquiring the lock at p_1' (or p_2') does not guarantee that the deadlock will be avoided.

Dimmunix shares ideas with [5,9], but uses a more accurate avoidance mechanism. Like in these approaches, Dimmunix's deadlock avoidance mechanism relies on temporarily suspending threads. Dimmunix has fewer false positives, compared to these techniques, thus alleviating the problem of lost parallelism. Finally, the efficiency of Dimmunix's critical-path computations is comparable to acquiring a gate lock.

6   Conclusion

In this paper, we presented the optimizations we brought to Dimmunix, a system that enables applications to defend themselves against deadlocks.

We reduce the overhead introduced by Dimmunix's deadlock detection by performing it offline, when the program terminates. We optimize the deadlock avoidance by (1) performing selective program instrumentation to confine monitoring to only lock statements previously involved in deadlocks, (2) inlining the matching of signatures, (3) reducing the number of false positives, and (4) aborting deadlock avoidance when the deadlock situation becomes unreachable.

We implemented these optimizations for the Dimmunix prototype targeting Java applications. Our evaluation shows that these optimizations significantly reduce the overhead Dimmunix incurs on Java applications.

References

[1] Boronat, P., Cholvi, V.: A transformation to provide deadlock-free programs. In: Intl. Conf. on Computational Science (2003)

[2] Fonseca, P., Li, C., Singhal, V., Rodrigues, R.: A study of the internal and external effects of concurrency bugs. In: Intl. Conf. on Dependable Systems and Networks (2010)

[3] Jula, H., Tralamazza, D., Zamfir, C., Candea, G.: Deadlock immunity: Enabling systems to defend against deadlocks. In: Symp. on Operating Sys. Design and Implem. (2008)

[4] Lu, S., Park, S., Seo, E., Zhou, Y.: Learning from mistakes – a comprehensive study on real world concurrency bug characteristics. In: Intl. Conf. on Architectural Support for Programming Languages and Operating Systems (2008)

[5] Nir-Buchbinder, Y., Tzoref, R., Ur, S.: Deadlocks: From Exhibiting to Healing. In: Leucker, M. (ed.) RV 2008. LNCS, vol. 5289, pp. 104–118. Springer, Heidelberg (2008)

[6] Pyla, H.K., Varadarajan, S.: Avoiding deadlock avoidance. In: Proceedings of the 19th International Conference on Parallel Architectures and Compilation Techniques, PACT (2010)

[7] Song, X., Chen, H., Zang, B.: Why software hangs and what can be done with it. In: Intl. Conf. on Dependable Systems and Networks (2010)

[8] Wang, Y., Kelly, T., Kudlur, M., Lafortune, S., Mahlke, S.A.: Gadara: Dynamic deadlock avoidance for multithreaded programs. In: Symp. on Operating Sys. Design and Implem. (2008)

[9] Zeng, F.: Pattern-driven deadlock avoidance. In: Workshop on Parallel and Distributed Systems: Testing, Analysis, and Debugging, PADTAD (2009)

[10] Zeng, F., Martin, R.P.: Ghost locks: Deadlock prevention for Java. In: Mid-Atlantic Student Workshop on Programming Languages and Systems (2004)

Permission Regions for Race-Free Parallelism

Edwin Westbrook, Jisheng Zhao, Zoran Budimlić, and Vivek Sarkar

Department of Computer Science, Rice University
{emw4,jisheng.zhao,zoran,vsarkar}@rice.edu

Abstract. It is difficult to write parallel programs that are correct. This is because of the potential for *data races*, when parallel tasks access shared data in complex and unexpected ways. A classic approach to addressing this problem is dynamic race detection, which has the benefits of working transparently to the programmer and not raising any false alarms. Unfortunately, dynamic race detection is very slow in practice; further, it can only detect low-level races, not high-level races which are also known as *atomicity violations*. In this paper, we present a new approach to dynamic detection of data races and atomicity violations based on the concept of *permission regions*, which are regions of code that have permission to read or write certain variables. Dynamic checks are used to ensure that no conflicting permission regions execute in parallel, thereby allowing the granularity of checks to be adjusted according to the size of permission regions. We demonstrate that permission regions can be used to achieve significantly better performance than past work on dynamic race detection, to the point where they could be used to enable always on race detection for both low- and high-level races in production code.

1 Introduction

As chip manufacturers turn towards multi-core processors for performance, parallel programming is becoming a critical bottleneck to future software performance. Unfortunately, it is difficult to write parallel programs that are correct because of the potential for *data races*, where parallel tasks can read and write shared data in complex and unexpected ways. Except rare cases of parallelism experts writing race-tolerant code, a data race is a bug, as it can cause code to run in ways that were not intended by the programmer. It is a more devious sort of bug than most, however, because data races are notoriously hard to detect and reproduce.

A classic approach to dealing with data races is dynamic race detection [32,17,28,16,30,35,14]. Under this approach, each memory access of a program is instrumented to check, at runtime, whether it conflicts with a parallel access. This approach has two powerful benefits: it works transparently to the programmer, since the instrumentation is done by the compiler or runtime system; and it can work with many patterns of synchronization, since the dynamic checks need not be aware of how synchronization is achieved. This last point is in contrast with many other approaches, such as static race detection [20,40,6,15,4], transactional memory [24], or approaches to deterministic parallelism [5,34], which

S. Khurshid and K. Sen (Eds.): RV 2011, LNCS 7186, pp. 94–109, 2012.

generally require very specific approaches to synchronization and parallelism. Unfortunately, past approaches to dynamic race detection have been very slow, limiting its usefulness in practice. In addition, dynamic race detection cannot detect *high-level* races, or atomicity violations, where a task modifies the data of another in the absence of standard, or *low-level*, data races[1]. High-level races are especially insidious because they depend on programmer intent, and can occur even in well-synchronized code.

In this paper, we introduce a new programming language model that enables a form of "always on" race detection for both low- and high-level races. More specifically, our approach enforces a property which we call the *permission property*, which ensures that no task is permitted to write to a memory location while another task has permission to access that location. The permission property is stronger than race-freedom, and in fact corresponds to the way most programmers write code. To enforce this "single-writer" property, we introduce a new construct called a *permission region*. These constructs mark a region of code with read and write sets of variables, to indicate that the region has permission to read or write those variables while it executes. Two permission regions are said to *conflict* when the write set of one overlaps the read or write set of the other. The runtime system then checks that no two conflicting permission regions execute in parallel, throwing an exception if a conflict is detected.

Permission regions can be seen as an extension of dynamic race detection that increases the granularity of dynamic checks to entire regions of code, instead of to individual memory accesses. One of the key differences from dynamic race-detection approaches is that permission regions are fundamentally a language-based approach, where the dynamic checks and exceptions are an explicit part of the language semantics; this is as opposed to dynamic race detection, where checks are inserted without changing the semantics of a program. Having a language-based approach has the following benefits: It allows the programmer to control the granularity of dynamic checks in a straightforward manner that does not require any knowledge of how the checks are actually performed; and it allows for compiler insertion (inference) of permission regions, which can be refined by the programmer as desired.

We demonstrate our approach with an implementation of permission regions in the Habanero Java (HJ) programming language, an extension of Java with task parallel constructs [9]. This implementation has successfully run 11 HJ benchmarks totaling more than 9,000 lines of code. Most of the benchmarks run less than 2.5× slower than their uninstrumented versions, with a geometric mean around 1.5×. Compared with most of the state-of-art data race detection implementations [32,28,16,3,30,35], which typically result in a slowdown of an order of magnitude or more, our overhead is relatively low especially for parallel runs. Further, the annotation burden of our approach is also low due to compiler inference of permission regions. The main source of programmer annotations observed in our approach is for array-based parallel loops that modify disjoint parts of an array in parallel; the programmer is required to create these disjoint

---

[1] We borrow the terms "low-level race" and "high-level race" from Artho et al. [3].

array pieces as array sub-views, which generally requires one call to be inserted per loop. Over our 11 benchmarks, this leads to an average of 3% of the lines of code being modified. In addition, there was exactly one false positive due to the compiler insertion algorithm. The annotation burden here is much lower than comparable approaches, such as Deterministic Parallel Java [34,5], which requires an average of 12% of the lines of code to be modified.

The rest of the paper is organized as follows. Section 2 introduces the Habanero Java (HJ) parallel programming language and the Java Memory Model. Section 3 introduces permission regions as an extension of HJ. Section 4 presents compiler techniques to automatically insert permission regions into HJ programs. Section 5 presents the implementation details of the language construct within the Habanero-Java compiler and runtime. Section 6 shows the performance evaluation of our implementation of permission regions on a set of HJ benchmarks. Section 7 discusses related work, and Section 8 presents conclusions and directions for future work.

2 Background: Data Races in Habanero-Java

In this section, we briefly introduce Habanero Java (HJ) [9] and explain low- and high-level races. HJ is an extension of Java with several constructs for parallelism and synchronization; in this paper, we consider **async** and **finish** which respectively spawn a child task and wait for all tasks spawned in a lexically-scoped block to complete[2], as well as **isolated** which ensures mutual exclusion among all instances of isolated statements (weak atomicity). The **async** and **finish** constructs are borrowed from X10 [10], and are more general that the spawn and sync constructs of Cilk, respectively. The **isolated** work is borrowed from early work on critical sections and recent work on transactions.

A low-level race in Java, and similarly in HJ, is defined by the Java Memory Model (JMM). We refer the reader to other work [18,26,41] for the technical details, but conceptually a low-level race occurs when two accesses to the same memory location, one of which is a write, occur in distinct tasks without some form of synchronization between them. The difficulty of low-level races is that, in their presence, the actions of a task can appear to happen in a different order to other tasks running in parallel. When a program has no low-level races, however, then the JMM ensures *sequential consistency* (SC) [23], meaning it behaves as if each instruction of each task appears to be atomic. When there are low-level races, however, the possible behavior can be quite complex, making the program difficult to understand.

As an example, consider the two tasks depicted in Figure 1, which perform push and a pop operations on a stack (**SNode**) object, **this**, in parallel. (**this** is assumed to be the same in both tasks.) Since there is no synchronization between them, the write of **this**.next in task 1 has a low-level race with the read of the same field in task 2. This means that, under the JMM, task 1 can appear to occur

---

[2] We use the term "task" here instead of "thread" to distinguish semantically parallel tasks from the OS threads to which they might be mapped by an implementation.

```
                                      SNode pop () {
                                        SNode tmp = this.next;
void push (SNode n) {                   if (tmp != null)
  n.next = this.next;                     this.next = tmp.next;
  this.next = n;                        return tmp;
}                                     }
```

(a) Task 1   (b) Task 2

Fig. 1. A Simple Data Race

in a different order to task 2, allowing task 2 to see the newly pushed node n with the old value of n.next. This execution can also be viewed as equivalent to rewriting the body of Task 1 to "temp = this.next; this.next = n; n.next = temp;", a transformation that is permitted by the JMM if n and this refer to distinct objects. In this scenario, the third line of pop() would set this.next to the old value of n.next, obliterating the remainder of the stack after this.

Even assuming SC with no low-level data races (e.g., if every instruction were protected by a lock), the code may still execute incorrectly if task 1 runs to completion directly after the read of this.next in task 2, since n would be removed from the stack when task 2 sets this.next. This represents a high-level race, or atomicity violation, as task 2 intuitively assumes that this.next does not change between the read and the write of this field.

3   Permission Regions

The syntax of a permission region is as follows:

permit read $(x_1, \ldots, x_m)$ **write** $(y_1, \ldots, y_n)$ { *BODY* }

This statement executes *BODY* under the assertion that, while *BODY* executes, no conflicting **permit** statement will execute in a different task at the same time. We call the variables x_i and y_j the *read* and *write variables* of the permission region, respectively, and the set of objects they refer to during execution the *read* and *write sets*[3]. Two dynamic instances of **permit** statements are said to be *conflicting* if the write set of one overlaps the read or write sets of the other. If a permission region begins executing while a conflicting permission region is already executing in parallel, an exception is thrown. Otherwise, the permission region's execution is guaranteed to be in isolation relative to its read and write sets. This means that the body cannot see any writes from another task after entering the permission region, nor can any parallel task see its writes until the permission region has completed. "Completion" includes both normal and exceptional exit from *BODY*.

As an example, Figure 2 shows how compiler annotates the racy example of Figure 1. (The algorithm used to place the annotations is discussed in Section 4.)

---

[3] Note that there can be no data races on local variables in Java or HJ.

```
                                      SNode pop () {
                                        permit write(this) {
                                          SNode tmp = next;
void push (SNode n) {                     if (tmp != null)
  permit write(this ,n) {                   permit read(n)
    n.next = next;                            next = n.next;
    next = n;                             return tmp;
  }                                     }
}                                     }
```

(a) Task 1   (b) Task 2

Fig. 2. Adding **permit** to Figure 1

The push() method is annotated with a permission region whose write variables include **this**, the stack on which a stack node is pushed, and n, the stack node being pushed onto the current stack. This permission region ensures that the call to push() must have write permission to these two objects while it executes. The pop() method is annotated with two permission regions: the first has write variable **this**, since **this** may possibly be modified to remove the next element of the stack; the second has read variable n, which represents the top node of the stack, since the next element of the stack after n must be read. Again, these permission regions ensure that pop() must have these permission on these two variables. Thus if one of push() and pop() begins executing before the other completes, then that method will throw a PermissionViolationException.

Permission regions represent a combination of static and dynamic checks. Checking that two conflicting permission regions do not run in parallel is in general an undecidable problem, and although there has been much work on static may-happen-in-parallel analysis (*e.g.,* [1]), such analysis must in general be conservative. Thus we leave happens-in-parallel checking as a dynamic check. To ensure the permissions property, however, we must also be sure that all reads and writes happen inside appropriate permission regions; i.e., writes to x.f may only occur inside a permission region whose write variables include x, and similarly, reads of x.f may only occur inside a permission region whose read or write variables include x. The algorithm used to insert these checks is discussed in Section 4. We now briefly summarize some of the salient points of the design of permission regions.

Read and Write Variables can be Modified: It is allowed for the variables in the variable set of a permission region to be modified in the body of the permission region. For example, the following code performs a loop inside a permission region which conditionally modifies the its write variable:

```
permit write(x) {
  while (...) {
    if (...) { x = ...; }
  }
}
```

This generalizes the semantics of permissions regions as follows: two **permit** statements are said to be conflicting if the *current values* of the write set of one overlaps the *current values* of the read or write sets of the other. Modifying a read or write variable can also cause a permission region to come into conflict with a concurrently executing permission region, and thus assignments to such variables, such as the assignment to x above, can cause data race exceptions to be thrown.

Final and Static Fields: Under the JMM, reading **final** fields do not is never considered a data race. Similarly, we allow such fields to be read without inserting any permission regions[4]. Fields marked as **static** are global, and are not associated with a particular object. Thus we also allow **static** fields to be read or write variables in permission regions, where conflicts involving **static** fields can only occur between regions that both use the field itself, not the value pointed to by the field. Permissions on objects pointed to by static fields can be obtained by reading the static field into local variables.

Constructors: The bodies of constructors are always implicitly contained inside a permission region with write variable **this**, as the purpose of a constructor is to initialize an object before it is used. Thus, although parallelism is allowed in constructors, passing **this** to another task in a constructor will cause an exception if the other task tries to access **this** before the constructor finishes.

Array Views: In order to support array-based parallelism, where tasks process pieces of an array in parallel, a permission region can specify pieces of an array in its read or write sets. This specification is supported by having users access arrays through *array views* [36,22], which are objects in HJ that represent pieces, or sets of cells, of an array. To create an array-based parallel loop, the programmer must create one *sub-view* of an array view per parallel task, to represent the piece of the array being processed by that task. This is illustrated by the code in Figure 3, which shows a simple array-based parallel loop using sub-views. The loop creates N sub-tasks, each of which creates a sub-view of the array-view A, where the syntax int [.] denotes the type of an array-view with element type int. Each task creates a sub-view subA of A and uses a **permit** to indicate that it will write to subA; it then iterates over all points p in the region r, writing to subA[p].

    This approach was chosen because allows programmer control and it fits nicely with the rest of the system. It does have some notational overhead, however, as it requires the programmer to explicitly create sub-views. In fact, this notational overhead is the main source of programmer effort required to port existing HJ benchmarks, as discussed in Section 6, since HJ itself does not require sub-views to be created. It is good programming practice, however, for the programmer to make explicit the pieces of the array that will be modified by each task. The only other approach would be to allow permission regions to explicitly state the pieces

---

[4] We ignore known issues with potential data races on final fields during object initialization.

```
int [.] A = ...;
for (int i = 0; i < N; ++i) { async {
    region r = ...; int [.] subA = A.subView (r);
    permit write(subA) {
        for (point p : r) { subA[p] = ...; }
} } }
```

Fig. 3. An Array-Based Parallel Loop using Sub-Views

of an array-view that are allowed to be accessed, but this would require some form of dependent types or dynamic checks to ensure that the array accesses inside the permission region fall inside the specified array piece, further complicated the system.

Inter-Method Permissions: It can often be useful to have permission regions cross method boundaries. For example, accessor methods are often used in the context of a more complex operation which is intended to be strongly isolated. To allow inter-method permission regions, we introduce *permission method annotations*. These take the form of two new keywords allowed in method signatures, **reading** and **writing**, which mark arguments in a method signature that must be in the read or write variables, respectively, of an enclosing permission region when the method is called. The implicit **this** argument can also be modified with these keywords by applying the keyword to an entire method, i.e., by listing the keyword in the method signature before the return type.

For example, we could change the signature of the push() method of Figure 2 as follows:

> **void writing** push (**writing** SNode n)

This states that any calls to p.push(q) must always occur inside permission regions for p and q. In turn, the compiler need not insert the permission regions for this method given in Figure 2. This can be useful to reduce the number of dynamic checks performed at runtime. It also allows the user to state stronger atomicity requirements; for example, code containing three consecutive calls to push() with this new signature is guaranteed to push all three elements in order with no intervening pushes or pops in parallel, since such parallel accesses would result in an exception.

4   Compiler Insertion of Permission Regions

In this section, we describe the algorithm our compiler uses to insert permission regions, to reduce the annotation burden for the programmer. The basic assumption of the algorithm is that, in general, a programmer does not intend for an object to be modified in parallel while that object is in scope. Thus our algorithm essentially tries to match permission regions to variable scopes. Naturally, this approach will not always exactly capture the programmer's intent;

i.e., this approach may lead to false alarms when the original code had no data races. However, this approach is always sound; i.e., an exception-free execution using compiler-inferred checks is guaranteed to be data-race-free. Further, this approach is *almost* always correct in practice: for the 11 benchmarks discussed in Section 6, totaling about 9k lines of code, only one case was found that led to a false positive, other than the requirement that regular parallel application use array views in the manner discussed in Section 3. Note also that our algorithm does not insert any of the method annotations of Section 3, as these could potentially change the semantics of a program in ways the user did not intend.

We proceed as follows. Section 4.1 gives our insertion algorithm, while Section 4.2 describes two cases where this algorithm gives incorrect results and describes why these cases are rare.

4.1   The Insertion Algorithm

As discussed above, our algorithm essentially tries to match permission regions to variable scopes. This goal is modified by a number of concerns. First, permission regions do not cross **async** statements; in fact, inserting an permission region for x outside an **async** statement is drastically different than inserting it inside the body of the **async** statement, since the former means the parent process can access x while the latter means the child task can access x. Second, if x is only accessed within the bodies of **isolated** statements — which specify critical sections in HJ (instead of using monitors like Java's **synchronized** keyword) — then the algorithm assumes that x should only be accessed inside critical sections, and permission regions for x are only inserted inside the body of **isolated** statements. Finally, if the programmer explicitly writes a **permit** statement then the algorithm respects the placement of that permission region.

The inference algorithm works on a per-method basis by considering the abstract syntax tree (AST) of a method body. The algorithm first finds all nodes n in the AST where read or write access to each variable x is required such that n does not already occur inside of an appropriate permission region. Read or write access could be required either because of access to a field x.f or because of a method call that specifies **reading** or **writing** for an argument position for which x is passed. Next, for each such node n that requires access to x in the AST, the algorithm finds the highest ancestor a of n such that the path from a to n does not contain an **async** or an **isolated**. A permission region for x is then inserted around a in the AST, with x in the appropriate variable set.

4.2   Limitations of the Insertion Algorithm

The inference algorithm presented above yields false positives in two potential programming patterns, which we call *intra-scope parallel access* and *task-dependent conditionals*. Intra-scope parallel access is when a region of code that accesses x somehow passes x to a parallel task, like this:

```
x.f = ...; compute(x); ... = x.f;
```

where `compute()` performs some parallel computation on its argument. In this case, the user does expect x to be accessed in parallel while `compute()` executes, and thus the proper placement of permission regions for x would be to have two regions, neither of which contains the call to `compute()`. Our algorithm, however, inserts a single region around the whole piece of code, yielding a false positive and requiring manual insertion by the user. This pattern occurred exactly once in our study of over 9000 lines of HJ benchmarks, specifically in the PDFS benchmark, so it is not incredibly common.

Task-dependent conditionals occur when accesses to an object are guarded by a conditional that picks out a specific task, like this:

```
if (isTask1) { x.f = ...; }
```

Our inference algorithm will insert the permission region around the entire conditional; however, if this code is called in parallel by multiple tasks, where only one task has `isTask1` set to true, then the proper place for the permission region is arguably inside the conditional. This is a very rare programming pattern, though, that we have not seen in any of our benchmarks. Further, the problem only appears when the condition is guaranteed to hold for at most one parallel task; otherwise, there really is a potential race, which should indeed be reported.

5   Implementation

Permission regions are implemented within the Habanero-Java (HJ) programming language. Figure 4(a) depicts the main components of the Habanero-Java compiler/runtime framework, with labels next to each component that had to be modified to support permission regions, indicating modifications were made. The parser was modified to support the new **permit** statement. The Analysis and Transformation phase was modified in two ways, by adding new sorts of AST nodes to the the parallel intermediate representation (PIR), to represent permission regions, and by adding the permission region insertion algorithm of Section 4 as a compiler pass. Finally, the HJ runtime was modified to track potential conflicting permission regions, as follows.

The default root object HJ, `hj.lang.Object`, has been extended with four new methods, `acquireR()`, `releaseR()`, `acquireW()`, `releaseW()`. These are called on an object when the current task needs to acquire or release read or write permission to that object; acquires happen on entry to a permission region and when a read or write variable is modified, while releases happen on exit from a permission region. These methods perform transitions on a state machine, maintained for each object, which is described in Figure 4(b). This includes the following states: Null means no permissions are being held; private read indicates that read permission are being held by one task; private write indicates that a task holds write permissions; and shared readonly indicates that multiple tasks hold read permissions. Any attempt to acquire conflicting permissions leads to a runtime exception in the current task, though in fact the state machine of the object is not modified. The state of an object is maintained by two fields: owner,

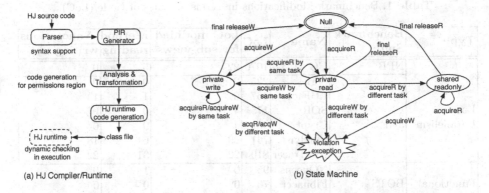

Fig. 4. The Implementation of Permission Regions in the HJ Compiler/Runtime

which contains the state as well as the associated task for private read and private write; and count, which maintains the nesting of the current state. Similar methods have been added to the objects implementing array views, which maintain lists of pieces of an array view in different states and compute intersections of array pieces to determine if there are conflicts.

6   Performance Evaluation

In this section we evaluate permission regions along two dimensions, performance and usability. To do this, we considered 11 benchmarks for HJ, including small- to large-scale benchmarks from the JavaGrande benchmark suite [39], the NAS Parallel Benchmark suite [13], the BOTS benchmark suite [11], and a Parallel Depth First Search application (PDFS). These are listed in Table 1, which also separates the benchmarks into loop vs functional parallelism.

For each benchmark, we performed the following experiment. We first converted any parallel array processing in the benchmark to use array views, as discussed in Section 3. Table 1 gives the number of lines of code that were modified in column 5. We then ran the code to determine if there were any false positives; as discussed above in Section 4, there was exactly one false positive in the PDFS benchmark. Next, we timed the benchmark with and without permission regions, to measure the slowdown of permission regions. Finally, for the 5 benchmarks with the biggest slowdowns, we added permission method annotations to key methods to increase performance and timed the results. The numbers of **reading** and **writing** keywords added to each benchmark are given in columns 6 and 7 of Table 1, respectively. All timing results were obtained on a 16-way (quad-socket, quad-core per socket) Intel Xeon 2.4GHz system with 30GB of memory, running Red Hat Linux (RHEL 5) and Sun JDK 1.6 64-bit version. We used the linux taskset command to physically restrict the number of cores involved in the experiment, from 1 to 16 cores, to measure scalability.

From a usability perspective, our results were promising. The biggest change required was modifying the benchmarks to use array views, requiring an average

Table 1. Benchmark Modifications in Terms of Lines of Code (LoC)

Type	Benchmark Suite	Name	LoC	LoC modified for sub-views	Method Annotations reading	writing
	NPB	CG	1070	22	5	0
		Series	225	2	0	0
		LUFact	467	0	1	1
Loop		SOR	175	4	0	0
Parallelism	JGF	Crypt	402	4	0	0
		Moldyn	741	29	6	18
		RayTracer	810	22	31	22
		NQueens	95	0	1	0
Functional	BOTS	Fibnacci	70	0	0	0
Parallelism		FFT	4480	209	0	0
		PDFS	537	0	0	2
total			9072	292	44	43

of 3% of the lines of code to be edited; this resulted from adding explicit creation of sub-views, as discussed in Section 3. Other work [37,22] has demonstrated that array views are useful for other reasons as well, so this cannot be held against permission regions too seriously. Otherwise, only one permission region had to be added to remove a false positive, and the "optimization" step of adding permission method annotation modified less than 1% of the code on average.

The timing results are given by the two graphs in Figure 5. These graphs give the slowdowns of each benchmark run with permission regions versus without permission regions, for 1, 2, 4, 8, and 16 cores. The first graph gives the slowdowns for the first timing experiment, after removing false positives, while the second gives those for the second timing experiment, including the permission method annotations. Most of the benchmarks run less than 2.5× slower than their uninstrumented versions, with a geometric mean around 1.5×. Compared with most of the state-of-art data race detection implementations [32,28,16,3,30,35], which typically result in a slowdown of an order of magnitude or more, our overhead is relatively low. The main reason for the relatively low overhead is granularity; we are checking object permissions once for each region rather than for each memory access. In addition, the permission method annotations significantly improved performance of 3 of the 5 benchmarks with which they were used, the lufact, moldyn, and RayTracer benchmarks.

One benchmark that deserves a separate discussion is the RayTracer benchmark which has a 27.49× slowdown when running on 8 threads. The reason for this drastic performance penalty is that RayTracer uses objects (3-dimensional Points) as the basic computation units, which forces the compiler to insert permission regions around each object access to ensure the correct permissions. These object accesses are done within the innermost loop of the main kernel, which does not have significant additional computation to hide the overhead. More advanced compiler optimizations such as loop interchange and loop unrolling should be able to enable the compiler to create large enough permission regions to eliminate a significant part of this overhead. This is future work.

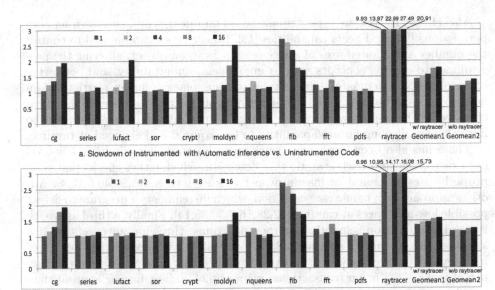

a. Slowdown of Instrumented with Automatic Inference vs. Uninstrumented Code

b. Slowdown of Instrumented with Automatic Inference and User Added Annotation vs. Uninstrumented Code

Fig. 5. Slowdown of Instrumented Code vs. Uninstrumented Code

7   Related Work

There have been significant recent work on runtime systems which detect low-level data races before they happen and throw exceptions, thus ensuring sequential consistency. DRFx [38,27] is similar to our work except that all the regions are automatically inserted by the compiler. This and similar [25,12] approaches cannot prevent high-level data races, which one of the main advantages of the permission regions described in this paper.

In Deterministic Parallel Java [34,5], each object has to be associated with a specific *data region* when allocated, which limits expressivity of the programming model. Also, methods must be annotated with effects, with an average of 12% of the lines of code requiring annotation.

In Transactional Memory [24], it is difficult to allow I/O within transactions since they may have to be restarted. Permission regions can have arbitrary code within them, including I/O code. The semantics of nested transaction and nested parallelism in transactional memory has also been a subject of much debate [2]. Permission regions offer a clear and intuitive semantic for nesting.

Dynamic race detection [32,28,16,3,30,35] is not efficient enough to be "always on" as it may result in an order of magnitude slowdown over original code.

Type systems and static analyses that ensure shared accesses are guarded by appropriate locks or other guards [33,20,40,29,6,15,4]; are often too restrictive or cumbersome to use in general, preventing many concurrency patterns that are safe and useful in practice. Static analyses and model-checking [31,21], in contrast, generally are incomplete and/or report false positives.

Also closely related are type systems based on linear types, such as fractional permissions [8,7] and Scala capabilities [19]. Linear types can be used to control the number and allowed uses of active references to an object, allowing the programmer to express concepts such as uniqueness, immutability, and borrowing of an object. Unfortunately, linear type systems place complex restrictions on how objects can be used, often making it difficult for programmers to use them effectively. The present work can be seen as a "partially dynamic" approach to linear types, allowing linear capabilities to be acquired and changed at runtime.

There has also been much prior work on techniques that eliminate low-level data races. One approach is static race detection, which either checks that code properly uses locks and/or inserts proper locking into code [20,40,6,15,4]. Another approach is dynamic race detection, which instruments a program to detect possible low-level races at runtime [32,28,16,3,30,35,14]. Finally, a third approach is to give a fail-stop semantics for racy programs, throwing an exception if a low-level race occurs at runtime [38,27]. Very little work exists that addresses high-level data races, however, and this work is either entirely based on correct use of locks [33,3] or on transactional memory [24,2]. The former is unsatisfactory because many concurrency patterns, such as those based on array tiling, do not use locks. Transactional memory, although promising in many aspects, has performance issues when transactions are too big, cannot perform certain non-transactional actions such as spawning parallel tasks or performing system calls inside transactions, and seems to require special hardware for good performance.

8   Conclusions and Future Work

In this paper, we introduced a construct called *permission regions* that enable application programmers to ensure that low-level or high-level data races will never occur during execution of their programs. The approach is based on the *permission property*: data should be only accessed by a single task in read-write mode, and any data that can be accessed by multiple tasks must be in read-only mode. Any violation of the permission property results in an exception being thrown at runtime prior to any data access that may participate in a data race.

The foundation of our approach lies in the insertion of *permission regions* in the program through a combination of 1) automatic inference, 2) manual insertion to avoid false positive exceptions, and 3) manual insertion to improve the performance of permission checks across method call boundaries. Of the 11 benchmarks studied in this paper, 4 required no modification by the programmer for 2) and 3), and the changes made in the remaining 7 benchmarks impacted fewer than 5% of the lines of code. Further, no parallel programming expertise is necessary to understand permission regions, since these permission annotations can enable useful runtime checking for invariants in sequential programs as well. Finally, the overhead for checking permissions in our approach is far lower than that of state-of-the-art approaches for dynamic race detection. The geometric mean of the slowdown relative to unchecked execution on 16 cores was only 1.58× when the outlying `raytracer` benchmark is included, and 1.26× if `raytracer` is excluded. Smaller slowdowns were observed for fewer numbers of cores.

In contrast, the average slowdown reported by the state-of-the-art FAST-TRACK dynamic low-level data race detector [17] for comparable benchmarks was 8.5× for fine-grained location-level analysis and 5.3× for coarse-grained object-level analysis. However, it is worth noting that the Permission Regions and FASTTRACK approaches address different problems *e.g.*, FASTTRACK does not require any user interaction but also offers no solution for high-level races.

Permission regions offer a number of opportunities for future research. One direction is to explore approaches that catch exceptions thrown by permission regions and perform some kind of remediation to avoid the problem entirely *e.g.*, by performing rollbacks and executing the conflicting tasks on a single worker. Another direction is to simply log permission conflicts instead of throwing an exception, and explore the use of conflict logs as debugging feedback at the end of program execution. Finally, as discussed in the paper, there is a natural complementarity between permission regions and software transactions that offers new opportunities to explore hybrid combinations of both approaches.

References

1. Agarwal, et al.: May-happen-in-parallel analysis of x10 programs. In: PPoPP 2007 (2007)
2. Agrawal, K., Fineman, J.T., Sukha, J.: Nested parallelism in transactional memory. In: PPoPP 2008, pp. 163–174 (2008)
3. Artho, C., Havelund, K., Biere, A.: High-level data races. In: STVR 2003, vol. 13(4), pp. 207–227 (2003)
4. Bacon, D.F., Strom, R.E., Tarafdar, A.: Guava: a dialect of java without data races. In: OOPSLA 2000, pp. 382–400 (2000)
5. Bocchino, J.R.L., et al.: A type and effect system for deterministic parallel java. In: OOPSLA 2009 (2009)
6. Boyapati, C., Lee, R., Rinard, M.: Ownership types for safe programming: preventing data races and deadlocks. In: OOPSLA 2002, pp. 211–230 (2002)
7. Boyland, J.: Checking Interference with Fractional Permissions. In: Cousot, R. (ed.) SAS 2003. LNCS, vol. 2694, Springer, Heidelberg (2003)
8. Boyland, J., Retert, W., Zhao, Y.: Comprehending annotations on object-oriented programs using fractional permissions. In: IWACO 2009 (2009)
9. Cavé, V., et al.: Habanero-Java: the New Adventures of Old X10. In: PPPJ 2011 (2011)
10. Charles, P., et al.: X10: an object-oriented approach to non-uniform cluster computing. In: OOPSLA 2005, pp. 519–538. ACM, New York (2005)
11. Duran, A., et al.: Barcelona openmp tasks suite: A set of benchmarks targeting the exploitation of task parallelism in openmp. In: ICPP 2009 (2009)
12. Elmas, T., Qadeer, S., Tasiran, S.: Goldilocks: a race and transaction-aware java runtime. In: PLDI 2007 (2007)
13. Bailey, D.H., et al.: The nas parallel benchmarks (1994)
14. Feng, M., Leiserson, C.E.: Efficient detection of determinacy races in cilk programs. In: SPAA 1997, pp. 1–11 (1997)
15. Flanagan, C., Freund, S.N.: Type-based race detection for java. In: PLDI 2000, pp. 219–232 (2000)

16. Flanagan, C., Freund, S.N.: Atomizer: a dynamic atomicity checker for multi-threaded programs. In: POPL 2004, pp. 256–267 (2004)
17. Flanagan, C., Freund, S.N.: Fasttrack: efficient and precise dynamic race detection. In: PLDI 2009, pp. 121–133. ACM, New York (2009)
18. Gosling, J., Joy, B., Steele, G., Bracha, G.: The Java^{TM} Language Specification, 3rd edn. Addison Wesley (2005)
19. Haller, P., Odersky, M.: Capabilities for Uniqueness and Borrowing. In: D'Hondt, T. (ed.) ECOOP 2010. LNCS, vol. 6183, pp. 354–378. Springer, Heidelberg (2010)
20. Hammer, C., et al.: Dynamic detection of atomic-set-serializability violations. In: ICSE 2008, pp. 231–240 (2008)
21. Henzinger, T.A., Jhala, R., Majumdar, R.: Race checking by context inference. In: PLDI 2004, pp. 1–13 (2004)
22. Joyner, M.: Array Optimizations for High Productivity Programming Languages. PhD thesis, Rice University (2008)
23. Lamport, L.: How to Make a Multiprocessor Computer that Correctly Executes Multiprocess Programs. IEEE Trans. on Computers C-28(9), 690–691 (1979)
24. Larus, J.R., Rajwar, R.: Transactional Memory. Morgan & Claypool (2006)
25. Lucia, B., et al.: Conflict exceptions: simplifying concurrent language semantics with precise hardware exceptions for data-races. In: ISCA 2010 (2010)
26. Manson, J., Pugh, W., Adve, S.V.: The java memory model. In: POPL 2005, pp. 378–391 (2005)
27. Marino, D., et al.: Drfx: a simple and efficient memory model for concurrent programming languages. In: PLDI 2010, pp. 351–362 (2010)
28. Marino, D., Musuvathi, M., Narayanasamy, S.: Literace: effective sampling for lightweight data-race detection. In: PLDI 2009, pp. 134–143 (2009)
29. Naik, M., Aiken, A., Whaley, J.: Effective static race detection for java. In: PLDI 2006, pp. 308–319 (2006)
30. O'Callahan, R., Choi, J.-D.: Hybrid dynamic data race detection. In: PPoPP 2003, pp. 167–178 (2003)
31. Qadeer, S., Rehof, J.: Context-Bounded Model Checking of Concurrent Software. In: Halbwachs, N., Zuck, L.D. (eds.) TACAS 2005. LNCS, vol. 3440, pp. 93–107. Springer, Heidelberg (2005)
32. Raman, R., Zhao, J., Sarkar, V., Vechev, M., Yahav, E.: Efficient Data Race Detection for Async-Finish Parallelism. In: Barringer, H., Falcone, Y., Finkbeiner, B., Havelund, K., Lee, I., Pace, G., Roşu, G., Sokolsky, O., Tillmann, N. (eds.) RV 2010. LNCS, vol. 6418, pp. 368–383. Springer, Heidelberg (2010)
33. Roberson, M., Boyapati, C.: A static analysis for automatic detection of atomicity violations in java programs. draft available on second author's websites (2010)
34. Robert, J., Bocchino, L., Heumann, S., Honarmand, N., Adve, S.V., Adve, V.S., Welc, A., Shpeisman, T.: Safe nondeterminism in a deterministic-by-default parallel language. In: POPL 2011 (2011)
35. Savage, S., Burrows, M., Nelson, G., Sobalvarro, P., Anderson, T.: Eraser: a dynamic data race detector for multithreaded programs. ACM Trans. Comput. Syst. 15, 391–411 (1997)
36. Shirako, J., Kasahara, H., Sarkar, V.: Language Extensions in Support of Compiler Parallelization. In: Adve, V., Garzarán, M.J., Petersen, P. (eds.) LCPC 2007. LNCS, vol. 5234, pp. 78–94. Springer, Heidelberg (2008)
37. Shirako, J., Kasahara, H., Sarkar, V.: Language Extensions in Support of Compiler Parallelization. In: Adve, V., Garzarán, M.J., Petersen, P. (eds.) LCPC 2007. LNCS, vol. 5234, pp. 78–94. Springer, Heidelberg (2008)

38. Singh, A., et al.: Efficient processor support for DRFx, a memory model with exceptions. In: ASPLOS 2011 (2011)
39. Smith, L.A., Bull, J.M., Obdržálek, J.: A parallel java grande benchmark suite. In: Proceedings of SC (2001)
40. Vaziri, M., Tip, F., Dolby, J.: Associating synchronization constraints with data in an object-oriented language. In: POPL 2006 (2006)
41. Ševčík, J., Aspinall, D.: On Validity of Program Transformations in the Java Memory Model. In: Ryan, M. (ed.) ECOOP 2008. LNCS, vol. 5142, pp. 27–51. Springer, Heidelberg (2008)

Dynamic Race Detection with LLVM Compiler

Compile-Time Instrumentation for ThreadSanitizer

Konstantin Serebryany, Alexander Potapenko,
Timur Iskhodzhanov, and Dmitriy Vyukov

Google LLC, 7 Balchug st., Moscow, 115035, Russia
{kcc,glider,timurrrr,dvyukov}@google.com

Abstract. Data races are among the most difficult to detect and costly
bugs. Race detection has been studied widely, but none of the existing
tools satisfies the requirements of high speed, detailed reports and wide
availability at the same time. We describe our attempt to create a tool
that works fast, has detailed and understandable reports and is available
on a variety of platforms. The race detector is based on our previous
work, ThreadSanitizer [1], and the instrumentation is done using the
LLVM compiler. We show that applying compiler instrumentation and
sampling reduces the slowdown to less than 1.5x, fast enough to use
instrumented programs interactively.

1   Introduction

Recently the growth of CPU frequencies has transformed into the growth of the
number of cores per CPU. As a result, multithreaded code became more popular
on desktops, and concurrency bugs, especially *data races*, became more frequent.
The classical approach to dynamic race detection assumes that program code
is instrumented and program events are passed to an analysis algorithm [8,11].
Some of the publicly available race detectors for native code [7,1,12] use *run-time
instrumentation*. There are also tools that use *compiler instrumentation* [3,6,10],
but none is publicly available on most popular operating systems.

In [1] we described ThreadSanitizer (TSan-Valgrind), a dynamic race detector
for native code based on *run-time instrumentation*. The tool has found hundreds
of harmful races in a number of C++ programs at Google, including some in
the Chromium browser [4]. Significant slowdown remains the largest problem
of ThreadSanitizer: for many tests we observed 5x–30x slowdown due to the
complex race detection algorithm; on heavy web applications the slowdowns
were even greater (50x and more) because of the underlying translation system
(Valgrind, [12])[1]. Another problem with Valgrind is that it serializes all threads;
with multicore machines this becomes a serious limitation. Finally, Valgrind is
not available on some platforms we are interested in (entirely unavailable on
Windows, hard to deploy on ChromiumOS).

---

[1] Mainly because Valgrind had to execute much single-threaded JavaScript code.

S. Khurshid and K. Sen (Eds.): RV 2011, LNCS 7186, pp. 110–114, 2012.

In this paper we present TSan-LLVM, a dynamic race detector that uses *compile-time instrumentation* based on a widely available LLVM compiler[2] [9]. The new tool shares the race detection logic with ThreadSanitizer, but has greater speed and portability. Our work resembles LiteRace [10] (both use compiler instrumentation and sampling, the performance figures are comparable), but the significant advantages of our tool are the more precise race detection algorithm [1], the granularity of sampling and public availability.

2   Compiler Instrumentation

The compiler instrumentation is implemented as a pass for the LLVM compiler. The resulting object files are linked against our runtime library.

2.1   Runtime Library

As opposed to a number of popular race detection algorithms [11,12,10], Thread-Sanitizer [1] tracks both locksets and the happens-before relation. This allows it to switch between the pure happens-before mode, which reports no false positives, but may miss potential bugs, and the hybrid mode, which finds more potential races, but may give false reports. In both modes the tool reports the call stacks of all the accesses constituting the race, along with the locks taken and the origin of memory involved. This is vital in order to give all the necessary information to the tool users.

The algorithm is basically a state machine – it receives program events, updates the internal state and, when appropriate, reports a potential race. The major events handled by the state machine are: READ, WRITE (memory accesses); SIGNAL, WAIT (happens-before events); LOCK, UNLOCK (locking events).

The runtime library provides entry points for the instrumented code, keeps all the information about the running program (e.g. the location and size of thread stacks and thread-local storage) and generates the events by wrapping the functions that are of interest for the race detector: synchronization primitives and thread manipulation routines, memory allocation routines, other functions that imply happens-before relations in the real world programs (e.g. `read()`/`write()`), and dynamic annotations [1].

2.2   Instrumentation

The instrumentation is done at the LLVM IR level. For each translation unit the following steps are done:

Call stack instrumentation. In order to report nearly precise contexts for all memory accesses that constitute a race, ThreadSanitizer has to maintain a correct call stack for every thread at all times. We keep a per-thread stack with

---

[2] We have also made an instrumentation plugin for GCC, but do not describe it here due to the limited space.

a pointer to its top; the stack is updated at every function entry and exit, as well as at every basic block start[3].

To keep the call stack consistent, the tool also needs to intercept `setjmp()` and instrument the LLVM `invoke` instruction to roll back the stack pointer when necessary. This is not done yet, because these features are rarely used at Google.

Memory access instrumentation. Each memory access event is a tuple of 5 attributes: *thread id*, *ADDR*, *PC*, *isWrite*, *size*. The last three are statically known. Memory accesses that happen in one basic block[4] are grouped together; for each block the compiler module creates a *passport* – an array of tuples representing each memory access. Every memory access is instrumented with the code that records the effective address of the access into a thread-local buffer. The buffer contents are processed by the ThreadSanitizer state machine [1] at the end of each block.

2.3   Sampling

In order to decrease the runtime overhead even more, we've experimented with sampling the memory accesses. We exploit the *cold-region hypothesis* [10]: data races are more likely to occur in cold regions of well-tested programs, because the races in hot regions either have been already found and fixed or are benign.

The technique we use for sampling is similar to that suggested in LiteRace [10]: ThreadSanitizer adapts the thread-local sampling rate per code region such that the sampling rate decreases logarithmically with the total number of executions of a particular region. Unlike in LiteRace, the instrumented code is always executed and the memory access addresses are put into the buffer, which is then either processed or ignored depending on the value of the execution counter. Another difference from LiteRace is that we apply sampling to smaller regions (basic blocks or superblocks, as opposed to whole functions), which allows to find races in cold regions of hot functions with higher probability.

2.4   Limitations and Further Improvements

The compiler-based instrumentation has some disadvantages over the run-time instrumentation: the races in the code which was not re-compiled with the instrumentation enabled (system libraries, JIT-ed code) will be missed, the tool usage is less convenient since it requires a custom build[5]. As we show in the next section, the benefit of much higher speed outweighs these limitations for our use cases.

Much could be done to decrease the overhead even further by reducing the number of instrumented memory accesses without losing races. A promising direction is to use compiler's static analysis to skip accesses that never escape the current thread. Another optimization is to instrument only one of the accesses to the same memory location on the same path.

---

[3] Optimizations may apply.

[4] We also extend this approach to handle larger acyclic regions of code (superblocks).

[5] Valgrind-based tools also usually require a custom build to avoid false positives.

3 Results

To estimate the performance of our tool, we ran it on two Chromium tests and a synthetic microbenchmark. We've already used TSan-Valgrind to test Chromium (see [1]) and were able to compare the results and assess the benefits of the compile-time instrumentation approach for a real-word application. cross_fuzz [5] is a cross-document DOM binding fuzzer that is known to stress the browser and reveal complex bugs, including races. net_unittests [4] is a set of nearly 2000 test cases that test various networking features and create many threads. The third test we ran just calls a simple non-inlined function[6] many times:

```
void IncrementMe(int *x) { (*x)++; }
```

One variant of the test is single-threaded, the other variant spawns 4 threads that access separate memory regions. The measurements were done on an HP Z600 machine (2 quad-core Intel Xeon E5620 CPUs, 12G RAM).

Table 1 contains execution times for uninstrumented binaries run natively and under TSan-Valgrind compared to the instrumented binaries tested in two modes: with full memory access analysis (TSan-LLVM, sampling disabled) and with race detection disabled (TSan-LLVM-null, an empty stub is called at the end of each block). We've also measured run times under Intel Inspector XE [7], Memcheck[7] and Helgrind version 3.6.1 [12]. The comparison shows that TSan-LLVM outperforms TSan-Valgrind by 1.7x–2.9x on the big tests. TSan-LLVM does not instrument libc and other system libraries, but we estimate their performance impact to be within 2%–3%.

Table 1. TSan-LLVM compared to other tools. Time in seconds.

tool	cross_fuzz	net_unittests	synthetic, 1 thread	synthetic, 4 threads
native run	71.6	87	0.9	0.9
Memcheck	1275	991	33	133
Inspector XE	failed	1064	130	480
Helgrind	failed	2529	40	154
TSan-Valgrind	325.2	592	49	191
TSan-LLVM	190.9	206	15.5	17
TSan-LLVM-null	78.6	119	2	2.1

Table 2 shows how the performance depends on the sampling parameter (a number k which means that the tool starts ignoring some memory accesses after executing the region 2^{32-k} times). Using the sampling value of 20 is 1.5x–2x faster than without sampling on the chosen benchmarks. In this mode the slowdown compared to the native run is less than 1.5x, and the tool is still capable

---

[6] Part of racecheck_unittest [2], a test suite for data race detectors.

[7] Memcheck, the Valgrind memory error detector, does different kind of instrumentation and can not ignore JavaScript, but its figures may still serve as a data point.

of finding a number of known races. We found over 15 races in Chromium while running `cross_fuzz` with TSan-Valgrind; these races (except one, which happens in a system library) are also detectable with TSan-LLVM, without sampling and even with sampling value 20.

Table 2. TSan-LLVM performance with various sampling values

test name	sampling parameter	-	10	20	30
cross_fuzz	time, sec	190.9	142.3	94.5	78.1
	accesses analyzed, %	100.0	77.8	16.2	3.6
net_unittests	time, sec	206	190	134	117
	accesses analyzed, %	100.0	33.7	14.1	13.4

4   Conclusions

We present a dynamic race detector based on low-level compiler instrumentation. This detector has a large speed advantage (1.7x–2.9x on the real-world applications) over our previous Valgrind-based tool, and a slowdown factor of 2.5x (less than 1.5x, if sampling is used), which is fast enough to run interactive UI tests on the instrumented Chromium browser. The achieved speedup can be improved even further if additional compile-time static analysis is employed.

References

1. Serebryany, K., Iskhodzhanov, T.: ThreadSanitizer: data race detection in practice. WBIA (2009)
2. ThreadSanitizer project: documentation, source code, dynamic annotations, unit tests, http://code.google.com/p/data-race-test
3. Sun Studio, http://developers.sun.com/sunstudio
4. Chromium browser, http://dev.chromium.org
5. Cross Fuzz, http://lcamtuf.coredump.cx/cross_fuzz
6. Duggal, A.: Stopping Data Races Using Redflag. Master's thesis, Stony Brook University (May 2010), technical Report FSL-10-02
7. Intel Inspector XE, http://software.intel.com/en/articles/intel-parallel-studio-xe
8. Lamport, L.: Time, clocks, and the ordering of events in a distributed system. Commun. ACM (1978)
9. The LLVM Compiler Infrastructure, http://llvm.org
10. Marino, D., Musuvathi, M., Narayanasamy, S.: Literace: effective sampling for lightweight data-race detection. In: PLDI (2009)
11. Savage, S., Burrows, M., et al.: Eraser: a dynamic data race detector for multi-threaded programs. ACM TOCS 15(4), 391–411 (1997)
12. Valgrind, Helgrind, http://www.valgrind.org

NORT: Runtime Anomaly-Based Monitoring of Malicious Behavior for Windows

Narcisa Andreea Milea[1], Siau Cheng Khoo[1],
David Lo[2], and Cristian Iuliu Pop[3],[*]

[1] National University of Singapore
{mileanar,khoosc}@comp.nus.edu.sg
[2] Singapore Management University
davidlo@smu.edu.sg
[3] Microsoft, Redmond USA
cristi.pop@gmail.com

Abstract. Protecting running programs from exploits has been the focus of many host-based intrusion detection systems. To this end various formal methods have been developed that either require manual construction of attack signatures or modelling of normal program behavior to detect exploits. In terms of the ability to discover new attacks before the infection spreads, the former approach has been found to be lacking in flexibility. Consequently, in this paper, we present an anomaly monitoring system, NORT, that verifies on-the-fly whether running programs comply to their expected normal behavior. The *model of normal behavior* is based on a rich set of discriminators such as minimal infrequent and maximal frequent iterative patterns of system calls, and relative entropy between distributions of system calls. Experiments run on malware samples have shown that our approach is able to effectively detect a broad range of attacks with very low overheads.

1 Introduction

Many techniques have been proposed to ensure the safety of computing systems. Security policies on the flow of sensitive information [2] and encryption target only the safety of highly sensitive data while neglecting the presence of malware and infections. Traditional antivirus system target infections by searching for known patterns of malware *statically*, within system files. Host-based intrusion detection systems (IDS), on the other hand, monitor the *dynamic* behavior of a computing system in order to detect infections.

Misuse IDS [11] are similar to traditional antivirus systems. They model *known* intrusions and scan running programs to detect signatures of attacks. While they benefit from a high degree of accuracy their main drawback is the inability to detect novel attacks. Consequently, attackers exploit this weakness by using various obfuscation techniques or developing new attacks. Built as a response, *anomaly-based IDS* learn the normal behavior of programs and protect

---

[*] Research conducted by co-author when attached to National University of Singapore.

S. Khurshid and K. Sen (Eds.): RV 2011, LNCS 7186, pp. 115–130, 2012.
© Springer-Verlag Berlin Heidelberg 2012

them by observing the events they generate and comparing them to the *expected* behavior, thus are capable of detecting new attacks. The models of *expected* behavior can be obtained either by static analysis [21, 8, 9] or dynamic analysis [7, 13, 23, 24, 18, 6]. Although conservative static analysis approaches do not exhibit false positives they suffer from generating and using imprecise models due to the need to handle non-determinism, non-standard control flows, function pointers, libraries, etc. Dynamic analysis, on the other hand, leverages specific program's input to yield more accurate models; it however admits false positives.

In this work we propose an *anomaly-based IDS*, called NORT, that models *dynamic* behavior of programs and detects attacks by discovering deviations from the expected behavior. Our motivation lies with the very nature of malware that will usually reach our computers by exploiting vulnerabilities in running programs, getting installed as a start-up service by using legitimate services and hiding itself by modifying legitimate programs.

We build upon the work of Forrest et al [7] that was the first to propose a simple yet effective model, based on contiguous sequences of system calls, to describe the behavior of programs. We add to their success and strive to attain better performance by considering arguments, return values and probability distributions of system calls (in addition to temporal information) in our model. More importantly, we capture *both frequent* and *infrequent system call patterns* and relative entropy between distributions of calls to distinguish between acceptable and unacceptable behavior. Compared to other techniques based on data mining [24, 13] one of our contributions is the richness of our feature set: NORT is the first work that uses *iterative patterns* (of system calls) to model normal behavior. Iterative patterns permit gaps between adjacent calls found in the patterns, allowing for faster convergence and both effective and efficient detection of variants of malware. They also succinctly capture repetitive call sequences, resulting in patterns of shorter length and far less overhead in pattern manipulations. We are also the first to employ relative entropy to detect anomalies in a host machine (previously, this has mostly been used in network IDS). By adding this extra layer of security we raise the likelihood of an intrusion being detected.

NORT addresses current security issues, including the zero-day attacks, and the emergence of more a advanced malware phenomenon also known as Malware 2.0. These new security situations entail the development of adaptive methods, such as NORT, that can detect attacks and intrusions without prior knowledge about the malware itself. The contributions of our work are:

1. A new mining algorithm of frequent and infrequent patterns and a practical application to runtime verification and malware detection.
2. An effective model to describe the dynamic behavior of programs, incorporating not only the temporal ordering of input events but also data-flow information. This differs from past work on pattern based specification mining[15].
3. A prototype system, implemented and tested on Windows, to verify that programs comply to their expected behavior. Most IDS so far focused on Unix systems. However recent attacks such as the one on Google [1] showed the need for an IDS for a commodity operating system such as Windows.

The experiments aimed at evaluating our prototype system have shown a good balance between the three main concerns of dynamically built program models: accuracy, training convergence, and efficiency. Accuracy makes the model useful while efficiency and the rate of convergence make it usable, especially on-the-fly. Our results showed fast training convergence for both simple applications such as the Windows printing service and complicated applications such as Internet Explorer and Adobe Reader. In terms of accuracy, NORT showed the ability to detect a broad range of attacks with runtime overhead of less than 10%.

2   Overall Picture

NORT is designed as a system that offers individual computers one more layer of security, besides the ones already used: firewall, network IDS and antivirus.

It relies on the fact that software is used in a consistent manner and it detects malicious changes by a two phase-system: first it learns the normal behavior of the system and then it monitors the dynamic system to detect deviations from normal. During the *learning* phase a stochastic vector capturing the distribution of system calls for each *program* is computed, frequent iterative call patterns discovered across programs are mined and minimal infrequent call patterns exhibited within each program are identified and stored in a *normal behavior database* (NBDB). When the *detection* mode is activated, NORT computes the relative entropy between the stochastic vectors of the *running processes* and the corresponding *learned programs* in the NBDB, mines maximal frequent and minimal infrequent iterative patterns and compares them against those stored in NBDB.

Similar to usual dynamic machine learning approaches, a major challenge that we face is with the **incompleteness** of the training data. In the ideal case the normal database would contain all variations in normal behavior and we could regard a single mismatch found to be significant. Unfortunately, in real environments, it is practically impossible to collect all normal variations. Our solution to this problem is to attach, to each process, a *trust barometer* that increases the trust level when normal behavior is observed and decreases when anomalies are detected. Different types of anomalies have different weights associated to them. The weights of high entropy and new frequent patterns are heavier since these are less likely to occur in traces while the weight of new infrequent patterns is lighter such that several anomalies must occur before an alert is raised. The weight associated with normal behavior is much smaller than those associated with anomalies and has the effect of ignoring isolated anomalies.

The **architecture** of NORT is modular, being comprised of a kernel-driver, an engine and the user interface, as seen in Figure 1(a). The *kernel instrumentation* module acts as a sensor, recording system calls with their parameters and passing them to the engine. Because these have to be done at real-time, kernel-level buffers are used. The *engine* consists of several modules and is the core of the system. The first module *preprocesses* the data and passes the results through the learner/detector modules: *entropy* and *data miner*. The learner/detector modules store or query information from the *storage* module. The graphical user interface allows the user to choose the programs to monitor and to view the reports of specifications learned or detected and alerts generated.

3   Data Preprocessing

For runtime systems that deal with an infinite sequence of input events, it is important to have efficient data collection and preprocessing techniques. This section is thus dedicated to describing the *kernel instrumentation module* that handles the interception of the input events (system calls) and the *data preprocessing module* where we structure the stream of system calls by considering call arguments and employing techniques such as aggregation.

3.1   System-Calls and Kernel Instrumentation

System calls represent the basic interaction unit between programs and the OS kernel. We assume that *any harmful attack to a system will require the compromised applications to interact with the OS*. Thus, we focus on inspecting system calls, their arguments and return values to discriminate between normal and abnormal dynamic program behaviors.

Several approaches have been proposed for intercepting system calls. User-level mechanisms [18, 6] are deemed unsuitable, as they usually incur run-time overheads in the range of 100% and 250% due to the additional task switching operation required at each interception. Techniques that intercept system calls *within* the kernel, through kernel modifications, incur much lower overheads. We therefore adopt the latter approach and use techniques from BindView's strace open-source application to install a kernel driver. We also provide users the option to monitor either all or part of the system calls and their parameters.

3.2   Handling Complex Behavior and Overcoming Obfuscation

Signature based antivirus programs easily become ineffective when viruses employ obfuscation techniques [4]. Several types of obfuscation techniques are described in [4] classifying viruses as either *polymorphic* or *metamorphic*. A polymorphic virus tries to avoid detection by encrypting itself and applying transformations to its decryption routine such as inserting instructions without effect (*nop, dead-code*), changing the order of instructions and inserting jump instructions to preserve the effect of the code (*code transposition*) or making use of other registers. Metamorphic viruses change their code to an equivalent one by employing more complex techniques such as code transposition, equivalent instruction sequence substitution, and code insertion to the entire host binary.

By performing data mining on system calls sequences, it is possible to eliminate threats from many of these obfuscation techniques. However, mining system call patterns naively may not be effective, as it may attempt to distinguish call patterns which differ by the ordering of calls made on different resources. For instance, when a program opens two files and mixes reads and writes from these two files, two call patterns describing this file operation behavior may deem distinct as they capture different orderings of file operations.

NORT performs clever data mining on system calls. It first overcomes the call ordering problem mentioned earlier by using system call's parameters. NORT groups together system calls that refer to the same resource, thus ignoring the order of operations that apply to different resources. Next, contiguous strings of the same repeating system calls are aggregated into one system call; cf. [5]. These techniques also help in learning more complex behaviors and speeding up the convergence rate of normal behavior as we will explain in the section on Experiments.

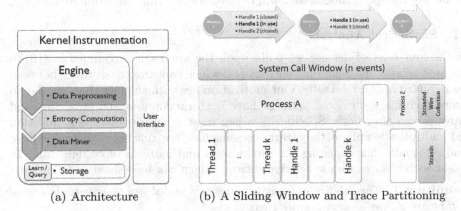

(a) Architecture   (b) A Sliding Window and Trace Partitioning

Fig. 1. NORT

3.3   Trace Partitioning

As NORT is required to analyze data in the form of possibly infinite sequences of calls, we apply a *sliding window model* to split the data and mine and compute relative entropy for windows of events. A definition of this model would be: each element arrives at time t and expires at time $t + w$, where w is the window size.

On top of splitting the stream of system calls into windows we further structure it by process ids and then in thinner strands by handle and thread ids (Figure 1(b)). We also apply an aggregation technique which involves adding a system call to a strand only if it differs from the previous one. A thread strand will contain all system calls generated by the thread execution and that are not related to a handle. A handle strand will contain system calls that act upon an object such as a file, socket, button (handles are some of the most important data objects in Win32). Because handles may be reused in the process context, they can be either *in use* (opened) or *old* (closed). Handles that are in use get special treatment when a window expires. Specifically, in order to avoid losing information, handles in use are kept beyond window expiration until they are closed or they have reached a certain age (in terms of number of windows).

During preprocessing we also check the return values of system calls. If a system call has executed successfully we will add its id to the preprocessing database. Otherwise we will add an anomaly score (greater than the highest id ever assigned to a system call) to its id and add this new value to the preprocessing database. By using this additional information the training convergence of normal behavior is not adversely affected. Also, we are able to detect more attacks such as the PDFKA attack on Adobe Reader.

4 Analysis Engine

To detect anomalous behavior we make use of both statistical analysis and a specification mining approach that extends the algorithm proposed by Lo et al [15]. In this section we describe these two layers of detection and the method for storing the specifications that will be used for real time detection of malware.

4.1 Statistical Analysis

As the first layer of defence we build upon the approach expounded in [16] to compute relative informational entropy [14] which captures the distance between the regularity of two datasets. Our motivation lies with the fact that, similar to Internet traffic, *system call patterns* have both randomness and structure, and malware can alter both. Specifically, when most malware enter their infection and multiplication phase, they start accessing files, creating network connections, sending emails thus changing the randomness and patterns of system calls. To detect such changes we use relative entropy which can be defined as follows:

Definition 1. *The relative entropy between two probability distributions P and Q that are defined over the same class C_x is:*

$$H_{rel}(P \mid Q) = \sum_{x \in C_X} P(x) \log \frac{P(x)}{Q(x)}.$$

In our interpretation of relative entropy, x represents a system call, the class C_X refers to the set of all system calls under consideration while the two probability distributions P(x) and Q(x) refer respectively to the *learned* and *current* distributions of system calls generated by a process. Specifically, Q(x) is implemented as a stochastic vector that captures the degree of randomness of a process in the *currently* processed window and P(x) is the corresponding stochastic vector computed and stored in the NBDB (for each program) during the *learning* phase by aggregating the results from *multiple* windows. These two vectors are used to compute the *relative entropy* between the current distribution for each process and window and the learned distribution of the corresponding program (found in NBDB). These relative entropies obtained during the learning phase are used to determine the maximum relative entropy exhibited during learning for each program. The relative entropies obtained during the *detecting* phase, on the other hand, are compared against a threshold and the trust levels of the appropriate programs are decremented or incremented according to the result. The threshold chosen is relative to the maximum relative entropy observed in the learning phase. It is thus unique for each program as a global absolute value would not be appropriate due to differences among programs.

As entropy only measures the randomness of system calls, not all malware could be detected via entropy measures. To further enhance the malware detection capability, we use a novel data mining algorithm that looks for both frequent and infrequent patterns in the call stream, as described in the next subsection.

4.2 Specification/Pattern Mining

To capture relevant patterns of software behavior we adapt two existing mining algorithms – *Efficient Mining of Iterative Patterns for Software Specification Discovery* [15] and *Towards Rare Itemset Mining* [20] – and obtain *FEELER: Frequent and infrEquent itErative sequentiaL pattErn mineR*. In this subsection we describe formally the notion of iterative patterns and how they are used by FEELER to detect malware.

Basic Definitions. Let I be a set of distinct events which are the system calls under consideration. Let a sequence S be an ordered list of events. We write S as $\langle e_1, e_2, \ldots, e_{end} \rangle$ where each e_i is an event from I. The input to the mining algorithm is a set of sequences also referred to as the sequence database (SeqDB).

A pattern P_1 $(\langle e_1, e_2, \ldots, e_n \rangle)$ is considered a *subsequence* of another pattern P_2 $(\langle f_1, f_2, \ldots, f_m \rangle)$ if there exist integers $1 \leq i_1 < i_2 < \ldots < i_n \leq m$ where $e_1 = f_{i_1}, \ldots, e_n = f_{i_n}$. We denote this subsequence relationship by $P_1 \subseteq P_2$.

Concatenation of two patterns $P_1(\langle e_1, \ldots, e_n \rangle)$ and $P_2(\langle f_1, \ldots, f_m \rangle)$ is defined as follows: $< e_1, \ldots, e_n > + + < f_1, \ldots, f_m > = < e_1, \ldots, e_n, f_1, \ldots, f_m >$.

Semantics of Iterative Patterns. For the rest of this section, we use *iterative pattern* and *pattern* interchangeably. An *iterative pattern* is a pattern the instances of which conform to a specific requirement, as defined below:

Definition 2. *(Iterative Pattern Instance) Given an iterative pattern $P = \langle e_1, e_2, \ldots, e_n \rangle$, a substring $SB = \langle sb_1, sb_2, \ldots, sb_n \rangle$ of a sequence S in the sequence database is an instance of P if SB can be described by the Quantified Regular Expression:*

$$e_1; [-e_1, \ldots, e_n]; e_2; [-e_1, \ldots, e_n]; \ldots; e_n$$

A Quantified regular expression is very similar to a standard regular expression with ; as the concatenation operator and [-] as the exclusion operator.

Definition 3. *(Support) The support of a pattern P (denoted as sup(P)) wrt. to a sequence database SeqDB is the number of its instances in SeqDB.*

Definition 4. *(Frequent and Infrequent Patterns) A pattern P is considered frequent in SeqDB when its support, sup(P) is greater or equal to a certain threshold (min_sup). Otherwise if sup(P) < min_sup, P is infrequent or rare.*

The following theorem, the proof of which is omitted, provides a valuable means to prune the search space during mining, rendering the mining process efficient.

Theorem 1. *(Anti-monotonicity Property) If a pattern Q is infrequent and $P = Q + + evs$ (where evs is a series of events), then P is also infrequent.*

As there may be too many frequent and infrequent patterns, we mine for two compact sets of patterns: maximal frequent and minimal infrequent.

Definition 5. *(Maximal Frequent Patterns) An iterative pattern P is considered maximal frequent in a sequence database SeqDB if P is frequent and there exists no super-sequence Q such that $P \subseteq Q$ and Q is frequent in SeqDB.*

Definition 6. *(Minimal Infrequent Patterns) An iterative pattern P is considered minimal infrequent (minimal rare) in a sequence database SeqDB if P is rare and there exists no sub-sequence R such that $R \subseteq P$ and R is rare in SeqDB.*

Generation of Iterative Patterns. Our algorithm for mining, FEELER, adopts a depth-first pattern growth and prune strategy to obtain maximal frequent and minimal infrequent *iterative patterns*. Its input comes from the pre-processing module in the form of all strands (handle and thread) of system calls corresponding to one process. These strands constitute the sequences in the *SeqDB*. The output of FEELER, the iterative patterns obtained for each running process in a window of calls, are stored in the NBDB during the learning phase and checked against the corresponding ones in the NBDB in the detection phase.

Procedure MinePat
Inputs : min_sup : Minimum Support Threshold
Outputs : $freqDB$: Max. Frequent Patterns, $infreqDB$: Min. Infreq. Patterns
1 : *Let FreqEv = All single events e where $sup(e) \geq min\_sup$*
2 : *Let infreqDB = All single events e where $0 < sup(e) < min\_sup$*
3 : *Let freqDB = {}*
4 : *For each f_ev in FreqEv do*
5 :   *Call GrowPat ($f\_ev, min\_sup, FreqEv, freqDB, infreqDB$)*

Procedure GrowPat
Inputs : *Pat* : A frequent pattern
         min_sup : Minimum Support Threshold
         EV : Frequent Events
         $freqDB$: Max. Frequent Patterns, $infreqDB$: Min. Infrequent Patterns
 6 : *Let $NxtFreq = \{Pat ++e \mid e \in EV \ \wedge (sup(Pat ++e) \geq min\_sup)\}$*
 7 : *Let $NxtInfreq = \{Pat ++e \mid e \in EV \ \wedge (0 < sup(Pat ++e) < min\_sup)\}$*
 8 : *For each $iPat \in NxtInfreq$*
 9 :   *If $(\nexists R. \ (R \in infreqDB \ \wedge \ R \subseteq iPat))$ then*
10 : $infreqDB = infreqDB \setminus \{Q \mid Q \in infreqDB \wedge \ (iPat \subseteq Q)\}$
11 : $infreqDB = infreqDB \ \cup \ \{iPat\}$
12 : *If $|NxtFreq| = 0$ then*
13 :   *If $(\nexists Q. \ (Q \in freqDB \ \wedge \ Pat \subseteq Q))$ then*
14 : $freqDB = freqDB \setminus \{R \mid R \in freqDB \ \wedge \ (R \subseteq Pat)\}$
15 : $freqDB = freqDB \ \cup \ \{Pat\}$
16 : *Else For each fPat in NxtFreq*
17 :   *Call GrowPat(fPat, min_sup, EV, freqDB, infreqDB)*

Fig. 2. FEELER Mining Algorithm

The main procedure of FEELER, *MinePat*, shown in Figure 2, will first find frequent patterns of length one (Line 1) and then call *GrowPat* which recursively grows each pattern (Line 5). The length-1 patterns that are infrequent (*support* < *min_sup*) and minimal are added to *infreqDB* (Line 2).

Procedure *GrowPat*, shown at the bottom of Figure 2, receives as inputs a frequent pattern *(Pat)*, the support threshold, the set of frequent events and the sets of maximal frequent *(freqDB)* and minimal infrequent *(infreqDB)* iterative patterns. The recursive algorithm will grow the current pattern *Pat* by a single event and collect the resultant frequent and infrequent patterns (Lines 6-7). For each infrequent pattern *iPat*, GrowPat will check if any of its subsequences is in *infreqDB* (Line 9) and will add *iPat* to *infreqDB* if no pattern is found. The patterns in *infreqDB* that are not minimal are also removed (Line 10). For each frequent pattern *fPat* it will try to grow further by calling *GrowPat* recursively (Line 17). If however the growth of *Pat* resulted in non-frequent patterns, *Pat* is added to *freqDB* if none of its super sequences is found in *freqDB*(Lines 12-15).

4.3 Storage

The Storage module interacts with the entropy and miner modules and manages the extracted specifications. The unique feature that enables this module to efficiently respond to queries is the use of bloom filters to store patterns [3](one bloom filter for the frequent patterns from *all* the running processes and one *per* process for the infrequent patterns). These data structures generate and store a unique binary hash of a pattern and allow us to query for patterns without having to enumerate them. However, depending on the bloom filter size and hashing, the queries might have false positives. We have determined empirically the size of all the bloom filters to be 4MB in order to reduce the false positives.

5 Experiments

Dynamically built program models for runtime intrusion detection can be evaluated on three criteria: accuracy, training convergence, and efficiency. Greater accuracy makes the model useful while efficiency and fast convergence make the model usable. In order to evaluate our model we gathered different types of real world exploits and legitimate applications and confronted them against our prototype. All the experiments were performed on a Quad Core i7 running Windows XP SP 2 with 2GB of RAM inside VMWare Player on a Windows 7 host.

We started the experiments by first constructing models of normal behavior for the internal components of the operating system (winlogon, explorer, spoolsv, services), the pre-installed programs (Internet Explorer, notepad), and several legitimate applications such as Adobe PDF Reader. The obtained models showed fast training convergence rates for both simple and complex applications. Second, we ran a series of cross-validation tests. These tests consisted of learning the models of normal behavior and then feeding Nort in detection mode with new data from a clean installation, data that has never been learned before. No false positives were exhibited at the end of the tests. We next experimented with a broad range of malware samples and observed significant changes caused by the exploits in legitimate applications (as exhibited by the introduction of new frequent and infrequent patterns and a significant increase in entropy) that resulted in all attacks being detected. Lastly, we evaluated the efficiency of NORT by computing the runtime overhead of the system.

During the course of the experiments we used a window size of 10,000, a minimum support of 20 for mining and a threshold of 150% for relative entropy. From the list of 284 system calls of Windows XP we monitored a subset of 274.

5.1 Training Convergence

All anomaly detection techniques factor the time required to train and the convergence of the model in their evaluation. The rate of convergence is of particular interest as it governs the training time needed to attain a given level of false positives. The faster the convergence rate the smaller the training time needs to be.

We ran experiments with Internet Explorer, Adobe PDF Reader, spoolsv, and the internals of the operating system (services such as explorer, svchost, etc.). Internet Explorer and Adobe Reader were chosen as we wanted to show how learning converges for complex applications with interfaces, and where user behavior is perceived to yield slow convergence. The spoolsv printing service, for which all executions differ, was chosen to demonstrate that fast convergence can be attained by aggregating multiple reads and multiple writes.

The rate of convergence was measured in terms of the number of *unique* frequent and infrequent patterns (as functions of the number of system calls) required to learn applications. As shown in Figure 3, despite the initial surge, the

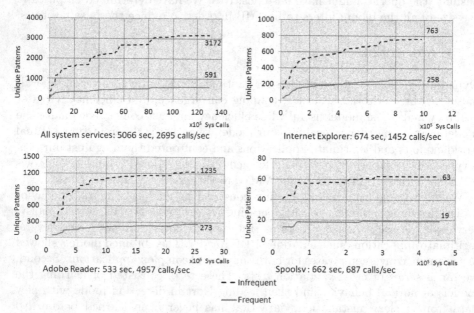

Fig. 3. Training convergence

increase in new patterns tapers off after reasonable amount of training time. We also ran alternative experiments that did not split the system calls by handles; there we observed a larger number of learned patterns (due to the interleaving of calls on resources such as keys, threads, etc.) and much longer times are needed for learning to converge.

5.2   Performance Study

An improvement in security comes at a cost: the performance degradation caused on a running system. As NORT has to continuously monitor legitimate applications without disrupting overall usability of the system, performance is critical. To evaluate the efficiency of NORT we measured the impact of on-the-fly monitoring on the runtime of 7-zip (a well known compression application) and on the startup time of three interactive applications (Figure 4). We also observed the system during viral tests, and found neither noticeable slow-down nor loss in usability.

As the runtime overhead caused by NORT depends on the type and rate of system calls it processes we ran experiments that would show a range of system usage scenarios. In the first 7-zip test, a simple compression benchmark was run mimicking the case in which an application is performing a CPU-bound computation. In the second test, a mixed workload scenario was simulated. Here, 7-zip was used to compress and archive a folder that contained 733 MB of data (404 files in 74 subfolders). The third test depicts an IO-bound workload scenario. Here, 7-zip was used to archive the same folder without performing compression. These results, as summarized in the left table in Figure 4, show that running NORT causes very low overhead (less than 10%) for all applications.

The other set of experiments we ran were aimed at measuring the impact of NORT on the startup time of Microsoft Office and Adobe Reader. To this end we used a program to launch the tested applications and monitor the initialization status through the WaitforInputIdle() API. The results – depicted at the right of Figure 4 – showed that the monitoring activities only incur a slight overhead on the tested applications although a higher rate of system calls was generated.

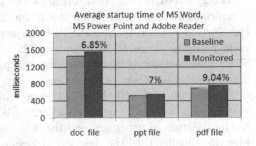

	Baseline	Monitored
7-zip Benchmark	5:29s	5:31s(0.6%)
7-zip Compress	2:43s	2:45s(1.22%)
7-zip Archive	18s	19s(5.55%)

Fig. 4. NORT monitoring runtime overhead

We also ran tests to find the rate of system calls NORT can intercept and process. During the course of these experiments we found that when the OS is not intensively used (cmd, notepad, calc, etc.) the average number of system calls/second is 1,600 whereas the peak is 26,000. When the system is used intensively (a Trend Micro Office scan or running MS Visual Studio while browsing the Web) the average number of calls/second is 12,476 and peaks at 65,000. These findings are shown in Figure 5. In addition, the last two bars in this figure also show NORT's processing capability in two running modes. In the online mode NORT was able to handle a high rate of calls while in the offline mode (all calls are written in a MySql file) NORT is able to handle a smaller rate.

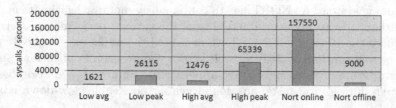

Fig. 5. NORT processing capability

During the course of all experiments NORT handled high rates of system calls with a small runtime impact. We attribute these results to the efficient interception of system calls, the small size of the window on which the algorithms are run, and the aggregation of calls.

5.3   Accuracy

In this subsection, we show that NORT is able to accurately detect attacks by real-world malware. Each viral experiment we performed involved, as the first step, the analysis of the malware to find information about the applications compromised and the nature of the changes. We then learned the behavior of legitimate applications and ran the malware and NORT (in detection mode) to capture the changes on legitimate applications. To avoid mixing malware, the virtual machine was brought to its initial installation before every experiment.

W32/Virut.n is a polymorphic virus that infects PE and HTML files and downloads other malware. In order to modify critical files the virus first disables the System File Protection (SFP) by injecting code into winlogon. The injected code modifies sfc_os.dll in memory (which allows it to infect files protected by SFP) and downloads malicious files such as worm_bobax.f and worm_bobax.bd. The observable effects of the intrusion are an increase in entropy, new frequent operations on files and the registry, new infrequent patterns containing unseen system calls related to network activity (as winlogon downloads malicious files), to the creation of processes and threads (as winlogon creates processes from the files downloaded), to the deletion of keys or values from the registry, etc.

PDFKA takes the form of an innocent PDF document and is accounted for 42.97% of all exploits detected by Kaspersky in the first quarter of 2010 [10]. In our experiments, running Win32.Pdfka.bo resulted in a large number of unseen frequent and infrequent patterns in AcroRd32Info, AcroRd32 and

AdobeARM. AcroRd32Info started exhibiting infrequent network activity and infrequent activity on processes, threads and virtual memory. The new behavior of AdobeARM was mostly related to activity on processes (virtual memory accesses and threads creation) as AdobeARM will open all running processes. The new patterns generated by AcroRd32 were detected from the anomalous return values reflecting the corrupted nature of the PDF file being opened.

Project Aurora surfaced in December 2009 when security experts at Google identified a highly sophisticated attack targeted on their corporate infrastructure and another 20 large companies such as Adobe, Yahoo, etc. The 0-Day widespread attack exploits a vulnerability in the way Internet Explorer handles a deleted object which results in IE referencing a memory location where the attacker dropped malicious code. In order to test this exploit we connected two virtual machines (the attacker and the victim) and used reverse tcp as payload. Employing the attack caused IE 6, running on the victim, to connect to the attacker and execute commands (getting the user id and a screenshot). The new patterns detected by NORT include system calls that create named pipes (the new code in IE initiates communication with the attacker) and system calls on threads, processes and virtual memory (memory is allocated for the payload).

Win32.Hydraq is a family of backdoor Trojans that was first used by the Aurora Project, as a payload. The carefully crafted attack takes advantage of the svchost process in Windows (a common technique used by malware to persist on a compromised computer) and can be detected by our approach due to a new service and the new patterns generated by it. The attack caused svchost to exhibit network activity directed to 360.homeunix.com and was detected by means of: new frequent patterns of network usage, of memory mapped IO and files; infrequent patterns on the registry that returned anomalously, etc.

Other attacks For a more thorough evaluation we tested several more malware taken from the *Top 10 malware list* [19]. *Z0mbie.MistFall.3*, one of the best metamorphic viruses, which infects other executables and causes many running programs to exhibit abnormal behavior, was detected by NORT. We are also able to detect *NetSky.y* and *Mytob.x* in different processes as these worms overwrite other executables and try to exploit components of the operating system (*services.exe* and *svchost.exe*). In the experiments with *Zhelatin.uq* (*aka Storm*), the newly installed malicious service component was detected as anomalous.

6 Related Work

Many models have been proposed that try to define normal system behavior in such a way that the models are sensitive to dangerous foreign activity.

Models of program behavior obtained by dynamic analysis. Forrest et al [7] were the first to propose the use of fixed length contiguous sequences of system calls (n-grams) to define the expected behavior of programs. Their results showed a fast convergence and good discrimination which made system calls based IDS the most popular approach in detecting novel attacks. The downfall of the simple n-gram model is that due to not allowing gaps between system calls forming sequences, one single misplaced system call will cause multiple mismatches. In our mining approach we mitigate this weakness by allowing for flexible gaps between system calls forming patterns of various sizes. We also consider the frequencies of patterns and split the stream of system calls by threads and handles to address the complexity due to concurrency.

Lee and Stolfo adopt a data mining approach by generalizing fixed length sequences of system calls as a set of concise association rules [13]. They reported a good degree of success in accurately detecting new attacks. We further improve their success by (1) mining on variable length sequences thus allowing for flexible gaps among call events and capturing long term correlations (2) involving call arguments and return values in our mining.

In [24] Wespi et al introduce a technique based on the Teiresias algorithm to create a table of *maximal* variable length patterns. While their model uses variable-length maximal patterns and aggregation, they do not allow gaps in patterns and do not consider using infrequent patterns and relative entropy.

Sekar et al [18] propose profiling normal system behavior via finite state automata with the states corresponding to the values of the innermost program counter located at a static location and the transitions to system calls. They thus are not able to characterize the behavior exhibited by dynamically linked libraries which, as demonstrated in [6], may significantly impair their accuracy.

Feng et al. use both program counters and stack history to capture normal behavior in [6]. This enables the detection of any attack that modifies the return address of a function. The overheads reported in [18, 6] are unfortunately in the range of 100 to 250%.

Pattern-Based Specification Mining. There have been a number of works on mining patterns as specifications of a program [15, 17, 12]. In our approach we leverage the efficiency of iterative patterns [15] and extend it to mine for both minimal infrequent and maximal frequent events. This new algorithm combined with a smart preprocessing of the input events and statistical analysis proved to be an expressive way of modeling behavior and effective in detecting malware.

7   Conclusions and Future Work

As Malware 2.0 threatens to be more adaptive than what we have experienced so far, we believe that data mining and artificial intelligence techniques will play more prominent roles in managing the new security problem.

This paper describes a prototype system (NORT [1] that integrates advanced pattern mining techniques and relative entropy to effectively and efficiently detect malware intrusions. By using these layers of defence our prototype attained a reasonably fast rate of training convergence for all applications and detected all malware intrusions with at most 10% slowdown. Although further investigation is required, we believe that by using frequencies, distributions, and relative entropy of system calls our system should be robust enough to mimicry attacks, an invention of Wagner and Soto [22] tasked at evading IDS detection.

---

[1] The prototype can be found at http://www.comp.nus.edu.sg/%7Especmine/nort/

NORT is not meant to be a substitute of an antivirus, but rather to complement one. The ability of NORT to detect malicious activity as anomalous behavior can prevent spreading of viruses or worms and provide a modern tool for security specialists to determine the installation of rootkits inside systems.

We envisage the use of NORT in an environment with multiple similar host systems. Here, distributed data mining can be used to better detect intrusions or to identify points of malware entry. Patterns discovered from all the machines will be gathered and then compared, taking in account the time-window and frequencies. Notifications can be redirected to a security specialist or a larger cross-institution knowledge base of known patterns.

Acknowledgment. We are thankful to the reviewers for their valuable comments. This work is partially supported by the research grants R-252-000-403-112 and R-252-000-318-422.

References

[1] Operation aurora (2010),
    http://en.wikipedia.org/wiki/Operation_Aurora#Response_and_aftermath
[2] Agency, N.S.: Security-enhanced linux (2008), http://www.nsa.gov/selinux
[3] Broder, A., Mitzenmacher, M.: Network applications of bloom filters: A survey. Internet Mathematics (2004)
[4] Christodorescu, M., Jha, S.: Static analysis of executables to detect malicious patterns. Tech. rep., University of Wisconsin, Madison (2003)
[5] Christodorescu, M., Jha, S., Kruegel, C.: Mining specifications of malicious behavior. In: India Software Engineering Conference. ACM (2008)
[6] Feng, H.H., Kolesnikov, O.M., Fogla, P., Lee, W., Gong, W.: Anomaly detection using call stack information. In: Proc. IEEE S&P (2003)
[7] Forrest, S., Hofmeyr, S.A., Somayaji, A., Longstaff, T.A.: A sense of self for unix processes. In: Proc. IEEE S&P (1996)
[8] Giffin, J.T., Jha, S., Miller, B.P.: Detecting manipulated remote call streams. In: Proc. USENIX Security Symposium (2002)
[9] Gopalakrishna, R., Spafford, E.H., Vitek, J.: Efficient intrusion detection using automaton inlining. In: Proc. IEEE S&P (2005)
[10] Kaspersky: Adobe: the number one target for hackers in the first quarter (2010), http://www.kaspersky.com/news?id=207576094
[11] Kumar, S., Spafford, E.: A pattern matching model for misuse intrusion detection. In: Proc. National Computer Security Conference (1994)
[12] Lee, C., Chen, F., Rosu, G.: Mining parametric specifications. In: Proc. ICSE (2011)
[13] Lee, W., Stolfo, S.J.: Data mining approaches for intrusion detection. In: Proc. USENIX Security Symposium (1998)
[14] Lee, W., Xiang, D.: Information-theoretic measures for anomaly detection. In: Proc. IEEE S&P (2001)
[15] Lo, D., Khoo, S.C., Liu, C.: Efficient mining of iterative patterns for software specification discovery. In: Proc. ACM SIGKDD (2007)
[16] Nucci, A., Bannerman, S.: Controlled chaos. IEEE Spectrum (December 2007), http://www.spectrum.ieee.org/dec07/5722

[17] Safyallah, H., Sartipi, K.: Dynamic analysis of software systems using execution pattern mining. In: Proc. IEEE ICPC (2006)

[18] Sekar, R., Bendre, M., Dhurjati, D., Bollineni, P.: A fast automaton-based method for detecting anomalous program behaviors. In: Proc. IEEE S&P (2001)

[19] Sophos: Top 10 malware (June 2008), http://www.sophos.com/security/top-10/

[20] Szathmary, L., Napoli, A., Valtchev, P.: Towards rare itemset mining. In: Proc. IEEE International Conference on Tools with Artificial Intelligence (2007)

[21] Wagner, D., Dean, D.: Intrusion detection via static analysis. In: Proc. S&P (2001)

[22] Wagner, D., Soto, P.: Mimicry attacks on host-based intrusion detection systems. In: Proc. CCS (2002)

[23] Warrender, C., Forrest, S., Pearlmutter, B.: Detecting intrusions using system calls: Alternative data models. In: Proc. IEEE S&P (1999)

[24] Wespi, A., Dacier, M., Debar, H.: Intrusion Detection Using Variable-Length Audit Trail Patterns. In: Debar, H., Mé, L., Wu, S.F. (eds.) RAID 2000. LNCS, vol. 1907, pp. 110–129. Springer, Heidelberg (2000)

Runtime Verification
of LTL-Based Declarative Process Models

Fabrizio Maria Maggi[1,*], Michael Westergaard[1,**],
Marco Montali[2,***], and Wil M.P. van der Aalst[1]

[1] Eindhoven University of Technology, The Netherlands
{f.m.maggi,m.westergaard,w.m.p.v.d.aalst}@tue.nl
[2] KRDB Research Centre, Free University of Bozen-Bolzano, Italy
montali@inf.unibz.it

Abstract. Linear Temporal Logic (LTL) on finite traces has proven to
be a good basis for the analysis and enactment of flexible constraint-
based business processes. The *Declare* language and system benefit from
this basis. Moreover, LTL-based languages like Declare can also be used
for runtime verification. As there are often many interacting constraints,
it is important to keep track of *individual constraints* and *combinations of
potentially conflicting constraints*. In this paper, we operationalize the notion of conflicting constraints and demonstrate how innovative automata-
based techniques can be applied to monitor running process instances.
Conflicting constraints are detected immediately and our toolset (realized using Declare and ProM) provides meaningful diagnostics.

Keywords: Monitoring, Linear Temporal Logic, Finite State Automata,
Declarative Business Processes, Operational Support, Process Mining.

1 Introduction

Linear Temporal Logic (LTL) provides a solid basis for design-time verification
and model checking. Moreover, LTL has also been used for the *runtime verification* of dynamic, event-based systems. In this latter setting, desired properties
are expressed in terms of LTL. These properties and/or their conjunction are
translated to a monitor which can be used to dynamically evaluate whether the
current trace, representing an evolving run of the system, complies with the
desired behavior or not.

Traditionally, LTL-based approaches were mainly used to verify or monitor running programs. However, the need for flexibility and a more declarative
view on work processes fueled the interest in the Business Process Management

---

* Research carried out as part of the Poseidon project at Thales under the responsibilities of the Embedded Systems Institute (ESI). The project is partially
supported by the Dutch Ministry of Economic Affairs under the BSIK program.
** Research supported by the Technology Foundation STW, applied science division
of NWO and the technology program of the Dutch Ministry of Economic Affairs.
*** Research supported by the NWO "Visitor Travel Grant" initiative and by the EU
Project FP7-ICT ACSI (257593).

S. Khurshid and K. Sen (Eds.): RV 2011, LNCS 7186, pp. 131–146, 2012.
© Springer-Verlag Berlin Heidelberg 2012

(BPM) field. The *Declare* language and system [11] show that it is possible to model LTL constraints graphically such that end user can understand them, while a workflow engine can enact the corresponding process. Constraints may be enforced by the Declare system or are monitored while the process unfolds.

Each graphical constraint in Declare is represented as an LTL formula, and the global process model is formalized as the conjunction of all such "local" formulas. Hence, there are two levels: (a) *individual constraints* well-understood by the end-user and (b) *global constraints* resulting from the interaction of local constraints. Runtime verification must provide *intuitive diagnostics* for every individual constraint, tracking its state as the monitored process instance evolves, but at the same time also provide diagnostics for the overall process model, giving a meaningful feedback obtained from the combination of different constraints.

In [6], we have investigated automata-based techniques for the runtime verification of LTL-based process models. In particular, we proposed *colored automata* to provide intuitive diagnostics for singular constraints and ways to continue verification even after a violation has taken place. Intuitively, a colored automaton is a finite state automaton built for the whole set of constraints composing a process model, where each state contains specific information (*colors*) indicating the state of individual constraints.

Here, we again use colored automata for runtime verification. However, now we focus on the *interplay of constraints*, i.e., we detect violations that cannot be attributed to a single constraint in isolation, but result from combinations of conflicting constraints. To do so, we extend a variant of the four-valued RV-LTL semantics [2] with the notion of *conflicting constraint set*, in effect adding a fifth truth value indicating that while a constraint is not violating the specification on its own, the interplay with other constraints makes it impossible to satisfy the entire system. Given the current trace of a system's instance, a set of constraints is conflicting if, for any possible continuation of the instance, at least one of such constraints will be eventually violated. Hence, our approach is able to *detect* constraint violations as early as possible. We show how to compute *minimal* conflicting sets, i.e., conflicting sets where the conflict disappears if one of the constraints is removed. We present our framework in the context of process models (as it was developed in that context), but it is applicable to any system described, directly or indirectly, using a set of finite automata.

Our approach has been implemented in the context of the Declare system[1] and ProM[2]. We provide diagnostics that assist end-users in understanding the nature of deviations and suggest recovery strategies focusing on the constraints that are truly causing the problem.

The remainder of this paper is organized as follows. Section 2 presents some background material, and, in Sect. 3, we introduce our runtime verification framework. Section 4 explains the core algorithms used in our approach. We have been applying our approach to various real-world case studies. In Sect. 5,

---

[1] www.win.tue.nl/declare/

[2] www.processmining.org

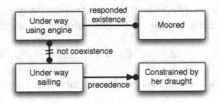

Fig. 1. Example Declare model

we report on the monitoring of Declare constraints in the context of maritime safety and security. Section 6 concludes the paper.

2 Background

In this section, we introduce some background material illustrating the basic components of our framework. Using a running example, we introduce Declare, present RV-FLTL, an LTL semantics for finite traces, and an approach to translate a Declare model to a set of automata for runtime verification.

2.1 Declare and Running Example

Declare is a declarative process modeling language and a workflow system based on constraints [9]. The language is grounded in LTL, but has an intuitive graphical representation. Differently from imperative models that are "closed", Declare models are "open", i.e., they specify undesired behavior and allow everything that is not explicitly forbidden. The Declare system is a full-fledged workflow management system that, being based on a declarative language, offers more flexibility than traditional workflow systems.

Figure 1 shows a simple Declare model used within the maritime safety and security field. We use this example to explain the main concepts. It involves four *events* (depicted as rectangles, e.g., Under way using engine) and three *constraints* (shown as arcs between the events, e.g., not coexistence). In our example, a vessel can be Under way, either using an engine or sailing but not both, as indicated by the not coexistence between the two events. A vessel can be Constrained by her draught, but only after being Under way sailing (as a vessel with an engine cannot be constrained by draught and a sailing vessel cannot be constrained before it is under way). This is indicated by the precedence constraint. Due to harbor policy, only vessels with an engine can be Moored (sailing ships are instead anchored). This is indicated by the responded existence, which says that if Moored occurs, Under way using engine has to occur before or after. Note that events represent changes in the navigational state of a ship and then are considered to be atomic.

Each individual Declare constraint can be formalized as an LTL formula talking about the connected events. Let us consider, for example, Fig. 1, naming the LTL formulas formalizing its different constraints as follows: φ_n is the not coexistence constraint, φ_p is the precedence constraint and φ_r is the responded existence constraint. Using M, S, E and C to respectively denote Moored, Under way sailing, Under way using engine and Constrained by her draught, we then have

$$\varphi_n = (\lozenge \mathsf{E}) \Rightarrow (\neg \lozenge \mathsf{S}) \qquad \varphi_p = (\lozenge \mathsf{C}) \Rightarrow (\neg \mathsf{C} \sqcup \mathsf{S}) \qquad \varphi_r = (\lozenge \mathsf{M}) \Rightarrow (\lozenge \mathsf{E})$$

The semantics of the whole model is determined by the conjunction of these formulas.

2.2 LTL Semantics for Constraint-Based Business Processes

Traditionally, LTL is used to reason over infinite traces. When focusing on runtime verification, reasoning is carried out on partial, ongoing traces, which describe a finite portion of the system's execution. Among the possible LTL semantics on finite traces, we use a variant of *Runtime Verification Linear Temporal Logic* (RV-LTL), a four-valued semantics proposed in [2]. Indeed, the four values used by RV-LTL capture in an intuitive way the possible states in which Declare constraints can be during the execution. Differently from the original RV-LTL semantics, which focuses on trace suffixes of infinite length, we limit ourselves to possible finite continuations (RV-FLTL). This choice is motivated by the fact that we consider process instances that need to complete eventually. This has considerable impact on the corresponding verification technique: reasoning on Declare models is tackled with standard finite state automata (instead of, say, Büchi automata).

We denote with $u \models \varphi$ the truth value of an LTL formula φ in a finite trace u, according to FLTL [5], a standard LTL semantics for dealing with finite traces.

Definition 1 (RV-FLTL). *The semantics of $[u \models \varphi]_{RV}$ is defined as follows:*

- $[u \models \varphi]_{RV} = \top$ *(φ permanently satisfied by u) if for each possible finite continuation σ of u: $u\sigma \models \varphi$;*
- $[u \models \varphi]_{RV} = \bot$ *(φ permanently violated by u) if for each possible finite continuation σ of u: $u\sigma \not\models \varphi$;*
- $[u \models \varphi]_{RV} = \top^p$ *(φ possibly satisfied by u) if $u \models \varphi$ but there is a possible finite continuation σ of u such that $u\sigma \not\models \varphi$;*
- $[u \models \varphi]_{RV} = \bot^p$ *(φ possibly violated by u) if $u \not\models \varphi$ but there is a possible finite continuation σ of u such that $u\sigma \models \varphi$.*

We denote $\mathbb{B}_4 = \{\top, \bot, \top^p, \bot^p\}$ and assume an order $\bot \prec \bot^p \prec \top^p \prec \top$.

We say a formula is satisfied (or violated), if it is permanently or possible satisfied (or violated).

As we have seen for Declare, we do not look at specifications that consist of a single formula, but rather at specifications including sets of formulas. We generalize this aspect by defining an LTL process model as a set of (finite trace) LTL formulas, each capturing a specific business constraint.

Definition 2 (LTL process model). *An LTL process model is a finite set of LTL constraints $\Phi = \{\varphi_1, \ldots, \varphi_m\}$.*

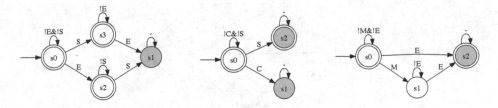

Fig. 2. Local automata for φ_n, φ_p, and φ_r from the example in Fig. 1

One way to verify at runtime an LTL process model $\Phi = \{\varphi_1, \ldots, \varphi_m\}$ is to test the truth value $[u \models \Phi]_{RV} = [u \models \bigwedge_{i=1,\ldots,m} \varphi_i]_{RV}$. This approach, however, does not give any information about the truth value of each member of Φ in isolation. A solution for that is to test the truth values $[u \models \varphi_i]_{RV}, i = 1, \ldots, m$ separately. This is, however, still not enough. Let us consider, for example, the Declare model represented in Fig. 1. After executing the trace Moored, Under way sailing, the conjunction $\varphi_n \wedge \varphi_p \wedge \varphi_r$ is permanently violated but each member of the conjunction is not (φ_n is possibly satisfied, φ_p is permanently satisfied, and φ_r is possibly violated). Therefore, to give insights about the state of each constraint of an LTL process model and still detect non-local violations, we need to check both global and local formulas.

2.3 Translation of an LTL Process Model to Automata

Taking advantage of finiteness of traces in the RV-FLTL semantics, we construct a *deterministic finite state automaton* showing the state of each constraint given a prefix (we simply refer to such an automaton as "automaton"). An automaton accepts a trace if and only if it does not violate the constraint, and is constructed by using the translation in [3].

For the constraints in the model in Fig. 1, we obtain the automata depicted in Fig. 2. In all cases, state 0 is the initial state and accepting states are indicated using a double outline. A gray background indicates that the state is permanent (for both satisfied and violated). As well as transitions labeled with a single letter (repesenting an event), we also have transitions labeled with one or more negated letters; they indicate that we can follow the transition for any event not mentioned. This allows us to use the same automaton regardless of the exact input language. When we replay a trace on an automaton, we know that if we are in an accepting state, the constraint is satisfied, and when we are in a non-accepting state, it is violated. We can distinguish between the possible/permanent cases by the background; states with a gray background indicate that the state is permanent.

We can use these *local automata* directly to monitor each constraint, but to detect non-local violations we also need a *global automaton*. This can be constructed as the automaton product of the local automata or equivalently as the automaton of the conjunction of the individual constraints [12].

The global automaton for our example is shown in Fig. 3. We use state numbers from each of the automata from Fig. 2 as state names, so state 202

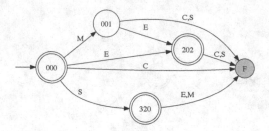

Fig. 3. Global automaton for our example

corresponds to constraint not coexistence being in state 2, constraint precedence being in state 0, and constraint responded existence being in state 2. These names are for readability only and do not indicate we can infer the states of local automata from the global states. To not clutter the diagram, we do not show self loops. These can be derived: every state also has a self-loop transition for any transition not otherwise explicitly listed. Accepting states in the global automaton correspond to states where all constraints are satisfied. In a non-accepting state, at least one constraint is possibly violated. State F corresponds to all situations where it is no longer possible to satisfy all constraints. We note that state 321 is not present in Fig. 3 even though none of the local automata is in a permanently violated state and it is in principle reachable from state 001 via a S. The reason is that from this state it is never possible to reach a state where all constraints together are satisfied. Indeed, by executing the trace Moored, Under way sailing, Under way with engine, for instance, we obtain the trace $000 \to^M 001 \to^S F \to^E F$. Hence, we correctly identify that after the first event, we possibly violate some constraints, and after Under way sailing there is a non-local violation and we cannot satisfy all constraints together anymore.

The global automaton in Fig. 3 allows us to detect the state of the entire system, but not for individual constraints. In [6], we introduced a more elaborate automaton, the *colored automaton*. This automaton is also the product of the individual local automata, but now we include information about the acceptance state for each individual constraint. The colored automaton for our example is shown in Fig. 4. We retain the state numbering strategy, but add a second line describing which constraints are satisfied. In this case, each state of the colored automaton really contains indications about the acceptance state for each individual constraint. If a constraint is satisfied in a state, we add the first letter of the name of the constraint in uppercase (e.g., R indicating that the constraint responded existence is permanently satisfied in state 202). If a constraint is only possibly satisfied, we put parentheses around the letter (e.g., (R) in state 320). If a constraint is possibly violated in a state, we add the letter in lowercase (e.g., r in state 001), and if a constraint is permanently violated, we omit it entirely (e.g., precedence is permanently violated in state 011). Executing the trace Moored, Under way sailing, Under way using engine on the colored automaton, we obtain the trace $000 \to^M 001 \to^S 321 \to^E 122$. We can see in state 122 that we have permanently violated the constraint not coexistence and permanently satisfied the others (PR). Note that the presence of an undesired situation, attesting an

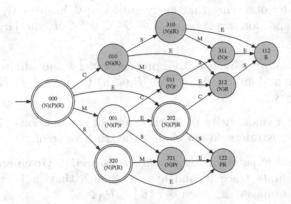

Fig. 4. Colored automaton for the example in Fig. 1

unavoidable future violation, is already detected in state 321. However, in 321, the problem cannot be attributed to a single constraint. The problem is non-local and is caused by the interplay between not coexistence and responded existence (the first forbidding and the other requiring the presence of event Under way using engine). We capture this kind of situation by introducing the notion of *conflicting* constraint sets.

3   Conflicting Constraint Sets

The colored automaton described in the previous section is able to detect both local and non-local violations. However, it does not provide enough information for user-friendly diagnostics. To do so, we have to identify the smallest parts of the original LTL process model that cause a problem. We tackle this issue by characterizing the relationship between the overall state of the system and the one of individual constraints. In particular, we show that the global state can be determined from the local states only when an explicit notion of *conflicting set* is defined and included in the semantics. In this respect, we first look at the truth value of subsets of the original specification:

Definition 3 (Monitoring evaluation). *Given an LTL process model Φ and a finite trace u, we define the sets $P_s(\Phi, u) = \{\Psi \subseteq \Phi \mid [u \models \Psi]_{RV} = s\}$ for $s \in \mathbb{B}_4$. The monitoring evaluation of trace u w.r.t. Φ is then $\mathcal{M}(\Phi, u) = (P_\perp(\Phi, u), P_{\perp^P}(\Phi, u), P_{\top^P}(\Phi, u), P_\top(\Phi, u))$*

As our goal is to deduce the global state of a system from the states of individual constraints, we need to analyze the structure of elements of $\mathcal{M}(\Phi, u)$. It can be observed that $\mathcal{M}(\Phi, u)$ is a partition of the powerset of Φ:

Property 1 (Partitioning). Given an LTL process model Φ and a finite trace u, $\mathcal{M}(\Phi, u)$ is a partition of the powerset of Φ, i.e., $\bigcup_{s \in \mathbb{B}_4} P_s(\Phi, u) = 2^\Phi$ and for $s, s' \in \mathbb{B}_4$ with $s \neq s'$: $P_s(\Phi, u) \cap P_{s'}(\Phi, u) = \emptyset$.

This is realized by observing that every subset of Φ has exactly one assigned truth value. Second, for two subsets of Φ, $\Psi' \subseteq \Psi'' \subseteq \Phi$, the larger one is not easier to satisfy:

Property 2 (Inclusion). Given an LTL process model Φ and a finite trace u, then for $\Psi' \subseteq \Psi'' \subseteq \Phi$ and an $s \in \mathbb{B}_4$, if $\Psi' \in P_s(\Phi, u)$ then $\Psi'' \in P_{s'}(\Phi, u)$ for some $s' \in \mathbb{B}_4$ with $s' \preceq s$.

This stems from monotonicity of truth values of conjunctions. Third, permanently satisfied constraints do not change the truth value of sets of constraints:

Property 3 (Effect of permanently satisfied constraints). Given an LTL process model Φ and a finite trace u, and a $\psi \in \Psi$ such that $[u \models \psi]_{RV} = \top$, if $\Psi \in P_s(\Phi, u)$ for some $s \in \mathbb{B}_4$, then $\Psi \setminus \{\psi\} \in P_s(\Phi, u)$.

This stems from the fact that for any extension, the permanently satisfied one reduces to true and can be removed using identity $\top \wedge \psi = \psi$ for any constraint ψ. This allows us to characterize the structure of sets with a given truth value:

Property 4 (Structure of global states). Given an LTL process model Φ and a finite trace u, for a subset of constraints $\Psi \subseteq \Phi$

1. $\Psi \in P_\top(\Phi, u)$ if and only if $\forall \psi \in \Psi$, $[u \models \psi]_{RV} = \top$,
2. $\Psi \in P_{\top^p}(\Phi, u)$ if and only if $\forall \psi \in \Psi$, $[u \models \psi]_{RV} \in \{\top, \top^p\}$ and $\exists \psi \in \Psi$ such that $[u \models \psi]_{RV} = \top^p$,
3. if $\Psi \in P_{\bot^p}(\Phi, u)$, then $\forall \psi \in \Psi$, $[u \models \psi]_{RV} \in \{\top, \top^p, \bot^p\}$ and $\exists \psi \in \Psi$ such that $[u \models \psi]_{RV} = \bot^p$, and
4. if $\Psi \in P_\bot(\Phi, u)$ and $\forall \psi \in \Psi$, $[u \models \psi]_{RV} \neq \bot$, then $\exists \psi \in \Psi$ such that $[u \models \psi]_{RV} = \bot^p$.

The first item is seen by assuming that some constraint exists in Φ that is not permanently satisfied for u. Equivalently, there exists a finite continuation of u where this constraint is not satisfied and the conjunction of all constraints in Φ is not satisfied for u. The second and third are seen by similar arguments. The last one is seen by observing that if a set has only possibly or permanently satisfied members, it is itself possibly or permanently satisfied.

Given an LTL process model Φ, a trace u, and a subset $\Psi \subseteq \Phi$, we can easily identify whether Ψ belongs to $P_\top(\Phi, u)$ or $P_{\top^p}(\Phi, u)$ by simple inspection of the state of individual constraints in the colored automaton mentioned earlier. For the first two items of Prop. 4, the states of the constraints in a node completely characterize, in this case, the global state of the system. However, we cannot determine whether a set belongs to $P_{\bot^p}(\Phi, u)$ or $P_\bot(\Phi, u)$ only by looking at the state of individual constraints: Prop. 4 only gives us implication in one direction in this case.

We introduce a fifth truth value of constraints $\bot^c$ that allows us to deduce the state of the entire system from the state of individual constraints. This reflects that a constraint is not permanently violated, but is in conflict with others so the entire system cannot be satisfied again. To better characterize the problem when a permanent violation occurs, we minimize the sets originating the violation. Therefore, we look at minimal subsets $\Psi \in P_\bot(\Phi, u)$. A first group of these minimal subsets are singletons $\{\psi\}$ with $\psi \in P_\perp(\Phi, u)$. A second group consists of *conflicting sets*:

Definition 4 (Conflicting set). *Given an LTL process model Φ and a finite trace u, $\Psi \subseteq \Phi$ is a* conflicting set *of Φ w.r.t. u if:*

1. $\Psi \in P_\perp(\Phi, u)$,
2. $\forall \psi \in \Psi$, $[u \models \psi]_{RV} \neq \perp$, and
3. $\forall \psi \in \Psi$, $[u \models \Psi \setminus \{\psi\}]_{RV} \neq \perp$.

We extend the semantics of RV-FLTL to capture conflicting sets:

Definition 5 (RVc-FLTL). *The semantics of $[u, \Phi \models \varphi]_{RVc}$ is defined as*

$$[u, \Phi \models \varphi]_{RVc} = \begin{cases} \perp^c & \text{if there is a conflicting set } \Psi \subseteq \Phi \text{ s.t. } \varphi \in \Psi \\ [u \models \varphi]_{RV} & \text{otherwise.} \end{cases}$$

Therefore, we can introduce a variant of Prop. 4 allowing us to determine the global state solely using local values:

Theorem 1 (Structure of global states). *Given an LTL process model Φ and a finite trace u, then*

1. $[u \models \Phi]_{RV} = \top$, *if and only if* $\forall \psi \in \Phi$, $[u, \Phi \models \psi]_{RVc} = \top$,
2. $[u \models \Phi]_{RV} = \top^p$, *if and only if* $\forall \psi \in \Phi$, $[u, \Phi \models \psi]_{RVc} \in \{\top, \top^p\}$ *and* $\exists \psi \in \Phi$ *such that* $[u, \Phi \models \psi]_{RVc} = \top^p$,
3. $[u \models \Phi]_{RV} = \perp^p$, *if and only if* $\forall \psi \in \Phi$, $[u, \Phi \models \psi]_{RVc} \in \{\top, \top^p, \perp^p\}$ *and* $\exists \psi \in \Phi$ *such that* $[u, \Phi \models \psi]_{RVc} = \perp^p$,
4. $[u \models \Phi]_{RV} = \perp$ *if and only if* $\exists \psi \in \Phi$ *such that* $[u, \Phi \models \psi]_{RVc} \in \{\perp^c, \perp\}$.

In [6], we explain how to modify the original LTL process model on the fly in an efficient way when a violation occurs. Therefore, when a non-local violation is detected, it can be useful to identify minimal sets of constraints to be removed in the original LTL process model to recover from the violation. We capture this as a *recovery set*:

Definition 6 (Recovery set). *Given an LTL process model Φ and a finite trace u such that $[u \models \Phi]_{RV} = \perp$, then $\Psi \subseteq \Phi$ is a recovery set of Φ' w.r.t. Φ and u if*

1. $[u \models \Phi \setminus \Psi]_{RV} \neq \perp$
2. $\forall \psi \subset \Psi$, $[u \models \Phi \setminus (\Psi \setminus \{\psi\})]_{RV} = \perp$.

Intuitively, we must remove exactly one constraint from each conflicting set in Φ, but if two (or more) conflicting sets overlap, we can remove one from the intersection to make a smaller recovery set.

Let us consider the Declare model represented in Fig. 1. We name the LTL constraints of this model as specified in Sect. 2.1. Figure 5 shows a graphical representation of the constraints' evolution: events are displayed on the horizontal

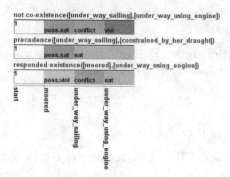

Fig. 5. One of the views provided by our monitoring system. Colors show the state constraints while the process instance evolves; *red* (*viol*) refers to $\bot$, *yellow* (*poss. viol*) to $\bot^p$, *green* (*poss. sat*) to $\top^p$, *blue* (*sat*) refers to $\top$, and *orange* (*conflict*) to $\bot^c$.

axis. The vertical axis shows the three constraints. Initially, all three constraints are possibly satisfied. Let $u_0 = \varepsilon$ denote the initial (empty) trace:

$$[u_0, \Phi \models \varphi_n]_{RVc} = \top^p \qquad [u_0, \Phi \models \varphi_p]_{RVc} = \top^p \qquad [u_0, \Phi \models \varphi_r]_{RVc} = \top^p$$

Event Moored is executed next ($u_1 = Moored$), we obtain:

$$[u_1, \Phi \models \varphi_n]_{RVc} = \top^p \qquad [u_1, \Phi \models \varphi_p]_{RVc} = \top^p \qquad [u_1, \Phi \models \varphi_r]_{RVc} = \bot^p$$

Note that $[u_1 \models \varphi_r]_{RV} = \bot^p$ because the responded existence constraint becomes possibly violated after the occurrence of Moored. The constraint is waiting for the occurrence of another event (execution of Under way using engine) to become satisfied again. Then, Under way sailing is executed ($u_2 = Moored, Under\ way\ sailing$), leading to a situation in which constraint precedence is permanently satisfied, but not coexistence and responded existence are in conflict.

$$[u_2, \Phi \models \varphi_n]_{RVc} = \bot^c \qquad [u_2, \Phi \models \varphi_p]_{RVc} = \top \qquad [u_2, \Phi \models \varphi_r]_{RVc} = \bot^c$$

Note that we have exactly one conflicting set, $\{\varphi_n, \varphi_r\}$. Indeed, if we look at the automaton in Fig. 4, from 321 it is not possible to reach a state where both these constraints are satisfied. Moreover, no supersets can be a conflicting set (due to minimality). $\{\varphi_n, \varphi_p\}$ is not a conflicting set as they are both satisfied in 122, and $\{\varphi_n, \varphi_p\}$ is not a conflicting set as it is temporarily satisfied. The next event is Under way using engine ($u_3 = Moored, Under\ way\ sailing, Under\ way\ using\ engine$), resulting in:

$$[u_3, \Phi \models \varphi_n]_{RVc} = \bot \qquad [u_3, \Phi \models \varphi_p]_{RVc} = \top \qquad [u_3, \Phi \models \varphi_r]_{RVc} = \top$$

not coexistence becomes permanently violated because Under way using engine and Under way sailing cannot coexist in the same trace. Note that this violation has been detected as early as possible by our monitoring system; already when

Under way sailing occurred, the conflicting set of constraints showed that it would be impossible to satisfy all constraints at the same time. However, it is still possible to see that the responded existence constraint becomes permanently satisfied by the Under way using engine event.

4   Deciding RVc-FLTL Using Automata

In this section, we give algorithms for detecting the state of sets of constraints. We start by giving algorithms for the extra information we have added to the automata in Sect. 2, and then focus on how to compute the information about conflicting sets contained in the colored automaton.

4.1   Local Automata

We get most of the information exhibited in the local automata in Fig. 2 from the standard translation in [3]. The only thing missing is the background color indicating whether a constraint is permanently/possibly satisfied or violated.

We get the background information by marking any state from which an accepting state is always/never reachable. We can do this efficiently using the strongly connected components (SCCs) of the automaton (this can be computed in linear time using Tarjan's algorithm [10]). We look at components with only outgoing arcs to components already processed (initially none), and we color a component gray only if i) it contains nodes that are all accepting/non-accepting and ii) all (if any) reachable components contain the same type states and are colored. This is also linear in the input automaton.

If the automaton we get is deterministic and minimal, we know that at most one accepting state will have gray background and at most one non-accepting state will have gray background. These can be identified as the (unique) accepting and non-accepting states with a self-loop allowing all events. All automata in Fig. 2 satisfy this, and we see they all have at most one gray state of each kind. Using these automata, we can decide the state of a constraint ($\top$, $\bot$, $\top^p$, or $\bot^p$) with respect to each trace, but we cannot detect non-local violations.

4.2   Global Automaton and Its Combination with Local Automata

We can compute the global automaton directly using the same approach adopted for local automata (following [12] for better performance). This is the approach used for the automaton in Fig. 3. Using this automaton, we compute the state of the global system, but not for individual constraints. In this way, we can detect non-local violations, but we cannot compute conflicting sets nor decide the state of individual constraints.

To infer the state of the entire system as well as of individual constraints, we can use at the same time the local and global automata. However, this forces us to replay the trace on many automata: the global one plus n local ones, where n is the number of constraints. Moreover, we cannot here detect exactly which constraints are conflicting, only that there are some, making this approach less useful for debugging.

4.3   Colored Automaton

To identify conflicting sets, we construct a colored automaton (like the one in Fig. 4) using the method described in [6]. We then post-process it to distinguish permanently/possibly satisfied or violated states (by computing SCCs, exactly like we did for the local automata).

To additionally compute conflicting sets, we notice that they are shared among states in an SCC (if a set of constraints cannot be satisfied in a state, it also cannot be satisfied in states reachable from it, and all states in an SCC are reachable from each other by definition). Furthermore, conflicting sets have to be built using possibly satisfied and possibly violated constraints of an SCC. We can ignore permanently satisfied constraints because of Prop. 3 and item 3 of Def. 4. We can ignore permanently violated constraints due to item 2 of Def. 4. In an SCC, all states share permanently violated and satisfied constraints as they can all reach each other, so we can obtain all interesting constraints by looking at one of the states in isolation.

Due to item 1 for Def. 4 and Prop. 2, we only have to consider states that are permanently violated for computation of conflicting sets (gray states with single outline in Fig. 4). We notice that the conflicting sets of an SCC have to be super-sets of conflicting sets of all successor SCCs or contain a constraint that in a successor SCC is permanently violated. This is seen by a weaker version of the argument for members of SCCs sharing conflicting sets, as reachability is only true in one direction. The inclusion may be strict due to minimality of conflicting sets (item 3 of Def. 4).

We thus start in terminal SCCs (SCCs with no successors) and compute the conflicting sets. This is done by considering all subsets composed of possibly violated/satisfied constraints with more than one member and checking whether they are satisfiable in the component. This can be done by examining all states of the SCC and checking if there is one where all members of the considered subset are (possibly) satisfied. We can perform this bottom-up or top-down. The bottom-up approach starts with sets with two elements and adds elements until a set become unsatisfiable, exploiting minimality (item 3 of Def. 4) in that no superset of a conflicting set is a conflicting set. Alternatively, we can compute the sets top-down, starting with all possible violated/satisfied constraints and removing constraints until the set becomes satisfied, exploiting that subsets of a set of satisfied constraints do not need to be considered due to monotonicity. Which one is better depends on the size of the conflicting sets.

For each globally unsatisfiable SCC we recursively compute for all successors and then build conflicting set bottom-up, starting with all possible (minimal) unions of conflicting sets or singleton permanently violated properties of successors. For the example in Fig. 4, state 112 has, for instance, no conflicting sets, but two permanently violated constraints (φ_n and φ_p). Computing conflicting sets for 311 only needs to consider sets containing (at least) one of these, and as φ_p is permanently violated, we can ignore it. The only possibility, $\{\varphi_n, \varphi_r\}$, is indeed a conflicting set. For state 310 we need to consider unions of the conflicting sets and permanently violated constraints of successors of 311 and 112, i.e., $\{C_1 \cup C_2 \mid C_1 \in \{\{\varphi_n\}, \{\varphi_p\}\},\ C_2 \in \{\{\varphi_n, \varphi_r\}, \{\varphi_p\}\}\} =$ $\{\{\varphi_n, \varphi_r\}, \{\varphi_n, \varphi_p\}, \{\varphi_p, \varphi_n, \varphi_r\}, \{\varphi_p\}\}$ which can be reduced by removing sets containing φ_p (which is permanently violated in 310) to $\{\{\varphi_n, \varphi_r\}\}$. We furthermore remove any supersets of contained sets (none in this case), and use the sets as basis for computing conflicting sets. As $\{\varphi_n, \varphi_r\}$ is satisfiable in 310, such constraints do not constitute a conflicting set, hence 310 has no conflicting sets.

Each SCC can have exponentially many conflicting sets in the number of constraints (assume we have n constraints and construct a SCC with all states possibly satisfying exactly $\frac{n}{2}$ constraints and possibly violating the remaining; as all sets have the same size, none can be subsets of the others, and we have $\frac{n!}{\frac{n}{2}!} \in O(2^{\frac{n}{2}})$ such sets). In our initial experiments, we have never seen examples with more than a few possibly violated/satisfied constraints, so in practice this is acceptable. Future work includes validating that this is also true for large real-life examples. If the pre-computation proves to be too expensive, we can also perform the algorithm at run-time, only computing conflicting sets when we reach a globally permanently violated state. By caching and sharing the results between instances (as well as intermediate results imposed by recursion), we should be able to provide acceptable runtime performance.

In our running example, executing the trace Moored, Under way sailing, we obtain the trace $000 \to^M 001 \to^S 321$. Using our algorithm to compute the conflicting sets, we see that in terminal SCC 122 in Fig. 4, we have no conflicting sets, but a single permanently violated constraint φ_n. In state 321, we have exactly one conflicting set, $\{\varphi_n, \varphi_r\}$.

5   Case Study

We now present a real case study focused on monitoring vessel behavior in the context of maritime safety and security. It has been provided by Thales, a global electronics company delivering mission-critical information systems and services for aerospace, defense, and security. For the sake of brevity, the results obtained in the case study are only partially illustrated in this section. Here, we only want to give an example of a possible application of our framework.

In our experiments, we use different logs describing the behavior of different types of vessels. These logs have been collected by a maritime Automatic Identification System (AIS) [4], which acts as a transponder that logs and sends events to an AIS receiver. Each log contains a set of process instances corresponding to the behavior of vessels of the same type (e.g., Passenger ship, Fishing boat, Dredger or Tanker). An event in a process instance is a change in the navigational state of the vessel (e g , Moored, Under way using engine, At anchor, Under way sailing, or Restricted maneuverability). The logs are one-week excerpts of larger logs tracing the behavior of each vessel in the long term.

Starting from these logs, exploiting process mining techniques [1], we discover Declare models representing the behavior of each vessel type. A fragment of the discovered model for Dredger is shown in Fig. 6. The ultimate goal is to consequently use these models to monitor new vessel behaviors, using the colored automata-based approach outlined in this contribution.

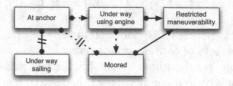

Fig. 6. Discovered model for vessel type Dredger; dashed constraints represent a conflicting set arising after the occurrence of At anchor

More specifically, to construct the model in Fig. 6, we apply the Declare discovery technique described in [7]. We fix the not coexistence and response constraints as possible candidate constraints (the response indicating that if the source event occurs, then the target event must eventually occur). The miner identifies all the not coexistence and response constraints that are satisfied in all the traces of the log. However, when the log is an excerpt of a larger log, it is possible to make the discovery process more flexible by accepting a constraint also if it is possibly violated in some traces: being each execution trace incomplete, such a constraint could be satisfied in the continuation of the trace.

Even though the miner only identifies constraints that never give rise to a permanent violation by themselves, it is possible that conflicting sets of constraints exist in the discovered model. The conflicting sets are caused by the fact that, to extract the reference models from the logs, the miner checks each constraint separately while accepting possibly violated constraints. This makes the approach presented in this paper relevant in the prompt identification of an actual conflict during the monitoring process. For example, Fig. 6 contains a conflict when At anchor is executed; the conflicting constraints are depicted with dashed lines. In this specific case, each constraint of the conflicting set is a recovery set: the conflict is solved by removing any of them from the model.

6   Conclusion

We have introduced the runtime verification of flexible, constraint-based process models formalized in terms of LTL on finite traces, focusing on violations arising from interference of multiple constraints. A conflicting set provides a minimal set of constraints with no continuation where all constraints can be satisfied.

To do so, we have exploited in a novel way established results achieved in the field of temporal logics and runtime verification. In particular, we have considered a finite-trace variation of the RV-LTL semantics [2], following the finite state automata approach of [3] and the optimized algorithms proposed in [12] for the generation of automata. Such automata are employed to provide intuitive diagnostics about the business constraints during execution of a model. More specifically, we have shown how local and/or global information can be provided by combining the use of local automata and of a global automaton, or using a single colored automaton to provide full information.

All the techniques presented in this paper have been fully implemented in Declare and ProM. In particular, we have developed an Operational Support (OS) provider for ProM [1,13], exploiting the recently introduced OS service. The OS service is the backbone for implementing process mining techniques that are not used in a post-mortem manner, i.e., on already completed process instances, but are instead meant to provide runtime support to running executions. Our provider takes in input a Declare model, and exploits the colored automata-based techniques presented here to track running instances and give intuitive diagnostics to the end users, graphically showing the status of each constraint, as well as reporting local and non-local violations (see Fig. 5 for an example). In the latter case, recovery sets are computed, showing the minimal possible modifications that can be applied to the model to alleviate the detected conflict.

Monitoring business constraints can be also tackled by using the Event Calculus (EC) [8]. The two approaches are orthogonal to each other: the EC can only provide diagnostics about local violations, but is easier to augment with other perspectives such as metric time constraints and data related aspects. We plan to investigate the incorporation of metric time aspects also in an automaton-based approach, relying on timed automata for verification.

References

1. van der Aalst, W.M.P.: Process Mining: Discovery, Conformance and Enhancement of Business Processes. Springer, Heidelberg (2011)
2. Bauer, A., Leucker, M., Schallhart, C.: Comparing LTL Semantics for Runtime Verification. In: Logic and Computation, pp. 651–674 (2010)
3. Giannakopoulou, D., Havelund, K.: Automata-Based Verification of Temporal Properties on Running Programs. In: Proc. ASE, pp. 412–416 (2001)
4. International Telecommunications Union. Technical characteristics for a universal shipborne Automatic Identification System using time division multiple access in the VHF maritime mobile band, Recommendation ITU-R M.1371-1 (2001)
5. Lichtenstein, O., Pnueli, A., Zuck, L.D.: The Glory of the Past. In: Proc. of Logic of Programs, pp. 196–218 (1985)
6. Maggi, F.M., Montali, M., Westergaard, M., van der Aalst, W.M.P.: Monitoring Business Constraints with Linear Temporal Logic: An Approach Based on Colored Automata. In: Rinderle-Ma, S., Toumani, F., Wolf, K. (eds.) BPM 2011. LNCS, vol. 6896, pp. 132–147. Springer, Heidelberg (2011)
7. Maggi, F.M., Mooij, A.J., van der Aalst, W.M.P.: User-Guided Discovery of Declarative Process Models. In: Proc. of CIDM, pp. 192–199 (2011)
8. Montali, M., Maggi, F.M., Chesani, F., Mello, P., van der Aalst, W.M.P.: Monitoring Business Constraints with the Event Calculus. Technical Report DEIS-LIA-002-11, University of Bologna, Italy, LIA Series no. 97 (2011)
9. Pesic, M., Schonenberg, H., van der Aalst, W.M.P.: DECLARE: Full Support for Loosely-Structured Processes. In: Proc. of EDOC, pp. 287–300 (2007)
10. Tarjan, R.: Depth-First Search and Linear Graph Algorithms. SIAM Journal on Computing, 146–160 (1972)

11. van der Aalst, W.M.P., Pesic, M., Schonenberg, H.: Declarative workflows: Balancing between flexibility and support. Computer Science - R&D (2009)
12. Westergaard, M.: Better Algorithms for Analyzing and Enacting Declarative Workflow Languages Using LTL. In: Rinderle-Ma, S., Toumani, F., Wolf, K. (eds.) BPM 2011. LNCS, vol. 6896, pp. 83–98. Springer, Heidelberg (2011)
13. Westergaard, M., Maggi, F.M.: Modelling and Verification of a Protocol for Operational Support using Coloured Petri Nets. In: Proc. of ATPN 2011 (2011)

Parametric Identification of Temporal Properties

Eugene Asarin[1], Alexandre Donzé[2], Oded Maler[2], and Dejan Nickovic[3]

[1] LIAFA, Université Paris Diderot / CNRS, Paris, France
[2] Verimag, Université Joseph Fourier / CNRS, Giéres, France
[3] IST Austria, Klosterneuburg, Austria

Abstract. Given a dense-time real-valued signal and a parameterized temporal logic formula with *both* magnitude and timing parameters, we compute the subset of the parameter space that renders the formula satisfied by the trace. We provide two preliminary implementations, one which follows the exact semantics and attempts to compute the validity domain by quantifier elimination in linear arithmetics and one which conducts adaptive search in the parameter space.

1 Introduction

Much of discrete verification is concerned with evaluating behaviors (traces) generated by a *system model* against *specifications* that classify behaviors as good or bad. A similar approach is used in other engineering domains, where the system model is described using some modeling and numerical simulation framework. Such models, which semantically correspond to continuous or hybrid systems, generate finite traces (trajectories, waveforms, signals). The simulation traces are then evaluated according to some *performance measures*, which are typically *quantitative* in nature. Such trace evaluation procedures are integrated in the development cycle of the system, where each time a specification violation is found or a behavior of a poor performance is observed, the systems is modified or fine-tuned to achieve its correctness or improve its performance.

The above description fits well the development of *engineered* systems constructed from components with known input-output behavior. Simulation and verification are required only because the outcome of the *interaction* between these components is hard to predict beyond a certain complexity. The specifications describe at a high-level the *intended* functionality that we want the system to achieve.

In this work we tackle the *inverse* problem, namely, given a trace or a set of traces, find a specification that it satisfies. The procedure used to resolve this problem consists in *learning* from examples (*system identification, inductive inference, parameter estimation*), and can be very useful in the context of *experimental science* such as Biology where one wants to come up with a succinct and human intelligible *description* of experimentally observed data. This approach can also help in the design of systems that admit physical parts whose properties are characterized experimentally, for example, analog components in digital circuits, and be integrated in a framework for compositional reasoning based on *assume-guarantee* principles.

As a specification formalism, we adopt *signal temporal logic* (STL) introduced in [17] to express and monitor temporal properties of *dense-time real-valued* signals. We introduce PSTL, a parametric extension of STL, where *threshold constants* in numerical

S. Khurshid and K. Sen (Eds.): RV 2011, LNCS 7186, pp. 147–160, 2012.
© Springer-Verlag Berlin Heidelberg 2012

inequalities as well as *delay bounds* in temporal operators can be replaced by parameters. Then, we solve the following problem: *Given a PSTL formula, find the range of parameters that render the formula satisfied by a given set of traces.* This work extends the pioneering work of Fages and Rizk [10] who identify parameter ranges for numerical predicates on top of the discrete-time temporal logic LTL [22]. Our use of a dense-time logic, where time is handled arithmetically, rather than as a sequence of "ticks", makes the whole framework more robust to changes in sampling rates or integration steps. More importantly, it allows us to use parameters in the temporal operators and compute trade-offs between timing and magnitude parameters.

The rest of the paper is organized as follows. In Sect. 2 we present PSTL and its semantics in terms of validity domains. In Sect. 3 we show that validity domains for PSTL formulae relative to (interpolated) piecewise-linear signals are semilinear and show that they can be computed, in principle, by quantifier elimination. In Sect. 4 we move to an approximate computation based on adaptive sampling of the parameter space using recently-developed techniques for approximating Pareto fronts. We demonstrate the viability of the approach by computing the validity domains on a non-trivial example of a stabilization property with 3 parameters relative to a signal with 1024 sampling points. We conclude with a discussion of past and future work.

2   Parametric Signal Temporal Logic

Parametric signal temporal logic (PSTL) is based on the logic STL introduced in [17,21,18] for specifying and monitoring properties of real-valued continuous time signals, in particular those produced by analog circuits [13]. In the rest of the paper, we assume a time domain $\mathbb{T} = [0, \infty)$ (or a finite prefix of it) and traces (signals) of the form $x : \mathbb{T} \to \mathbb{R}^n$. We use $x[t]$ to denote the value of x at time t and $x_i[t]$ for the value of its ith coordinate.

We abuse the same variables $\{x_1, \ldots, x_n\}$ to speak of the value of the signal in the logical formulae. In addition we use two types of parameters, *magnitude* parameters $\{p_1, \ldots, p_g\}$ and *timing* parameters $\{s_1, \ldots, s_h\}$, ranging over their respective domains $\mathcal{P}$ and $\mathcal{S}$, say hyper-rectangles in $\mathbb{R}^g$ and $\mathbb{R}^h$, respectively. We use p and s for the vectors of all parameters. A *numerical predicate* μ is an inequality of the form $f(x) < \theta$ or $f(x) > \theta$ where f is a function from $\mathbb{R}^n$ to $\mathbb{R}$ and θ is a threshold which is either a constant c or a magnitude parameter p_i. We use I to denote an interval of the form (a, b), $(a, b]$, $[a, b)$, $[a, b]$, (a, ∞) or $[a, \infty)$ where each of a, b can be either a non-negative constant or a timing parameter s_i. When both bounds are constants we require $0 \leq a < b$. A PSTL formula is then defined by the grammar

$$\varphi := \mu \,|\, \neg\varphi \,|\, \varphi_1 \wedge \varphi_2 \,|\, \varphi_1 \, \mathcal{U}_I \varphi_2$$

The usual *always* and *eventually* operators are defined as: $\Diamond_I \varphi \triangleq$ true $\mathcal{U}_I \varphi$ and $\Box_I \varphi \triangleq \neg\Diamond_I \neg\varphi$. For example, $\varphi = \Diamond_{[0,s_2]}\Box_{[0,s_1]}(x < p)$ is a PSTL formula with one magnitude parameter p, and two temporal parameters s_1 and s_2.

A parameter valuation $(u, v) \in \mathbb{R}^g \times \mathbb{R}^h$ transforms a PSTL formula φ into an STL formula $\varphi_{u,v}$ obtained by substituting the values (u, v) in the parameters (p, s). We use the notation $\theta_{u,v}$ to denote the threshold obtained from θ by such a substitution and $I_{u,v}$ for the similar operation on the interval I.

The *polarity* $\pi(p, \varphi)$ of a parameter p with respect to a formula φ is positive if it is easier to satisfy φ as we increase the value of p and is negative if it is harder. Intuitively, magnitude parameters satisfy

$$\pi(p, f(x) < p) = + \quad \pi(p, f(x) > p) = -$$

and timing parameters satisfy

$$\pi(s, \varphi \, \mathcal{U}_{[b,s]} \psi) = + \quad \pi(s, \varphi \, \mathcal{U}_{[s,b]} \psi) = -$$

We now formally define the polarity of a parameter. Let $\top, +, -$ and $\perp$ indicate, respectively, undefined, positive, negative and mixed polarities. The polarity of a magnitude parameter p in a formula φ is defined inductively as follows.

$$\pi(p, f(x) < c) = \pi(p, f(x) > c) = \top$$
$$\pi(p, f(x) < p) = + \quad \pi(p, f(x) > p) = -$$
$$\pi(p, \neg\varphi) = \sim \pi(p, \varphi)$$
$$\pi(p, \varphi \, \mathcal{U}_I \psi) = \pi(p, \varphi \wedge \psi) = \pi(p, \varphi) \circ \pi(p, \psi)$$

For a timing parameter s we have

$$\pi(s, \mu) = \top$$
$$\pi(s, \varphi \, \mathcal{U}_I \psi) = u \circ (\pi(p, \varphi) \circ \pi(p, \psi))$$

where

$$u = \begin{cases} + & \text{when } I = [a, s] \\ - & \text{when } I = [s, b] \\ \top & \text{otherwise} \end{cases}$$

The rules for negation and conjunction are identical to the rules for magnitude parameters. Operations $\sim$ and $\circ$ are defined as

$\circ$	$\top$	$+$	$-$	$\perp$		$\sim$	
$\top$	$\top$	$+$	$-$	$\perp$		$\top$	$\top$
$+$	$+$	$+$	$\perp$	$\perp$		$+$	$-$
$-$	$-$	$\perp$	$-$	$\perp$		$-$	$+$
$\perp$	$\perp$	$\perp$	$\perp$	$\perp$		$\perp$	$\perp$

A formula is fine if the polarity of every parameter is either $+$ or $-$. We consider only fine formulae.

The semantics of a PSTL formula φ with respect to a signal x is given, following [10], in terms of a *validity domain* $D(x, \varphi) \subseteq \mathcal{P} \times \mathcal{S}$ consisting of all tuples (u, v) such that x satisfies $\varphi_{u,v}$ in the usual sense of STL satisfaction. To compute it we will need at intermediate stages extended validity domains of the form $d(x, \varphi) \subseteq \mathbb{T} \times \mathcal{P} \times \mathcal{S}$ consisting of all tuples (t, u, v) such that $(x, t) \models \varphi_{u,v}$. Then $D(x, \varphi) = \{(u, v) : (0, u, v) \in d(x, \varphi)\}$ consists of all parameter values that yield satisfaction at time zero.

Definition 1 (Validity Domain). *The validity domain of a formula φ with respect to a signal x is defined inductively as follows.*

$$
\begin{aligned}
d(x, f(x) < \theta) &= \{(t, u, v) : f(x(t)) < \theta_{u,v}\} \\
d(x, \varphi \wedge \psi) &= d(x, \varphi) \cap d(x, \psi) \\
d(x, \neg\varphi) &= \overline{d(x, \varphi)} \\
d(x, \varphi\, \mathcal{U}_I \psi) &= \{(t, u, v) : \exists t' \in t \oplus I_{u,v} \text{ s.t. } (t', u, v) \in d(x, \psi) \wedge \\
&\qquad \forall t'' \in [t, t'] (t'', u, v) \in d(x, \varphi)\}
\end{aligned}
$$

where $t \oplus I = (t + I) \cap \mathbb{T}$.

Note that in the terminology of machine learning and inductive inference, our whole setting is that of learning from *positive* examples: we observe traces that occur but nobody gives us impossible traces. Hence it is natural to look for the *minimal*[1] elements of the validity domain that yield the tightest (strongest) formulae satisfied by the traces.

3   Computing Validity Domains

In this section, we present a procedure for exact computation of validity domains for a given trace and PSTL formula, and illustrate it with a simple example. Finally, we present experimental results that indicate how this exact technique scales both with respect to the size of the input traces and the size of the PSTL formula.

3.1   Semilinear Validity Domains

To start with, observe that the semantics of STL formulae is defined in terms of *dense-time* real-valued signals, but in reality the signals that one can observe, either experimentally or via numerical simulators, are *sampled* signals consisting of sequences of time stamped values of the form

$$(t_0, x[t_0]), (t_1, x[t_1]), \ldots, (t_k, x[t_k]). \tag{1}$$

for an increasing sequence of time stamps with $t_0 = 0$. We interpret these sampled signals as continuous-time signals using linear interpolation as in [18]. In each interval of the form $[t_j, t_{j+1}]$ we consider the value of $x[t]$ to be

$$x[t] = x[t_j] + \frac{x[t_{j+1}] - x[t_j]}{t_{j+1} - t_j} \cdot t = \beta_j + \alpha_j t.$$

It follows that the validity domain of a formula φ with respect to a piecewise-linear signal x, can be defined inductively as follows:

$$
\begin{aligned}
d(x, f(x) < p) &= \{(t, u, v) : \bigvee_{j=0}^{k-1} (t_j < t < t_{j+1}) \wedge (\alpha_j t + \beta_j < u)\} \\
d(x, \varphi \wedge \psi) &= \{(t, u, v) : (t, u, v) \in d(x, \varphi) \wedge (t, u, v) \in d(x, \psi)\} \\
d(x, \neg\varphi) &= \{(t, u, v) : (t, u, v) \notin d(x, \varphi)\} \\
d(x, \varphi\, \mathcal{U}_I \psi) &= \{(t, u, v) : \exists t' \, (t + v_1 \le t' \le t + v_2) \wedge (t', u, v) \in d(x, \psi) \wedge \\
&\qquad \forall t'' (t \le t'' \le t') \Rightarrow (t'', u, v) \in d(x, \varphi)\} \\
D(x, \varphi) &= \{(t, u, v) : t = 0 \wedge (t, u, v) \in d(x, \varphi)\}
\end{aligned}
$$

---

[1] Or maximal, depending on the parameter polarity.

We next show that the above rules for computing the validity domain φ with respect to a piecewise-linear signal x result in a Boolean combination of linear inequalities.

Definition 2 (Semilinear Validity Domains). *A subset of the parameter space is semilinear if it can be written as a Boolean combination of linear inequalities on the corresponding variables.*

Proposition 1. *For every PSTL formula φ and piecewise-linear signal x, the validity domain $D(x, \varphi)$ is semilinear.*

Proof. We first prove that $d(x, \varphi)$ is semilinear for every φ by a simple induction on the structure of the formula. For the base case of a predicate $f(x) < p$ we first construct from x a derived sampled signal $y = (t_0, y[t_0]), (t_1, y[t_1]), \ldots$ with $y[t_j] = f(x[t_j])$ that by interpolation is extended to the real time axis to obtain $y[t] = \alpha_j t + \beta_j$ whenever $t \in [t_j, t_{j+1}]$. Then, we have seen that the validity domain can be written as

$$d(x, f(x) < p) = \{(t, u, v) : \bigvee_{j=0}^{k-1} (t_j < t < t_{j+1}) \wedge (\alpha_j t + \beta_j < u)\}$$

which is semilinear. For the inductive case, closure under Boolean operations is immediate. For the *until* operator, we remind the reader that $d(x, \varphi \, \mathcal{U}_{[s_1, s_2]} \psi)$ can be written as

$$\{(t, u, v) : \exists t' \, (t + v_1 \leq t' \leq t + v_2) \wedge (t', u, v) \in d(x, \psi) \wedge \\ \forall t''(t \leq t'' \leq t') \Rightarrow (t'', u, v) \in d(x, \varphi)\}$$

and since semilinear sets are closed under universal and existential projection (quantifier elimination) and $d(x, \varphi)$ and $d(x, \psi)$ are semilinear by the inductive hypothesis, the result follows. Finally, transforming d to D by projecting on $t = 0$ also preserves semilinearity. ∎

Note that a function f appearing in a predicate need not be necessarily linear. The result also holds when each f is linear and parameters are allowed as coefficients. In the discrete time logic used in [10], the restriction of parameters to threshold will lead to rectangular validity domains. The extension of Proposition 1 to validity domains associated with *several* signals is trivial: $D(\{x, x'\}, \varphi) = D(x, \varphi) \cap D(x', \varphi)$.

We note that the validity domain computed by this procedure provides the exact representation of all parameters for which the piecewise-linear signal x satisfies the formula φ. Given that the validity domain is semilinear, i.e. can be represented as a Boolean combination of linear inequalities, it follows that the problem of finding a vector of parameters that satisfy φ with respect to x can be reduced to a constraint satisfaction problem. However, given a validity domain, a user may not be interested only in a vector of parameters that satisfy the formula φ with respect to x, but in such "optimal" parameters, where the notion of optimality depends on the particular application. Given that in this paper we consider only fine formulas, it makes sense to search for *tightest* parameters, that is parameters with negative (positive) polarity whose increase (decrease) of their value would make the formula φ violated. Tightest parameters give the most precise specification that matches the observed traces, and are in particular useful for learning the model from the simulated behaviors. In that case, the problem of searching such parameters reduces to the identification of multi-dimensional Pareto fronts, that will be discussed in more detail in Section 4.

3.2 Example

Let us illustrate the computation of validity domains on the formula $\varphi = \Diamond_{[0,s_2]} \Box_{[0,s_1]}(x < p)$ and some of its variants and subformulas relative to the signal x of Fig. 1-(a). The formula admits two temporal parameters s_1 and s_2 and a magnitude parameter p. The validity domain $V_1 = d(x, x < p)$, depicted in Fig. 1-(b), is

$$V_1 = (t \geq 0 \wedge t < 2 \wedge 2p > 4t) \qquad \vee$$
$$(t \geq 2 \wedge t < 4 \wedge 2p + 4t > 16) \vee$$
$$(t \geq 4 \wedge t < 5 \wedge p > 2t - 8) \qquad \vee$$
$$(t \geq 5 \wedge t < 6 \wedge p + 2t > 12)$$

The validity domain $V_2 = d(x, \Box_{[0,s_1]}(x < p))$, which by definition is the set $\{(t, p, s_1) \mid \forall t' \in [t, t+s_2] \cap [0, 6), (t', p, s_1) \in d(x, x < p)\}$, is obtained by eliminating the universal quantifier, yielding a validity domain expressed by:

$$V_2 = (p + 2s_1 + 2t < 12 \vee p + 2t > 12 \vee p > 0 \vee p \leq 0) \wedge$$
$$(p + 2s_1 + 2t < 8 \vee p + 2t > 8 \vee p + 4 \leq 0 \vee p > 4) \wedge$$
$$(s_1 + t \geq 6 \vee (p - 2s_1 - 2t > 0 \wedge s_1 + t < 2) \vee$$
$$(p + 2s_1 + 2t > 8 \wedge s_1 + t \geq 2 \wedge s_1 + t < 4) \vee$$
$$(p - 2s_1 - 2t + 8 > 0 \wedge s_1 + t \geq 4 \wedge s_1 + t < 5) \vee$$
$$(p + 2s_1 + 2t > 12 \wedge s_1 + t \geq 5)) \wedge (p \geq 2 \vee s_1 + t < 5 \vee t \geq 5) \wedge$$
$$(p > 0 \vee s_1 + t < 4 \vee t \geq 4) \wedge (p \geq 4 \vee s_1 + t < 2 \vee t_1 \geq 2) \wedge$$
$$(p > 0 \vee s_1 + t < 6 \vee t \geq 6)$$

Figures 1-(c,d) depict the projections of V_2 on $p = 1$ and $p = 2$, respectively. Finally the validity domain of the top-level formula, $V_3 = d(x, \Diamond_{[0,s_2]} \Box_{[0,s_1]}(x < p))$, which is the set $\{(t, p, s_1, s_2) \mid \exists t' \in [t, t + s_2] \cap [0, 6) \text{ s.t. } (t', p, s_1, s_2) \in V_2\}$, is obtained by eliminating the existential quantifier. The projection of V_3 on $t = 0$ and $p = 2$ yields the domain expressed by the following quantifier-free formula:

$$V_3 = (s_1 + s_2 \geq 5 \wedge 0 \leq s_1 < 2 \wedge s_2 \geq 0) \vee$$
$$(s_1 + s_2 > 5 \wedge s_1 \geq 0 \wedge s_2 > 5) \vee$$
$$(s_1 + s_2 \geq 4 \wedge s_1 + s_2 < 5 \wedge s_1 \geq 0 \wedge s_2 > 3) \vee$$
$$(s_1 + s_2 > 3 \wedge s_1 + s_2 < 4 \wedge s_1 \geq 0 \wedge s_2 > 3) \vee$$
$$(s_1 \geq 0 \wedge s_2 \geq 6) \vee (s_1 < 1 \wedge s_1 \geq 0 \wedge s_2 \geq 0) \vee$$
$$(s_1 + s_2 < 1 \wedge s_1 \geq 0 \wedge s_2 \geq 0)$$

The projections of V_3 on $(s_1 = 1.5 \wedge p = 2)$ and on $(t = 0 \wedge p = 2)$ are shown in Figures 1-(e) and 1-(f), respectively.

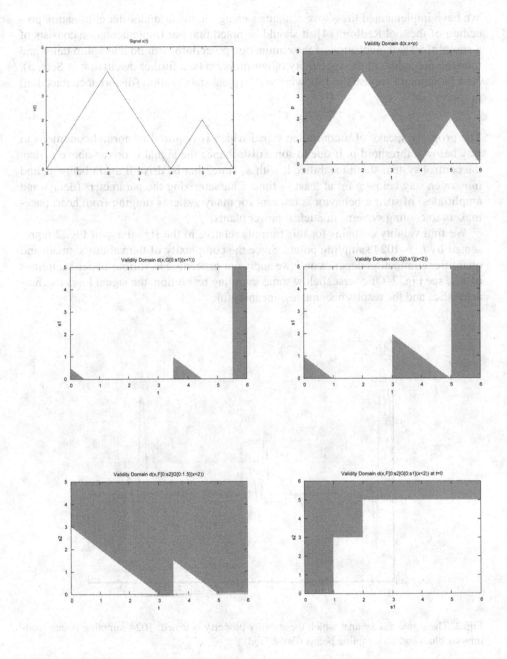

Fig. 1. (a) Signal x; (b) $d(x, x < p)$; (c) $d(x, \Box_{[0,s_1]}(x < 1))$; (d) $d(x, \Box_{[0,s_1]}(x < 2))$; (e) $d(x, \Diamond_{[0,s_2]}\Box_{[0,1.5]}(x < 2))$; and (f) $D(x, \Diamond_{[0,s_2]}\Box_{[0,s_1]}(x < 2))$

3.3   Experimental Results for Exact Computation of Validity Domains

We have implemented the above semantics using the linear quantifier elimination procedure of the tool Redlog [14]. It should be noted that our implementation consists of
a straightforward invocation of the elimination procedure with no attempt to tailor and
tune the procedure to the specificity of our problem (see further discussion in Sect. 5).
As a benchmark we use the following very typical stabilization (disturbance rejection)
property:

$$\varphi_{st} : \Box((x \geq p) \rightarrow \Diamond_{[0,s_2]}\Box_{[0,s_1]}(x < p)). \tag{2}$$

The property speaks of a controlled signal which is required in normal conditions to
stay below a threshold p. If due to some disturbance the signal is driven above p, than
the control system should stabilize it with s_1 time, that is, drive it again below p, and
moreover, stay below p for at least s_2 time. Characterizing the parameters (delays and
amplitudes) of such a behavior is relevant for many systems ranging from heart pacemakers to cooling systems in nuclear power plants.

We find validity domains for this formula relative to the signal x_{st} of Fig. 2 represented by $k = 1024$ sampling points. Since the complexity of the validity domain and
quantifier elimination depends on k we apply our procedure to various under-samplings
of x_{st}, see Fig. 2. Of course, below some sampling resolution, the signal loses its characteristics and the results become less meaningful.

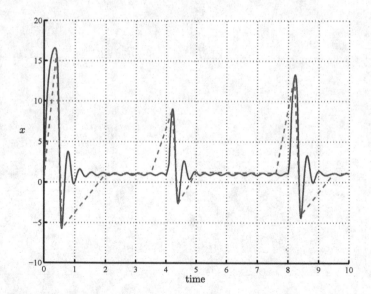

Fig. 2. The signal x_{st} against which the stability property is tested: 1024 sampling points (continuous blue) and 16 sampling points (dashed red)

Table 1 shows some statistics on computation time and description size of the validity domain for the formula φ_{st} and its subformulae

$$\varphi_1 : \square_{[0,s_1]}(x < p)$$
$$\varphi_2 : \lozenge_{[0,s_2]}\square_{[0,s_1]}(x < p)$$
$$\varphi_3 : (x \geq p) \rightarrow \lozenge_{[0,s_2]}\square_{[0,s_1]}(x < p)$$

against various sampled versions of x_{st}. The size of the solution corresponds to the number of linear inequalities used for its representation (no redundancy elimination applied at this point) and the symbol $*$ denotes a time-out after 10 minutes.

Table 1. Computation time and description size for the stabilization formula φ_{st} and its subformulas for different sampling of signal x_{st}

formula	φ_1		φ_2		φ_3		φ_{st}	
k	time(s)	size	time(s)	size	time(s)	size	time(s)	size
8	0.02	38	0.11	197	0.17	207	3	4219
16	0.10	66	0.81	855	0.74	375	83.79	37709
32	0.26	86	19.07	6553	18.27	2885	*	*
64	4.16	144	341.95	23103	308.93	10258	*	*
128	68.29	895	*	*	*	*	*	*
256	386.72	3098	*	*	*	*	*	*

Note that in the worst case, the Fourier-Motzkin quantifier elimination procedure may square the number of constraints which gives a description size of k^{2^m} where m is the number of nested simple ($\square$ or $\lozenge$) temporal operators, not counting the normalization of the formula after each iteration.

4   Approximating Validity Domains

The limitations of the exact method motivate us to apply an alternative approximation technique based on intelligent search in the parameter space. For every point (u, v) in the parameter space we can pose a *query* concerning its membership in $D(x, \varphi)$ by constructing the STL formula $\varphi_{u,v}$ and checking whether $x \models \varphi_{u,v}$. This approach to parameter space exploration has been implemented in a tool [5] and applied to embedded [7] and biological [6] case studies. To conduct this exploration efficiently we will take advantage of an additional property of our validity domains due to the use of a fixed polarity for each parameter.

Definition 3 (Monotonic Validity Domains). *A subset $V \subseteq \mathcal{P} \times \mathcal{S}$ is monotonic if for every i, whenever a parameter valuation $(v_1, \ldots, v_i, \ldots, v_{g+h})$ is in V so is any $(v_1, \ldots, v_i', \ldots, v_{g+h}) \in \mathcal{P} \times \mathcal{S}$ satisfying $v_i' > v_i$ (when $\pi(p_i, \varphi) = +$) or $v_i' < v_i$ (when $\pi(p_i, \varphi) = -$).*

To facilitate the discussion we apply a coordinate transformation to the parameter space and replace every negative polarity parameter p by its complement $-p$ and thus deal with validity domains which are *upward closed* relative to the parameter space, namely $v \in V$ implies $v' \in V$ for every $v' > v$. The set of minimal parameter values that render the formula satisfied is the boundary between the validity domain and its complement relative to the parameter space. Such sets are known in the context of multi-criteria optimization [9] as *Pareto surfaces* or *Pareto fronts*, see Fig. 3-(a). An ϵ-approximation of the surface is a set of points $S \subseteq V$ such that each point on the surface admits an ϵ-close point in S. In other words, the set S consists of a representative sample of the optimal trade-offs available in the problem. In the following we describe briefly the exploration technique developed in [15] for efficient approximation of Pareto fronts, which constitutes a multi-dimensional generalization of binary search.

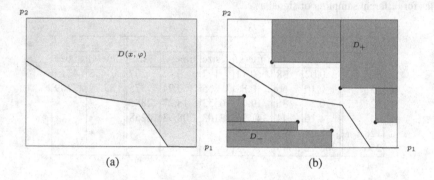

(a)   (b)

Fig. 3. (a) An upward-closed validity domain in 2 dimensions and its lower boundary (thick line); (b) state of knowledge after 3 positive and 3 negative queries in the parameter space

Figure 3-(b) depicts our state of knowledge after performing 3 positive and 3 negative queries in the parameter space. Since the set is upward closed, we know that the upward closure of the positive points (the set D_+) is included in $D(x, \varphi)$ while the downward closure of the negative points (the set D_-) is included in the the complement of $D(x, \varphi)$. The frontier that we look for is situated between these two sets, and the *distance* between their boundaries gives and upper bound the quality of the approximation (ϵ) provided by the set of positive points. Orienting subsequent queries to points in the parameter space that reduce this distance provides for focusing the queries on the boundary, see more details in [15]. Exponentiality in the dimension of the parameter space cannot be, of course, avoided but the time for each query is linear in k. We have implemented a search based approach to the example, and Fig. 4 depicts the surface obtained for φ_{st} and the 1024-points version of x_{st}.

4.1 Experimental Results for the Approximate Computation of Validity Domains

The approximation technique for computing validity domains by parameter search exploration was evaluated by using the tool Breach [5]. This approach cannot be directly

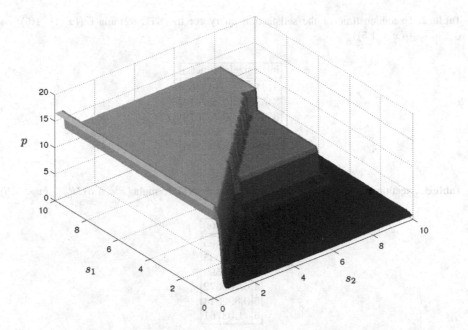

Fig. 4. Approximate boundary of the validity domain $D(x_{st}, \varphi_{st})$ for the stabilization formula φ_{st} with parameters s_1, s_2 and p, for signal x_{st} of Fig. 2 with $k = 1024$

compared to the exact method presented in Section 3. Unlike the exact method, the approximation algorithm does not compute the validity domain precisely. However, the exact validity domain can be approximated to an arbitrary precision, of course at a price of the number of queries required, and consequently the increased computation time.

In Table 2, we first show the computation time for checking the satisfaction query of an STL formula with respect to an input signal of increasing size (where the input size is expressed in terms of the number of sample points). The STL formula that we use is an instantiation of the PSTL formula $\Box((x \geq p) \to \Diamond_{[0,s_2]}\Box_{[0,s_1]}(x < p))$, used in Section 3.3, with parameter values $p = 1.5$, $s_1 = 5$ and $s_2 = 5$. We can observe that for a single query, the computation time grows linearly with the size of the inputs, and that we are able to deal with much larger input traces than in the case of the exact method.

In Table 3, we study the computation time for checking satisfaction query with respect to the size of the STL formulas. For this, we fix the input size, and consider an artificial STL formula $(x < 1.5)\,\mathcal{U}^i_{[0,10]}(x < 1.5)$ with increasing number of nested temporal operators, where $\varphi\,\mathcal{U}^1_I\psi = \varphi\,\mathcal{U}_I\psi$ and $\varphi\,\mathcal{U}^i_I\psi = \varphi\,\mathcal{U}_I(\varphi\,\mathcal{U}^{i-1}_I\psi)$, for $i > 1$. We can see from the experimental results that the computation time also increases linearly with the size of the STL formula.

These experimental results suggest that the approximate technique for computing validity domains can be used to efficiently find parameters that satisfy the PSTL specification with respect to the given set of input traces, and additionally offers to the user the possibility to decide the trade-off between the tightness of the parameters and the computation time needed to compute them.

Table 2. Execution time of the satisfaction query for the STL formula $\Box((x \geq 1.5) \rightarrow \Diamond_{[0,5]}\Box_{[0,5]}(x < 1.5))$

input size	time(s)
31416	0.18402
345566	0.407612
659716	0.755079
973866	1.09268
1288016	1.45865

Table 3. Execution time of the satisfaction query for the STL formula $(x < 1.5)\,\mathcal{U}^i_{[0,10]}(x < 1.5)$

i	time(s)
1	0.347465
2	0.46335
3	0.60599
4	0.760672
5	0.892014
6	1.03761

5   Discussion

We have shown how to synthesize magnitude and timing parameters in a quantitative temporal logic formula so that it fits observed data. The only similar work we are aware of is that of [10] that we extend by making the temporal dimension quantitative and hence parameterizable. This line of work should not be confused with other types of "temporal queries", e.g. [4] where a parametric temporal formula contains a "place-holder" that needs to be replaced by a proposition resulting in a formula that satis-fies a given model. In the context of real-time model checking, the decision problems for parametric timed automata and parametric extension of a real-time temporal logic MITL were studied in [12,3].

We consider the following extensions of this work in order to enlarge its scope both in terms of problem size and richer settings. We are investigating specialized ways to organize the quantifier elimination process so as to proceed along the time axis, in the same manner as qualitative [18] and quantitative [8] satisfaction is computed. A par-ticular difficulty here is that validity domains do not decompose naturally into time segments, that is, a disjunction where each disjuncts admits a distinct term of the form $a < t < b$, but rather segments of the from $a < t + s < b$ for a temporal parameters s. Another technical problem to solve is the efficient derivation of the semilinear for-mula characterizing the minimal facets of a non-convex validity domain. To this end we intend to employ the novel quantifier elimination techniques of [19,20].

Although the restriction to parameters of fixed polarity is justified in many cases and simplifies life, one can imagine situations where it should be dropped, for example in a predicate of the form $p + a < x < p + b$ where the value of x is constrained to be in an interval of a fixed size but a parameterized displacement. Likewise we may have parameterized temporal intervals of the form $[s + a, s + b]$. In such situations, semilinearity is preserved but not monotonicity. Other relaxation of fixed polarity may be required in the context of parameters in nonlinear functions. In the absence of monotonicity, finding the minimal set of parameters is not the only natural choice. In fact, one my argue on the contrary, that it is safer to pick parameters which are deep inside the validity domain as they provide for more *robust* [23,11,8] satisfaction. Since tightness and robustness are conflicting goals perhaps the best solution would be to provide trade-offs (Pareto points) between the two.

The work presented in this paper was fully parametric in the sense that the template formula φ is given and only parameters were sought. A more ambitious goal would be to combine it with a search in the space of formula templates. While such a solution will bring us closer to the science fiction scenario of automatic derivation of theories from experiments, it is clear that it is very easy to face a combinatorial explosion if the search space is not restricted to some small class of property templates. For example one may consider response properties of the form $\Box(\varphi \Rightarrow \Diamond_I \psi)$ where both φ and ψ are Boolean combinations of a small number of simple predicates.

In the more general context, the technique presented here may occupy an interesting niche in all domains that deal with this kind of reverse engineering, e.g. *system identification* [16], machine learning [2] or *inductive inference* [1]. In all these areas one wants to generalize from observations and find a mathematical model compatible with them. In the context of signals, one can think of two extreme classes of target models: detailed models of *dynamical systems* that produce traces which are close to the observed ones or more abstract *logical theories* that define logical dependencies between observations. Temporal logic [22], which is a logic tailored for describing dynamic behaviors, augmented with *quantitative* constructs in time and space as in STL, can offer an interesting tradeoff between the over determination of dynamic models and the quantitative vagueness of too abstract logical statements such as *A causes B* that are sometimes used to summarize experimental findings in the life sciences. A temporal formula expressing the quantitative temporal constraints between the evolution of real-valued observed quantities might provide an optimal level of detail in some application domains.

References

1. Angluin, D., Smith, C.H.: Inductive inference: Theory and methods. ACM Comput. Surv. 15(3), 237–269 (1983)
2. Bishop, C.M.: Pattern Recognition and Machine Learning. Springer, Heidelberg (2006)
3. Bozzelli, L., La Torre, S.: Decision Problems for Lower/Upper Bound Parametric Timed Automata. In: Arge, L., Cachin, C., Jurdziński, T., Tarlecki, A. (eds.) ICALP 2007. LNCS, vol. 4596, pp. 925–936. Springer, Heidelberg (2007)
4. Chan, W.: Temporal-Locig Queries. In: Emerson, E.A., Sistla, A.P. (eds.) CAV 2000. LNCS, vol. 1855, pp. 450–463. Springer, Heidelberg (2000)

5. Donzé, A.: Breach, A Toolbox for Verification and Parameter Synthesis of Hybrid Systems. In: Touili, T., Cook, B., Jackson, P. (eds.) CAV 2010. LNCS, vol. 6174, pp. 167–170. Springer, Heidelberg (2010)

6. Donzé, A., Clermont, G., Langmead, C.J.: Parameter synthesis in nonlinear dynamical systems: Application to systems biology. Journal of Computational Biology 17(3), 325–336 (2010)

7. Donzé, A., Krogh, B.H., Rajhans, A.: Parameter Synthesis for Hybrid Systems with an Application to Simulink Models. In: Majumdar, R., Tabuada, P. (eds.) HSCC 2009. LNCS, vol. 5469, pp. 165–179. Springer, Heidelberg (2009)

8. Donzé, A., Maler, O.: Robust Satisfaction of Temporal Logic over Real-Valued Signals. In: Chatterjee, K., Henzinger, T.A. (eds.) FORMATS 2010. LNCS, vol. 6246, pp. 92–106. Springer, Heidelberg (2010)

9. Ehrgott, M.: Multicriteria optimization. Springer, Heidelberg (2005)

10. Fages, F., Rizk, A.: From Model-Checking to Temporal Logic Constraint Solving. In: Gent, I.P. (ed.) CP 2009. LNCS, vol. 5732, pp. 319–334. Springer, Heidelberg (2009)

11. Fainekos, G.E., Pappas, G.J.: Robustness of temporal logic specifications for continuous-time signals. Theoretical Computer Science 410(42), 4262–4291 (2009)

12. Di Giampaolo, B., La Torre, S., Napoli, M.: Parametric Metric Interval Temporal Logic. In: Dediu, A.-H., Fernau, H., Martín-Vide, C. (eds.) LATA 2010. LNCS, vol. 6031, pp. 249–260. Springer, Heidelberg (2010)

13. Jones, K.D., Konrad, V., Nickovic, D.: Analog property checkers: a ddr2 case study. Formal Methods in System Design 36(2), 114–130 (2010)

14. Lasaruk, A., Sturm, T.: Effective Quantifier Elimination for Presburger Arithmetic with Infinity. In: Gerdt, V.P., Mayr, E.W., Vorozhtsov, E.V. (eds.) CASC 2009. LNCS, vol. 5743, pp. 195–212. Springer, Heidelberg (2009)

15. Legriel, J., Le Guernic, C., Cotton, S., Maler, O.: Approximating the Pareto Front of Multi-criteria Optimization Problems. In: Esparza, J., Majumdar, R. (eds.) TACAS 2010. LNCS, vol. 6015, pp. 69–83. Springer, Heidelberg (2010)

16. Ljung, L.: System Identification - Theory For the User. Prentice Hall (1999)

17. Maler, O., Nickovic, D.: Monitoring Temporal Properties of Continuous Signals. In: Lakhnech, Y., Yovine, S. (eds.) FORMATS 2004 and FTRTFT 2004. LNCS, vol. 3253, pp. 152–166. Springer, Heidelberg (2004)

18. Maler, O., Nickovic, D., Pnueli, A.: Checking Temporal Properties of Discrete, Timed and Continuous Behaviors. In: Avron, A., Dershowitz, N., Rabinovich, A. (eds.) Trakhtenbrot/Festschrift. LNCS, vol. 4800, pp. 475–505. Springer, Heidelberg (2008)

19. Monniaux, D.: A Quantifier Elimination Algorithm for Linear Real Arithmetic. In: Cervesato, I., Veith, H., Voronkov, A. (eds.) LPAR 2008. LNCS (LNAI), vol. 5330, pp. 243–257. Springer, Heidelberg (2008)

20. Monniaux, D.: Automatic modular abstractions for linear constraints. In: POPL 2009, pp. 140–151. ACM (2009)

21. Nickovic, D., Maler, O.: AMT: A Property-Based Monitoring Tool for Analog Systems. In: Raskin, J.-F., Thiagarajan, P.S. (eds.) FORMATS 2007. LNCS, vol. 4763, pp. 304–319. Springer, Heidelberg (2007)

22. Pnueli, A.: The Temporal Semantics of Concurrent Programs. Theoretical Computer Science 13, 45–60 (1981)

23. Rizk, A., Batt, G., Fages, F., Soliman, S.: On a Continuous Degree of Satisfaction of Temporal Logic Formulae with Applications to Systems Biology. In: Heiner, M., Uhrmacher, A.M. (eds.) CMSB 2008. LNCS (LNBI), vol. 5307, pp. 251–268. Springer, Heidelberg (2008)

Marathon: Detecting Atomic-Set Serializability Violations with Conflict Graphs

William N. Sumner[1], Christian Hammer[1,2], and Julian Dolby[3]

[1] Purdue University, West Lafayette, IN, USA
wsumner@cs.purdue.edu
[2] Utah State University, Logan, UT, USA
hammer@usu.edu
[3] IBM T.J. Watson Research Center Hawthorne, NY, USA
dolby@us.ibm.com

Abstract. Recent research has proposed several analyses to mitigate the fact that finding concurrency bugs in multi-threaded software is notoriously hard. This work proposes a new analysis based on a correctness criterion called "atomic-set serializability", which incorporates both race conditions and traditional atomicity/serializability. We present a novel analysis based on conflict cycle detection that is guaranteed to find all violations in the intercepted execution trace. A set of heuristics automatically determines all annotations required for atomic-set serializability. We implemented the analysis and evaluated it on a suite consisting of real programs and benchmarks. The evaluation demonstrates the usefulness of our heuristics by finding a number of known (as well as new) violations with competitive overhead and a very low false positive rate.

Keywords: Serializability, Atomicity, Data Races, Concurrent Object-Oriented Programming, Dynamic Analysis.

1 Introduction

Multi-threaded programs have become more and more predominant as processor speeds cease to rise significantly, and manufacturers put multiple cores onto one processor. However, writing correct multi-threaded code is notoriously hard, which gave rise to several analyses that statically or dynamically enforce certain correctness criteria. These criteria range from the weakest form, data races on single memory locations, to atomicity for all memory involved in a given transaction. Data races occur when two threads access the same shared variable without synchronization, where one of the accesses is a write. Yet in general, data-race freedom does not guarantee the absence of concurrency-related bugs [1, 2, 7]. A remedy has been found in various definitions of serializability (or atomicity) [13, 23, 33, 38, 39]. According to these definitions, an execution performed by a collection of threads is *serializable* if it is equivalent to a serial execution, in which each thread's transactions (or atomic sections) are executed in some serial order. However, serializability/atomicity ignores invariants and consistency

S. Khurshid and K. Sen (Eds.): RV 2011, LNCS 7186, pp. 161–176, 2012.

properties that may exist between shared memory locations, and therefore may not accurately reflect the intentions of the programmer for correct behavior, resulting in missed errors and false positives.

A more flexible correctness criterion that takes such relationships into account has been explored recently: *Atomic-set serializability* defines *atomic sets* of memory locations related by some correctness constraint. It further defines *units of work*, operations that preserve these invariants. Since the sets can range from a single location to the entire heap atomic-set serializability subsumes low level data races as well as atomicity [36]. Like serializability, atomic-set serializability disallows concurrency-related errors [1, 2, 7], but it also permits certain non-problematic interleaving scenarios. Atomic-set serializability is based on a declarative specification about data, which can be checked independent from the actual synchronization code, permitting the code to be checked against the programmer's intention, in particular it can be checked independently of specific synchronization constructs such as locks. Therefore, it can be used in settings where many existing approaches cannot, such as classes from the Java 5 `java.util.concurrent` library and lock-free algorithms.

To detect concurrency errors, the intent of the programmer must still be known in terms of the atomic sets of related locations and their corresponding units of work. Declaring them explicitly could impose a significant burden; hence, we explore whether they can be inferred using heuristics based on the assumption that object-oriented code associates units of consistency with objects. We present a set of heuristics (Sect. 4.1) and show that they generate very few false positives (between 2–4%) in terms of our best manual understanding of what the evaluated programs are meant to do.

This work presents a new approach for checking atomic-set serializability based on cycle detection in conflict graphs. The new approach is guaranteed not to miss errors in a given execution with respect to the given atomic sets and units of work, while providing all advantages of atomic-set serializability over previous correctness criteria. Key steps of our technique include:

- Using a simple static escape analysis to detect fields of objects that may be accessed by multiple threads,
- Encoding the dynamic call stack of each thread efficiently [35] based on a static approximation of the call graph,
- Maintaining a conflict graph of units of work in order to detect cycles during execution, which indicates a serializability violation.

Note that all static analyses are for optimization purposes only, our analysis is independent of these preprocessing steps. We implemented the analysis using the *Shrike* bytecode instrumentation component of the WALA program analysis infrastructure. Our tool instruments the bytecodes of an application in order to: (i) intercept accesses to shared data, (ii) maintain a dynamic call graph [35] to determine the units of work to which these accesses belong, and (iii) update the conflict graph accordingly. To encourage problematic interleavings, we optionally instrumented the code with yields, a technique also known as *noise making* [3]. To determine the units of work we made the heuristic assumptions that method boundaries delineate units of work, and that there is one atomic set for (each instance of) each class, containing all the instance fields of that class.

We evaluated our tool on a number of benchmarks, including classes from the Java Collections Framework, and applications from the ConTest suite [11]. We found a significant number of violations, including known problems [11, 13], as well as problems not previously reported. Our technique does not miss errors in a given execution, provided our heuristics determine the atomic sets and units of work appropriately. On average over all benchmarks, the instrumentation inserted by our tool slows down program execution by a factor of 4, which is similar to, or better than, the performance overhead incurred by other dynamic serializability violation detection tools [13, 14, 19, 23, 30, 38–40]

In summary, this paper makes the following contributions:

1. We present a dynamic analysis guaranteed to detect all atomic-set serializability violations in the intercepted execution trace based on discovering cycles in a conflict graph. This graph is based on atomic sets and units of work, rather than low-level memory and locking operations in prior work.
2. We incorporated an efficient dynamic call graph encoding scheme that computes the callstack as a small number of integers, and still encompasses all the complexities of object-oriented systems such as exceptions. This uses both less time and less space than traditional approaches.
3. We model the semantics of Object.wait in the context of atomic sets, which leads to a drastic reduction of the false positive rate.
4. We present a set of heuristics that automatically determine the atomic sets and units of work of an application. We demonstrate the usefulness of these heuristics by using them to find many known races and simultaneously keeping the set of false positives very low (2–4%).
5. We implemented this analysis using the WALA infrastructure and show its effectiveness on a number of Java benchmarks. We found known bugs as well as bugs not detected by our previous approach.

2   Background

Our work is based on atomic-set serializability, a correctness criterion for concurrent programs defined by Vaziri et al. [36] which exploits that invariants typically exist between *specific* memory locations; a well-encapsulated data structure will have operations that update only its own memory locations. Atomic-set serializability assumes the existence of *atomic sets* of memory locations that must be updated atomically, and *units of work*, code fragments that preserve consistency of the atomic set, when executed sequentially. Intuitively, the atomic set denotes the elements of a specific data structure, and units of work are the operations for manipulating that data structure.

For cases where an operation needs to happen across multiple data structures, the language offers two more keywords. A parameter declared unitfor signifies that the method is a unit of work for that parameter, and hence this method

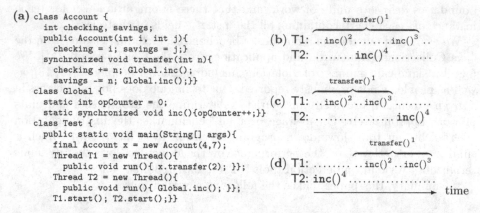

(a)
```
class Account {
  int checking, savings;
  public Account(int i, int j){
    checking = i; savings = j;}
  synchronized void transfer(int n){
    checking += n; Global.inc();
    savings -= n; Global.inc();}}
class Global {
  static int opCounter = 0;
  static synchronized void inc(){opCounter++;}}
class Test {
  public static void main(String[] args){
    final Account x = new Account(4,7);
    Thread T1 = new Thread(){
      public void run(){ x.transfer(2); }};
    Thread T2 = new Thread(){
      public void run(){ Global.inc(); }};
    T1.start(); T2.start();}}
```

Fig. 1. (a) Example program. (b)–(d) Three different thread executions.

must appear atomic with respect to units of work upon that parameter. For example, the ArrayList constructor from the JDK 1.5.0.18 takes another collection c as parameter without synchronizing on it. Thus, another thread could add or remove elements to c between retrieving the size of c and copying the elements of c to the ArrayList, which results in an inconsistent value of the ArrayLists size. Declaring c unitfor expresses the consistency requirement between the two calls.

The owned keyword conceptually declares that a given field is "part of" its containing object by merging the respective atomic sets; this allows composition of more-complex data structures from simpler ones. For example, in the Java Collections, a HashSet is implemented with a backing HashMap stored in a field called map that would be declared owned to express the invariant between the state of the set itself and the backing map.

2.1 Example

Figure 1(a) shows a class Account that declares fields checking and savings, as well as a method to transfer money from one to the other. Also shown is a class Global declaring a field opCounter that counts the number of transactions that have taken place. For the purposes of this example, we assume that the programmer intends the following behavior: (1) Intermediate states in which the deposit to checking has taken place without the accompanying withdrawal from savings cannot be observed. (2) Concurrent executions of inc() are allowed provided that variable opCounter is updated atomically. To this end, transfer() and inc() are protected by separate locks. The class Test creates two threads that execute Account.transfer() and Global.inc() concurrently.

Figure 1(b)-(d) depicts executions in which two threads, T1 and T2, concurrently execute the transfer() and inc() methods, respectively. For convenience, each method execution is labeled with a distinct number (1 through 4). Observe that, in Figure 1(b), the execution of inc() by T2 occurs interleaved between that of the two calls to inc() by T1.

2.2 Atomicity/Serializability

For brevity, we only describe these notions on a high level. For a more detailed comparison and the details concerning the example in Figure 1 the reader is referred to our previous work [19].

Atomicity. Atomicity is a non-interference property in which a method or code block is classified as being *atomic* if its execution is not affected by and does not interfere with that of other threads. In our example, the idea is to show that checking and savings are updated atomically by demonstrating that the transfer() method is an atomic section or a transaction. Lipton's theory of reduction [22] defines a pattern of operations that can be reduced to an equivalent serial execution. However, method transfer() does not correspond to this pattern, so the theory cannot show that no intermediate states are exposed to other threads.

View-serializability. Two executions are *view-equivalent* [4, 38] if they contain the same events, each read operation reads the result of the same write operation in both executions, and both executions have the same final write for any location. An execution is *view-serializable* if it is view-equivalent to a serial execution. It is easy to see that execution (b) is neither view-equivalent to serial execution (c), nor to serial execution (d). Hence, execution (b) is not view-serializable.

Conflict-serializability. Two events that are executed by different threads are *conflicting* if they operate on the same location and one of them is a write. Two executions are *conflict-equivalent* [4, 38] iff they contain the same events, and each pair of conflicting events appears in the same order. An execution is *conflict-serializable* iff it is conflict-equivalent to a serial execution. Conflict-serializability implies view-serializability [4, 38] as they only differ on how they treat *blind writes*. Hence, execution (b) is not conflict-serializable.

2.3 Atomic-Set Serializability

Given assumption (1) stated above, we assume that checking and savings form an atomic set S_1, and that transfer()[1] is a unit of work on S_1. Moreover, from assumption (2) stated above, we infer that opCounter is another atomic set S_2 and Global.inc()[2], Global.inc()[3], and Global.inc()[4] are units of work on S_2. Atomic-set serializability is equivalent to conflict serializability *after projecting the original execution onto each atomic set*, i.e., only events from one atomic set are included when determining conflicts. The projection of execution (b) onto atomic set S_1 is trivially serial, because events from only one thread are included. Furthermore, the projection onto atomic set S_2 is also serial because the events of units of work Global.inc()[2], Global.inc()[3], and Global.inc()[4] are not interleaved. Therefore, execution (b) is atomic-set serializable.

In conclusion, by taking the relationships between shared memory locations (atomic sets) into account, atomic-set serializability provides a more fine-grained correctness criterion than the traditional notions of atomicity, conflict- and view-serializability. In practice, those would classify execution (b) as having a bug,

(a)
```
x=3; y=2; z=1
fork;
```

```
//Unit of Work u1 (T₁):  //Unit of Work u2 (T₂):  //Unit of Work u3 (T₃):
x = 4; y = 3              z = x                     print(z, y)
```

(b) $W_{u1}(x), R_{u2}(x), W_{u2}(z), R_{u3}(z), R_{u3}(y), W_{u1}(y)$

Fig. 2. (a) Example threads. (b) Non-serializable execution

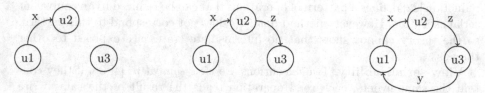

Fig. 3. Conflict graph development for Fig. 2(b) showing a serializability violation as a cycle of conflicts on variables x, y and z between the units of work $u1$, $u2$, and $u3$

but atomic-set serializability correctly reveals that there is none. Yet, if a coarser granularity of data is desired, all three locations can be placed in a single atomic set, in which case our method reverts to conflict-serializability.

2.4   Overview of Our Approach

The goal of this work is to check atomic-set serializability violations dynamically during program execution. To that end our technique leverages a data structure from database theory called a *conflict graph*. A conflict graph consists of nodes representing the units of work (transactions), and edges modeling conflicts between those. Intuitively, a conflict between two nodes occurs when both units of work access a memory location in an associated atomic set, where one access is a write (see Sect. 3 for formal definitions.) The theory asserts that an execution is serializable if and only if the conflict graph is acyclic.

As an example, consider Fig. 2(a), taken from Wang and Stoller [39, Sect. 6.3], which displays a serializability violation involving 3 threads in part (b). Looking at Fig. 3 reveals the nature of this serializability violation: The execution of Fig. 2(b) induces a conflict graph involving three threads in units $u1, u2$ and $u3$ and the conflict edges are labeled with all three variables involved, so reasoning about this bug is very natural.

3   Algorithm

This section presents the theory behind our new algorithm based on the definition of atomic-set serializability.

Let $\mathcal{L}$ be the set of all memory locations. A subset $L \subseteq \mathcal{L}$ is an *atomic set*, indicating that there *exists* a consistency property between those locations. An *event* is a read $R(l)$ or a write $W(l)$ to a memory location $l \in L$, for some atomic set L. We assume that each access to a single memory location is uninterrupted. Given an event e, the notation $loc(e)$ denotes the location accessed by e.

A unit of work u is a sequence of events, and is *declared on* a set of atomic sets. Let $\mathcal{U}$ be the set of all units of work. We write $sets(u)$ for the set of atomic sets corresponding to u. We say that $\bigcup_{L \in sets(u)} L$ is the *dynamic atomic set* of u. Units of work may be nested, and we write $u \leftarrow u'$ to indicate that u' is nested in u. Units of work form a forest via the $\leftarrow$ relation.

An access to a location $l \in L$ appearing in unit of work u *belongs* to the top-most (with respect to the $\leftarrow$ forest) unit of work u' within u such that $L \in sets(u')$. The notation $R_u(l)$ denotes a read belonging to u, and similarly for writes. So if a method foo calls another method bar, where both are declared units of work for the atomic set L_1 and bar reads a location $l \in L_1$ in bar, then this read belongs to foo, as foo $\leftarrow$ bar. Given an event e, the notation $unit(e)$ denotes the unit of work of e.

A *thread* is a sequence of units of work. The notation $thread(u)$ denotes the thread corresponding to u. An *execution* is a sequence of events from one or more threads. Given an execution E and an atomic set L, the *projection of E on L* is an execution that has all events on L in E in the same order, and only those events.

Definition 1 (Atomic-set serializability [36]). *An execution is called* atomic-set serializable *if its projections on each atomic set are serializable.*

Definition 2 (Conflict). *Let L be an atomic set, $l \in L$, and u and u' be two units of work for L. Unit u conflicts with u' ($u \rightsquigarrow u'$) if and only if both u and u' access l, at least one of these accesses is a write, and the access in u either reads from or performs the first write of l temporally preceding the access in u'.*

A *conflict graph* is a directed graph where the vertices are the units of work, $\mathcal{U}$, and there exists an edge from u to u' if and only if $u \rightsquigarrow u'$. Figure 3 depict the development of the conflict graph for the executions in Fig. 2(b), with the code shown in part (a).

Lemma 1. *An execution is atomic-set serializable iff its conflict graph is acyclic*

Proof. Follows from our definition of conflict together with previous serializability results [5, 12, 15, 28].

Corollary 1 ([Serializability Violation). *An execution has an atomic-set serializability violation iff there exists a cycle in the conflict graph of the execution.*

According to this corollary, the cycles in the conflict graphs of Fig. 3 establish an atomic-set serializability violation in the respective executions of Fig. 2(b).

4   Implementation

This section presents details of our implementation. We first present our choice of defaults for atomic sets and units of work (Sect. 4.1). We then discuss how we perform instrumentation to capture events (Sect. 4.2).

4.1   Automatic Detection of Atomic Sets and Units of Work

We assume that all (including inherited) non-final, non-volatile instance fields of an object are members of an atomic set. All accessible non-static public and protected methods of that object are considered initial units of work declared on this atomic set. All its non-final, non-volatile static fields form another per-class atomic set with all non-private methods of the class as initial units of work.

In order to satisfy that each access to an atomic set is done within a corresponding unit of work [36, Sect. 4.1], we assume that a method containing a direct access to a field (or using a simple getter/setter function) is an additional unit of work for the atomic set the field belongs to. A unit of work declared on multiple atomic sets must be a unit of work on their union. Therefore, we merge the original atomic set and the set accessed directly during the execution of the additional unit of work. We support two modi for merging atomic sets: When the direct access is accessing a field of a member of the atomic set, we assume that field is *owned*, so we merge the current atomic set with the one of that member field and propagate that atomic set to the top-most unit of work (see Sect. 3). For direct access to any other field, we do not propagate to the top-most unit, as we assume *unitfor* semantics. Our previous work supported only the owned semantics, which may result in more false positives [19].

Apart from that, we model inner classes. Inner classes indirectly leak access to fields of an enclosing class. For example, in Java Collections, Iterators expose access to an ArrayList's internals to a caller of the iterator() method. Thus, we make the caller a *unitfor* the the enclosing ArrayList as well, protecting access to its internal fields.

These heuristics have been found very effective. They deal correctly with a huge number of access patterns in Java programs.Therefore, we did not add any manual annotations to the programs. We also implemented an intra-procedural static analysis that determines whether a method call is a simple getter/setter.

Modeling wait/notify. A call to a.wait() releases the lock associated with a and waits for another thread to signal a certain condition (usually involving a's atomic set). The other thread changes shared state and calls notify(All). When the first thread resumes, it re-evaluates the condition, which would lead to a benign cycle in the conflict graph with a naïve heuristics of units of work. We break a unit of work into two at a call to wait() due to its non-atomic semantics, which is essential for a low false positive rate as shown by our experiments.

Discussion. These heuristics are designed to discover atomic sets that cover individual data structures; for many applications, such as building concurrent libraries, this is precisely what is required; however, it is certainly possible to have atomicity violations across data structures. Such races imply dependences between memory locations across data structures that are not isolated behind abstraction boundaries. This suggests a severe breakage of modularity, of which atomicity violations are merely one of many deleterious consequences. Much work, e.g. alias control such as ownership types [10], has focused on helping programmers eliminate such errors.

4.2 Program Instrumentation

We instrument the program to intercept field access and to determine what unit of work each access belongs to. To this end, we use the Shrike bytecode instrumentor of the WALA program analysis infrastructure.[1] For all benchmarks other than those testing the collections, we did *not* instrument the Java library. All inter-procedural static analyses are purely optimizations to reduce runtime overhead, and we have fallback mechanisms if these analyses fail to complete.

Before instrumentation, our tool performs a simple static escape analysis that determines a conservative set of possibly-escaping fields by computing the set of all types that are transitively reachable from a static field or are passed to a thread constructor. We instrument all non-final and non-volatile fields of such types, as well as access to arrays.

Our tool uses a non-blocking queue similar to [17, Sect. 15.4.2] to store and serialize events of different threads, keeping the *probe effect* [16] (i.e., changes to the system behavior due to observation) as low as possible, and as, under contention, blocking will show degraded performance due to context-switching overhead and scheduling delays. Serializing events in a sequential order is a prerequisite for detecting cycles in the conflict graph. As a field access and its recording do not happen atomically, the scheduler could activate another thread in-between. Nevertheless, the obtained execution is always a valid execution of the program, as the recording takes place in the same thread, and any synchronization that applies to the access also applies to the recording. Thus, the intercepted execution must be consistent with the program's synchronization scheme, i.e., it might happen with a possible scheduling.

To determine in which unit of work each access belongs, we keep track of a *dynamic call graph*, essentially a call stack, for each called method. An access to a location in an atomic set belongs to its top-most unit of work. To maintain the dynamic call graph, we exploit a technique from Sumner et al. that uses simple arithmetic operations at the invocation points in the program [35]. A call stack corresponds to a path in the static call graph. Using static analysis, we number paths in the call graph and then compute the number of the current path at runtime through addition and subtraction. To handle callbacks and recursion, we represent the dynamic call graph as a list of numbers, saving the last computed id to the list before such a callback and restoring it from the list afterward. We further extend the technique to handle exceptions in Java by saving the id before a try and restoring it within a catch or finally.

As an option, our instrumentation adds yields at certain points in the program to achieve more interleavings, a technique is called *noise making*. Ben-Asher et al. found that, with a more elaborate noise strategy, the probability of producing a bug increases considerably [3].

---

[1] http://wala.sf.net

To reduce the memory overhead of our technique, we additionally garbage collect old units of work that can no longer lead to cycles in the conflict graph. When a unit of work completes and has no incoming conflict edges, it cannot participate in a conflict and may be safely collected. This further allows any terminated units of work conflicting only with the collected one to also be collected.

5   Evaluation

We evaluated our new analysis on the same set of benchmarks as the previous analysis [19] and additional real world programs, including ConTest [11], Java Collections, the Jigsaw webserver, and the Jspider and Weblech web crawlers from [29]. We ran all benchmarks on a 64-bit 2.8GHz 4-core Intel machine with 6GB memory and used the Sun Hotspot JVM version 1.6.0_24-b07.

Table 1 shows the results of our analysis, where each benchmark was executed twice. The column "Program" lists the name of each benchmark. We first list benchmarks from the ConTest suite and then other benchmarks. The "LOC" column contains the number of static lines of code. While the ConTest benchmarks are small kernel programs, others range from a few thousand to more than 100K LOC, showing the applicability of the technique to real world programs. The "#Threads" column lists the configured number of threads in the benchmark. For the ConTest and Collections benchmarks, these are the same as in previous work.

We evaluated the reported violations along several dimensions: The *unique* cycles are counted in the "Cycle Sizes" column according to the number of units of work that the cycle comprises. When multiple accesses (on possibly different fields of an atomic set) can induce the same cycle in the conflict graph, they are considered parts of the same violation and only counted once. However, we listed cycles involving the same atomic set with different sizes separately.

The column "FP" displays the ratio of benign violations (false positives) and the total violations reported based on manual inspection of the programmer's intentions. With our model of Object.wait, only few violations did not in fact indicate a bug. For example, the programs BufWriter, Lottery and Manager had cases where our heuristics for units of work were too coarse grained. Exploring further options for splitting up units of work at certain places like thread fork or join points is subject to future work. Overall, our false positive rate is just under 2%. The Collections benchmarks are admittedly pathological in the number of violations they observe, but even excluding them, our false positive rate is 4%. It was interesting to see the number of violations found for Piper reduce from 75 to 0 when we introduced splitting of the unit of work at Object.wait callsites (see Sect. 4.1). Also BoundedBuffer, JSpider and Weblech would have had several false positives without splitting. These numbers show that faithfully modeling the semantics of wait reduces the false positive rate considerably.

The "New Vio" column compares the current technique with our previous approach [19]. It lists the number of new serializability violations detected. Programs not previously evaluated are denoted by –. We interpret the substantial

Table 1. For each benchmark, the table indicates the number of different violations detected by cycle length, false positives, new violations, slowdown factor, max. size of the conflict graph, and the avg. call stack size

Program	LOC	Cycle Sizes								FP	New Vio	SF Mem	SF Disk	|CG|	Stack Depth	#Threads
		2	3	4	5	6	7	8	9+							
Account	155	1	0	0	0	0	0	0	0	0/1	0	1.0	1.0	14	2.0	10
AirlineTickets	95	1	1	0	0	0	0	0	0	0/2	0	1.5	1.5	94	2.0	100
AllocationV	286	0	0	0	0	0	0	0	0	0/0	0	1.0	1.0	4	2.0	2
BoundedBuffer	328	0	0	1	0	0	0	0	0	0/1	–	1.0	1.0	10	2.0	3
BubbleSort	362	2	3	1	0	0	0	0	0	0/6	0	1.0	1.0	17	2.0	8
BubbleSort 2	130	1	1	1	1	1	1	1	27	0/34	34	10.4	1.4	201	2.0	200
BufWriter	255	1	2	0	0	0	0	0	0	2/3	2	–	–	8	2.0	6
Critical	68	1	0	0	0	0	0	0	0	0/1	0	1.0	1.0	2	2.0	2
DCL	183	1	1	1	0	0	0	0	0	0/1	0	1.3	1.3	31	2.0	20
FileWriter	325	0	0	0	0	0	0	0	0	0/0	0	1.0	1.0	6	2.0	N/A
LinkedList	416	1	0	0	0	0	0	0	0	0/1	0	1.0	1.0	9	2.0	2
Lottery	359	2	1	1	1	1	0	0	0	1/6	5	1.5	1.5	98	2.0	33
Manager	188	4	0	0	0	0	0	0	0	2/4	2	1.0	1.0	7	2.0	3
MergeSort	375	1	0	0	0	0	0	0	0	1/1	0	1.1	1.1	12	3.4	4
MergeSortBug	257	2	1	2	1	1	0	0	0	0/7	1	8.7	1.1	27	3.6	4
PingPong	272	1	0	0	0	0	0	0	0	0/1	0	1.0	1.0	124	2.0	120
Piper	116	0	0	0	0	0	0	0	0	0/0	–	–	–	83	2.0	40
ProducerConsumer	223	3	3	0	0	0	0	0	0	0/6	–	1.0	1.0	12	2.0	6
Shop	273	2	1	1	1	1	1	1	17	0/25	1	1.0	1.0	122	2.0	7
SunsAccount	144	2	1	1	1	1	1	1	31	0/39	1	1.0	1.0	7613	2.0	N/A
Jigsaw	142K	1	0	0	0	0	0	0	0	0/1	0	3.9	3.9	94	8.0	3
Jspider	56K	4	0	0	0	0	0	0	0	0/4	–	1.2	1.2	128	3.4	6
Weblech	1874	2	0	0	0	0	0	0	0	0/2	–	1.1	1.0	12	2.0	9
ArrayBlockingQ	1576	1	1	0	0	0	0	0	0	0/7	2	26.6	14.12	725	4.1	10
ArrayList (sync)	2266	24	37	10	5	3	0	0	0	0/60	60	48.9	19.6	429	4.1	10
LinkedBlockingQ	1620	1	0	0	0	0	0	0	0	0/1	1	20.1	16.9	605	4.0	10
DelayQueue	1961	25	13	3	1	1	0	0	0	0/43	20	23	17.5	155	4.2	10
Vector	2636	18	38	36	24	11	4	0	0	0/131	131	52.8	10.4	63	4.0	10

number of new violations as an indication of the benefit over the old technique, stemming from the fact that the new technique does not miss violations in the intercepted execution. We note that the newly found violations also mean that our technique has no false negatives with respect to the known bugs in the ConTest and Collections benchmarks except for in AllocationV, FileWriter, and Merge-Sort. In these benchmarks, poor object orientation as discussed in Sect. 4 and an inability to reproduce a failing run prevented us from detecting violations.

The "SF" columns indicate the slowdown factor of the instrumented version compared to the uninstrumented version of the program. "SF Mem" is the slowdown when the conflict graph is maintained online during program execution, and "SF Disk" is the slowdown when all accesses are logged to disk and cycle detection is performed postmortem. Note that Piper exhibits a bug that prevented it from terminating and being timed, and BufWriter terminates its threads predictably after 10 seconds. We excluded these from the average, denoted by –. For Jigsaw, we measured the slowdown in response time for client requests, as a web server runs in an infinite loop. Our technique is comparable or better than previous approaches, which range from 10x-200x [13, 14, 19, 23, 30, 38–40], having a 8.5x average overhead factor when performed online. This, however, is biased by the pathological Collection benchmarks. When only the programs with more realistic behavior are considered, the overhead diminishes to 1.9x. When cycle detection is performed postmortem, these numbers diminish to 4x and 1.1x respectively. Some benchmarks, in particular our synthetic test harness for the Collections exhibit pathological behavior such that every field access must be checked for potential conflicts, resulting in atypical overhead. We include the Collections data to show that out technique works even on degenerate programs. In particular, most techniques checking atomicity or serializability violations depend on a particular locking discipline and are thus not suitable for the highly concurrent data structures of the package java.util.concurrent.

Taken from our cycle detection algorithm [18], our technique has a theoretical time complexity of $O(n^{3/2})$ where n is the number of accesses to shared variables. In reality, our technique is efficient and practical because real world programs do not have such degenerate behavior. In practice, conflict graphs do not grow very large, as seen in Table 1. This is the result of the pruning from Sect. 4.2, and it reduces the practical cost of cycle detection. That is, the practical running time of the algorithm is no longer proportional to an execution's length. In addition, the number of variables that escape across multiple threads is limited, ensuring that much of an execution can usually be ignored by the analysis.

The column "$|CG|$" shows the maximum size of the conflict graph before each garbage collection, given as the number of units of work in the graph. "Stack depth" shows the number of integers required for our compact stack encoding. There is no consistent correspondence between these statistics and the apparent slowdown factor, which supports our argument on the algorithm's complexity.

6   Related Work

A data race occurs when there are two concurrent accesses to a shared memory location not ordered by synchronization, at least one of which is a write. Dynamic analyses for detecting data races include those based on the lockset algorithm [32, 34], on the happens-before relation [25], or on a combination of the two [27]. Dynamic approaches to detecting races scale reasonably well for real applications and have detected a large number of bugs in real software [27, 32, 33].

Narayanasamy et al. [26] present a dynamic race detection tool and an automated technique for classifying the races found by the tool as benign or malign. This classification is based on replaying the execution of a piece of code that exhibits a race according to two different executions, and observing whether or not the resulting executions produce different results.

A program without data races may not be free of concurrency bugs as shown in [2, 7]. Atomic-set serializability captures these forms of high-level data races as a correctness criterion based on the programmer's intentions for correct behavior directly. Unlike these techniques, our approach is independent of any synchronization mechanism.

Atomizer [13] , is a dynamic atomicity checker based on Lipton's theory of reduction. Wang and Stoller present a number of different algorithms for detecting atomicity violations [38, 39]. The Block-Based Algorithm [39] is based on nonserializable interleaving patterns. In addition, they view the heap as a single atomic set, whereas our approach is parameterized by a partitioning of the heap into multiple atomic sets. Wang and Stoller also [38] present two Commit-Node Algorithms for checking view serializability and conflict serializability (detailed comparison presented in [19]).

Lu et al. [23] detect atomicity violations in C programs. They observe many correct "training" executions of a concurrent application and record nonserializable interleavings of accesses to shared variables. Then, nonserializable interleavings that *only* arise in incorrect executions are reported as atomicity violations. They only detect atomicity violations that involve a single shared variable, whereas our approach can handle multiple locations.

Another serializability violation detector was presented by Xu et al. [40]. It dynamically detects atomic regions (called Computation Units or CUs) using a *region hypothesis*, which proved useful in their experiments but is not sound in general. Thus, their analysis produces both false positives and negatives. Nonserializability checking is done using a heuristic based on strict two-phase locking. Like us, it does not rely on the possibly buggy locking structure of the program.

Recently, Park et al. correlated access patterns with the observed likelihood or suspicion that they cause a program to behave incorrectly [30]. They ignore such problems as stale writes and inconsistent reads, and they do not handle unserializable behaviors between more than two threads.

Other recent work uses cycle detection to find atomicity violations: Farzan et al. use postmortem cycle detection to find atomicity violations requiring user specified transactions [12]. Velodrome dynamically detects atomicity violations [14]. It uses a similar mechanism for safely garbage collecting terminated transactions. Atomicity does not take the consistency properties between data into account and thus may ignore the programmer's intentions as exemplified in Sect. 2.2. While Velodrome's analysis should be both sound and complete, their implementation is neither. This is due to slightly unsound optimizations, and because Velodrome makes the heuristic assumption that all methods are atomic, which is not generally the case, like for Thread's run() methods. We argue that our heuristics based on OO principles and the declarative approach to synchronization models the programmer's intentions better. As for false positives, they report none; however, that is with respect to their very strong assumptions. In contrast, our reports of false positives are with respect to the programmer's intentions as measured by potential to produce wrong answers. Finally, Velodrome does not instrument array access for reasons of complexity, which would have resulted in more than 22% missed violations in our ConTest benchmarks.

Related work also explores alternative thread schedules that might cause atomicity violations to occur [6, 8, 9, 14, 20, 21, 31]. We leave this orthogonal problem as future work. The work of Burnim et al. [6] also extends to such difficult data structures as those in java.util.concurrent.

Martin et al. [24] propose dynamic ownership policy checking for shared objects in C/C++. Their approach requires manual ownership annotations and imposes an average runtime overhead of 26%. Working on a very fine granularity level, their annotations could in theory be used to check atomic-set serializability, however, by annotating code instead of data their approach is not data-centric.

A previous approach of Hammer et al. [19] matches an intercepted execution trace against a set of problematic interleaving patterns. Unlike conflict graphs, that approach cannot find all possible atomic-set serializability violations in an intercepted execution trace. Apart from that, that work used a different heuristics to determine units of work and atomic sets. In particular it only supported the owned annotation, did not infer direct field access in accessor methods, needed to retain the exact index of array access for maximal precision and could not optimize away events accessing the same atomic set and unit of work.

7   Conclusions

This work presents a new mechanism to dynamically detect atomic-set serializability violations. It is both more powerful than previous atomic-set serializability violation detectors, for identifying all violations present in the intercepted execution, as well as detectors of other correctness criteria like race freedom, serializability, and atomicity, as these are subsumed by the notion of atomic-set serializability. We have shown that our new algorithm scales to realistic program sizes. We also proposed a set of heuristics to determine atomic sets and units of work and demonstrate their effectiveness in the evaluation where they successfully find many known concurrency bugs with a very low false positive rate. Even though our analysis already finds a high number of violations due to noise making, we envisage prediction of atomic-set serializability violations in alternative schedules of the program as a possible extension, to mitigate coverage of the huge test space of concurrent programs.

Acknowledgement. We are grateful to Frank Tip, Mandana Vaziri, and Pavel Avgustinov for discussions on this approach. This work was supported in part by NSF grant CCF 1048398.

References

1. Artho, C., Havelund, K., Biere, A.: High-level data races. Journal on Software Testing, Verification and Reliability (STVR) 13(4), 207–227 (2003)
2. Artho, C., Havelund, K., Biere, A.: Using Block-Local Atomicity to Detect Stale-Value Concurrency Errors. In: Wang, F. (ed.) ATVA 2004. LNCS, vol. 3299, pp. 150–164. Springer, Heidelberg (2004)
3. Ben-Asher, Y., Eytani, Y., Farchi, E., Ur, S.: Noise makers need to know where to be silent - producing schedules that find bugs. In: ISOLA 2006 (2006)
4. Bernstein, P., Hadzilacos, V., Goodman, N.: Concurrency Control and Recovery in Database Systems. Addison-Wesley (1987)
5. Bernstein, P.A., Goodman, N.: Concurrency Control in Distributed Database Systems. ACM Comput. Surv. 13(2), 185–221 (1981)
6. Burnim, J., Necula, G., Sen, K.: Specifying and checking semantic atomicity for multithreaded programs. In: ASPLOS 2011 (2011)

7. Burrows, M., Leino, K.R.M.: Finding stale-value errors in concurrent programs. Concurrency and Computation: Practice and Experience 16(12), 1161–1172 (2004)
8. Chen, Q., Wang, L.: An Integrated Framework for Checking Concurrency-Related Programming Errors. In: COMPSAC 2009 (2009)
9. Chen, Q., Wang, L., Yang, Z., Stoller, S.D.: HAVE: Detecting Atomicity Violations via Integrated Dynamic and Static Analysis. In: Chechik, M., Wirsing, M. (eds.) FASE 2009. LNCS, vol. 5503, pp. 425–439. Springer, Heidelberg (2009)
10. Clarke, D.G., Noble, J., Potter, J.M.: Simple Ownership Types for Object Containment. In: Lee, S.H. (ed.) ECOOP 2001. LNCS, vol. 2072, pp. 53–76. Springer, Heidelberg (2001)
11. Eytani, Y., Ur, S.: Compiling a benchmark of documented multi-threaded bugs. In: IPDPS 2004 (2004)
12. Farzan, A., Madhusudan, P.: Monitoring Atomicity in Concurrent Programs. In: Gupta, A., Malik, S. (eds.) CAV 2008. LNCS, vol. 5123, pp. 52–65. Springer, Heidelberg (2008)
13. Flanagan, C., Freund, S.N.: Atomizer: a dynamic atomicity checker for multi-threaded programs. In: POPL 2004 (2004)
14. Flanagan, C., Freund, S.N., Yi, J.: Velodrome: a sound and complete dynamic atomicity checker for multithreaded programs. In: PLDI 2008 (2008)
15. Fle, M.P., Roucairol, G.: On serializability of iterated transactions. In: PODC 1982 (1982)
16. Gait, J.: A probe effect in concurrent programs. Software: Practice and Experience 16(3), 225–233 (1986)
17. Goetz, B., Peierls, T., Bloch, J., Bowbeer, J., Holmes, D., Lea, D.: Java Concurrency in Practice. Addison Wesley Professional (May 2006)
18. Haeupler, B., Kavitha, T., Mathew, R., Sen, S., Tarjan, R.E.: Faster Algorithms for Incremental Topological Ordering. In: Aceto, L., Damgård, I., Goldberg, L.A., Halldórsson, M.M., Ingólfsdóttir, A., Walukiewicz, I. (eds.) ICALP 2008, Part I. LNCS, vol. 5125, pp. 421–433. Springer, Heidelberg (2008)
19. Hammer, C., Dolby, J., Vaziri, M., Tip, F.: Dynamic detection of atomic-set-serializability violations. In: ICSE 2008 (2008)
20. Kahlon, V., Wang, C.: Universal Causality Graphs: A Precise Happens-Before Model for Detecting Bugs in Concurrent Programs. In: Touili, T., Cook, B., Jackson, P. (eds.) CAV 2010. LNCS, vol. 6174, pp. 434–449. Springer, Heidelberg (2010)
21. Lai, Z., Cheung, S.C., Chan, W.K.: Detecting atomic-set serializability violations in multithreaded programs through active randomized testing. In: ICSE 2010 (2010)
22. Lipton, R.J.: Reduction: a method of proving properties of parallel programs. Commun. ACM 18(12), 717–721 (1975)
23. Lu, S., Tucek, J., Qin, F., Zhou, Y.: AVIO: Detecting Atomicity Violations via Access Interleaving Invariants. In: ASPLOS 2006 (2006)
24. Martin, J.P., Hicks, M., Costa, M., Akritidis, P., Castro, M.: Dynamically checking ownership policies in concurrent C/C++ programs. In: POPL 2010 (2010)
25. Min, S.L., Choi, J.D.: An efficient cache-based access anomaly detection scheme. In: ASPLOS 1991 (1991)
26. Narayanasamy, S., Wang, Z., Tigani, J., Edwards, A., Calder, B.: Automatically classifying benign and harmful data races using replay analysis. In: PLDI 2007 (2007)
27. O'Callahan, R., Choi, J.D.: Hybrid dynamic data race detection. In: PPoPP 2003 (2003)
28. Papadimitriou, C.: The theory of database concurrency control. Computer Science Press, Inc., New York (1986)

29. Park, C., Sen, K.: Randomized active atomicity violation detection in concurrent programs. In: FSE 2008 (2008)
30. Park, S., Vuduc, R.W., Harrold, M.J.: Falcon: fault localization in concurrent programs. In: ICSE 2010 (2010)
31. Park, S., Lu, S., Zhou, Y.: CTrigger: exposing atomicity violation bugs from their hiding places. In: ASPLOS 2009 (2009)
32. von Praun, C., Gross, T.R.: Object race detection. In: OOPSLA 2001 (2001)
33. von Praun, C., Gross, T.R.: Atomicity Violations in Object-Oriented Programs. Journal of Object Technology 3(6), 103–122 (2004)
34. Savage, S., Burrows, M., Nelson, G., Sobalvarro, P., Anderson, T.: Eraser: a dynamic data race detector for multithreaded programs. ACM Trans. Comput. Syst. 15(4), 391–411 (1997)
35. Sumner, W.N., Zheng, Y., Weeratunge, D., Zhang, X.: Precise calling context encoding. In: ICSE 2010 (2010)
36. Vaziri, M., Tip, F., Dolby, J.: Associating synchronization constraints with data in an object-oriented language. In: POPL 2006 (2006)
37. Vaziri, M., Tip, F., Dolby, J., Hammer, C., Vitek, J.: A Type System for Data-Centric Synchronization. In: D'Hondt, T. (ed.) ECOOP 2010. LNCS, vol. 6183, pp. 304–328. Springer, Heidelberg (2010)
38. Wang, L., Stoller, S.D.: Accurate and Efficient Runtime Detection of Atomicity Errors in Concurrent Programs. In: PPoPP 2006 (2006)
39. Wang, L., Stoller, S.D.: Runtime Analysis of Atomicity for Multithreaded Programs. IEEE Transactions on Software Engineering 32(2), 93–110 (2006)
40. Xu, M., Bodík, R., Hill, M.D.: A serializability violation detector for shared-memory server programs. In: PLDI 2005 (2005)

Coverage Metrics for Saturation-Based and Search-Based Testing of Concurrent Software

Bohuslav Křena, Zdeněk Letko, and Tomáš Vojnar

FIT, Brno University of Technology, Czech Republic
{krena,iletko,vojnar}@fit.vutbr.cz

Abstract. Coverage metrics play a crucial role in testing. They allow one to estimate how well a program has been tested and/or to control the testing process. Several concurrency-related coverage metrics have been proposed, but most of them do not reflect concurrent behaviour accurately enough. In this paper, we propose several new metrics that are suitable primarily for saturation-based or search-based testing of concurrent software. Their distinguishing feature is that they are derived from various dynamic analyses designed for detecting synchronisation errors in concurrent software. In fact, the way these metrics are obtained is generic, and further metrics can be obtained in a similar way from other analyses. The underlying motivation is that, within such analyses, behavioural aspects crucial for occurrence of various bugs are identified, and hence it makes sense to track how well the occurrence of such phenomena is covered by testing. Next, coverage tasks of the proposed as well as some existing metrics are combined with an abstract identification of the threads participating in generation of the phenomena captured in the concerned tasks. This way, further, more precise metrics are obtained. Finally, an empirical evaluation of the proposed metrics, which confirms that several of them are indeed more suitable for saturation-based and search-based testing than the previously known metrics, is presented.

1 Introduction

Despite the constant development of various approaches to verification and bug finding based on formal roots, *software testing* still belongs among the most common ways of discovering errors in programs. However, it has to face new challenges related to the changes in programming paradigms commonly used in practice. In particular, in the past years, *concurrent programming* has become much more common than before. Testing concurrent software is much more difficult due to the non-determinism present in scheduling executions of concurrent threads. Various ways how to improve testing of concurrent software have been proposed, including, e.g., the use of noise injection or various dynamic analyses.

In testing, a crucial role is played by the so-called *coverage metrics*. A coverage metric is based on a *coverage domain* that is a set of *coverage tasks* representing different phenomena (such as reachability of a certain line, reachability of a situation in which a certain variable has a certain value, etc.) whose occurrence in the behaviour of a tested program is considered to be of interest. One can then measure how many of the phenomena corresponding to the coverage tasks have been seen in the witnessed

S. Khurshid and K. Sen (Eds.): RV 2011, LNCS 7186, pp. 177–192, 2012.

behaviours of the tested program. Such a measurement can be used to asses how well the program has been tested. Moreover, in the so-called *saturation-based testing* [16], one looks for the moment when the obtained coverage stops growing, and hence the testing can be stopped. Further, in *search-based testing* [12], a fitness function driving an optimisation algorithm used to control the testing process can be based on the values of a coverage metric.

For metrics used in saturation-based or search-based testing, one can identify several specific properties that they should exhibit. First, within the testing process, the obtained coverage should as often as possible grow for a while and then stabilise. Hence, it should not immediately jump to some value and stabilise on it. On the other hand, it should not take too much time for the coverage to stabilise. Also, to enable a reliable detection of stabilisation, the coverage should grow as smoothly as possible, i.e., without growing through a series of distinctive shoulders. Next, in case of testing an erroneous program, the stabilisation should ideally not happen before an error is detected. Finally, the increase in coverage should be linked with witnessing more and more behaviours that differ in their potential of exhibiting a bug.

In this paper, we propose several *new coverage metrics* suitable for saturation-based or search-based testing of concurrent programs. These metrics are based on coverage tasks derived from the information about program behaviour that is gathered or computed by various *dynamic analyses* that have been proposed for *discovering synchronisation-related errors in concurrent programs*. In fact, the idea of inferring new metrics from these analyses is rather generic and can be applied to other dynamic as well as static analyses (even those that will appear in the future) too. The proposal is motivated by the idea that within the development of such analyses, behavioural aspects of concurrent programs that are highly relevant for the existence of synchronisation-related errors have been identified. Hence, it makes sense to measure how well the aspects of the behaviour tracked by such analyses have been covered during testing.

Further, we also combine coverage tasks of the newly proposed as well as some existing metrics with *abstract identifiers of the threads* involved in generating the phenomena reflected in the concerned tasks. The identifiers abstract away the concrete numerical identifiers of the threads, but preserve information on their type, the history of their creation, etc. This way, an increased number of coverage tasks is obtained, forming a new, more precise variant of the original metric.

We have performed an *empirical comparison* of the use of the newly proposed metrics against three common concurrency-related metrics. We show that several of the newly proposed metrics indeed meet the criteria of suitability for saturation-based and search-based testing in a significantly better way than the previously known metrics.

Plan of the paper. In Section 2, we discuss the related work. Section 3 details the proposed way of deriving new coverage metrics and presents several concrete new metrics. For comparison purposes, the section then also presents in a uniform way several existing metrics (one of these metrics is slightly extended too). Section 4 presents the techniques we use for an abstract identification of objects and threads. Section 5 describes our experimental setting and provides our experimental results. Finally, Section 6 concludes the paper and provides some notes on the possible future work.

2   Related Work

As said already in the previous section, testing is one of the most common approaches used for discovering concurrency bugs. The testing process is typically empowered in some way to cope with the fact that concurrency bugs often appear only under very special scheduling circumstances. To increase chances of spotting a concurrency bug, various ways of *influencing the scheduling* are often used. An example of this approach is random or heuristic noise injection used in the IBM Concurrency Testing Tool (Con-Test) [4] or a systematic exploration of all schedules up to some number of context switches as used in the Microsoft CHESS tool [13].

Another way to improve traditional concurrency testing is to try to extrapolate the behaviour seen within a testing run and to warn about a possible error even if such an error was not in fact seen in the test execution. Such approaches are called *dynamic analyses*. Many dynamic analyses have been proposed for detecting special classes of bugs, such as data races [2,5,14,15], atomicity violations [10], or deadlocks [1,7]. These techniques may find more bugs than classical testing, but on the other hand, their com-putational complexity is usually higher, and they can also produce false alarms.

An alternative to testing and dynamic analyses is the use of *static analyses*. They avoid execution of the given program or execute it on a highly abstract level only. Various static analyses of concurrent software exist, including light-weight analyses that look for specific patterns in the code that might lead to a bug [6] or, e.g., various dataflow-based analyses that try to identify bugs like data races [8] or deadlocks [20]. *Model checking* [3] (sometimes viewed as a heavy-weight static analysis too) tries to systematically analyse all possible interleavings of threads in a given program (the CHESS approach can, in fact, be seen as a form of bounded model checking). Light-weight static analyses may produce many false alarms and heavy-weight approaches may have troubles with scalability. There also exist approaches that combine static and dynamic analyses in an attempt to suppress their deficiencies.

We build our new coverage metrics on the information that is gathered or com-puted by several different dynamic analyses mentioned above, namely, Eraser [15], GoldiLocks [5], AVIO [10], and GoodLock [1]. In our experiments with these metrics, we use ConTest and its noise injection mechanisms to generate different legal interleav-ing scenarios in repeated executions of the considered test cases. Although not explored in this paper, new coverage metrics could be derived from various static analyses too.

Many different coverage metrics have been proposed targeting probably all areas of testing in the past decades. Testing of concurrent software is not an exception. Out of the existing *concurrency-related metrics*, among the ones that we find as the probably most promising from the point of view of their practical applicability there is the metric based on du-pairs proposed in [21], the metric based on concurrent pairs of events from [2], and the synchronisation coverage [18]. We discuss these metrics in more detail in Section 3.3, and we experimentally compare our metrics with them in Section 5.

The idea of extending coverage tasks of metrics by further information has also been presented in [16] where saturation-based testing of concurrent programs is introduced. The authors propose three types of context information which can be used to refine existing metrics. The *pair context* handles situations where two events in the concurrent programs interact and makes this information explicit for the metric. The *group context* makes explicit the type of thread that performed an event (this is a special case of our abstract thread identifiers). Finally, the *thread context* explicitly identifies the thread which performed the event.

3   Concurrency Coverage Metrics

Our goal is to create metrics that are suitable for saturation-based and search-based testing of concurrent software. As we have already said in the introduction, metrics to be used in this context should have some special properties. In particular, during testing, the coverage should as often as possible first increase for some reasonable amount of time and then stabilise. The stabilisation should not happen too early nor too late. This typically implies that the number of coverage tasks should not be too small nor too large. The growth should not generate distinctive shoulders so that saturation can be reasonably detected. In case of testing an erroneous program, the stabilisation should as often as possible happen after the error is detected. Finally, a growth of coverage should be in some relation to witnessing more and more behaviours distinct from the point of view of their potential for generating some concurrency error. In addition, one should also consider a generic requirement for the metrics not to be too costly to use

We now first discuss a methodology how metrics satisfying the above can be obtained, and then propose several new concrete metrics. Finally, for comparison purposes, we describe (and in one case also extend) some existing metrics too.

3.1   Methodology of Deriving Suitable Coverage Metrics

To derive metrics satisfying the criteria set up above, we propose to get inspired by various existing *dynamic (and possibly even static) concurrency error detection techniques*. This is motivated by two observations: (1) These detection techniques focus on those events occurring in runs of the analysed programs that appear relevant for detection of various concurrency-related errors. (2) The techniques build and maintain a representation of the context of such events that is important for detection of possible bugs in the program. Hence, trying to measure how many of such events have been seen, and possibly in how many different contexts, seems promising from the point of view of relating the growth of a metric to an increasing likelihood of spotting an error.

The described idea is very generic, and we can speak about a new class of concurrency coverage metrics that can be obtained in the described manner. A crucial step in the creation of a new coverage metric based on some error detection algorithm is to choose suitable pieces of information available to or computed by the detection algorithm, which are then used to construct the domain of the new coverage metric such that the other, above mentioned criteria are met. This leads to a trade off among the precision of the metric and the amount of information tracked, the associated computational complexity, and speed of saturation. One extreme is to build a coverage metric directly on warnings about concurrency errors issued by the detection algorithm. In this case, we need to implement the detection algorithm entirely. Another extreme is to build a coverage metric counting just the events tracked by the detection algorithm, without their context. In such a case, we often obtain very similar metrics to already existing metrics. Within this process—which can hardly be made algorithmic and which requires certain ingenuity and also experimental evidence, it can also of course turn out that some detection algorithms are not suitable as a basis of a coverage metric at all.

Let us demonstrate the described problem on an example of two dynamic data race detection algorithms. The *vector-clock-based algorithms*, e.g., [14], maintain for each thread an internal clock which is an integer value representing the number of synchronisation events that the thread executed so far. The algorithm then also maintains for each thread, each lock, and each variable vectors of clocks representing synchronisation bindings among events performed on these program elements. The goal is to obtain the so-called *happens-before relation* that says which events are *guaranteed* to happen before other events, meaning that such events cannot participate on a data race (where the order of the events must not be fixed). Nevertheless, vectors of clocks are not suitable for our purposes because they encode the history context using a too large number of values. This would lead to a huge number of coverage tasks, a slow progress towards saturation, and also a high cost of measuring the obtained coverage.

On the other hand, the Eraser algorithm [15] computes the so-called *locksets*. For each thread, the algorithm computes a set of locks currently held by the thread, and for each variable access, the algorithm uses these sets to derive the set of locks that were held by each thread that had so far accessed the variable. These so-called locksets are maintained according to a *state* assigned to each variable which represents how the variable has been operated so far (e.g., exclusively within one thread, shared among threads, for reading only, etc.). This algorithm is more suitable for our purposes because the history context used by it gives rise to a reasonable number of coverage tasks (as we show below).

Finally, we note that, according to our experimental evidence mentioned later on, the precision of the constructed metrics can further be suitably adjusted by combining their coverage tasks with some *abstract identification of the threads* involved in generating the phenomena reflected in the concerned tasks. The identification should of course not be based on the unique thread identifiers, but it can preserve information on their type, the history of their creation, etc. A similar identification can then also be used whenever the coverage tasks contain some dynamically instantiated objects (e.g., locks).

3.2   New Coverage Metrics

We are now going to derive several new concrete coverage metrics. As we have already said, they are all based on some dynamic analyses used for detecting errors in synchronisation of concurrent programs. In order to allow for a quick comparison among the metrics, Table 1 presents an overview of all the proposed metrics, together with some other metrics that we will consider in our experiments. For each metric, the second column shows a tuple defining coverage tasks of the metric, and the third column contains information whether the metric is new (N), already existing (E), or whether it is our modification of some already known metric (M). The first item of each of the tuples representing a coverage task (denoted as pl_1) gives a primary program location which generates the given task when reached by some thread. The rest of the tuples can then be viewed as a context under which the location is reached. For most of the metrics, we provide two versions: a basic version and a version with an extended context, denoted by *. In the following paragraphs, the versions with the extended context are described only. The basic versions can easily be derived from them by dropping some elements of the context.

Table 1. The considered coverage metrics

metric	coverage task	note
Avio	(pl_1, pl_2, pl_3)	N
Avio*	$(pl_1, pl_2, pl_3, var, t_1, t_2)$	N
Eraser	$(pl_1, state, lockset)$	N
Eraser*	$(pl_1, var, state, lockset, t_1)$	N
GoldiLock	$(pl_1, goldiLockSetSC)$	N
GoldiLock*	$(pl_1, var, goldiLockSetSC, t_1)$	N
GoodLock	(pl_1, pl_2, l_1, l_2)	N
GoodLock*	$(pl_1, pl_2, l_1, l_2, t_1)$	N
HBPair	$(pl_1, pl_2, syncObj)$	N
HBPair*	$(pl_1, pl_2, syncObj, t_1, t_2)$	N
ConcurPairs	$(pl_1, pl_2, switch)$	E
DUPairs	(pl_1, pl_2, var)	E
DUPairs*	$(pl_1, pl_2, var, t_1, t_2)$	M
Sync	$(pl_1, mode)$	E

In order to make the description more concrete, in the rest of the paper, we assume the *Java memory model* [11]. In the text below, we use the following notation. V is a set of identifiers of instances of non-volatile variables (i.e., non-volatile fields of objects) that may be used in the tested program at hand, O is a set of identifiers of instances of volatile variables used in the program, L is a set of identifiers of locks used in the program, T is a set of identifiers of all threads that may be created by the program, and P is a set of all program locations in the program. We discuss one possible concrete way how the needed identifiers may be obtained in Section 4.

A coverage metric based on Eraser. The coverage metric Eraser* is based on the Eraser algorithm [15] whose basics have been sketched above. Its coverage tasks have the form of a tuple $(pl_1, var, state, lockset, t_1)$ where $pl_1 \in P$ identifies the program location of an instruction accessing a shared variable $var \in V$, $state \in \{virgin, exclusive, exclusive', shared, modified, race\}$ gives the state in which the Eraser's finite control automaton is when the given location is reached (we consider the extended version of Eraser using the $exclusive'$ state as introduced in [19], which is more suitable for the Java memory model), and $lockset \subseteq L$ denotes a set of locks currently guarding the variable var. Finally, $t_1 \in T$ represents the thread performing the access operation.

A coverage metric based on GoldiLocks. GoldiLocks [5] is one of the most advanced lockset-based algorithms. The main idea of this algorithm is that it combines the use of locksets with computing the happens-before relation. In GoldiLocks, locksets are allowed to contain not only locks but also volatile variables and threads. If a thread t appears in the lockset of a shared variable when the variable is accessed, it means that t is properly synchronised for using the given variable because all other accesses that might cause a data race are guaranteed to happen before the current access. The algorithm uses a limited number of elements placed in the lockset to represent an important part of the synchronisation history preceding an access to a shared variable. This is in contrast with the vector-clocks-based algorithms mentioned above. The basic GoldiLocks algorithm is still relatively expensive but can be optimised by the so-called *short circuit checks* (SC) which are three cheap checks that are sufficient for deciding race freedom between the two last accesses to a variable. The original algorithm is then used only when SC cannot prove race freedom. Our GoldiLock-based metric GoldiLock* is based on coverage tasks having the form of tuples $(pl_1, var, goldiLockSet, t_1)$ where $pl_1 \in P$ gives the location of an instruction accessing a variable $var \in V$ within a thread $t_1 \in T$, and $goldiLockSet \subseteq O \cup L \cup T$ represents the lockset computed by GoldiLocks.

A coverage metric based on Avio. The Avio algorithm that detects atomicity violation over one variable is presented in [10]. We choose this algorithm because it does not require any additional information from the user about instructions that should be executed atomically. The algorithm considers any two consecutive accesses a_1 and a_2 from one thread to a shared variable var to form an atomic block B. Serialisability is then defined based on an analysis of what can happen when B is interleaved with some read or write access a_3 from another thread to the variable var. Out of the eight total cases arising in this way, four (namely, r/w/r, w/w/r, w/r/w, r/w/w) are considered to lead to an unserialisable execution. Tracking of all accesses that occur concurrently to a block B can be very expensive. Therefore, we define our criterion to consider only the last interleaving access to the concerned variable from a different thread. Our Avio* metric uses coverage tasks in the form of tuples $(pl_1, pl_2, pl_3, var, t_1, t_2)$ where $var \in V$, $pl_1, pl_2, pl_3 \in P$, and $t_1, t_2 \in T$. The considered atomic block B spans between pl_1 and pl_2, and it is executed by a thread t_1. Finally, pl_3 gives a location of an instruction executed in a thread t_2 that interferes with the block B.

A coverage metric based on GoodLock. GoodLock is a popular deadlock detection algorithm that exists in several modifications—we, in particular, build on its modification published in [1]. The algorithm builds the so-called *guarded lock graph* which is a labelled oriented graph where nodes represent locks, and edges represent nested locking within which a thread that already has some lock asks for another one. Labels over edges provide additional information about the thread that creates the edge. The algorithm searches for cycles in the graph wrt. the edge labels in order to detect deadlocks. Our metric focuses on occurrence of nested locking that is considered interesting by GoodLock. We omit collection of the locksets of the threads which the original algorithm uses as one element of the edge label because this information is used in the algorithm to suppress certain false alarms only. Our GoodLock* metric is therefore based on coverage tasks in the form of tuples $(pl_1, pl_2, l_1, l_2, t_1)$ where $pl_1, pl_2 \in P$, $l_1, l_2 \in L$, and $t_1 \in T$. Such a task is covered when the thread t_1 has obtained the lock l_1 at pl_1, and now the same thread is obtaining the lock l_2 at pl_2.

A coverage metric based on happens-before pairs. This coverage metric is motivated by observations we get from the GoldiLocks algorithm and the vector-clock algorithms, both of them depending on computation of the happens-before relation. In order to get rid of the possibly huge number of coverage tasks produced by the vector-clock algorithms and trying to decrease the computational complexity needed when the full GoldiLocks algorithm is used, we focus on pieces of information the algorithms use for creating their representations of the analysed program behaviours (without actually computing and using these representations). All of these algorithms rely on synchronisation events observed along the execution path. Inspired by this, we propose the HBPair* metric that tracks successful synchronisation events based on locks, volatile variables, wait-notify operations, and thread start and join operations used in Java. A coverage task is defined as a tuple $(pl_1, pl_2, syncObj, t_1, t_2)$ where $pl_1 \in P$ is a program location in a thread $t_1 \in T$ that was synchronised with the location $pl_2 \in P$ of the thread $t_2 \in T$ using the synchronisation objects $syncObj \in L \cup O \cup \{\bot\}$. Here, $\bot$ represents a thread start or a successful join synchronisation where no synchronisation object is needed.

3.3 Existing Metrics

In order to compare our metrics with already existing metrics, we further consider—and in one case also extend—the following metrics.

Coverage based on concurrently executing instructions (ConcurPairs). The coverage of concurrent pairs of events proposed in [2] is a metric in which each coverage task is composed of a pair of program locations that are assumed to be encountered consecutively in a run and a third item that is $true$ or $false$. It is $false$ iff the two locations are visited by the same thread and $true$ otherwise—that is, $true$ means that there occurred a context switch between the two program locations. This metric provides statement coverage information (using the $false$ flag) and interleaving information (using the $true$ flag) at once. In our notation, each task of the metric is a tuple $(pl_1, pl_2, switch)$ where $pl_1, pl_2 \in P$ represent the consecutive program locations (only concurrency primitives and variable accesses are monitored), and $switch \in \{true, false\}$ denotes whether the context switch occurs in between of them. Since this metric produces a large number of coverage tasks even for small programs, we decided not to enrich it with any further context information.

Definition-use coverage. This coverage metric is based on the *all-du-path* coverage metric for parallel programs described in [21]. This metric considers coverage tasks in the form of triples (var, d, u) where var is a shared variable, d is a node in the parallel program flow graph (PPFG) where the value of var is defined, and u is a node in the PPFG where the value is read. The du-pair therefore denotes an existing path in the PPFG from a node d to a node u where the value of var from d is still available, i.e., there is no node redefining the value of var on the path between d and u. We consider the original all-du-pair coverage metric (denoted as DUPairs), and we also extend it to a metric which adds more context information to the coverage tasks. Our metric DUPairs* is based on coverage tasks in the form of tuples $(pl_1, pl_2, var, t_1, t_2)$ where $pl_1, pl_2 \in P$ represent program locations where the value of the variable $var \in V$ is defined and used, respectively, $t1 \in T$ denotes the thread that performed the definition of var at pl_1, and $t_2 \in T$ denotes the thread that subsequently uses the value at pl_2.

Synchronisation coverage (Sync). The synchronisation coverage [18] focuses on the use of synchronisation primitives and does not directly consider thread interleavings. Coverage tasks of the metric are defined based on various distinctive situations that can occur when using each specific type of synchronisation primitives. For instance, in the case of a synchronised block (defined using the Java keyword `synchronised`), the obtained tasks are: *synchronisation visited, synchronisation blocking*, and *synchronisation blocked*. The synchronisation visited task is basically just a code coverage task. The other two are reported when there is an actual contention between synchronised blocks—when a thread t_1 reaches a synchronised block A and stops because another thread t_2 is inside a block B synchronised on the same lock. In this case, A is reported as blocked, and B as blocking (both, in addition, as visited). In our notation, the metric is defined using tuples of the form $(pl_1, mode)$ where $pl_1 \in P$ represents the program location of a synchronisation primitive, and $mode$ represents an element from the set of the distinctive situations relevant for the given type of synchronisation.

4   Abstract Object and Thread Identification

Our coverage metrics introduced in Section 3 are based on tasks that include identification of threads and instances of variables and locks. The Java virtual machine (JVM) generates identifiers of objects and threads dynamically. Such identifiers are, however, not suitable for our purposes: (1) In long runs, too many of them may be generated. (2) We would like to be able to match semantically equivalent tasks generated in different runs (may be not precisely, but at least with a reasonable precision), and the identifiers generated by JVM for the same threads (from the semantical point of view) in different runs will quite likely be different.

Previous works, such as [16], used Java types to identify threads. We consider this type-based identification of elements as too rough. Our goal is to create identifiers which distinguish behaviour of objects and threads within the program more accurately, but still keeping a reasonable level of abstraction so the set of such abstract identifiers remains of a moderate size.

The abstract *object identification* that we consider in this work (to identify locks as well as instances of variables[1]) is based on the observation that, usually, objects created in the same place in the program are used in a similar way. For instance, there are usually many instances of the class `String` in an average Java program, but all strings that are created within invocations of the same method will probably be manipulated similarly. Therefore, we define an object identifier as a tuple $(type, loc)$ where $type$ refers to the type of the object, and loc refers to the top of the stack (excluding calls to constructors) when the object is created. The record at top of the stack contains a method, source file, and line of code.

Next, our abstract *thread identification* is based on an observation that the type and place of creation are not sufficient to build a thread identifier. Several threads created at the same program location (e.g., in a loop) can subsequently process different data and therefore behave differently. We need more information concerning the thread execution trace to better capture the behaviour of threads. Therefore, we use as the identifier a tuple $(type, hash)$ where $type$ denotes the type of the object implementing the thread,

---

[1] Instances of variables are identified by an object identifier and the appropriate field of the object.

and *hash* contains a hash value computed over a sequence of n first method identifiers that the thread executed after its creation (if the thread terminates sooner, then all methods it executed are taken into account). The value of n influences precision of the abstraction. Of course, when a pool of threads (a set of threads started once and used for several tasks) is used, the computation of the hash value must be restarted immediately after picking the thread up from the pool.

5   Experiments

Our architecture for collecting concurrency related coverage is built upon the IBM Java Concurrency Testing Tool (ConTest) [4]—an advanced tool for testing, debugging, and measuring test coverage for concurrent Java programs. The tool provides a facility for bytecode instrumentation and a listeners infrastructure allowing one to create *plug-ins* for collecting various pieces of information about the multi-threaded Java programs being executed as well as to easily implement various algorithms for dynamic analyses. The tool is itself able to collect structural coverage metrics (basic blocks, methods) and some concurrency-related metrics (ConcurPairs, Sync) too. ConTest further provides a noise injection facility which injects the so-called noise into the execution of a tested application and so allows us to observe different legal interleavings if the test is executed repeatedly. We use our platform called SearchBestie [9] to set up and execute tests with ConTest, and to collect, maintain, and export results produced by ConTest and its plug-ins from multiple executions of a test.

5.1   Test Cases

We have evaluated the metrics discussed in Section 3 on four small test cases (Dining philosophers, Airlines, Crawler, FtpServer) and one large test case (TIDOrbJ).

The *Dining philosophers* test case is an implementation of the well-known synchronisation problem of dining philosophers. Our implementation is taken from the distribution of the Java PathFinder model checker. The program generates a set of 6 philosophers (each represented by a thread) and the same number of shared objects representing forks. A deadlock can occur when executing the test case.

The *Airlines* test case is a simple artificial program simulating an air ticket reservation system. It generates a database of air tickets and then allows 2 resellers (each represented by a separate thread) to sell tickets to 4 sets of 10 customers (each set is represented by a separate thread). Finally, a check whether the number of customers with tickets is equal to the number of sold tickets is done. The program contains a high-level atomicity violation whose occurrence makes the final check fail.

The three other considered programs are real-life case studies. *Crawler* is a part of an older version of a major IBM production software. It demonstrates a tricky concurrency bug detected in this software. The crawler creates a set of threads waiting for a connection. If a connection simulated by a testing environment is established, a worker thread serves it. There is a bug in a method that is called when the crawler shuts down. The bug causes an exception sometimes leading to a deadlock. The trickiness of the bug can be seen from its very low error probability shown in Table 2.

Our second real-life case study is an early development version of an open-source *FtpServer* produced by Apache. This case study has 120 classes. The server creates a new worker thread for each new incoming connection to serve it. The version of the server we used contains several data races that can cause exceptions during the shut down process when there is still an active connection. The probability of spotting an error when noise injection is enabled is quite high in this example because there are multiple places in the test where an exception can be thrown.

Our biggest test case is *TIDOrbJ*—a CORBA-compliant ORB (Object Request Broker) product that is a part of the MORFEO Community Middleware Platform [17]. The instrumented part of the middleware has 1399 classes. We have used the *Echo concurrent* test which checks how the infrastructure handles multiple concurrent simple requests. The test starts an instrumented server and then 10 clients, each sending 5 requests to the server. There was originally no error in this test, and therefore we introduced one by commenting one `synchronised` statement in the part of code that is executed by the test. This way, we introduced a high-level atomicity violation that leads to a null pointer exception.

5.2   Experimental Setup

We used our infrastructure introduced above to collect relevant data from 10,000 executions of the small test cases and 4,000 executions of TIDOrbJ. In order to see as many different legal interleaving scenarios as possible, we set up ConTest to randomly inject noise into the executions. We have implemented ConTest plug-ins to collect coverage information and set up SearchBestie to detect occurrences of errors (deadlocks were detected using a timeout, other errors by detection of unhandled exceptions). All further studies of the metrics were done using the collection of executions obtained this way. For instance, we often needed to evaluate the behaviour of the metrics on series of executions. To generate the needed series of executions, we used SearchBestie to randomly select a needed number of executions out of the recorded collection and to compute accumulated values of the chosen metrics on such series. All tests were executed on a computer with an Intel 6600 processor and 2 GB of memory, running Sun Java version 1.6 under GNU Linux.

5.3   Results of Experiments

Object and Thread Abstract Identification. Table 2 summarises information on our test cases (both from the point of view of the source code as well as the runtime behaviour) and—most importantly—it illustrates the effect of our abstract object and thread identifiers. In particular, the second column of Table 2 shows the number of instrumented classes for each test case. The following column shows the probability of spotting an error during a test execution when random noise injection is used (computed as the number of executions where an error occurs divided by the total number of executions). The rest of the columns provide information about the size of the case studies in terms of the numbers of threads and objects created in them. These columns also illustrate precision of our abstract identifiers of objects and threads. The *Real* column contains the total number of distinct objects (or threads) we encountered in 10

Table 2. Test cases and abstract identifiers

	Classes	Error Ratio	ObjectAbstraction Real	Type	Abs	ThreadAbstraction Real	Type	Abs$_{10}$	Abs$_{20}$
Dining phil.	2	0.4151	130	3	3	7	2	2	2
Airlines	8	0.0333	15 210	6	6	60	3	3	4
Crawler	19	0.0006	1 828	13	14	180	4	9	12
FtpServer	120	0.4032	26 110	27	29	1 641	5	5	6
TIDOrbJ echo	1 399	0.0170	180 320	98	129	79	5	9	11

performed executions of the tests. The *Type* column shows the total number of distinct object (or thread) types we have spot, and the *Abs* columns show the total number of distinct abstract objects (or threads) we distinguish using our abstract identifiers introduced in Section 4. For the thread abstraction, two values are given showing the influence of the length n of the considered sequence of methods called by the threads.

Typical Saturation Behaviour of the Metrics. To decide whether a coverage metric is suitable for saturation-based testing or not, one needs to evaluate several aspects of its behaviour. The typical behaviour of the considered coverage metrics can be seen in Figure 1. All four sub-figures show the cumulative number of coverage tasks of the metrics covered during one randomly chosen series of the Crawler test case executions (with the thread abstraction variable n set to 20).

Figure 1(a) shows the behaviour of the metrics that, according to our opinion, do not capture the concurrent behaviour accurately enough. One coverage metric for non-concurrent code measuring the number of *basic blocks* covered during tests is added to demonstrate the difference between classical and concurrency-related coverage metrics. The coverage obtained under the metric based on basic blocks is nearly constant all the time because we are repeatedly executing the same code with the same inputs. For the rest of the metrics shown in Figure 1(a), the cumulative number of tasks covered during test executions increases only within approximately the 200 first executions, and then a saturation is reached. The only metrics which slightly differ from the others in this group are Eraser and DUPairs. The Eraser metric has a similar behaviour to the *Avio* metric (and the metrics close to it) but approximately four times higher numbers of covered tasks. This is caused by the fact that the tracked shared variables usually get to four Eraser states. The DUPairs metric has also higher numbers of covered tasks but it is almost all the time stabilised.

The most interesting part of Figure 1(a) between 0 and 200 executions is zoomed in Figure 1(b). One can see that the saturation effect occurs earlier (at about 100 executions) for the HBPair and Sync metrics which both focus on synchronisation events only. The Avio metric (and also the Eraser metric which is not shown) that focus on accesses to shared variables saturate a bit later. The depicted curves demonstrate one further disadvantage of the concerned metrics—a presence of distinctive shoulders. A repeated execution of the test case does examine different concurrent behaviours (which is indicated by the later discussed metrics) but the metrics concerned in the figure are not able

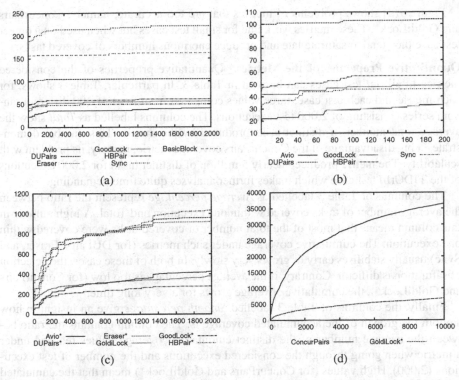

Fig. 1. Saturation of different metrics on the Crawler test case (the horizontal axis gives the number of executions, the vertical axis gives the cumulative number of covered tasks)

to distinguish differences in these behaviours, and therefore we can see clear shoulders in the curves (i.e., sequences of constant values). The presence of such shoulders makes automatic saturation detection harder.

Figure 1(c) demonstrates a positive effect of considering an extended context of the tracked events as proposed in Section 3. The metrics concerned in this sub-figure (i.e., Avio*, Eraser*, DUPairs*, HBPair*, GoodLock*, and GoldiLock) are able to distinguish differences in the behaviour of the executed tests more accurately, leading to shorter shoulders, bigger differences in the cumulated values, and a later occurrence of the saturation effect—indicating that the concerned metrics behave in a way much better for saturation-based testing. As can be seen from a similar jump in the obtained coverage of the HBPair*, Eraser*, and Avio* metrics at around 1300 executions, the extended context can sometimes have a dramatic influence. The jump is caused by the abstract thread identifiers. At the given point, a thread with a new abstract identifier appears, and all tasks involving this thread are different to those already known. This leads to a much more significant increase in the cumulative coverage. A special attention should be paid to the GoldiLock metric. This metric does not suffer from shoulders nor sudden, dramatic increases of the obtained coverage, and it reaches saturation near the saturation points of the other metrics. This is a very positive behaviour, and the GoldiLock metric is clearly winning here.

Figure 1(d) shows problems of metrics that are too accurate, namely, ConcurPairs and GoldiLock*. These metrics work fine for small test cases but when used on a bigger test case they tend to saturate late and produce enormous numbers of covered tasks.

Quantitative Properties of the Metrics. Quantitative properties of the considered metrics in all our test cases can be seen in Table 3. In particular, Table 3 shows, for each metric and each test case, three values computed from a set of 100 different random series consisting of 2,000 test executions. The columns labelled as *Total* show the average total number of distinct tasks produced by the metric. This number demonstrates a big disadvantage of the ConcurPairs coverage metric, namely, its problem with scalability. The metric produced nearly 5 million of distinct tasks for 2,000 executions of the TIDOrbJ test case which makes further analyses quite time demanding.

The columns of Table 3 labelled as *Average percentage* represent the ratio between the average number of tasks covered within one execution and Total. A high number in this column means that most of the total number of covered tasks were covered within one execution. The cumulative coverage under such metrics (for DUPairs, Eraser, and Sync) usually stabilises early or grows very slowly. In both of these cases, the detection of saturation is difficult. Contrary, if the average percentage is too low (for ConcurPairs and GoldiLock*), the cumulative coverage grows for a very long time.

Finally, the columns of Table 3 labelled *Smooth percentage* give an insight in how smooth the growth of the accumulated coverage is. The column contains the ratio between the average number of the distinct cumulative coverage values reached under a metric when going through the considered executions and the number of test executions (2,000). High values (for ConcurPairs and GoldiLock*) mean that the cumulated

Table 3. A quantitative comparison of the metrics

| | Dining phil. | | | Airlines | | | Crawler | | | FtpServer | | | TIDOrbJ echo | | |
	Total	Average %	Smooth %	Total	Average %	Smooth %	Total	Average %	Smooth %	Total	Average %	Smooth %	Total	Average %	Smooth %
Avio	6	47	0	17	60	1	40	22	1	529	45	10	822	50	8
Avio*	30	10	0	490	2	10	418	3	9	1 023	33	16	3 280	29	22
ConcurP.	4 059	6	38	16 730	6	85	20 866	3	83	526 280	6	100	4 908 100	2	100
DUPairs	18	76	0	43	97	0	105	81	1	330	92	2	1 933	98	2
DUPair*	72	19	0	1 401	3	9	921	11	8	646	82	3	3 092	90	4
Eraser	29	76	0	73	96	0	217	64	2	684	88	4	2 978	90	4
Eraser*	89	25	0	1 429	5	8	861	19	5	1 086	79	4	4 886	83	6
GoldiLock	26	73	0	102	64	2	384	20	12	1 091	61	9	6 265	51	29
GoldiLock*	119	16	0	4 217	1	20	3 335	3	26	2 210	47	12	10 434	41	46
GoodLock	9	56	0	0	-	0	57	52	1	0	-	0	321	63	3
GoodLock*	22	23	0	0	-	0	258	17	4	0	-	0	915	34	6
HBPair	6	62	0	25	79	0	61	39	1	13	73	0	131	70	2
HBPair*	29	13	0	1 013	2	13	984	4	12	28	49	0	420	46	5
Sync	8	56	0	27	78	0	49	46	1	22	66	0	172	79	2

coverage under the metric changed many times, and therefore there was contiguously growing. Low values (for Avio, DUPairs, Eraser, GoodLock, and Sync) mean that the cumulated coverage changed only a few times, and therefore there either occurred a fast saturation or there appeared long shoulders. Both of these phenomena are problematic for a good metric to be used in saturation-based testing.

The table also shows a disadvantage of the GoodLock* metric. The metric focuses on nested locking as was described in Section 3.2. If such a phenomenon does not occur in the tested program, the metric provides no information as can be seen in the Airlines and FtpServer test cases. On the other hand, the metric can provide additional information which cannot be directly inferred by other metrics in programs which contains this phenomenon. In total, the evaluation in Table 3 gives similar champions for a good metric to be used in saturation-based testing as what we saw in Figure 1(c). Namely, this is the case of the Avio*, Eraser*, DUPairs*, HBPair*, and GoldiLock metrics.

6   Conclusions and Future Work

We have proposed a methodology of deriving new coverage metrics to be used in testing of concurrent software from dynamic (and possibly also static) analyses designed for discovering bugs in concurrent programs. Using this idea, we have derived several new concrete metrics. We have performed an empirical evaluation of these metrics, which has shown that several of them are indeed better for use in saturation-based and search-based testing than various previously known metrics.

As an additional advantage of the metrics that we have proposed, we can mention their better applicability in debugging. For debugging, understandability of each coverage task is important. We believe that tasks generated by our metrics provide much more problem-related information to the tester than existing metrics such as ConcurPairs or DUPairs. The tester can track the threads and objects that appear in the covered tasks to their place of creation or use some additional information (e.g., a lockset) present in the tasks to better understand what happened during the witnessed executions.

In the future, more experimental evidence about the proposed metrics should be obtained to further explore their properties. Metrics based on other dynamic as well as static analyses could be considered too. Finally, an evaluation of the metrics within the entire framework of search-based testing should be done.

Acknowledgement. This work was supported by the Czech Science Foundation (projects P103/10/0306 and 102/09/H042), the Czech Ministry of Education (projects COST OC10009 and MSM 0021630528), the EU/Czech IT4Innovations Centre of Excellence project CZ.1.05/1.1.00/02.0070, and the internal BUT project FIT-11-1.

References

1. Bensalem, S., Havelund, K.: Dynamic Deadlock Analysis of Multi-threaded Programs. In: Ur, S., Bin, E., Wolfsthal, Y. (eds.) HVC 2005. LNCS, vol. 3875, pp. 208–223. Springer, Heidelberg (2006)

2. Bron, A., Farchi, E., Magid, Y., Nir, Y., Ur, S.: Applications of Synchronization Coverage. In: Proc. of PPoPP 2005. ACM Press (2005)
3. Clarke, E., Grumberg, O., Peled, D.: Model Checking. MIT Press (1999)
4. Edelstein, O., Farchi, E., Goldin, E., Nir, Y., Ratsaby, G., Ur, S.: Framework for Testing Multi-threaded Java Programs. Concurrency and Computation: Practice and Experience 15(3-5), 485–499 (2003)
5. Elmas, T., Qadeer, S., Tasiran, S.: Goldilocks: A Race and Transaction-aware Java Runtime. In: Proc. of PLDI 2007. ACM Press (2007)
6. Hovemeyer, D., Pugh, W.: Finding Concurrency Bugs in Java. In: Proc. of PODC 2004. ACM Press (2004)
7. Joshi, P., Park, C.-S., Sen, K., Naik, M.: A Randomized Dynamic Program Analysis Technique for Detecting Real Deadlocks. In: Proc. of PLDI 2009. ACM Press (2009)
8. Kahlon, V., Yang, Y., Sankaranarayanan, S., Gupta, A.: Fast and Accurate Static Data-Race Detection for Concurrent Programs. In: Damm, W., Hermanns, H. (eds.) CAV 2007. LNCS, vol. 4590, pp. 226–239. Springer, Heidelberg (2007)
9. Křena, B., Letko, Z., Vojnar, T., Ur, S.: A Platform for Search-based Testing of Concurrent Software. In: Proc. of PADTAD 2010. ACM Press (2010)
10. Lu, S., Tucek, J., Qin, F., Zhou, Y.: Avio: Detecting Atomicity Violations via Access Interleaving Invariants. In: Proc. of ASPLOS 2006. ACM Press (2006)
11. Manson, J., Pugh, W., Adve, S.V.: The Java Memory Model. In: Proc. of POPL 2005. ACM Press (2005)
12. McMinn, P.: Search-based Software Test Data Generation: A Survey: Research Articles. Software Testing, Verification, and Reliability 14(2), 105–156 (2004)
13. Musuvathi, M., Qadeer, S., Ball, T., Basler, G., Nainar, P.A., Neamtiu, I.: Finding and Reproducing Heisenbugs in Concurrent Programs. In: Proc. of OSDI 2008. USENIX Association (2008)
14. Pozniansky, E., Schuster, A.: Efficient On-the-fly Data Race Detection in Multithreaded C++ Programs. In: Proc. of PPoPP 2003. ACM Press (2003)
15. Savage, S., Burrows, M., Nelson, G., Sobalvarro, P., Anderson, T.: Eraser: A Dynamic Data Race Detector for Multi-threaded Programs. In: Proc. of SOSP 1997. ACM Press (1997)
16. Sherman, E., Dwyer, M.B., Elbaum, S.: Saturation-based Testing of Concurrent Programs. In: Proc. of ESEC/FSE 2009. ACM Press (2009)
17. Soriano, J., Jimenez, M., Cantera, J.M., Hierro, J.J.: Delivering Mobile Enterprise Services on Morfeo's MC Open Source Platform. In: Proc. of MDM 2006. IEEE CS (2006)
18. Trainin, E., Nir-Buchbinder, Y., Tzoref-Brill, R., Zlotnick, A., Ur, S., Farchi, E.: Forcing Small Models of Conditions on Program Interleaving for Detection of Concurrent Bugs. In: Proc. of PADTAD 2009. ACM Press (2009)
19. von Praun, C., Gross, T.R.: Object Race Detection. In: Proc. of OOPSLA 2001. ACM Press (2001)
20. Williams, A., Thies, W., Ernst, M.D.: Static Deadlock Detection for Java Libraries. In: Gao, X.-X. (ed.) ECOOP 2005. LNCS, vol. 3586, pp. 602–629. Springer, Heidelberg (2005)
21. Yang, C.-S.D., Souter, A.L., Pollock, L.L.: All-du-path Coverage for Parallel Programs. In: Proc. of ISSTA 1998. ACM Press (1998)

Runtime Verification with State Estimation

Scott D. Stoller[1], Ezio Bartocci[2], Justin Seyster[1], Radu Grosu[1],
Klaus Havelund[3], Scott A. Smolka[1], and Erez Zadok[1]

[1] Department of Computer Science, Stony Brook University, USA
[2] Department of Applied Math and Statistics, Stony Brook University, USA
[3] Jet Propulsion Laboratory, California Institute of Technology, USA

Abstract. We introduce the concept of *Runtime Verification with State Estimation* and show how this concept can be applied to estimate the probability that a temporal property is satisfied by a run of a program when monitoring overhead is reduced by sampling. In such situations, there may be *gaps* in the observed program executions, thus making accurate estimation challenging. To deal with the effects of sampling on runtime verification, we view event sequences as observation sequences of a Hidden Markov Model (HMM), use an HMM model of the monitored program to "fill in" sampling-induced gaps in observation sequences, and extend the classic forward algorithm for HMM state estimation (which determines the probability of a state sequence, given an observation sequence) to compute the probability that the property is satisfied by an execution of the program. To validate our approach, we present a case study based on the mission software for a Mars rover. The results of our case study demonstrate high prediction accuracy for the probabilities computed by our algorithm. They also show that our technique is much more accurate than simply evaluating the temporal property on the given observation sequences, ignoring the gaps.

1 Introduction

Runtime verification (RV) is the problem of, given a program P, execution trace τ of P, and temporal logic formula ϕ, decide whether τ satisfies ϕ. To perform RV, one typically transforms ϕ into a *monitor* (a possibly parametrized finite state machine) M_ϕ and *instruments* P so that it emits *events* of interest to M_ϕ. This allows M_ϕ to *process* these events and determine whether the event sequence satisfies ϕ.

RV does not come for free. The *overhead* associated with RV is a measure of how much longer a program takes to execute due to runtime monitoring. If the original program executes in time R, and the instrumented program executes in time $R + M$ with monitoring, we say that the monitoring overhead is $\frac{M}{R}$.

Recently, a number of techniques have been developed to mitigate the overhead due to RV [13,9,1,14,5]. Common to these approaches is the use of *event sampling* to reduce overhead. Sampling means that some events are not processed at all, or are processed in a limited (and thus less expensive) manner than other events. A natural question is: *how does sampling affect the results of RV?* This

S. Khurshid and K. Sen (Eds.): RV 2011, LNCS 7186, pp. 193–207, 2012.
© Springer-Verlag Berlin Heidelberg 2012

issue has been largely ignored in prior work: the monitor simply reports the result of processing the observed events, without indicating how sampling might have affected the results.

For example, let ϕ be the formula $\Box(a \Rightarrow \Diamond c)$ (invariably, a is eventually followed by c) and let τ be the trace $a\,b\,c\,a\,b\,c\,a\,b\,c$. Clearly τ satisfies ϕ. Suppose now that τ is an *incomplete* trace of an execution with implicit gaps due to sampling. Although we cannot decisively say whether the execution satisfies ϕ (for example, there could be an unobserved a event after the last c event), we would like to compute a confidence measure that the execution satisfies ϕ.

In this paper, we introduce the concept of *runtime verification with state estimation* (RVSE), and show how this concept can be applied to estimate the probability that a temporal property is satisfied by a run of a program when monitoring overhead is reduced by sampling. In such situations, there may be *gaps* in observed program executions, making accurate estimation challenging.

The main idea behind our approach is to use a statistical model of the monitored system to "fill in" sampling-induced gaps in event sequences, and then calculate the probability that the property is satisfied. In particular, we appeal to the theory of Hidden Markov Models [17]. An HMM is a Markov model in which the system being modeled is assumed to be a Markov process with unobserved (hidden) states. In a regular Markov model, states are directly visible to the observer, and therefore state transition probabilities are the only required parameters. In an HMM, states cannot be observed; rather, each state has a probability distribution for the possible observations (formally called *observation symbols*). The classic *state estimation* problem for HMMs is to compute the most likely sequence of states that generated a given observation sequence.

The main contributions of this paper are:

- We use HMMs to formalize the RVSE problem as follows. Given an HMM system model H, temporal property ϕ, and observation sequence O (an execution trace that may have gaps due to sampling), compute $\Pr(\phi \mid O, H)$, i.e., the probability that the system's behavior satisfies ϕ, given O and H. Note that we use *Hidden* Markov Models, meaning that the states of the system are hidden from the observer. This is because we intend to use machine learning to learn the HMM from traces that contain only observable actions of the system, not detailed internal states of the system.

- The *forward algorithm* [17] is a classic recursive algorithm for computing the probability that, given an observation sequence O, an HMM ended in a particular state. This problem is the so-called *filtering* version of the state estimation problem for HMMs. We present an extension of the forward algorithm for the RVSE problem that computes a similar probability, but in this case for the paired execution of an HMM system model and a monitor automaton for the temporal property ϕ. We first present a version of the algorithm that does not consider gaps; in this case, the states of the monitor are completely determined by O, because the monitor is deterministic.

- We then present an algorithm that handles gaps. We use a special symbol to mark gaps, i.e., points in the observation sequence where unobserved events might have occurred. Gap symbols may be inserted in the trace by the instrumentation when it temporarily disables monitoring; or, if gaps may occur everywhere, a gap symbol can be inserted at every point in the trace. When the algorithm processes a gap, no observation is available, so the state of the monitor automaton is updated probabilistically based on the current state estimation for the HMM and the observation probability distribution for the HMM. Since the length of a gap (i.e., the number of consecutive unobserved events) might be unknown, we allow the gap length to be characterized by a probability distribution.

– We evaluate our RVSE methodology using a case study based on human operators in a ground station issuing commands to a Mars rover [3]. Sampling of execution traces is simulated using SMCO-style overhead control [14]. Our evaluation demonstrates high prediction accuracy for the probabilities computed by our algorithm. It also shows that our technique is much more accurate than simply evaluating the temporal property on the given observation sequences, ignoring the gaps.

2   Related Work

To the best of our knowledge, Runtime Verification with State Estimation has not been studied before, and our HMM-based technique to support the calculation of the conditional probability that a system satisfies a temporal logic formula given a sampled event trace (observation sequence) is new. In this section, we discuss related work on runtime verification of statistical properties and on probabilistic model checking.

Sammapun et al. [18] consider runtime verification of probabilistic properties of the form: given a condition A, does the probability that an outcome B occurs fall within a given range? Their technique determines statistically, and with an adequate level of confidence, whether a system satisfies a probabilistic property. Wang et al. [19] apply a similar statistical RV technique, in conjunction with Monte Carlo simulation, to analog and mixed signal designs. Recent work on the runtime verification of probabilistic properties [11,21] uses acceptance sampling and sequential hypothesis testing to outperform these approaches. In contrast, we perform runtime verification of traditional *non-probabilistic* properties, but in the presence of sampling.

Finkbeiner et al. [10] extend LTL to perform statistical experiments over runtime traces, but they do not consider sampling. For example, their methodology can be used to determine the percentage of positions in a trace at which the trace satisfies a temporal property. This is a different statistic than the conditional probabilities we compute. LarvaStat [7] incrementally computes statistical information about runtime executions, but it, too, does not consider sampling.

Probabilistic model checking [15,2] can be used to compute the probability that a Markov model, such as a Discrete-Time or Continuous-Time Markov Chain, satisfies a probabilistic temporal logic formula. Zhang et al. [20] extend probabilistic model checking to HMMs, so that the probability that an HMM produces a given sequence of observations can be computed. In contrast, we use HMMs to probabilistically fill in gaps in sampled event traces, enabling us to estimate the probability that a (non-probabilistic) temporal property is satisfied by a trace that contains gaps due to sampling. It is important to note that for filling in the gaps, a considerably less accurate HMM model is acceptable.

3   Case Study: A Mars Rover Scenario

We illustrate and evaluate our approach on a software model of a planetary rover mission. The model is written in the SCALA programming language,[1] allowing for fast prototyping. Its architecture, depicted in Figure 1, is representative, in general terms, of actual rover missions, such as the current Mars Science Laboratory[2] (MSL) mission. The scenario we consider consists of a rover operating on the surface of Mars, controlled by commands from ground-based human operators. The rover consists of a collection of instruments (e.g., camera, drill, temperature sensor) performing specialized tasks. For this case study, the rover hosts two generic instruments, A and B. Furthermore, every event of importance occurring on the rover is recorded in a log, which is maintained on the ground. A ground-based logger module receives and stores such events.

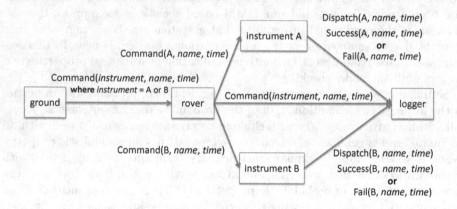

Fig. 1. Mission architecture

We consider four kinds of events, presented in Figure 2 and inspired by the scenario explained by Barringer et al. [3]. Commands are issued from ground to the rover and are characterized by three parameters: instrument id (A or B), command name, and a time stamp indicating when the event occurred. The other three events have similar parameters. Upon receipt of a command, the rover reports this event to the logger (by sending the command to the logger),

[1] http://www.scala-lang.org

[2] http://mars.jpl.nasa.gov/msl

Command(*instrument, name, time*)	commands submitted to rover
Dispatch(*instrument, name, time*)	dispatch of command from rover to instrument
Success(*instrument, name, time*)	success of command on instrument
Fail(*instrument, name, time*)	failure of command on instrument

Fig. 2. Events observed

and then sends the command to the relevant instrument. The instrument, upon receipt of the command, issues a dispatch event to the logger (recording that it was dispatched to the instrument). The instrument then executes the command. If the execution is successful, a success is reported to the logger. If execution fails, a fail status is reported. It is possible that neither a success nor a fail occur, and that the command is simply lost for some reason. An example log collected during the execution of this system could be: Command(A, START, 1008), Command(B, RESET, 2303), Success(A, START, 4300), Success(B, RESET, 5430).

One aspect of the desired behavior of the rover system is expressed by the requirement: Every Command(i, n, t_1) event should eventually be followed by a Success(i, n, t_2) event, with no Fail(i, n, t_3) event occurring in between.

The above trace satisfies this property. The following trace does not satisfy the property, because the first command fails explicitly, and the second command fails implicitly (neither success nor failure occurs): Command(A, START, 1008), Command(B, RESET, 2303), Fail(A, START, 4520).

This property can be expressed in LTL as follows, where $\Box$ means "always", $\mathcal{U}$ means "until", underscore means "don't care", and the subscript "cs" is mnemonic for "command success".

$$\phi_{cs} = (\forall\, i : Instrument, n : Name. \tag{1}$$
$$\Box(\text{Command}(i, n, \_) \Rightarrow \neg \text{Fail}(i, n, \_)\ \mathcal{U}\ \text{Success}(i, n, \_)))$$

The property was formulated and checked with TRACECONTRACT [4], a SCALA API for trace analysis supporting parameterized state machines and temporal logic. In TRACECONTRACT, the property is expressed as follows, where SCALA keywords are in bold, TRACECONTRACT features are underlined, and the *hot* state waits for an event that matches the pattern in one of the **case** statements and represents the requirement that such an event eventually occurs:

```
class Contract extends Monitor[Event] {
    require {
        case Command(i,n,_) ->
            hot {
                case Fail(`i`, `n`, _) => error
                case Success(`i`, `n`, _) => ok
            }
    }
}
```

4   Background

Hidden Markov Models. A Hidden Markov Model (HMM) [17] is a tuple $H = \langle S, A, V, B, \pi \rangle$ containing a set S of states, a transition probability matrix A, a set V of observation symbols, an observation probability matrix B (also called "emission probability matrix" or "output probability matrix"), and an initial state distribution π. The states and observations are indexed (i.e., numbered), so S and V can be written as $S = \{s_1, s_2, \ldots, s_{N_s}\}$ and $V = \{v_1, \ldots, v_{N_o}\}$, where N_s is the number of states, and N_o is the number of observation symbols. Let $\Pr(c_1 \mid c_2)$ denote the probability that c_1 holds, given that c_2 holds. The transition probability distribution A is an $N_s \times N_s$ matrix indexed by states in both dimensions, such that $A_{i,j} = \Pr(\text{state is } s_j \text{ at time } t + 1 \mid \text{ state is } s_i \text{ at time } t)$. The observation probability distribution B is an $N_s \times N_o$ matrix indexed by states and observations, such that $B_{i,j} = \Pr(v_j \text{ is observed at time } t \mid \text{ state is } s_i \text{ at time } t)$. π_i is the probability that the initial state is s_i.

An example of an HMM is depicted in the left part of Figure 3. Each state is labeled with observation probabilities in that state; for example, P(Succ)=.97 in state s_3 means $B_{3,Succ} = 0.97$, i.e., an observation made in state s_3 has probability 0.97 of observing a Success event. Edges are labeled with transition probabilities; for example, .93 on the edge from s_2 to s_3 means that $A_{2,3} = 0.93$, i.e., in state s_2, the probability that the next transition leads to state s_3 is 0.93.

An HMM generates observation sequences according to the following five-step procedure [17]. (1) Choose the initial state q_1 according to the initial state distribution π. (2) Set $t = 1$. (3) Choose the tth observation O_t according to the observation probability distribution in state q_t. (4) Choose the next state q_{t+1} according to the transition probability distribution in state q_t. (5) Increment t and return to step (3), or stop.

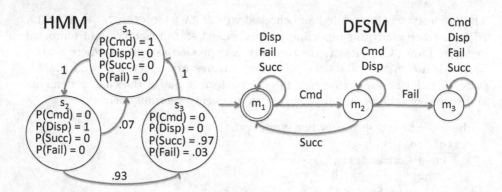

Fig. 3. Left: an example of an HMM. The initial state distribution is: $\pi_1 = 1$, $\pi_2 = 0$, $\pi_3 = 0$. Right: M_{cs}, an example of a DFSM. States with a double border are accepting states. In both machines, Cmd abbreviates Command(i, n, _), Disp abbreviates Dispatch(i, n, _), Succ abbreviates Success(i, n, _), and Fail abbreviates Fail(i, n, _).

The *forward algorithm* [17] is a classic algorithm for computing the probability that an HMM ended in a particular state, given an observation sequence $O = \langle O_1, O_2, \ldots, O_T \rangle$. Let $Q = \langle q_1, q_2, \ldots, q_T \rangle$ denote the (unknown) state sequence that the system passed through, i.e., q_t denotes the state of the system when observation O_t is made. Let $\alpha_t(i) = \Pr(O_1, O_2, \ldots, O_t, q_t = s_i \mid H)$, i.e., the probability that the first t observations yield $O_1, O_2, \ldots, O_t$ and that q_t is s_i, given the model H. To hide the notational clutter from indexing of V, we access the B matrix using the traditional notation [17]:

$$b_i(v_k) = B_{i,k} \tag{2}$$

The forward algorithm for computing α is:

$$\alpha_1(j) = \pi_j b_j(O_1) \quad \text{for } 1 \leq j \leq N_s \tag{3}$$
$$\alpha_{t+1}(j) = \left(\sum_{i=1..N_s} \alpha_t(i) A_{i,j} \right) b_j(O_{t+1}) \tag{4}$$
$$\text{for } 1 \leq t \leq T-1 \text{ and } 1 \leq j \leq N_s$$

In the base case, $\alpha_1(j)$ is the joint probability of starting in state s_j and emitting O_1. Similarly, the recursive case calculates the joint probability of reaching state s_j and emitting O_T. The probability of reaching s_j is calculated by summing over the immediate predecessors s_i of s_j; the summand $\alpha_t(i) A_{i,j}$ is the joint probability of reaching s_i while observing O_1 through O_{T-1} and then transitioning from s_i to s_j. The cost of computing α using these equations is $O(N_s^2 T)$.

Learning an HMM. One can obtain an HMM for a system automatically, by learning it from complete traces using standard HMM learning algorithms [17]. These algorithms require the user to specify the desired number of states in the HMM. These algorithms allow (but do not require) the user to provide information about the structure of the HMM, specifically, that certain entries in the transition probability matrix and the observation probability matrix are zero. This information can help the learning algorithm converge more quickly and find globally (instead of locally) optimal solutions. If the temporal property or properties to be monitored are known before the HMM is learned, then the set of observation symbols can be limited to contain only events mentioned in those properties, and the number of states can be chosen just large enough to be able to model the relevant aspects of the system's behavior. Note that we use *Hidden* Markov Models, meaning that the states of the system are hidden from the observer, because we intend to learn H from traces that contain only observable actions of the system, not detailed internal states of the system.

Deterministic Finite State Machines. Our algorithm assumes that the temporal property ϕ to be monitored is expressed as a parametrized deterministic finite state machine (DFSM). The DFSM could be written directly or obtained by translation from a language such as LTL. A DFSM is a tuple $M = \langle S_M, m_{init}, V, \delta, F \rangle$, where S_M is the set of states, m_{init} in S_M is the initial state, V is the alphabet (also called the set of input symbols), $\delta : S_M \times V \to S_M$ is the transition function, and F is the set of accepting states (also called "final states"). Note that δ is a total function. A trace O satisfies the property iff it leaves M in an accepting state.

For example, a DFSM M_{cs} that expresses the property ϕ_{cs} in Equation 1 is depicted in the right part of Figure 3. The Dispatch event is not in the alphabet of the TRACECONTRACT property ϕ and hence normally would be omitted from the alphabet of the DFSM; we include it in this DFSM for illustrative purposes, so that the alphabets of the HMM and DFSM are the same.

5   Algorithm for RVSE

The first subsection defines the problem more formally and presents our algorithm for RVSE. Our algorithm is based on the forward algorithm in Section 4 and hence can be used for on-line or post-mortem analysis. The second subsection describes how we handle parameterized properties.

5.1   Problem Statement and Algorithm

A problem instance is defined by an observation sequence O, an HMM H, and a temporal property ϕ over sequences of actions of the monitored system.

The observation sequence O contains events that are occurrences of actions performed by the monitored system. In addition, O may contain the symbol $gap(L)$ denoting a possible gap with an unknown length. The length distribution L is a probability distribution on the natural numbers: $L(\ell)$ is the probability that the gap has length ℓ.

If no information about the location of gaps is available (and hence no gap events appear in the trace obtained from the runtime monitor), we insert a gap event at the beginning of the trace and after every event in the trace, to indicate that gaps may occur everywhere.

The HMM $H = \langle S, A, V, B, \pi \rangle$ models the monitored system, where $S = \{s_1, \ldots, s_{N_s}\}$ and $V = \{v_1, \ldots, v_{N_o}\}$. Observation symbols of H are observable actions of the monitored system. H need not be an exact model of the system.

The property ϕ is represented by a DFSM $M = \langle S_M, m_{init}, V, \delta, F \rangle$. For simplicity, we take the alphabet of M to be the same as the set of observation symbols of H. It is easy to allow the alphabet of M to be a subset of the observation symbols of H, by modifying the algorithm so that observations of symbols outside the alphabet of M leave M in the same state.

The goal is to compute $\Pr(\phi \mid O, H)$, i.e., the probability that the system's behavior satisfies ϕ, given observation sequence O and model H.

First, we extend the forward algorithm in Section 4 to keep track of the state of M. Let m_t denote the state of M immediately after observation O_t is made. Let $\alpha_t(i, m) = \Pr(O_1, O_2, \ldots, O_t, q_t = s_i, m_t = m \mid H)$, i.e., the joint probability that the first t observations yield $O_1, O_2, \ldots, O_t$ and that q_t is s_i and that m_t is m, given the model H. Let $\text{pred}(n, v)$ be the set of predecessors of n with respect to v, i.e., the set of states m such that M transitions from m to n on input v. A conditional expression $c\,?\,e_1 : e_2$ equals e_1 if c is true, and it equals e_2 if c

is false. The extended forward algorithm appears below. The main changes are introduction of a conditional expression in equation (6), reflecting that the initial state of M is m_{init}, and introduction of a sum over predecessors m of n with respect to O_{t+1} in equation (7), analogous to the existing sum over predecessors i of j, so that the sum takes into account all ways of reaching the configuration in which H is in state s_i and M is in state m.

$$\text{pred}(n, v) = \{m \in S_M \mid \delta(m, v) = n\} \tag{5}$$

$$\alpha_1(j, n) = (n = \delta(m_{init}, O_1)) \,?\, \pi_j b_j(O_1) : 0 \tag{6}$$
$$\text{for } 1 \leq j \leq N_s \text{ and } n \in S_M$$

$$\alpha_{t+1}(j, n) = \left(\sum_{\substack{i \in [1..N_s] \\ m \in \text{pred}(n, O_{t+1})}} \alpha_t(i, m) A_{i,j} \right) b_j(O_{t+1}) \tag{7}$$
$$\text{for } 1 \leq t \leq T - 1 \text{ and } 1 \leq j \leq N_s \text{ and } n \in S_M$$

Now we extend the algorithm to handle gaps. The result appears in Figure 4. An auxiliary function p_i is used to calculate the probability of transitions of M during gaps. When H is in state s_i and M is in state m, $p_i(m, n)$ is the probability that the next observation (i.e., the observation in state s_i) causes M to transition to state n. Since we do not know which event occurred, we sum over the possibilities, weighting each one with the appropriate observation probability from B.

Another auxiliary function g_ℓ, called the gap transition relation, is used to compute the overall effect of a gap of length ℓ. Specifically, $g_\ell(i, m, j, n)$ is the probability that, if H is in state s_i and M is in state m and a gap of length ℓ occurs, then the H is in state s_j and M is in state n after the gap. The definition of $g_{\ell+1}$ uses a recursive call to g_ℓ to determine the probabilities of states reached after a gap of length ℓ (these intermediate states are represented by i' and m'), and then calculates the effect of the $(\ell + 1)^{\text{th}}$ unobserved event as follows: $A_{i',j}$ is the probability that H transitions from state $s_{i'}$ to state s_j, and $p_j(m', n)$ is the probability that M transitions to state n.

In the definition of α_1, for the case $O_1 = gap(L)$, there is a probability $L(0)$ that no gap occurred, in which case M remains in its initial state m_{init} and the probability distribution for states of H remains as π_j; furthermore, for each $\ell > 0$, there is a probability $L(\ell)$ of a gap of length ℓ, whose effect is computed by a call to y_ℓ, and π_i is the probability that H is in state s_i at the beginning of the gap.

In the definition of α_{t+1}, for the case $O_{t+1} = gap(L)$, there is a probability $L(0)$ that no gap occurred, in which case the state of the HMM and the DFSM remain unchanged, so $\alpha_{t+1}(j, n) = \alpha_t(j, n)$; furthermore, for each $\ell > 0$, there is a probability $L(\ell)$ of a gap of length ℓ, whose effect is computed by a call to g_ℓ, and $\alpha_t(i, m)$ is the probability that H is in state s_i and M is in state m at the beginning of the gap.

$$p_i(m, n) = \sum_{v \in V \text{ s.t. } \delta(m,v)=n} b_i(v) \tag{8}$$

$$g_0(i, m, j, n) = (i = j \wedge m = n) ? 1 : 0 \tag{9}$$

$$g_{\ell+1}(i, m, j, n) = \sum_{i' \in [1..N_s], m' \in S_M} g_\ell(i, m, i', m') A_{i',j} p_j(m', n) \tag{10}$$

$$\alpha_1(j, n) = \tag{11}$$

$$\begin{cases} (n = \delta(m_{init}, O_1)) ? \pi_j b_j(O_1) : 0 & \text{if } O_1 \neq gap(L) \\ L(0)(n = m_{init} ? \pi_j : 0) + \sum_{\ell > 0, i \in [1..N_s]} L(\ell) \pi_i g_\ell(i, m_{init}, j, n) & \text{if } O_1 = gap(L) \end{cases}$$

for $1 \leq j \leq N_s$ and $n \in S_M$

$$\alpha_{t+1}(j, n) = \begin{cases} \left(\displaystyle\sum_{\substack{i \in [1..N_s] \\ m \in \text{pred}(n, O_{t+1})}} \alpha_t(i, m) A_{i,j} \right) b_j(O_{t+1}) & \text{if } O_{t+1} \neq gap(L) \\ L(0)\alpha_t(j, n) + \displaystyle\sum_{\ell > 0} L(\ell) \sum_{\substack{i \in [1..N_s] \\ m \in S_M}} \alpha_t(i, m) g_\ell(i, m, j, n) & \text{if } O_{t+1} = gap(L) \end{cases} \tag{12}$$

for $1 \leq t \leq T - 1$ and $1 \leq j \leq N_s$ and $n \in S_M$

Fig. 4. Forward algorithm modified to handle gaps

Although the algorithm involves a potentially infinite sum over ℓ, typically $L(\ell)$ is non-zero for only a finite number of values of ℓ, in which case the sum contains only a finite number of non-zero terms. For example, if the system uses lightweight instrumentation to count events during gaps, then the position and length of all gaps are known. In this case, for each gap, $L(\ell)$ is non-zero only for the value of ℓ that equals the number of unobserved events (i.e., the gap length). If counts of unobserved events are unavailable (because monitoring is completely disabled during gaps), it is sometimes possible to determine (based on characteristics of the system and how long monitoring was disabled) a threshold such that $L(\ell)$ is non-zero only below that threshold. Even if no such threshold exists, $L(\ell)$ typically approaches 0 as ℓ becomes large, so the sum can be approximated by truncating it after an appropriate number of terms.

5.2   Handling Parameterized Temporal Properties

Our approach supports parameterized temporal properties. Specified events trigger creation of a new instance of the parameterized property, and parameters of the trigger event are used as parameters of the property. For example, the property ϕ_{cs} in equation (1), and the corresponding DFSM M_{cs} in Figure 3, are parameterized by the instrument i and the name n. The parameters of the

DFSM may be used in the definition of the alphabet of the DFSM; in other words, the alphabet is also parameterized. For example, the alphabet of M_{cs} is $\{\texttt{Command}(i, n, \_), \texttt{Dispatch}(i, n, \_), \texttt{Success}(i, n, \_), \texttt{Fail}(i, n, \_)\}$.

For a parameterized property, we decompose (or "demultiplex") a given trace into a set of subtraces by projecting it onto the alphabet of each instance of the property. The HMM is learned from these subtraces; thus, the HMM represents the slice of the system's overall behavior relevant to a single instance of the property. When learning the HMM, we abstract from the specific values of the parameters in each subtrace, because the values are, of course, different in each subtrace, and we do not aim to learn the distribution of parameter values.

When applying our modified forward algorithm for a parameterized property, we run the algorithm separately for each instance of the property, and use the corresponding subtrace (i.e., the projection of the trace onto the alphabet of that property instance) as the observation sequence O.

When projecting a trace containing gaps onto the alphabet of a property instance, it is typically unknown whether the unobserved event or events that occurred during a gap are in that alphabet. This can be reflected by modifying the length distribution parameter of the gap symbol appropriately before inserting the gap in the subtrace for that property instance. Developing a method to modify the length distribution appropriately, based on the nearby events in the trace and the HMM, is future work. Lee et al.'s work on trace slicing [16] might provide a basis for this.

The above approach does not assume any relationship between the property parametrization and the sampling strategy. An alternative approach is to adopt a sampling strategy in which, for each property instance, either all relevant events are observed, or none of them are. For example, when QVM [1] checks properties of Java objects, it selects some objects for checking, monitors all events on those objects, and monitors no events on other objects. With this approach, the property is checked with 100% confidence for the selected objects, but it is not checked at all for other objects. This trade-off might be preferable in some applications but not in others. Also, this property-directed sampling may incur more overhead than property-independent sampling, because it must ensure that all events relevant to the selected property instances are observed.

6   Evaluation

6.1   Evaluation Methodology

We used the following methodology to evaluate the accuracy of our approach for a given system.

1. Produce a set T_L of traces by monitoring the system without sampling, and learn an HMM H from them.
2. Produce another set T_E of traces by monitoring the system without sampling, and use them for evaluation as follows.

3. Produce a sampled version $\breve{O}$ of each trace O in T_E. If the system is deterministic, $\breve{O}$ can be produced by re-running the system on the same input as for O while using sampling. An alternative approach, applicable regardless of whether the system is deterministic, is to write a program that reads a trace, simulates the effect of sampling, and outputs a sampled version of the trace.

4. For each trace O in T_E, apply our algorithm to compute the probability $\Pr(\phi|\breve{O}, H)$.

5. Compare the probabilities from the previous step to reality, by partitioning the traces in T_E into "bins" (i.e., sets) based on $\Pr(\phi|\breve{O}, H)$, and checking whether the expected fraction of the traces in each set actually satisfy ϕ. Specifically, using $B + 1$ bins, for $b \in [0..B]$, the set of traces placed in bin b is $T_E(b) = \{O \in T_E \mid b/B \leq \Pr(\phi|\breve{O}, H) < (b+1)/B\}$. Let $sat_{act}(b)$ denote the fraction of traces in bin b that actually satisfy ϕ. Based on the results from our algorithm, $sat_{act}(b)$ is expected to be approximately $sat_{est}(b) = \text{average}(\{\Pr(\phi|\breve{O}, H) \mid O \in T_E(b)\})$. The subscript "est" is mnemonic for "estimation", i.e., "expected based on state estimation".

6. Quantify the overall inaccuracy as a single number I between 0 and 1, where 0 means perfect accuracy (i.e., no inaccuracy), by summing the differences between the actual and expected fractions from the previous step for non-empty bins and normalizing appropriately ("ne" is mnemonic for "non-empty"):

$$B_{\mathrm{ne}} = \{b \in [0..B] \mid T_E(b) \neq \emptyset\} \tag{13}$$

$$I = \frac{1}{|B_{\mathrm{ne}}|} \sum_{b \in B_{\mathrm{ne}}} |sat_{act}(b) - sat_{est}(b)|. \tag{14}$$

7. Put this inaccuracy into perspective by comparing it with the inaccuracy of the naive approach that ignores the effect of sampling and simply evaluates the property on sampled traces, ignoring gaps. Specifically, $sat_{naive}(b)$ is the fraction of traces in $T_E(b)$ such that the sampled trace satisfies ϕ, i.e., $sat_{naive}(b) = |\{O \in T_E(b) \mid \breve{O} \models \phi\}|/|T_E(b)|$, and

$$I_{naive} = \frac{1}{B_{\mathrm{ne}}} \sum_{b \in B_{\mathrm{ne}}} |sat_{act}(b) - sat_{naive}(b)|. \tag{15}$$

If the sampling strategy has a parameter that controls how many events are observed, then the inaccuracy I can be graphed as a function of that sampling parameter. For example, SMCO has a parameter o_t, the target overhead. We expect the inaccuracy to approach 0 as the fraction of events that are observed approaches 1. Similarly, for a particular trace O, $\Pr(\phi|\breve{O}, H)$ can be graphed as a function of that sampling parameter; if the trace O satisfies ϕ, this curve should monotonically increase towards 1 as the fraction of events that are observed approaches 1.

6.2   Experiments

We applied the above methodology to the rover case study described in Section 3. The SCALA model was executed to generate 200 traces, each containing 200 issued commands. The average length of the traces is 587 events. To facilitate evaluation of our approach, the model was modified to pseudo-randomly introduce violations of the requirement ϕ_{cs} in Equation 1. Approximately half of the traces satisfy the requirement. In the other half of the traces, the requirement is violated by approximately 30% of the commands; among those commands, approximately half have an explicit Fail event, and the other half do not have a Success or Fail event. We wrote a program that reads a trace, simulates the sampling performed by SMCO with a global controller [14], and then outputs the trace with some events replaced by $gap(L_0)$, where $L_0(0) = 0$, $L_0(1) = 1$, and $L_0(\ell) = 0$ for $\ell > 1$. Note that $gap(L_0)$ represents a definite gap of length 1. The use of a definite gap reflects that the SMCO controller knows when it disables and enables monitoring, and that (in an actual implementation) lightweight instrumentation would be used to count the number of unobserved events when monitoring is (mostly) disabled. With the target overhead that we specified, the SMCO simulator replaced 47% of the events with gaps.

Based on the parameters of the property ϕ_{cs}, each sampled trace was decomposed into a separate subtrace for each instrument and command, following the approach in Section 5.2. When decomposing the trace, we assigned each gap to the appropriate subtrace by referring to the original (pre-sampling) trace. Although it is generally unrealistic to assume that the monitor can assign gaps to subtraces with 100% accuracy, this assumption allows us to isolate this source of inaccuracy and defer consideration of it to future work, in which we plan to introduce uncertain gaps into subtraces corresponding to nearby events in the full trace, using the HMM to compute probabilities for the uncertain gaps.

To obtain the HMM H, we manually specified the number of states (six) and the structure of the HMM, and then learned the transition probability matrix and observation probability matrix from half of the generated traces. We used the other half of the generated traces for evaluation.

We measured the inaccuracy of our approach using $B = 10$, and obtained $I = 0.0205$. This level of inaccuracy is quite low, considering the severity of the sampling: recall that sampling replaced 47% of the events with gaps. In comparison, the inaccuracy of the naive approach is $I_{naive} = 0.3135$; this is approximately a 15× worse I.

7   Conclusions and Future Work

This paper introduces the new concept of *Runtime Verification with State Estimation* (RVSE) and shows how this concept can be applied to estimate the probability that a temporal property is satisfied by a run of a system given a sampled execution trace. An initial experimental evaluation of this approach shows encouraging results.

One direction for future work, mentioned in Section 5.2, is to determine the probability that a gap belongs to each subtrace of a parameterized trace, in order to more accurately determine the length distribution parameter for gap events inserted in subtraces. Because the parameters of events in gaps are unknown, it is impossible to directly determine the subtrace to which a gap belongs.

Although our Mars rover case study is based on actual rover software, due to ITAR restrictions, our evaluation used parametrized event traces synthetically produced by a simulator. We plan to conduct additional case studies involving actual traces obtained from publicly available real-world software. Likely target software systems include the GCC compiler suite and the Linux kernel.

Another direction for further study is RVSE of quantitative properties. For example, the goal of integer range analysis [9,14] is to compute the range (upper and lower bounds) of each integer variable in the program. Performing this kind of analysis on traces with gaps can lead to inaccuracies in the ranges computed, due to unobserved updates to integer variables. In this case, we would like to extend our RVSE algorithm to adjust (improve) the results of the analysis as well as provide a confidence level in the adjusted results. Similar comments apply to other quantitative properties, such as runtime analysis of NAPs (non-access periods) for heap-allocated memory regions [13,14].

Our broader goal is to use probabilistic models of program behavior, learned from traces, for multiple purposes, including program understanding [6], program visualization [8], and anomaly detection [12] (by checking future runs of the program against the model).

Acknowledgements. We would like to thank the anonymous reviewers for their valuable comments. Part of the research described in this publication was carried out at the Jet Propulsion Laboratory (JPL), California Institute of Technology, under a contract with the National Aeronautics and Space Administration. Research supported in part by AFOSR Grant FA9550-09-1-0481, NSF Grants CCF-1018459, CCF-0926190, CNS-0831298, and ONR Grant N00014-07-1-0928.

References

1. Arnold, M., Vechev, M., Yahav, E.: QVM: An efficient runtime for detecting defects in deployed systems. In: Proc. 23rd ACM SIGPLAN International Conference on Object-Oriented Programming, Systems, Languages, and Applications (OOPSLA 2008), pp. 143–162. ACM (October 2008)
2. Baier, C., Katoen, J.P.: Principles of Model Checking. MIT Press (2008)
3. Barringer, H., Groce, A., Havelund, K., Smith, M.: Formal analysis of log files. Journal of Aerospace Computing, Information, and Communication 7(11), 365–390 (2010)
4. Barringer, H., Havelund, K.: TRACECONTRACT: A Scala DSL for Trace Analysis. In: Butler, M., Schulte, W. (eds.) FM 2011. LNCS, vol. 6664, pp. 57–72. Springer, Heidelberg (2011)
5. Bonakdarpour, B., Navabpour, S., Fischmeister, S.: Sampling-Based Runtime Verification. In: Butler, M., Schulte, W. (eds.) FM 2011. LNCS, vol. 6664, pp. 88–102. Springer, Heidelberg (2011)

6. Buss, E., Henshaw, J.: Experiences in program understanding. In: Proc. Second Conference of the Centre for Advanced Studies on Collaborative Research (CAS-CON 1992), pp. 157–189. IBM Press (1992)
7. Colombo, C., Gauci, A., Pace, G.J.: LarvaStat: Monitoring of Statistical Properties. In: Barringer, H., Falcone, Y., Finkbeiner, B., Havelund, K., Lee, I., Pace, G., Roşu, G., Sokolsky, O., Tillmann, N. (eds.) RV 2010. LNCS, vol. 6418, pp. 480–484. Springer, Heidelberg (2010)
8. Diehl, S.: Software Visualization: Visualizing the Structure, Behavior, and Evolution of Software. Springer, Heidelberg (2007)
9. Fei, L., Midkiff, S.P.: Artemis: Practical runtime monitoring of applications for execution anomalies. In: Proc. 2006 ACM SIGPLAN Conference on Programming Language Design and Implementation (PLDI 2006), pp. 84–95. ACM, Ottawa (2006)
10. Finkbeiner, B., Sankaranarayanan, S., Sipma, H.B.: Collecting statistics over runtime executions. Form. Methods Syst. Des. 27, 253–274 (2005)
11. Grunske, L.: An effective sequential statistical test for probabilistic monitoring. Information and Software Technology 53, 190–199 (2011)
12. Hangal, S., Lam, M.S.: Tracking down software bugs using automatic anomaly detection. In: Proc. 24th International Conference on Software Engineering (ICSE 2002), pp. 291–301. ACM (2002)
13. Hauswirth, M., Chilimbi, T.M.: Low-overhead memory leak detection using adaptive statistical profiling. In: Proc. 11th International Conference on Architectural Support for Programming Languages and Operating Systems (ASPLOS 2004), pp. 156–164 (October 2004)
14. Huang, X., Seyster, J., Callanan, S., Dixit, K., Grosu, R., Smolka, S.A., Stoller, S.D., Zadok, E.: Software monitoring with controllable overhead. International Journal on Software Tools for Technology Transfer (2011)
15. Kwiatkowska, M., Norman, G., Parker, D.: Stochastic Model Checking. In: Bernardo, M., Hillston, J. (eds.) SFM 2007. LNCS, vol. 4486, pp. 220–270. Springer, Heidelberg (2007)
16. Lee, C., Chen, F., Roşu, G.: Mining parametric specifications. In: Proc. 33rd International Conference on Software Engineering (ICSE 2011), pp. 591–600. ACM (2011)
17. Rabiner, L.R.: A tutorial on hidden Markov models and selected applications in speech recognition. Proceedings of the IEEE 77(2), 257–286 (1989)
18. Sammapun, U., Lee, I., Sokolsky, O., Regehr, J.: Statistical Runtime Checking of Probabilistic Properties. In: Sokolsky, O., Taşiran, S. (eds.) RV 2007. LNCS, vol. 4839, pp. 164–175. Springer, Heidelberg (2007)
19. Wang, Z., Zaki, M., Tahar, S.: Statistical runtime verification of analog and mixed signal designs. In: Proc. Third International Conference on Signals, Circuits and Systems (SCS 2009), pp. 1–6. IEEE (November 2009)
20. Zhang, L., Hermanns, H., Jansen, D.N.: Logic and Model Checking for Hidden Markov Models. In: Wang, F. (ed.) FORTE 2005. LNCS, vol. 3731, pp. 98–112. Springer, Heidelberg (2005)
21. Zhang, P., Ki, W., Wan, D., Grunske, L.: Monitoring of probabilistic timed property sequence charts. Software: Practice and Experience 41, 841–866 (2011)

Efficient Techniques for Near-Optimal Instrumentation in Time-Triggered Runtime Verification

Samaneh Navabpour[1], Chun Wah Wallace Wu[1],
Borzoo Bonakdarpour[2], and Sebastian Fischmeister[1]

[1] Department of Electrical and Computer Engineering
University of Waterloo
200 University Avenue West
Waterloo, Ontario, Canada, N2L 3G1
{snavabpo,cwwwu,sfischme}@uwaterloo.ca
[2] School of Computer Science
University of Waterloo
200 University Avenue West
Waterloo, Ontario, Canada, N2L 3G1
borzoo@cs.uwaterloo.ca

Abstract. *Time-triggered* runtime verification aims at tackling two defects associated with runtime overhead normally incurred in event-triggered approaches: *unboundedness* and *unpredictability*. In the time-triggered approach, a monitor runs in parallel with the program and periodically samples the program state to evaluate a set of properties. In our previous work, we showed that to increase the sampling period of the monitor (and hence decrease involvement of the monitor), one can employ auxiliary memory to build a history of state changes between subsequent samples. We also showed that the problem of optimization of the size of history and sampling period is NP-complete.

In this paper, we propose a set of heuristics that find near-optimal solutions to the problem. Our experiments show that by employing negligible extra memory at run time, we can solve the optimization problem significantly faster, while maintaining a similar level of overhead as the optimal solution. We conclude from our experiments that the NP-completeness of the optimization problem is not an obstacle when applying time-triggered runtime verification in practice.

Keywords: Runtime monitoring, instrumentation, optimization, verification, time-triggered, predictability.

1   Introduction

Runtime verification [1, 2, 4, 7, 9, 12] refers to a technique where a system under inspection is continually checked by a *monitor* at run time with respect to its specification. In the literature, deploying runtime verification involves instrumenting

S. Khurshid and K. Sen (Eds.): RV 2011, LNCS 7186, pp. 208–222, 2012.
© Springer-Verlag Berlin Heidelberg 2012

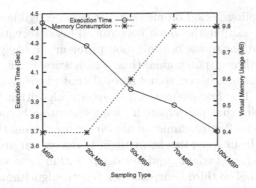

Fig. 1. Memory usage vs. sampling period [3]

the program under inspection, so that upon occurrence of events (e.g., change of value of a variable) that may change the truthfulness of a property, the monitor is called to re-evaluate the property. We call this method *event-triggered* runtime verification, because each change prompts a re-evaluation. Event-triggered runtime verification suffers from two drawbacks: (1) *unpredictable* overhead, and (2) possible *bursts* of events at run time. These defects can lead to undesirable transient overload situations in time-sensitive systems such as real-time embedded safety-critical systems. To address these issues, in [3], we introduced the notion of *time-triggered* runtime verification, where a monitor runs in parallel with the program and samples the program state periodically to evaluate a set of system properties.

The main challenge in time-triggered runtime verification is to guarantee accurate program state reconstruction at sampling time. To this end, we introduced an optimization problem where the objective is to find the minimum number of critical events that need to be buffered for a given sampling period [3]. Consequently, the time-triggered monitor can successfully reconstruct the state of the program between two successive samples. We showed that this optimization problem is NP-complete and proposed a transformation of this problem to an *integer linear program* (ILP). This transformation enables us to employ powerful ILP-solvers to identify the minimum buffer size and instrumentation instructions for state reconstruction. It is possible to solve the corresponding ILP model for some applications, but for larger applications, the exponential complexity poses a serious stumbling block.

With this motivation, in this paper, we focus on developing polynomial time algorithms that find near-optimal solutions to the optimization problem. Our algorithms are inspired by an observation made in [3]. Figure 1, taken from [3], shows the decrease in execution time and increase in total memory usage of a program (y-axis) when the sampling period (denoted *MSP* in Figure 1) is increased by factors of 20, 50, 70, and 100 (x-axis). Increasing the sampling period requires storing more events, and hence, requiring larger buffers. However, Figure 1 shows that when we increase the sampling period even by a factor of 100, the increase in memory usage is only 4%. In other words, the impact of increasing the sampling period on memory usage is negligible. Our experiments on other programs exhibit the same behavior. This observation suggests that nearly optimal solutions to the optimization problem are likely to be effective.

We propose three polynomial-time heuristics. All heuristics are over-approximations and, hence, sound (they do not cause overlooking of events to be monitored). The first heuristic is a greedy algorithm that aims at instrumenting variables that participate in many execution branches. The second heuristic is based on a 2-approximation algorithm for solving the minimum vertex cover problem. Intuitively, this heuristic instruments variables that are likely to cover all cases where variable updates occur within time intervals less than the sampling period. The third heuristic uses genetic algorithms, where the population generation aims at minimizing the number of variables that need to be instrumented and buffered.

The results of our experiments show that our heuristics are significantly faster than the ILP-based solution proposed in [3]. More importantly, the solutions returned by all three algorithms lead to a negligible increase in instrumentation overhead and total memory usage at run time as well as negligible increase in the total execution time of the monitored program. We also observe that in general, extra instrumentation instructions are evenly distributed between samples. Moreover, our genetic algorithm generally produces instrumentation schemes closest to the optimal solution as compared to the other heuristics. Based on the results of our experiments, we conclude that the NP-completeness of the optimization problem is not an obstacle when applying time-triggered runtime verification in practice.

2   Preliminaries

Time-triggered runtime verification [3] consists of a monitor and an application program under inspection. The monitor runs in parallel with the application program and interrupts the program execution at regular time intervals to observe the state of the program. The state of the program is determined by evaluating the value of a set of variables being monitored. The key advantage of this technique is *bounded* and *predictable* overhead incurred during program execution. This overhead is inversely proportional to the sampling period at which the monitor samples the program.

Formally, let P be a program and Π be a logical property (e.g., in LTL), where P is expected to satisfy Π. Let $\mathcal{V}_\Pi$ denote the set of variables that participate in Π. In time-triggered runtime verification, a monitor reads the value of variables in $\mathcal{V}_\Pi$ at certain time intervals and evaluates Π. The main challenge in this mechanism is accurate reconstruction of states of P between two consecutive samples; i.e., if the value of a variable in $\mathcal{V}_\Pi$ changes more than once between two consecutive samples, then the monitor may fail to detect violations of Π. Control flow analysis helps us to reconstruct the states of P. To reason about the control-flow of programs at run time, we utilize the notion of *control-flow graphs* (CFG).

```
1:      a = scanf(...);
2:      if (a % 2 == 0) goto 9
3:      else {
4:          printf(a + "is odd");
5:*         b = a/2;
6:*         c = a/2 + 1;
7:          goto 10;
8:      }
9:      printf(a + "is even");
10:     end program
```

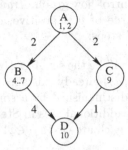

(a) A simple C program   (b) Control-flow graph

Fig. 2. A C program and its control-flow graph

Definition 1. *The* control-flow graph *of a program P is a weighted directed simple graph* $CFG_P = \langle V, v^0, A, w \rangle$, *where:*

- *V: is a set of vertices, each representing a basic block of P. Each basic block consists of a sequence of instructions in P.*
- v^0: *is the* initial vertex *with in-degree 0, which represents the initial basic block of P.*
- *A: is a set of* arcs (u, v), *where* $u, v \in V$. *An arc* (u, v) *exists in A, if and only if the execution of basic block u immediately leads to the execution of basic block v.*
- *w: is a function* $w : A \to \mathbb{N}$, *which defines a* weight *for each arc in A. The weight of an arc is the* best-case execution time *(BCET) of the source basic block.* □

For example, consider the C program in Figure 2(a) (taken from [3]). If each instruction takes one time unit to execute in the best case, then the resulting control-flow graph is the one shown in Figure 2(b). Vertices of the graph in Figure 2(b) are annotated by the corresponding line numbers of the C program in Figure 2(a).

In order to accurately reconstruct program states between two samples, we modify CFG_P in three steps.

Step 1: Identifying Critical Vertices
We ensure that each *critical instruction* (i.e., an instruction that modifies a variable in V_Π) is in a basic block that contains no other instructions. We refer to such a basic block as a *critical basic block* or *critical vertex*. For example, in Figure 2(a), if variables b and c are of interest for verification of a property at run time, then instructions 5 and 6 will be critical and we will obtain the control-flow graph shown in Figure 3(a).

Step 2: Calculating the Minimum Sampling Period
Since uncritical vertices play no role in determining the sampling period, in the second step, we collapse uncritical vertices as follows. Let $CFG = \langle V, v^0, A, w \rangle$

be a control-flow graph. *Transformation* $T(CFG, v)$, where $v \in V \setminus \{v^0\}$ and the out-degree of v is positive, obtains $CFG' = \langle V', v^0, A', w' \rangle$ via the following ordered steps:

1. Let A'' be the set $A \cup \{(u_1, u_2) \mid (u_1, v), (v, u_2) \in A\}$. Observe that if an arc (u_1, u_2) already exists in A, then A'' will contain parallel arcs (such arcs can be distinguished by a simple indexing or renaming scheme). We eliminate the additional arcs in Step 3.
2. For each arc $(u_1, u_2) \in A''$,

$$
w'(u_1, u_2) = \begin{cases} w(u_1, u_2) & \text{if } (u_1, u_2) \in A \\ w(u_1, v) + w(v, u_2) & \text{if } (u_1, u_2) \in A'' \setminus A \end{cases}
$$

3. If there exist parallel arcs from vertex u_1 to u_2, we will only include the one with minimum weight in A''.
4. Finally, $A' = A'' \setminus \{(u_1, v), (v, u_2) \mid u_1, u_2 \in V\}$ and $V' = V \setminus \{v\}$.

We clarify a special case of the above transformation, where u and v are two uncritical vertices with arcs (u, v) and (v, u) between them. Deleting one of the vertices, say u, results in a self-loop (v, v), which we can safely remove. This is simply because a loop that contains no critical instructions does not affect the sampling period.

We apply the above transformation on all uncritical vertices. We call the result a *critical control-flow graph*. Such a graph includes (1) an uncritical initial basic block, (2) possibly an uncritical vertex with out-degree 0 (if the program is terminating), and (3) a set of critical vertices. Figure 3(b) shows the critical control-flow graph of the graph in Figure 3(a).

Definition 2. *Let* $CFG = \langle V, v^0, A, w \rangle$ *be a critical control-flow graph. The minimum sampling period for* CFG *is* $MSP_{CFG} = \min\{w(v_1, v_2) \mid (v_1, v_2) \in A \land v_1 \text{ is a critical vertex}\}$. $\square$

Intuitively, the minimum sampling period is the minimum timespan between two successive changes to any two variables in $\mathcal{V}_{\Pi}$. For example, the minimum sampling period of the control-flow graph in Figure 3(b) is $MSP = 1$. By applying this sampling period, all property violations can be detected [3].

Step 3: Increasing the Sampling Period using Auxiliary Memory

To increase the sampling period (and, hence, the involvement of the monitor), we use auxiliary memory to build a history of critical state changes between consecutive samples. More specifically, let (u, v) be an arc and v be a critical vertex in a critical control-flow graph CFG, where critical instruction *inst* changes the value of a variable a. We apply transformation $T(CFG, v)$ and append an instruction $inst' : a' \leftarrow a$, where a' is an auxiliary memory location, to the sequence of instructions in vertex u. We call this process *instrumenting transformation* and denote it by $IT(CFG, v)$. Observe that deleting a critical vertex v results in incorporating an additional memory location.

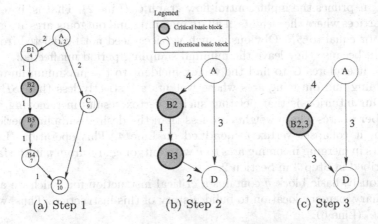

Fig. 3. Steps for obtaining optimized instrumentation and sampling period

Unlike uncritical vertices, the issue of loops involving critical vertices needs to be handled differently. Suppose u and v are two critical vertices with arcs (u, v) and (v, u) between them and we intend to delete u. This results in a self-loop (v, v), where $w(v, v) = w(u, v) + w(v, u)$. Since we do not know how many times the loop may iterate at run time, it is impossible to determine the upper bound on the size of auxiliary memory needed to collapse vertex v. Hence, to ensure correctness, we do not allow applying the transformation IT on critical vertices that have self-loops.

Given a critical control-flow graph, our goal is to optimize two factors through a set of IT transformations: (1) minimizing auxiliary memory, and (2) maximizing sampling period. In [3], we showed that this optimization problem is NP-complete.

3   Heuristics for Optimizing Instrumentation and Auxiliary Memory

An interesting observation from the ILP-based experiments conducted in [3] is that increasing the sampling period even by a factor 100 resulted in at most a 4% increase in total memory usage for tested programs. This observation strongly suggests that for a fixed sampling period, even nearly optimal solutions to the problem (in terms of the size of auxiliary memory) are likely to be quite acceptable. With this intuition, in this section, we propose two polynomial-time heuristics. Both heuristics take a control-flow graph G and a desired sampling period SP as input and return a set U of vertices to be deleted as prescribed by Step 3 (i.e., $IT(CFG, v)$) in Section 2. This set identifies the extra memory locations and the corresponding instrumentation instructions.

3.1   Heuristic 1

Our first heuristic is a simple greedy algorithm (see Heuristic 1):

- First, it prunes the input control-flow graph G (Line 2). That is, it removes all vertices where the weights of all its incoming and outgoing arcs are greater than or equal to SP. Obviously, such vertices need not be deleted from the graph, because they leave the minimal sampling period unaffected.
- Next, it explores G to find the vertex incident to the maximum number of incoming and outgoing arcs whose weights are strictly less than SP (Line 4). Our intuition is that deleting such a vertex results in removing a high number of arcs whose weights are less than the desired sampling period.
- Then, it collapses vertex v identified on Line 4. This operation (Line 5) results in merging incoming arcs to v with outgoing arcs from v in the fashion described in Step 3 in Section 2.
- Obviously, basic block v contains a critical instruction for which we add an auxiliary memory location to build history of this instruction. Thus, we add v to U (Line 6).
- We repeat Lines 3-7 until the minimum arc weight of G is greater than or equal to SP (the while-loop condition in Line 3).
- If the graph cannot be collapsed further (i.e., all vertices are collapsed), then the graph's structure will not permit increasing the sampling period to SP and the algorithm declares failure.

3.2   Heuristic 2

Our second heuristic is an algorithm based on a solution to the *minimum vertex cover* problem: Given a (directed or undirected) graph $G = \langle V, E \rangle$, our goal is to find the minimum set $U \subseteq V$, such that each edge in E is incident to at least one vertex in U. The minimum vertex cover problem is NP-complete, but there exists several approximation algorithms that find nearly optimal solutions (e.g., the 2-approximation in [5]).

Our algorithm (see Heuristic 2) works as follows:

- First, it prunes G (Line 2). That is, it removes all vertices where the weights of all its incoming and outgoing arcs are greater than or equal to SP. Obviously, such vertices can remain in the graph.
- Next, we compute an approximate vertex cover of graph G (Line 4), denoted as vc. Our intuition is that since the graph is pruned and the vertex cover vc covers all arcs of the graph, collapsing all vertices in vc may result in removing all arcs whose weights are strictly less than SP. We note that the approximation algorithm in [5] is a non-deterministic randomized algorithm and may produce different covers for the same input graph. To improve our solution, we run Line 4 multiple times and select the smallest vertex cover. This is abstracted away from the pseudo-code.
- Then, similar to Heuristic 1, we collapse each vertex $v \in vc$ (Lines 5-7). This operation (Lines 5-7) results in merging incoming arcs to v with outgoing arcs from v in the fashion described in Step 3 in Section 2. Basic block v contains a critical instruction for which we add an auxiliary memory location to build history of this instruction. Thus, we add v to U (Line 7).

Heuristic 1. Greedy

Input: A critical control-flow graph $G = \langle V, v^0, A, w \rangle$ and desired sampling period SP.

Output: A set U of vertices to be deleted from G.

1: $U := \{\}$;
2: $G := \mathsf{PruneCFG}(G, SP)$;

3: **while** $(MW(G) < SP \wedge U \neq V)$ **do**
4:    $v := \mathsf{GreedySearch}(G)$;
5:    $G := \mathsf{CollapseVertex}(G, v)$;
6:    $U := U \cup \{v\}$;
7: **end while**

8: **if** $(U = V)$ **then** declare failure;
9: **return** U;

Heuristic 2. Vertex Cover Based

Input: A critical control-flow graph $G = \langle V, v^0, A, w \rangle$ and desired sampling period SP.

Output: A set U of vertices to be deleted from G.

1: $U := \{\}$;
2: $G := \mathsf{PruneCFG}(G, SP)$;

3: **while** $(MW(G) < SP \wedge U \neq V)$ **do**
4:    $vc :=$ Approximate-Vertex-Cover(G);
5:    **for each** vertex $v \in vc$ **do**
6:       $G := \mathsf{CollapseNode}(G, v)$;
7:       $U := U \cup \{v\}$;
8:    **end for**
9: **end while**

10: **if** $(U = V)$ **then** declare failure;
11: **return** U;

- We repeat Lines 3-8 until the minimum arc weights of G are greater than or equal to SP (the while-loop condition in Line 3).
- If the graph cannot be collapsed further (i.e., all vertices are collapsed), then the graph's structure will not permit increasing the sampling period to SP and the algorithm declares failure.

4   Optimization Using a Genetic Algorithm

In our genetic model, we define a desirable sampling period SP and aim at collapsing a minimum number of vertices in a given critical control-flow graph G, so that we achieve a sampling period of at least SP.

We map our optimization problem to the following genetic model and will describe it in detail in the following subsections:

1. *Chromosomes*: Each chromosome represents the list of vertices in a critical control-flow graph, G. Each vertex in a chromosome is flagged by either the value *true* or *false*. The value *true* represents the condition where the vertex has been chosen to be collapsed in G.
2. *Fitness Function*: The fitness function of a chromosome is the number of collapsed vertices represented by the chromosome.

3. *Reproduction*: To create a new generation of chromosomes, we use both mutation and crossover.
4. *Termination*: The genetic algorithm terminates when a chromosome with the optimal number of collapsed vertices is found, or the upper limit on creating new generations is reached.

4.1   The Chromosomes

Let $G = \langle V, v^0, A, w \rangle$ be a critical control-flow graph. Each chromosome in the genetic model has a static length of $|V|$. Each entry of the chromosome is a tuple $\langle$vertex id, min-SP, value$\rangle$ that represents a vertex in G. *Vertex id* is the vertex identifier, *min-SP* is the minimum weight of the incoming and outgoing arcs of the vertex and *value* indicates whether the vertex is collapsed in G. If *value* $=$ *true* for a vertex v, then v is collapsed and we add an auxiliary memory location to build a history of the instruction in v. The sampling period of the control-flow graph resulting from the collapsed vertices identified by the chromosome must always be at least SP. We refer to the sampling period of the resulting control-flow graph as the chromosome's sampling period.

Upon initialization, we create the initial generation. First, We choose the size $|\mathcal{G}|$ (i.e., number of chromosomes) of the generations. Second, we randomly create $|\mathcal{G}|$ chromosomes for the initial generation. To create a chromosome, we randomly collapse a set of vertices resulting in a control-flow graph with a sampling period of at least SP. Our genetic algorithm executes the following steps to generate such a chromosome:

- First, it finds the set of vertices, SV, in G where *min-SP* is less than SP for each vertex in SV.
- Second, it randomly chooses a vertex $v \in SV$ and collapses v from G and produces a new control-flow graph $G' = T(G, v)$.
- Third, it calculates the sampling period of G'. If the sampling period is less than SP, it returns back to the first step and chooses the next vertex to collapse.

4.2   Selection/Fitness Function

Since we aim at increasing the sampling period to SP with the least number of collapsed vertices, the chromosome is more fit when the number of collapsed vertices in the chromosome is closer to the optimal number of collapsed vertices. Hence, we define the fitness function as: $\mathcal{F} = \mathcal{C}_{chr}$, where $\mathcal{C}_{chr}$ is the number of collapsed vertices in chromosome chr. Consequently, if $\mathcal{F}$ is smaller, then the chromosome will be more fit.

4.3   Reproduction

We use both *mutation* and *crossover* to evolve the current generation into a new generation. First, we use a *one-point* crossover to create new chromosomes for the next generation. The choice of parents is random. In the crossover, we cut the two parents into half and create two children by swapping halves between the parents. We check both children to see if their sampling period is at least SP. If so, the child will be added to the set of chromosomes of the next generation; if not, the child will be passed on to the mutation step.

Second, the mutation process takes the children passed over by the crossover process and processes each child by the following steps:

1. It finds the set of vertices, SV, where $min\text{-}SP$ is less than SP for each vertex in SV.
2. It randomly chooses a vertex $v \in SV$ to collapse by using $T(G, v)$.
3. It finds the set of collapsed vertices, PV, in the child chromosome for vertices where $min\text{-}SP$ is larger than SP.
4. It randomly chooses a vertex $u \in PV$ to un-collapse, meaning that u is restored to the control-flow graph represented by the child chromosome.
5. It will check if the minimum sampling period of the new child chromosome is at least SP. If the sampling period is less than SP, it will return to the first step and repeat the steps again, until the sampling period of the child chromosome is at least SP or when it exhausts the limit we set for the number of times a chromosome can be mutated.
6. If a new child chromosome with a sampling period of at least SP is reached at step five, it is added to the next generation.

Sometimes the crossover and mutation processes fails to create $|\mathcal{G}|$ chromosomes to populate the next generation, since fewer than $|\mathcal{G}|$ children satisfy the sampling period restriction for chromosomes. In this case, our genetic algorithm chooses the most fit chromosomes from the current generation and adds them to the next generation to create a population of $|\mathcal{G}|$ chromosomes. In the case that duplicates chromosomes appear in this process, it discards the duplicates and randomly creates new chromosomes as described in Section 4.1.

4.4 Termination

Two conditions can terminate the process of creating a new generation: (1) when we find a chromosome with a sampling period of at least SP and has collapsed the same number of vertices as the optimal solution; (2) when we reach an upper bound on the number of generations. In the second case, we choose from all generations the chromosome with the lowest fitness value $\mathcal{F}$.

5   Experimental Results

Our tool chain consists of the following: We generate the control-flow graph of a given C program using the tool CIL [11]. Next, we generate the critical control-flow graph and either transform it into an ILP model using the method in [3] and solve the model using lp_solve [10] or we feed the critical control-flow graph into our heuristics. In either case, we obtain the set of instructions and variables

Table 1. Performance of different optimization techniques

	CFG Size($|V|$)	ILP time (s)	SOF	Heuristic 1 (Greedy) time (s)	SOF	Heuristic 2 (VC) time (s)	SOF	Genetic Algorithm time (s)	SOF
Blowfish	177	5316	–	0.0363	7.8	0.8875	8	383	2.5
CRC	13	0.35	–	0.0002	3.5	0.0852	3	0.254	1.5
Dijkstra	48	1808	–	0.0064	1.2	0.1400	1.2	116	1.7
FFT	47	269	–	0.0042	1.7	0.1737	1.8	74	1.1
Patricia	49	2084	–	0.0054	1.4	0.1369	1.6	140	1.5
Rijndael	70	3096	–	0.0060	1.6	0.2557	2.1	370	1.9
SHA	40	124	–	0.0039	2.2	0.1545	2.2	46	1.3
Susan	20 259	∞	–	3 181	N/A	26 211	N/A	923	N/A

in the program that need to be instrumented using auxiliary memory. We use the breakpoint mechanism of **gdb** [6] to implement time-triggered monitors. Finally, a Python script controls **gdb**. Our case studies are from the MiBench [8] benchmark suite. We fix a sampling period of $40 \times MSP$, where MSP is the minimum sampling period of the program (see Definition 2). All experiments in this section are conducted on a personal computer with a 2.26 GHz Intel Core 2 Duo processor and 6 GB of main memory.

5.1 Performance of Heuristics

Table 1 compares the performance of the ILP-based solution [3] with the heuristics presented in Section 3 and the genetic algorithm proposed in Section 4 for different programs from MiBench. The first column shows the size of the critical control-flow graph of programs in terms of the number of vertices. With each approach, we record the time spent to solve the optimization problem (in seconds) and the suboptimal factor (SOF). SOF is defined as $\frac{sol}{opt}$, where sol and opt are the number of vertices requiring instrumentation returned by a heuristic and the ILP-based solution (i.e., the optimal solution), respectively.

Clearly from Table 1, all three heuristic algorithms perform substantially faster than solving the exact ILP problem. On average, Heuristic 1, Heuristic 2, and the genetic algorithm yield in speedups of 200 000, 7 000, and 9, respectively, where the speedup is defined as the ratio between the execution time required to solve the ILP problem and the time required to generate an approximate solution using one of the heuristics. The execution times of Heuristic 2 are based on running Approximate-Vertex-Cover 500 times to cope with the randomized vertex cover algorithm (see Line 4 in Heuristic 2). Table 1 shows that for large programs, such as Susan, solving for the optimal solution becomes infeasible because of the problem's intractability. However, we see that all three heuristics are able to generate some approximate solution that can be used to instrument the program for time-triggered runtime verification.

In general, the genetic algorithm produces results that are closer to the optimal solution than Heuristics 1 and 2. The spread of the SOFs for the conducted experiments is small for the genetic algorithm. For the conducted experiments,

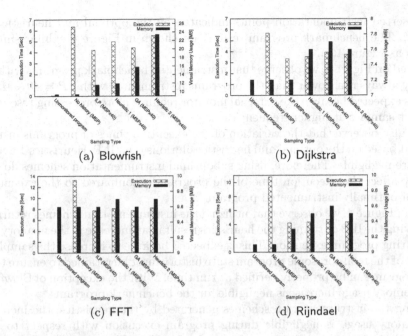

Fig. 4. The impact of different instrumentation schemes on memory usage and total execution time

the worst SOF for the genetic algorithm is 2.5 (i.e., for Blowfish), which indicates that this solution will collapse 2.5 times more vertices in the critical control-flow graph than the optimal solution. With the exception of Blowfish, Heuristics 1 and 2 also perform well, where the SOF ranges from 1.2 to 3.5. We cannot conclude that the performance of Heuristics 1 and 2 suffers as the size of the problem increases because for Susan, Heuristics 1 and 2 indicate that SP may be satisfied by collapsing 104 and 180 vertices, respectively, while the genetic algorithm produces a solution where 222 vertices must be collapsed. The SOFs for Dijkstra also indicate an anomaly in the overall trend. Therefore, the performance of the heuristics likely depends on the structure of the critical control-flow graph. For Susan, the number of vertices being collapsed is approximately 0.5% to 1% of $|V|$, which indicates that the instrumentation overhead should be small.

5.2   Analysis of Instrumentation Overhead

We also collected the execution times and memory usage of the instrumented benchmark programs during experimentation. Figure 4 shows the execution times and memory usage of four of the eight benchmark programs (for reasons of space) we used for our experiments. Each plot in Figure 4 contains the execution times and memory usage for the unmonitored program, the program monitored with a sampling period of MSP, and the program monitored at $40 \times MSP$ with the inserted instrumentation points indicated by the optimal and heuristic solutions. The benchmark program results not shown in Figure 4 exhibit similar trends as Figure 4(c).

Based on Figure 4, we observe that instrumented benchmark programs with no history always run slower than the programs instrumented with $SP = 40 \times MSP$. This is expected because the external monitor requires more processing resources when it samples at higher frequencies.

We also observe that the variation of the execution times of programs instrumented based on the optimal and heuristic solutions (i.e., ILP, Heuristics 1 and 2, GA) are negligible. Therefore, using suboptimal instrumentation schemes do not greatly affect the execution time of the program as compared to the execution time of optimally instrumented program.

From Figure 4, we observe that utilizing the instrumentation schemes returned by solving the ILP or running the heuristics result in an increase in the memory usage during program execution. This is expected because to increase the sampling period of the monitor, some program state history must be retained to ensure that the program can be properly verified at run time. With the exception of Blowfish, the memory usage increase is negligible for the benchmark programs.

Using the instrumentation schemes generated by the heuristics, the increase in memory usage is negligible during program execution with respect to the optimally instrumented program, except for Blowfish. The variation of memory usage for all benchmark programs except for Blowfish generally spans from 0 MB to 0.1 MB. Even though the memory usage of Blowfish instrumented with the schemes produced by Heuristic 2 and the genetic algorithm is relatively larger than the optimal scheme, an increase of 15 MB of virtual memory is still negligible to the amount of memory that is generally available on the machine used to verify a program. Of the three heuristics, we cannot conclude which heuristic generally produces the best instrumentation scheme, as each heuristic behaves differently for different types of control-flow graphs.

Figure 5 shows the percentage increase in the number of instrumentation instructions executed and the percentage increase in the maximum size of history between two consecutive samples with respect to the optimally instrumented benchmark programs. Note that logarithmic scales are used in the charts in Figure 5. Observe that Susan is not shown in the figure, because solving for the optimal solution is infeasible. Blowfish performed the poorest with respect to the two measures when the instrumentation schemes generated by Heuristics 1 and 2 were used. In most cases, the percentage increase in the number of instrumentation instructions that are executed and the maximize size of history are below 50% if we remove the two largest percentages from each set. If we ignore a few more outliers, then most of the percentage increases for both measures will be below 20%. We also observe that the percentage increase in the number of instrumentation instructions executed is proportional to the increase in the maximum size of the history between two consecutive samples. This implies that the extra instrumentation instructions (as compared to the optimal solution) are evenly distributed among sampling points.

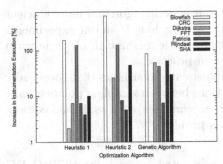 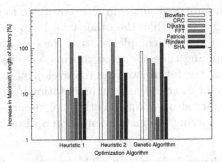

(a) Increase in the number of execution of instrumentation instructions.

(b) Increase in the maximum size of history between two samples.

Fig. 5. The impact of sub-optimal solutions on execution of instructions to build history and its maximum size

Recall that the collapsed vertices during the transformation IT (see Section 2) determine the instrumentation instructions added to the program under inspection. These instructions in turn store changes in critical variables to the history. Although one may argue that auxiliary memory usage at run time must be in direct relationship with the number of collapsed vertices (i.e., instrumentation instructions), this is not necessarily true. This is because the number of added instrumentation instructions differs in different execution paths. For example, one execution path may include no instrumentation instruction and another path may include all such instructions. In this case, the first path will build no history and the second will consume the maximum possible auxiliary memory. This observation also holds in our analysis on other types of overheads as well as the total execution time. This is why in Table 1, the genetic algorithm does the best job of optimizing the Blowfish benchmark for the fewest critical instructions, but in Figure 4(a), the benchmark uses substantially more memory than the greedy heuristic. This is also why in Figure 5, the amount of auxiliary memory used by a monitored program is not proportional to the number of instrumented critical instructions.

6   Conclusion

In this paper, we proposed three efficient algorithms to address the NP complete problem of optimizing the instrumentation of programs in the context of time-triggered runtime verification [3]. This instrumentation is needed for constructing history to record events between two consecutive samples at run time. Our algorithms are inspired by different techniques, such as greedy heuristics, finding the minimum vertex cover, and biological evolution. We rigorously benchmarked eight different programs using our algorithms. The results show that the solutions returned by all three algorithms lead to negligible increase in instrumentation overhead and total memory usage at run time as well as the total execution time of monitored program. Moreover, we found our genetic algorithm more efficient and robust than the other two. In summary, we conclude from our experiments that the NP-completeness of the optimization problem is not an obstacle when applying time-triggered runtime verification in practice.

In the future, we plan to develop more sophisticated heuristics that specifically aim at distributing instrumentation instructions between sampling points evenly. We are also working on other polynomial-time techniques, such as ILP relaxation, for solving the instrumentation optimization problem.

Acknowledgement. This research was supported in part by NSERC DG 357121-2008, ORF RE03-045, ORE RE-04-036, and ISOP IS09-06-037.

References

1. Bauer, A., Leucker, M., Schallhart, C.: Runtime Verification for LTL and TLTL. ACM Transactions on Software Engineering and Methodology, TOSEM (2009) (in press)
2. Bauer, A., Leucker, M., Schallhart, C.: Comparing LTL Semantics for Runtime Verification. Journal of Logic and Computation 20(3), 651–674 (2010)
3. Bonakdarpour, B., Navabpour, S., Fischmeister, S.: Sampling-Based Runtime Verification. In: Butler, M., Schulte, W. (eds.) FM 2011. LNCS, vol. 6664, pp. 88–102. Springer, Heidelberg (2011)
4. Colin, S., Mariani, L.: 18 Run-Time Verification. In: Broy, M., Jonsson, B., Katoen, J.-P., Leucker, M., Pretschner, A. (eds.) Model-Based Testing of Reactive Systems. LNCS, vol. 3472, pp. 525–555. Springer, Heidelberg (2005)
5. Cormen, T.H., Leiserson, C.E., Rivest, R.L., Stein, C.: Introduction to Algorithms, 3rd edn. The MIT Press (2009)
6. GNU debugger, http://www.gnu.org/software/gdb/
7. Giannakopoulou, D., Havelund, K.: Automata-Based Verification of Temporal Properties on Running Programs. In: Automated Software Engineering (ASE), pp. 412–416 (2001)
8. Guthaus, M.R., Ringenberg, J.S., Ernst, D., Austin, T.M., Mudge, T., Brown, R.B.: MiBench: A Free, Commercially Representative Embedded Benchmark Suite. In: IEEE International Workshop on In Workload Characterization (WWC), pp. 3–14 (2001)
9. Havelund, K., Goldberg, A.: Verify your Runs, pp. 374–383 (2008)
10. ILP solver lp_solve, http://lpsolve.sourceforge.net/5.5/
11. Necula, G.C., McPeak, S., Rahul, S., Weimer, W.: CIL: Intermediate language and tools for analysis and transformation of c programs. In: Proceedings of Conference on Compilier Construction (2002)
12. Pnueli, A., Zaks, A.: PSL Model Checking and Run-Time Verification Via Testers. In: Misra, J., Nipkow, T., Karakostas, G. (eds.) FM 2006. LNCS, vol. 4085, pp. 573–586. Springer, Heidelberg (2006)

CoMA: Conformance Monitoring of Java Programs by Abstract State Machines

Paolo Arcaini[1], Angelo Gargantini[2], and Elvinia Riccobene[1]

[1] Dip. di Tecnologie dell'Informazione,
Università degli Studi di Milano, Italy
{paolo.arcaini,elvinia.riccobene}@unimi.it
[2] Dip. di Ing. dell'Informazione e Metodi Matematici,
Università di Bergamo, Italy
angelo.gargantini@unibg.it

Abstract. We present *CoMA* (Conformance Monitoring by Abstract State Machines), a specification-based approach and its supporting tool for runtime monitoring of Java software. Based on the information obtained from code execution and model simulation, the conformance of the concrete implementation is checked with respect to its formal specification given in terms of Abstract State Machines. At runtime, undesirable behaviors of the implementation, as well as incorrect specifications of the system behavior are recognized.

The technique we propose makes use of Java annotations, which link the concrete implementation to its formal model, without enriching the code with behavioral information contained only in the abstract specification. The approach fosters the separation between implementation and specification, and allows the reuse of specifications for other purposes (formal verification, simulation, model-based testing, etc.).

1 Introduction

Runtime software monitoring has been used for software fault-detection and recovery, as well as for profiling, optimization, performance analysis. Software fault detection provides evidence whether program behavior conforms with its desired or specified behavior during program execution. While other formal verification techniques, such as model checking and theorem proving, aim to ensure universal correctness of programs, the intention of runtime software-fault monitoring is to determine whether the current execution behaves correctly; thus, monitoring aims to be a lightweight verification technique that can be used to provide additional defense against failures and confidence of the system correctness.

In most approaches dealing with runtime monitoring of software, the required behavior of the system is formalized by means of correctness properties [11] (often given as temporal logic formulae) which are then translated into *monitors*. The monitor is then used to check if the properties are violated during the execution of a system. The properties specify all admissible individual executions of a system and may be expressed using a great variety of different formalisms. Some of

S. Khurshid and K. Sen (Eds.): RV 2011, LNCS 7186, pp. 223–238, 2012.

these approaches are, for example, language oriented formalisms like extended regular expressions or tracematches by Allan et al. [1]. Temporal logic-based formalisms, which are well-known from model checking, are also very popular in runtime verification, especially variants of linear temporal logic, such as LTL, as seen for example in [13,5].

Our approach requires a shift from a *declarative* style of monitoring to an *operational* style. Declarative specifications are used to state the desired properties of a software system by using a descriptive language. Examples of such notations are logic formulae, JML [16] or the LTL temporal logic. An *operational* specification describes the desired system behavior by providing a model implementation or model program of the system, generally executable. Examples of operational specifications are abstract automata and state machines. In [19], for instance, the specification is given in the Z language and it describes the system state and the ways in which it changes.

Specification styles (and languages) may differ in their expressiveness and very often their use depends on the preference and taste of the specifier, the availability of supporting tools, and so forth. Up to now, descriptive languages have been preferred for runtime software monitoring, while the use of operational languages has not been investigated with the same strength. Section 2 presents the current state of the art.

In this paper, we assume that the desired system behavior is given in an *operational* way by means of an Abstract State Machine (ASM), whose notation is presented in Section 3. We also assume that the implementation is a Java program and the technique we propose makes use of Java annotations. However, annotations do not contain the specification of the correct behavior (like in JML [16]) but they are used only to link the concrete implementation to its formal model, keeping separated the implementation of the system and its high-level specification. The approach has, therefore, the advantage of allowing the reuse of abstract formal specifications for other purposes, like formal verification, model simulation, model-based testing, and so forth. Indeed, the result of this work has to be also viewed towards the goal of engineering and building an environment able to support the major software life cycle activities by means of the integration of several tools that can be used for different purposes on the base of the same specification model. We are trying to achieve this goal through the open project ASMETA (ASM mETAmodeling) [3], which permits the integrated use of different tools for ASM model development and manipulation. Currently, the ASMETA tool-set allows creation, storage, interchange, Java representation, simulation, testing, scenario-based validation, model checking, and model review of ASM models for software systems[1].

In Section 4, we present the theoretical framework of *CoMA* (Conformance Monitoring by ASMs), in which we explain the relationship between the Java implementation and its ASM specification. This relationship defines syntactical links or mappings between Java and ASM elements and a semantical relation which represents the conformance. In Section 5, we introduce the actual

---

[1] See the Asmeta web site http://asmeta.sourceforge.net, 2011.

implementation of our conformance monitoring approach which is based on Java annotations and AspectJ. A particular form of non-determinism is dealt with in Section 6. In Section 7, we discuss some advantages and limits of our approach; by means of diverse examples, we evaluate performance, expressiveness and usability of different ways (*compiled* vs *built-in*) of using CoMA, as well as w.r.t. other approaches for runtime monitoring, while Section 8 concludes the paper.

2 Related Work

Complete surveys about runtime verification can be found in [9,18,11].

Our work has been inspired by the work presented in [19], in which the authors describe a *formal specification-based software monitoring system*. In their system they check that the behavior of a concrete implementation (a Java code) complies with its formal specification (a Z model). We share with their work the fact that the concrete implementation is separated from the specification. In their monitoring system, a user of the Java program must use a specific tool to define the sequence of methods to execute. Therefore, their monitoring system is useful at testing and debugging time, but can not be used in the deployed system in which the monitoring system should be hidden to the final user. The final user, indeed, could be different from the developer of the code: he could be a normal user who wants to execute the code or another developer who wants to reuse the code. In both cases the user should be unaware of the formal specification; he could only be aware that some kind of monitoring is performed. In our system, instead, a developer can deploy a Java code linked with its formal specification. The final user can use the monitored code without knowing anything about the formal specification; the only thing that he must know is that, if he wants to enable the monitoring to the code, he must execute it with AspectJ.

Monitored-oriented programming (MOP) [7] permits to execute runtime monitoring by means of annotating the code with formal property specifications. The specifications can be written in any formalism for which a logic plug-in has been developed (LTL, ERE, JML, ...). The formal specifications are translated (in two steps) in the target programming language. The obtained monitoring code can be used in an *in-line* mode in which the monitoring code is placed in the monitored program, and in an *out-line* mode in which it is used to check traces recorded by adequate probes. Similarly to us, they use AspectJ to weave the monitoring code into the monitored code; in particular AspectJ gives them the ability to execute the monitoring code before or after some methods invocations. A similar approach is taken by *Lime* [15]. This tool permits to monitor the invocations of the methods of an interface by defining *pre* and *post* conditions, called *call specifications* (CS) and *return specifications* (RS). Specifications can be written as past/future LTL formulas, as regular expressions and as nondeterministic finite automata. The specifications are then translated into deterministic finite state automata encoded in Java that function as observers. AspectJ is used to weave the observer code into the original program that is being tested.

Another approach that uses ASMs as formal specification for system monitoring purpose is presented in [4]. That approach shares with ours many common features as using operational specifications (called model programs) and dealing with method calls ordering. However, the approach is mainly applied to specify all of the traditional design-by-contract concepts of pre- and post-conditions and invariants. The technological framework is completely different, since .NET components are considered.

Different approaches exist for system monitoring that are based on runtime verification of temporal properties. In [5], traces of programs are examined in order to check if they satisfy some temporal properties expressed in LTL_3, a linear-time temporal logic designed for runtime verification.

3   Abstract State Machines

Abstract State Machines (ASMs), whose complete presentation can be found in [6], are an extension of FSMs, where unstructured control states are replaced by states with arbitrary complex data. The *states* of an ASM are multi-sorted first-order structures, i.e. domains of objects with functions and predicates defined on them. ASM states are modified by *transition relations* specified by "rules" describing the modification of the function interpretations from one state to the next one. There is a limited but powerful set of *rule constructors* that allow to express guarded actions (`if-then`), simultaneous parallel actions (`par`) or sequential actions (`seq`). Appropriate rule constructors also allow non-determinism (existential quantification `choose`) and unrestricted synchronous parallelism (universal quantification `forall`).

An ASM state is a set of *locations*, namely pairs (*function-name, list-of-parameter-values*). Locations represent the abstract ASM concept of basic object containers (memory units). Location *updates* represent the basic units of state change and they are given as assignments, each of the form $loc := v$, where loc is a location and v its new value.

Functions may be *static* (never change during any run of the machine) or *dynamic* (may change as a consequence of agent actions or *updates*). Dynamic functions are distinguished between *monitored* (only read by the machine and modified by the environment), and *controlled* (read and written by the machine).

A *computation* of an ASM is a finite or infinite sequence $s_0, s_1, \ldots, s_n, \ldots$ of states of the machine, where s_0 is an initial state and each s_{n+1} is obtained from s_n by executing its (unique) *main rule*. An ASM can have more than one *initial state*. It is possible to specify state *invariants*. Because of the non-determinism of the choose rule and of moves of the environment, an ASM can have several different runs starting in the same initial state.

Code in Fig. 1 reports the ASM specification of a counter limited to 10 (according to the invariant) and initialized to the monitored value *initValue*; *counter* and *initValue* are both 0-ary functions.

The ASMETA tool set is a set of tools around the ASMs [3]. They can assist the user in developing specifications and proving model correctness by checking

```
asm counterMax10
signature:          dynamic controlled counter: Integer
                    dynamic monitored initValue: Integer

definitions:        invariant inv_a over counter: counter <= 10

  main rule r_Main = if counter < 10 then       counter := counter + 1 endif

// initizialize   counter
default init s0:        function counter = initValue
```

Fig. 1. ASM Counter in AsmetaL

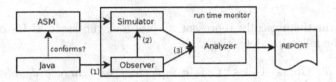

Fig. 2. The CoMA runtime monitor for Java

state invariants and temporal logic properties. For instance, the invariant in Fig. 1 can be proved invalid if *initValue* is greater than 10 by model checking.

Among the ASMETA tools, those involved in our conformance analysis process are: the textual notation *AsmetaL*, used to encode fragments of ASM models, and the simulator *AsmetaS*, used to execute ASM models.

4   Runtime Conformance Monitoring Based on ASMs

A *runtime software-fault monitor*, or simply a *monitor*, is a system that observes and analyzes the states of an executing software system. The monitor checks the correctness of the system behavior by comparing an *observed* state of the system with an *expected* state. The expected behavior is generally provided in terms of a formal specification. We here intend runtime monitoring as conformance analysis at runtime and we propose *CoMA*, runtime *Conformance Monitoring* of Java code *by ASM specifications*.

The CoMA monitor allows *online* monitoring, namely it considers executions in an incremental fashion. It takes as input an executing Java software system and an ASM formal model. The monitor observes the behavior of the Java system and determines its correctness w.r.t. the ASM specification working as an oracle of the expected behavior. While the software system is executing, the monitor checks conformance between the observed state and the expected state.

As shown in Fig. 2, the monitor is, therefore, composed of: an *observer* that evaluates when the Java (observed) state is changed (1), and leads the abstract ASM to perform a machine step (2), and an *analyzer* that evaluates the step conformance between the Java execution and the ASM behavior (3). When the monitor detects a violation of conformance, it reports the error. It can also produce a trace in form of couterexample, which may be useful for debugging. Note that the use of CoMA can be twofold: also faults in the specification can be discovered by monitoring software. For instance, by analysing and re-executing counterexamples, faults in the model can be exposed.

In the following sections, we introduce the theoretical basis of our monitoring system. We, therefore, formally define what is an observed Java state, how to establish a conformance relation between Java and ASM states, and, therefore, step conformance and runtime conformance between Java and ASM executions.

4.1   Observable Java Elements and Their Link with ASM Entities

In order to mathematically represent a class and the state of its objects, we introduce the following definitions.

Definition 1. *Class* *A class C is a tuple $\langle c, f, m \rangle$ where c denotes the non-empty set of constructors, f is the set of all the fields, m is the set of methods.*

We denote the public fields of C as f^{pub} while the public methods are denoted as m^{pub}. Among the methods of a class, we distinguish also the *pure* methods:

Definition 2. *Pure method* *Pure methods m_{pure} are side effect free, with respect to the object/program state. They return a value but do not assign values to fields. m_{pure}^{pub} denotes the set of all pure public methods in m.*

Pure methods [10] are useful and common specification constructs. By marking a method as pure, the specifier indicates that it can be treated as a function of the state (as in JML [16]). We consider only pure methods without arguments.

Definition 3. *Virtual State* *Given a class $C = \langle c, f, m \rangle$, the virtual state, $VS(C)$, is given by $VS(C) = f^{pub} \cup m_{pure}^{pub}$.*

Definition 4. *Observed State* *We define observed state, $OS(C) \subseteq VS(C)$, as the subset of the virtual state consisting of all public fields, and pure public methods of the class C the user wants to observe.*

Therefore, $OS(C)$ is the set of Java elements monitored at runtime. For convenience, we can see $OS(C) = OF(C) \cup OM(C)$ to distinguish between the subset of *observed fields* $OF(C)$ and the subset of *observed methods* $OM(C)$ of $OS(C)$. Note that $OF(C) \subseteq f^{pub}$ and $OM(C) \subseteq m_{pure}^{pub}$. The (returned) values of the elements of $OS(C)$ can change by executing any not pure method (in $m_{\neg pure} = m - m_{pure}$).

Definition 5. *Changing Method* *Given a Java class C, we define changing methods, $changingMethods(C) \subseteq m_{\neg pure}$, all methods of C whose execution is responsible for changing an element of $OS(C)$ and that the user wants to observe.*

Linking observable Java elements to ASM entities. In order to be runtime monitored, a Java class $C = \langle c, f, m \rangle$ should have a corresponding ASM model, ASM_C, abstractly specifying the behavior of an instance of the class C.

Observable elements of a class C must be linked to the dynamic functions $Funcs\_ASM_C$ of the ASM model ASM_C. The function

$$link : OS(C) \rightarrow Funcs\_ASM_C \qquad (1)$$

yields the set of the ASM dynamic functions linked to the observable Java elements of C. The function $link$ is not surjective because there are ASM dynamic functions that are not used in the conformance analysis.

Execution step in Java and ASM. In order to define a step of a Java class execution, we rely on the concept of *machine step* and *last state* of execution sequence defined in the Unifying Theories of Programming (UTP) [14]. A Java *state* of an instance of a class C is the set of the actual values of its fields.

Definition 6. *Java Step Let m be a method of a Java class. A Java step is defined as the relation (s,m,s') where s is the starting state of the execution of m and s' the last state of this execution.*

Definition 7. *Change Step Let C be a Java class. A change step is defined as a Java step for $m \in changingMethods(C)$.*

Note that, choosing the granularity of the Java step at the level of class method and not at the level of single assignment, allows the designer to tune the desired granularity of the monitoring.

ASM *state* and ASM computation *step* have been defined in Section 3.

4.2   State Conformance, Step Conformance and Run Conformance

We have formally related a Java class and the execution of a Java class instance with the corresponding abstract ASM model and relative execution(s). In the following definitions, let C be a Java class, O_C any instance of C, and ASM_C its corresponding ASM abstract model.

We assume that the function $val_{Java}(e, s)$ yields the value of a Java element $e \in VS(C)$ of C in a given state s of O_C, while the value of an ASM function l in a state S is given by $val_{ASM}(l, S)$. Moreover we assume that there exists a conformance $\overset{conf}{=}$ relation among Java and ASM values [2].

Definition 8. *State Conformance We say that a state s of O_C conforms to a state S of ASM_C if all observed elements of C have values in O_C conforming to the values of the locations in ASM_C linked to them; i.e.*

$$conf(s, S) \equiv \forall e \in OS(C) : val_{Java}(e, s) \overset{conf}{=} val_{ASM}(link(e), S) \qquad (2)$$

Definition 9. *Step   Conformance*
We say that a change step (s, m, s')
of an instance O_C, with m a method
of C, conforms with a step (S, S') of
ASM_C if $conf(s, S) \wedge conf(s', S')$.

$$ASM_C \qquad S \xrightarrow{\ step\ } S'$$
$$\qquad\qquad \uparrow conf \qquad\quad \uparrow conf$$
$$O_C \qquad\quad s \xrightarrow{\ m\ } s'$$

Definition 10. *Runtime Conformance Given an observed computation of*
a Java instance O_C, we say that C is runtime conforming to its specification
ASM_C if the following conditions hold:
— the initial state s_0 of the computation of O_C conforms to the initial state
S_0 of the computation of ASM_C, i.e. it yields $conf(s_0, S_0)$;
— every observed change step (s, m, s') with s the current state of O_C, con-
forms with the step (S, S') of ASM_C with S the current state of ASM_C;
— no specification invariant of ASM_C is ever violated.

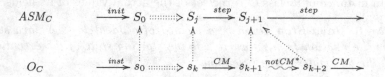

Fig. 3. Runtime conformance

Fig. 3 depicts the co-simulation of an instance O_C and its specification ASM_C.
Def. 10 requires conformance between s_0 and S_0. If O_C is in state s_k, executes
a change method CM, and moves to state s_{k+1}, then s_k must conform to the
current ASM state S_j and s_{k+1} must conform to the next ASM state S_{j+1}. Then,
no conformance check is performed until the next observed state s_{k+2} when a
changing method is invoked again. Note that the final state of a Java change step
and the initial state of the subsequent change step are both *state conforming* to
the same abstract state of the ASM.

5   Monitor Implementation

We here describe how CoMA works. We provide technical details on how the runtime monitor is implemented by exploiting the mechanism of Java annotations
to link observable Java elements to corresponding ASM entities, and AspectJ to
observe code execution and establish conformance relation.

5.1   Using Java Annotations

Java annotations are meta-data tags that can be used to add some information
to code elements as class declarations, field declarations, etc.

In addition to the standard ones, annotations can be defined by the user similarly as classes. For our purposes we have defined a set of annotations in order to link the Java code to its abstract specification. The retention policy, i.e. the way to signal how and when the annotation can be accessed, of all of our annotations is *runtime* – annotations can be read by the compiler and by the monitor at run-time through reflection.

In order to link a Java class C with its corresponding ASM model ASM_C, the class must be annotated with the @Asm annotation having the path of the ASM model as string attribute. Fig. 4 reports the Java class `Counter` linked to its ASM specification (see Fig. 1).

To establish the mapping defined by the function *link*, we annotate each observed field $f \in OF(C)$ by @FieldToFunction, and each observed method $m \in OM(C)$ by @MethodToFunction; both these annotations have a string attribute yielding the name of the corresponding ASM function. In the example, the Java field `counter` and the Java pure method `getCounter` are both linked to the *counter* ASM function.

All methods of *changingMethods(C)* are annotated with the @RunStep. In the example, the observed method is `inc()` that simply increments the counter.

Finally, the user has to decide the starting point of the monitoring. The annotation @StartMonitoring is used to select a proper (not empty) subset of constructors[2]. All or some constructor parameters (if any) can be annotated with the @Init annotation that permits to link a parameter with a monitored function (i.e. only read, as events provided by the environment) of the ASM model. This allows initializing the ASM model with the same values used to create the Java instance. In the example there is just one constructor whose parameter is linked with the ASM monitored function *initValue* which fixes the initial value of the counter (see the specification in Fig. 1).

Our use of the annotation mechanism requires a very limited code modification and differs from that usually exploited in other approaches for system monitoring. Usually annotations are used to enrich the code with extra formal specifications to obtain behavioral information about the target program [7,15]. This leads to the lack of separation between the implementation of the system and its high-level requirements specification. In our approach, the few annotations are

```
@Asm("counterMax10.asm")
class Counter {

@FieldToFunction("counter")
public int counter;

@StartMonitoring
Counter(@Init("initValue") int x){counter = x}

@MethodToFunction("counter")
public int getCounter(){ return counter;}

@RunStep
public void inc(){ counter ++; }}
```

Fig. 4. Java Counter Annotated

---

[2] We do not consider the default constructor. If the class does not have any constructor, the user has to specify an empty constructor and annotate it with @StartMonitoring.

only used to link the code to its specification, but keeping them separate. Furthermore, annotations are statically type checked and since the annotations are read reflectively at runtime, the monitoring setup can be carried out very easily. This is much more convenient than inserting special comments (like JML) and writing our own parser for them. Moreover, Java annotations make the links more robust when code refactoring is applied. Our approach fosters the reuse of specifications when code changes.

5.2   Runtime Monitor and AspectJ

The *runtime monitor* (see Fig. 2) is implemented through the facilities of AspectJ that permits to easily observe the execution of Java objects. AspectJ allows programmers to define special constructs called *aspects*.

(1)   Observer. By means of an aspect, AspectJ allows to specify different *pointcuts*, that are points of the program execution one wants to capture; for each pointcut it is possible to specify an *advice*, that is the actions that must be executed when a pointcut is reached. AspectJ permits to specify when to execute the *advice*: *before* or *after* the execution of the code specified by the pointcut.

The CoMA tool supports two different ways, *built-in* and *compiled*, of developing an aspect.

Built-in. In this approach there is just one aspect that permits to monitor all the objects of the classes that must be monitored: (i) the pointcuts are general enough to capture the instantiations and the method executions of all the objects that must be monitored; (ii) the advices are able to dynamically inspect the Java and the ASM state in order to do the conformance checking.

The main advantage of this approach is that the developer does not have to care about building the aspect: after having written the Java class and the ASM specification, and after having linked them properly, he/she can execute the code immediately.

The main disadvantage of this approach is that, since the aspects are very general, they introduce an overhead in the pointcuts and in the advices that execute the conformance checking. For instance, the pointcuts to detect the creation of an observed object and to capture the execution of a *changing method* (we do not consider changing methods that are executed in the scope of other changing methods) are reported below.

```
pointcut objCreated(): call(@StartMonitoring *.new(..));
pointcut runStepCalled(): call(@RunStep * *.*(..))
                    && !cflowbelow(call(@RunStep * *.*(..)));
```

In order to read the values of the fields that are monitored, we have implemented two techniques: (i) reading them through reflection at the beginning and at the end of the execution of a changing method; (ii) using the AspectJ pointcut *set* in order to capture all their updates.

The main advantage of using reflection is that we can get their values just once for each changing method execution; using the *set* pointcut, instead, every time a monitored field is updated we collect its value: if a field is updated frequently (e.g. in a loop), using the *set* pointcut the performances of the monitoring module can get worse. However, the *set* pointcut can read private fields without programmatically changing their visibility.

Compiled. In this approach, for each Java class that must be monitored, a suitable aspect is built. The main advantage of this approach is that the aspect definitions (pointcuts and advices) can be more precise (e.g. the pointcut that captures the execution of the changing methods can specify exactly the methods whose execution must be captured: in the *built-in* approach, instead, we must capture all the methods annotated with @RunStep). The main disadvantage is that the developer, before running his code, must build the aspect: if the Java code and/or the ASM specification change, the aspect may need to be rebuilt. For instance, the pointcuts for the CounterDec class are:

pointcut objCreated(): **call**(CountercDec.**new**(..));
pointcut methodCalled(): **call**(@RunStep **public void** CountercDec.inc()) ||
               call(@RunStep **public void** CountercDec.dec()));
pointcut runStepCalled(CountercDec target): methodCalled() &&
               !cflowbelow(methodCalled()) && target(target);

(2) Simulator. Upon a Java change step signaled by the observer, the *simulator* performs an ASM step by AsmetaS [12]. Before a change step, an advice reads the values of the *monitored* fields, sets the ASM monitored functions, and executes a state conformance check ($conf(s, S)$ in Def. 9). After a change step, another advice simulates a step of the ASM and forces the Analyzer to check again the state conformance ($conf(s', S')$ in Def. 9).

(3) Analyzer. The *analyzer* compares the Java and the ASM state. To check state conformance (see Def. 8), we have implemented the conformance relation $\stackrel{conf}{=}$ among Java and ASM values as a string comparison. Therefore, the Java and the ASM values are both transformed into strings for comparison.

```
@Asm("CounterDec.asm")
class CounterDec {
@FieldToLocation("counter")
public int counter;

@RunStep(setFunction = "action", toValue = "dec")
public void dec() {
   counter --; }

@RunStep(setFunction = "action", toValue = "inc")
public void inc() {
   counter ++; } }
```

```
asm CounterDec
signature:
   controlled counter: Integer
   monitored action: String

definitions:
   main rule r_Main =
      if action = "inc" then
         counter := counter + 1
      else if action = "dec" then
         counter := counter - 1
      endif endif
```

Fig. 5. Counter with decrement

6 Dealing with Multiple Changing Methods

Definition 10 is adequate for runs where the next state of a Java class C and of its specification ASM_C are unique. Thus, nondeterminism is limited to monitored quantities, which, once not deterministically fixed by the environment, make the evolution of the system deterministic. In this Section, we extend our conceptual framework to deal with a limited form of nondeterminism due to the presence of more than one changing method, each of which takes C to a possible different correct next state in a deterministic way; however, the choice of the changing method that causes a change step is non-deterministic.

In this case, the observer must signal to the ASM under simulation, which step has been chosen by the program. To this scope, we introduce two fields in the @RunStep annotation: *setFunction* permits to specify the name of a monitored function of the ASM model, and *toValue* the value to whom it must be set.

In the Java code in Fig. 5, the @RunStep annotations of the changing methods *dec()* and *inc()* specify that the monitored function *action* must be set, respectively, to *dec* and *inc*.

7 Evaluation

In order to assess the viability of our approach, we have taken several examples in literature and checked whether we were able to apply our approach to existing runtime case studies, including the Railroad Gate [9], the Initialization Fiasco problem [5], a robotic assembly system [19], the Knight's Tour problem [20]. We have written the Java code, if not available, and their ASM specifications (see [2] for details). We applied also CoMA to several Java programs borrowed from JavaMOP [7], like Iterator and FileWriter. Overall we found our approach applicable to all the considered case studies.

Execution time. In order to evaluate the runtime overhead of our approach, we have considered three examples, the *Counter*, the *Iterator* and the *Initialization Fiasco*, and we have monitored them with CoMA, JavaMOP (FSM or LTL), and JML, when applicable. A comparison with [19] is not possible. They use, like CoMA, interpretation of formal specifications, but their tool is not available and no time data are published.

Table 1 reports the average of the time required for 20 runs with 100 instances running in parallel for 1000 steps. JML cannot be used with the *Iterator* and the *Initialization Fiasco*. For the CoMA, Table 1 reports the time for the three kinds of aspects described in Section 5.2; we have divided the overall time between the time taken by the simulator (column AsmetaS) and the time taken by the code under analysis and the monitor module.

It is apparent that most of the time is taken by the simulator, which is based on the Eclipse Modelling Framework, widely uses reflection and visitor design

Table 1. Execution time in the experiments (in secs)

	Java	JML	JavaMOP	CoMA			
				AsmetaS	compiled	set	reflection
Counter	4	280	(FSM) 109	4837	+ 783	+ 825	+ 898
Iterator	8	N/A	(FSM) 91	866306	+ 1439	+ 1812	+ 1820
Initialization Fiasco	7	N/A	(LTL) 72	870719	+1914	+ 2235	+ 2366

patterns, and has never been optimized for performance. On the average, using reflection or using the *set* pointcut is almost equivalent. However, *set* point-cuts may perform worst when an observed field is updated frequently. Instead, *compiled* pointcuts provide the best results.

Although our approach seems not competitive with others in terms of time overhead, we believe that it provides several advantages (explained below) and it can be used when performances are not critical. As a future work, we plan to decrease the running time of the simulation by translating the ASM machine directly into Java code (similarly of what is done in JavaMOP and in Lime). However, encoding ASM into Java would require the semantic correctness proof of the translation. Approaches translating to Java/AspectJ are more efficient but the preservation of the semantics by the translation may become an issue.

At the current development stage of our framework, we have been more inter-ested in assessing the usability and expressiveness of our approach than its time performance.

Usability and expressiveness. Although any comparison of our approach with others in terms of usability and expressiveness may be disputable, since it may depend on the expertise and taste of the user, some general considerations follow.

In comparison with JML, CoMA can be used to express the behavior of a single method call and also the interaction among calls, while JML concentrates on single methods. There exist JML extensions that allow the specification of temporal aspects of Java interfaces (like LIME [15] and trace assertions of Jass). Another difference is that CoMA has a model separated from the implemen-tation, while JML follows a unique model paradigm in which the code itself contains its specification. The advantage of CoMA is that the specification can exist even before its implementation and can be used for several preliminary activities (like model simulation, model review, and formal verification).

The expressiveness of CoMA is greater than approaches using plain FSMs, since ASMs can have infinite states and can be viewed as pseudo-code over abstract data type. In many approaches, like in JavaMOP and in JavaMAC (which uses automata with auxiliary variables) [17], FSMs are enriched with state variables. For instance, the FSM for the counter in JavaMOP becomes:

```
CheckCounter(Counter c) {
// counter value
int count = 0;
// inc call  event
event inc before(Counter c): call(* Counter.inc()) && target(c) {count ++;}
// error event
event err after(Counter c): call(* Counter.inc()) && target(c) &&
                 condition(c.getCounter() != count) {}
// the FSM
fsm: safe [inc -> safe    err -> error]       error []

@error { System.out.println("Counter not incremented"); }}
```

Since JavaMOP specifications are compiled into AspectJ, JavaMOP can include and use all the power of AspectJ. However, we believe that mixing implementation and specification notations may encourage the user to insert implementation details in the specification at the expense of abstractness. An important feature of our methodology is the clear separation between the monitored implementation and the high level specification also in terms of notation, as in [17,19].

Comparison with property-based approaches. An objective comparison with approaches based on the use of properties is more questionable. In this paper, we assume that the specification is given in operational style instead of the more classical declarative style. There has been an endless debate about which style fits better the designer needs: some argue that with an operational style the designers tend to insert implementation details in the abstract specifications, others observe that practitioners feel uncomfortable with declarative notations like temporal logics. The scope of this paper is to provide evidence that also abstract operational notation can be effectively used for runtime monitoring. Sometimes, operational specifications are easier to write and understand; other times, declarative specifications are preferable. For instance, LTL and PLTL can describe correct sequences of method calls with ease. The correct order of calls for an `Iterator`, is specified by the following PLTL formula: $\Box(next \implies \odot hasNext)$, where the operator $\odot$ means in the previous time step. However, properties about states are more difficult (and sometimes impossible) to write. For instance, the fact that an unbounded counter is correctly incremented is not expressible by LTL. Indeed, LTL does not allow variable quantifiers and, therefore, formulas like $\forall x \; \Box(counter = x \implies \bigcirc(counter = x + 1))$ are incorrect.

8   Conclusions and Future Work

We have presented and briefly evaluated CoMA, a framework for runtime conformance monitoring of Java code with respect to its specification given in terms of Abstract State Machines. The source code must be annotated to link Java elements to ASM elements. The CoMA monitor, based on AspectJ, checks runtime conformance between Java executions and ASM specifications. While the software executes, the monitor simulates step by step the ASM specification and checks the state conformance.

Our approach has some limits. The use of an operational specification can lead the designer into inserting implementation details in the specification. Since each class is linked to its specification, monitoring safety properties involving collections of two or more objects [8] is not possible, but we plan to extend CoMA to support also these scenarios. We deal only with restricted forms of nondeterminism, but we are working on supporting more generic forms of it [2]. Monitoring real time requirements seems problematic: we believe that a monitored function *time* may model the real time and would allow its measurement, but further experiences are needed and the runtime overhead may be an issue. Since CoMA currently checks conformance by interpreting the ASM, it performs much slower than other approaches. We plan to optimize the monitoring process to reduce the temporal overhead.

Despite these limits, we believe that our approach presents a viable technique for checking conformance of an implementation (as Java program) with respect to its formal and abstract operational specification (as ASM). Although it is difficult to give a definitive evaluation, we believe that the operational style should be appealing for those preferring executable models instead of properties and that an operational abstract style of describing system behavior may be more easy to write and understand. In our approach, specifications are developed independently from the implementations and they are linked by Java annotations which however contain minimal behavioral information.

There are some advantages not related to runtime verification in using executable specifications (as also discussed in [4]), including that a specification can be executed in isolation, even before its implementation exists. CoMA fosters the reuse of specifications for further purposes thanks to its integration in the ASMETA framework [3], which supports editing, type checking, simulation, review, formal verification, and test case generation for ASMs.

References

1. Allan, C., Avgustinov, P., Christensen, A.S., Hendren, L.J., Kuzins, S., Lhoták, O., de Moor, O., Sereni, D., Sittampalam, G., Tibble, J.: Adding trace matching with free variables to AspectJ. In: Johnson, R.E., Gabriel, R.P. (eds.) OOPSLA, pp. 345–364 (2005)
2. Arcaini, P., Gargantini, A., Riccobene, E.: Runtime monitoring of Java programs by Abstract State Machines. TR 131, DTI Dept., Univ. of Milan (2010)
3. Arcaini, P., Gargantini, A., Riccobene, E., Scandurra, P.: A model-driven process for engineering a toolset for a formal method. Softw., Pract. Exper. 41(2), 155–166 (2011)
4. Barnett, M., Schulte, W.: Runtime verification of.NET contracts. The Journal of Systems and Software 65(3), 199–208 (2003)
5. Bauer, A., Leucker, M., Schallhart, C.: Runtime verification for LTL and TLTL. ACM Transactions on Software and Methodology (TOSEM) 20 (2011)

6. Börger, E., Stärk, R.: Abstract State Machines: A Method for High-Level System Design and Analysis. Springer, Heidelberg (2003)
7. Chen, F., D'Amorim, M., Roşu, G.: A Formal Monitoring-Based Framework for Software Development and Analysis. In: Davies, J., Schulte, W., Barnett, M. (eds.) ICFEM 2004. LNCS, vol. 3308, pp. 357–372. Springer, Heidelberg (2004)
8. Chen, F., Roşu, G.: Mop: an efficient and generic runtime verification framework. In: Proceedings of the 22nd Annual ACM SIGPLAN Conference on Object Oriented Programming Systems and Applications - OOPSLA 2007, Montreal, Quebec, Canada, page 569 (2007)
9. Colin, S., Mariani, L.: 18 Run-Time Verification. In: Broy, M., Jonsson, B., Katoen, J.-P., Leucker, M., Pretschner, A. (eds.) Model-Based Testing of Reactive Systems. LNCS, vol. 3472, pp. 525–555. Springer, Heidelberg (2005)
10. Darvas, A., Leino, K.R.M.: Practical Reasoning About Invocations and Implementations of Pure Methods. In: Dwyer, M.B., Lopes, A. (eds.) FASE 2007. LNCS, vol. 4422, pp. 336–351. Springer, Heidelberg (2007)
11. Delgado, N., Gates, A.Q., Roach, S.: A taxonomy and catalog of runtime software-fault monitoring tools. IEEE Transactions on Software Engineering 30(12), 859–872 (2004)
12. Gargantini, A., Riccobene, E., Scandurra, P.: A metamodel-based language and a simulation engine for Abstract State Machines. Journal of Universal Computer Science (JUCS) 14(12), 1949–1983 (2008)
13. Havelund, K., Roşu, G.: Efficient monitoring of safety properties. Int. J. Softw. Tools Technol. Transf. 6, 158–173 (2004)
14. Hoare, C.A.R., He, J.: Unifying Theories of Programming. Prentice-Hall International, Englewood Cliffs (1998)
15. Kähkönen, K., Lampinen, J., Heljanko, K., Niemelä, I.: The LIME Interface Specification Language and Runtime Monitoring Tool. In: Bensalem, S., Peled, D.A. (eds.) RV 2009. LNCS, vol. 5779, pp. 93–100. Springer, Heidelberg (2009)
16. Leavens, G.T., Baker, A.L., Ruby, C.: Preliminary design of JML: a behavioral interface specification language for Java. SIGSOFT Softw. Eng. Notes 31, 1–38 (2006)
17. Lee, I., Kannan, S., Kim, M., Sokolsky, O., Viswanathan, M.: Runtime assurance based on formal specifications. In: Parallel and Distributed Processing Techniques and Applications, pp. 279–287 (1999)
18. Leucker, M., Schallhart, C.: A brief account of runtime verification. Journal of Logic and Algebraic Programming 78(5), 293–303 (2009)
19. Liang, H., Dong, J., Sun, J., Wong, W.: Software monitoring through formal specification animation. Innovations in Systems and Soft. Eng. 5, 231–241 (2009)
20. Weisstein, E.W.: Knight's tour. from MathWorld–A Wolfram Web Resource

Automated Test-Trace Inspection
for Microcontroller Binary Code

Thomas Reinbacher[1], Jörg Brauer[2], Daniel Schachinger[1],
Andreas Steininger[1], and Stefan Kowalewski[2]

[1] Embedded Computing Systems Group, Vienna University of Technology, Austria
[2] Embedded Software Laboratory, RWTH Aachen University, Germany

Abstract. This paper presents a non-intrusive framework for runtime
verification of executable microcontroller code. A dedicated hardware
unit is attached to a microcontroller, which executes the program under scrutiny, to track atomic propositions stated as assertions over program variables. The truth verdicts over the assertions are the inputs to a
custom-designed μCPU unit that evaluates past-time LTL specifications
in parallel to program execution. To achieve this, the instruction set of
the μCPU is tailored to determining satisfaction of specifications.

1 Introduction

Real software runs on real machines. Ideally, verification should thus take place
on the execution level. A main advantage of this approach is that it eliminates the
need for compiler correctness, which is extremely difficult to establish. However,
analyzing programs on the machine-level poses other challenges, even more so
in the embedded systems domain where there is heavy interaction between the
software and its environment. As a consequence, in practice, only certain parts
of the program may be backed up with a formal correctness argument. For the
remaining part of the program, testing is often the technique of choice to increase
confidence in correctness of the program without proving absence of errors.

Testing is based on a guess-and-check paradigm: one (a) *guesses* a configuration of the program's inputs (the test-case) and (b) *checks* the result of the
individual test runs. While the former can — to a large extent — be automated by automated test-case generation [1], the latter often turns out to be
a time-consuming and manual activity, remaining a core task of test engineers.
With respect to test automation, it is therefore highly desirable to automatically
evaluate the validity of a single test trace when running in the intended execution environment. Runtime verification further ties verification to testing: The
intended behavior of the system is described in some suitable temporal logic
formula, the validity of which is monitored dynamically, while the test case is
executed. Yet, in the context of safety-critical embedded systems, the application of runtime verification on execution level is hampered by the fact that code
instrumentation — which is required by traditional techniques — is likely to affect certain real-time and memory constraints of the system. This is specifically
serious in applications where the design tightly fits into the available resources.

S. Khurshid and K. Sen (Eds.): RV 2011, LNCS 7186, pp. 239–244, 2012.

In previous work [8], we synthesized VHDL code representing a monitor for a past-time LTL [4] (ptLTL) formulae. The truth values of the atomic propositions (APs) as well as the validity of the specification were evaluated in a pure hardware solution. The approach proves feasible in a *static* setting, where one checks a fixed set of properties at every run of the program, e.g., after the product is shipped. However, in a *dynamic* setting such as testing, the specification is likely to change with every single test execution. Since generating a hardware observer from VHDL requires invoking a logic synthesis tool (which may take several minutes), this approach is infeasible for testing. To make runtime verification amenable to real-world testing, this paper proposes a more general approach that relies on a μCPU to determine satisfaction of ptLTL properties on-the-fly. APs are (still) evaluated by a dedicated, configurable hardware unit.

2   Runtime Verification for Microcontroller Binary Code

This section presents our framework for non-intrusive runtime verification of microcontroller binary code (see Fig. 1). APs are evaluated in a component called the atChecker, whereas satisfaction of a ptLTL formula is determined by a μCPU unit, the μMonitor. A control unit wiretaps the memory of the microcontroller that executes the software under investigation. To illustrate our (mostly generic) approach, we employ an off-the-shelf Intel MCS-51 microcontroller IP-core for our experiments. Since verification is performed on the binary program, this approach does not impose any constraints on the high-level implementation language.

Specification. Our framework supports specifications in ptLTL augmented with monitoring operators [7]. A GUI-based host application compiles a specification (consisting of a set of formulae) into a pair $\langle \Pi, \mathcal{C} \rangle$, where $\mathcal{C}$ is a configuration for the atChecker and Π is a set of native programs for the μMonitor. To do so, we instantiate an algorithm proposed by Havelund and Roşu [7] to generate observers for ptLTL. If available, we parse debug information generated during compilation to relate program symbols to memory locations on the microcontroller. This allows us to use high-level program symbols in specifications, for example, $\psi : \uparrow (\text{foo} = 20) \Rightarrow \text{bar} \leq 50$; where foo and bar are variables.

Evaluating Assertions On-The-Fly. The atChecker supports a subclass of two-variable inequalities, namely those of the form $\alpha \cdot m_1 + \beta \cdot m_2 \bowtie C$ where $\alpha, \beta \in \{0, \pm 2^n \mid n \in \mathbb{N}\}$, m_1, m_2 are locations within RAM, $\bowtie \in \{<, >, \leq, \geq, =, \neq\}$, and $C \in \mathbb{Z}$ is a constant. These assertions are easily evaluated in hardware using shifters and adders. One unit is used for each AP of the specification.

Evaluating ptLTL specifications. The μMonitor is a non-pipelined, RISC-based microcomputer featuring an instruction set that supports sequential evaluation of ptLTL specifications. It has separate address spaces for program and

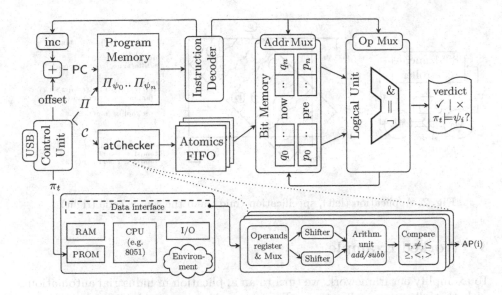

Fig. 1. μMonitor (top), atChecker (bottom right), and the SUT (bottom left)

data memory, i.e., represents a Harvard architecture. The data memory consists of two registers, one holding the evaluations (true, false) of all subformulae of the formula ψ in the current execution cycle $q[0 \dots n]$ and one the results of the previous cycle $p[0 \dots n]$. All bits in the data memory are directly addressable. The program memory, in turn, is partitioned into n sections, each holding a program $\pi_\psi \in \Pi$ compiled from ψ. The host computer selects an individual program by setting an offset that is added to the current program counter. This easily allows to change the specification on-the-fly, e.g., whenever a new test-case is loaded.

Each program π_ψ is executed in cycles. A cycle starts with the first address belonging to π_ψ and ends when the last instruction was executed. At the end of a cycle, the verdict is updated to indicate whether ψ holds up to the current state of the program. The start of a cycle is triggered whenever any of the APs change their truth values. To illustrate, consider again $\psi : \uparrow (\text{foo} = 20) \Rightarrow \text{bar} \leq 50$. A cycle of π_ψ is triggered iff [foo = 20] or [bar $\leq$ 50] toggle their truth values.

The *instruction set* features 16 opcodes to handle the ptLTL operators, where each opcode is three bytes long. An instruction decoder allows to address individual bits in the data memory and set the operator for the *logical unit*. A multi-way multiplexer (the logical unit) connects bits, originating from either $p[0 \dots n]$ or $q[0 \dots n]$, with a Boolean operator $op \in \{\neg, \wedge, \vee\}$ and transfers the result back to memory. The whole framework results in an efficient hardware design. The μMonitor unit synthesizes down to 367 logic cells (with $f_{max} = 145\,\text{MHz}$) and a single atChecker unit to 290 logic cells (with $f_{max} = 80\,\text{MHz}$) on an Altera Cyclone III EP3C16 FPGA device. By way of comparison, the Intel MCS-51 core consumes roughly 4000 logic cells on the same device and runs at clock speed of up to 16 MHz.

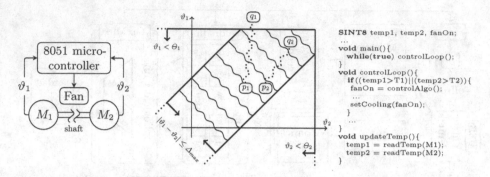

Fig. 2. Application (left), specification (mid), and the source code (right)

3   Worked Example

To exemplify our framework, we turn to an application in industrial automation with the following specification: "The program under scrutiny is a digital controller implementation controlling the temperature of two DC motors M_1 and M_2 by driving a fan. The motors have a maximum operating temperature Θ_1 and Θ_2, respectively. The target application continuously reads the current operating temperatures ϑ_1 and ϑ_2. The applications invokes cooling whenever either $\vartheta_1 > T_{on_1}$ or $\vartheta_2 > T_{on_2}$. To avoid damage of the motors along with functional deficiency, the fan needs to be turned on before the temperature of the motors reaches their critical temperature. Both motors operate on the same shaft, thus, an additional sanity check is that the absolute temperature difference $|\vartheta_1 - \vartheta_2|$ remains within Δ_{max}, otherwise, we could assume that one of the motors is blocking while the other needs to apply an unusually high torque."

The implementation consists of approx. 250 lines of C (compiled with Keil μVision3). An outline of the code structure is shown in Fig. 2 (right). The function updateTemp() is periodically called from a timer interrupt, whereas controlAlgorithm() holds the controller implementation. Intuitively, the different temperature bounds describe four hyper-planes as shown in Fig. 2 (mid). Consider the temperature pattern from $\boxed{p_1}$ to $\boxed{q_1}$. The controlLoop turns on the cooling in $\boxed{p_1}$ after one of the thresholds is reached. After returning from controlAlgorithm() and turning on the fan, the temperatures are already at $\boxed{q_1}$, violating the temperature requirement of M_1. However, the pattern from $\boxed{p_2}$ to $\boxed{q_2}$ is valid wrt. the specification as the temperature curve never leaves the hatched area until the fan is turned on. It is thus straightforward to come up with the specification:

$$\psi : \mathsf{Inv}(|\vartheta_1 - \vartheta_2| \leq \Delta_{max}) \quad \bigwedge$$
$$\uparrow (\mathsf{fanOn} = \mathsf{\#F\_ON}) \Rightarrow [\vartheta_1 > T_{on_1} \vee \vartheta_2 > T_{on_2} ; \ \vartheta_1 \geq \Theta_1 \vee \vartheta_2 \geq \Theta_2)_s$$

The symbols ϑ_1 and ϑ_2 in ψ refer to the variables temp1 and temp2. ψ requires that: (a) The absolute temperature difference between M_1 and M_2 shall never be greater than Δ_{max} and (b) whenever the fan is turned on then one of the motor temperatures exceeded its threshold in the past, and since then none of the temperatures exceeded its critical temperature. Inv stands for *invariant*, i.e., holds in every state, ↑ means *rising* (false in the previous state but true in the current), and $[p; q)_s$ is the *strong interval operator* [7] (q was never true since the last time p was observed to be true, including the state when p was true). The bounds are set to $\Delta_{max} = 40°C$, $T_{on_1} = 30°C$, $T_{on_2} = 35°C$, $\Theta_1 = 100°C$, and $\Theta_2 = 90°C$. For ψ, the host application generates a program consisting of 13 instructions for the μMonitor and a configuration to evaluate the 7 APs of ψ for the atChecker. The application as well as the monitor execute at full clock rate.

4 Concluding Discussion

This paper presents a custom-designed μCPU unit for non-intrusive runtime monitoring of ptLTL. The μCPU as well as hardware circuits for checking APs are wiretapped to an FPGA running the target hardware. The force of this approach is that the μCPU can be reprogrammed dynamically, depending on the specification to be checked, whereas previous approaches evaluated formulae using fixed hardware circuits, which is clearly not as flexible. In contrast to software-based solutions such as TEMPORAL ROVER [3], JPAX [5], or RMOR [6], our framework does not require instrumentation. Existing hardware-based approaches [2, 9] require sophisticated monitoring devices, whereas our framework simply wiretaps the microcontroller's memory on an FPGA. Future work will be the integration of our framework with binary code analysis frameworks that generate the actual test cases, rather than using randomly generated executions as done currently.

References

1. Belinfante, A., Frantzen, L., Schallhart, C.: 14 Tools for Test Case Generation. In: Broy, M., Jonsson, B., Katoen, J.-P., Leucker, M., Pretschner, A. (eds.) Model-Based Testing of Reactive Systems. LNCS, vol. 3472, pp. 391–438. Springer, Heidelberg (2005)
2. Chen, F., Roşu, G.: MOP: An efficient and generic runtime verification framework. In: OOPSLA, pp. 569–588. ACM (2007)
3. Drusinsky, D.: The Temporal Rover and the ATG Rover. In: Havelund, K., Penix, J., Visser, W. (eds.) SPIN 2000. LNCS, vol. 1885, pp. 323–330. Springer, Heidelberg (2000)
4. Emerson, E.A.: Temporal and modal logic. In: Handbook of Theoretical Computer Science, vol. B, pp. 995–1072. MIT Press (1990)
5. Havelund, K., Roşu, G.: An Overview of the Runtime Verification Tool Java PathExplorer. Form. Methods Syst. Des. 24(2), 189–215 (2004)
6. Havelund, K.: Runtime Verification of C Programs. In: Suzuki, K., Higashino, T., Ulrich, A., Hasegawa, T. (eds.) TestCom/FATES 2008. LNCS, vol. 5047, pp. 7–22. Springer, Heidelberg (2008)

7. Havelund, K., Roşu, G.: Synthesizing Monitors for Safety Properties. In: Katoen, J.-P., Stevens, P. (eds.) TACAS 2002. LNCS, vol. 2280, pp. 342–356. Springer, Heidelberg (2002)
8. Reinbacher, T., Brauer, J., Horauer, M., Steininger, A., Kowalewski, S.: Past Time LTL Runtime Verification for Microcontroller Binary Code. In: Salaün, G., Schätz, B. (eds.) FMICS 2011. LNCS, vol. 6959, pp. 37–51. Springer, Heidelberg (2011)
9. Tsai, J.J.P., Fang, K.Y., Chen, H.Y., Bi, Y.D.: A Noninterference Monitoring and Replay Mechanism for Real-Time Software Testing and Debugging. IEEE Trans. Softw. Eng. 16, 897–916 (1990)

What Is My Program Doing?
Program Dynamics in Programmer's Terms

Steven P. Reiss and Alexander Tarvo

Department of Computer Science, Brown University, Providence RI
{spr,alexta}@cs.brown.edu

Abstract. Programmers need to understand their systems. They need to understand how their systems work and why they fail; why they perform well or poorly, and when the systems are behaving abnormally. Much of this involves understanding the dynamic behavior of complex software systems. These systems can involve multiple processes and threads, thousands of classes, and millions of lines of code. These systems are designed to run continuously, often running for months at a time. We consider the problem of using dynamic analysis and visualization to help programmers achieve the necessary understanding. To be effective this needs to be done on running applications with minimal overhead and in the high-level terms programmers use to think about their system. After going over past efforts in this area we look at our current work and then present a number of challenges for the future.

Keywords: program understanding, visualization.

1 Introduction

Today's software is complex. It involves multiple threads and processes, complex locking behavior, large code bases, nondeterminism, and long-running systems. It is often reactive, responding to external or user events in an asynchronous manner. The software is often written by teams of programmers, uses a variety of external libraries, and interacts asynchronously with existing hardware and software. Understanding the static structure of several millions of lines of code is a daunting task. Understanding the dynamic behavior of complex interacting systems is often worse.

The goal of our research is to provide programmers with an understanding of the dynamics of their complex systems. While there are a wide variety of tools for analysis and understanding the static structure of software systems, there are few tools for understanding the dynamic behavior. Moreover, these tools are generally inadequate for dealing with today's systems and the actual problems that programmers face. To fully appreciate why this is so, we need to understand why programmers want to understand the dynamics of their systems, what understanding really means, how current tools address the issues, and why programmers don't use these tools.

S. Khurshid and K. Sen (Eds.): RV 2011, LNCS 7186, pp. 245–259, 2012.

There are several reasons for looking at and trying to understand the behavior of today's software. The simplest is just to understand what is happening. This can be a prelude to rewriting the system, to adding new features, or simply to verify that the system behaves correctly. Another reason is to understand unusual behavior such as performance problems, bugs that only show up occasionally and are difficult to reproduce, or locking problems. A third reason is to facilitate system evolution and maintenance. Here programmers might want to know what triggers certain behaviors of the system or what might happen if a portion of the code changes. They might also want to understand how setting various system parameters such as the number of threads in a thread pool or the number of active connections might affect system behavior, effectively asking "what if" questions about their systems.

What does it mean for programmers to understand their systems? As programmers, we want to understand the system in our terms. We typically have a model of the system in our heads and want to understand the system in terms of that model. While that model might correspond to the actual system, more likely it represents an abstraction of the system. This might be the simple high-level model of the system; it might be the more complex model that was used initially but became obscured in the process of translating the design into code; or it might be a skewed model of a programmer who only knows one portion of the system and effectively abstracts away all others.

Programmers also need to understand their system's behavior as it happens. When abnormal behavior occurs, they want to correlate it with the external events that are currently happening; when the program seems to be running slowly, they need to look at its behavior right then and there.

Finally, programmers need to understand real problems in real systems. They need to understand the behavior of long-running production systems when the requisite behaviors only arise occasionally and can't be easily reproduced. They need to understand interactive systems and still have those systems interact.

Our research attempts to build tools that satisfy these goals. We want tools that describe the system in the programmers terms. We want tools that work on production systems in real time. Moreover, we want a variety of tools to address the different types of problems that programmers face. Most importantly, however, we want tools that will actually be used.

2   Examples

Every programmer working on complex systems faces run time problems. While many of these problems are simple, the more complex problems are the most interesting ones. Below we describe some of the problems that we have encountered over the past several years. These problems serve in part as our motivation for dynamic analysis tools.

One simple program we wrote as a prelude to a class project, was a multithreaded web crawler. It kept a queue of URLs to look at, and had a pool of threads each of which would repeatedly take an URL off the queue, get the corresponding page, process the page, save the results, and possibly add more URLs to the queue. We had two basic problems with the system. The first was deciding what is the optimum number of threads for a machine with a given number of CPU cores. The second problem was that the system would occasionally (every five minutes or so), pause; all the threads would either be waiting or doing I/O and no work would be done. While this could have been due to the time to access a web page, but with 32 or 64 threads it seemed unlikely to be the case. Analysis with our preliminary tools showed that the bottleneck was in accessing robots.txt files to determine if pages should be crawled or not.

A somewhat more complex system involved a peer-to-peer network designed for Internet-scale programming [21]. We still have two outstanding problems on this system that we eventually hope to use dynamic analysis to solve. The first problem occurs rarely, generally after the system has been running for a month or two. Here one of the nodes will suddenly run out of memory for no apparent reason. The second problem occurs sometimes where there are severe network glitches that affect multiple nodes. In this case, the ring of nodes in the network becomes malformed.

Another system we have does a gravity-based simulation of large numbers of particles. This system was originally written as single threaded but was then retrofitted to work with multiple threads. The problem here is that we are only getting about half of the expected speed up. Detailed analysis using our tools showed that we did a good job of parallelizing the gravity computations, but a poor job of parallelizing the task of adding up the forces.

A web service we built does semantics based-code search [26]. The server for this is uses multiple thread pools (for getting source, for doing code transformations, and for testing) with overlapping threads. The system can easily consider tens or hundreds of thousands of potential solutions for a particular request. We had two problems here for which we used our dynamic analysis tools. The first involved excessive memory use, with the system using over 24G of memory to process what we though was a moderately complex request. The second was that when the server got multiple requests, it seemed to only handle one at a time.

Our current work is centered around the Code Bubbles programming environment. This is a multithreaded user interface for programming that runs Eclipse as a background process. It uses a message bus and has separate processes running to deal with version management and testing.

The workings of this system can be quite complex. Even something as simple and common as typing a character into an editor is difficult to understand. Typing a character edits the underlying document; changes to the document result in callbacks that update the document structure to reflect the updated line, send a message to Eclipse describing the edit, update the caret position, update the locations of annotations (e.g. breakpoints), and update the editor's title bar (in case the edit changed the name of the method). At some point, Eclipse sends back two messages which are processed by separate threads. One describes the modified syntax tree for the method being edited, which then has to be analyzed to update the document structure a second time. Another contains the set of error and warning messages for the changed file which affect annotations in the editor as well as the display of tokens. These messages will not be sent if there is another edit within a given time limit. Moreover, additional message with errors for other files might also be sent. Changes to the editor document or new error messages will generate repaint requests which then result in a recomputation of line reflows and line elisions, which might require updating the location of annotations on the side of the editor. This process is complicated in that the document for an editor on a single method is actually a virtual document referring to another document for the file containing the method; in that both documents require read/write locking; in that messages from Eclipse are handled by a thread pool and queue; and in that much of the work is done through vaguely ordered callbacks registered on the documents, Eclipse messages, or Java Swing.

In working with this system we have had and continue to have a wide range of dynamic problems. One outstanding problem is that occasionally, there will be an access to the structured view of an editor document that has invalid positions. This happens infrequently and under a variety of different conditions. We presume this is a timing problem, but haven't been able to understand the exact sequence of events that leads to it. In addition to this, we have encountered (and hopefully fixed) a variety of locking problems, most of which involved complex interactions of java locks both in our code and in the Java libraries, the read/write locks implemented for Swing documents, and messages to Eclipse that require responses. Another set of problems that are timing dependent are display anomalies, for example the squiggle under an undefined identifier, that sometimes don't go away until the user moves the mouse or does more editing. Another set of issues we have and continue to deal with are performance problems. Typing text at the editor, even as complex as it is, is now fast enough. However, the system seems to occasionally pause for no apparent reason (we blame Eclipse, but that's probably wrong), and some operations such as selecting an identifier occasionally take much longer than expected.

3   Current Tools

Dynamic program understanding is a topic of continuing interest to developers. A good survey of work in this area can be found in [4]. Our own efforts over the past twenty-five years are a significant part of this [24].

3.1   Related Current Work

A variety of techniques are being used to help programmers understand the behavior of their systems. Run time anomaly detection techniques treat bugs as anomalies and use programming rules, either explicitly specified by the user [5] or automatically extracted using statistical, mining techniques [11], [13] to cross-check their presence.

Thereska collects dynamic information in order to predict program behavior of complex distributed services consisting of multiple interacting processes

and I/O systems under different circumstances [34]. Ko's Whyline collects trace
data during a program run and then lets the user ask questions about specific
behaviors that are answered from the trace [9].

Barham and Isaacs use Magpie for request extraction and workload modeling [2]. Magpie builds the model of the software using existing instrumentation
mechanisms in the OS and the applications being analyzed, with the data points
being chosen manually. A similar framework is used by Hellerstein in the ETE
system, with manual instrumentation used to define event probes. Their output is then glued together to form a request using a user-provided schema [7].
The resultant request is visualized and the visualization can be used to detect
problems such as bottlenecks in the application.

Aguilera, et al. does performance analysis of large distributed systems built
from legacy components by monitoring network traffic between the components
[1]. This work builds a call tree among the system components and annotates
each node with the expected time for processing. BorderPatrol takes a similar
approach, but uses a variety of instrumentation techniques to isolate particular
messages and their corresponding processing [10].

Chen's Pinpoint system uses instrumentation and a statistical framework to
look for path-based models of programs [3]. Software health management uses a
formal definition of normal behavior and then uses techniques such as Bayesian
analysis and fault trees to detect anomalies [33]. Widely used programs can be
also monitored statistically [14].

Program analysis is also used for performance prediction. Pace uses static
analysis to infer a control flow of a parallel or distributed program that uses
MPI or PVM for communication, and then generates its analytical performance
model [15]. The Same system relies on program traces to construct performance
models of message passing programs using a layered queuing network [8].

Another technique used for performance prediction is statistical modeling.
Gupta et al. uses classifiers to predict query running times in DBMS [6]. Lee et
al. used non-linear regressions and neural networks to predict the running time
of scientific computing applications on the grid [12].

3.2   Our Work on Dynamic Analysis

Our early work on Garden [17], and Field [18] attempted to illustrate program
dynamics by showing program execution in terms of source constructs. In Field,
this was extended to show execution in more abstract terms, using both call
graph and class hierarchy displays to show what is currently executing. Field
also included views to look at I/O activity, memory behavior, and both general
and line-specific performance as the program executed.

Our first attempt at dynamic monitoring and model building was with the
Bloom system [29]. Here we collected full traces of multithreaded C/C++ and
Java systems on a variety of platforms. The trace data was analyzed off-line to
build a variety of probabilistic finite-state and context-free models of program

behavior mainly for the purpose of program visualization. We also used the trace data to find event handlers in the code based on dynamic behavior, and then to trace and model transactions [19]. Finally, we used control flow traces from C programs as a means for fault localization [32], [31].

The off-line approach that we took in Bloom is quite common among dynamic analysis tools. It has several advantages. First, the tool can have access to a large amount of potential information by collecting a broad range of detailed trace data. Second, the displays and the underlying analysis can be more sophisticated since they don't have to be done in real time as the program executes. Third, once the run is complete, programmers can use the resultant visualization at their leisure, spending time appropriate to understanding their problem. An industrial example of such a system is Jinsight [16].

Having worked on and with such tools, we have come to the conclusion that they are not going to work for the types of problems and programs we want to address. There are several reasons for this. First, these tools tend to generate a significant amount of trace data. The cost of generating and storing this data

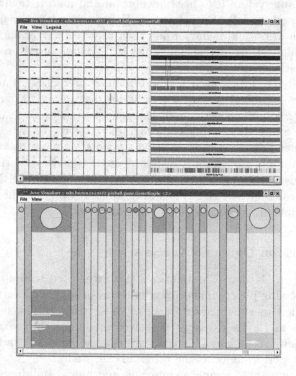

Fig. 1. Jive and Jove dynamic visualizations. The first window shows Jive with the lefthand panel shows execution time and allocations by class or package; the right hand panel shows thread activity and interactions. The second window shows Jove which provides line-level usage information for the classes in a system.

significantly slows the execution of the program, making it difficult to analyze programs that are interactive and long running. Second, because the trace files are large, the analyses that need to be done can also take a significant amount of time; the cost of just getting to the point of being able to see the analysis is high and is discouraging to potential users. Third, the tools typically model the whole run and show the result after execution is over. This makes it difficult for the user to correlate a particular external event with the analysis or even to remember what was going on at a point where the analysis might look interesting. Fourth, the collection of large amounts of trace data tends to significantly perturb the behavior of the program, making problems involving timing, threads, or process interaction difficult to reproduce.

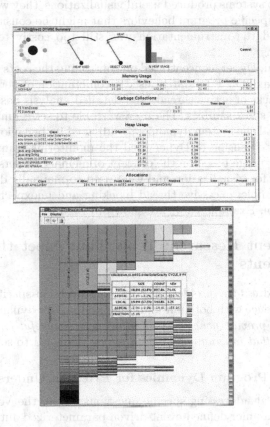

Fig. 2. Dyper visualizations. The first window shows a performance analysis summary, with the dots showing different performance aspects and their priorities; the gauges showing detailed information about what is currently happening, and the bottom details providing summary information. The second window shows a summary of memory ownership information, with color showing the classes that are using most of the space and the right hand bar showing usage over time.

Our next attempt at dynamic analysis tried to overcome the complexities and difficulties of full tracing. Here we developed two systems, Jive and Jove, shown in Figure 1, that provided dynamic information about program behavior as the program ran. Jive provided an overview of the number of method calls and allocations by class, and time view of thread state changes and thread blocking interactions [20]. Jove provided basic-block level execution counts [30]. Both operated by accumulating data over a short time interval and only reporting summary data. They were able to run without slowing the application by more than a factor of two. In addition to providing dynamic visualizations of the above information, we did on-line analysis of the data to build a program phase model [22] where we demonstrated the ability to dynamically detect phases using the accumulated information as a statistical model.

While these two systems produced useful visualizations, they were not detailed enough to model specific program behaviors that might be considered abnormal or interesting, and the instrumentation was still too costly to be used with production systems.

Our next system, Dyper, concentrated on controlling the costs associated with dynamic monitoring [25]. This system used a combination of periodically exam- inations of the stacks of active threads and detailed analysis based on problems detected from the stack samples. The user was able to set a limit on the moni- toring overhead and the system dynamically adjusted its behavior to stay within this limit. A later extension of Dyper used the monitoring framework to build models of memory usage based on the concept of memory ownership [27]. Dyper models were built for visualization and were used to manually detect abnormal behaviors, for example, excessive thread blocking and unexpected or excessive memory utilization. Example views are shown in Figure 2.

4   Our Current Research: Tools That Meet the Requirements

Dyper did not address the problem of collecting question-specific information. Indeed, our experience with both our and other systems for dynamic analysis was that *generic tools provide generic results that are not useful for answering the specific questions that programmers actually have.* This led to several projects.

4.1   Analyzing Program Dynamics for Program Understanding

Our first attempt at addressing specific questions was in the Veld system [23]. In Veld, the programmer defined event-driven parameterized automata that de- scribed the expected program behavior. Veld would then instrument the program with a small set of high-level calls corresponding to the programmer's defined events, and then monitor instances of the defined automata dynamically, both to visualize the program and to detect unexpected behavior.

The problem with the approach taken in Veld was that the program models were difficult for the programmer to define and get right. Many of the behaviors of interest to the programmer do not correspond directly to simply defined events. Programmers often have models of program behavior that are not directly reflected in the underlying code. Finally, while we were able to construct some relatively complex models (with 20-30 events and a corresponding set of states), we noted that the actual program models are significantly more complex, often involving a hundred or more events and automata that are too complex for the programmer to easily create or understand.

As a result of this analysis, we built a successor system, Dyview, based on the monitoring technology provided by Dyper [28]. Dyview addressed a limited goal, understanding the behavior of threads, transactions and tasks in an event-based system. The notions of transaction and task are flexible to accommodate many type of applications and to provide differing views of those applications based on programmer needs. Typically *transactions* correspond to requests in the program, while *tasks* are actions performed to process transactions.

Dyview first asks programmers to specify the class or set of classes that represent transactions, any classes they want to explicitly consider as separate tasks,

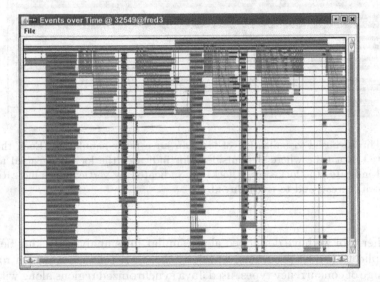

Fig. 3. Visualization of the search server in action. The scroll bar on the bottom allows the user to select the time span to be visualized. The scroll bar on the right lets the users restrict the display to different threads. Each row in the display corresponds to a thread in the application. Colored bars in the rows indicate processing. The outside colors of the bar represent the transaction being processed. The inside color represents the task. Gray lines show where tasks are created and then first used. This particular visualization illustrates a problem with the search server in dealing with multiple transactions simultaneously. For the latter half of the time, there are always two transactions being processed at once. However, the processing shows that most of the time one transaction dominates and the other can make little progress.

and any classes that represent specific threads of interest. It then uses a combination of static and dynamic analysis to find the event handlers, task and transaction processing points, and significant processing events in the tasks. Finally, Dyview associates thread activity with a corresponding transaction and, optionally, with a task. This analysis is done *automatically* without user intervention. Its results are used to build a simple model of program behavior, which, in turn, is used to derive an appropriate set of high-level instrumentation points. Information collected by instrumentation is used to visualize program execution in terms of threads, transactions and tasks. An example can be seen in Figure 3. Dyview's visualizations have been used to answer difficult run time problems such as unexpected behaviors, poor thread performance, and unusual interactions between transactions in a variety of event-based systems.

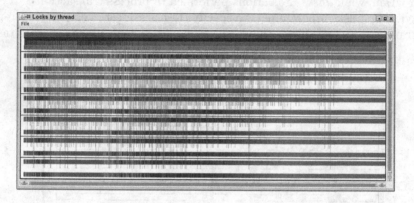

Fig. 4. Thread-based visualization of locks in an n-body simulation. Each thread is represented as a tube where the outside color indicates the lock being used and the inside fill indicates the lock state. Blocks are indicated by vertical lines indicating the from (green) thread and to (red) thread.

Another tool we have developed along similar lines analyzes locking behavior in an application. Java programs, especially those written before Java introduced a full range of concurrency types, used Java synchronized regions along with wait and notify to implement a variety of high-level lock types such as semaphores and barriers. Our system uses the JVMTI for low-overhead instrumentation of locking operations in an application. It then does an off-line analysis of the resultant trace to find those locks which play a significant part in the application and to characterize those locks as mutexes, semaphores, delays, barriers, producer-consumer locks, read-write locks, latches, and conditional locks according to their use. Then it does byte-code instrumentation of the application using the locking information to track and then visualize the use of locks as the application is run. An example can be seen in Figure 4.

4.2   Analyzing Program Dynamics for Performance Prediction

Currently, we are working on a more ambitious effort that combines static and dynamic analysis in an attempt to build performance prediction models. These models will predict performance of various multithreaded applications based on values of their configuration parameters. Parameters include configuration options of the program such as the number of working threads and workload characteristics, parameters of the OS such as limits on the number of file descriptors and the type of I/O scheduler, and parameters of the hardware such as the number of CPU cores and hard drive and network performance.

Building such models by hand is difficult. The models must simulate functioning of the system on various levels, including the program itself, the underlying OS, and the hardware. Although certain components of the system, such as hard drives or networking can be simulated by analytical or statistical models, computer programs are much more diverse in their structure and behavior. They must be simulated with more sophisticated modeling techniques, such as stochastic automata and queuing networks. To be useful, such models must be also built automatically.

Our automatic approach to generating these models involves a combination of static and dynamic analysis. We start by using static analysis to find information on hierarchy of classes and packages, information on types (types of class fields, global fields, local variables, and the types allocated by each method), and synchronization information.

Next we run the program and collect stack samples using the low-overhead instrumentation. Stack samples are used to build a trie that contains all the paths detected during the program's execution. The trie is then analyzed off-line to find thread pools; routines that represent callbacks (which can be either calls to user code from system routines or calls from a low level of the package hierarchy to a higher level); event handlers (routines that are invoked after data is read or after a wait); and significant program states. Program states are defined as a particular region of the program and are flagged either as a CPU-bound, I/O bound, or WAIT-bound state.

Using data from both the static and dynamic analysis, we next determine what user objects represent transactions. Transactions objects correspond to requests in the program; they are accessible from event handlers and callbacks and are central to building the model. Currently we can automatically determine only candidate classes that might represent transactions, and we let the user select the appropriate classes from the set of candidates.

Once we know the transactions classes, we instrument the byte code of the program and run it again to generate a more detailed view of program's execution. This view contains a per-thread trace of all uses of event handlers, callbacks, synchronization routines, and program states. We also instrument the OS kernel to obtain data on I/O operations initiated by the program. We use this data to define properties of I/O-bound program states, which include number and properties of the disk I/O requests for each state. Because the set of items traced is selective, this new round of instrumentation can also be done with relatively low overhead.

The generated trace is then analyzed off-line to actually build the model. This includes determining the types and parameters of synchronization mechanisms that exist in the program, finding the transition diagram between program states, determining computation requirements for CPU-bound states, and associating wait states with the corresponding synchronization calls.

5   Challenges

Dynamic analysis is useful only if it is used. While the research community has produced many dynamic analysis tools, they are generally not being used by programmers to investigate complex run time bugs or unexpected behaviors. The primary reason for this is that programmers will learn and use only those tools that can answer *real* questions about *real* systems in a way that is more effective and more efficient than existing tools such as debuggers or print statements. The mission of our community should be to develop this kind of analysis tools.

This is a multipart problem. We first have to be able to address real systems, especially those systems where programmers are likely to have problems. This means our tools have to address production systems that may run for days or weeks before showing the unexpected behavior; systems that involve multiple communicating processes each of which involves multiple threads. Designing tools that can handle yesterday's simpler systems won't work. We need to think about tools that can handle tomorrow's systems.

The key challenges here are devising very efficient and lightweight dynamic analysis, coordinating dynamic analysis from multiple threads and multiple processes, doing automatic instrumentation, automatically building high-level models of systems that match the programmers models, and determining how to use sampling and heuristic techniques to infer detailed information from sparse input.

The second part of the problem involves addressing real questions. Most current dynamic tools provide information about the system at a fixed level, typically at the level provided by either the underlying system or by the programming language. For example, tools for Java locking look at locking in terms of Java's synchronized regions. Similarly, tools for performance analysis look at performance in terms of code blocks or methods executed.

Programmers, however, tend to work with the higher-level abstractions they used to design and code the system. For example, instead of synchronized regions, they might think in terms of the semaphores, producer-consumer locks, or read-write locks that they implemented and treat as primitives in their code. Similarly, rather than looking at performance of individual blocks and methods, they want to understand performance of individual transactions and tasks, where a task is typically a programmer-defined concept.

Moreover, the actual questions that programmers have about run time behavior of their systems do not fall into nice, simple categories that can be addressed easily by a single tool. Examples of such questions presented in Section 2 are quite diverse and require different types of analysis and different levels of modeling. A useful tool suite will need to handle a wide variety of problems and be able to map those problems into the abstractions that the programmer actually uses.

The challenges here involve mapping low level information to an appropriate level of abstraction; obtaining a wide variety of different types of information, possibly using the same information sources; combining appropriate static and dynamic analyses along with heuristics; and determining what types of information might be the most relevant to the programmer.

The next problem here is producing a tool that is effective and easy to use from the programmer's perspective. Programmers typically know that they have a run time problem and have some sense of what information they might need to understand the unexpected or abnormal behavior. However, they think of that problem in terms of higher-level abstractions they used in developing and working on that application. An effective tool needs to elicit this information from the programmer in terms the programmer can easily express and understand.

Just as important, an effective tool needs to provide output in a way that actually addresses the programmers' problems. This means providing output in high level terms that clearly distinguishes the abnormal behavior that is interesting to a programmer.

The challenges here involve building models of the types of problems that programmers are likely to have and then parameterizing these models in ways that make it easy for the programmer to state their problem. They also include creating visualizations and other data presentations that can show the large amounts of data while highlighting the cases that are of interest. Finally, they involve building heuristics, possibly with the help of the programmer, that would allow the system to sift through the dynamic information that is gathered to determine what is actually relevant to the programmer.

Acknowledgements. Our current work is funded by NSF grant CCF1130822, and support from Microsoft and Google.

References

1. Aguilera, M.K., Mogul, J.C., Wiener, J.L., Reynolds, P., Muthitacharoen, A.: Performance debugging for distributed systems of black boxes. In: SOSP 2003, pp. 74–89 (October 2003)
2. Barham, P., Donnelly, A., Isaacs, R., Mortier, R.: Using magpie for request extraction and workload modelling. In: Proceedings of the Sixth USENIX Symposium on Operating Systems Design and Implementation (OSDI) (December 2004)
3. Chen, M.Y., Accardi, A., Kiciman, E., Lloyd, J., Patterson, D., Fox, A., Brewer, E.: Path-based failure and evolution management. In: NSDI 2004 (2004)

4. Cornelissen, B., Zaidman, A., van Deursen, A., Moonen, L., Koschke, R.: A systematic survey of program comprehension through dynamic analysis. Technical Report TUD-SERG-2008-033, Delft University of Technology (2008)

5. Engler, D., Chen, D.Y., Hallem, S., Chou, A., Chelf, B.: Bugs as deviant behavior: a general approach to inferring errors in systems code. In: Proc. 18th ACM Symp. on Operating Systems Principles, pp. 57–72 (2001)

6. Gupta, C., Mehta, A., Dayal, U.: PQR: predicting query execution times for autonomous workload management. In: Proceedings of the 2008 International Conference on Autonomic Computing, pp. 13–22 (June 2008)

7. Hellerstein, J.L., Maccabee, M., Mills, W.N., Turek, J.J.: ETE: a customizable approach to measuring end-to-end response times and their components in distributed systems. In: International Conference on Distributed Computing Systems (1999)

8. Israr, T.A., Lau, D.H., Franks, G., Woodside, M.: Automatic generation of layered queuing software performance models from commonly available traces. In: Proceedings of the 5th International Workshop on Software and Performance, pp. 147–158 (July 2005)

9. Ko, A.J., Myers, B.A.: Debugging reinvented: asking and answering why and why not questions about program behavior. In: ICSE 2008, pp. 301–310 (May 2008)

10. Koskinen, E., Jannotti, J.: Borderpatrol: isolating events for black-box tracing. In: EuroSys 2008, pp. 191–203 (2008)

11. Kremenek, T., Twohey, P., Back, G., Ng, A.Y., Engler, D.: From uncertainty to belief: inferring the specification within. In: Proc. OSDI 2006, pp. 161–176 (2006)

12. Lee, B.C., Brooks, D.M., de Supinski, B.R., Schulz, M., Singh, K., McKee, S.A.: Methods of inference and learning for performance modeling of parallel applications. In: Proceedings of the 12th ACM SIGPLAN Symposium on Principles and Practice of Parallel Programming (March 2007)

13. Li, Z., Zhou, Y.: PR-miner: automatically extracting implicit programming rules and detecting violations in large software code. In: Proc. ESEC/FSE 2005, pp. 306–315 (September 2005)

14. Liblit, B., Aiken, A., Zheng, A.X., Jordan, M.I.: Bug isolation via remote program sampling. In: PDLI 2003, pp. 141–154 (June 2003)

15. Nudd, G.R., Kerbyson, D.J., Papaefstathiou, E., Perry, S.C., Harper, J.S., Wilcox, D.V.: Pace - a toolset for the performance prediction of parallel and distributed systems. International Journal of High Performance Computing Applications 14(3), 228–251 (2000)

16. De Pauw, W., Kimelman, D., Vlissides, J.: Visualizing object-oriented software execution. In: Stasko, J., Domingue, J., Brown, M.H., Price, B.A. (eds.) Software Visualization: Programming as a Multimedia Experience, pp. 329–346. MIT Press (1998)

17. Reiss, S.P.: Working in the garden environment for conceptual programming. IEEE Software 4(6), 16–27 (1987)

18. Reiss, S.P.: FIELD: A Friendly Integrated Environment for Learning and Development. Kluwer (1994)

19. Reiss, S.P.: Event-based performance analysis. In: Proc. 11th IEEE Intl. Workshop on Program Comprehension, pp. 74–81 (2003)

20. Reiss, S.P.: Visualizing java in action. In: Proc. IEEE International Conference on Software Visualization, pp. 123–132 (2003)

21. Reiss, S.P.: A component model for internet-scale applications. In: Proc. ASE 2005, pp. 34–43 (November 2005)

22. Reiss, S.P.: Dynamic detection and visualization of software phases. In: Proc. Third International Workshop on Dynamic Analysis (May 2005)
23. Reiss, S.P.: Visualizing program execution using user abstractions. In: SOFTVIS 2006, pp. 125–134 (September 2006)
24. Reiss, S.P.: Visual representations of executing programs. Journal of Visual Languages and Computing 18(2), 126–148 (2007)
25. Reiss, S.P.: Tracking source locations. In: Proc. ICSE 2008, pp. 11–20 (May 2008)
26. Reiss, S.P.: Semantics-based code search. In: ICSE 2009, pp. 243–253 (May 2009)
27. Reiss, S.P.: Visualizing the java heap to detect memory problems. In: Proc. VIS-SOFT 2009, pp. 73–80 (September 2009)
28. Reiss, S.P., Karumuri, S.: Visualizing threads, transactions, and tasks. In: PASTE 2010, pp. 9–16 (June 2010)
29. Reiss, S.P., Renieris, M.: Languages for dynamic instrumentation. In: Proc. WODA 2003, ICSE Workshop on Dynamic Analysis, pp. 41–45 (2003)
30. Reiss, S.P., Renieris, M.: JOVE: Java as it happens. In: Proc. SoftVis 2005, pp. 115–124 (May 2005)
31. Renieris, M.: A Research Framework for Software-Fault Localization Tools. Ph.D. dissertation, Department of Computer Science, Brown University (2005)
32. Renieris, M., Reiss, S.P.: Fault localization with nearest neighbor queries. In: Proc. 18th Intl. Conf. on Automated Software Engineering, pp. 30–39 (2003)
33. Schumann, J., Mengshoel, O.J., Srivastava, A.N., Darwiche, A.: Towards software health management with bayesian networks. In: Proceedings of the FSE/SDP Workshop on Future of Software Engineering Research (FoSER 2010), pp. 331–336 (2010)
34. Thereska, E., Salmon, B., Strunk, J., Wachs, M., Abd-El-Malek, M., Lopex, J., Granger, G.R.: Stardust: tracking activity in a distributed sotrage system. In: Proc. SIGMETRICS 2006 (June 2006)

Algorithms for Monitoring Real-Time Properties*,**

David Basin, Felix Klaedtke, and Eugen Zălinescu

Computer Science Department, ETH Zurich, Switzerland

Abstract. We present and analyze monitoring algorithms for a safety fragment of metric temporal logics, which differ in their underlying time model. The time models considered have either dense or discrete time domains and are point-based or interval-based. Our analysis reveals differences and similarities between the time models for monitoring and highlights key concepts underlying our and prior monitoring algorithms.

1 Introduction

Real-time logics [2] allow us to specify system properties involving timing constraints, e.g., every request must be followed within 10 seconds by a grant. Such specifications are useful when designing, developing, and verifying systems with hard real-time requirements. They also have applications in runtime verification, where monitors generated from specifications are used to check the correctness of system behavior at runtime [10]. Various monitoring algorithms for real-time logics have been developed [4, 5, 7, 12, 14, 15, 17, 20] based on different time models. These time models can be characterized by two independent aspects. First, a time model is either point-based or interval-based. In point-based time models, system traces are sequences of system states, where each state is time-stamped. In interval-based time models, system traces consist of continuous (Boolean) signals of state variables. Second, a time model is either dense or discrete depending on the underlying ordering on time-points, i.e., whether there are infinitely many or finitely many time-points between any two distinct time-points.

Real-time logics based on a dense, interval-based time model are more natural and general than their counterparts based on a discrete or point-based model. In fact, both discrete and point-based time models can be seen as abstractions of dense, interval-based time models [2, 18]. However, the satisfiability and the model-checking problems for many real-time logics with the more natural time model are computationally harder than their corresponding decision problems when the time model is discrete or point-based. See the survey [16] for further discussion and examples.

In this paper, we analyze the impact of different time models on monitoring. We do this by presenting, analyzing, and comparing monitoring algorithms

---

* This work was supported by the Nokia Research Center, Switzerland.
** Due to space restrictions, some proof details have been omitted. They can be found in the full version of the paper, which is available from the authors' web pages.

S. Khurshid and K. Sen (Eds.): RV 2011, LNCS 7186, pp. 260–275, 2012.
© Springer-Verlag Berlin Heidelberg 2012

for real-time logics based on different time models. More concretely, we present monitoring algorithms for the past-only fragment of propositional metric temporal logics with a point-based and an interval-based semantics, also considering both dense and discrete time domains. We compare our algorithms on a class of formulas for which the point-based and the interval-based settings coincide. To define this class, we distinguish between event propositions and state propositions. The truth value of a state proposition always has a duration, whereas an event proposition cannot be continuously true between two distinct time-points.

Our analysis explains the impact of different time models on monitoring. First, the impact of a dense versus a discrete time domain is minor. The algorithms are essentially the same and have almost identical computational complexities. Second, monitoring in a point-based setting is simpler than in an interval-based setting. The meaning of "simpler" is admittedly informal here since we do not provide lower bounds. However, we consider our monitoring algorithms for the point-based setting as conceptually simpler than the interval-based algorithms. Moreover, we show that our point-based monitoring algorithms perform better than our interval-based algorithms on the given class of formulas on which the two settings coincide.

Overall, we see the contributions as follows. First, our monitoring algorithms simplify and clarify key concepts of previously presented algorithms [4, 13–15]. In particular, we present the complete algorithms along with a detailed complexity analysis for monitoring properties specified in the past-only fragment of propositional metric temporal logic. Second, our monitoring algorithm for the dense, point-based time model has better complexity bounds than existing algorithms for the same time model [20]. Third, our comparison of the monitoring algorithms illustrates the similarities, differences, and trade-offs between the time models with respect to monitoring. Moreover, formulas in our fragment benefit from both settings: although they describe properties based on a more natural time model, they can be monitored with respect to a point-based time model, which is more efficient.

2   Preliminaries

Time Domain and Intervals. If not stated differently, we assume the dense time domain[1] $\mathbb{T} = \mathbb{Q}_{\geq 0}$ with the standard ordering $\leq$. Adapting the following definitions to a discrete time domain like $\mathbb{N}$ is straightforward.

A *(time) interval* is a non-empty set $I \subseteq \mathbb{T}$ such that if $\tau < \kappa < \tau'$ then $\kappa \in I$, for all $\tau, \tau' \in I$ and $\kappa \in \mathbb{T}$. We denote the set of all time intervals by $\mathbb{I}$. An interval is either left-open or left-closed and similarly either right-open or right-closed. We denote the left margin and the right margin of an interval $I \in \mathbb{I}$ by $\ell(I)$ and

---

[1] We do not use $\mathbb{R}_{\geq 0}$ as dense time domain because of representation issues. Namely, each element in $\mathbb{Q}_{\geq 0}$ can be finitely represented, which is not the case for $\mathbb{R}_{\geq 0}$. Choosing $\mathbb{Q}_{\geq 0}$ instead of $\mathbb{R}_{\geq 0}$ is without loss of generality for the satisfiability of properties specified in real-time logics like the metric interval temporal logic [1].

$r(I)$, respectively. For instance, the interval $I = \{\tau \in \mathbb{T} \mid 3 \leq \tau\}$, which we also write as $[3, \infty)$, is left-closed and right-open with margins $\ell(I) = 3$ and $r(I) = \infty$.

For an interval $I \in \mathbb{I}$, we define the extension $I^{\geq} := I \cup (\ell(I), \infty)$ to the right and its strict counterpart $I^{>} := I^{\geq} \setminus I$, which excludes I. We define ${}^{\leq}I := [0, r(I)) \cup I$ and ${}^{<}I := ({}^{\leq}I) \setminus I$ similarly. An interval $I \in \mathbb{I}$ is *singular* if $|I| = 1$, *bounded* if $r(I) < \infty$, and *unbounded* if $r(I) = \infty$. The intervals $I, J \in \mathbb{I}$ are *adjacent* if $I \cap J = \emptyset$ and $I \cup J \in \mathbb{I}$. For $I, J \in \mathbb{I}$, $I \oplus J$ is the set $\{\tau + \tau' \mid \tau \in I \text{ and } \tau' \in J\}$.

An *interval partition* of $\mathbb{T}$ is a sequence $\langle I_i \rangle_{i \in N}$ of time intervals with $N = \mathbb{N}$ or $N = \{0, \ldots, n\}$ for some $n \in \mathbb{N}$ that fulfills the following properties: (i) I_{i-1} and I_i are adjacent and $\ell(I_{i-1}) \leq \ell(I_i)$, for all $i \in N \setminus \{0\}$, and (ii) for each $\tau \in \mathbb{T}$, there is an $i \in N$ such that $\tau \in I_i$. The interval partition $\langle J_j \rangle_{j \in M}$ *refines* the interval partition $\langle I_i \rangle_{i \in N}$ if for every $j \in M$, there is some $i \in N$ such that $J_j \subseteq I_i$. We often write $\bar{I}$ for a sequence of intervals instead of $\langle I_i \rangle_{i \in N}$. Moreover, we abuse notation by writing $J \in \langle I_i \rangle_{i \in N}$ if $J = I_i$, for some $i \in N$.

A *time sequence* $\langle \tau_i \rangle_{i \in \mathbb{N}}$ is a sequence of elements $\tau_i \in \mathbb{T}$ that is strictly increasing (i.e., $\tau_i < \tau_j$, for all $i, j \in \mathbb{N}$ with $i < j$) and progressing (i.e., for all $\tau \in \mathbb{T}$, there is $i \in \mathbb{N}$ with $\tau_i > \tau$). Similar to interval sequences, $\bar{\tau}$ abbreviates $\langle \tau_i \rangle_{i \in \mathbb{N}}$.

Boolean Signals. A *(Boolean) signal* γ is a subset of $\mathbb{T}$ that fulfills the following finite-variability condition: for every bounded interval $I \in \mathbb{I}$, there are intervals $I_0, \ldots, I_{n-1} \in \mathbb{I}$ such that $\gamma \cap I = I_0 \cup \cdots \cup I_{n-1}$, for some $n \in \mathbb{N}$. The least such $n \in \mathbb{N}$ is the *size* of the signal γ on I. We denote it by $\|\gamma \cap I\|$.

We use the term "signal" for such a set γ because its characteristic function $\chi_\gamma : \mathbb{T} \to \{0, 1\}$ represents, for example, the values over time of an input or an output of a sequential circuit. Intuitively, $\tau \in \gamma$ iff the signal of the circuit is high at the time $\tau \in \mathbb{T}$. The finite-variability condition imposed on the set γ prevents switching infinitely often from high to low in finite time. Note that $\|\gamma \cap I\|$ formalizes how often a signal γ is high on the bounded interval I, in particular, $\|\gamma \cap I\| = 0$ iff $\gamma \cap I = \emptyset$.

A signal γ is *stable* on an interval $I \in \mathbb{I}$ if $I \subseteq \gamma$ or $I \cap \gamma = \emptyset$. The *induced interval partition* $\overline{\mathsf{ip}}(\gamma)$ of a signal γ is the interval partition $\bar{I}$ such that γ is stable on each of the intervals in $\bar{I}$ and any other stable interval partition refines $\bar{I}$. We write $\overline{\mathsf{ip}}^1(\gamma)$ for the sequence of intervals I in $\overline{\mathsf{ip}}(\gamma)$ such that $I \cap \gamma \neq \emptyset$. Similarly, we write $\overline{\mathsf{ip}}^0(\gamma)$ for the sequence of intervals I in $\overline{\mathsf{ip}}(\gamma)$ such that $I \cap \gamma = \emptyset$. Intuitively, $\overline{\mathsf{ip}}^1(\gamma)$ and $\overline{\mathsf{ip}}^0(\gamma)$ are the sequences of maximal intervals on which the signal is γ is high and low, respectively.

Metric Temporal Logics. To simplify the exposition, we restrict ourselves to monitoring the past-only fragment of metric temporal logic in a point-based and an interval-based setting. However, future operators like $\Diamond_I$, where the interval I is bounded, can be handled during monitoring by using queues that postpone the evaluation until enough time has elapsed. See [4], for such a monitoring algorithm that handles arbitrary nesting of past and bounded future operators.

Let P be a non-empty set of *propositions*. The syntax of the past-only fragment of metric temporal logic is given by the grammar $\phi ::= p \mid \neg \phi \mid \phi \wedge \phi \mid \phi \, \mathsf{S}_I \, \phi$, where $p \in P$ and $I \in \mathbb{I}$. In Figure 1, we define the satisfaction relations $\models$ and $\overset{\bullet}{\models}$,

$$\hat{\gamma}, \tau \models p \qquad \text{iff } \tau \in \gamma_p$$
$$\hat{\gamma}, \tau \models \neg\phi \qquad \text{iff } \hat{\gamma}, \tau \not\models \phi$$
$$\hat{\gamma}, \tau \models \phi \wedge \psi \quad \text{iff } \hat{\gamma}, \tau \models \phi \text{ and } \hat{\gamma}, \tau \models \psi$$
$$\hat{\gamma}, \tau \models \phi \mathsf{S}_I \psi \text{ iff there is } \tau' \in [0, \tau] \text{ with}$$
$$\tau - \tau' \in I,$$
$$\hat{\gamma}, \tau' \models \psi, \text{ and}$$
$$\hat{\gamma}, \kappa \models \phi, \text{ for all } \kappa \in (\tau', \tau]$$

(a) interval-based semantics

$$\hat{\gamma}, \bar{\tau}, i \models p \qquad \text{iff } \tau_i \in \gamma_p$$
$$\hat{\gamma}, \bar{\tau}, i \models \neg\phi \qquad \text{iff } \hat{\gamma}, \bar{\tau}, i \not\models \phi$$
$$\hat{\gamma}, \bar{\tau}, i \models \phi \wedge \psi \quad \text{iff } \hat{\gamma}, \bar{\tau}, i \models \phi \text{ and } \hat{\gamma}, \bar{\tau}, i \models \psi$$
$$\hat{\gamma}, \bar{\tau}, i \models \phi \mathsf{S}_I \psi \text{ iff there is } i' \in [0, i] \cap \mathbb{N} \text{ with}$$
$$\tau_i - \tau_{i'} \in I,$$
$$\hat{\gamma}, \bar{\tau}, i' \models \psi, \text{ and}$$
$$\hat{\gamma}, \bar{\tau}, k \models \phi, \text{ for all } k \in (i', i] \cap \mathbb{N}$$

(b) point-based semantics

Fig. 1. Semantics of past-only metric temporal logic

where $\hat{\gamma} = (\gamma_p)_{p \in P}$ is a family of signals, $\bar{\tau}$ a time sequence, $\tau \in \mathbb{T}$, and $i \in \mathbb{N}$. Note that $\models$ defines the truth value of a formula for every $\tau \in \mathbb{T}$. In contrast, a formula's truth value with respect to $\models$ is defined at the "sample-points" $i \in \mathbb{N}$ to which the "time-stamps" $\tau_i \in \mathbb{T}$ from the time sequence $\bar{\tau}$ are attached.

We use the standard binding strength of the operators and standard syntactic sugar. For instance, $\phi \vee \psi$ stands for the formula $\neg(\neg\phi \wedge \neg\psi)$ and $\blacklozenge_I \psi$ stands for $(p \vee \neg p) \mathsf{S}_I \psi$, for some $p \in P$. Moreover, we often omit the interval $I = [0, \infty)$ attached to a temporal operator. We denote the set of subformulas of a formula ϕ by $\mathsf{sf}(\phi)$. Finally, $|\phi|$ is the number of nodes in ϕ's parse tree.

3   Point-Based versus Interval-Based Time Models

3.1   State Variables and System Events

State variables and system events are different kinds of entities. One distinguishing feature is that events happen at single points in time and the value of a state variable is always constant for some amount of time. In the following, we distinguish between these two entities. Let P be the disjoint union of the proposition sets S and E. We call propositions in S *state propositions* and propositions in E *event propositions*. Semantically, a signal $\gamma \subseteq \mathbb{T}$ is an *event signal* if $\gamma \cap I$ is finite, for every bounded interval I, and the signal γ is a *state signal* if for every bounded interval I, the sets $\gamma \cap I$ and $(\mathbb{T} \setminus \gamma) \cap I$ are the finite unions of non-singular intervals. Note that there are signals that are neither event signals nor state signals. A family of signals $\hat{\gamma} = (\gamma_p)_{p \in S \cup E}$ is *consistent* with S and E if γ_p is a state signal, for all $p \in S$, and γ_p is an event signal, for all $p \in E$.

The point-based semantics is often motivated by the study of real-time systems whose behavior is determined by system events. Intuitively, a time sequence $\bar{\tau}$ records the points in time when events occur and the signal γ_p for a proposition $p \in E$ consists of the points in time when the event p occurs. The following examples, however, demonstrate that the point-based semantics can be unintuitive in contrast to the interval-based semantics.

Example 1. A state proposition $p \in S$ can often be mimicked by the formula $\neg f \mathsf{S} s$ with corresponding event propositions $s, f \in E$ representing "start" and "finish." For the state signal γ_p, let γ_s and γ_f be the event signals where γ_s and γ_f consist of the points in time of γ_p when the Boolean state variable starts and respectively finishes to hold. Then $(\gamma_s, \gamma_f), \tau \models \neg f \, \mathsf{S} \, s$ iff $\gamma_p, \tau \models p$, for any $\tau \in \mathbb{T}$, under the assumption that $I \cap \gamma_p$ is the finite union of left-closed and right-open intervals, for every bounded left-closed and right-open interval I.

However, replacing p by $\neg f \, \mathsf{S} \, s$ does not always capture the essence of a Boolean state variable when using the point-based semantics. Consider the formula $\blacklozenge_{[0,1]} \, p$ containing the state proposition p and let $\gamma_p = [0, 5)$ be a state signal. Moreover, let (γ_s, γ_f) be the family of corresponding event signals for the event propositions s and f, i.e., $\gamma_s = \{0\}$ and $\gamma_f = \{5\}$. For a time sequence $\bar{\tau}$ with $\tau_0 = 0$ and $\tau_1 = 5$, we have that $(\gamma_s, \gamma_f), \bar{\tau}, 1 \not\models \blacklozenge_{[0,1]}(\neg f \, \mathsf{S} \, s)$ but $\gamma_p, \tau_1 \models \blacklozenge_{[0,1]} \, p$. Note that $\bar{\tau}$ only contains time-stamps when an event occurs. An additional sample-point between τ_0 and τ_1 with, e.g., the time-stamp 4 would result in identical truth values at time 5.

Example 2. Consider the (event) signals $\gamma_p = \{\tau \in \mathbb{T} \mid \tau = 2n, \text{ for some } n \in \mathbb{N}\}$ and $\gamma_q = \emptyset$ for the (event) propositions p and q. One might expect that these signals satisfy the formula $p \rightarrow \blacklozenge_{[0,1]} \, \neg q$ at every point in time. However, for a time sequence $\bar{\tau}$ with $\tau_0 = 0$ and $\tau_1 = 2$, we have that $\hat{\gamma}, \bar{\tau}, 1 \not\models p \rightarrow \blacklozenge_{[0,1]} \, \neg q$. The reason is that in the point-based semantics, the $\blacklozenge_I$ operator requires the existence of a previous point in time that also occurs in the time sequence $\bar{\tau}$.

As another example consider the formula $\blacklozenge_{[0,1]} \, \blacklozenge_{[0,1]} \, p$. One might expect that it is logically equivalent to $\blacklozenge_{[0,2]} \, p$. However, this is not the case in the point-based semantics. To see this, consider a time sequence $\bar{\tau}$ with $\tau_0 = 0$ and $\tau_1 = 2$. We have that $\hat{\gamma}, \bar{\tau}, 1 \not\models \blacklozenge_{[0,1]} \, \blacklozenge_{[0,1]} \, p$ and $\hat{\gamma}, \bar{\tau}, 1 \models \blacklozenge_{[0,2]} \, p$ if $\tau_0 \in \gamma_p$.

The examples above suggest that adding additional sample-points restores a formula's intended meaning, which usually stems from having the interval-based semantics in mind. However, a drawback of this approach for monitoring is that each additional sample-point increases the workload of a point-based monitoring algorithm, since it is invoked for each sample-point. Moreover, in the dense time domain, adding sample-points does not always make the two semantics coincide. For instance, for $\gamma_p = [0, 1)$ and $\tau \geq 1$, we have that $\gamma_p, \tau \not\models \neg p \, \mathsf{S} \, p$ and $\gamma_p, \bar{\tau}, i \models \neg p \, \mathsf{S} \, p$, for every time sequence $\bar{\tau}$ with $\tau_0 < 1$ and every $i \in \mathbb{N}$.

3.2   Event-Relativized Formulas

In the following, we identify a class of formulas for which the point-based and the interval-based semantics coincide. For formulas in this class, a point-based monitoring algorithm can be used to soundly monitor properties given by formulas interpreted using the interval-based semantics. We assume that the propositions are typed, i.e., $P = S \cup E$, where S contains the state propositions and E the event propositions, and a family of signals $\hat{\gamma} = (\gamma_p)_{p \in S \cup E}$ is consistent with S and E. Moreover, we assume without loss of generality that there is always at least one event signal γ in $\hat{\gamma}$ that is the infinite union of singular intervals, e.g., γ is the signal of a clock event that regularly occurs over time.

We inductively define the sets $rel_\forall$ and $rel_\exists$ for formulas in negation normal form. Recall that a formula is in negation normal form if negation only occurs directly in front of propositions. A logically-equivalent negation normal form of a formula can always be obtained by eliminating double negations and by pushing negations inwards, where we consider the Boolean connective $\vee$ and the temporal operator "trigger" T_I as primitives. Note that $\phi\,\mathsf{T}_I\,\psi = \neg(\neg\phi\,\mathsf{S}_I\,\neg\psi)$.

$$\neg p \in rel_\forall \quad \text{if} \quad p \in E \tag{$\forall$1}$$
$$\phi_1 \vee \phi_2 \in rel_\forall \quad \text{if} \quad \phi_1 \in rel_\forall \text{ or } \phi_2 \in rel_\forall \tag{$\forall$2}$$
$$\phi_1 \wedge \phi_2 \in rel_\forall \quad \text{if} \quad \phi_1 \in rel_\forall \text{ and } \phi_2 \in rel_\forall \tag{$\forall$3}$$
$$p \in rel_\exists \quad \text{if} \quad p \in E \tag{$\exists$1}$$
$$\phi_1 \wedge \phi_2 \in rel_\exists \quad \text{if} \quad \phi_1 \in rel_\exists \text{ or } \phi_2 \in rel_\exists \tag{$\exists$2}$$
$$\phi_1 \vee \phi_2 \in rel_\exists \quad \text{if} \quad \phi_1 \in rel_\exists \text{ and } \phi_2 \in rel_\exists \tag{$\exists$3}$$

A formula ϕ is *event-relativized* if $\alpha \in rel_\forall$ and $\beta \in rel_\exists$, for every subformula of ϕ of the form $\alpha\,\mathsf{S}_I\,\beta$ or $\beta\,\mathsf{T}_I\,\alpha$. We call the formula ϕ *strongly* event-relativized if ϕ is event-relativized and $\phi \in rel_\forall \cup rel_\exists$.

The following theorem relates the interval-based semantics and the point-based semantics for event-relativized formulas.

Theorem 1. *Let* $\hat{\gamma} = (\gamma_p)_{p\in S\cup E}$ *be a family of consistent signals and* $\bar{\tau}$ *the time sequence listing the occurrences of events in* $\hat{\gamma}$, *i.e.,* $\bar{\tau}$ *is the time sequence obtained by linearly ordering the set* $\bigcup_{p\in E}\gamma_p$. *For an event-relativized formula* ϕ *and every* $i \in \mathbb{N}$, *it holds that* $\hat{\gamma},\tau_i \models \phi$ *iff* $\hat{\gamma},\bar{\tau},i \overset{\bullet}{\models} \phi$. *Furthermore, if* ϕ *is strongly event-relativized, then it also holds that* (a) $\hat{\gamma},\tau \not\models \phi$ *if* $\phi \in rel_\exists$ *and* (b) $\hat{\gamma},\tau \models \phi$ *if* $\phi \in rel_\forall$, *for all* $\tau \in \mathbb{T} \setminus \{\tau_i \mid i \in \mathbb{N}\}$.

Observe that the formulas in Example 1 and 2 are not event-relativized. The definition of event-relativized formulas and Theorem 1 straightforwardly extend to richer real-time logics that also contain future operators and are first-order. We point out that most formulas that we encountered when formalizing security policies in such a richer temporal logic are strongly event-relativized [3].

From Theorem 1, it follows that the interval-based semantics can simulate the point-based one by using a fresh event proposition sp with its signal $\gamma_{sp} = \{\tau_i \mid i \in \mathbb{N}\}$, for a time sequence $\bar{\tau}$. We then event-relativize a formula ϕ with the proposition sp, i.e., subformulas of the form $\psi_1\,\mathsf{S}_I\,\psi_2$ are replaced by $(sp \to \psi_1)\,\mathsf{S}_I\,(sp \wedge \psi_2)$ and $\psi_1\,\mathsf{T}_I\,\psi_2$ by $(sp \wedge \psi_1)\,\mathsf{T}_I\,(sp \to \psi_2)$.

4   Monitoring Algorithms

In this section, we present and analyze our monitoring algorithms for both the point-based and the interval-based setting. Without loss of generality, the algorithms assume that the temporal subformulas of a formula ϕ occur only once in ϕ. Moreover, let P be the set of propositions that occur in ϕ.

4.1   A Point-Based Monitoring Algorithm

Our monitoring algorithm for the point-based semantics iteratively computes the truth values of a formula ϕ at the sample-points $i \in \mathbb{N}$ for a given time

```
step•(φ, Γ, τ)                          init•(φ)
  case φ = p                              for each ψ ∈ sf(φ) with ψ = ψ₁ S_I ψ₂ do
    return p ∈ Γ                            L_ψ := ⟨⟩
  case φ = ¬φ'
    return not step•(φ', Γ, τ)
  case φ = φ₁ ∧ φ₂                       update•(φ, Γ, τ)
    return step•(φ₁, Γ, τ) and step•(φ₂, Γ, τ)    let φ₁ S_I φ₂ = φ
  case φ = φ₁ S_I φ₂                       b₁ = step•(φ₁, Γ, τ)
    update•(φ, Γ, τ)                        b₂ = step•(φ₂, Γ, τ)
    if L_φ = ⟨⟩ then return false          L = if b₁ then drop•(L_φ, I, τ) else ⟨⟩
                else return τ − head(L_φ) ∈ I    in if b₂ then L_φ := L ⧺ ⟨τ⟩
                                                    else L_φ := L
```

Fig. 2. Monitoring in a point-based setting

sequence $\bar{\tau}$ and a family of signals $\hat{\gamma} = (\gamma_p)_{p \in P}$. We point out that $\bar{\tau}$ and $\hat{\gamma}$ are given incrementally, i.e., in the $(i+1)$st iteration, the monitor obtains the time-stamp τ_i and the signals between the previous time-stamp and τ_i. In fact, in the point-based setting, we do not need to consider "chunks" of signals; instead, we can restrict ourselves to the snapshots $\Gamma_i := \{p \in P \mid \tau_i \in \gamma_p\}$, for $i \in \mathbb{N}$, i.e., Γ_i is the set of propositions that hold at time τ_i.

Each iteration of the monitor is performed by executing the procedure step•. At sample-point $i \in \mathbb{N}$, step• takes as arguments the formula ϕ, the snapshot Γ_i, and i's time-stamp τ_i. It computes the truth value of ϕ at i recursively over ϕ's structure. For efficiency, the procedure step• maintains for each subformula ψ of the form $\psi_1 S_I \psi_2$ a sequence L_ψ of time-stamps. These sequences are initialized by the procedure init• and updated by the procedure update•. These three procedures[2] are given in Figure 2 and are described next.

The base case of step• where ϕ is a proposition and the cases for the Boolean connectives $\neg$ and $\wedge$ are straightforward. The only involved case is where ϕ is of the form $\phi_1 S_I \phi_2$. In this case, step• first updates the sequence L_ϕ and then computes ϕ's truth value at the sample-point $i \in \mathbb{N}$.

Before we describe how we update the sequence L_ϕ, we describe the elements that are stored in L_ϕ and how we obtain from them ϕ's truth value. After the update of L_ϕ by update•, the sequence L_ϕ stores the time-stamps τ_j with $\tau_i - \tau_j \in {}^{\leq}I$ (i.e., the time-stamps that satisfy the time constraint now or that might satisfy it in the future) at which ϕ_2 holds and from which ϕ_1 continuously holds up to the current sample-point i (i.e., ϕ_2 holds at $j \leq i$ and ϕ_1 holds at each $k \in \{j+1, \ldots, i\}$). Moreover, if there are time-stamps τ_j and $\tau_{j'}$ with $j < j'$ in L_ϕ with $\tau_i - \tau_j \in I$ and $\tau_i - \tau_{j'} \in I$ then we only keep in L_ϕ the time-stamp of the later sample-point, i.e., $\tau_{j'}$. Finally, the time-stamps in L_ϕ are ordered increasingly. Having L_ϕ at hand, it is easy to determine ϕ's truth value. If L_ϕ is the empty sequence then obviously ϕ does not hold at sample-point i. If L_ϕ is non-empty then ϕ holds at i iff the first time-stamp κ in L_ϕ fulfills the timing constraints given by the interval I, i.e., $\tau_i - \kappa \in I$. Recall that ϕ holds at i iff

---

[2] Our pseudo-code is written in a functional-programming style using pattern matching. $\langle\rangle$ denotes the empty sequence, $\mathbin{+\!\!+}$ sequence concatenation, and $x :: L$ the sequence with head x and tail L.

$\mathsf{drop}^{\bullet}(L, I, \tau)$
  case $L = \langle\rangle$
    return $\langle\rangle$
  case $L = \kappa :: L'$
    if $\tau - \kappa \notin {}^{\leq}I$ **then return** $\mathsf{drop}^{\bullet}(L', I, \tau)$
      else return $\mathsf{drop}'^{\bullet}(\kappa, L', I, \tau)$

$\mathsf{drop}'^{\bullet}(\kappa, L', I, \tau)$
  case $L' = \langle\rangle$
    return $\langle\kappa\rangle$
  case $L' = \kappa' :: L''$
    if $\tau - \kappa' \in I$ **then return** $\mathsf{drop}'^{\bullet}(\kappa', L'', I, \tau)$
      else return $\kappa :: L'$

Fig. 3. Auxiliary procedures

there is a sample-point $j \leq i$ with $\tau_i - \tau_j \in I$ at which ϕ_2 holds and since then ϕ_1 continuously holds.

Initially, L_ϕ is the empty sequence. If ϕ_2 holds at sample-point i, then $\mathsf{update}^{\bullet}$ adds the time-stamp τ_i to L_ϕ. However, prior to this, it removes the time-stamps of the sample-points from which ϕ_1 does not continuously hold. Clearly, if ϕ_1 does not hold at i then we can empty the sequence L_ϕ. Otherwise, if ϕ_1 holds at i, we first drop the time-stamps for which the distance to the current time-stamp τ_i became too large with respect to the right margin of I. Afterwards, we drop time-stamps until we find the last time-stamp τ_j with $\tau_i - \tau_j \in I$. This is done by the procedures $\mathsf{drop}^{\bullet}$ and $\mathsf{drop}'^{\bullet}$ shown in Figure 3.

Theorem 2. *Let* ϕ *be a formula,* $\hat{\gamma} = (\gamma_p)_{p \in P}$ *be a family of signals,* $\bar{\tau}$ *be a time sequence, and* $n > 0$. *The procedure* $\mathsf{step}^{\bullet}(\phi, \Gamma_{n-1}, \tau_{n-1})$ *terminates, and returns* **true** *iff* $\hat{\gamma}, \bar{\tau}, n - 1 \models \phi$, *whenever* $\mathsf{init}^{\bullet}(\phi)$, $\mathsf{step}^{\bullet}(\phi, \Gamma_0, \tau_0)$, $\ldots$, $\mathsf{step}^{\bullet}(\phi, \Gamma_{n-2}, \tau_{n-2})$ *were called previously in this order, where* $\Gamma_i = \{p \in P \mid \tau_i \in \gamma_p\}$, *for* $i < n$.

We end this subsection by analyzing the monitor's computational complexity. Observe that we cannot bound the space that is needed to represent the time-stamps in the time sequence $\bar{\tau}$. They become arbitrarily large as time progresses. Moreover, since the time domain is dense, they can be arbitrarily close to each other. As a consequence, operations like subtraction of elements from $\mathbb{T}$ cannot be done in constant time. We return to this point in Section 4.3.

In the following, we assume that each $\tau \in \mathbb{T}$ is represented by two bit strings for the numerator and denominator. The representation of an interval I consists of the representations for $\ell(I)$ and $r(I)$ and whether the left margin and right margin is closed or open. We denote the maximum length of these bit strings by $\|\tau\|$ and $\|I\|$, respectively. The operations on elements in $\mathbb{T}$ that the monitoring algorithm performs are subtractions and membership tests. Subtraction $\tau - \tau'$ can be carried out in time $\mathcal{O}(m^2)$, where $m = \max\{\|\tau\|, \|\tau'\|\}$.[3] A membership test $\tau \in I$ can also be carried out in time $\mathcal{O}(m^2)$, where $m = \max\{\|\tau\|, \|I\|\}$.

The following theorem establishes an upper bound on the time complexity of our monitoring algorithm.

---

[3] Note that $\frac{p}{q} - \frac{p'}{q'} = \frac{p \cdot q' - p' \cdot q}{q \cdot q'}$ and that $\mathcal{O}(m^2)$ is an upper bound on the multiplication of two m bit integers. There are more sophisticated algorithms for multiplication that run in $\mathcal{O}(m \log m \log \log m)$ time [19] and $\mathcal{O}(m \log m 2^{\log^* m})$ time [8]. For simplicity, we use the quadratic upper bound.

Theorem 3. *Let* ϕ, $\hat{\gamma}$, $\bar{\tau}$, n, *and* $\Gamma_0, \ldots, \Gamma_{n-1}$ *be as in Theorem 2. Executing the sequence* $\mathsf{init}^\bullet(\phi)$, $\mathsf{step}^\bullet(\phi, \Gamma_0, \tau_0)$, $\ldots$, $\mathsf{step}^\bullet(\phi, \Gamma_{n-1}, \tau_{n-1})$ *requires* $\mathcal{O}(m^2 \cdot n \cdot |\phi|)$ *time, where* $m = \max(\{\|I\| \mid \alpha\, \mathsf{S}_I\, \beta \in \mathsf{sf}(\phi)\} \cup \{\|\tau_0\|, \ldots, \|\tau_{n-1}\|\})$.

4.2 An Interval-Based Monitoring Algorithm

Our monitoring algorithm for the interval-based semantics determines, for a given family of signals $\hat{\gamma} = (\gamma_p)_{p \in P}$, the truth value of a formula ϕ, for any $\tau \in \mathbb{T}$. In other words, it determines the set $\gamma_{\phi, \hat{\gamma}} := \{\tau \in \mathbb{T} \mid \hat{\gamma}, \tau \models \phi\}$. We simply write γ_ϕ instead of $\gamma_{\phi, \hat{\gamma}}$ when the family of signals $\hat{\gamma}$ is clear from the context. Similar to the point-based setting, the monitor incrementally receives the input $\hat{\gamma}$ and incrementally outputs γ_ϕ, i.e., the input and output signals are split into "chunks" by an infinite interval partition $\bar{J}$. Concretely, the input of the $(i+1)$st iteration consists of the formula ϕ that is monitored, the interval J_i of $\bar{J}$, and the family $\hat{\Delta}_i = (\Delta_{i,p})_{p \in P}$ of sequences of intervals $\Delta_{i,p} = \overline{\mathsf{IP}}^1(\gamma_p \cap J_i)$, for propositions $p \in P$. The output of the $(i+1)$st iteration is the sequence $\overline{\mathsf{IP}}^1(\gamma_\phi \cap J_i)$.

Observe that the sequence $\overline{\mathsf{IP}}^1(\gamma_p \cap J_i)$ only consists of a finite number of intervals since the signal γ_p satisfies the finite-variability condition and J_i is bounded. Moreover, since γ_p is stable on every interval in $\overline{\mathsf{IP}}(\gamma_p)$ and an interval has a finite representation, the sequence $\overline{\mathsf{IP}}^1(\gamma_p \cap J_i)$ finitely represents the signal chunk $\gamma_p \cap J_i$. Similar observations are valid for the signal chunk $\gamma_\phi \cap J_i$.

Each iteration is performed by the procedure step. To handle the since operator efficiently, step maintains for each subformula ψ of the form $\psi_1\, \mathsf{S}_I\, \psi_2$, a (possibly empty) interval K_ψ and a finite sequence of intervals Δ_ψ. These global variables are initialized by the procedure init and updated by the procedure update. These three procedures are given in Figure 4 and are described next.

The procedure step computes the signal chunk $\gamma_\phi \cap J_i$ recursively over the formula structure. It utilizes the right-hand sides of the following equalities:

$$\gamma_p \cap J_i = \bigcup_{K \in \overline{\mathsf{IP}}^1(\gamma_p \cap J_i)} K \tag{1}$$

$$\gamma_{\neg \phi'} \cap J_i = J_i \setminus \left(\bigcup_{K \in \overline{\mathsf{IP}}^1(\gamma_{\phi'} \cap J_i)} K\right) \tag{2}$$

$$\gamma_{\phi_1 \wedge \phi_2} \cap J_i = \bigcup_{\substack{K_1 \in \overline{\mathsf{IP}}^1(\gamma_{\phi_1} \cap J_i) \\ K_2 \in \overline{\mathsf{IP}}^1(\gamma_{\phi_2} \cap J_i)}} (K_1 \cap K_2) \tag{3}$$

$$\gamma_{\phi_1 \mathsf{S}_I \phi_2} \cap J_i = \bigcup_{\substack{K_1 \in \overline{\mathsf{IP}}^1(\gamma_{\phi_1})\ \text{with}\ K_1 \cap J_i \neq \emptyset \\ K_2 \in \overline{\mathsf{IP}}^1(\gamma_{\phi_2})\ \text{with}\ (K_2 \oplus I) \cap (J_i^{\geq}) \neq \emptyset}} \left(((K_2 \cap {}^+K_1) \oplus I) \cap K_1 \cap J_i\right) \tag{4}$$

where ${}^+K := \{\ell(K)\} \cup K$, for $K \in \mathbb{I}$, i.e., making the interval K left-closed.

The equalities (1), (2), and (3) are obvious and their right-hand sides are directly reflected in our pseudo-code. The case where ϕ is a proposition is straightforward. For the case $\phi = \neg \phi'$, we use the procedure invert, shown in Figure 5, to compute $\overline{\mathsf{IP}}^1(\gamma_\phi \cap J_i)$ from $\Delta' = \overline{\mathsf{IP}}^1(\gamma_{\phi'} \cap J_i)$. This is done by "complementing" Δ' with respect to the interval J_i. For instance, the output of $\mathsf{invert}(\langle [1, 2]\, (3, 4)\rangle, [0, 10))$ is $\langle [0, 1)\, (2, 3]\, [4, 10)\rangle$. For the case $\phi = \phi_1 \wedge \phi_2$, we use the procedure $\mathsf{intersect}$, also shown in Figure 5, to compute $\overline{\mathsf{IP}}^1(\gamma_\phi \cap J_i)$ from $\Delta_1 = \overline{\mathsf{IP}}^1(\gamma_{\phi_1} \cap J_i)$ and $\Delta_2 = \overline{\mathsf{IP}}^1(\gamma_{\phi_2} \cap J_i)$. This procedure returns the

```
step(φ, Δ̂, J)                              init(φ)
  case φ = p                                  for each ψ ∈ sf(φ) with ψ = ψ₁ S_I ψ₂ do
    return Δ_p                                  K_ψ := ∅
  case φ = ¬φ'                                  Δ_ψ := ⟨⟩
    let Δ' = step(φ', Δ̂, J)
    in return invert(Δ', J)                  update(φ, Δ̂, J)
  case φ = φ₁ ∧ φ₂                             let φ₁ S_I φ₂ = φ
    let Δ₁ = step(φ₁, Δ̂, J)                     Δ₁ = step(φ₁, Δ̂, J)
        Δ₂ = step(φ₂, Δ̂, J)                     Δ₂ = step(φ₂, Δ̂, J)
    in return intersect(Δ₁, Δ₂)                 Δ'₁ = prepend(K_φ, Δ₁)
  case φ = φ₁ S_I φ₂                             Δ'₂ = concat(Δ_φ, Δ₂)
    let (Δ'₁, Δ'₂) = update(φ, Δ̂, J)          in K_φ := if Δ'₁ = ⟨⟩ then ∅ else last(Δ'₁)
    in return merge(combine(Δ'₁, Δ'₂, I, J))     Δ_φ := drop(Δ'₂, I, J)
                                                return (Δ'₁, Δ'₂)
```

Fig. 4. Monitoring in an interval-based setting

```
cons(K, Δ)                                 intersect(Δ₁, Δ₂)
  if K = ∅ then                              if Δ₁ = ⟨⟩ or Δ₂ = ⟨⟩ then
    return Δ                                   return ⟨⟩
  else                                       else
    return K :: Δ                             let K₁ :: Δ'₁ = Δ₁
invert(Δ, J)                                     K₂ :: Δ'₂ = Δ₂
  case Δ = ⟨⟩                                 in if K₁ ∩ (K₂^≥) = ∅ then
    return ⟨J⟩                                     return cons(K₁ ∩ K₂, intersect(Δ'₁, Δ₂))
  case Δ = K :: Δ'                            else
    return cons(J ∩ <K, invert(Δ', J ∩ (K^>)))    return cons(K₁ ∩ K₂, intersect(Δ₁, Δ'₂))
```

Fig. 5. The auxiliary procedures for the Boolean connectives

sequence of intervals that have a non-empty intersection of two intervals in the input sequences. The elements in the returned sequence are ordered increasingly.

The equality (4) for $\phi = \phi_1 \, S_I \, \phi_2$ is less obvious and using its right-hand side for an implementation is also less straightforward since the intervals K_1 and K_2 are not restricted to occur in the current chunk J_i. Instead, they are intervals in $\overline{\text{ITp}}^1(\gamma_{\phi_1})$ and $\overline{\text{ITp}}^1(\gamma_{\phi_2})$, respectively, with certain constraints.

Before giving further implementation details, we first show why equality (4) holds. To prove the inclusion $\subseteq$, assume $\tau \in \gamma_{\phi_1 S_I \phi_2} \cap J_i$. By the semantics of the since operator, there is a $\tau_2 \in \gamma_{\phi_2}$ with $\tau - \tau_2 \in I$ and $\tau_1 \in \gamma_{\phi_1}$, for all $\tau_1 \in (\tau_2, \tau]$.

- Obviously, $\tau_2 \in K_2$, for some $K_2 \in \overline{\text{ITp}}^1(\gamma_{\phi_2})$. By taking the time constraint I into account, K_2 satisfies the constraint $(K_2 \oplus I) \cap (J_i^{\geq}) \neq \emptyset$. Note that even the more restrictive constraint $(K_2 \oplus I) \cap J_i \neq \emptyset$ holds. However, we employ the weaker constraint in our implementation as it is useful for later iterations.
- Since $\overline{\text{ITp}}(\gamma_{\phi_1})$ is the coarsest interval partition of γ_{ϕ_1}, there is an interval $K_1 \in \overline{\text{ITp}}^1(\gamma_{\phi_1})$ with $(\tau_2, \tau] \subseteq K_1$. As $\tau \in J_i$, the constraint $K_1 \cap J_i \neq \emptyset$ holds.

It follows that $\tau \in K_1$ and $\tau_2 \in {}^+K_1$, and thus $\tau_2 \in K_2 \cap {}^+K_1$. From $\tau - \tau_2 \in I$, we obtain that $\tau \in (K_2 \cap {}^+K_1) \oplus I$. Finally, since $\tau \in K_1 \cap J_i$, we have that $\tau \in ((K_2 \cap {}^+K_1) \oplus I) \cap K_1 \cap J_i$. The other inclusion $\supseteq$ can be shown similarly.

```
prepend(K, Δ)                              combine(Δ'₁, Δ'₂, I, J)
   if K = ∅ then                              if Δ'₁ = ⟨⟩ or Δ'₂ = ⟨⟩ then return ⟨⟩
      return Δ                                 else
   else                                           let K₂ :: Δ''₂ = Δ'₂
      case Δ = ⟨⟩                                 in if (K₂ ⊕ I) ∩ J = ∅ then return ⟨⟩
         return ⟨K⟩                                  else
      case Δ = K' :: Δ''                                let K₁ :: Δ''₁ = Δ'₁
         if adjacent(K, K') or K ∩ K' ≠ ∅ then            Δ = if K₂⁼ ∩ ⁺K₁ = ∅ then
            return K ∪ K' :: Δ'                                combine(Δ''₁, Δ'₂, I, J)
         else                                               else
            return K :: Δ                                      combine(Δ'₁, Δ''₂, I, J)
                                                    in return (K₂ ∩ ⁺K₁) ⊕ I) ∩ K₁ ∩ J :: Δ


concat(Δ₁, Δ₂)                             merge(Δ)
   case Δ₁ = ⟨⟩                               case Δ = ⟨⟩
      return Δ₂                                  return Δ
   case Δ₁ = Δ'₁ ++ ⟨K₁⟩                      case Δ = K :: Δ'
      return Δ'₁ ++ prepend(K₁, Δ₂)             return prepend(K, merge(Δ'))


drop(Δ'₂, I, J)                            drop'(K, Δ'₂, I, J)
   case Δ'₂ = ⟨⟩                              case Δ'₂ = ⟨⟩
      return ⟨⟩                                  return ⟨K⟩
   case Δ'₂ = K₂ :: Δ''₂                      case Δ'₂ = K₂ :: Δ''₂
      let K = (K₂ ⊕ I) ∩ (J⁼)                   let K' = (K₂ ⊕ I) ∩ (J⁼)
      in if K = ∅ then return drop(Δ''₂, I, J)   in if K ⊆ K' then return drop'(K', Δ''₂, I, J)
               else return drop'(K, Δ'₂, I, J)          else return Δ'₂
```

Fig. 6. The auxiliary procedures for the since operator

For computing the signal chunk $\gamma_{\phi_1 S_I \phi_2} \cap J_i$, the procedure step first determines the subsequences Δ'_1 and Δ'_2 of $\overline{\mathrm{iip}}^1(\gamma_{\phi_1})$ and $\overline{\mathrm{iip}}^1(\gamma_{\phi_2})$ consisting of those intervals K_1 and K_2 appearing in the equality (4), respectively. This is done by the procedure update. Afterwards, step computes the sequence $\overline{\mathrm{iip}}^1(\gamma_\phi \cap J_i)$ from Δ'_1 and Δ'_2 by using the procedures combine and merge, given in Figure 6. We now explain how merge(combine($\Delta'_1, \Delta'_2, I, J$)) returns the sequence $\overline{\mathrm{iip}}^1(\gamma_{\phi_1 S_I \phi_2} \cap J_i)$. First, combine($\Delta'_1, \Delta'_2, I, J$) computes a sequence of intervals whose union is $\gamma_{\phi_1 S_I \phi_2} \cap J_i$. It traverses the ordered sequences Δ'_1 and Δ'_2 and adds the interval $((K_2 \cap {}^+K_1) \oplus I) \cap K_1 \cap J_i$ to the resulting ordered sequence, for K_1 in Δ'_1 and K_2 in Δ'_2. The test $K_2^\geqq \cap {}^+K_1 = \emptyset$ determines in which sequence (Δ'_1 or Δ'_2) we advance next: if the test succeeds then $K'_2 \cap {}^+K_1 = \emptyset$ where K'_2 is the successor of K_2 in Δ'_2, and hence we advance in Δ'_1. The sequence Δ'_2 is not necessarily entirely traversed: when $(K_2 \oplus I) \cap J_i = \emptyset$, one need not inspect other elements K'_2 of the sequence Δ'_2, as then $((K'_2 \cap {}^+K_1) \oplus I) \cap K_1 \cap J_i = \emptyset$. The elements in the sequence returned by the combine procedure might be empty, adjacent, or overlapping. The merge procedure removes empty elements and merges adjacent or overlapping intervals, i.e., it returns the sequence $\overline{\mathrm{iip}}^1(\gamma_{\phi_1 S_I \phi_2} \cap J_i)$.

Finally, we explain the contents of the variables K_ϕ and Δ_ϕ and how they are updated. We start with K_ϕ. At the $(i+1)$st iteration, for some $i \geq 0$, the following invariant is satisfied by K_ϕ: before the update, the interval K_ϕ is the last interval of $\overline{\mathrm{iip}}^1(\gamma_{\phi_1} \cap {}^{\leq}J_{i-1})$ if $i > 0$ and this sequence is not empty, and K_ϕ is the empty set otherwise. The interval K_ϕ is prepended to the sequence $\overline{\mathrm{iip}}^1(\gamma_{\phi_1} \cap J_i)$ using the prepend procedure from Figure 6, which merges K_ϕ with the first interval of $\Delta_1 = \overline{\mathsf{np}}^1(\gamma_{\phi_1} \cap J_i)$ if these two intervals are adjacent. The obtained sequence Δ_1' is the maximal subsequence of $\overline{\mathsf{np}}^1(\gamma_{\phi_1} \cap {}^{\leq}J_i)$ such that $K_1 \cap J_i \neq \emptyset$, for each interval K_1 in Δ_1'. Thus, after the update, K_ϕ is the last interval of $\overline{\mathsf{np}}^1(\gamma_{\phi_1} \cap {}^{\leq}J_i)$ if this sequence is not empty, and K_ϕ is the empty set otherwise. Hence the invariant on K_ϕ is preserved at the next iteration.

The following invariant is satisfied by Δ_ϕ at the $(i + 1)$st iteration: before the update, the sequence Δ_ϕ is empty if $i = 0$, and otherwise, if $i > 0$, it stores the intervals K_2 in $\overline{\mathsf{np}}^1(\gamma_{\phi_2} \cap {}^{\leq}J_{i-1})$ with $(K_2 \oplus I) \cap (J_{i-1}^{\geq}) \neq \emptyset$ and $(K_2 \oplus I) \cap (J_{i-1}^{\geq}) \not\subseteq (K_2' \oplus I) \cap (J_{i-1}^{\geq})$, where K_2' is the successor of K_2 in $\overline{\mathsf{np}}^1(\gamma_{\phi_2} \cap {}^{\leq}J_{i-1})$. The procedure concat concatenates the sequence Δ_ϕ with the sequence $\Delta_2 = \overline{\mathsf{np}}^1(\gamma_{\phi_2} \cap J_i)$. Since the last interval of Δ_ϕ and the first interval of Δ_2 can be adjacent, concat might need to merge them. Thus, the obtained sequence Δ_2' is a subsequence of $\overline{\mathsf{np}}^1(\gamma_{\phi_2} \cap {}^{\leq}J_i)$ such that $(K_2 \oplus I) \cap (J_i^{\geq}) \neq \emptyset$, for each element K_2. Note that $J_{i-1}^{\geq} = J_i^{\geq}$. The updated sequence Δ_ϕ is obtained from Δ_2' by removing the intervals K_2 with $(K_2 \oplus I) \cap (J_i^{\geq}) = \emptyset$, i.e., the intervals that are irrelevant for later iterations. The procedure drop from Figure 6 removes these intervals. Moreover, if there are intervals K_2 and K_2' in Δ_ϕ with $(K_2 \oplus I) \cap (J_i^{\geq}) \subseteq (K_2' \oplus I) \cap (J_i^{\geq})$ then only the interval that occurs later is kept in Δ_ϕ. This is done by the procedure drop'. Thus, after the update, the sequence Δ_ϕ stores the intervals K_2 in $\overline{\mathsf{np}}^1(\gamma_{\phi_2} \cap {}^{\leq}J_i)$ with $(K_2 \oplus I) \cap (J_i^{\geq}) \neq \emptyset$ and $(K_2 \oplus I) \cap (J_i^{\geq}) \not\subseteq (K_2' \oplus I) \cap (J_i^{\geq})$, where K_2' is the successor of K_2 in $\overline{\mathsf{np}}^1(\gamma_{\phi_2} \cap {}^{\leq}J_i)$. Hence the invariant on Δ_ϕ is preserved at the next iteration.

Theorem 4. *Let ϕ be a formula, $\hat{\gamma} = (\gamma_p)_{p \in P}$ a family of signals, $\bar{J}$ an infinite interval partition, and $n > 0$. The procedure $\mathsf{step}(\phi, \hat{\Delta}_{n-1}, J_{n-1})$ terminates and returns the sequence $\overline{\mathsf{np}}^1(\gamma_\phi \cap J_{n-1})$, whenever $\mathsf{init}(\phi)$, $\mathsf{step}(\phi, \hat{\Delta}_0, J_0)$, $\ldots$, $\mathsf{step}(\phi, \hat{\Delta}_{n-2}, J_{n-2})$ were called previously in this order, where $\hat{\Delta}_i = (\Delta_{i,p})_{p \in P}$ with $\Delta_{i,p} = \overline{\mathsf{np}}^1(\gamma_p \cap J_i)$, for $i < n$.*

Finally, we analyze the monitor's computational complexity. As in the point-based setting, we take the representation size of elements of the time domain $\mathbb{T}$ into account. The basic operations here in which elements of $\mathbb{T}$ are involved are operations on intervals like checking emptiness (i.e. $I = \emptyset$), "extension" (e.g. $I^{>}$), and "shifting" (i.e. $I \oplus J$). The representation size of the interval $I \oplus J$ is in $\mathcal{O}(\|I\| + \|J\|)$. The time to carry out the shift operation is in $\mathcal{O}(\max\{\|I\|, \|J\|\}^2)$. All the other basic operations that return an interval do not increase the representation size of the resulting interval with respect to the given intervals. However, the time complexity is quadratic in the representation size of the given intervals whenever the operation needs to compare interval margins.

The following theorem establishes an upper bound on the time complexity of our monitoring algorithm.

Theorem 5. *Let ϕ, $\hat{\gamma}$, $\bar{J}$, n, and $\hat{\Delta}_i$ be given as in Theorem 4. Executing the sequence $\mathsf{init}(\phi)$, $\mathsf{step}(\phi, \hat{\Delta}_0, J_0)$, $\ldots$, $\mathsf{step}(\phi, \hat{\Delta}_{n-1}, J_{n-1})$ requires $\mathcal{O}(m^2 \cdot (n + \delta \cdot |\phi|) \cdot |\phi|^3)$ time, where $m = \max(\{\|I\| \mid \alpha\, \mathsf{S}_I\, \beta \in \mathsf{sf}(\phi)\} \cup \{\|J_0\|, \ldots, \|J_{n-1}\|\} \cup \bigcup_{p \in P}\{\|K\| \mid K \in \overline{\mathsf{np}}^1(\gamma_p \cap ({}^{<}J_n))\})$ and $\delta = \sum_{p \in P} \|\gamma_p \cap ({}^{<}J_n)\|$.*

We remark that the factor $m^2 \cdot |\phi|^2$ is due to the operations on the margins of intervals. With the assumption that the representation of elements of the time domain is constant, we obtain the upper bound $\mathcal{O}((n + \delta \cdot |\phi|) \cdot |\phi|)$.

4.3   Time Domains

The stated worst-case complexities of both monitoring algorithms take the representation size of the elements in the time domain into account. In practice, it is often reasonable to assume that these elements have a bounded representation, since arbitrarily precise clocks do not exist. For example, for many applications it suffices to represent time-stamps as Unix time, i.e., 32 or 64 bit signed integers. The operations performed by our monitoring algorithms on the time domain elements would then be carried out in constant time. However, a consequence of this practically motivated assumption is that the time domain is discrete and bounded rather than dense and unbounded.

For a discrete time domain, we must slightly modify the interval-based monitoring algorithm, namely, the operator ^+K used in the equality (4) must be redefined. In a discrete time domain, we extend K by one point in time to the left if it exists, i.e., $^+K := K \cup \{k - 1 \mid k \in K \text{ and } k > 0\}$. No modifications are needed for the point-based algorithm. If we assume a discrete and unbounded time domain, we still cannot assume that the operations on elements from the time domain can be carried out in constant time. But multiplication is no longer needed to compare elements in the time domain and thus the operations can be carried in time linear in the representation size. The worst-case complexity of both algorithms improves accordingly.

When assuming limited-precision clocks, which results in a discrete time domain, a so-called fictitious-clock semantics [2, 18] is often used. This semantics formalizes, for example, that if the system event e happens strictly before the event e' but both events fall between two clock ticks, then we can distinguish them by temporal ordering, not by time. In a fictitious-clock semantics, we time-stamp e and e' with the same clock value and in a trace e appears strictly before e'. For ordering e and e' in a trace, signals must be synchronized. Our point-based monitoring algorithm can directly be used for a fictitious-clock semantics. It iteratively processes a sequence of snapshots $\langle \Gamma_0, \Gamma_1, \dots \rangle$ together with a sequence of time-stamps $\langle \tau_0, \tau_1, \dots \rangle$, which is increasing but not necessarily strictly increasing anymore. In contrast, our interval-based monitoring algorithm does not directly carry over to a fictitious-clock semantics.

4.4   Comparison of the Monitoring Algorithms

In the following, we compare our two algorithms when monitoring a strongly event-relativized formula ϕ. By Theorem 1, the point-based setting and the interval-based setting coincide on this formula class.

First note that the input for the $(i+1)$th iteration of the point-based monitoring algorithm can be easily obtained online from the given signals $\hat{\gamma} = (\gamma)_{p \in S \cup E}$. Whenever an event occurs, we record the time $\tau_i \in \mathbb{T}$, determine the current truth values of the propositions, i.e., $\Gamma_i = \{p \in P \mid \tau_i \in \gamma_p\}$, and invoke the monitor by executing $\mathsf{step}^\bullet(\phi, \Gamma_i, \tau_i)$. The worst-case complexity of the point-based monitoring algorithm of the first n iterations is $\mathcal{O}(m^2 \cdot n \cdot |\phi|)$, where m is according to Theorem 3.

When using the interval-based monitoring algorithm, we are more flexible in that we need not invoke the monitoring algorithm whenever an event occurs. Instead, we can freely split the signals into chunks. Let $\bar{J}$ be a splitting in which the n'th interval $J_{n'-1}$ is right-closed and $r(J_{n'-1}) = \tau_{n-1}$. We have the worst-case complexity of $\mathcal{O}\big(m'^2 \cdot (n' + \delta \cdot |\phi|) \cdot |\phi|^3\big)$, where m' and δ are according to Theorem 5. We can lower this upper bound, since the formula ϕ is strongly event-relativized. Instead of the factor $m'^2 \cdot |\phi|^2$ for processing the interval margins in the n' iterations, we only have the factor m'^2. The reason is that the margins of the intervals in the signal chunks of subformulas of the form $\psi_1 \mathsf{S}_I \psi_2$ already appear as interval margins in the input.

Note that $m' \geq m$ and that δ is independent of n'. Under the assumption that $m' = m$, the upper bounds on the running times for different splittings only differ by n', i.e., how often we invoke the procedure step. The case where $n' = 1$ corresponds to the scenario where we use the monitoring algorithm offline (up to time τ_{n-1}). The case where $n' = n$ corresponds to the case where we invoke the monitor whenever an event occurs. Even when using the interval-based monitoring algorithm offline and assuming constant representation of the elements in $\mathbb{T}$, the upper bounds differ by the factors n and $\delta \cdot |\phi|$. Since $\delta \geq n$, the upper bound of the point-based monitoring algorithm is lower. In fact, there are examples showing that the gap between the running times matches our upper bounds and that $\delta \cdot |\phi|$ can be significantly larger than n.

5   Related Work

We only discuss the monitoring algorithms most closely related to ours, namely, those of Basin et al. [4], Thati and Roşu [20], and Nickovic and Maler [14, 15].

The point-based monitoring algorithms here simplify and optimize the monitoring algorithm of Basin et al. [4] given for the future-bounded fragment of metric first-order temporal logic. We restricted ourselves here to the propositional setting and to the past-only fragment of metric temporal logic to compare the effect of different time models on monitoring.

Thati and Roşu [20] provide a monitoring algorithm for metric temporal logic with a point-based semantics, which uses formula rewriting. Their algorithm is more general than ours for the point based setting since it handles past and future operators. Their complexity analysis is based on the assumption that operations involving elements from the time domain can be carried out in constant time. The worst-case complexity of their algorithm on the past-only fragment is worse than ours, since rewriting a formula can generate additional formulas. In particular, their algorithm is not linear in the number of subformulas.

Nickovic and Maler's [14, 15] monitoring algorithms are for the interval-based setting and have ingredients similar to our algorithm for this setting. These ingredients were first presented by Nickovic and Maler for an offline version of their monitoring algorithms [13] for the fragment of interval metric temporal logic with bounded future operators. Their setting is more general in that their signals are continuous functions and not Boolean values for each point in time. Moreover, their algorithms also handle bounded [15] and unbounded [14] future operators by delaying the evaluation of subformulas. The algorithm in [14] slightly differs from the one in [15]: [14] also handles past operators and before starting monitoring, it rewrites the given formula to eliminate the temporal operators until and since with timing constraints. The main difference to our algorithm is that Maler and Nickovic do not provide algorithmic details for handling the Boolean connectives and the temporal operators. In fact, the worst-case complexity, which is only stated for their offline algorithm [13], seems to be too low even when ignoring representation and complexity issues for elements of the time domain.

We are not aware of any work that compares different time models for runtime verification. The surveys [2, 6, 16] on real-time logics focus on expressiveness, satisfiability, and automatic verification of real-time systems. A comparison of a point-based and interval-based time model for temporal databases with a discrete time domain is given by Toman [21]. The work by Furia and Rossi [9] on sampling and the work on digitization [11] by Henzinger et al. are orthogonal to our comparison. These relate fragments of metric interval temporal logic with respect to a discrete and a dense time domain.

6   Conclusions

We have presented, analyzed, and compared monitoring algorithms for real-time logics with point-based and interval-based semantics. Our comparison provides a detailed explanation of trade-offs between the different time models with respect to monitoring. Moreover, we have presented a practically relevant fragment for the interval-based setting by distinguishing between state variables and system events, which can be more efficiently monitored in the point-based setting.

As future work, we plan to extend the monitoring algorithms to handle bounded future operators. This includes analyzing their computational complexities and comparing them experimentally. Another line of research is to establish lower bounds for monitoring real-time logics. Thati and Roşu [20] give lower bounds for future fragments of metric temporal logic including the next operator. However, we are not aware of any lower bounds for the past-only fragment.

References

1. Alur, R., Feder, T., Henzinger, T.: The benefits of relaxing punctuality. J. ACM 43(1), 116–146 (1996)
2. Alur, R., Henzinger, T.: Logics and Models of Real Time: A Survey. In: Huizing, C., de Bakker, J.W., Rozenberg, G., de Roever, W.-P. (eds.) REX 1991. LNCS, vol. 600, pp. 74–106. Springer, Heidelberg (1992)
3. Basin, D., Klaedtke, F., Müller, S.: Monitoring security policies with metric first-order temporal logic. In: SACMAT 2010, pp. 23–33 (2010)
4. Basin, D., Klaedtke, F., Müller, S., Pfitzmann, B.: Runtime monitoring of metric first-order temporal properties. In: FSTTCS 2008, pp. 49–60 (2008)

5. Bauer, A., Leucker, M., Schallhart, C.: Monitoring of Real-Time Properties. In: Arun-Kumar, S., Garg, N. (eds.) FSTTCS 2006. LNCS, vol. 4337, pp. 260–272. Springer, Heidelberg (2006)
6. Bouyer, P.: Model-checking times temporal logics. In: 5th Workshop on Methods for Modalities. ENTCS, vol. 231, pp. 323–341 (2009)
7. Drusinsky, D.: On-line monitoring of metric temporal logic with time-series constraints using alternating finite automata. J. UCS 12(5), 482–498 (2006)
8. Fürer, M.: Faster integer multiplication. In: STOC 2007, pp. 55–67 (2007)
9. Furia, C., Rossi, M.: A theory of sampling for continuous-time metric temporal logic. ACM Trans. Comput. Log. 12(1) (2010)
10. Goodloe, A., Pike, L.: Monitoring distributed real-time systems: A survey and future directions. Tech. rep. CR-2010-216724, NASA Langley Research Center (2010)
11. Henzinger, T., Manna, Z., Pnueli, A.: What Good are Digital Clocks? In: Kuich, W. (ed.) ICALP 1992. LNCS, vol. 623, pp. 545–558. Springer, Heidelberg (1992)
12. Kristoffersen, K., Pedersen, C., Andersen, H.: Runtime verification of timed LTL using disjunctive normalized equation systems. In: RV 2003. ENTCS, vol. 89, pp. 210–225 (2003)
13. Maler, O., Nickovic, D.: Monitoring Temporal Properties of Continuous Signals. In: Lakhnech, Y., Yovine, S. (eds.) FORMATS 2004 and FTRTFT 2004. LNCS, vol. 3253, pp. 152–166. Springer, Heidelberg (2004)
14. Ničković, D.: Checking Timed and Hybrid Properties: Theory and Applications. PhD thesis, Université Joseph Fourier, Grenoble, France (2008)
15. Nickovic, D., Maler, O.: AMT: A Property-Based Monitoring Tool for Analog Systems. In: Raskin, J.-F., Thiagarajan, P.S. (eds.) FORMATS 2007. LNCS, vol. 4763, pp. 304–319. Springer, Heidelberg (2007)
16. Ouaknine, J., Worrell, J.: Some Recent Results in Metric Temporal Logic. In: Cassez, F., Jard, C. (eds.) FORMATS 2008. LNCS, vol. 5215, pp. 1–13. Springer, Heidelberg (2008)
17. Pike, L., Goodloe, A., Morisset, R., Niller, S.: Copilot: A Hard Real-Time Runtime Monitor. In: Barringer, H., Falcone, Y., Finkbeiner, B., Havelund, K., Lee, I., Pace, G., Roşu, G., Sokolsky, O., Tillmann, N. (eds.) RV 2010. LNCS, vol. 6418, pp. 345–359. Springer, Heidelberg (2010)
18. Raskin, J.-F., Schobbens, P.-Y.: Real-time Logics: Fictitious Clock as an Abstraction of Dense Time. In: Brinksma, E. (ed.) TACAS 1997. LNCS, vol. 1217, pp. 165–182. Springer, Heidelberg (1997)
19. Schönhage, A., Strassen, V.: Schnelle Multiplikation großer Zahlen. Computing 7(3-4), 281–292 (1971)
20. Thati, P., Roşu, G.: Monitoring algorithms for metric temporal logic specifications. In: RV 2004. ENTCS, vol. 113, pp. 145–162 (2005)
21. Toman, D.: Point vs. interval-based query languages for temporal databases. In: PODS 1996, pp. 58–67 (1996)

Runtime Monitoring of Stochastic Cyber-Physical Systems with Hybrid State*

A. Prasad Sistla, Miloš Žefran, and Yao Feng

University of Illinois at Chicago
{sistla,mzefran,yfeng9}@uic.edu

Abstract. Correct functioning of cyber-physical systems is of critical importance. This is more so in the case of safety critical systems such as in medical, automotive and many other applications. Since verification of correctness, in general, is infeasible and testing is not exhaustive, it is of critical importance to monitor such system during their operation and detect erroneous behaviors to be acted on. A distinguishing property of cyber-physical systems is that they are described by a mixture of integer-valued and real-valued variables. As a result, approaches that assume countable number of states are not applicable for runtime monitoring of such systems. This paper proposes a formalism, called Extended Hidden Markov systems, for specifying behavior of systems with such hybrid state. Using measure theory, it exactly characterizes when such systems are monitorable with respect to a given property. It also presents monitoring algorithms and experimental results showing their effectiveness.

1 Introduction

As traditional control systems are replaced by ever more powerful networks of microprocessors, cyber-physical systems are becoming an integral part of modern society. Their correct functioning is of paramount importance since a malfunction can lead to a serious injury or a loss of life. Monitoring at run time and shutting the system down safely in case of malfunctioning can thus provide a mechanism for safe operation of such systems.

The monitor observes the inputs and outputs of the component and checks whether the behavior of the system is consistent with the expected behavior. The fundamental advantage of monitors is that they are in principle easy to implement, and they are independent of the design procedures used to develop a component. While wrong assumptions might lead to a faulty design, the monitor is independent of design decisions and can therefore easily detect that the component is failing to perform its function.

In our earlier works [10, 29], we addressed the problem of monitoring a system, modeled as a Hidden Markov Chain (HMC) H, when the correctness specification is given by a deterministic Streett automaton A on the outputs generated

---

* This research was supported in part by NSF grants IIS-0905593, CNS-0910988, CCF-0916438 and CNS-1035914.

S. Khurshid and K. Sen (Eds.): RV 2011, LNCS 7186, pp. 276–293, 2012.

by the system. In these works, we defined two measures, called *Acceptance Accuracy (AA)* and *Rejection Accuracy (RA)* that capture the effectiveness of the monitor. Here $(1 - AA)$ and $(1 - RA)$ give measures of false alarms and missed alarms, respectively. Monitoring algorithms for achieving arbitrary high values of accuracies were presented when H and $\mathcal{A}$ are finite state systems.

In a more recent paper [31], we considered the case of internal monitoring, i.e., when the property $\mathcal{A}$ to be monitored is specified on the states of the system and when both the system H and the automaton $\mathcal{A}$ may have countably infinite number of states. In this setting, we defined a notion of monitorability, which states that a system is monitorable with respect to a property if arbitrary high levels of accuracy, close to one, can be achieved. We proved a fundamental theorem, called *monitorability theorem*, that exactly characterizes when a system is monitorable with respect to a property. The paper also gave monitoring algorithms that achieve high accuracies for monitorable cases. We applied the algorithms to systems modeled by probabilistic hybrid automata by approximating its hybrid state space by a discrete state space through quantization.

In this paper, we consider Extended Hidden Markov Systems (EHMS), which are like HMCs, but in which the state space is a hybrid state space. In these systems, the system variables and the output variables are partitioned into discrete and continuous variables. We consider probability functions over such hybrid state spaces. A probability function can be considered as a set of sub-probability density functions on the continuous part of the state space where each density function is indexed by a discrete part of the state. An EHMS is given by a next state function and an output function that give the probability functions on the next state and outputs, given the current state. We extend the monitorability theorem to EHMSes. This extension is non-trivial, and relies on results from measure theory, as we have to deal with continuous as well as discrete probability distributions. We present monitoring algorithms and experimental results showing the effectiveness of our approach for a more complex version of the example considered in [31].

In summary the main contributions of the paper are as follows: (1) an Extended Hidden Markov model for modeling cyber-physical systems, without discretization; (2) exact characterizations of systems that are monitorable with respect to a property; (3) monitoring algorithms when the system and property automata are specified by probabilistic hybrid automata; and (4) experimental results showing the effectiveness of our approach.

2   Related Work

A wealth of literature is available for the modeling and control of hybrid systems and we refer the reader to the overview articles [1, 5] and the books [20, 33]. In these systems, safety requirements are described by a set of system states which are permissible, or equivalently, by a set of system states that are forbidden. A closely related problem is checking liveness properties, where in general we require that a set of states is visited infinitely often. Formally, safety and liveness properties can be described using temporal logic [16, 18]. Safety and liveness verification thus becomes a verification problem for a hybrid automaton modeling the robotic system [12, 24]. It was shown that except for the simplest hybrid automata this verification problem is undecidable [12].

A problem that has been extensively studied is monitoring and diagnosis of hybrid automata [2, 3, 9, 13, 17, 19, 23, 34], where the aim is to detect when the automaton enters a fail state so that the system can appropriately react. Similar work has been done in the Artificial Intelligence community on failure detection and recovery from failures using Hidden Markov models [27]. In most cases, these works employ techniques that depend on the specific possible modes of failure. Furthermore, even if such methods are employed, one still needs to monitor the correct functioning of the overall system for correct functioning. None of the above works addresses this general problem of monitoring system behaviors against specifications given in an expressive formal system such as the hybrid automata. Furthermore, they do not address the problem of monitoring liveness properties.

An alternative to verification is to directly incorporate the safety requirements into the design process itself so that no verification step is necessary [16, 18, 21]. These approaches are not yet able to adequately address systems with complex continuous dynamics, nor can they deal with stochastic phenomena such as sensor and actuator failures.

There has been much work done in the literature on monitoring violations of safety properties in distributed systems, for example [4]. This work assumes that it can fully observe the system state and it instruments the program with commands to gather its state information and use it for monitoring. In contrast, we assume that the system is not directly observable. A method for monitoring and checking quantitative and probabilistic properties of real-time systems has been given in [11, 28]. These works take specifications in a probabilistic temporal logic (called CSL) and monitor for its satisfaction. The probabilities are deduced from the repeated occurrence of events in a computation. The work presented in [25] considers monitoring interfaces for faults using game-theoretic framework. Run-time monitoring is used to verify that the interface has a winning strategy. *Conservative* run time monitors were proposed in [22, 30]. In this scheme, one identifies a safety property that implies the given property f (in general, f is the intersection/conjunction of a safety and a liveness property). None of these works is intended for monitoring of hybrid systems.

3 Definitions and Notation

Sequences. Let S be a set. Let $\sigma = s_0, s_1, \ldots$ be a possibly infinite sequence over S. The length of σ, denoted as $|\sigma|$, is defined to be the number of elements in σ if σ is finite, and ω otherwise. For any $i \geq 0$, $\sigma[0, i]$ denotes the prefix of σ up to s_i. If α_1 is a finite sequence and α_2 is either a finite or an ω-sequence then $\alpha_1\alpha_2$ denotes the concatenation of the two sequences in that order. We let

S^*, S^ω denote the set of finite sequences and the set of infinite sequences over S. If $C \subseteq S^\omega$ and $\alpha \in S^*$ then αC denotes the set $\{\alpha\beta : \beta \in C\}$.

Safety Properties. For any $\sigma \in S^\omega$, let prefixes(σ) denote the set of prefixes of σ and for any $C \subseteq S^\omega$, let prefixes$(C) = \cup_{\sigma \in C}(\text{prefixes}(\sigma))$. We say that $C \subseteq S^\omega$ is a *safety* property if the following condition holds: for any $\sigma \in S^\omega$, if prefixes$(\sigma) \subseteq$ prefixes(C) then $\sigma \in C$. For any $C \subseteq S^\omega$, let *closure*(C) be the smallest safety property such that $C \subseteq closure(C)$.

Extended Hidden Markov systems. We assume that the reader is familiar with basic probability theory, random variables and Markov chains. We consider stochastic systems over discrete time with both discrete and continuous states. Let $\mathbf{R}, \mathbf{N}$ denote the set of real numbers and non-negative integers, respectively. Throughout the paper, we will be using integrals over measurable functions which are taken to be Lebesgue integrals (see [26] for definitions).

Let $\sigma = (\sigma_0, ..., \sigma_{n-1})$ be a vector in $\{0,1\}^n$. For each such σ, we define the hybrid domain $S_\sigma = T_0 \times T_1 \times ... \times T_{n-1}$ where $T_i = \mathbf{N}$ or $T_i = \mathbf{R}$ depending on whether $\sigma_i = 0$ or $\sigma_i = 1$, respectively. We define a class $\mathcal{D}_\sigma$ of measurable subsets of S_σ as follows. Let I be the set of all values of i such that $\sigma_i = 0$ and J be the set of all values of j such that $\sigma_j = 1$. Let n_1, n_2 be the cardinalities of I, J respectively. Clearly $n_1 + n_2 = n$. For any $s \in S_\sigma$, let $s|I$ and $s|J$,respectively, be the projections of s on to the coordinates in I and J. That is, $s|I$, $s|J$ give the values of discrete and continuous elements in s. For any $a \in \mathbf{N}^{n_1}$ and any $C \subseteq \mathbf{R}^{n_2}$, let $D_{a,C} = \{s : s|I = a, s|J \in C\}$. Now, we define $\mathcal{D}_\sigma$ to be the σ-algebra generated by the sets in $\{D_{a,C} : a \in \mathbf{N}^{n_1}, C \subseteq \mathbf{R}^{n_2} \text{ is a Borel set}\}$. A function $\mu : S_\sigma \to [0, \infty)$ is called a *probability function* if it is a measurable function and $\sum_{x \in \mathbf{N}^{n_1}} \int_{\mathbf{R}^{n_2}} \mu(x, x')dx' = 1$, where x is a vector of n_1 variables ranging over $\mathbf{N}$, and x' is a vector of n_2 variables ranging over $\mathbf{R}$. Note that, we first integrate over the continuous variables, keeping the discrete variables constant, and then sum over all possible values for the discrete variables. Note that, if σ has no 0s, i.e., $S_\sigma = \mathbf{R}^n$, then μ will be the standard probability density function. We say that μ is a *sub probability function* if it is a measurable function and $\sum_{x \in \mathbf{N}^{n_1}} \int_{\mathbf{R}^{n_2}} \mu(x, x')dx' \leq 1$.

Let $n_1, n_2, m_1, m_2 \geq 0$ be integers and σ_1, σ_2 be the vectors $0^{n_1}1^{n_2}$ and $0^{m_1}1^{m_2}$, respectively. Intuitively, n_1, n_2 give the number of discrete and continuous state variables, while m_1, m_2 give the number of discrete and continuous outputs of the system being described. An Extended Hidden Markov System (EHMS) H of dimensions (n_1, n_2, m_1, m_2), is a triple (f, g, μ) where $f : (S_{\sigma_1} \times S_{\sigma_1}) \to [0, \infty)$, $g : (S_{\sigma_1} \times S_{\sigma_2}) \to [0, \infty)$ and μ are functions, satisfying the following properties. Let x, y be sequences of $n_1 + n_2$ variables each and z be a sequence of $m_1 + m_2$ variables. The function $f(x, y)$, called *next state function*, is a probability function in the arguments in y; that is, for any appropriate fixed values for variables in x, f is a probability function on S_{σ_1} in the argument y. Similarly $g(x, z)$, called *output function*, is a probability function in the arguments in z. Finally, μ is a probability function on S_{σ_1}.

Intuitively, the first set of arguments in $f()$ and $g()$ give the discrete and continuous parts of the current state. In $f()$ the last set of arguments give discrete and continuous parts of the next state, while in $g()$ they give the discrete and continuous parts of the output values.

For convenience, from here onwards, we let S denote S_{σ_1} and Σ denote S_{σ_2} which represent the set of possible system states and outputs respectively. Intuitively, H describes a dynamic stochastic system with n_1, n_2 discrete, continuous state variables respectively, and with m_1, m_2 discrete,continuous output values respectively. The state of such a system, at any instance of time, is given by a value in S, denoting the values of the state variables. The outputs generated by the system at any instance is given by an element in Σ denoting the values of the $m_1 + m_2$ outputs. Essentially, given that the current state of the system is given by x, $f(x,y)$ denotes the probability density that the system is in state given by y at the next time instance. Similarly, $g(x,z)$ denotes the probability function in variables in z denoting the probability that the system generates the output values given by z. The function μ gives the probability distribution on the initial state. Many times we write the function $f()$ to be over four vectors of variables, i.e., $f(x, x', y, y')$ where x, x' denote the discrete and continuous part of the current state, and y, y' denote the discrete and continuous parts of the next state. Similar convention is followed for $g()$ and $\mu()$ as well.

We consider an ω-sequence over S as a computation/trajectory of H. The semantics of the EHMS H are given by three probability spaces $(S^\omega, \mathcal{E}_H, \phi_H)$, $(\Sigma^\omega, \mathcal{F}_H, \psi_H)$ and $((S \times \Sigma)^\omega, \mathcal{P}_H, \zeta_H)$ defined as follows.

First, we define the following notation. Let $n', n'' \geq 0$ be integers. For a finite sequence $a = (a_0, ..., a_{l-1})$ of elements from $\mathbf{N}^{n'}$ and a finite sequence $C = (C_0, C_1, ..., C_{l-1})$ of Borel subsets of $\mathbf{R}^{n''}$, let $E_{(a,C)}$ be the set of all ω-sequences $(s_0, ..., s_i, ...)$ of states in $S_{0^{n'}1^{n''}}$ such that $s_i \in \{a_i\} \times C_i$ for $0 \leq i < l$. Note that, if a, C are empty sequences, i.e., sequences of length zero, then $E_{(a,C)} = (S_{0^{n'}1^{n''}})^\omega$. Note that $E_{a,C}$ is well defined, for any $n', n'' \geq 0$, if a, C are of the same length.

Now, $\mathcal{E}_H$ is the smallest σ-algebra which contains the class of sets $\{E_{(a,C)} : \exists l \geq 0, a \in (\mathbf{N}^{n_1})^l$ and C is a finite sequences of Borel sets in $\mathbf{R}^{n_2}$ of length $l\}$.

For any μ', which is a probability function or is a sub-probability function, we define a unique probability measure $\Theta(\mu')$ on $\mathcal{E}_H$ such that for any $a \in (\mathbf{N}^{n_1})^l$, and any finite sequence $C = (C_0, ..., C_{l-1})$ of Borel sets in $\mathbf{R}^{n_2}$,

$$\Theta(\mu')(E_{(a,C)}) = \int_{\mathcal{C}} \mu'(a_0, x_0)(\prod_{0 \leq i < l-1} f(a_i, x_i, a_{i+1}, x_{i+1}) \, dx_{i+1}) \, dx_0,$$

where the integral is taken over the region $\mathcal{C}$ in which variables in x_i range over the region C_i, for $0 \leq i < l - 1$. The probability measure ϕ_H is defined to be $\Theta(\mu)$.

The class $\mathcal{F}_H$ is the smallest σ-algebra which contains the class of sets $\{E_{(b,C)} : \exists l \geq 0, b \in (\mathbf{N}^{m_1})^l, C = (C_0, ..., C_{l-1})$ is a sequence of Borel sets in $\mathbf{R}^{m_2}\}$. ψ_H is the unique probability measure on $\mathcal{F}_H$ such that

$$\psi_H(E_{(b,C)}) = \sum_{a_i \in \mathbf{N}^{n_1}, i < l} \int_{\mathcal{D}} \int_{\mathcal{C}} \mu(a_0, x_0) g(a_0, x_0, b_0, y_0)(\prod_{0 \leq i < l-1} F_i \, dx_{i+1} dy_{i+1}) \, dx_0 dy_0,$$

where $F_i = f(a_i, x_i, a_{i+1}, x_{i+1})g(a_{i+1}, x_{i+1}, b_{i+1}, y_{i+1})$, and $\mathcal{C}$ is the region in which the variables in $x_0, ..., x_{l-1}$ range over $\mathbf{R}^{n_2}$ and $\mathcal{D}$ is the region where the variables in $y_0, ..., y_{l-1}$ range over $C_0, ..., C_{l-1}$, respectively.

For any $l \geq 0$ and $a \in (\mathbf{N}^{n_1+m_1})^l$ and any finite sequence $C = (C_0, ..., C_{l-1})$ of Borel sets of $\mathbf{R}^{n_2+m_2}$, let $F_{a,C}$ be the set of all ω-sequences in $(S \times \Sigma)^\omega$ of the form $((s_0, t_0), ..., (s_i, t_i), ...)$ such that, for $i \geq 0$, $s_i = (b_i, u_i)$, $t_i = (c_i, v_i)$ where b_i, c_i are, respectively, the vectors consisting of the first n_1 and the last m_1 elements of a_i, and u_i, v_i are, respectively, the vectors consisting of the fist n_2 and the last m_2 elements of a vector in C_i.

The class $\mathcal{P}_H$ is the smallest σ-algebra which contains the class of sets $\{F_{(a,C)} : \exists l \geq 0, a \in (\mathbf{N}^{n_1+m_1})^l, C = (C_0, ..., C_{l-1})$ is a finite sequence of open sets in $\mathbf{R}^{n_2+m_2}\}$. ζ_H is the unique probability measure on $\mathcal{F}_H$ such that

$$\zeta_H(F_{(a,C)}) = \int_C \mu(b_0, x_0)g(b_0, x_0, c_0, y_0)dx_0 dy_0 \prod_{0 \leq i < l-1} G_i \, dx_{i+1} dy_{i+1},$$

where $G_i = f(b_i, x_i, b_{i+1}, x_{i+1})g(b_{i+1}, x_{i+1}, c_{i+1}, y_{i+1})$, and b_i is the vector consisting of the first n_1 values and c_i is the vector consisting of the last m_1 values of the vector a_i and C is the region in which the $n_2 + m_2$ variables in x_i and y_i range over C_i, for each $i = 0, ..., l-1$.

For any $s = (s_0, s_1, ...s_{n_1+n_2-1}) \in S$ and $t = (t_0, t_1, ...t_{m_1+m_2-1}) \in \Sigma$, let $s \otimes t$ denote the vector obtained by concatenating elements of s, t in that order. For any $u \in S^\omega$ and $v \in \Sigma^\omega$, given by $u = (u_0, ..., u_i, ...)$ and $v = (v_0, ..., v_i, ...)$, let $u \otimes v$ denote the unique $w = (w_0, ..., w_i, ...)$ where $w_i = u_i \otimes v_i$, for each $i \geq 0$. Now, for any $X \subseteq S^\omega$ and $Y \subseteq \Sigma^\omega$, let $X \otimes Y = \{u \otimes v : u \in X, v \in Y\}$. Observe that $X \otimes Y \subseteq (S \times \Sigma)^\omega$.

The following lemma is fairly straightforward to prove.

Lemma 1. *If $X \in \mathcal{E}_H$ and $Y \in \mathcal{F}_H$ then $X \otimes Y \in \mathcal{P}_H$.*

Probabilistic Hybrid Automata. Probabilistic Hybrid Automata (PHA) were defined in [13, 14]. They provide a convenient formalism for specifying systems. A probabilistic hybrid automaton $\mathcal{A}$ is a tuple $(Q, V, \Delta t, \mathcal{E}, \mathcal{T}, c_0)$ where Q is a countable set of *discrete* states (modes); V is a disjoint union of three sets V_1, V_2 and V_3 called the continuous state variables, output variables and noise variables, respectively, that all take values in $\mathbf{R}$; Δt is the sampling time; $\mathcal{E}$ is a function that with each $q \in Q$ associates a set $\mathcal{E}(q)$ of discrete-time state equations [8] describing the evolution of the continuous state (value of the variables in V_1) and the output (value of the variables in V_2) at time $t + \Delta t$ as functions of the state at t and the noise variables[1]; $\mathcal{T}$ is a function that assigns to each $q \in Q$ a set of *transitions* (ϕ, p), where the *guard* ϕ is a measurable predicate over the set of continuous (and possibly discrete) state variables and p is a probability distribution over Q; and c_0 is a pair giving the initial discrete state and an initial

---

[1] Additional explicit discrete state variables can be added to the variables in V provided their update equations only involve deterministic functions of such discrete state variables.

continuous probability distribution on the variables in V_1. We require that for each $q \in Q$, the state equations in $\mathcal{E}(q)$ have noise variables on the right hand side and that the set of guards on the transitions in $\mathcal{T}(q)$ be mutually exclusive and exhaustive.

We next give the semantics of the PHA. Within each mode q, the evolution of the PHA is given by the difference equations. When the guard ϕ of a transition $(\phi, p) \in \mathcal{T}(q)$ becomes satisfied, a transition takes place from q to some target mode q' according to the probability distribution p. Since there are no deterministic resets to variables in the transitions, it is quite easy to see that the semantics of $\mathcal{A}$ can be given in terms of an EHMS system $H_{\mathcal{A}}$.

Monitors. We consider monitors that take outputs Σ, generated by a EHMC H, as inputs and accept or reject them. Formally, a monitor $M : \Sigma^* \to \{0, 1\}$ is a function with the property that, for any $\alpha \in \Sigma^*$, if $M(\alpha) = 0$ then $M(\alpha\beta) = 0$ for every $\beta \in \Sigma^*$. For an $\alpha \in \Sigma^*$, we say that M rejects α, if $M(\alpha) = 0$, otherwise we say M accepts α. Thus if M rejects α then it rejects all its extensions. For an infinite sequence $\sigma \in \Sigma^\omega$, we say that M rejects σ iff there exists a prefix α of σ that is rejected by M; we say M accepts σ if it does not reject it. Let $L(M)$ denote the set of infinite sequences accepted by M. It is not difficult to see that $L(M)$ is a safety property. We require that $L(M)$ is a measurable set, i.e., is in $\mathcal{F}_H$.

It is to be noted that, in practice, a monitor is given as an algorithm that takes a finite sequence of elements from Σ as input, and raises an alarm or not. Here raising an alarm is considered as rejection. Associated with such an algorithm, there is a monitor function as defined above. Note that such a function is computable. Thus, for a monitor M to be feasible it has to be computable.

Accuracy Measures. Let $H = (f, g, \mu)$ be a EHMC over (n_1, n_2, m_1, m_2)-dimensions. Let S, Σ be the states and outputs of H as defined earlier. Let $GOOD$ be a set in $\mathcal{E}_H$ denoting a measurable set. We fix $GOOD$ and call its members as good computations of H. Let $M : \Sigma^* \to \{0, 1\}$ be a monitor as given above. The *acceptance accuracy* of M for $GOOD$ with respect to H, denoted by $AA(M, H, GOOD)$, is defined to be the conditional probability that M accepts the output generated by H given that the computation of H is in $GOOD$. Formally, it is defined to be the value given by

$$AA(M, H, GOOD) = \frac{\zeta_H(GOOD \otimes L(M))}{\zeta_H(GOOD \otimes \Sigma^\omega)}.$$

Note that $\zeta_H(GOOD \otimes L(M))$ denotes the probability that a computation in $GOOD$ generates an output in $L(M)$, while $\zeta_H(GOOD \otimes \Sigma^\omega)$ denotes the probability that the system generates a computation in $GOOD$. Also note that the later value is same as $\phi_H(GOOD)$.

All computations that are not in $GOOD$ are called bad and we denote this set by BAD, i.e., $BAD = S^\omega - GOOD$. The *rejection accuracy* of M for $GOOD$ with respect to H, denoted by $RA(M, H, GOOD)$, is defined to be the conditional probability that M rejects the output generated by a bad computation of H. Formally, it is defined to be the value given by

$$RA(M, H, GOOD) = \frac{\zeta_H(BAD \otimes (\Sigma^\omega - L(M)))}{\zeta_H(BAD \otimes \Sigma^\omega)}.$$

Note that the $\zeta_H(BAD \otimes (\Sigma^\omega - L(M)))$ denotes the probability that a bad computation is rejected by M, while $\zeta_H(BAD \otimes \Sigma^\omega)$ denotes the probability that the system generates a bad computation. Clearly, both the above accuracies are defined only when $0 < \phi_H(GOOD) < 1$.

Monitorability. We say that a system H is *monitorable* with respect to $GOOD$ if for every $x \in [0, 1)$ there exists a monitor M such that $AA(M, H, GOOD) \geq x$ and $RA(M, H, GOOD) \geq x$. In the next section, we give necessary and sufficient conditions for these properties to be satisfied.

It is worth noting that monitorability, while related to the classical notion of observability, is fundamentally different from it. It is not difficult to construct cyber-physical systems that are not observable or even discrete-state observable but are monitorable.

4   Monitorability

In this subsection, we give necessary and sufficient conditions for monitorability. Let $H = (f, g, \mu)$ be the given EHMS over (n_1, n_2, m_1, m_2)-dimensions. Let $GOOD$ be a member of $\mathcal{E}_H$, i.e., is a measurable subset of S^ω such that $0 < \phi_H(GOOD) < 1$.

Consider an integer $l > 0$ and let $O = (y_0, ..., y_l)$ denote a sequence of variables denoting an output sequence of elements from Σ^m; each y_i consists of $m_1 + m_2$ variables corresponding to discrete as well as continuous outputs. Define a function $I(y_0, ..., y_l)$ as follows.

$$I(y_0, ..., y_l) = \sum \int \mu(u_0, x_0')g(u_0, x_0', y_0)(\prod_{0 \leq i < l} F_i \, dx_{i+1}')dx_0'$$

where $F_i = f(u_i, x_i', u_{i+1}, x_{i+1}')g(u_{i+1}, x_{i+1}', y_{i+1})$.

In the above equation, u_i, x_i' denote n_1 discrete state variables and n_2 continuous state variables, respectively. The integration is over variables in x_i', for $i = 0, ...,$, where each such variable ranges over $\mathbf{R}$. The summation is over all discrete variables in u_i, for $i = 0, ..., l$. Each such variable ranges over $\mathbf{N}$.

Essentially, $I(y_0, ..., y_l)$ defines a probability function, over $(l+1)m_1$ discrete variables and $(l+1)m_2$ continuous variables, giving the probability of generation of the output sequence O by all the computations of the system. Using the fact that sums and products of measurable functions are also measurable, and using Fubini's theorem (see [26]) we see that $I(y_0, ..., y_l)$ is a measurable function.

Now, we define sub-probability function $J(y_0, ..., y_l)$ for the probability of generation of the output sequence O by computations of H that are in GOOD. For any sequence $\alpha = (x_0, ..., x_l)$ of states of the system, let $GOOD|\alpha$ denote the set of all sequences $\beta \in S^\omega$ such that $\alpha\beta \in GOOD$. For $i = 0, ..., l$, each x_i has n_1 discrete and n_2 continuous variables. Intuitively, $GOOD|\alpha$ is the set of sequences obtained by dropping the prefix α from those sequences in $GOOD$ that have α as a prefix. It is easy to show that $GOOD|\alpha$ is a measurable set. Now, let $\mu'_{O,\alpha}(z)$ be a probability function on S defined by:

$$\mu'_{O,\alpha}(z) = \mu(x_0)(\prod_{0 \leq i < l} g(x_i, y_i)f(x_i, x_{i+1}))g(x_l, y_l)f(x_l, z)$$

Essentially, it gives the probability that the output sequence O is generated by the sequence of states given by α followed by the state given by z. Note that, in the above equation each x_i has n_1 discrete variables and n_2 continuous variables. Let $U_O(\alpha)$ be the measure of the set $GOOD|\alpha$ defined by the initial probability density function $\mu'_{O,\alpha}$, i.e., $U_O(\alpha) = \Theta(\mu'_{O,\alpha})(GOOD|\alpha)$. Now, define

$$J(y_0, ..., y_l) = \sum \int U_O(u_0, x'_0, ..., u_l, x'_l)dx_0...dx_l$$

In the above equation, for each $i = 0, ..., l$, each u_i denotes n_1 discrete variables and each x'_i denotes n_2 continuous variables. Furthermore, the integration is over all variables in x'_i, for $i = 0, ..., l$, while the summation is over all variables in u_i, for $i = 0, ..., l$. Each continuous variable ranges over $\mathbf{R}$, while each discrete variable ranges over $\mathbf{N}$. Notice that $J(y_0, ..., y_l)$ is the probability function for the probability of generation of outputs given by O by computations of the system that are in $GOOD$. It should be easy to see that $J(y_0, ..., y_l) \leq I(y_0, ..., y_l)$ for all appropriate values for variables in y_i, $i = 0, ..., l$.

Lemma 2. *$GOOD|\alpha$ is a measurable set and $J(y_0, ..., y_l)$ is a measurable function.*

Let $GoodProb(O)$ be the value defined by

$$GoodProb(O) = \frac{J(y_0, ..., y_l)}{I(y_0, ..., y_l)}$$

Observe that $GoodProb(O) \leq 1$. Essentially $GoodProb(O)$ gives the conditional probability that the computation of the system is good, i.e. in $GOOD$, given that the output generated in the first $l+1$ states is given by O. It is not difficult to see that $GoodProb(y_0, ..., y_l)$ is a measurable function since $I(y_0, ..., y_l)$, $J(y_0, ..., y_l)$ are measurable functions.

Recall that for any $\beta \in \Sigma^\omega$ and integer $i \geq 0$, $\beta[0, i]$ denotes the prefix of β of length $i + 1$. Now, let $OneSeq(H, GOOD)$ be the set of all $\beta \in \Sigma^\omega$ such that $\lim_{i \to \infty} GoodProb(\beta[0, i])$ exists and it's value is 1. Similarly, let $ZeroSeq(H, GOOD)$ be the set of all $\beta \in \Sigma^\omega$ such that the above limit exists and is equal to 0. Let $ZeroOneSeq(H, GOOD) = OneSeq(H, GOOD) \cup ZeroSeq(H, GOOD)$. The following lemma states that the sets $OneSeq(H, GOOD)$ and $ZeroSeq(H, GOOD)$ are measurable. It also states that the measure of the computations of H that generate output sequences in $OneSeq(H, GOOD)$ (sequences in $ZeroSeq(H, GOOD)$) and that are bad (that are good) is zero.

Lemma 3. *The sets $OneSeq(H, GOOD)$ and $ZeroSeq(H, GOOD)$ are measurable (both are members of $\mathcal{F}_H$). Furthermore,*

$$\zeta_H(BAD \otimes OneSeq(H, GOOD)) = 0 \quad and$$
$$\zeta_H(GOOD \otimes ZeroSeq(H, GOOD)) = 0.$$

The following *monitorability theorem* gives a necessary and sufficient condition for the monitorability of H with respect to $GOOD$ and is a generalization of the corresponding theorem for HMCs, i.e.,discrete state systems proved in [31]. The theorem states that H is monitorable with respect to $GOOD$ iff with probability 1, any random infinite output sequence generated by H is in $ZeroOneSeq(H, GOOD)$.

Theorem 1. *For any EHMS H and measurable set $GOOD$ in $\mathcal{E}_H$, H is monitorable with respect to $GOOD$ iff $\psi_H(ZeroOneSeq(H, GOOD)) = 1$.*

Proof. Let $H = (f, g, \mu)$ be a EHMS of dimension (n_1, n_2, m_1, m_2) and $GOOD$ be a measurable set in $\mathcal{E}_H$. Assume that H is monitorable with respect to $GOOD$.

Suppose that $\psi_H(ZeroOneSeq(H, GOOD)) < 1$. Let $F = \Sigma^\omega - ZeroOneSeq(H, GOOD)$. Clearly $\psi_H(F) > 0$. Consider any $\beta \in F$. It should be easy to see that for some $u > 0$, the following property (*) holds:
(*) For infinitely many values of i, $GoodProb(\beta[0, i]) < (1 - \frac{1}{2^u})$ and for infinitely many values of j, $GoodProb(\beta[0, j]) > \frac{1}{2^u}$.

For each $u > 0$, define F_u to be the set of sequences $\beta \in F$ such that u is the smallest integer that satisfies (*). It is easy to see that the set $\{F_u : u > 0\}$ is a partition of F. It should also be easy to see that $F_u \in \mathcal{F}_H$, i.e., is measurable, for each $u > 0$. Since $\psi_H(F) > 0$, it follows that for some $u > 0$, $\psi_H(F_u) > 0$. Fix such an u and let $x = \psi_H(F_u)$. From property (*), it can be shown that for any $C \in \mathcal{F}_H$, such that $C \subseteq F_u$ and $y = \psi_H(C) > 0$, the following property (**) holds:

$$(**) \quad \zeta_H(GOOD \otimes C) \geq \frac{y}{2^u} \text{ and } \zeta_H(BAD \otimes C) \geq \frac{y}{2^u}.$$

Now, consider any monitor M. Recall that $L(M)$ is the set of infinite sequences in Σ^ω that are accepted by M. Further more, $L(M)$ is a safety property and is measurable, i.e., $L(M) \in \mathcal{F}_H$. Now, since $x = \psi_H(F_u)$ and $F_u = (F_u \cap L(M)) \cup (F_u - L(M))$, it is the case that either $\psi_H(F_u \cap L(M)) \geq \frac{x}{2}$ or $\psi_H(F_u - L(M)) \geq \frac{x}{2}$. In the former case, by taking $C = F_u \sqcap L(M)$ and using property (**), we see that the measure of bad computations of the system (i.e., those in BAD) that are accepted by the monitor is $\geq \frac{x}{2^{u+1}}$ and in the later case, by taking $C = (F_u - L(M))$, the measure of good computations of the system (i.e., those that are in $GOOD$) that are rejected is $\geq \frac{x}{2^{u+1}}$. Now, let $z = \max\{\phi_H(GOOD), \phi_H(BAD))\}$. From the above arguments, we see that , for every monitor M, either $RA(M, H, GOOD) \leq 1 - \frac{x}{z \cdot 2^{u+1}}$ or $AA(M, H, GOOD) \leq 1 - \frac{x}{z \cdot 2^{u+1}}$. This contradicts our assumption that H is monitorable with respect to $\mathcal{A}$.

Now, assume that $\psi_H(ZeroOneSeq(H, GOOD)) = 1$. Let $z \in (0,1)$. Let $M_z : \Sigma^* \to \{0,1\}$ be a function such that for any $\alpha \in \Sigma^*$, $M_z(\alpha) = 0$ iff there exists a prefix α' of α such that $GoodProb(\alpha') < 1 - z$. Clearly M_z is a monitor. When extended to infinite sequences $M_z(\beta) = 0$ for every $\beta \in ZeroSeq(H, GOOD)$, i.e., it rejects all of them. The second part of Lemma 3 implies that $\zeta_H(GOOD \otimes ZeroSeq(H, GOOD)) = 0$, and it can further be deduced that $\zeta_H(BAD \otimes ZeroSeq(H, GOOD)) = 1$. From these observations, it follows that $RA(M_z, H, GOOD) = 1$. It should be easy to see that the measure of good computations of H that are rejected by M_z is $\leq \min\{y, 1 - z\}$ where $y = \phi_H(GOOD)$. Therefore, $AA(M_z, H, GOOD) \geq 1 - \frac{\min\{y, 1-z\}}{y}$. Now, for any given $x \in (0,1)$, we can chose a value of z such that $AA(M_z, H, GOOD) \geq x$ and $RA(M_z, H, GOOD) = 1$. This implies that H is monitorable with respect to $GOOD$. □

5   Monitoring Algorithms

In this section we describe how the formal methodology developed above can be used in applications. We assume that the system to be monitored is specified by a probabilistic hybrid automaton (PHA) [13, 14] as described in Sec. 3. Let the system under consideration be specified by a PHA $\mathcal{A}$. Recall that $\mathcal{H}_\mathcal{A}$ denotes the EHMS capturing the behavior of $\mathcal{A}$.

Property Automaton. We consider traditional deterministic Buchi automata to specify properties over sequences of states of $H_\mathcal{A}$. We allow these automata to have possibly infinite, but countable, number of states. It is well known that the set of inputs accepted by a Buchi automaton $\mathcal{P}$ is a measurable set, i.e., is a member of $\mathcal{E}_{H_\mathcal{A}}$. A safety automaton is a property automaton having a special absorbing state called *error* state with all the other states being the accepting states. The set of sequences accepted by a safety automaton is a safety property.

Product Automaton. In order to monitor whether the system specified by $\mathcal{A}$ satisfies the property specified by $\mathcal{P}$, we construct the product of $\mathcal{A}$ and $\mathcal{P}$ in a natural way. This product is a hybrid automaton and we designate it by $\mathcal{B}$. The formal specification of $\mathcal{B}$ is left out due to space limitations. Each discrete state of $\mathcal{B}$ is a pair (q, q') where q is the discrete state of $\mathcal{A}$ and q' is a state of $\mathcal{P}$. Essentially, $\mathcal{B}$ behaves like $\mathcal{A}$ and at the same time runs $\mathcal{P}$ on the sequence of states of $\mathcal{A}$. Observe that the outputs generated by $\mathcal{A}$ and $\mathcal{B}$ are same.

5.1   Monitoring Safety Properties

Let $\mathcal{A}$ be a system automaton, $\mathcal{P}$ be a safety property automaton specified on $\mathcal{A}$ and $\mathcal{B}$ be the product hybrid automaton. Let $GOOD$ be the set of all input sequences accepted by $\mathcal{P}$. Consider an infinite sequence α of outputs generated by the EHMS $H_\mathcal{A}$. Recall that $\alpha[0, i]$ denotes the prefix of α of length $i+1$. For EHMS $H_\mathcal{A}$, let $u_i = 1 - GoodProb(\alpha[0, i])$ and v_i be the probability that the EHMS $H_\mathcal{B}$ is in an error state given that $\alpha[0, i]$ is the sequence of outputs generated by it. The following lemma shows that u_i and v_i converge to the same value.

Lemma 4. *For all $i \geq 0$, $v_i \leq u_i$ and $\lim_{i \to \infty} (v_i) = \lim_{i \to \infty} (u_i)$.*

Assume that $\mathcal{A}$ is monitorable with respect to $\mathcal{P}$. For any $z > 0$, let M_z be a monitor that works as follows. On any infinite sequence α of outputs generated by the system given by $\mathcal{A}$ and at instance of time $i \geq 0$, M_z estimates the probability v_i using the product system $\mathcal{B}$, and rejects if $v_i > z$. Using the proof of Theorem 1 and Lemma 4, we see that by increasing z arbitrarily close to 1, we can get monitors whose accuracies are arbitrarily close to 1.

5.2   Liveness Monitoring

Now we give an approach for monitoring properties specified by liveness automata using the methods given in [22, 30]. Let $\mathcal{P}$ be a property automaton which is a liveness automaton. We convert it into a safety automaton $\mathcal{P}'$ by using timeouts as follows. Let T be a large time constant. We modify $\mathcal{P}$ so that it goes to a special error state q_{error} if it does not reach an accepting state with in T steps initially, and also after each occurrence of an accepting state. It is fairly straightforward to obtain such an automaton $\mathcal{P}'$. $\mathcal{P}'$ is a safety automaton. It is fairly easy to show that any input sequence that is rejected by $\mathcal{P}$ is also rejected by $\mathcal{P}'$; however $\mathcal{P}'$ rejects more input sequences. Thus, $\mathcal{P}'$ is an approximation of $\mathcal{P}$. Note that we get better approximations by choosing larger values of T.

We can also construct a safety automaton $\mathcal{P}'$ that is even a better approximation by increasing the time outs after each occurrence of an accepting state. Let h be a monotonically increasing function from $\mathbf{N}^+$ to $\mathbf{N}^+$ where $\mathbf{N}^+$ is the set of natural numbers. We construct $\mathcal{P}'$ which behaves like $\mathcal{P}$ except that it goes to the errors state q_{error} if the next accepting state is not reached with in $h(i)$ steps after the ith occurrence of an accepting state, for each $i \geq 0$. Such an automaton can be defined using countable number of states or concisely using the hybrid automata formalism using discrete state variables. When h is a constant function then we get constant time outs; when it is a linear function we get linearly increasing time outs. By using functions h that start with high initial values and that grow fast, we can get monitors with higher accuracies.

6   Example

Consider the operation of a train with electronically-controlled pneumatic (ECP) brakes [7]. In this case, a braking signal is sent to each of the N cars ($N = 5$ for the simulations) of the train that subsequently engage their own brakes. We consider the case when the braking systems of individual cars can fail. If this happens to more than a given number of cars ($2N/3$ in our example) the train might not be able to stop and it should start an emergency stopping procedure (for example, engaging the brakes using the traditional pneumatic system). Furthermore, when some of the brakes can fail, the links that connect the cars can be subject to excessive levels of stress. To prevent possible damage to the links we also want to trigger the emergency stopping procedure if any of the links are subject to a stress force above a safe threshold. We would thus like to develop a monitor that can correctly trigger the emergency stopping procedure when either the number of failed brakes is excessive, or when the braking pattern might result in unsafe level of stress on links between the cars, allowing the train operators to take the advantage of the superior braking performance of the ECP while not sacrificing the safety of the train.

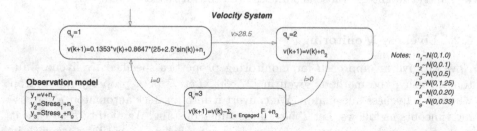

Fig. 1. Velocity subsystem and measured outputs for the train with ECP brakes

Figure 1 describes how the train velocity v evolves. The train starts in the discrete state $q_v = 1$ and remains in that state until the velocity exceeds a threshold $V_U = 28.5$, when it switches to the discrete state $q_v = 2$. The train remains in the state $q_v = 2$ until one of the brakes engages and it switches to state $q_v = 3$. The velocity in states $q_v = 2$ and $q_v = 3$ depends on the number of brakes that have been engaged through the braking force term $- \sum_{j \in Engaged} F_j$, where F_j is the braking force of car j and $Engaged$ is the set of indeces of the cars whose brakes are engaged. When all the brakes disengage, the velocity system switches back to the state $q_v = 1$. When in the state $q_v = 1$, the train accelerates to a constant velocity $V_C = 25$ and oscillates around it with the amplitude 2.5. The measured variables are the velocity v and the link forces $Stress_1$ and $Stress_4$. All the measurements are corrupted by a measurement noise. It can be shown that the link forces $Stress_i$ depend on the braking pattern but not on the velocity of the train.

It is worth noting that the dynamics of the system (and thus statistical properties of output sequences) are different for $q_v = 1$ and $q_v = 3$. We assume that the braking forces have the form $F_j = \kappa_n + \kappa_p b^j$ for some appropriate constants κ_n, κ_p and b (for simulations, $\kappa_n = 11.7$, $\kappa_p = 9.6$ and $b = 1.2$). These two properties can be used to show that the system is monitorable. If the braking forces were all equal, it is not difficult to see that it would not be possible to determine the braking pattern from the measurements.

Figure 2 describes the operation of the braking system of each of the cars. The braking system starts in the discrete state $q_b = 1$ and remains in that state until the velocity exceeds a threshold $V_U = 28.5$, when it switches to the discrete state $q_b = 2$. The braking system remains in the state $q_b = 2$ until the timer c_1 reaches $L_1 = 1$ (modeling delays in actuation and computational delays). Note that the initial value of the timer c_1 in the state $q_b = 2$ is not deterministic, so

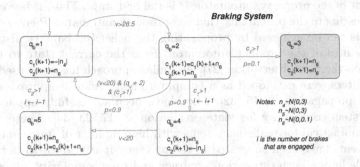

Fig. 2. ECP braking subsystem of each car of the train

the duration of time the system remains in $q_b = 2$ is a random variable. After the timer reaches L_1, the braking system can fail with a probability $p = 0.1$ and permanently switch to $q_b = 3$. With the probability $p = 0.9$ it either returns to state $q_b = 1$ if the velocity already fell below the threshold $V_L = 20$, or switches to $q_b = 4$ and engages in braking sequence otherwise. When the brake engages the variable i is increased by 1, thereby affecting the velocity of the train as described above. When the velocity falls below $V_L = 20$, the brake disengages after a random amount of time (modeled by the timer c_2 in the state $q_b = 5$), when it switches to the state $q_b = 1$.

Since the braking system is defined for each car, the overall model of the system is roughly a product of N copies of the braking system with the velocity system. For $N = 5$, the number of discrete states of the resulting automaton is more than 9000. Observe that if the system above is allowed to run forever then all the breaks will eventually fail with probability one. To prevent this, we assume that the brakes can only fail in the first τ units of time. To capture this, we add an additional counter in the breaking subsystem that allows the transition from $q_b = 2$ to the $q_b = 3$ only if this counter is less than τ; this is not shown in the figure. For the simulations, $\tau = 500$.

The desired behavior of the train is given by the following specification: (1) every time the train velocity increases beyond V_U, the train should brake so that the velocity decreases below V_L; and (2) the link force $Stress_k$ for any link k should never stay above the safe threshold $Stress_{max}$ for more than T_2 ($T_2 = 4$ for simulations). The first property can be described by a liveness automaton that can be converted to a safety automaton using a static time out T_1 according to the approach given in Section 5.2. For the simulations, the force threshold was set to $Stress_{max} = 30$. Out of 32 possible braking patterns, 5 cause the link force to exceed this threshold, however the forces that exceed the threshold are not those that are directly measured.

State estimation. Let S be the system automaton and P the property automaton . We construct the product of S and P to obtain the product automaton $S \times P$. Using this product automaton and using the outputs generated by the actual system, our Monitor M estimates the probability that the state component of the property automaton $\mathcal{P}$ is the bad state. Thus, it becomes necessary to estimate the probability that the property automaton $\mathcal{P}$ enters the bad state. This can be achieved by propagating the belief (probability distribution over the states of the product automaton) from the current state to the next state, given the new observation [27]. A similar approach has been used in [35]. Particle filters were developed as a computationally efficient approximation of the belief propagation [6, 15, 32]. They have been successfully applied in the hybrid system community for state estimation [3, 17, 23, 34]. These methods become impractical for realistic systems with high number of states and several improvements have been suggested in recent years. It is also worth noting that for particle filters, both estimation accuracy and time complexity increase with the number of particles. The exact relationships depend on the structure of the system and transition probabilities and are difficult to characterize. All these issues are beyond the scope of the present paper.

Experimental results. As described in Section 4, the monitor M computes the probability that the property automaton $\mathcal{P}$ is in a bad state and raises an alarm when this probability surpasses a given threshold z. In order to evaluate the performance of the monitor numerically, the system was run 500 times. Particle filter was used to estimate the probability of each state of the product automaton $\mathcal{S} \times \mathcal{P}$. The number of particles for the particle filter was $\eta = 2000$. The simulation was terminated when either an alarm was raised, or the discrete time (number of steps the system has taken) reached $T_d = 700$. As explained above, the brakes can only fail during the first $\tau = 500$ units of time. For each run, the state of the property automaton was recorded, as well as the state of the monitor. The acceptance and rejection accuracies, respectively, denoted by $AA(M, \mathcal{S}, \mathcal{P})$ and $RA(M, \mathcal{S}, \mathcal{P})$ were computed according to:

$$AA(M, \mathcal{S}, \mathcal{P}) = \frac{g_a}{g_a + g_r} \qquad RA(M, \mathcal{S}, \mathcal{P}) = \frac{b_r}{b_a + b_r},$$

where g_a (resp., g_r) is the number of good runs that were accepted (resp., rejected), and b_r (resp., b_a) is the number of bad runs that were rejected (resp., accepted). Note that g_r corresponds to the number of false alarms, and b_a to the number of missed alarms; accuracies approach 1 as these numbers approach 0. A run was considered good if the state of the property automaton at $T_d = 700$ was not an error state, and bad otherwise.

An example of the monitor performance for $T_1 = 30$ and different values of the threshold probability z is shown in Table 1a. In general, if z increases the number of false alarms (g_r) decreases while the number of missed alarms (b_a) increases as it becomes more difficult for the particle filter to estimate that the property automaton entered the fail state with such a high probability.

Table 1b shows accuracy measures of the monitor for different values of the probability threshold z and time out value T_1. As z increases the acceptance accuracy in general increases and the rejection accuracy decreases. The reason for this is that as z increases, the estimate of the probability that the state of the property automaton $\mathcal{P}$ is bad must be higher before the monitor raises an

Table 1. Monitor performance for different values of z and T_1 (500 runs)

(a) Monitor outcomes for $T_1 = 30$.

z	$T_1 = 30$					
	g_a	g_r	b_a	b_r	RA	AA
0.050	313	76	7	104	0.937	0.805
0.100	313	75	7	105	0.938	0.807
0.300	314	73	7	106	0.938	0.811
0.500	314	72	8	106	0.930	0.813
0.750	314	72	8	106	0.930	0.813
0.875	315	70	8	107	0.930	0.818
0.950	315	70	8	107	0.930	0.818

(b) Monitor accuracies. The last two columns assume correct braking mode estimation (67% of the runs).

z	$T_1 = 30$		$T_1 = 60$		$T_1 = 80$		$T_1 = 80^*$	
	RA	AA	RA	AA	RA	AA	RA	AA
0.050	0.937	0.805	0.853	0.824	0.838	0.845	0.982	0.978
0.100	0.938	0.807	0.853	0.826	0.838	0.845	0.982	0.978
0.300	0.938	0.811	0.853	0.826	0.838	0.847	0.982	0.982
0.500	0.930	0.813	0.853	0.828	0.838	0.847	0.982	0.982
0.750	0.930	0.813	0.840	0.828	0.838	0.847	0.982	0.982
0.875	0.930	0.818	0.840	0.828	0.838	0.847	0.982	0.982
0.950	0.930	0.818	0.840	0.828	0.838	0.847	0.982	0.982

alarm. Clearly for $z_1 < z_2$, if the monitor with the threshold z_2 would raise an alarm so would the monitor with the threshold z_1, while the reverse is not true. So with lower z, the probability that a false alarm is declared is higher. Similar argument applies to rejection accuracy. On the other hand, for our example this effect is not that pronounced since the particle filter quickly converges to either zero probability or probability one for the braking pattern. This is because the link force measurements strongly correlate with the braking pattern.

Recall that T_1 is the time out used to (conservatively) approximate a liveness property with a safety property. As T_1 increases, the acceptance accuracy for monitoring the liveness property (and therefore overall acceptance accuracy) increases. The rejection accuracy decreases since we run the experiment for a finite time and the estimator does not have enough time to converge to the correct value of the state.

Due to the high number of possible discrete states, particle filter faces the problem of particle depletion [32]. In fact, in our experiments the particle filter only correctly estimated the braking pattern in 67% of the cases. The last two columns in Table 1b thus show monitor performance when only these runs are considered; it is clearly much improved.

It is worth noting that while Theorem 1 provides necessary and sufficient conditions for monitorability, in order for the monitor to be implementable, the system also needs to allow robust state estimation. When state estimation can not be performed reliably, a system designer might use additional sensors that provide more information about the system and thus better state estimation.

7   Conclusion

In this paper, we introduced Extended Hidden Markov Systems as models for cyber physical systems and considered the monitoring problem for them. This model does not discretize continuous variables. We exactly characterized when such systems are monitorable. We presented highly accurate monitoring algorithms when the system is specified by probabilistic hybrid automata and when it is monitorable with respect to the given property.

The monitors have been implemented for an automotive example using particle filters as state estimators. Experimental results showing the effectiveness of our approach are presented.

We used certain class of probabilistic hybrid automata for specifying systems. However, we required such automata should not contain resets of continuous variables on transitions. Removing this restriction, will be part of future work.

References

1. Alur, R., Henzinger, T.A., Lafferriere, G., Pappas, G.J.: Discrete abstractions of hybrid systems. Proceedings of the IEEE 88(7), 971–984 (2000)
2. Balluchi, A., Benvenuti, L., Di Benedetto, M., Sangiovanni-Vincentelli, A.: Design of Observers for Hybrid Systems. In: Tomlin, C.J., Greenstreet, M.R. (eds.) HSCC 2002. LNCS, vol. 2289, pp. 76–80. Springer, Heidelberg (2002)
3. Blom, H., Bloem, E.: Particle filtering for stochastic hybrid systems. In: 43rd IEEE Conference on Decision and Control, CDC 2004, vol. 3 (2004)
4. D'Amorim, M., Roşu, G.: Efficient Monitoring of ω-Languages. In: Etessami, K., Rajamani, S.K. (eds.) CAV 2005. LNCS, vol. 3576, pp. 364–378. Springer, Heidelberg (2005)
5. DeCarlo, R.A., Branicky, M.S., Pettersson, S., Lennartson, B.: Perspectives and results on the stability and stabilizability of hybrid systems. Proceedings of the IEEE 88(7), 1069–1082 (2000)
6. Doucet, A., de Freitas, N., Murphy, K., Russell, S.: Rao-Blackwellised particle filtering for dynamic Bayesian networks. In: Proceedings of the Sixteenth Conference on Uncertainty in Artificial Intelligence, pp. 176–183 (2000)
7. Federal Railroad Administration. ECP brake system for freight service (2006), http://www.fra.dot.gov/downloads/safety/ecp_report_20060811.pdf
8. Franklin, G., Powell, J., Workman, M.: Digital control of dynamic systems. Addison-Wesley world student series. Addison-Wesley (1998)
9. Funiak, S., Williams, B.: Multi-modal particle filtering for hybrid systems with autonomous mode transitions. In: Workshop on Principles of Diagnosis (2003)
10. Gondi, K., Patel, Y., Sistla, A.P.: Monitoring the Full Range of ω-Regular Properties of Stochastic Systems. In: Jones, N.D., Müller-Olm, M. (eds.) VMCAI 2009. LNCS, vol. 5403, pp. 105–119. Springer, Heidelberg (2009)
11. Grunske, L., Zhang, P.: Monitoring probabilistic properties. In: Proceedings of 7th Joint meeting of European Software Engineering Conference and ACM Symposium on Foundations of Software Engineering ESEC-FSE 2009, pp. 183–192. ACM (2009)
12. Henzinger, T.A., Kopke, P.W., Puri, A., Varaiya, P.: What's decidable about hybrid automata? Journal of Computer and System Sciences 57(1), 94–124 (1998)
13. Hofbaur, M.W., Williams, B.C.: Mode Estimation of Probabilistic Hybrid Systems. In: Tomlin, C.J., Greenstreet, M.R. (eds.) HSCC 2002. LNCS, vol. 2289, pp. 253–266. Springer, Heidelberg (2002)
14. Hofbaur, M.W.: Hybrid Estimation of Complex Systems. LNCIS, vol. 319. Springer, Heidelberg (2005)
15. Isard, M., Blake, A.: Condensation–conditional density propagation for visual tracking. International Journal of Computer Vision 29(1), 5–28 (1998)
16. Kloetzer, M., Belta, C.: A Fully Automated Framework for Control of Linear Systems from LTL Specifications. In: Hespanha, J.P., Tiwari, A. (eds.) HSCC 2006. LNCS, vol. 3927, pp. 333–347. Springer, Heidelberg (2006)

17. Koutsoukos, X., Kurien, J., Zhao, F.: Estimation of Distributed Hybrid Systems Using Particle Filtering Methods. In: Maler, O., Pnueli, A. (eds.) HSCC 2003. LNCS, vol. 2623, pp. 298–313. Springer, Heidelberg (2003)
18. Kress-Gazit, H., Fainekos, G., Pappas, G.: Where's Waldo? Sensor-based temporal logic motion planning. In: IEEE Int. Conf. on Robotics and Automation, pp. 3116–3121 (2007)
19. Lerner, U., Moses, B., Scott, M., McIlraith, S., Koller, D.: Monitoring a complex physical system using a hybrid dynamic bayes net. In: Proceedings of the 18th Annual Conference on Uncertainty in AI (UAI), pp. 301–310 (2002)
20. Liberzon, D.: Switching in Systems and Control. Birkhäuser, Boston (2003)
21. Lygeros, J., Godbole, D.N., Sastry, S.S.: A Game Theoretic Approach to Hybrid System Design. In: Alur, R., Sontag, E.D., Henzinger, T.A. (eds.) HS 1995. LNCS, vol. 1066, pp. 1–12. Springer, Heidelberg (1996)
22. Margaria, T., Sistla, A., Steffen, B., Zuck, L.: Taming Interface Specifications. In: Abadi, M., de Alfaro, L. (eds.) CONCUR 2005. LNCS, vol. 3653, pp. 548–561. Springer, Heidelberg (2005)
23. McIlraith, S., Biswas, G., Clancy, D., Gupta, V.: Hybrid Systems Diagnosis. In: Lynch, N.A., Krogh, B.H. (eds.) HSCC 2000. LNCS, vol. 1790, pp. 282–295. Springer, Heidelberg (2000)
24. Pnueli, A.: Verifying Liveness Properties of Reactive Systems. In: Maler, O. (ed.) HART 1997. LNCS, vol. 1201, Springer, Heidelberg (1997)
25. Pnueli, A., Zaks, A., Zuck, L.D.: Monitoring interfaces for faults. In: Proceedings of the 5th Workshop on Runtime Verification, RV 2005 (2005); To appear in a special issue of ENTCS
26. Rudin, W.: Real and Complex Analysis. McGrawHill, NewYork (1987)
27. Russell, S.J., Norvig, P.: Artificial Intelligence: A Modern Approach, 2nd edn. Prentice Hall (December 2002)
28. Sammapun, U., Lee, I., Sokolsky, O.: Rt-mac:runtime monitoring and checking of quantitative and probabilistic properties. In: Proc. of 11th IEEE International Conference on Embedded and Real-time Computing Systems and Applications (RTCSA 2005), pp. 147–153 (2005)
29. Sistla, A.P., Srinivas, A.R.: Monitoring Temporal Properties of Stochastic Systems. In: Logozzo, F., Peled, D.A., Zuck, L.D. (eds.) VMCAI 2008. LNCS, vol. 4905, pp. 294–308. Springer, Heidelberg (2008)
30. Sistla, A., Zhou, M., Zuck, L.: Monitoring Off-the-Shelf Components. In: Emerson, E.A., Namjoshi, K.S. (eds.) VMCAI 2006. LNCS, vol. 3855, pp. 222–236. Springer, Heidelberg (2005)
31. Sistla, A.P., Žefran, M., Feng, Y.: Monitorability of Stochastic Dynamical Systems. In: Gopalakrishnan, G., Qadeer, S. (eds.) CAV 2011. LNCS, vol. 6806, pp. 720–736. Springer, Heidelberg (2011)
32. Thrun, S., Fox, D., Burgard, W., Dellaert, F.: Robust Monte Carlo localization for mobile robots. Artificial Intelligence 128(1-2), 99–141 (2001)
33. van der Schaft, A.J., Schumacher, J.M.: An Introduction to Hybrid Dynamical Systems. LNCIS, vol. 251. Springer, Heidelberg (1999)
34. Verma, V., Gordon, G., Simmons, R., Thrun, S.: Real-time fault diagnosis. IEEE Robotics & Automation Magazine 11(2), 56–66 (2004)
35. Wilcox, C., Williams, B.: Runtime Verification of Stochastic, Faulty Systems. In: Barringer, H., Falcone, Y., Finkbeiner, B., Havelund, K., Lee, I., Pace, G., Roşu, G., Sokolsky, O., Tillmann, N. (eds.) RV 2010. LNCS, vol. 6418, pp. 452–459. Springer, Heidelberg (2010)

Combining Time and Frequency Domain Specifications for Periodic Signals[*]

Aleksandar Chakarov[1], Sriram Sankaranarayanan[1], and Georgios Fainekos[2]

[1] University of Colorado, Boulder, CO
firstname.lastname@colorado.edu
[2] Arizona State University, Tempe, AZ
fainekos@asu.edu

Abstract. In this paper, we investigate formalisms for specifying periodic signals using time and frequency domain specifications along with algorithms for the signal recognition and generation problems for such specifications. The time domain specifications are in the form of hybrid automata whose continuous state variables generate the desired signals. The frequency domain specifications take the form of an "envelope" that constrains the possible power spectra of the periodic signals with a given frequency cutoff. The combination of time and frequency domain specifications yields mixed-domain specifications that constrain a signal to belong to the intersection of the both specifications.

We show that the signal recognition problem for periodic signals specified by hybrid automata is NP-complete, while the corresponding problem for frequency domain specifications can be approximated to any desired degree by linear programs, which can be solved in polynomial time. The signal generation problem for time and frequency domain specifications can be encoded into linear arithmetic constraints that can be solved using existing SMT solvers. We present some preliminary results based on an implementation that uses the SMT solver Z3 to tackle the signal generation problems.

1 Introduction

The combination of time and frequency domain specifications often arises in the design of analog or mixed signal circuits [16], digital signal processing systems [20] and control systems [3]. Circuits such as filters and modulators often specify time-domain requirements on the input signal. Common examples of time domain specifications include setup time and hold time requirements for flip-flops, the slew rate for clocks and bounds on the duty cycle for pulse width modulators [16]. Likewise, the behavior of many components are also specified in terms of their frequency responses. Such requirements concern the effect of a subsystem on the various frequency components of a input signal. The problem of combining these specification styles is therefore of great interest, especially in the runtime verification setting.

---

[*] This work was supported, in part, by the US National Science Foundation (NSF) awards CNS-1017074 and CNS-1016994.

S. Khurshid and K. Sen (Eds.): RV 2011, LNCS 7186, pp. 294–309, 2012.

In this paper, we study models for specifying real-valued *periodic signals* using *mixed-domain specifications*. Such specifications combine commonly used automata-theoretic models that can specify the characteristics of a signal over time with frequency-domain specifications that constrain the distribution of amplitude (or the power) of the sinusoidal components over some range of frequencies. Given such a mixed-domain specification, we consider the signal recognition and generation problems. The signal generation problem seeks test cases for an analog or a mixed-signal circuit from its input specifications. Since specifications are often non-deterministic, an *exhaustive generator* explores all the possible cases encoded in the specification by generating a set of representative signals. Likewise, the signal recognition or monitoring problem decides whether a given signal conforms to specifications.

In this paper, we present an encoding that reduces both problems to constraints in linear arithmetic. While such an encoding is easily obtained time domain specifications, a naive encoding of the frequency domain constraints yields a system of non-linear constraints that are hard to solve. We demonstrate how such non-linear constraints can be systematically approximated to arbitrary precision using constraints from linear arithmetic. Finally, we present some preliminary results on a prototype implementation of our technique that uses the SMT solver Z3 to solve the resulting constraints [5]. Owing to space restrictions, we have omitted some of the finer details including proofs of key lemmas. An extended version containing proofs along with supplementary material containing the source code and models for our experiments are available upon request.

Related Work. Automata, especially timed and hybrid automata, are quite natural formalisms for specifying the behavior of signals over time [1,12]. Likewise, the study of Fourier transforms and power spectra of signals forms the basis for specifying analog and mixed signal systems [20]. The problem of matching observations to runs for timed and hybrid automata was studied by Alur et al. [2]. Whereas Alur et al. study the problem of matching a trace consisting of a set of events generated by discrete transitions, the traces here are partial observations over the run, sampled discretely. Therefore, while the timestamp generation problem is shown to be polynomial time by Alur et al., its analog in our setting is NP-complete.

Monitoring algorithms for discrete-time Boolean valued signals have been well-studied [26,13,10,9,7]. Such specifications can capture Boolean abstractions of discrete-time signals sampled over the output signals generated by hybrid/embedded systems. An off-line algorithm for temporal logic analysis of continuous-time signals was proposed by Nickovic et al. [15] and extended to an on-line algorithm [19]. Thati et al. [26] and Kristoffersen et al. [13] presented algorithms for monitoring timed temporal logics over timed state sequences. While fragments temporal logics and a restricted class of automata are well known to be efficiently monitorable, it is not easy to express properties of oscillators such as periodicity, rise times, duty cycles and bounds on derivatives in these fragments without introducing extraneous constraints or quantifiers. Fainekos et al. [6], considered the problem of monitoring continuous-time temporal logic properties of a signal based solely on discrete-time analysis of its sampling points. Tan et al. [24,25] consider hybrid automaton specifications for synthesizing monitors for embedded systems, wherein the monitor's execution is synchronized with the model of the system during run-time. Specification and verification of the periodicity of oscillators has been considered by Frehse et al. [8] and Steinhorst et al.[23].

On the other hand, specification formalisms for frequency domain properties of systems have not received as much attention. Hedrich et al. [11] study the problem of verifying frequency domain properties of systems with uncertain parameters. Our encoding for frequency domain specifications is similar to techniques used in regression, wherein the goal is to find a function from a given family that best fits a given set of points, wherein the "best fit" can be defined as the sum of the distances between the data points and the function under some norm. The connection between regression and optimization is discussed in many standard textbooks on convex optimization [4].

2 Signals and Automata

Let $\mathbb{R}$ denote the set of real numbers. A signal $f(t)$ is a function $f : \mathbb{R} \mapsto \mathbb{R}$. A signal is *periodic* iff there is a time period $T > 0$ such that for all $t \geq 0$, $f(t + T) = f(t)$. Let Σ represent the set of all signals $f : \mathbb{R} \mapsto \mathbb{R}$. Note that in most applications, the domain of a signal is the continuous time domain $t \in \mathbb{R}_{\geq 0}$. Let $\tau = \langle t_0, t_1, \ldots, t_k \rangle$ be some set of time instants such that $0 \leq t_0 < t_1 \ldots < t_k$. A sample of a signal f at the time instants τ is given by $f(\tau) = \langle f(t_0), f(t_1), \ldots, f(t_k) \rangle$.

Hybrid Automaton: Our discussion will focus mostly on hybrid automata with dynamics specified by rectangular differential inclusions.

Definition 1 (Linear Hybrid Automata). *A Linear Hybrid Automaton $\mathcal{H}$ consists of a tuple $\langle Q, \boldsymbol{x}, \mathcal{T}, \mathcal{D}, \mathcal{I}, q_0, \Theta \rangle$:*

1. *Q is a finite set of discrete modes,*
2. *$\boldsymbol{x}$ is a vector of finitely many continuous system variables.*
3. *$\mathcal{T}$ is a set of discrete transitions. Each transition $\tau \in \mathcal{T}$ is a tuple $\tau : \langle s, t, \rho_\tau \rangle$ where $s, t \in Q$ are the pre- and the post-modes respectively and $\rho_\tau[\boldsymbol{x}, \boldsymbol{x}']$ is a transition relation that relates the current value of $\boldsymbol{x}$ with the next state values $\boldsymbol{x}'$.*
4. *$\mathcal{D}$ maps each $q \in Q$ to a rectangular differential inclusion $\boldsymbol{\ell}(q) \leq \frac{d\boldsymbol{x}}{dt} \leq \boldsymbol{u}(q)$.*
5. *$\mathcal{I}$ maps each mode $q \in Q$ to a mode invariant set $\mathcal{I}(q)$.*
6. *q_0 is the start state and Θ is a logical assertion over $\boldsymbol{x}$ that specifies the initial conditions for the continuous variables.*

A state of the hybrid automaton is a pair $(s, \boldsymbol{x})$ consisting of a discrete mode $s \in Q$ and a continuous state $\boldsymbol{x} \in \mathcal{I}(q)$. The semantics of a hybrid automaton are defined in terms of runs. In this paper, we will describe periodic signals by means of finite runs of a hybrid system.

Definition 2 (Runs). *A finite run of a linear hybrid automaton $\mathcal{H}$ is a finite sequence of states and actions: $\sigma : (s_0, \boldsymbol{x}_0) \xrightarrow{a_1} (s_1, \boldsymbol{x}_1) \xrightarrow{a_2} (s_2, \boldsymbol{x}_2) \xrightarrow{a_3} \cdots \xrightarrow{a_N} (s_N, \boldsymbol{x}_N),$ wherein each action a_i is of the form τ for some discrete transition or $(\mathrm{tick}(\delta_i), f_i)$, for some time interval $\delta_i \geq 0$ and function $f_i : [0, \delta_i) \mapsto \mathbb{R}^n$, such that:*

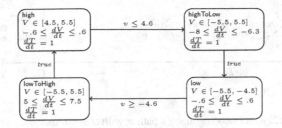

Fig. 1. Hybrid automaton model for example signal specification

- *If action a_i is a discrete transition τ_i then τ_i must be of the form $\langle s_{i-1}, s_i, \rho_i \rangle$ (i.e, the transition must take us from state s_{i-1} to state s_i) and $(x_{i-1}, x_i) \models \rho_i$, i.e., the continuous variables change according to the transition relation.*
- *If a_i is a "tick" of the form $(\mathrm{tick}(\delta_i), f_i)$, wherein $s_i = s_{i-1}$ (i.e., no mode change can occur). The function $f_i : [0, \delta_i] \mapsto \mathbb{R}^n$ is a continuous and piecewise differentiable function such that: (1) $f_i(0) = x_i$, $f_i(\delta_i) = x_{i+1}$, (2) $f_i(t)$ satisfies the mode invariant $\mathcal{I}(s_i)$ for all $t \in [0, \delta)$, and (3) $\frac{df_i}{dt} \in [\ell(s_i), u(s_i)]$ at all instances $t \in [0, \delta)$ where f_i is differentiable.*

Example 1. Consider the following signal specification for a square wave generator: (1) The signal has two stable phases: high $(5 \pm 0.5V)$ or low $(-5 \pm 0.5V)$. (2) If the signal transitions from one phase to another, the value of v at the start of the transition must be in the range $[-4.6, 4.6]$. (3) The signal remains a minimum of 0.5 seconds in each mode. (4) The rate of signal rise during transition from low to high lies within $[5, 7.5]V/s$. (5) The rate of signal fall during transition from high to low lies within $[-6.3, -8]V/s$. (6) In any stable phase, the rate of change lies between $[-.6, .6]V/s$.

Figure 1 shows a hybrid automaton that specifies the signal. The modes high and low specify the stable phases for the signal. Similarly, the modes highToLow and lowToHigh represent the transitions.

3   Periodic Signals in Time Domain

We will now explore the use of hybrid automata with piecewise constant dynamics to specify periodic signals. We will observe that the problem of checking if a sampled signal can be generated by some run of a hybrid automaton is NP-Complete. In fact, the problem of checking if *a given path through the automaton* generates the samples of a given signal is itself NP-complete. As a result, barring restrictions, linear hybrid automata by themselves are too rich a formalism for use in monitoring of signals. Thereafter, we focus on signal generation, presenting techniques for generating runs using a systematic exploration of the state-space of the automaton using LP solvers.

We augment the basic hybrid automaton by designating a set of modes as *final modes* and an output function $y = f(x)$ that specifies the output signal as a function of the continuous state variables. Additionally, we require that the runs of the automaton σ : $(x_0, s_0) \to (x_1, s_1) \to \cdots \to (x_N, s_N)$, satisfy the following constraints:

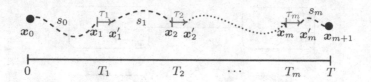

Fig. 2. Run Encoding along a path π with transitions $\tau_1, \ldots, \tau_m$

Constraints	Remarks
$\Theta[\boldsymbol{x}_0]$	Initial condition
$f(\boldsymbol{x}_0) = f(\boldsymbol{x}_{m+1})$	Periodicity of the trace
$\bigwedge_{i=1}^{m} T_i - T_{i-1} \geq \delta_{\min}$	Minimum Dwell Time.
$\bigwedge_{k=1}^{m} \left(\begin{array}{c} \boldsymbol{\ell}(\boldsymbol{s}_k)(T_{k+1} - T_k) \leq (\boldsymbol{x}_{k+1} - \boldsymbol{x}_k') \\ (\boldsymbol{x}_{k+1} - \boldsymbol{x}_k' \leq \boldsymbol{u}(\boldsymbol{s}_k)(T_{k+1} - T_k) \end{array} \right)$	$\boldsymbol{x}_k'$ reachable from $\boldsymbol{x}_k$ in mode s_k
$\bigwedge_{k=1}^{m} \left[\mathcal{I}_{s_{k-1}}(\boldsymbol{x}_k) \wedge \mathcal{I}_{s_k}(\boldsymbol{x}_k') \right]$	Invariants for mode s_k

Fig. 3. Constraints encoding the existence of a run along a path. **Note:** The guards, invariant sets, initial conditions of $\mathcal{H}$ are convex polyhedra. The function f is affine.

1. There is a *minimum dwell time* $\delta_{\min}$ for each mode such that whenever a run enters a mode q, it will remain in that mode for time at least $\delta_{\min}$ before taking a transition.
2. The terminal mode $s_N \in F$.
3. The initial state $(s_0, \boldsymbol{x}_0)$ and the terminal state $(s_N, \boldsymbol{x}_N)$ yield the same output $f(\boldsymbol{x}_0) = f(\boldsymbol{x}_N)$, so that the signal is periodic.

The minimum dwell time requirement seems quite natural for signal specifications, and furthermore, it considerably simplifies the complexity of signal membership checking and generation problems that we will discuss subsequently (also Cf. [2]). As a result of the requirements above, the output $\boldsymbol{y}(t)$ obtained on any finite run of the automaton can be thought of as constituting a single period of the signal. Repeating this output with time shifted yields the overall periodic signal.

Definition 3 (Time Domain Periodic Signal Specification). *A time domain period signal specification consists of a hybrid automaton* $\mathcal{H}$ *with a set of final modes* $F \subseteq Q$, *an output function* $\boldsymbol{y} = f(\boldsymbol{x})$ *and a minimum dwell time* $\delta_{\min}$.

3.1   Run Encoding

Let $\langle \mathcal{H}, F, f, \delta_{\min} \rangle$ be a hybrid automaton for a signal specification. Consider a syntactic path through $\pi : s_0 \xrightarrow{\tau_1} s_1 \xrightarrow{\tau_2} \cdots s_{m-1} \xrightarrow{\tau_m} s_m$ such that s_0 is initial, $s_m \in F$ and $m \leq \left\lfloor \frac{T}{\delta_{\min}} \right\rfloor$. We wish to encode the (possibly empty) set of runs that yield a periodic signal of time period T along the path π in terms of a linear program (LP) $\Psi_{T,\pi}$. We describe the variables that will be used in our encoding, as depicted in Figure 2. (A)

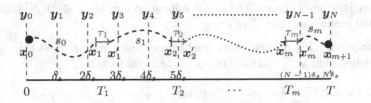

Fig. 4. Encoding membership of a sampled trace

$T_1, \ldots, T_m$ represent the transition times. We add two constants $T_0 = 0$ and $T_{m+1} = T$ to denote the start and end times of the trace, respectively. (B) x_0 and x_{m+1} denote the initial and terminal values for continuous variables. (C) $x_1, x_1', \ldots, x_m, x_m'$ encode the continuous states before and after each of the m discrete transitions. The overall encoding is a conjunction of linear inequalities as described in Figure 3. This encoding is similar to the timestamp generation encoding provided by Alur et al. [2].

Note that the encoding yields a linear program $\Psi_{T,\pi}$, assuming that all transition relations, mode invariants are polyhedral and the output function f is affine. Note that models of $\Psi_{T,\pi}$, if they exist, do not fully specify a run of the hybrid automaton. A run σ of $\mathcal{H}$ corresponds to a model $(x_0, x_1', T_1, x_1, \ldots, x_m', T_m, x_m, x_{m+1})$ of $\Psi_{T,\pi}$ if the initial, terminal states, switching times and states before/after the discrete transitions of σ coincide with those specified by the model.

Theorem 1. *The encoding of a run $\Psi_{T,\pi}$ is a linear assertion such that (a) each model of $\Psi_{T,\pi}$ corresponds to a run σ of duration T, and (b) conversely, every run σ of duration T along the path π corresponds to a model of $\Psi_{T,\pi}$.*

3.2 Testing Membership

We first consider the problem of deciding signal membership given N samples of periodic signal $g(t)$ with time period T, sampled at some fixed rate $\delta_s = \frac{T}{N}$ for a single time period. Let $g_0, \ldots, g_{N-1}$ be the signal values at times $0, \delta_s, \ldots, (N-1)\delta_s$, respectively. Since the signal is periodic, we have $g_N = g(N\delta_s) = g_0$. We assume that δ_s the sampling time, is strictly less than $\delta_{\min}$, the minimum dwell time.

We use the following strategy to search for a run σ of the hybrid automaton $\mathcal{H}$ that coincides with the samples of $g(t)$.

1. Explore paths from s_0 to a final state $s_m \in F$ explicitly [1]
2. For each path π with transitions $\tau_1, \ldots, \tau_m$, we encode the existence of a run along the path using $\Psi_{T,\pi}$, and
3. We conjoin $\Psi_{T,\pi}$ with a formula $\Gamma_{\pi,g}$ that encodes that the samples $g_0, \ldots, g_{N-1}$ conform to the run encoded in Ψ.

We encode the unknown continuous state at time $t = i\delta_s$ by variable y_i. The encoding for $\Gamma_{\pi,g}$ will contain the following clauses:

---

[1] This search can also be encoded implicitly as a SAT formula.

Continuous State and Output: The signal value g_i at $t = i\delta_s$, $i \in [0, N]$ must correspond to the continuous state: $f(\boldsymbol{y}_i) = g_i$.

Mode change rule: If a discrete transition happens between time $((i-1)\delta_s, i\delta_s)$ then $\boldsymbol{x}_j$ is reachable from $\boldsymbol{y}_{i-1}$ and likewise, $\boldsymbol{y}_i$ is reachable from $\boldsymbol{x}'_j$.

$$\bigwedge_{i,j=1}^{m} \begin{bmatrix} (i-1)\delta_s \leq T_j \wedge \\ T_j < i\delta_s \end{bmatrix} \Rightarrow \begin{bmatrix} (i\delta_s - T_j)\ell(s_j) \leq (\boldsymbol{y}_i - \boldsymbol{x}'_j) \leq u(s_j)(i\delta_s - T_j) \wedge \\ (T_j - (i-1)\delta_s)\ell(s_{j-1}) \leq (\boldsymbol{x}_j - \boldsymbol{y}_{i-1}) \leq u(s_{j-1})(T_j - (i-1)\delta_s) \end{bmatrix}$$

On the other hand, if no mode change happens in the interval $[(i-1)\delta_s, i\delta_s)$ then the mode at time $i\delta_s$ is the same as that at time $(i+1)\delta_s$. Furthermore, it is possible to reach the state $\boldsymbol{y}_i$ from $\boldsymbol{y}_{i-1}$ by evolving according to the dynamics at this mode:

$$\bigwedge_{i=1}^{N} \bigwedge_{j=1}^{m} \left[\begin{pmatrix} T_j < (i-1)\delta_s \wedge \\ T_{j+1} \geq i\delta_s \end{pmatrix} \right] \Rightarrow [\delta_s \ell(s_j) \leq (\boldsymbol{y}_i - \boldsymbol{y}_{i-1}) \leq \delta_s u(s_j)]$$

Simplifying the Encoding: The encoding presented above can be simplified considerably by noting the minimum dwell time requirement on the runs. As a result of this requirement, we may deduce that the switching time for the jth transition T_j must lie in the range $[j\delta_{\min}, T - (m + 1 - j)\delta_{\min}]$, wherein $\delta_{\min}$ is the minimum dwell time. As a result, some of the antecedents of the implications for the mode change rule are always false. This allows us to reduce the size of the encoding, in practice.

Let $g_0, \ldots, g_{N-1}$ be the signal samples at times $0, \delta_s, 2\delta_s, \ldots, (N-1)\delta_s$, wherein we assume that δ_s is smaller than the minimum dwell time. Let us assume that $\Gamma_{g,\pi}$ is the formula obtained over variables $\boldsymbol{x}_0, \ldots, \boldsymbol{x}_{m+1}, \boldsymbol{y}_0, \ldots, \boldsymbol{y}_N, T_1, \ldots, T_m$ using the encoding presented in this section.

Theorem 2. *The samples $g_0, \ldots, g_{N-1}$ of a periodic signal with sample time $\delta_s < \delta_{\min}$ are generated by some run of the hybrid automaton $\mathcal{H}$ if and only if the linear arithmetic formula $\Gamma_\pi \wedge \Psi_{T,\pi}$ is satisfiable for some path π from an initial mode s_0 to a final mode $s_m \in F$ with $m \leq \lfloor \frac{T}{\delta} \rfloor$ discrete transitions.*

Given samples $g_0, \ldots, g_N$ of a signal, the algorithm thus far searches for a path π, a sequence of switching times and values of continuous states $\boldsymbol{x}_0, \ldots, \boldsymbol{x}_{m+1}, \boldsymbol{y}_0, \ldots, \boldsymbol{y}_N$ by solving a linear arithmetic formula using a SMT solver. Naturally, it is worth asking if there is an efficient algorithm for signal recognition using hybrid automata. We show that this is unlikely by proving the NP-completeness of the signal recognition problem. We observe the following surprising result for the seemingly simply problem of deciding if a given feasible path π can yield a run generating the samples $g_0, \ldots, g_N$.

Theorem 3. *Let $g_0, \ldots, g_N$ be samples of a periodic signal $g(t)$ and π be a path from initial to final mode in $\mathcal{H}$. Deciding if the given samples are generated by some run of along path π is NP-complete.*

Membership in NP is clear from the SMT encoding to a linear arithmetic formula which can be solved by a non-deterministic polynomial time TM coupled with a LP solver which operates in polynomial time. The proof of NP-hardness is by reduction from

CNF-SAT problem and is presented in an extended version of this paper available upon request. Our results show that significant restrictions are required on the linear hybrid automaton model to make it suitable for signal monitoring. For instance, such restrictions have to go beyond simply restricting the number of paths from the initial to the final mode.

3.3 Signal Generation

We will now consider the problem of generating signals *at random* from a given hybrid automaton specification. The signal generator explores all the paths in the hybrid automaton up to a depth bound. For each path π, the set of signals form a convex set given by the convex polyhedron $\Psi_{T,\pi}$ (Cf. Section 3.1). The notion of sampling uniformly at random from a convex set is defined rigorously in most standard textbooks [21]. Our generator samples a fixed number of solutions uniformly at random.

1. Systematically explore paths of length $m \leq \lfloor \frac{T}{\delta} \rfloor$ from initial to a final mode.
2. For each path π, encode the formula $\Psi_{T,\pi}$ to generate switching times and continuous state values x_i, x_i' before and after transitions (Cf. Section 3.1).
3. Extract solutions uniformly at random from $\Psi_{T,\pi}$.
4. For each solution, generate sampled signals according the dynamics of each mode.

Extracting Random Solutions from Linear Programs

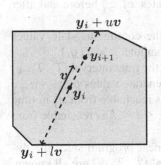

Fig. 5. Hit-and-run sampling

As shown in Section 3.1, let $\Psi_{T,\pi}$ be the LP corresponding to a path π over variables $(x_0, x_1, x_1', \ldots, T_1, \ldots, T_m)$ that we shall collectively refer to as y. We assume that Ψ is feasible. Our goal is to extract solutions at random from the polyhedron that represents all feasible solutions of Ψ. This is achieved by a simple Monte-Carlo sampling scheme known as hit-and-run sampling [21]. Let y_0 be some feasible point in Ψ obtained by using a LP solver. At each step, we generate a new solution y_{i+1}, at random, from the current sample y_i (Cf. Fig. 5):

(1) Choose a random unit vector v uniformly. A simple scheme is to generate a vector h whose entries are uniform random numbers in $[0, 1]$ and compute $v = \frac{1}{\|h\|_2} h$.

(2) Discover the interval $[l, u]$, such that $\forall \lambda \in [l, u]$, $y_i + \lambda v \in [[\Psi]]$. In other words, v yields a line segment containing the point x along the directions $\pm v$ and $[l, u]$ represent the minimum and maximum offsets possible along the direction v starting from y_i. Since $[[\Psi]]$ is a polyhedron, bounds $[l, u]$ may be obtained by simply by substituting $x \mapsto y_i + \lambda v$ in each inequality wherein λ is an unknown. This yields upper and lower bounds on λ.

(3) Finally, we choose a value $\lambda \in [l, u]$ uniformly at random. The new solution sample is $y_{i+1} = y_i + \lambda v$.

The analysis of this scheme and proof of convergence to the uniform distribution follows from the theory of Markov Chain Monte Carlo sampling [21,22]. However,

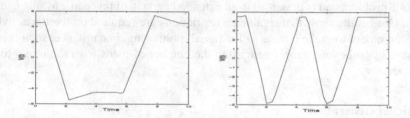

Fig. 6. Periodic signals generated for the automaton in Example 1

care must be taken to ensure that the polyhedron Ψ is not *skewed* along some direction r. In the worst case, we may imagine Ψ as a straight line segment. In such cases, it is essential to ensure that random unit vectors at each step belong to any subspace that Ψ itself is contained in. Finally, the scheme works best if the initial point y_0 is an interior point. Lovasz et al. [14] analyze the convergence of hit-and-run samplers for generating uniformly distributed points belonging to a convex set.

From Switching Times To Sampled Signal

Thus far, we have presented a scheme for encoding runs by means of a linear program $\Psi_{T,\pi}$ and choosing solutions at random efficiently from the polyhedron representing Ψ by means of hit-and-run samplers. The next step is to construct signal samples $g_0, \ldots, g_{N-1}$ given the switching times $T_1, \ldots, T_m$, the continuous states x_0, x_{m+1} at the beginning and end of the run, and the continuous states x_j, x'_j before and after transition τ_j, respectively.

Let δ_s be the sampling time. We will first generate the continuous state values $y_0, \ldots, y_N$ corresponding to the samples and thereafter, compute $g_i = f(y_i)$.

From the switching times, it is known that all samples in the time interval (T_j, T_{j+1}) will belong to the mode s_j (Cf. Figure 2). Our goal is to generate values $y_i, \ldots, y_{i+k}$ that lie between these time intervals, to ensure that (A) y_i is reachable from x'_j in time $i\delta_s - T_j$ evolving according to the mode s_j; (B) y_{i+l} for $1 \leq l \leq k$ is reachable from y_{i+l-1} in time δ_s; and (C) x_{j+1} is reachable from y_{i+k}.

Once again, these requirements can be encoded as a linear program since the dynamics at mode s_j and the number of samples in the interval (T_j, T_{j+1}) are all known. We may then use hit-and-run sampler to choose values for the continuous variables $y_i, \ldots, y_{i+k}$ and thereafter, the signal samples by applying the function f.

Example 2. Consider the signal in Example 1. We will designate the state high as both the start and the end states. Figure 6 plots two signals that were generated using the models obtained for two paths π_1, π_2 of lengths 4 and 8 going around the cycle once and twice, respectively. For each path, we generate one solution for the switching times and one set of samples.

4   Frequency Domain Specifications

We will now consider the specification of periodic signals in the frequency domain by specifying constraints on its power spectrum. Let $g(t)$ be a continuous signal with time period $T > 0$. Its unique frequency domain representation can be derived by its Fourier series representation:

$$g(t) = a_0 + \sum_{k=1}^{\infty} \left(a_k \sin\left(\frac{2k\pi t}{T}\right) + b_k \cos\left(\frac{2k\pi t}{T}\right) \right)$$

The coefficient a_0 represents D.C component of the signal and coefficients a_k, b_k represent the amplitude variable for the components at frequency $f = \frac{k}{T} = kf_0$. We will term $f_0 = \frac{1}{T}$ as the fundamental frequency. The amplitude at frequency $f_k = kf_0$ is given by $\sqrt{a_k^2 + b_k^2}$.

Let $G : [0, f_{max}] \mapsto \mathbb{R}_{\geq 0}$ be a function mapping each frequency $f \in [0, f_{max}]$ to a non-negative number $G(f)$. We assume that G is a computable function so that $G(f)$ can be computed for any given f to arbitrary precision. The function G along with the maximum frequency f_{max} are said to form a *power spectral envelope*. Consider periodic signal $g(t)$ with fundamental frequency f_0 and Fourier coefficients $a_0, a_1, b_1, \ldots, a_n, b_n$.

Definition 4 (Membership in Power Spectral Envelope). *The signal g belongs to the power spectral envelope $\langle f_{max}, G \rangle$, defined by $G : [0, f_{max}] \mapsto \mathbb{R}_{\geq 0}$ if and only if:*

1. *The amplitudes vanish for all frequency components in (f_{max}, ∞): $\forall k \in \mathbb{N}, (k \cdot f_0 > f_{max}) \Rightarrow a_k = b_k = 0$.*
2. *The amplitudes for all frequency components in $(0, f_{max}]$ are bounded by $G(f)$:*

$$\forall k \in \mathbb{N}, \ 0 < kf_0 < f_{max} \Rightarrow \sqrt{a_k^2 + b_k^2} \leq G(kf_0).$$

In other words, the possible values of a_k, b_k lie inside a circle of radius $G(kf_0)$ centered at $(0, 0)$.

3. *The D.C component is bounded by $G(0)$, i.e, $-G(0) \leq a_0 \leq G(0)$.*

In many situations, we are interested in signals being approximated within some tolerance limit by a signal that belongs to a given power spectral envelope $\langle f_{max}, G \rangle$. Therefore, we define membership with ϵ-tolerance for some $\epsilon \geq 0$.

Definition 5 (Membership with ϵ-tolerance). *A signal $s(t)$ satisfies $\langle f_{max}, G \rangle$ with a tolerance $\epsilon \geq 0$ iff s has a time period T and there exists a signal g that satisfies the frequency domain specification $\langle f_{max}, G \rangle$ such that the distance between s and g is bounded by ϵ, i.e, $(\forall t \in [0, T]), |s(t) - g(t)| \leq \epsilon$.*

Let δ_s be a sampling time period. We say that $s(t)$ satisfies to a specification with a sample tolerance of ϵ iff $|s(k\delta_s) - g(k\delta_s)| < \epsilon, \forall k \in [0, \lfloor \frac{T}{\delta_s} \rfloor]$

It is possible to relate continuous time tolerance to sample tolerance, provided absolute bounds may be placed on the derivatives of the signals s and g.

Theorem 4. *Let s, g be two signals with sample distance of ϵ and sample time δ_s. Let $|\frac{ds}{dt}| \leq D_s$ and $|\frac{dg}{dt}| \leq D_g$. For all $t \geq 0, |g(t) - s(t)| \leq \epsilon + \frac{\delta_s}{2}(D_s + D_g)$.*

A proof is provided in the extended version. Likewise, we prove that any signal belonging to a frequency domain specification $\langle f_{max}, G \rangle$ has absolute bounds on its derivative.

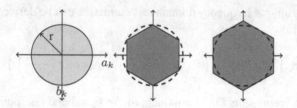

Fig. 7. Relaxations and restrictions of amplitude constraint by polyhedral constraints

Theorem 5. *The derivative of a signal s with time period $T > 0$, whose Fourier series representation belongs to $\langle f_{\max}, G \rangle$, is bounded:*

$$\left| \frac{ds}{dt} \right| \leq \pi G_{\max} f_{\max} (1 + T f_{\max}), \text{ where } G_{\max} = \sup_{0 \leq f \leq f_{\max}} G(f).$$

Example 3. Consider the function $G(f) = \begin{cases} 1 + 8f & f \in [0, 0.5] \\ 7 - 4f & f \in [0.5, 1] \\ 0 & f > 1 \end{cases}$. We specify the set of all periodic signals whose time periods are in the range $T \in [5, 100]$ seconds, belonging to the envelope $\langle 1Hz, G \rangle$ with a tolerance of 0.01.

4.1   Encoding Membership

Let g be some periodic signal with time period $T > 0$, sampled with time period $\delta > 0$. We represent s in terms of its $N = \frac{T}{\delta}$ samples $g_0, g_1, \ldots, g_{N-1}$ wherein $g_k = g(k\delta)$. The sampling frequency $\frac{1}{\delta}$ is assumed to be at least $2 f_{\max}$, the Nyquist limit to enable reconstruction of the original signal from its samples [20]. We wish to ascertain whether g belongs to a given power spectral envelope $\langle f_{\max}, G \rangle$, with a given sample tolerance of $\epsilon \geq 0$. Membership is encoded in terms of linear inequality constraints over the unknown coefficients of the Fourier series representation of the signal $g(t)$.

Let $f_0 = \frac{1}{T}$ be the fundamental frequency. We will assume that $f_0 < f_{\max}$ (otherwise, membership is trivial). Let $m = \left\lfloor \frac{f_{\max}}{f_0} \right\rfloor$ represent the total number of potentially non-zero frequency components. We introduce the variables $a_0, a_1, \ldots, b_m$. The encoding consists of the following constraints:

Sample Tolerance: We encode that at each time instant $t = j\delta$, where $0 \leq j < N$, s_j is approximated by the Fourier series:

$$\bigwedge_{j=0}^{N-1} -\epsilon \leq \left(g_j - \sum_{k=1}^{m} [a_k \sin(2\pi k f_0 j\delta) + b_k \cos(2\pi k f_0 j\delta)] - a_0 \right) \leq \epsilon.$$

Note that since j and δ are known, the values of the trigonometric terms can be computed to arbitrary precision. As a result, the constraints above are linear inequalities over the unknowns $a_0, a_1, b_1, \ldots, b_m$.

Table 1. Running times for signal generation benchmarks with various sets of time periods and sampling times. Legend: **#M:** # discrete modes, **#Tr:** # transitions, **#Samp:** # samples per period, **TP:** Time Period, **#FC:** Fourier Coefficients, **Time:** Signal generation time (Seconds), **#Path:** Paths explored, **#Sat:** satisfiable paths.

Name	Time		Freq.			Time Domain Only			Time + Freq Domain		
	#M	#Tr	#Samp	TP	#FC	Time	#Path	#Sat	Time	#Path	#Sat
SquareWave	4	4	10	10	7	0	5	1	0.2	5	1
			15	15	13	.2	7	2	30	7	0
			20	20	13	.5	10	3	1300	10	0
PulseWidth	6	8	10	10	7	.7	10	8	6.9	10	8
			15	15	11	8.7	15	13	391	15	7
			20	20	13	71.5	20	15	-	T/O	-
Sq+SawtoothWave	8	12	10	10	21	2.7	255	127	4.9	255	40
			15	15	31	149	8191	4095	1097	8191	32
			20	20	41	6349	262143	131071	-	T/O	-
RoomHeater	5	6	40	76	-	136	38	4	-	n/a	-

D.C. Component: We encode requirements on a_0, $-G(0) \leq a_0 \leq G(0)$

Amplitude Constraint: For each $k \in [1, m]$, we wish to encode $\sqrt{a_k^2 + b_k^2} \leq G(kf_0)$. However, such a constraint is clearly non-linear. We present linear approximations of this constraints such that if any solution can be found for the linear restriction, then the solution satisfies the amplitude constraint above.

Geometrically, the constraint $\sqrt{a_k^2 + b_k^2} \leq G(kf_0)$ encodes that the feasible values of (a_k, b_k) belong to the circle centered at origin of radius $G(kf_0)$ (see Figure 7). Let $P(r)$ be a polygon that under-approximates the circle of radius r centered at the origin, and $Q(r)$ be a polygon that over-approximates the unit circle. It is well-known [2] that such polygons can approximate the circle to any desired accuracy. Therefore, we may restrict the constraint above by linear constraints $(a_k, b_k) \in P(G(kf_0))$, or relax it by linear constraints $(a_k, b_k) \in Q(G(kf_0))$. The overall encoding yields a linear program by conjoining the constraints above. The under approximate encoding is given by choosing $(a_k, b_k) \in P(r_k)$, wherein $r_k = G(kf_0)$, whereas the over approximate encoding is given by choosing the constraints $(a_k, b_k) \in Q(r_k)$.

Signal Recognition: Given a power spectral envelope $\langle f_{max}, G \rangle$, a time period T and signal samples $g_0, \ldots, g_{N-1}$ with timestep δ, let $U_\epsilon(f_{max}, G, T, g, \delta)$ be the restricted system and $O_\epsilon(f_{max}, G, T, g, \delta)$ represent the relaxed constraints.

Theorem 6. *If U_ϵ is satisfiable then the signal $g(t)$ belongs to $\langle f_{max}, G \rangle$ with sample tolerance ϵ. If O_ϵ is unsatisfiable, then the signal $g(t)$ does not belong to $\langle f_{max}, G \rangle$ with sample tolerance ϵ.*

---

[2] Going back to the Greek mathematician Archimedes and the ancient Egyptians before him!

Signal Generation: Signal generation uses the same encoding (O_ϵ, U_ϵ) with $g_0, \ldots, g_{N-1}$ as unknown variables as opposed to known samples of a signal. Once again, the hit-and-run sampling scheme used for choosing solutions at random can be employed to generate multiple samples.

Mixed Domain Specifications The problem of signal recognition can be solved by considering signal membership individually, in the time and frequency domains.

The encodings presented can be combined to generate signals. Let us assume that we are interested in generating a signal $g(t)$ with a fixed time period T. We choose some fixed sampling interface δ_s, satisfying the Nyquist sampling criteria such that $\delta_s < \frac{1}{2f_{\max}}$. Let $g_i, i \in [0, N-1]$ denote the unknown signal sample to be generated at time $i\delta_s$. Once again, we generate the encodings $\Psi_{T,\pi}$ along paths π to generate switching times and states before/after switching (Cf. Section 3.1). Next we generate LP $\Gamma_{g,\pi}$ that encodes the time domain correspondence of the signal samples w.r.t the run along path π (Cf. Section 3.2). The sampled values from $\Psi_{T,\pi}$ are used to simplify $\Gamma_{g,\pi}$. The overall signal samples are generated by picking solutions from the LP $\Gamma_{g,\pi} \wedge U_\epsilon$ using a hit-and-run sampler.

5   Experiments

We will now report on our implementation, as a preliminary proof-of-concept for the ideas in this paper and some initial experimental results using these ideas.

Implementation: Our implementation reads in a hybrid automaton specification along with a frequency domain specification. The envelope function G is specified by pairs $f_j, G(f_j)$ for a finite set of frequencies f_j. The value of $G(f)$ for $f \in (f_j, f_{j+1})$ is computed by linear interpolation. Our implementation first searches over paths in the hybrid automaton from the initial to the final states, constructing the LP $\Psi_{T,\pi}$ for each path. If this is found to be feasible, our approach constructs a SMT formula Γ that encodes the existence of a signal sample corresponding to π. Currently, our approach uses Yices to obtain a single solution. Once such a solution is obtained, we may use the hit-and-run sampler to obtain other solutions. In fact, this process does not need further calls to the solver. The alternative and potentially less expensive strategy of fixing a set of switching times by sampling from $\Psi_{T,\pi}$ and checking the conjunction of the time and frequency domain constraints remains to be implemented. The resulting samples are printed out in a suitable format that can be loaded into an environment such as Matlab. The encoding used in our implementation supports signal recognition as well.

We collected a set of benchmarks for commonly used specifications of various waveforms that are used in circuits including square waves that are commonly used to clock digital circuits (Cf. Example 1), sawtooth waves that are used in video monitors, the specification of a pulse-width modulator (PWM) waveform and a specification of an external disturbance temperature signal for testing the room heating benchmark available in Simulink/Stateflow(tm).

Pulse-Width Modulator Waveform: Figure 8 shows time domain and frequency domain specifications for signals generated by a PWM waveform. The waveform consists of a square pulse represented by v that alternates between on and off. An associated signal x

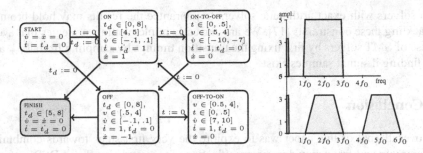

Fig. 8. PWM signal time + frequency domain specification along with generated signals

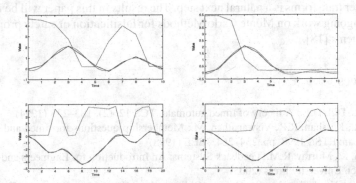

Fig. 9. Some signals generated for the PWM specification in Figure 8. The time domain samples (blue) and the frequency domain samples (red) are overlaid on each other.

rises whenever the v is high and falls when v is low. In effect, x represents the waveform v by a sequence of 1s and 0s represented by v. We add two requirements (a) the % of time period v must be high (also known as the duty cycle) must be between $50\% - 80\%$, and (b) the waveform v must belong to one of the two power-spectral envelopes shown in Fig. 8(right). Note that while the former is a time domain constraint on v, the latter is a frequency domain constraint on x. Fig 9 shows some of the waveforms output by our implementation. The sample tolerance between time and frequency domain signals was specified to be 0.1 and the sampling rate was chosen to be roughly $2.5 f_{\max}$ (slightly larger than the Nyquist rate).

Table 1 shows some of the results obtained by running the benchmark examples. Three of the examples have frequency domain specifications while the room heating benchmark had no frequency domain part. Overall, the benchmarks show that it is possible to exhaustively explore relatively small time domain specifications to obtain sample signals. Nevertheless, the complexity of exploration using SMT solvers is quite sensitive to the sampling rate. The addition of frequency domain constraints increases the complexity of these specifications many-fold. We believe that the handling of large floating point coefficients using exact arithmetic in tools such as Yices and Z3 is a bottleneck for frequency domain constraints and also to a limited extent for time domain constraints. A new generation of SMT solvers that combine the efficiency of floating point solvers with exact arithmetic solvers to guarantee the results may hold promise for tackling these constraints [17]. We are currently implementing strategies that avoid the use of SMT solvers by first fixing the transition timings by sampling from $\Psi_{T,\pi}$ and then finding if signal samples exist.

6   Conclusion

The overall goal of this paper was to explore the very first steps towards combining time domain and frequency domain specifications for mixed signal and DSP systems. In the future, we wish to consider restrictions of the time domain specifications for efficient monitoring. The generation of non-periodic signals by specifying the shape of their Fourier transforms is a natural next step. The results in this paper will be integrated into our ongoing work on Monte Carlo Methods for falsification of safety properties for hybrid systems [18].

References

1. Alur, R., Dill, D.L.: A theory of timed automata. TCS 126(2), 183–235 (1994)
2. Alur, R., Kurshan, R.P., Viswanathan, M.: Membership questions for timed and hybrid automata. In: RTSS 1998, pp. 254–264. IEEE (1998)
3. Åstrom, K., Murray, R.M.: Feedback Systems: An Introduction for Engineers and Scientists. Princeton University Press (2005)
4. Boyd, S., Vandenberghe, S.: Convex Optimization. Cambridge University Press (2004), http://www.stanford.edu/~boyd/cvxbook.html
5. de Moura, L., Bjørner, N.: Z3: An Efficient SMT Solver. In: Ramakrishnan, C.R., Rehof, J. (eds.) TACAS 2008. LNCS, vol. 4963, pp. 337–340. Springer, Heidelberg (2008)
6. Fainekos, G.E., Pappas, G.J.: Robustness of temporal logic specifications for continuous-time signals. Theoretical Computer Science 410(42), 4262–4291 (2009)
7. Finkbeiner, B., Sipma, H.: Checking finite traces using alternating automata. Form. Methods Syst. Des. 24, 101–127 (2004)
8. Frehse, G., Krogh, B.H., Rutenbar, R.A., Maler, O.: Time domain verification of oscillator circuit properties. Electron. Notes Theor. Comput. Sci. 153, 9–22 (2006)
9. Geilen, M.: On the construction of monitors for temporal logic properties. In: Proceedings of the 1st Workshop on Runtime Verification. ENTCS, vol. 55, pp. 181–199 (2001)
10. Havelund, K., Rosu, G.: Monitoring programs using rewriting. In: Proceedings of the 16th IEEE International Conference on Automated Software Engineering (2001)
11. Hedrich, L., Barke, E.: A formal approach to verification of linear analog circuits with parameter tolerances. In: Proceedings of the Conference on Design, Automation and Test in Europe (DATE), pp. 649–655. IEEE Computer Society, Washington, DC (1998)
12. Henzinger, T.A.: The theory of hybrid automata. In: LICS 1996, pp. 278–292. IEEE (1996)
13. Kristoffersen, K.J., Pedersen, C., Andersen, H.R.: Runtime verification of timed LTL using disjunctive normalized equation systems. In: Proceedings of the 3rd Workshop on Run-time Verification. ENTCS, vol. 89, pp. 1–16 (2003)
14. Lovasz, L.: Hit-and-run is fast and run. Mathematical Programming 86, 443–461 (1999)
15. Maler, O., Nickovic, D.: Monitoring Temporal Properties of Continuous Signals. In: Lakhnech, Y., Yovine, S. (eds.) FORMATS 2004 and FTRTFT 2004. LNCS, vol. 3253, pp. 152–166. Springer, Heidelberg (2004)

16. Millman, J., Halkias, C.C.: Electronic Devices and Circuits. McGraw-Hill Inc. (1967)
17. Monniaux, D.: On Using Floating-Point Computations to Help an Exact Linear Arithmetic Decision Procedure. In: Bouajjani, A., Maler, O. (eds.) CAV 2009. LNCS, vol. 5643, pp. 570–583. Springer, Heidelberg (2009)
18. Nghiem, T., Sankaranarayanan, S., Fainekos, G.E., Ivancic, F., Gupta, A., Pappas, G.J.: Monte-carlo techniques for falsification of temporal properties of non-linear hybrid systems. In: Proceedings of the 13th ACM International Conference on Hybrid Systems: Computation and Control, pp. 211–220 (2010)
19. Nickovic, D., Maler, O.: AMT: A Property-Based Monitoring Tool for Analog Systems. In: Raskin, J.-F., Thiagarajan, P.S. (eds.) FORMATS 2007. LNCS, vol. 4763, pp. 304–319. Springer, Heidelberg (2007)
20. Oppenheim, A.V., Schafer, R.W.: Digital Signal Processing. Prentice Hall (1975)
21. Rubinstein, R.Y., Kroese, D.P.: Simulation and the Monte Carlo Method. Wiley Series in Probability and Mathematical Statistics (2008)
22. Smith, R.L.: The hit-and-run sampler: a globally reaching markov chain sampler for generating arbitrary multivariate distributions. In: Proceedings of the 28th Conference on Winter Simulation, pp. 260–264. IEEE Computer Society (1996)
23. Steinhorst, S., Hedrich, L.: Model checking of analog systems using an analog specification language. In: Proceedings of the Conference on Design, Automation and Test in Europe, DATE 2008, pp. 324–329. ACM, New York (2008)
24. Tan, L., Kim, J., Lee, I.: Testing and monitoring model-based generated program. In: Proceedings of the 3rd Workshop on Run-time Verification. ENTCS, vol. 89, pp. 1–21 (2003)
25. Tan, L., Kim, J., Sokolsky, O., Lee, I.: Model-based testing and monitoring for hybrid embedded systems. In: Proceedings of the 2004 IEEE International Conference on Information Reuse and Integration, pp. 487–492 (2004)
26. Thati, P., Rosu, G.: Monitoring algorithms for metric temporal logic specifications. In: Runtime Verification. ENTCS, vol. 113, pp. 145–162. Elsevier (2005)

Runtime Verification for Ultra-Critical Systems

Lee Pike[1], Sebastian Niller[2], and Nis Wegmann[3]

[1] Galois, Inc.
leepike@galois.com
[2] National Institute of Aerospace
sebastian.niller@nianet.org
[3] University of Copenhagen
wegmann@diku.dk

Abstract. Runtime verification (RV) is a natural fit for ultra-critical systems, where correctness is imperative. In ultra-critical systems, even if the software is fault-free, because of the inherent unreliability of commodity hardware and the adversity of operational environments, processing units (and their hosted software) are replicated, and fault-tolerant algorithms are used to compare the outputs. We investigate both software monitoring in distributed fault-tolerant systems, as well as implementing fault-tolerance mechanisms using RV techniques. We describe the Copilot language and compiler, specifically designed for generating monitors for distributed, hard real-time systems, and we describe a case study in a Byzantine fault-tolerant airspeed sensor system.

1 Introduction

One in a billion, or 10^{-9}, is the prescribed safety margin of a catastrophic fault occurring in the avionics of a civil aircraft [1]. The justification for the requirement is essentially that for reasonable estimates for the size of an aircraft fleet, the number of hours of operation per aircraft in its lifetime, and the number of critical aircraft subsystems, a 10^{-9} probability of failure per hour ensures that the overall probability of failure for the aircraft fleet is "sufficiently small." Let us call systems with reliability requirements on this order *ultra-critical* and those that meet the requirements *ultra-reliable*. Similar reliability metrics might be claimed for other safety-critical systems, like nuclear reactor shutdown systems or railway switching systems.

Neither formal verification nor testing can ensure system reliability. Contemporary ultra-critical systems may contain millions of lines of code; the functional correctness of approximately ten thousand lines of code represents the state-of-the-art [2]. Nearly 20 years ago, Butler and Finelli showed that testing alone cannot verify the reliability of ultra-critical software [3].

Runtime verification (RV), where monitors detect and respond to property violations at runtime, holds particular potential for ensuring that ultra-critical systems are in fact ultra-reliable, but there are challenges. In ultra-critical systems, RV must account for both software and hardware faults. Whereas software

S. Khurshid and K. Sen (Eds.): RV 2011, LNCS 7186, pp. 310–324, 2012.

faults are design errors, hardware faults can be the result of random failure. Furthermore, assume that characterizing a system as being *ultra-critical* implies it is a distributed system with replicated hardware (so that the failure of an individual component does not cause system-wide failure); also assume ultra-critical systems are embedded systems sensing and/or controlling some physical plant and that they are *hard real-time*, meaning that deadlines are fixed and time-critical.

Contributions. Despite the relevance of RV to ultra-critical systems, there has been relatively little research on RV in that context. One of the primary contributions of this paper is to place RV within that context, particularly describing the constraints any RV solution must satisfy. A second contribution is the introduction of the notion of "easy fault-tolerance", where the machinery for implementing fault-tolerance resides in the monitor rather than the system under observation. Our third contribution is Copilot: a Haskell-based open-source language, compiler, and associated verification tools for generating RV monitors. Copilot answers two questions: (1) "Is RV possible for ultra-critical systems?" and (1) "Can functional programming be leveraged for embedded system RV?" We attempt to answer these questions by presenting the use of Copilot in a case-study replicating airspeed sensor failures in commercial aircraft.

Outline. We describe three recent software-related aircraft and Space Shuttle incidents motivating the need for RV in Section 2. In Section 3, we describe the constraints of RV implementations in the context of ultra-reliable systems.We describe the language Copilot in section 4; specifically, we describe how Copilot provides "easy" fault-tolerance, and we describe our approach to generating highly-reliable monitors. We present our use of Copilot in a case study simulating an ultra-reliable air speed system in Section 5. The remaining two sections present related work and conclusions, respectively.

2   When Ultra-Critical Is *Not* Ultra-Reliable

Well-known, albeit dated, examples of the failure of critical systems include the Therac-25 medical radiation therapy machine [4] and the Ariane 5 Flight 501 disaster [5]. However, more recent events show that critical-system software safety, despite certification and extensive testing, is still an unmet goal. Below, we briefly overview three examples drawing from faults in the Space Shuttle, a Boeing 777, and an Airbus A330, all occurring between 2005 and 2008.

Space Shuttle. During the launch of shuttle flight Space Transportation System 124 (STS-124) on May 31, 2008, there was a pre-launch failure of the fault diagnosis software due to a "non-universal I/O error" in the Flight Aft (FA) multiplexer de-multiplexer (MDM) located in the orbiter's aft avionics bay [6]. The Space Shuttle's data processing system has four general purpose computers (GPC) that operate in a redundant set. There are also twenty-three MDM units aboard the orbiter, sixteen of which are directly connected to the GPCs via shared buses. The GPCs execute redundancy management algorithms that include a fault detection, isolation, and recovery function. In short, a diode failed on the serial multiplexer interface adapter of the FA MDM. This failure was manifested as a *Byzantine fault* (i.e., a fault in which different nodes interpret a single broadcast message differently [7]), which was not tolerated and forced an emergency launch abortion.

Boeing 777. On August 1, 2005, a Boeing 777-120 operated as Malaysia Airlines Flight 124 departed Perth, Australia for Kuala Lumpur, Malaysia. Shortly after takeoff, the aircraft experienced an in-flight upset, causing the autopilot to dramatically manipulate the aircraft's pitch and airspeed. A subsequent analysis reported that the problem stemmed from a bug in the Air Data Inertial Reference Unit (ADIRU) software [8]. Previously, an accelerometer (call it A) had failed, causing the fault-tolerance computer to take data from a backup accelerometer (call it B). However, when the backup accelerometer failed, the system reverted to taking data from A. The problem was that the fault-tolerance software assumed there would not be a simultaneous failure of both accelerometers. Due to bugs in the software, accelerometer A's failure was never reported so maintenance could be performed.

Airbus A330. On October 7, 2008, an Airbus A330 operated as Qantas Flight QF72 from Singapore to Perth, Australia was cruising when the autopilot caused a pitch-down followed by a loss of altitude of about 200 meters in 20 seconds (a subsequent less severe pitch was also made) [9]. The accident required the hospitalization of fourteen people. Like in the Boeing 777 upset, the source of this accident was an ADIRU. The ADIRU appears to have suffered a transient fault that was not detected by the fault-management software of the autopilot system.

3   RV Constraints

Ideally, the RV approaches that have been developed in the literature could be applied straightforwardly to ultra-critical systems. Unfortunately, these systems have constraints violated by typical RV approaches. We summarize these constraints using the acronym "FaCTS":

- **F**unctionality: the RV system cannot change the target's behavior (unless the target has violated a specification).
- **C**ertifiability: the RV system must not make re-certification (e.g., DO-178B [10]) of the target onerous.
- **T**iming: the RV system must not interfere with the target's timing.
- **S**WaP: The RV system must not exhaust size, weight, and power (SWaP) tolerances.

The functionality constraint is common to all RV systems, and we will not discuss it further. The certifiability constraint is at odds with aspect-oriented programming techniques, in which source code instrumentation occurs across the code base—an approach classically taken in RV (e.g., the Monitor and Checking (MaC) [11] and Monitor Oriented Programming (MOP) [12] frameworks). For codes that are certified, instrumentation is not a feasible approach, since it requires costly reevaluation of the code. Source code instrumentation can modify both the control flow of the instrumented program as well as its timing properties. Rather, an RV approach must isolate monitors in the sense of minimizing or eliminating the effects of monitoring on the observed program's control flow.

Timing isolation is also necessary for real-time systems to ensure that timing constraints are not violated by the introduction of RV. Assuming a fixed upper bound on the execution time of RV, a worst-case execution-time analysis is used to determine the exact timing effects of RV on the system—doing so is imperative for hard real-time systems.

Code and timing isolation require the most significant deviations from traditional RV approaches. We have previously argued that these requirements dictate a *time-triggered* RV approach, in which a program's state is periodically sampled based on the passage of time rather than occurrence of events [13]. Other work at the University of Waterloo also investigates time-triggered RV [14,15].

The final constraint, SWaP, applies both to memory (embedded processors may have just a few kilobytes of available memory) as well as additional hardware (e.g., processors or interconnects).

4   Copilot: A Language for Ultra-Critical RV

To answer the challenge of RV in the context of fault-tolerant systems, we have developed a stream language called *Copilot*.[1] Copilot is designed to achieve the "FaCTS" constraints described in Section 3.

While a preliminary description of the language has been presented [13], significant improvements to the language have been made and the compiler has been fully reimplemented. In any event, the focus of this paper is the unique properties of Copilot for implementing hardware fault-tolerance and software monitoring in the context of an ultra-critical system. Copilot is a language with stream semantics, similar to languages like Lustre [16]; we mention advantages of Copilot over Lustre in Section 6.

To briefly introduce Copilot, we provide an example Copilot specification in Figure 1. A Copilot monitor program is a sequence of *triggers*. A trigger is comprised of a name (shutoff), a Boolean guard (not overHeat), and a list of arguments (in this case, one argument, maj, is provided). If and only if the condition holds is the function shutoff called with the arguments. What a trigger does is implementation-dependent; if Copilot's C code generator is used, then a raw C function with the prototype

```
void shutoff(uint8_t maj);
```

---

[1] Copilot is released under the BSD3 license and pointers to the compiler and libraries can be found at http://leepike.github.com/Copilot/.

> If the majority of the three engine temperature probes has exceeded 250 degrees,
> then the cooler is engaged and remains engaged until the temperature of the
> majority of the probes drop to 250 degrees or less. Otherwise, trigger an immediate
> shutdown of the engine.
>
> ```
> engineMonitor = do
>   trigger "shutoff" (not overHeat) [arg maj]
>   where
>   vals     = map externW8 ["tmp_probe_0", "tmp_probe_1", "tmp_probe_2"]
>   exceed   = map (< 250) vals
>   maj      = majority exceed
>   checkMaj = aMajority exceed maj
>   overHeat = (extern "cooler" || (maj && checkMaj)) `since` not maj
> ```

Fig. 1. A safety property and its corresponding Copilot monitor specification

should be defined. Within a single Copilot program, triggers are scheduled to fire
synchronously, if they fire at all. Outside of triggers, a Copilot monitor is side-
effect free with respect to non-Copilot state. Thus, triggers are used for other
events, such as communication between monitors, as described in Section 4.2.

A trigger's guard and arguments are *stream* expressions. Streams are infinite
lists of values. The syntax for defining streams is nearly identical to that of
Haskell list expressions; for example, the following is a Copilot program defining
the Fibonacci sequence.

```
fib = [0, 1] ++ fib + drop 1 fib
```

In Copilot streams, operators are automatically applied point-wise; for example,
negation in the expression `not overHeat` is applied point-wise over the elements
of the stream `overHeat`. In Figure 1, the streams are defined using library functions. The functions `majority`, `aMajority`, and `since` are all Copilot library
functions. The functions `majority` (which determines the majority element from
a list, if one exists—e.g., `majority [1, 2, 1, 2, 1] == 1`) and `aMajority`
(which determines if any majority element exists) come from a majority-vote
library, described in more detail in Section 4.1. The function `since` comes
from a a past-time linear temporal logic library. Libraries also exist for defining
clocks, linear temporal logic expressions, regular expressions, and simple statistical characterizations of streams.

Copilot is a typed language, where types are enforced by the Haskell type
system to ensure generated C programs are well-typed. Copilot is *strongly typed*
(i.e., type-incorrect function application is not possible) and *statically typed* (i.e.,
type-checking is done at compile-time). We rely on the type system to ensure
the Copilot compiler is type-correct. The base types are Booleans, unsigned and
signed words of width 8, 16, 32, and 64, floats, and doubles. All elements of a
stream must belong to the same base type.

To sample values from the "external world", Copilot has a notion of *external variables*. External variables include any value that can be referenced by a C variable (as well as C functions with a non-void return type and arrays of values). In the example, three external variables are sampled: tmp_probe_0, tmp_probe_1, tmp_probe_2. External variables are lifted into Copilot streams by applying a typed "extern" function. For example, An expression externW8 "var" is a stream of values sampled from the variable var, which is assumed to be an unsigned 8-bit word.

Copilot is implemented as an *embedded domain-specific language* (eDSL). An eDSL is a domain-specific language in which the language is defined as a sublanguage of a more expressive host language. Because the eDSL is embedded, there is no need to build custom compiler infrastructure for Copilot—the host language's parser, lexer, type system, etc. can all be reused. Indeed, Copilot is *deeply embedded*, i.e., implemented as data in the host language that can be manipulated by "observer programs" (in the host language) over the data, implementing interpreters, analyzers, pretty-printers, compilers, etc. Copilot's host language is the pure functional language Haskell [17]. In one sense, Copilot is an experiment to answer the question, "To what extent can functional languages be used for ultra-critical system monitoring?"

One advantage of the eDSL approach is that Haskell acts as a powerful macro language for Copilot. For example, in Figure 1, the expression

```
map externW8 ["tmp_probe_0", "tmp_probe_1", "tmp_probe_2"]
```

is a *Haskell* expression that maps the external stream operator externW8 over a list of strings (variable names). We discuss macros in more detail in Section 4.1.

Additionally, by reusing Haskell's compiler infrastructure and type system, not only do we have stronger guarantees of correctness than we would by writing a new compiler from scratch, but we can keep the size of the compiler infrastructure that is unique to Copilot small and easily analyzable; the combined front-end and core of the Copilot compiler is just over two thousand lines of code. Our primary back-end generating C code is around three thousand lines of code.

Copilot is designed to integrate easily with multiple back-ends. Currently, two back-ends generate C code. The primary back-end uses the Atom eDSL [18] for code generation and scheduling. Using this back-end, Copilot compiles into constant-time and constant-space programs that are a small subset of C99. By *constant-time*, we mean C programs such that the number of statements executed is not dependent on control-flow[2] and by *constant-space*, we mean C programs with no dynamic memory allocation.

The generated C is suitable for compiling to embedded microprocessors: we have tested Copilot-generated specifications on the AVR (ATmega328 processor) and STM32 (ARM Cortex M3 processor) micro-controllers. Additionally, the

---

[2] We do not presume that a constant-time C program implies constant execution time (e.g., due to hardware-level effects like cache misses), but it simplifies execution-time analysis.

compiler generates its own static periodic schedule, allowing it to run on bare hardware (e.g., no operating system is needed). The language follows a sampling-based monitoring strategy in which variables or the return values of functions of an observed program are periodically sampled according to its schedule, and properties about the observations are computed.

4.1   Easy Fault-Tolerance

Fault-tolerance is hard to get right. The examples given in Section 2 can be viewed as fault-tolerance algorithms that failed; indeed, as noted by Rushby, fault-tolerance algorithms, ostensibly designed to prevent faults, are often the source of systematic faults themselves [19]! One goal of Copilot is to make fault-tolerance easy—easy for experts to specify algorithms without having to worry about low-level programming errors and easy for users of the functions to integrate the algorithms into their overall system. While Copilot cannot protect against a designer using a fault-tolerant algorithm with a weak fault-model, it increases the chances of getting fault-tolerance right as well as decoupling the design of fault-tolerance from the primary control system. Finally, it separates the concerns of implementing a fault-tolerance algorithm from implementing the algorithm as a functionally correct, memory-safe, real-time C program.

As noted, because Copilot is deeply embedded in Haskell, Haskell acts as a meta-language for manipulating Copilot programs. For example, the streams maj, check, and overHeat in Figure 1 are implemented by Haskell functions that generate Copilot programs.

To see this in more detail, consider the Boyer-Moore Majority-Vote Algorithm, the most efficient algorithm for computing a majority element from a set[3] [20]. The majority library function implements this algorithm as a Copilot macro as follows:

```
majority (x:xs) = majority' xs x (1 :: Stream Word32)
  where
  majority' []     candidate _   = candidate
  majority' (x:xs) candidate cnt =
    majority' xs (if cnt == 0 then x else candidate)
              (if cnt == 0 || x == candidate then cnt+1 else cnt-1)
```

The macro specializes the algorithm for a fixed-size set of streams at compile-time to ensure a constant-time implementation, even though the algorithm's time-complexity is data-dependent. (Our library function ensures sharing is preserved to reduce the size of the generated expression.)

As an informal performance benchmark, for the majority algorithm voting over five streams of unsigned 64-bit words, we compare C code generated from Copilot and constant-time handwritten C. Each program is compiled using

---

[3] Due to space limitations, we will not describe the algorithm here, but an illustration of the algorithm can be found at
http://www.cs.utexas.edu/~moore/best-ideas/mjrty/example.html.

gcc -O3, with a `printf` statement piped to /dev/null (to ensure the function is not optimized away). The hand-written C code is approximately nine percent faster.

While the Boyer-Moore algorithm is not complicated, the advantages of the Copilot approach over C are (1) `majority` is a polymorphic library function that can be applied to arbitrary (Copilot-supported) data-types and sizes of voting sets; with (2) constant-time code, which is tedious to write, is generate automatically; (3) the Copilot verification and validation tools (described in Section 4.3) can be used.

4.2 Distributed Monitoring

Our case study presented in Section 5 implements distributed monitors. In a distributed monitor architecture, monitors are replicated, with specific parameters per process (e.g., process identifiers). The meta-programming techniques described in Section 4.1 can be used to generate distributed monitors by parameterizing programs over node-specific data, reducing a tedious task that is traditionally solved with makefiles and C macros to a few lines of Haskell.

Copilot remains agnostic as to how the communication between distinct processes occurs; the communication can be operating system supported (e.g., IPC) if the monitors are processes hosted by the same operating system, or they can be raw hardware communication mechanisms (e.g., a custom serial protocol and processor interrupts). If the monitors are on separate processors, the programmer needs to ensure either that the hardware is synchronized (e.g., by using a shared clock or by executing a clock synchronization protocol). Regardless of the method, triggers, described above, are also used to call C functions that implement the platform-specific protocol. Incoming values are obtained by sampling external variables (or functions or arrays).

4.3 Monitor Assurance

"Who watches the watchmen?" Nobody. For this reason, monitors in ultra-critical systems are the last line of defense and cannot fail. Here, we outline our approach to generate high-assurance monitors. First, as mentioned, the compiler is statically and strongly typed, and by implementing an eDSL, much of the infrastructure of a well-tested Haskell implementation is reused. Copilot contains a custom QuickCheck [21]-like test harness that generates random Copilot programs and tests the interpreted output against the compiler to ensure correspondence between the two. We have tested millions of randomly-generated programs between the compiler and interpreter.

We use the CBMC model checker [22] to verify C code generated by Copilot specifications. CBMC provides an independent check on the compiler. CBMC can prove that the C code is memory-safe, including proving there are no arithmetic underflows or overflows, no division by zero, no not-a-number floating-point values, no null-pointer dereferences, and no uninitialized local variables.

Some of these potential violations are impossible for the Copilot compiler to generate (e.g., null-pointer dereferences), provided it is bug-free. Sometimes CBMC cannot prove that a C program is memory-safe, since it requires the program to be loop-free. The C code generated by Copilot implements a state machine that generates the next values of the stream equations (see [13] for details). CBMC can symbolically unroll the state machine a small fixed number of steps. A separate (so far informal) proof must be given that the program has been unrolled sufficiently to prove memory-safety.

5   Case Study

In commercial aircraft, airspeed is commonly determined using pitot tubes that measure air pressure. The difference between total and static air pressure is used to calculate airspeed. Pitot tube subsystems have been implicated in numerous commercial aircraft incidents and accidents, including the 2009 Air France crash of an A330 [23], motivating our case study.

We have developed a platform resembling a real-time air speed measuring system with replicated processing nodes, pitot tubes, and pressure sensors to test distributed Copilot monitors with the objective of detecting and tolerating software and hardware faults, both of which are purposefully injected.

The high-level procedure of our experiment is as follows: (1) we sense and sample air pressure from the aircraft's pitot tubes; (2) apply a conversion and calibration function to accommodate different sensor and analog-to-digital converter (ADC) characteristics; (3) sample the C variables that contain the pressure values on a hard real-time basis by Copilot-generated monitors; and (4) execute Byzantine fault-tolerant voting and fault-tolerant averaging on the sensor values to detect arbitrary hardware component failures and keep consistent values among good nodes.

We sample five pitot tubes, attached to the wings of an Edge 540 subscale aircraft. The pitot tubes provide total and static pressure that feed into one

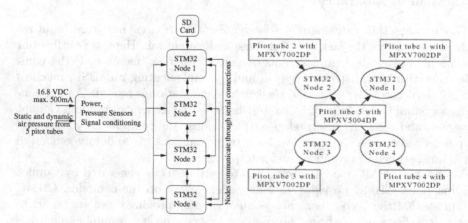

Fig. 2. Hardware stack and pitot tube configuration

MPXV5004DP and four MPXV7002DP differential pressure sensors (Figure 2). The processing nodes are four STM 32 microcontrollers featuring ARM Cortex M3 cores which are clocked at 72 Mhz (the number of processors was selected with the intention of creating applications that can tolerate one Byzantine processing node fault [7]). The MPXV5004DP serves as a shared sensor that is read by each of the four processing nodes; each of the four MPXV7002DP pressure sensors is a local sensor that is only read by one processing node.

Monitors communicate over dedicated point-to-point bidirectional serial connections. With one bidirectional serial connection between each pair of nodes, the monitor bus and the processing nodes form a complete graph. All monitors on the nodes run in synchronous steps; the clock distribution is ensured by a master hardware clock. (The clock is a single point of failure in our prototype hardware implementation; a fully fault-tolerant system would execute a clock-synchronization algorithm.)

Each node samples its two sensors (the shared and a local one) at a rate of 16Hz. The microcontroller's timer interrupt that updates the global time also periodically calls a Copilot-generated monitor which samples the ADC C-variables of the monitored program, conducts Byzantine agreements, and performs fault-tolerant votes on the values. After a complete round of sampling, agreements, and averaging, an arbitrary node collects and logs intermediate values of the process to an SD-card.

We tested the monitors in five flights. In each flight we simulated one node having a permanent Byzantine fault by having one monitor send out pseudo-random differing values to the other monitors instead of the real sampled pressure. We varied the number of injected benign faults by physically blocking the dynamic pressure ports on the pitot tubes. In addition, there were two "control flights", leaving all tubes unmodified.

The executed sampling, agreement, and averaging is described as follows:

1. Each node samples sensor data from both the shared and local sensors.
2. Each monitor samples the C variables that contain the pressure values and broadcasts the values to every other monitor, then relays each received value to monitors the value did not originate from.
3. Each monitor performs a majority vote (as described in Section 4.1) over the three values it has for every other monitor of the shared sensor (call this $maj_i(S)$ for node i) and the local sensor (call this $maj_i(L)$ for node i).
4. Copilot-generated monitors then compute a *fault-tolerant average*. In our implementation, we remove the least and greatest elements from a set, and average the remaining elements. For each node i and nodes $j \neq i$, fault-tolerant averages are taken over four-element sets: (1) $ftAvg(S) = \{S_i\} \cup \{maj_j(S)\}$ where S_i is i's value for the shared sensor.
5. Another fault-tolerant average is taken over a five-element set, where the two least and two greatest elements are removed (thus returning the median value). The set contains the fault-tolerant average over the shared sensor described in the previous step ($ftAvg(S)$), the node's local sensor value L_i, and $\{maj_j(L)\}$, for $j \neq i$. Call this final fault-tolerant average $ftAvg$.

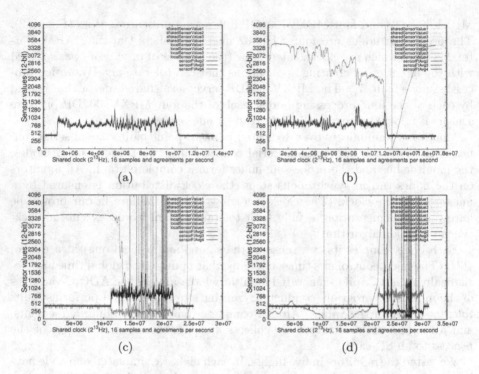

Fig. 3. Logged pressure sensor, voted and averaged data

6. Finally, time-stamps, sensor values, majorities and their existences are collected by one node and recorded to an SD card for off-line analysis.

The graphs in Figure 3 depict four scenarios in which different faults are injected. In each scenario, there is a software-injected Byzantine faulty node present. What varies between the scenarios are the number of physical faults. In Figure 3(a), no physical faults are introduced; in Figure 3(b), one benign fault has been injected by putting a cap over the total pressure probe of one local tube.[4] In Figure 3(c), in addition to the capped tube, sticky tape is placed over another tube, and in Figure 3(d), sticky tape is placed over two tubes in addition to the capped tube.

The graphs depict the air pressure difference data logged at each node and the voted and averaged outcome of the 3 non-faulty processing nodes. The gray traces show the recorded sensor data $S_1, \ldots, S_4$, and the calibrated data of the local sensors $L_1, \ldots, L_4$. The black traces show the final agreed and voted values $ftAvg$ of the three good nodes.

In every figure except for Figure 3(d), the black graphs approximate each other, since the fault-tolerant voting allows the nodes to mask the faults. This is despite wild faults; for example, in Figure 3(b), the cap on the capped tube creates a positive offset on the dynamic pressure as well as turbulences and low

---

[4] Tape left on the static pitot tube of Aeroperú Flight 603 in 1996 resulted in the death of 70 passengers and crew [24].

pressure on the static probes. At 1.2E7 clock ticks, the conversion and calibration function of the stuck tube results in an underflowing value. In Figure 3(d), with only two non-faulty tubes out of five left, *ftAvg* is not able to choose a non-faulty value reliably anymore. All nodes still agree on a consistent—but wrong—value.

Discussion. The purpose of the case-study is to test the feasibility of using Copilot-generated monitors in a realistic setting to "bolt on" fault-tolerance to a system that would otherwise be lacking that capability. The Copilot agreement monitor is around 200 lines. The generated real-time C code is nearly 4,000 lines.

Copilot reduced the effort to implement a non-trivial real-time distributed fault-tolerant voting scheme as compared to implementing it directly in C. While a sampling-based RV approach works for real-time systems, one major challenge encountered is ensuring the monitor's schedule corresponds with that of the rest of the system. Higher-level constructs facilitating timing analysis would be beneficial. Furthermore, it may be possible to reduce the size of the monitor's C code using more aggressive optimizations in the Copilot compiler.

6   Related Work

Using RV to implement fault-tolerance can be considered to be a "one-out-of-two" (1oo2) architecture [25], similar in spirit to the idea of the Simplex architecture [26]. In a 1oo2 architecture, one component may be an arbitrarily complex control system, and the other component is a monitor.

Copilot shares similarities with other RV systems that emphasize real-time or distributed systems. Krüger, Meisinger, and Menarini describe their work in synthesizing monitors for a automobile door-locking system [27]. While the system is distributed, it is not ultra-reliable and is not hard real-time or fault-tolerant via hardware replication. The implementation is in Java and focuses on the aspect-oriented monitor synthesis, similar in spirit to JavaMOP [28]. SYNCRAFT is a tool that takes a distributed program (specified in a high-level modeling language) that is fault-intolerant and given some invariant and fault model, transforms the program into one that is fault-tolerant (in the same modeling language). [29].

There are few instances of RV focused on C code. One exception is RMOR, which generates constant-memory C monitors [30]. RMOR does not address real-time behavior or distributed system RV, though.

Research at the University of Waterloo also investigates the use of time-triggered RV (i e , periodic sampling). Unlike with Copilot, the authors do not make the assumptions that the target programs are hard real-time themselves, so a significant portion of the work is devoted to developing the theory of efficiently monitoring for state changes using time-triggered RV for arbitrary programs, particularly for testing [14,15]. On the other hand, the work does not address issues such as distributed systems, fault-tolerance, or monitor integration.

With respect to work outside of RV, other research also addresses the use of eDSLs for generating embedded code. Besides Atom [18], which we use as a back-end, Feldspar is an eDSL for digitial signal processing [31]. Copilot is similar in spirit to other languages with stream-based semantics, notably represented by the Lustre family of languages [16]. Copilot is a simpler language, particularly with respect to Lustre's clock calculus, focused on monitoring (as opposed to developing control systems). Copilot can be seen as an generalization of the idea of Lustre's "synchronous observers" [32], which are Boolean-valued streams used to track properties about Lustre programs. Whereas Lustre uses synchronous observers to monitor Lustre programs, we apply the idea to monitoring arbitrary periodically-scheduled real-time systems. The main advantages of Copilot over Lustre is that Copilot is implemented as an eDSL, with the associated benefits; namely Haskell compiler and library reuse the ability to define polymorphic functions, like the `majority` macro in Section 4.1, that get monomorphised at compile-time.

7   Conclusions

Ultra-critical systems need RV. Our primary goals in this paper are to (1) motivate this need, (2) describe one approach for RV in the ultra-critical domain, (3) and present evidence for its feasibility.

Some research directions that remain include the following. Stochastic methods might be used to distinguish random hardware faults from systematic faults, as the strategy for responding to each differs [33]. We have not addressed the *steering* problem of how to address faults once they are detected. Steering is critical at the application level, for example, if an RV monitor detects that a control system has violated its permissible operational envelop. Because we have a sampling-based monitoring strategy, we would also like to be able to infer the periodic sampling rate required to monitor some property.

Research developments in RV have potential to improve the reliability of ultra-critical systems, and we hope a growing number of RV researchers address this application domain.

Acknowledgements. This work is supported by NASA Contract NNL08AD13T. We thank Ben Di Vito and Alwyn Goodloe at NASA Langley for their advice. Robin Morisset contributed to an earlier version of Copilot. NASA Langley's AirSTAR Rapid Evaluation and Prototyping Group graciously provided resources for our case study.

References

1. Rushby, J.: Software verification and system assurance. In: IEEE Intl. Conf. on Software Engineering and Formal Methods (SEFM), pp. 3–10 (2009)
2. Klein, G., Andronick, J., Elphinstone, K., Heiser, G., Cock, D., Derrin, P., Elkaduwe, D., Engelhardt, K., Kolanski, R., Norrish, M., Sewell, T., Tuch, H., Winwood, S.: seL4: Formal verification of an OS kernel. Communications of the ACM (CACM) 53, 107–115 (2010)

3. Butler, R.W., Finelli, G.B.: The infeasibility of quantifying the reliability of life-critical real-time software. IEEE Transactions on Software Engineering 19, 3–12 (1993)
4. Leveson, N.G., Turner, C.S.: An investigation of the Therac-25 accidents. Computer 26, 18–41 (1993)
5. Nuseibeh, B.: Soapbox: Ariane 5: Who dunnit? IEEE Software 14(3), 15–16 (1997)
6. Bergin, C.: Faulty MDM removed. NASA Spaceflight.com, May 18 (2008), http://www.nasaspaceflight.com/2008/05/sts-124-frr-debate-outstanding-issues-faulty-mdm-removed/
7. Lamport, L., Shostak, R., Pease, M.: The Byzantine generals problem. ACM Transactions on Programming Languages and Systems 4, 382–401 (1982)
8. Australian Transport Safety Bureau: In-flight upset event 240Km North-West of Perth, WA Boeing Company 777-200, 9M-MRG August 1, 2005. ATSB Transport Safety Investigation Report (2007)
9. Macaulay, K.: ATSB preliminary factual report, in-flight upset, Qantas Airbus A330, 154 Km West of Learmonth, WA, October 7, 2008. Australian Transport Safety Bureau Media Release, November 14 (2008), http://www.atsb.gov.au/newsroom/2008/release/2008_45.aspx
10. RTCA: Software considerations in airborne systems and equipment certification. RTCA, Inc., RCTA/DO-178B (1992)
11. Kim, M., Viswanathan, M., Ben-Abdallah, H., Kannan, S., Lee, I., Sokolsky, O.: Formally specified monitoring of temporal properties. In: 11th Euromicro Conference on Real-Time Systems, pp. 114–122 (1999)
12. Chen, F., Roşu, G.: Java-MOP: A Monitoring Oriented Programming Environment for Java. In: Halbwachs, N., Zuck, L.D. (eds.) TACAS 2005. LNCS, vol. 3440, pp. 546–550. Springer, Heidelberg (2005)
13. Pike, L., Goodloe, A., Morisset, R., Niller, S.: Copilot: A Hard Real-Time Runtime Monitor. In: Barringer, H., Falcone, Y., Finkbeiner, B., Havelund, K., Lee, I., Pace, G., Roşu, G., Sokolsky, O., Tillmann, N. (eds.) RV 2010. LNCS, vol. 6418, pp. 345–359. Springer, Heidelberg (2010)
14. Fischmeister, S., Ba, Y.: Sampling-based program execution monitoring. In: ACM International Conference on Languages, Compilers, and Tools for Embedded Systems (LCTES), pp. 133–142 (2010)
15. Bonakdarpour, B., Navabpour, S., Fischmeister, S.: Sampling-Based Runtime Verification. In: Butler, M., Schulte, W. (eds.) FM 2011. LNCS, vol. 6664, pp. 88–102. Springer, Heidelberg (2011)
16. Mikáč, J., Caspi, P.: Formal system development with Lustre: Framework and example. Technical Report TR-2005-11, Verimag Technical Report (2005), http://www-verimag.imag.fr/index.php?page=techrep-list&lang=en
17. Jones, S.P. (ed.): Haskell 98 Language and Libraries: The Revised Report (2002), http://haskell.org/
18. Hawkins, T.: Controlling hybrid vehicles with Haskell. Presentation. Commercial Users of Functional Programming, CUFP (2008), http://cufp.galois.com/2008/schedule.html
19. Rushby, J.: Formalism in safety cases. In: Dale, C., Anderson, T. (eds.) Making Systems Safer: Proceedings of the Eighteenth Safety-Critical Systems Symposium, pp. 3–17. Springer, Bristol (2010), http://www.csl.sri.com/users/rushby/papers/sss10.pdf
20. Boyer, R.S., Moore, J.S.: Mjrty: A fast majority vote algorithm. In: Automated Reasoning: Essays in Honor of Woody Bledsoe, pp. 105–118 (1991)

21. Claessen, K., Hughes, J.: Quickcheck: A lightweight tool for random testing of haskell programs. ACM SIGPLAN Notices, 268–279 (2000)
22. Clarke, E., Kroning, D., Lerda, F.: A Tool for Checking ANSI-C Programs. In: Jensen, K., Podelski, A. (eds.) TACAS 2004. LNCS, vol. 2988, pp. 168–176. Springer, Heidelberg (2004)
23. Aviation Today: More pitot tube incidents revealed. Aviation Today (February 2011),
    http://www.aviationtoday.com/regions/usa/More-Pitot-Tube-Incidents-Revealed_72414.html
24. Ladkin, P.B.: News and comment on the Aeroperu b757 accident; AeroPeru Flight 603, October 2, 1996 (2002), Online article RVS-RR-96-16,
    http://www.rvs.uni-bielefeld.de/publications/Reports/aeroperu-news.html
25. Littlewood, B., Rushby, J.: Reasoning about the reliability of diverse two-channel systems in which one channel is "possibly perfect". Technical Report SRI-CSL-09-02, SRI (January 2010)
26. Sha, L.: Using simplicity to control complexity. IEEE Software, 20–28 (July/August 2001)
27. Krüger, I.H., Meisinger, M., Menarini, M.: Runtime Verification of Interactions: From MSCs to Aspects. In: Sokolsky, O., Taşıran, S. (eds.) RV 2007. LNCS, vol. 4839, pp. 63–74. Springer, Heidelberg (2007)
28. Chen, F., d'Amorim, M., Roşu, G.: Checking and correcting behaviors of java programs at runtime with Java-MOP. Electronic Notes in Theoretical Computer Science 144, 3–20 (2006)
29. Bonakdarpour, B., Kulkarni, S.S.: SYCRAFT: A Tool for Synthesizing Distributed Fault-Tolerant Programs. In: van Breugel, F., Chechik, M. (eds.) CONCUR 2008. LNCS, vol. 5201, pp. 167–171. Springer, Heidelberg (2008)
30. Havelund, K.: Runtime Verification of C Programs. In: Suzuki, K., Higashino, T., Ulrich, A., Hasegawa, T. (eds.) TestCom/FATES 2008. LNCS, vol. 5047, pp. 7–22. Springer, Heidelberg (2008)
31. Axelsson, E., Claessen, K., Dvai, G., Horvth, Z., Keijzer, K., Lyckegrd, B., Persson, A., Sheeran, M., Svenningsson, J., Vajda, A.: Feldspar: a domain specific language for digital signal processing algorithms. In: 8th ACM/IEEE Int. Conf. on Formal Methods and Models for Codesign (2010)
32. Halbwachs, N., Raymond, P.: Validation of Synchronous Reactive Systems: From Formal Verification to Automatic Testing. In: Thiagarajan, P.S., Yap, R.H.C. (eds.) ASIAN 1999. LNCS, vol. 1742, pp. 1–12. Springer, Heidelberg (1999)
33. Sammapun, U., Lee, I., Sokolsky, O.: RT-MaC: runtime monitoring and checking of quantitative and probabilistic properties. In: 11th IEEE Intl. Conf. on Embedded and Real-Time Computing Systems and Applications, pp. 147–153 (2005)

Runtime Verification of Data-Centric Properties in Service Based Systems

Guoquan Wu[1], Jun Wei[1], Chunyang Ye[1,2], Xiaozhe Shao[1],
Hua Zhong[1], and Tao Huang[1]

[1] Institute of Software, Chinese Academy of Sciences
[2] University of Toronto, Canada
{gqwu,wj,cyye,xiaozheshao09,zhongh,tao}@otcaix.iscas.ac.cn

Abstract. For service-based systems which are composed of multiple independent stakeholders, correctness cannot be ascertained statically. Continuous monitoring is required to assure that runtime behavior of the systems complies with specified properties. However, most existing work considers only the temporal constraints of messages exchanged between services, ignoring the actual data contents inside the messages. As a result, it is difficult to validate some dynamic properties such as how message data of interest is processed between different participants. To address this issue, this paper proposes an efficient, online monitoring approach to dynamically analyze data-centric properties in service-based systems. By introducing *Par*-BCL - a Parametric Behavior Constraint Language for Web services - various data-centric properties can be specified and monitored. To keep runtime overhead low, we statically analyze the monitored properties to generate parameter state machine, and combine two different indexing mechanisms to optimize the monitoring. The experiments show that the proposed approach is efficient.

1   Introduction

Service oriented architecture (SOA) is an emerging software paradigm which provides support to dynamically evolving software systems (e.g., context-aware applications, pervasive computing, ambient intelligence), where both components and their bindings may change at runtime. In this paradigm, individual service providers develop their Web services, and publish them at service registries. Service consumers can then discover the required services from the service registries and compose them to create new services. WS BPEL [1] now represents the de-facto standard for the Web services composition, in which a central node called the composition process usually coordinates the interactions of distributed, autonomous Web services. An instance of the process is the actual running process that follows the logic described in the process specification.

For service-based systems which are composed of multiple independent stakeholders, correctness cannot be ascertained statically [5]. Instead, it requires continuous monitoring to assure that the runtime behavior of the systems complies with the specified properties, because both the agents interacting with the system or

S. Khurshid and K. Sen (Eds.): RV 2011, LNCS 7186, pp. 325–341, 2012.

the involved third-party service that constitute it may change or behave unpredictably. Runtime monitoring also provides a chance of recovery once serious problems are discovered, e.g., by terminating execution or trying to return to a stable state.

The need to runtime monitoring of service-based system has inspired a lot of research projects in recent years [2][3][4][5][6][7]. However, most existing work concentrates on properties related to the control flow of systems. These constraints consider the orders of messages only. As a result, some dynamic properties such as how data contents inside the message are processed between different participants are not supported. For example, in an online shopping system, to constrain the behavior of a customer who has made a commitment to one transaction, a property specifying that the purchased items should eventually appear in the final payment bill is needed. In this paper, we refer to this class of properties as *data-centric properties*. In section 2 we will provide a representative example where data-centric properties arise for a variety of reasons.

To validate data-centric properties at runtime, previous approaches [2][3][4][6][7] which rely only on one unique identifier (e.g., process instance id or session id) to dispatch system events to right monitor instance, are not adequate when multiple data inside a message need to be monitored. These data may flow through different activities that are within or across different process instances.

To overcome these limitations, this paper developed an efficient, online monitoring approach that allows for dynamic analysis of data-centric properties in service-based system, from the point of the view of composition process. We introduce *Par*-BCL - a Parametric Behavior Constraint Language for Web service - to specify various data-centric properties. Specifically, in *Par*-BCL, parameters are introduced to specify a set of message data that needs to be monitored during the system execution. Moreover, *Par*-BCL extends Specification Pattern System (*SPS*) [8] proposed by Dwyer et al. with first-order quantification over message contents and introduces parameterized event to support the expression of properties that are related to a set of message data.

To verify data-centric properties, this paper broadens the monitored patterns to include not only message exchange orders, but also data contents bound to the parameters. In this way, dataflow information between different participants can be tracked timely. The main challenge of this approach is how to reduce monitoring overhead: since a large number of monitor instances are generated at runtime, each observing a set of related data, it's difficult to locate the relevant monitor instances that need to be updated quickly. To keep runtime overhead of monitoring and event observation low, we devise an efficient implementation of *Par*-BCL. Particularly, the implementation generates parameter state machine resulted from a static analysis of the desired property, and combines two different indexing mechanisms (static and dynamic) to optimize monitoring. To evaluate the effectiveness of our proposal, we conducted several empirical experiments. The results show that our approach is promising: in most cases, the runtime overhead of monitoring is very low and can be negligible.

The major contributions of this paper are: (1) we propose a parametric behavior constraint language for Web services, which provides an easy and intuitive way to express various data-centric properties; (2) we propose an online parametric monitoring approach to validate data-centric properties, which overcomes the limitation of existing work and can track dataflow within or across process instances; (3) we develop an efficient monitoring algorithm, which generates parameter state machine by making use of the static knowledge about properties, and combines two indexing mechanisms to facilitate the optimization of monitoring process.

The rest of this paper is organized as follows: Section 2 motivates the research problem using a real-life example. Section 3 elaborates the proposed *Par*-BCL language. Section 4 introduces the monitoring model adopted by *Par*-BCL. Section 5 introduces an efficient monitoring process. Section 6 presents an implementation of runtime framework through an aspect-oriented extension to WS-BPEL engine. Section 7 evaluates the feasibility and effectiveness of our approach. Section 8 reviews related work. Section 9 concludes this paper.

2   Motivation Example

To investigate the necessity of runtime verification of data-centric properties in service-based systems, we introduce a representative scenario. Similar properties can be found in the literature [9][10].

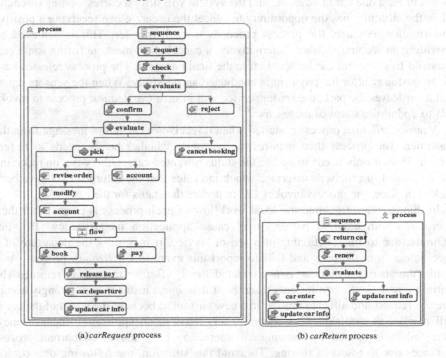

(a) *carRequest* process   (b) *carReturn* process

Fig. 1. CarRental System

This example is taken and adapted from [5]. As depicted in Fig.1, two processes are deployed in the *CarRental* system to provide car rental services for customers. *CarRequest* process is responsible for renting cars to customers and *CarReturn* process collects cars returned from customers. Both processes interact with the following partner services to provide the required functionalities:

Car Information Service (CIS). It maintains the registry of cars and allocates them to customers. It also provides operations to check and update the stock of cars.

Sensor Service (SS). It tracks cars in the parking lot automatically. There are several parking lots in *CarRental* system. When a car enters or leaves the parking lot, the sensor service will report this information to *CarRequest* and *CarReturn* processes.

User Interaction Service (UIS). It is responsible for interacting with customers.

Payment Service (PS). It transfers money between the car rental company and the customer.

In a typical car rental scenario, a new *CarRequest* process is launched when a car rental request is received from *UIS*. Then the process checks whether the requested cars are available by invoking *CIS*. If all cars are available, it will ask for a confirmation by producing a bill. At this step, the customer can make a commitment to rent at least one car in advance, and the system will offer a corresponding discount. Also, the customer has the opportunity to cancel the order. When receiving a positive confirmation message, the process proceeds to cash transfer. This is achieved by providing an account number. Alternatively, a cancellation message listing some cars removed from the bill can be sent before the final payment. The process releases keys to the customer after the payment is conducted successfully. When the sensors report that a car leaves the park, the sensor service will inform *CarRequest* process to invoke *CIS* to update the status of these cars.

A new *CarReturn* process is started when it receives a car return message from the customer. The process then inquires the customer whether he/she needs to re-rent the car. If so, it only needs to update the status of rented cars. Otherwise, on receiving the message from the sensor service which indicates that the returned cars have been parked in place, the process invokes *CIS* to update the status for the car.

In this paper, we assume the local workflow of each process is correct, but their interaction with external partners may cause application inconsistency [11]. For example, due to malfunctioning of a sensor service, it may miss the departure of a specific car from the park and fails to report this event to *CarRequest* process. As a result, the status of this car is not updated timely. Before this car is returned (by starting a new *CarReturn* instance), another *CarRequest* instance may wrongly accept a rental request and allocate this car to a new customer, because the status of the car is still marked as available. Consequently, this leads to an application inconsistency. This failure is caused by the implicit interaction [12] among concurrent process instances due to resource sharing. To avoid this situation, the following data-centric property can be specified and monitored at runtime:

Data-centric property 1. *for each rented car, there must be a departure event between two consecutive entrances to the park.*

This constraint is defined across the processes, involving *CarRequest* and *CarReturn*. It considers the universal temporal constraint of each rented car moving in and out of the park. Fig.2 shows the message definition of *senseCar* (see Fig.2(a)) and typical message content (see Fig.2(b)) transmitted at runtime.

```
<message name="senseCar">
   <part name="sensor" type="tns:departure" />
   <part name="session" type="xsd:integer" />
</message>
<complextType name="departure">
   <sequence>
      <element name="parkInfo" maxOccurs="unbounded" />
      <complexType>
         <sequence>
            <element name="carID" type="xsd:string"
                     maxOccurs="unbounded" />
            <element name="parkID" type="xsd:string" />
         </sequence>
      </complexType>
   </element>
   </sequence>
</complexType>
```

```
<senseCar>
   <sensor>
      <parkInfo>
         <carID> c_1 </carID>
         <parkID> p_1 </parkID>
      </parkInfo>
      <parkInfo>
         <carID> c_2 </carID>
         <carID> c_3 </carID>
         <parkID> p_2 </parkID>
      </parkInfo>
   </sensor>
   <session>10001</session>
</senseCar>
```

(a)   (b)

Fig. 2. senseCar Message

Besides the properties related to system correctness, some business related policies are also data-centric. For example, to constrain the running behavior of a customer who has made the commitment, one can specify that at the end of the transaction, the customer will be charged for at least one car in the final payment, shown as follows:

Data-centric property 2. *For the cars rented from the customer who has made the commitment, there must exist a car, which eventually appears in the final payment.*

This property has only relation with *CarRequest* process. It involves the data *user account*, *rented cars* and *bill*, and specifies the existential temporal constraints for the rented cars.

To check behavior correctness properties at runtime, there is already a lot of work in the area of dynamic analysis of service-based system [2][3][4][5][6][7]. However, most existing property specifications abstract away the actual data contents inside the messages and define the properties considering only the constraints on sequences of messages. They are propositional and not appropriate to express data-centric properties mentioned above. Although Hallé and Villemaire proposed LTL-FO+ [22], an extension to LTL with first order quantification over the message data, and an online monitoring algorithm to validate data-aware Web services properties, their approach does not support the checking of inter-process properties, nor does the approach consider the optimization of the monitoring process.

3   A Language for Specifying Data-Centric Properties

3.1   Syntax of *Par*-BCL

To address the problem of existing works, this paper proposes *Par*-BCL, a Parametric Behavior Constraint Language for Web service to specify data-centric behavior properties. Our approach to defining data-centric properties builds upon the property Specification Pattern System (*SPS*) [8], which is a pattern-based approach to representing, codifying, and reusing property specification. We choose *SPS* to specify the temporal relation of the events due to the following two reasons: it is easier to understand and write, compared to some formal logic (e.g. LTL, QRE), and has been shown to capture a majority of system properties.

```
Monitor Car_Behavior($car, $park) {
  scope = inter-proc;
  event rent: ? CIS. book binding <$car> with ($msg.sensor//carID);
  event initial_enter: ? Sensor. enter
      binding <$car, $park> with ($msg.sensor//carID, $msg.sensor//parkID);
  event depart : ? Sensor. depart
      binding <$car, $park> with ($msg.sensor//carID, $msg.sensor//parkID);
  event again_enter: ? Sensor. enter
      binding <$car> with ($msg.sensor//carID);

  forall ($car,$park)
   between_and (seq(rent<$car>,initial_enter<$car,$park>),
                      again_enter<$car>)
    exist (depart<$car, $park>);
}
```

Fig. 3. Data-centric property 1

Based on *SPS*, *Par*-BCL further allows first-order quantification over message contents. In addition, it introduces the concept of *parameterized event*, and can define constraints of the pattern "for a set of message data, parameterized properties cannot be violated at runtime" in a declarative way.

Fig.3 shows the example of data-centric property 1 using *Par*-BCL. *Rent*, *initial_enter*, *depart* and *again_enter* are the symbols representing the message of interest. *$car* and *$park* store the message data that need to be monitored. "**scope** = *inter-proc*" means the monitored data may flow across different process instances at runtime. The last part of this example specifies that for each rented car *$car*, there must be a departure event between two consecutive entrance records.

Fig.4 presents, in a semi-formal way, the syntax for the proposed *Par*-BCL language. In the following, we will explain the main elements of *Par*-BCL.

Event. As service providers may not release the details of their services, runtime monitoring of service-based systems is usually based on the messages exchanged between involved services. The event in *Par*-BCL is thus defined based on the WSDLs of all involved services. To ease the presentation, we use the following notation "**?** *Partner. operation*" to represent that process receives an invocation request (denoted by *operation*) from *Partner*, and "*! Partner. operation*" to represent that process sends an invocation request (denoted by *operation*) to *Partner*.

```
        <Specification> →  Monitor <Head> <Body>
              <Head> →  <Name > (<Parameters>)
              <Body> →  <Scope> <EventDecl>*
                         <Quant> <<Parameters>>
                         <Range > <Pattern>
            <Scope> →  scope = [inter-proc| intra-proc];
      <Parameters> →  <Var> [,<Var>]*
      <EventDecl > →  event <Symbol>: <Event > [<Binding>]
         <Binding> →  binding <<Var> [,<Var>]*> with (<XPath>, [,<XPath>]*);
          <Symbol> →  <Identifier>
        <EventRef> →  <Symbol>|< Symbol> (<Var>[,<Var>]*)
           <Event> →  [ ! |?] <Partner>.<Operation>[&&<FilterCondtion>]*
           <Quant> →  forall | exist
         <Pattern> →  absent (<Tracecut>)| occurs (<Tracecut> [, at least |at most, <n>] )
                      |precedes (<Tracecut>, <Tracecut>) | leadsto (<Tracecut>,<Tracecut>)
        <Tracecut> →  <EventRef> | seq (<Tracecut> [, <Tracecut>]*)
                      |all (<Tracecut> [, <Tracecut>]*) | any (<Tracecut> [, <Tracecut>]*)
           <Range> →  global | after (<Tracecut>) | after_until (<Tracecut>, <Tracecut>)
                      |between_and (<Tracecut>, <Tracecut>) | before (<Tracecut>)
```

Fig. 4. Semi-formal syntax of *Par*-BCL

Parameter&Binding. Parameter keeps message data that needs to be monitored. Since the same data can be expressed differently in different messages, to track the flow of a set of message data across different participants, *Par*-BCL uses parameter binding "**binding** <<*Var*>[,<*Var*>]*> **with** (<*XPath*>[,<*XPath*>*])" to bind concrete message data to the parameters. $msg denotes the exchanged xml message content between composition process and its partners. At runtime, these parameters will be instantiated and the "behavior" of each group of the data values will be monitored.

Scope. The scope defines how specified properties will be monitored. It can be two values: *intra-proc* and *inter-proc*. *Intra-proc* means the monitoring only needs to track the dataflow within individual process instance, while *inter-proc* needs to track dataflow across different process instances.

Body. The body part of *Par*-BCL is based on *SPS*, which allows expression of properties in the form "the *pattern* of interest can't be violated within a *range*". An example property expressed in *SPS* is like "event *P* is *absent between Q* and *S*". This is an *absence* pattern with *between* range. More details about *SPS* can be found in [8].

Although there already exists some *SPS* based property specifications in the area of service based systems [13][14], they are all propositional. This paper concentrates on the specification of data-centric properties. We extend *SPS* with first-order quantification over the parameters. To describe the "behavior" of a group of data values across different partner services, we introduce the concept of *parameterized event* to express the operation of each partner service on the message data of interest.

For example, consider the property "**forall** ($car, $park) ϕ" in Fig.3 (ϕ here represents the expression "**between_end**(…) **exist**(…)"). This property is true *iff* for all the groups of $car and $park value, ϕ is not violated. The event in ϕ can be a non-parametric symbol, called *base event* or a symbol with parameters, called *parameterized event*. Event *initial_enter* <$car, $park> is parametric in both $car and $park. This parameterized event is generated when $car enters $park from the received entering message.

Tracecut. Based on primitive event, we define three composite event operators: *any*, *seq* and *all* to capture the complex event during the system execution. *Tracecut* addresses the *SPS* limitation by supporting the specification of concurrent and sequential behavior that can be applied to the behavior patterns. Also, more complex events can be defined based on the combination of these operators.

- *any* operator. This operator takes a set of tracecuts as input. The complex event is captured when any event of them occurs.
- *seq* operator. *seq* takes a list of n ($n>1$) *tracecuts* as its parameter, such as *seq* ($<E_1>$, $<E_2>$, . . . , $<E_n>$). It specifies an order in which the events of interest should occur sequentially.
- *all* operator. This operator takes a list of *tracecuts* as input. If all specified events occur, the complex event is captured. This operator doesn't specify the order of events occurrence.

4   Monitoring Model of *Par*-BCL

Par-BCL supports to monitor the behavior of each group of related message data at the same time. We propose a parametric monitoring model to verify data-centric properties. It performs three orthogonal mechanisms: filtering, parameter binding and verification. Fig.5 illustrates the monitoring model of *Par*-BCL.

4.1   Filtering

First, filtering mechanism observes the current trace and extracts property-relevant messages. Note that, as we use *XPath* to extract data elements inside a message, multiple data values can be returned each btime. To extract the monitored data elements efficiently, we adopt the path sharing approach proposed by Diao et al. [15], which encodes multiple path expressions using a single NFA and can provide tremendous performance improvements. After filtering, an event containing a set of k-tuple data (k is the number of parameters that need to be bound for a message of interest) will be returned.

We do not use the *XPath* engine (which is adopted by work [22]) to extract message contents for the following reasons: First, as stated by Charfi [16], using *XPath* engine to navigate *xml* document is time-consuming. Second, if a message has multiple parameters to bind, it will be evaluated more than once, making the extraction more time-consuming. Finally, the extracted data elements may not preserve the same relation as in the original message after filtering.

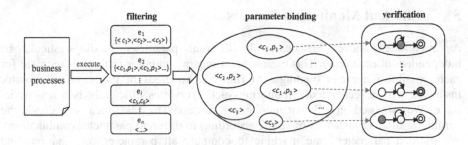

Fig. 5. Monitoring Model of *Par*-BCL

For instance, to evaluate *senseCar* message (see Fig.2) with binding clause "**binding** <$*car*, $*park*> **with** ($*msg*//carID, $*msg*//parkID)", if data values inside $*msg* are extracted respectively, $\{c_1,c_2,c_3\}$ will be returned for XPath expression "$*msg*//carID", and $\{p_1, p_2\}$ will be returned for "$*msg*//parkID". Based on $\{c_1,c_2,c_3\}$ and $\{p_1,p_2\}$, it is difficult to maintain the same relation of c_i and p_i as in the original message. While using the path sharing approach proposed in [15], we can easily preserve the relation of different elements. After filtering, the set of *k*-tuple data $\{<c_1, p_1>, <c_2, p_2>, <c_3, p_2>\}$ can be correctly returned. Note that, here we simplify the representation of *k*-tuple data by hiding its parameter name, e.g., $<c_1, p_1>$ means $<$ (*car*, c_1), (*park*, p_1)$>$.

4.2   Parameter Binding

After filtering, the events will construct a parametric trace. Our approach to monitoring parametric trace against data-centric properties is inspired by the observation of Chen and Rosu that "each parametric trace actually contains multiple non-parametric trace slices, each for a particular parameter binding instance" [18]. Whenever a parameter is bound more than once in a trace (by the same or different events), the parameter is not rebound to a new set of data. Rather, this step checks, for each group of old data that the parameter bound before, whether there is data in the new binding which is equal to the old one. If this is not the case, the new event symbol is ignored for this particular trace.

Note that, different from [18][19], as we concentrate on the dataflow across different partner services, the parameter binding instance of a sub-trace can be changed to include more binding values. More details about this will be introduced in Section 5.

4.3   Verification

The verification mechanism checks whether each sub-trace obtained after parameter binding violates the specified property. As sub-trace has already no parameter information, this step is the same as the ordinary propositional event pattern matching. To enable automated online monitoring, we formally define the semantics of *tracecut*, *pattern* and *range* operators using automata. Details about how to validate *SPS* based Web services properties can be found in [7].

5   Efficient Monitoring Process

As mentioned above, matches with different parameter bindings should be independent of each other. This means that a separate monitor instance is required for each possible parameter bindings. At runtime, hundreds of thousands of monitor instances will be generated. Monitoring such properties efficiently is a non-trivial issue. We proposed an efficient monitoring process. The basic idea is to divide the parameter binding instances of step 2 according to different parameter combinations. We build a parameter state machine to compute all parameter combinations and maintain their association. Then each state in the parameter state machine will contain lots of monitor instances that share the same parameters but with different binding values. When receiving an event, our monitoring process first locates the states that need to be updated in the parameter state machine. Then for each state, indexing mechanism is adopted to locate monitor instances that need to be updated quickly. Note that, to enable online monitoring, besides the parameter binding value, each monitor instance also records the active state in the behavior automata. In the following, we detail our efficient monitoring approach to reduce runtime overhead.

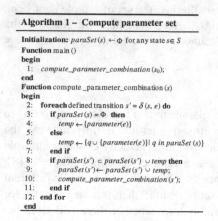

Algorithm 1 – Compute parameter set
Initialization: $paraSet(s) \leftarrow \Phi$ for any state $s \in S$
Function main ()
begin
1:    $compute\_parameter\_combination(s_0)$;
end
Function compute _parameter_combination (s)
begin
2:    **foreach** defined transition $s' = \delta(s, e)$ **do**
3:        **if** $paraSet(s) = \Phi$ **then**
4:            $temp \leftarrow \{parameter(e)\}$
5:        **else**
6:            $temp \leftarrow \{q \cup \{parameter(e)\} \mid q \ in \ paraSet(s)\}$
7:        **end if**
8:        **if** $paraSet(s') \subset paraSet(s') \cup temp$ **then**
9:            $paraSet(s') \leftarrow paraSet(s') \cup temp$;
10:           $compute\_parameter\_combination(s')$;
11:       **end if**
12:   **end for**
end

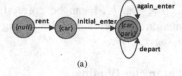

(a)

key	parameter state list
rent	{null}
initial_enter	{car}
depart	{car, park}
again_enter	{car, park}

(b)

Fig. 6. Compute Parameter Set   **Fig. 7.** Example of *PSM* and Index table

5.1   Parameter State Machine

To find all possible parameter combinations, our approach fully utilizes the specified properties through static analysis of the monitored property. By traversing the constructed behavior automata, we build a **Parameter State Machine (PSM)**, in which each parameter state stores one possible parameter combination, except the initial state with *null* value. The transition between parameter states is triggered by event symbol. Thus *PSM* describes the possible dataflow for a specified property.

To build a corresponding *PSM*, we maintain a *parameter set* for each state in the constructed behavior automata [7]. Parameter set stores the possible parameter combinations that can appear at specified state. Fig.6 shows the algorithm of computing parameter set for each state. The condition "if $enable(s') \subset enable\ (s') \cup temp$" ensures that we only call the recursive step on line 8, if new possible parameter combination can be added. After that, we construct a *PSM* by traversing each state again and merging the same parameter combination into a separate parameter state. Fig.7 (a) gives an example of parameter state machine of property 1.

To locate parameter states that need to be updated quickly, based on constructed *PSM*, we further build an index table which uses event symbol as key, and returns a parameter state list. Fig.7 (b) gives the indexing according to constructed *PSM*.

5.2   Monitor Instance

At runtime, each parameter state may contain a large number of monitor instances, making it time-consuming to locate monitor instances that needs to be updated. To locate monitor instances efficiently, we use the partition technique proposed by Avgustinov et al. [20] for indexing monitor instances. Generally, for each parameter state, the strategy for choosing index parameters is found by intersecting the corresponding parameter set with the parameters that event binds to benefit as many outgoing transition as possible. For example, to parameter state {*car,park*} in Fig.7(a), the set of parameters that can be used as index is found by intersecting {*car, park*} with {*car*} and {*car,park*} (for event *againt_enter* and *depart* respectively). Therefore, monitor instances at this state would be indexed by their binding for *car*. If the result of intersection is *null*, we can mark some event as "frequent", and repeat above process by just use of the "frequent" event to find parameters that can be indexed.

5.3   Monitoring Algorithm

Using proposed static parameter state indexing and dynamic monitor instance indexing mechanism, we present an efficient monitoring algorithm (see Fig. 8).

For a received event $<e,d>$, firstly, function *query_ parameter_state* (line 1) will query the index table of parameter state using e as a key, which returns a list of parameter states that needs to be updated. For each data element u in d, the algorithm traverses all possible parameter state s and computes next state s' when e occurs (line 2-4). If s is *initial state* and e is a start event, it will create a new monitor instance and the active state is updated according to behavior automata (line 5-8). When a violation state is entered, an *ERROR_EVENT_BINDING* exception will be thrown (line 10).

If s is not the initial state, function *look_up* uses internal index tree to locate all monitor instances that are associated with data element u (line 15). If s is not transferred to a new state $s'(s=s')$, then for each monitor instance β, its active state will be updated according to the behavior automata (line 17). If a new parameter state s' is entered, the binding value and active state of β will be updated (line 19-20). After that, the instance will be appended to the monitor instance list that the monitor of state s' manages and removed from state s at the same time (line 21-22). Then the algorithm will check the active state of β. If a violation state is entered, an *ERROR_EVENT_ BINDING* exception will be thrown (line 25).

Algorithm 2 – Locate and update monitor instances

Input: *e*: event symbol, *d*: set of *k*-tuple data
begin:
```
 1:  List states ← query_parameter_state (e);
 2:  foreach data u in d do
 3:     foreach parameter state s in states do
 4:        s' ← s. transition (e);
 5:        if (s is initial state and e is a start event) then
 6:           create monitor instance m;
 7:           m.binding_value ← u;
 8:           update active state of m according to behavior automata;
 9:           if active state is violation state then
10:              throw ERROR_EVENT_BINDING;
11:           else
12:              add m to the monitor instance list of s';
13:           end if
14:        else
15:           foreach monitor instance β in s.lookup (u)  do
16:              if (s' = s)  then
17:                 update active state of β according to behavior automata;
18:              else
19:                 β.binding_value ← β.binding_value ∪ u ;
20:                 update active state of β according to behavior automata;
21:                 remove β to the monitor instance list of s;
22:                 add β to the monitor instance list of s';
23:              end if
24:              if active state is violated then
25:                 throw ERROR_EVENT_BINDING;
26:              end if
27:           end for
28:        end if
29:     end for
30:  end for
end
```

Fig. 8. Locate and update monitor instance

However, the monitor needs to further decide whether the specified property is violated. For the universal quantifier, if any monitor instance enters into a violation state, the property is violated. For the existential quantifier, our approach maintains a bit vector to record whether the monitor instance created by a start event is violated. Each monitor instance makes a reference to the corresponding entry in the bit vector. When a monitor instance needs to bind more parameters (i.e., a new monitor instance is generated and the old monitor instance is deleted), the reference will also be modified. At runtime, if all monitor instances that the bit vector represents enter into the violation states, the specified property is violated.

Note that, during the phase of building index for parameter state, when a new state is needed to add, it should be inserted into the head of list. Thus we ensure the monitor instances are updated correctly. For example, consider the following situation: when an event $<e, \{(v=1, i=2)\}>$ is received, according to the parameter state list of event e (see Fig.9), monitors of state $\{u, v\}$ and $\{u, v, i\}$ are both needed to update. However, if the monitor of $\{u, v\}$ is updated first, according to the algorithm, it can cause the creation of new monitor instance $<u=3, v=1, i=2>$. When the monitor of $\{u, v, i\}$ is updated, the new monitor instance $<u=3, v=1, i=2>$ created by the monitor of $\{u, v\}$ will be updated again, which can incur wrong result.

5.4 Management of Monitor Instances

Another performance-related concern in our proposal is the memory overhead. As stated above, a large number of monitor instances will co-exist at runtime and become very large in the end. However, monitor instances can be no longer used when it is transferred to the new parameter state. To avoid memory leak, the data structure of monitor instance list should be carefully designed further.

We use an array structure to store monitor instances, as shown in Table 1. To manage these monitor instances, a new column *pointer* is introduced for each monitor instance. Using this index, a *free list* is maintained, as shown in Table 1. Initially, the list is traversed sequentially and the index of each element is assigned with the subscript value of next element. The head of *free list* is assigned with 0, the subscript of first element. With *free list*, new monitor instance can be created by visiting the head of this list and allocating corresponding entry to it. When the monitor instance is no longer used, it is inserted into the head of *free list*.

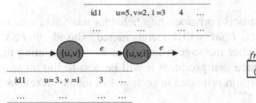

Fig. 9. Segment of a *PSM*

Table 1. Monitor instances llist

parameter binding	active state	pointer
u = 1, v = 2	3	1
u = 2, v = 3	4	2
...	...	...

6 Architecture and Implementation

In the previous section, we elaborate the design of proposed *Par*-BCL language. To monitor data-centric properties, we present an implementation of runtime framework through an aspect oriented extension to WS-BPEL engine. In this solution, business process logic and properties are defined and treated separately, since we advocate separation of concerns, which facilitates both the process design and later management. Fig.10 shows its overall architecture based on our developed OnceBPEL engine [21]. Similar extensions can be considered for other engines. In what follows, we describe the core components:

Aspect Manager. It represents the main advice that is weaved into the execution environment. As the implementation of WS-BPEL engine revolves around the runtime visitor design pattern and it also maintains an internal AST (abstract syntax tree), after a thorough study, we define our pointcuts (using AspectJ) as (1) after the engine visits a *Receive* node; (2) before and after it visits an *Invoke* node; (3) after it visits a *Pick* node and (4) before it visits a *Reply* node, to capture the message interaction between the process and partner services. After weaving, this component has direct access to the context information of current activity.

Configuration Manager. It's a persistent component in which we store the basic description information about the property, such as the events of interest, the binding clause, and optional filtering condition. At runtime, the aspect manager will query this component to extract the property-relevant events and send it to monitor manager.

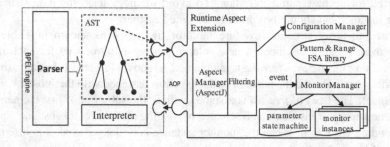

Fig. 10. Overall Architecture

Monitor Manager. This module constructs corresponding behavior automata when a property is deployed. As a side-effect, *PSM* will be constructed. Based on *PSM*, parameter state index is further built. After message filtering, an event containing the identifier ($*processid*) of process instance that produces it will be sent to the monitor manager, which then executes the algorithm provided in section 4 to locate all relevant monitor instances efficiently.

Note that, for *inter-proc* properties, one *PSM* is maintained to track dataflow across different process instances. For *intra-proc* properties, as it only checks dataflow within individual process instance, one *PSM* is generated for each monitored process instance. However, in order to unify the monitoring approach, for *intra-proc* properties, we choose $*processid* as an additive index for each parameter state. As a result, only one *PSM* is enough to monitor *intra-proc* properties.

7   Experiments

To evaluate the feasibility and effectiveness of the proposed parametric monitoring approach, we conducted several initial experiments.

In [22], Hallé and Villemaire proposed an online monitoring algorithm to check temporal properties with data parameterization. To compare with their work, in the first experiment, the processing time per message required by *Par*-BCL and LTL-FO+ is measured. We implemented the monitoring algorithm in [22]. By traversing possible execution paths of property 1, we used a simulator to generate 50 traces of length ranging from 10 to 1000 events, respectively. Each event manipulates 20 cars from a pool of 5000 possible car IDs and 1 park from 250 park IDs. The experiments were run on Windows XP with P4 2.53 GHZ and 1GB RAM.

Fig.11 shows the processing time per message of two algorithms for various trace lengths. It indicates that our algorithm to process each message has lower overhead.

The processing time is under 0.3 ms using our algorithm, while the time is about 3ms using the algorithm in [22]. The main reason is that in our work, the behavior automata is constructed completely when the property is deployed, while in [22], the automata is computed and generated at runtime. Also, using our monitoring algorithm, the length of event trace has no impact on the performance as the adoption of index. However, using non-optimized algorithm in [22], processing time per message grows with the increase of trace length, as a large number of "monitor instances" will be generated, making it time-consuming to locate monitor instances.

The first experiment mainly evaluated the performance of proposed monitoring algorithm. To evaluate the overall overhead incurred by monitoring during the process execution, in second experiment, we use *CarRental* system as a case study, in which properties 1-2 were deployed. *CarRequest* and *CarReturn* processes were deployed at a Windows server 2003 with P4 2.8 GHZ and 2GB RAM. Three Web services were implemented to simulate the functionality of partner services. They were deployed at Windows XP with P4 2.8 GHZ and 500MB RAM.

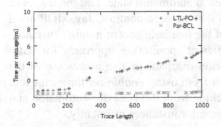

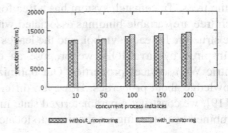

Fig. 11. Property 1   **Fig. 12.** Execution time

We measured the average execution time for different concurrent process instances within two configurations. Fig.12 shows the average execution time of process *CarRequest*. The first column in each set shows the process execution time without plug-in the runtime aspect extension module. The second column shows the process execution time when the properties were deployed. Clearly, the overhead due to monitoring is very low. The average execution time of *CarRequest* process under being monitored is only around 3% higher. Obviously, the results are affected by the scalability of the WS-BPEL engine itself. We can see that the execution time grows linearly with the number of concurrent process instances.

8   Related Work

As far as we know, the work done by Hallé and Villemaire [9][22] is most similar to ours. Hallé and Villemaire presented LTL-FO+, an extension to LTL that includes first order quantification over the message data. Although LTL-FO+ allows unrestricted use of universal and existential quantifier with message contents and *Par-BCL* only allows quantification outside the property operator for consideration of efficient monitoring, we find that all properties listed in the work [9][22] can be expressed in *Par*-BCL. We intend to investigate and compare the expressive power of LTL-FO+ and *Par*-BCL, our hypothesis is that two languages has the equal power. In addition, *Par*-BCL can preserve the relationship of multiple data elements after filtering and track dataflow across different process instances. Both these are not considered by LTL-FO+. Besides above mentioned differences, the approach proposed by Hallé and Villemaire is mainly used for client-side monitoring [9], and they do not consider the optimization of the monitoring process.

In [23], we propose an approach to monitor data-centric properties. This paper proposes new index mechanism and monitoring algorithm to locate monitor instances more efficiently. In addition, we modify *Par*-BCL notation (especially binding clause) to make it intuitive to express data-centric properties. Also, a new filtering mechanism based on path sharing approach [15] is adopted.

There is some work which aims to generate feasible trace monitor used with object-oriented languages [17][20]. To deal with parameter bindings, Tracematch [20] and JavaMOP [17] both use multi-level trees for indexing, but they differ in structure of the trees. Tracematch system has a tree for each automaton state, and the leaves of each tree are variable bindings associated with that state. In contrast, JavaMOP has a tree structure for each symbol, and the leaves of the tree hold sets of monitor instance.

Inspired by JavaMOP, we propose an efficient monitoring approach for data-centric Web services properties. Our optimization mechanism also makes use of the knowledge about properties. However, different from using *enable set* for each event in [19], we construct a parameterized state machine from the behavior automaton and combined two indexing mechanisms to locate monitor instances efficiently.

9   Conclusion

In this paper, we have proposed an efficient online monitoring approach to dynamically analyze service-based system involving multiple participants. We plan to conduct more experiments to further check the feasibility of our approach in the future work.

Acknowledgments. This work is supported by the National Natural Science Foundation of China under Grant Nos. 60903052, 61003029; the National Basic Research Program of China under Grant No.2009CB320704; the National Science and Technology Major Project of China under Grant No. 2010ZX01045-001-010-4.

References

1. OASIS. Web services business process execution language (ws-bpel) v2.0, http://docs.oasis-open.org/wsbpel/2.0/wsbpel-v2.0.pdf
2. Beeri, C., Eyal, A., Milo, T., Pilberg, A.: Monitoring business processes with queries. In: VLDB, pp. 603–614 (2007)

3. Baresi, L., Guinea, S.: Towards Dynamic Monitoring of WS-BPEL Processes. In: Benatallah, B., Casati, F., Traverso, P. (eds.) ICSOC 2005. LNCS, vol. 3826, pp. 269–282. Springer, Heidelberg (2005)
4. Barbon, F., Traverso, P., Pistore, M., Trainotti, M.: Runtime monitoring of instances and classes of web service compositions. In: ICWS, pp. 63–71 (2006)
5. Mahbub, K., Spanoudakis, G.: A framework for requirements monitoring of service based systems. In: ICSOC, pp. 84–93 (2004)
6. Simmonds, J., Gan, Y., Chechik, M., et al.: Runtime Monitoring of Web Service Conversation. TSC 2(3), 223–244 (2009)
7. Wu, G.Q., Wei, J., Huang, T.: Flexible pattern monitoring for WS-BPEL through stateful aspect extension. In: ICWS, pp. 577–584 (2008)
8. Dwyer, M.B., Avrunin, G.S., Corbett, J.C.: Patterns in property specifications for finite-state verification. In: ICSE, pp. 411–420 (1999)
9. Hallé, S., Villemaire, R.: Runtime enforcement of web service message contracts with data. IEEE Transaction on Service Computing (preprint)
10. Hallé, S., Villemaire, R., Cherkaoui, O.: Specifying and validating data-aware temporal web service properties. TSE 35(5), 669–683 (2009)
11. Greenfield, P., Kuo, D., Nepal, S., Fekete, A.: Consistency of web services applications. In: VLDB, pp. 1199–1203 (2005)
12. Ye, C.Y., Cheung, S.C., Chan, W.K., Xu, C.: Detection and resolution of atomicity violation in service composition. In: FSE, pp. 235–244 (2007)
13. Li, Z., Han, J., Jin, Y.: Pattern-Based Specification and Validation of Web Services Interaction Properties. In: Benatallah, B., Casati, F., Traverso, P. (eds.) ICSOC 2005. LNCS, vol. 3826, pp. 73–86. Springer, Heidelberg (2005)
14. Wang, Q.X., Shao, J., Deng, F., et al.: An online monitoring approach for web services requirements. TSC 2, 338–351 (2009)
15. Diao, Y.L., Altinel, M., et al.: Path Sharing and Predicate Evaluation for High-Performance XML Filtering. TODS 28(4), 467–516 (2003)
16. Charfi, A.: Aspect-oriented Workflow Languages: AO4BPEL and Applications (thesis)
17. Chen, F., Rosu, G.: MOP: An efficient and generic runtime verification framework. In: OOPSLA, pp. 569–588 (2007)
18. Chen, F., Rosu, G.: Parametric Trace Slicing and Monitoring. In: Kowalewski, S., Philippou, A. (eds.) TACAS 2009. LNCS, vol. 5505, pp. 246–261. Springer, Heidelberg (2009)
19. Chen, F., Meredith, P.O., Jin, D.Y., Rosu, G.: Efficient Formalism-Independent monitoring of Parametric Properties. In: ASE, pp. 383–394 (2009)
20. Avgustinov, P., Tibble, J., de Moor, O.: Making Trace Monitors Feasible. In: OOPSLA, pp. 589–608 (2007)
21. Chen, W., Wei, J., Wu, G., Qiao, X.: Developing a Concurrent Service Orchestration Engine Based on Event-Driven Architecture. In: Meersman, R., Tari, Z. (eds.) OTM 2008, Part I. LNCS, vol. 5331, pp. 675–690. Springer, Heidelberg (2008)
22. Hallé, S., Villemaire, R.: Runtime monitoring of message based workflows with data. In: EDOC, pp. 63–72 (2008)
23. Wu, G.Q., Wei, J., Ye, C.Y., et al.: Runtime monitoring of data-centric temporal properties for web services. In: ICWS (to appear, 2011)

Cooperative Concurrency for a Multicore World

(Extended Abstract)

Jaeheon Yi[1], Caitlin Sadowski[1], Stephen N. Freund[2], and Cormac Flanagan[1]

[1] University of California at Santa Cruz
[2] Williams College

Developing reliable multithreaded software is notoriously difficult, due to the potential for unexpected interference between concurrent threads. Even a familiar construct such as "x++" has unfamiliar semantics in a multithreaded setting, where it must in general be considered a non-atomic read-modify-write sequence, rather than a simple atomic increment. Understanding where thread interference may occur is a critical first step in understanding or validating a multithreaded software system.

Much prior work has addressed this problem, mostly focused on verifying the correctness properties of race-freedom and atomicity (see, for example, [6,13,10,3,4,1,9,11,7,14,15,8,5]). Race-freedom guarantees that software running on relaxed memory hardware behaves as if running on sequentially consistent hardware [2]. Atomicity guarantees that a program behaves as if each atomic block executes serially, without interleaved steps of concurrent threads. Unfortunately, neither approach is entirely sufficient for ensuring the absence of unintended thread interference.

We propose an alternative approach whereby all thread interference must be specified with explicit yield annotations. For example, if multiple threads intentionally access a shared variable x concurrently, then the above increment operation would need to rewritten as "int t=x; yield; x=t+1" to explicate the potential interference.

These yield annotations enable us to decompose the hard problem of reasoning about multithreaded program correctness into two simpler subproblems:

- **Cooperative correctness:** Is the program correct when run under a *cooperative scheduler* that context switches only at yield annotations?
- **Cooperative-preemptive equivalence:** Does the program exhibit the same behavior under a cooperative scheduler as it would under a traditional preemptive scheduler that can context switch at any program point?

A key benefit of this decomposition is that cooperative-preemptive equivalence can be mechanically verified, for example, via a static type and effect system that reasons about synchronization, locking, and commuting operations [17,16]. Alternatively, cooperative-preemptive equivalence can be verified dynamically by showing that the transactional happens-before relation for each observed trace is acyclic (where a transaction is the code between two successive yield annotations) [18].

S. Khurshid and K. Sen (Eds.): RV 2011, LNCS 7186, pp. 342–344, 2012.

The remaining subproblem of cooperative correctness is significantly more tractable than the original problem of preemptive correctness. In particular, cooperative scheduling provides an appealing concurrency semantics with the following desirable properties:

– Sequential reasoning is correct by default (in the absence of yield annotations), and so for example "x++" is always an atomic increment operation.
– Thread interference is always highlighted with yields, which remind the programmer to allow for the effects of interleaved concurrent threads.

Experimental results on a standard benchmark suite show that surprisingly few yield annotations are required—only 13 yields per thousand lines of code [16]. In addition, a preliminary user study showed that the presence of these yield annotations produced a statistically significant improvement in the ability of programmers to identify concurrent defects during code reviews [12]. These experimental results suggest that cooperative concurrency is a promising foundation for the development of reliable multithreaded software.

Acknowledgements. This work was supported by NSF grants CNS-0905650, CCF-1116883 and CCF-1116825.

References

1. Abadi, M., Flanagan, C., Freund, S.N.: Types for safe locking: Static race detection for Java. ACM Transactions on Programming Languages and Systems 28(2), 207–255 (2006)
2. Adve, S.V., Gharachorloo, K.: Shared memory consistency models: A tutorial. IEEE Computer 29(12), 66–76 (1996)
3. Bond, M.D., Coons, K.E., McKinley, K.S.: PACER: Proportional detection of data races. In: Conference on Programming Language Design and Implementation (PLDI), pp. 255–268 (2010)
4. Erickson, J., Musuvathi, M., Burckhardt, S., Olynyk, K.: Effective data-race detection for the kernel. In: Operating Systems Design and Implementation (OSDI), pp. 1–16 (2010)
5. Farzan, A., Madhusudan, P.: Monitoring Atomicity in Concurrent Programs. In: Gupta, A., Malik, S. (eds.) CAV 2008. LNCS, vol. 5123, pp. 52–65. Springer, Heidelberg (2008)
6. Flanagan, C., Freund, S.N.: Fasttrack: efficient and precise dynamic race detection. Commun. ACM 53(11), 93–101 (2010)
7. Flanagan, C., Freund, S.N., Lifshin, M., Qadeer, S.: Types for atomicity: Static checking and inference for Java. Transactions on Programming Languages and Systems (TOPLAS) 30(4), 1–53 (2008)
8. Flanagan, C., Freund, S.N., Yi, J.: Velodrome: A sound and complete dynamic atomicity checker for multithreaded programs. In: Conference on Programming Language Design and Implementation (PLDI), pp. 293–303 (2008)
9. Naik, M., Aiken, A., Whaley, J.: Effective static race detection for Java. In: Proceedings of the ACM Conference on Programming Language Design and Implementation, pp. 308–319 (2006)

10. O'Callahan, R., Choi, J.-D.: Hybrid dynamic data race detection. In: Symposium on Principles and Practice of Parallel Programming (PPoPP), pp. 167–178 (2003)
11. Pratikakis, P., Foster, J.S., Hicks, M.: Context-sensitive correlation analysis for detecting races. In: Proceedings of the ACM Conference on Programming Language Design and Implementation, pp. 320–331 (2006)
12. Sadowski, C., Yi, J.: Applying usability studies to correctness conditions: A case study of cooperability. In: Onward! Workshop on Evaluation and Usability of Programming Languages and Tools (PLATEAU), pp. 2:1–2:6 (2010)
13. Savage, S., Burrows, M., Nelson, G., Sobalvarro, P., Anderson, T.E.: Eraser: A dynamic data race detector for multi-threaded programs. ACM Transactions on Computer Systems (TOCS) 15(4), 391–411 (1997)
14. von Praun, C., Gross, T.R.: Static detection of atomicity violations in object-oriented programs. Journal of Object Technology, 103–122 (2003)
15. Wang, L., Stoller, S.D.: Runtime analysis of atomicity for multithreaded programs. IEEE Transactions on Software Engineering 32, 93–110 (2006)
16. Yi, J., Disney, T., Freund, S.N., Flanagan, C.: Types for precise thread interference. Technical Report UCSC-SOE-11-22, The University of California at Santa Cruz (2011)
17. Yi, J., Flanagan, C.: Effects for cooperable and serializable threads. In: Workshop on Types in Language Design and Implementation (TLDI), pp. 3–14 (2010)
18. Yi, J., Sadowski, C., Flanagan, C.: Cooperative reasoning for preemptive execution. In: Symposium on Principles and Practice of Parallel Programming (PPoPP), pp. 147–156 (2011)

Monitoring Data Structures
Using Hardware Transactional Memory*

Shakeel Butt[1], Vinod Ganapathy[1], Arati Baliga[2], and Mihai Christodorescu[3]

[1] Rutgers University, Piscataway, New Jersey, USA
{shakeelb,vinodg}@cs.rutgers.edu
[2] AT&T Security Research Center, Middletown, New Jersey, USA
arati.baliga@att.com
[3] IBM TJ Watson Research Center, Hawthorne, New York, USA
mihai@us.ibm.com

Abstract. The robustness of software systems is adversely affected by programming errors and security exploits that corrupt heap data structures. In this paper, we present the design and implementation of TxMon, a system to detect such data structure corruptions. TxMon leverages the concurrency control machinery implemented by hardware transactional memory (HTM) systems to additionally enforce programmer-specified consistency properties on data structures at runtime. We implemented a prototype version of TxMon using an HTM system (LogTM-SE) and studied the feasibility of applying TxMon to enforce data structure consistency properties on several benchmarks. Our experiments show that TxMon is effective at monitoring data structure properties, imposing tolerable runtime performance overheads.

Keywords: Data structure properties, Hardware transactional memory.

1 Introduction

Modern software systems manage a vast amount of data on the heap. Programming errors in such software systems can lead to data structure corruptions that adversely affect their robustness. These errors may result in data structures that violate well-accepted correctness criteria (*e.g.*, dangling pointer errors and heap metadata corruptions) or application-specific data structure consistency properties. Such programming errors are often hard to debug because their effect is delayed, *e.g.*, a dangling pointer error does not result in a crash until the pointer in question is dereferenced.

In this paper, we present the design and evaluation of TxMon, a system that uses hardware transactional memory (HTM) [18,20] to detect data structure corruptions. HTM systems (*e.g.*, [26,23,16,9,10,14]) provide a set of mechanisms in hardware and software to support *memory transactions*, and have been proposed as a mechanism to ease the development of parallel programs. To use transactional memory for concurrency control, programmers use instructions provided by the hardware to demarcate critical sections in a program. The HTM system speculatively executes transactions,

---

* Funded in part by NSF CNS grants 0728937, 0831268, 0915394 and 0952128. Most of this work was done when A. Baliga was affiliated with Rutgers University.

S. Khurshid and K. Sen (Eds.): RV 2011, LNCS 7186, pp. 345–359, 2012.

and ensures that the memory operations performed within these transactions are *atomic*, *i.e.*, they appear to execute in their entirety or not at all, and *isolated*, *i.e.*, their effects are not visible to other concurrently-executing threads until the transaction completes. By ensuring these properties, the HTM system allows transactions to synchronize access to shared data structures.

TxMon is based upon the insight that the mechanisms in HTM systems to implement transactions can also be used to detect data structure corruptions. HTM systems maintain bookkeeping information to track the set of memory locations accessed by each transaction. For example, in the LogTM-SE HTM system [26], speculative values computed by the transaction are written to memory, and the original values at these memory locations are stored in a per-thread *transaction log*, which is used to restore the contents of memory if the transaction aborts as the result of a race condition. Similar bookkeeping information is also available in other HTM systems [23,16,9,14,10].

TxMon interposes on the standard workflow of an HTM system to monitor data structure properties. It inspects the HTM system's bookkeeping information to identify data structures that were modified during a transaction and automatically triggers callbacks that check properties of these data structures, which can include both well-accepted correctness conditions as well as application-specific assertions. We show that in HTM systems that expose their bookkeeping information to software, *e.g.*, LogTM-SE and Rock [10][1], TxMon can be implemented with no hardware modifications. This ensures that applications on these platforms can readily benefit from TxMon.

Contributions. To sum up, this paper makes the following contributions:

(**1**) *Design of TxMon.* We present the design of TxMon, which uses the concurrency control machinery implemented in HTM systems to monitor data structure properties. Among the key features in the design of TxMon are *address maps*, which are a representation of complex data structures. We also present a novel technique to update address maps as the data structures that they represent are modified.

(**2**) *Implementation in LogTM-SE.* We implemented a prototype of TxMon by leveraging the LogTM-SE HTM system. Because LogTM-SE exposes transaction logs to software, our implementation required *no* modifications to the HTM system.

(**3**) *Evaluation of TxMon.* We used TxMon to monitor data structure properties on multi-threaded benchmarks from the Splash-2 suite [25], and two real-world applications, namely ClamAV and Memcached. Our evaluation shows that TxMon is effective at monitoring complex properties and that it imposes an acceptable runtime overhead.

More broadly, TxMon demonstrates that transactional memory hardware can provide additional benefits beyond providing concurrency control. There is still a debate in the community about the correct abstraction to ease parallel programming. In the long term, additional benefits of HTM systems as demonstrated by TxMon and similar recent and ongoing efforts [11,12,7,17,19] can serve as the catalyst that will lead to more research on transactions and their adoption by hardware and software vendors.

---

[1] We reference Rock although it is abandoned now (for economic reasons) because its design substantially resembles LogTM-SE, which we used for our prototype implementation.

```
(1)  struct item { ...
(2)    rel_time_t time;    //last access time
(3)    unsigned refcount; //reference count
(4)    struct item *next, *prev; ...
(5)  };
(6)  struct item *heads[255], *tails[255];
(7)  process_get_command (key) { ...
(8)    struct item *it = search(key);
(9)    if (it) {
(10)      it->refcount++;
(11)      it->time = curr_time;
(12)      move_to_head(it);
(13)   } ...
(14)   return it;
(15)  }
(16) process_add_command (key, value) { ...
(17)   struct item *it = alloc_item(key, value);
(18)   ...
(19) }
```

Fig. 1. Motivating example. This figure shows a simplified code snippet from Memcached.

2 Motivation and Overview

We use the example in Figure 1 to motivate the key requirements that a data structure monitor must satisfy, and then illustrate how TxMon satisfies these requirements. The snippet in Figure 1 is a simplified version of code drawn from Memcached [2], a distributed object caching server that has been adapted by Web services such as Livejournal, Slashdot and Wikipedia.

Memcached is a multi-threaded server that stores key/value pairs. Clients can invoke commands on the server to perform a variety of functionalities, such as fetching the value corresponding to a key, adding a new key/value pair, deleting an existing pair, and so on. Figure 1 shows snippets from the implementation of two such commands that fetch and add key/value pairs. Each key/value pair is stored in exactly one of 255 doubly-linked lists depending upon the size of the value. The arrays heads and tails store pointers to the heads and tails of these lists. Each element of these lists includes a timestamp field, which denotes the last access time (get or set) of an item, and a reference count field, which stores the number of active clients that are currently accessing that item.

As an object caching system, Memcached employs several complex policies to decide which key/value pairs to cache on the server, and how to organize these pairs in its linked lists. The code of process_get_command in Figure 1 depicts one such policy, which ensures that the most recently accessed object is placed at the head of the corresponding list. This property allows Memcached to employ a variant of the LRU algorithm[2] to evict items from the cache.

Even for this simple eviction policy to work correctly, several data structure properties must hold. First, all modifications to the linked lists must ensure that the items of each list are sorted in order of their access times. Second, it must ensure that the heads

---

[2] The actual eviction policy considers reference counts, access times, and other fields of item objects to decide upon a victim.

of linked lists are reachable from tails, and vice versa. Failure to ensure these data structure properties can result in incorrect operation. In particular, Memcached searches for victims from the tails of linked lists. If the first property fails to hold, the choice of the resulting victim will violate the LRU policy. Similarly, if the second property fails to hold, the eviction algorithm may not explore all elements in a linked list.

However, Memcached has a large code base and could contain programming errors; indeed the defect history of Memcached [1] shows over a hundred reports since October 2008. These programming errors could corrupt Memcached's data structures, which in turn may cause the server to malfunction. These errors may not manifest during testing, and deployed code can malfunction when these errors are encountered in the field. In fact, a recent version of Memcached contained an error that failed to decrement reference counts of items properly, thereby leading to memory leaks under rare conditions (because objects with non-zero reference counts are not reclaimed). Such errors can be detected using a framework to monitor data structures. For example, this framework could ensure that linked lists that are modified by a client continue to satisfy the sortedness property. It could also track "old" items with non-zero reference counts, thereby identifying items that leak.

This example motivates four design requirements for a data structure monitor:

(**1**) *Ability to monitor complex data structures.* Verifying properties of a complex data structure may require traversing the data structure. For instance, in the example above, ensuring that the list at `heads[i]` is sorted involves traversing it fully.

(**2**) *Extensibility.* In Memcached, a programmer may wish to verify that the list `heads[i]` is doubly-linked, in addition to verifying sortedness of the list. The monitor must be extensible, and allow the programmer to supply a checker for additional properties.

(**3**) *Applicability to low-level code.* Data structure corruptions are common in applications written in low-level memory-unsafe languages, such as C and C++. The monitor must therefore be applicable to programs written in such languages as well.

(**4**) *Low runtime overhead.* To monitor data structure properties in deployed software, the monitor must ideally be an "always-on" tool, and must impose an acceptable runtime performance overhead.

As we show in Section 4, TxMon satisfies all four requirements. To motivate how TxMon monitors data structure properties, consider an approach in which a programmer *inlines* checks at key locations in the program. For example, to ensure that the linked lists in Memcached are sorted by access time, the code snippet in Figure 1 can include inline checks to ensure this property as a post-condition of the functions `move_to_head` and `alloc_item` (which also adds elements to linked lists). Although apparently simple, an approach that inlines checks must overcome two challenges. First, appropriate data structure checks must be placed at locations where key data structures (*e.g.*, the linked lists in Memcached) are accessed. This requires the programmer to identify all such locations in the program and to identify the set of data structure checks that must be triggered at each of those locations. Identifying data structures accessed can be challenging, especially in the presence of pointer aliasing. This problem is exacerbated as software evolves, because data structure checks must also

```
(1)    struct item { ...                              Implementation of TxMon's monitor
(2)      rel_time_t time;//last access time      (m1)  txmon_entry (void) {
(3)      unsigned refcount;//reference count     (m2)    retval = true;
(4)      struct item *next, *prev; ...           (m3)    accset = Get accessed memory locations from HTM;
(5)    };                                        (m4)    for (each addr ∈ accset)
(6)    struct item *heads[255], *tails[255];     (m5)      for (each ds ∈ registered data structures)
(7)    process_get_command (key) {               (m6)        if (addr ∈ address_map(ds))
(8)      transaction (txmon_entry) { ...         (m7)          retval &= value returned by callback for ds;
(9)        struct item *it = search(key);        (m8)    if (!retval) invoke transaction_abort;
(10)       if (it) {                             (m9)  }
(11)         it->refcount++;                     (m10) void register_ds (void *dsptr, void *cback, ...) {
(12)         it->time = curr_time;               (m11)   // register cback as checking callback for dsptr
(13)         move_to_head(it);                   (m12)   // optionally register arguments for the callback
(14)       } ...                                 (m13) }
(15)     }                                       (m14) bool check_sort (struct item *hd) {
(16)     return it;                              (m15)   if (list not sorted by item->time) return false;
(17)   }                                         (m16)   /* update address_map(hd) */
(18)   process_add_command (key, value) {        (m17)   for (it = hd; it ≠ NULL; it = it->next) {
(19)     transaction (txmon_entry) { ...         (m18)     add &(it->next), &(it->prev) and &(it->time)
(20)       struct item *it =                                 to address_map(&hd);
(21)       alloc_item(key, value); ...           (m19)   return true;
(22)     }                                       (m20) }
(23)   }
(24)   //Server initialization code
(25)   for (i = 0; i < 255; i++) {
(26)     register_ds(&heads[i],
             check_sort, &heads[i]);
(27)     initialize address_map(&heads[i])
(28)   }
```

Fig. 2. Using TxMon. Code snippet from Figure 1 modified to use TxMon to monitor the lists headed at heads[0], ..., heads[254]. Lines m1-m13 are part of the TxMon monitor. The lines in bold-faced font show the code that a programmer must add.

be modified to reflect changes in the program. Second, in multi-threaded software, the placement of checks must avoid time-of-check to time-of-use errors (race conditions), in which a concurrently-executing thread may modify a data structure in the interval between property verification and use of the data structure.

The TxMon system developed in this paper eases the task of placing such data structure checks in the program. Rather than requiring a programmer to manually inline checks, TxMon instead requires code that manipulates key data structures to be embedded in *transactions*. In Figure 2 for instance, all operations on the linked lists with heads in the array heads[] happen within transactions. In multi-threaded code that uses transactional memory for synchronization, such transactions will naturally be placed around code that manipulates shared data structures. However, TxMon also applies to single-threaded programs. In such cases, transactions must be placed around the code where data structures are updated. In both cases, TxMon triggers property checks on data structures that were modified when the transaction completes execution.

In addition to placing transactions, the programmer has three key responsibilities:

(1) *Register data structures to be monitored.* The programmer must use an API supplied by TxMon to register data structures that must be monitored. In Figure 2, the register_ds calls placed in the initialization code of Memcached notify TxMon that the lists headed by heads[] are data structures that must be monitored.

(**2**) *Supply address maps.* The programmer must supply an *address map* for each registered data structure. The address map is an abstraction that stores the set of all memory addresses associated with that data structure. We defer an overview of how address maps are computed and maintained to Section 4.3.

(**3**) *Supply checker callbacks.* The programmer specifies the properties to be verified in *checker callbacks* associated with each data structure. TxMon ensures that if a data structure is modified in a transaction, then the corresponding callback executes at the end of the transaction and verifies that the data structure's properties hold. In Figure 2, the same checker callback (check_sort) is associated with each of the 255 linked lists. This function checks the property that these lists are sorted by last access time.

Upon completion of a transaction, control transfers to the entrypoint of TxMon's data structure monitor. As shown in Figure 2, the entrypoint (txmon_entry) is a function pointer that is registered using an argument to the transaction{...} keyword. TxMon obtains the set of memory locations accessed by the transactions from the bookkeeping information maintained by the HTM system—in our implementation, we obtain these locations from the transaction's undo log (see Section 3). TxMon's data structure monitor determines whether the memory addresses accessed during the transaction are also contained in the address maps of any of the data structures registered with it. If so, it triggers the checker callback associated with the corresponding data structure, which verifies the properties of that data structure.

The key point to note is that unlike the approach that inlines data structure checks, *the programmer need not specify which checker callbacks must be invoked at the end of a transaction.* Rather, TxMon uses the HTM system's bookkeeping information (*i.e.,* the undo log) to infer which callbacks must be invoked.

3   HTM Systems

In this section, we provide background on hardware transactional memory, focusing on the features relevant to the design of TxMon. HTM systems typically extend hardware instruction sets with new primitives that define the start (begin_tx) and end of transactions (end_tx). They ensure atomicity and isolation for all executing transactions, but vary widely in how they do so [20]. Nevertheless, all HTM systems implement mechanisms for *conflict detection* and *version management*.

Conflict detection mechanisms allow the HTM system to detect race conditions between concurrently executing transactions. An HTM system detect conflicts by intersecting the memory locations read/written by a transaction with those of other in-flight transactions. If a conflict is detected, the HTM must abort at least one conflicting transaction. Version management mechanisms allow the HTM system to record the set of data modifications made by a transaction. When a transaction is committed (or aborted), the HTM system consults the version manager to commit (or discard) the changes made by the transaction. For instance, LogTM-SE logs the old values of the memory locations modified by a transaction (in a per-transaction log), and uses the log to restore memory if the transaction aborts.

Both the conflict detection and version management mechanisms of an HTM system thus maintain a record of the memory locations modified by a transaction. TxMon can use the information from either mechanism to trigger data structure checks. However, in this paper, we focus on a system design that obtains memory access information from the version management mechanism of an HTM system. Our choice was motivated by the observation that HTM systems often store more precise version management information than they do conflict detection information. This is because conflict detection mechanisms need only conservatively determine if two transactions are in conflict. A false conflict wrongly aborts a transaction, but does not affect the correctness of the system. In turn, this allows HTM systems to maintain read/write sets using fixed-size hardware structures, such as Bloom filters, which over-approximate the set of memory locations accessed by a transaction.

In contrast, version management information is used to determine the values of memory locations at the end of a transaction (either upon a commit or an abort), and must therefore be precise. Precision is important because it affects the performance of Tx-Mon. If TxMon leverages imprecise read/write sets to identify the set of memory locations accessed by a transaction, it may trigger checks on data structures that were not otherwise accessed within the transaction. In turn, the execution of these additional checks may result in poor performance and spurious reports of failed data structure checks. Indeed, a preliminary design of TxMon that relied on a Bloom filter implementation of read/write sets had overheads in excess of 800% on the benchmarks reported in Section 5.

Our prototype implementation of TxMon, described in the following section, uses LogTM-SE [26]. This HTM system implements read/write sets as Bloom filters, uses a software-accessible undo log for version management, and allows transactions of unbounded length. Because version management information is accessible from software, LogTM-SE offers the additional benefit of allowing TxMon to be implemented *without any hardware modifications*.

4 Design and Implementation

TxMon enforces data structure properties by interposing on the standard workflow of an HTM system, as shown in Figure 3. In a standard HTM system, a transaction that has completed execution is passed to the conflict detection module, which determines whether to commit or abort the transaction. Our modifications to the HTM system's workflow ensure that TxMon's *data structure monitor* is first invoked upon the completion of the transaction.

The data structure monitor, which is implemented in software, verifies properties of the data structures that were accessed in the transaction. To identify the data structures accessed in the transaction, the monitor consults the transaction's undo log, which is stored in software. If the monitor returns successfully, it passes control to the conflict detection module, which then proceeds as before. If the monitor detects a data structure that violates a programmer-specified property, it invokes the HTM's mechanisms to abort the transaction. Thus, a transaction is committed only if it does not conflict with other transactions *and* the data structures that it modifies satisfy all programmer-specified properties. While TxMon's data structure monitor is invoked at the end of transactions by default, it can optionally be triggered at any point during the execution of a transaction using a function call, *e.g.,* a call to txmon_entry. We modified the

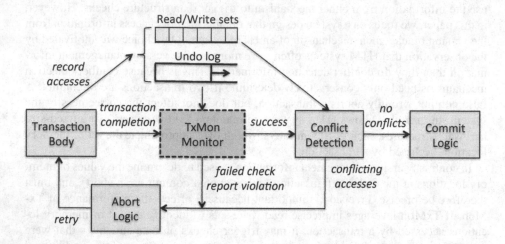

Fig. 3. Workflow of a TxMon-enhanced HTM

transaction{...} construct to additionally accept a parameter, which specifies the entrypoint of TxMon's data structure monitor, *e.g.*, as shown in Figure 2.

4.1   Implementation in LogTM-SE

We implemented TxMon using the LogTM-SE HTM system. This system is built for the SPARC architecture, and the HTM hardware has been simulated using the Virtutech Simics full system simulator. LogTM-SE employs eager conflict detection, *i.e.*, conflicts between transactions are detected as soon as they happen, and supports nested transactions. LogTM-SE also supports strong atomicity [20], *i.e.*, it can detect conflicting data accesses even if one of them was generated by non-transactional code.

Our choice of LogTM-SE as the implementation platform was motivated by three reasons. First, as a practical matter, LogTM-SE is a mature, freely-available, state of the art HTM system. Rather than building a new HTM system from scratch, using LogTM-SE allowed us to evaluate what changes would be necessary to an existing HTM system to monitor data structure properties. Second, LogTM-SE supports transactions of unbounded length. This feature is important for real-world applications, such as ClamAV and Memcached, in which data structures are modified by complex functions. Third, and most significant, LogTM-SE implements version management using a software-accessible undo log. Applications that use LogTM-SE transactions allocate memory for the log in their address space during startup. During execution, LogTM-SE eagerly updates memory locations modified within each transaction with speculative values, and checkpoints the original values at these locations within a per-transaction undo log. The log itself is stored in software, but is updated by the HTM hardware. TxMon's data structure monitor, which is implemented in software and is loaded into the application's address space, can also access the undo log to obtain the set of memory locations accessed by the transaction. As a result, we were able to implement TxMon with *no modifications* to the proposed LogTM-SE hardware.

While the design of LogTM-SE eased the implementation of TxMon, it may also be possible to design TxMon-like monitors for HTM systems that use alternative designs. For instance, some HTM systems (*e.g.*, [3]) buffer speculative updates and commit them at the end of the transaction (if there are no conflicts). In such systems, it suffices to expose the buffer that stores these updates to the data structure monitor. In some cases, hardware changes may be necessary to expose such state to the monitor (*e.g.*, the addition of new instructions to the ISA), but we expect that such changes will be relatively minor.

4.2 TxMon's Data Structure Monitor

The main responsibility of TxMon's data structure monitor is to trigger checks to verify the properties of all data structures accessed by a transaction. At the heart of the monitor is a table that stores *address maps* of data structures to be monitored, and the checking callback associated with each data structure. Programmers can register/unregister data structures to be monitored using an API exported by the monitor (*e.g.*, the function `register_ds` shown in Figure 2). The address map of a data structure contains the set of all memory locations of the data structure that are relevant to the property to be checked. The programmer must also supply the address map of each data structure (or specify how the address map must be computed) when he registers the data structure. For the example considered in Section 2 (*i.e.*, verifying the sortedness of the lists `heads[0]`, ..., `heads[254]`) the address map of each of these lists should at least contain the memory locations of all `next`, `prev` and `time` fields of each `struct item` node in the list. This is because any code that mistakenly violates the sortedness property must modify at least one of these fields of a `struct item` node.

In our implementation, address maps are implemented using hash tables that store the set of memory locations in a data structure. When the application invokes the TxMon monitor, the monitor fetches the set of memory locations accessed by the transaction from its undo log. It then queries address maps to determine data structures that were accessed by the application and triggers the callbacks associated with those data structures. The address map table also stores the arguments to be passed to the callback, *e.g.*, the argument `head[0]` is passed to the `check_sort` callback when triggered on the first linked list in Memcached.

Recall that TxMon's data structure monitor is triggered via a function call at the end of a transaction. As a result, the monitor and all the data structure checks that it triggers execute in the context of the transaction. This feature is useful for:

(1) *Detecting concurrent data structure modifications.* The property checks triggered by the monitor may need to traverse the data structures being monitored. In multi-threaded software, the monitored data structures may be shared, and may be modified by concurrently executing threads as the property checker traverses them. If the checker traverses a data structure when it is temporarily in an inconsistent state, it will report spurious property violations. By executing the property checks in the context of the transaction itself, TxMon ensures that any concurrent modifications of monitored data structures by other transactions will conflict with the current transaction. These conflicts are detected automatically by the HTM system's machinery, which will then abort one of the conflicting transactions. The LogTM-SE HTM system can also detect conflicting

accesses to monitored data structures from *non-transactional* code because it offers strong atomicity.

(2) *Protecting monitor state.* The monitor itself stores address maps, which are shared data structures. As explained below, address maps may be updated as data structures evolve. Executing TxMon's monitor in the context of the transaction ensures that concurrent modifications of monitor state will be identified by the HTM system's conflict detection machinery.

4.3   Computing and Maintaining Address Maps

Because the monitor detects accesses to a data structure by comparing the entries in the undo log to its address map, this map must be updated periodically to reflect changes to the data structure. For example, the addition of a new node or the deletion of an existing node in `heads[0]` must appropriately modify its address map in the TxMon monitor. One way to achieve this goal is to register/unregister elements of a data structure as they are allocated/destroyed. In the example shown in Figure 1, this would require the programmer to register each new item `it` when it is created in `process_add_command`. However, this approach is impractical for large code bases, because it requires the programmer to update address maps at several locations in the code.

We alleviate this problem by automating the creation of address maps. During program startup, we only require that the *heads* of data structures be registered with the TxMon monitor, to indicate which data structures must be monitored. For example, in Figure 1, the programmer only registers pointers to the heads of each of the 255 linked lists `heads[0],…, heads[254]`.

To create address maps, we leverage the insight that the callback associated with each data structure *must* access all its memory addresses that are relevant for the verification of that property. We can therefore piggyback address map creation with data structure property verification. To do so, we require the programmer to specify how the address map of a data structure must be updated within the callback of that data structure. In Figure 2, code that updates the address maps of the list passed as an argument to `check_sort` is supplied in lines `m16-m18`. As this callback executes, TxMon can update its address map for the data structures visited. The size of the address map is proportional to the size of the data structure.

The architecture of TxMon allows arbitrary C functions to be registered as callbacks for a data structure. The programmer can check the data structure specific properties in these functions e.g. the sortedness property of the linked lists `heads[0],…, heads[254]`. We have also implemented a library that allows programmers to easily create checker callbacks for properties inferred by Daikon [13].

5   Evaluation

We evaluated TxMon using two macrobenchmarks, namely Memcached and ClamAV, and three microbenchmarks from the Splash-2 suite. Figure 4 summarizes the benchmarks and workloads, and the corresponding data structures and properties monitored. Our experiments used the default configuration of Simics, which simulates an n-core

Benchmark	Workload	#Tx-S	#DS	#Prop	#Tx-D
(1) Memcached-1.4.0	Insert/query 100 pairs	7	255 linked lists	3	500
(2) Clamscan-0.95.2	Scan 356 files	23	engine	22	374
(3) Barnes	16K particles	3	Octree	1	68,819
(4) Radiosity	batch	44	Task queues	1	239,949
(5) Raytrace	teapot (small image)	10	Task queues	1	47,751

Fig. 4. Summary of benchmarks, workloads, data structures and number of properties monitored. The "#Tx-S" column shows the number of transactions added to the code of the benchmark, "#DS" shows the number of data structures monitored, "#Prop" shows the number of properties enforced, while "#Tx-D" shows the number of transactions executed at runtime.

Version	Ops/sec
(1) Unmodified (baseline)	7052
(2) Ported to LogTM-SE (no TxMon)	7066 (1×)
(3) With TxMon enabled	5937 (1.18×)
....	....
(4) TxMon/Walking log only	6,615 (1.06×)

Fig. 5. Performance of Memcached

UltraSPARC-III-plus processor running at 75MHz (we varied n for different benchmarks, as described in the subsections that follow), with $n \times 256$MB RAM (*i.e.,* we scaled memory proportional to the number of available cores), a 32KB instruction cache, 64KB data cache, and an 8MB L2 cache, running a Solaris 10 operating system. We extended Simics with the Wisconsin GEMS suite (version 2.1) to simulate a LogTM-SE HTM system. Our implementation of TxMon used 1024-bit Bloom filters to store read/write sets for conflict detection.

5.1 Memcached

This section presents a detailed performance evaluation of TxMon on Memcached. As discussed earlier, Memcached stores key/value pairs and supports operations such as inserting new key/value pairs and querying the value associated with a key. We converted Memcached to use transactional memory for synchronization by replacing each use of lock-based synchronization to use transactions instead. We registered each of the 255 linked lists that it uses to store key/value pairs with the TxMon monitor. We wrote checkers to enforce the following properties: (a) the tail of each list is reachable from the head by following next fields; (b) the head of each list is reachable from the tail by following prev fields; (c) items in each list are stored sorted in decreasing order of the last access time.

We used Memcached version 1.4.0 for our experiments and ran a workload that inserted 100 key/value pairs, and then queried Memcached for the values corresponding to each of the 100 keys that were just inserted. We measured average performance of Memcached as it performed these 200 operations. For this benchmark, we used an 8-core configuration of our Simics testbed, with 4 Memcached server threads processing requests received from a client thread.

As Figure 5 shows, TxMon imposed a moderate ($1.18\times$) overhead as it enforced data structure properties. We conducted another experiment to better understand the source of this overhead. We modified TxMon's data structure monitor to walk the undo log and fetch the set of memory locations accessed, but did not trigger any data structure checks using this information. That is, using the monitor shown in Figure 2 as an example, lines m5-m7 did not execute. Entry (4) of Figure 5 show the performance of Memcached of this experiment. As this figure shows, the operation of walking the undo log to fetch addresses imposed an overhead of $1.06\times$. TxMon cannot avoid this overhead, because it must read the undo log to decide which data structure checks to trigger.

The cost of performing checks depends on a number of factors, such as the type of workload, the number and size of the data structures being monitored, and the time-complexity of performing checks. For instance, the overheads of performing data structure checks in Memcached increased to $1.37\times$ when the workload was modified to insert and query 200 key/value pairs and to $1.73\times$ for 500 key/value pairs. As another example, it may well be that a workload consists of a number of $O(1)$ operations on Memcached's linked lists (*e.g.*, modifications to the heads of the lists), but that each of these operations triggers data structure checks that cost $O(n)$ (*e.g.*, traversal of the entire list). In such cases, the overhead of TxMon will be significantly higher if data structure checks are triggered naïvely. One way to reduce the overhead is to trigger checks with a probability $1/p$ at the end of trasaction, thus data structure checks will only be triggered once every p modifications to the data structure.

5.2   ClamAV

We evaluated TxMon's ability to monitor complex data structure properties on Clam-scan, a command line version of ClamAV. Clamscan uses a virus definition database to scan a set of input files, and determines if any of these files contain patterns in the database. Clamscan maintains several data structures to represent the virus definition database. Clamscan may potentially contain vulnerabilities that can be exploited by malware to hijack its execution and evade detection (*e.g.*, [4]). It is therefore critical to protect the integrity of Clamscan's data structures, such as those that represent the virus definition database.

We used Clamscan version-0.95.2 with its default virus definition database. We ran Clamscan on a uniprocessor configuration of our Simics testbed, and used it to scan the contents of a directory containing 356 files. We modified Clamscan so that code that accesses critical data structures is embedded in transactions. In all, we modified the code to place 23 transactions. We identified one critical data structure, called `engine` (of type `struct cl_engine`). This data structure has several fields, which store scan settings, file types to be scanned, and a pointer to an internal representation of the virus database, stored as a trie, as specified by the Aho-Corasick algorithm [6]. We wrote checkers for a total of 22 properties for this data structure.

As the Figure 6 shows, TxMon imposes an overhead of $1.03\times$ on Clamscan. Although Clamscan manages several complex data structures that can be expensive to traverse, the low runtime overhead observed is because most of these data structures are not modified during normal execution of Clamscan. However, a memory corruption bug or a security exploit that modifies monitored data structures will trigger TxMon to

Version	Time
(1) Unmodified (baseline)	10.95s
(2) Ported to LogTM-SE (no TxMon)	10.99s (1×)
(3) With TxMon enabled	11.30s (1.03×)

Fig. 6. Performance of Clamscan

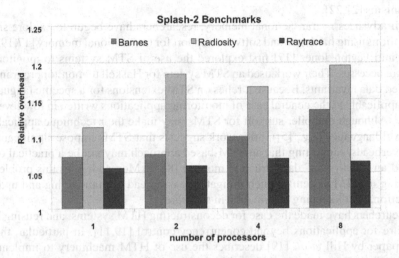

Fig. 7. Performance of Splash-2 benchmarks. This figure shows the overhead of a transactional-ized TxMon-enhanced benchmark relative to one that does not employ data structure checks.

traverse those data structures. This experiment shows that TxMon can be adopted as an "always on" tool to monitor the integrity of Clamscan's data structures.

5.3 Splash-2 Benchmarks

The Splash-2 suite [25] contains several multi-threaded benchmarks that have previously been used in transactional memory research. We used three benchmarks from this suite, namely Barnes, Radiosity and Raytrace, which were converted in prior work [26,23] to use transactions for synchronization. For each benchmark, we identified a complex data structure used by the benchmark (see Figure 4). The checking callback for each data structure simply traversed the data structure and updated its address map.

Figure 7 shows the overheads that TxMon imposed on the execution of each of these benchmarks on various testbed configurations (in which we varied the number of cores). For each benchmark, we calculated overheads relative to a version that employed transactions only for concurrency control, *i.e.*, TxMon was disabled, so no data structure checks were performed. The overheads ranged from about 1.05× for Raytrace to about 1.20× for Radiosity. These experiments again show that the overheads imposed by Tx-Mon are tolerable even if it is configured to be an "always-on" monitoring tool.

6   Related Work

The use of transactions to monitor data integrity was first suggested by the relational database community [24,15]. The idea was to use the transaction machinery implemented by database systems to additionally check data consistency when the database is modified. Recent work has adapted these ideas to isolate and recover from faults in software by creating custom implementations of transactions and speculative execution mechanisms [21,22].

With advances in transactional memory, researchers have begun to explore similar applications using hardware and software support for transactional memory [17,19,11,7]. Harris and Peyton Jones [17] first explored the use of STM systems to monitor data structure accesses. Their work used an STM system for Haskell to monitor programmer-specified data invariants. Because it relies on STM extensions for a specific language, it is not applicable to the general case of monitoring applications written in low-level languages. Although compiler support for STMs may make their technique applicable to low-level languages (e.g., [5]), prior work suggests that STMs impose significant runtime overheads, suggesting that an STM-based approach may not be a practical option to build an "always-on" data structure monitor [8]. TxMon addresses this problem by migrating to HTM systems, which mitigate the overhead of maintaining and updating transactional bookkeeping information in software.

Researchers have made the case for deconstructing HTM systems, and reusing HTM hardware for applications beyond concurrency control [19,11]. In particular, the position paper by Hill et al. [19] describes the use of HTM machinery to implement a data watchpoint framework. Although the ideas outlined in that paper are similar to those adopted by TxMon, our work explores the challenges of building a data structure integrity monitor using the basic watchpoint framework outlined in that paper.

7   Summary

This paper presented TxMon, a system that uses hardware transactional memory to monitor data structure properties. TxMon applies to software written in low-level languages, and can ensure that complex data structures satisfy a rich set of correctness properties. Experiments with both microbenchmarks and application benchmarks show that TxMon imposes tolerable runtime overheads.

References

1. Issues – memcached – project hosting on Google code,
   http://code.google.com/p/memcached/issues
2. Memcached: A distributed memory object caching system, http://memcached.org
3. Stanford transactional coherence and consistency project, http://tcc.stanford.edu
4. ClamAV multiple vulnerabilities, Secunia Advisories – SA28117 (December 2007)
5. Adi-Tabatabai, A., Lewis, B.T., Menon, V., Murphy, B.R., Saha, B.: Compiler and runtime support for efficient software transactional memory. In: ACM Conf. on Prog. Lang. Design & Impl. (June 2006)

6. Aho, A.V., Corasick, M.J.: Efficient string matching: An aid to bibliographic search. Comm. ACM (1975)

7. Bobba, J., Xiong, W., Yen, L., Hill, M.D., Wood, D.A.: StealthTest: Low overhead online software testing using transactional memory. In: Intl. Symp. Parallel Architectures and Compilation Techniques (September 2009)

8. Cascaval, C., Blundell, C., Michael, M., Cain, H.W., Wu, P., Chiras, S., Chatterjee, S.: Software transactional memory: Why is it only a research toy? Comm. ACM (2008)

9. Ceze, L., Tuck, J., Cascaval, C., Torrellas, J.: Bulk disambiguation of speculative threads in multiprocessors. In: Intl. Symp. Comp. Arch. (June 2006)

10. Chaudhry, S.: Rock: A third generation 65nm, 16-core, 32 thread + 32 scout-threads CMT SPARC processor. In: HotChips (2008)

11. Chung, J., Baek, W., Bronson, N.G., Seo, J., Kozyrakis, C., Olukotun, K.: ASeD: Availability, security, and debugging using transactional memory (poster). In: SPAA (June 2008)

12. Chung, J., Dalton, M., Kannan, H., Kozyrakis, C.: Thread-safe dynamic binary translation using transactional memory. In: IEEE Symp. High Perf. Comp. Arch. (February 2008)

13. Ernst, M.D., Perkins, J.H., Guo, P.J., McCamant, S., Pacheco, C., Tschantz, M.S., Xiao, C.: The Daikon system for dynamic detection of likely invariants. Sci. Comp. Prog. (December 2007)

14. Goetz, B.: Optimistic thread concurrency: Breaking the scale barrier, Azul Systems Technical Whitepaper (2009)

15. Hammer, M., McLeod, D.: A framework for data base semantic integrity. In: Intl. Conf. Soft. Engg. (1976)

16. Hammond, L., Wong, V., Chen, M., Carlstrom, B.D., Davis, J.D., Hertzberg, B., Prabhu, M.K., Wijaya, H., Kozyrakis, C., Olukotun, K.: Transactional memory coherence and consistency. In: Intl. Symp. Comp. Arch. (June 2004)

17. Harris, T., Peyton-Jones, S.: Transactional memory with data invariants. In: TRANSACT (June 2006)

18. Herlihy, M., Moss, J.E.B.: Transactional support for lock free data structures. In: Intl. Symp. Comp. Arch. (1993)

19. Hill, M.D., Hower, D., Moore, K.E., Swift, M.M., Volos, H., Wood, D.A.: A case for deconstructing hardware transactional memory systems. In: UW-Madison Computer Sciences Technical Report CS-TR-2007-1594 (2007)

20. Larus, J.R., Rajwar, R.: Transactional Memory. Synthesis Lectures on Comp. Arch. Morgan Claypool (2006)

21. Lenharth, A., Adve, V., King, S.T.: Recovery domains: An organizing principle for recoverable operating systems. In: ACM Conf. Architectural Support for Programming Languages and Operating Systems (March 2009)

22. Locasto, M.E., Stavrou, A., Cretu, G.F., Keromytis, A.D.: From STEM to SEAD: Speculative execution for automated defense. In: USENIX Annual Tech. Conf. (June 2007)

23. Moore, K.E., Bobba, J., Moravan, M.J., Hill, M.D., Wood, D.A.: LogTM: Log-based transactional memory. In: IEEE Symp. High Perf. Comp. Arch. (February 2006)

24. Stonebraker, M.: Implementation of integrity constraints and views by query modification. In: ACM SIGMOD (1975)

25. Woo, S.C., Ohara, M., Torrie, E., Singh, J.P., Gupta, A.: The SPLASH-2 programs: Characterization and methodological considerations. In: Intl. Symp. on Comp. Arch. (June 1995)

26. Yen, L., Bobba, J., Marty, M.R., Moore, K.E., Volos, H., Hill, M.D., Swift, M.M., Wood, D.A.: LogTM-SE: Decoupling hardware transactional memory from caches. In: IEEE Symp. High Perf. Comp. Arch. (February 2007)

MONPOLY: Monitoring Usage-Control Policies*

David Basin, Matúš Harvan, Felix Klaedtke, and Eugen Zălinescu

Computer Science Department, ETH Zurich, Switzerland

1 Introduction

Determining whether the usage of sensitive, digitally stored data complies with regulations and policies is a growing concern for companies, administrations, and end users alike. Classical examples of policies used for protecting and preventing the misuse of data are history-based access-control policies like the Chinese-wall policy and separation-of-duty constraints. Other policies from more specialized areas like banking involve retention, reporting, and transaction requirements. Simplified examples from this domain are that financial reports must be approved at most a week before they are published and that transactions over $10,000 must be reported within two days.

In the context of IT systems, compliance checking amounts to implementing a process that monitors, either online or offline, other processes. Such a monitor needs to temporally relate actions performed by the other processes and the data involved in these actions. Since the number of data items processed in IT systems is usually huge at each point in time and cannot be bounded over time, prior monitoring algorithms, in particular for propositional temporal logics, are of limited use for compliance checking.

In this paper, we present our monitoring tool MONPOLY for compliance checking. Policies are given as formulas of an expressive safety fragment of metric first-order temporal logic (MFOTL). The first-order fragment is well suited for formalizing relations on data, while the metric temporal operators can be used to specify properties depending on the times associated with past, present, and even future system events. MONPOLY processes a stream of system events with identifiers representing the data involved and reports policy violations. In the following, we describe MONPOLY and its features in more detail. We also briefly report on case studies and discuss related tools.

2 Tool Description

We describe MONPOLY's input and output and its theoretical underpinnings. Afterwards we give an overview of its implementation.

Input and Output. MONPOLY takes as command-line input a signature file, a policy file, and a log file. It outputs violations of the specified policy. We illustrate MONPOLY's input and output with an example.

---

* This work was funded by the Nokia Research Center, Switzerland. The authors thank the Nokia team in Lausanne for their support.

S. Khurshid and K. Sen (Eds.): RV 2011, LNCS 7186, pp. 360–364, 2012.

An MFOTL formalization of the policy that financial reports must be approved at most a week before they are published is

$$\Box \, \forall r. \; publish(r) \rightarrow \blacklozenge_{\leq 7 \, \text{days}} \; approve(r) \, . \tag{1}$$

We use $\Box$ for the temporal operator "always in the future" and $\blacklozenge$ for "sometimes in the past." Moreover, to express timing constraints, we attach metric constraints to these operators like ≤ 7 days for "within 7 days." The concrete textual input to MONPOLY for the policy (1) is

```
publish(?r) IMPLIES ONCE[0,7d] approve(?r),
```

where the arities of the predicates and the types of the arguments are specified in a signature file. The outermost temporal operator $\Box$ is implicit in the input to MONPOLY, since policies should hold at every point in time. Moreover, in our example the variable ?r is free. This is because MONPOLY should output the reports that were published but either not approved at all or the approval was too early. That is, MONPOLY outputs for every time-point the satisfying valuations of the negated formula

```
publish(?r) AND HISTORICALLY[0,7d] NOT approve(?r).
```

A log file consists of a sequence of time-stamped system events, which are ordered by their time-stamps. Events assumed to have happened simultaneously are grouped together. For example, according to the log file

```
@1307532861 approve (52)
@1307955600 approve (63)
            publish (60)
@1308477599 approve (87)
            publish (63) (52)
```

the report with the number 52 was approved at time-point 0 with the time-stamp 1307532861 (2011-06-08, 11:34:21 in UNIX time) and it was published at time-point 2 with the time-stamp 1308477599 (i.e., on 2011-06-19) together with the report 63, which was approved on 2011-06-13.

MONPOLY processes the log file incrementally and outputs for each time-point all policy violations. For the above input, MONPOLY reports the following violations:

```
@1307955600 (time-point 1): (60)
@1308477599 (time-point 2): (52)
```

Publishing the reports 60 and 52 each violates the policy (1). Report 60 was never approved and report 52 was approved too early. MONPOLY does not produce an output for time-point 0, since there is no policy violation at this time-point.

Foundations. MONPOLY implements our monitoring algorithm [7] for time-stamped temporal structures with finite relations. To effectively monitor properties specified in MFOTL, this algorithm only handles a safety fragment of MFOTL. Namely, the formulas must be of the form $\Box \, \Phi$, where the temporal future operators occurring in Φ are bounded, i.e., the attached metric constraints restrict these operators so that they range only over finitely many time-points. Roughly speaking, the monitoring algorithm iteratively processes the log file and determines for each given time-point the satisfying valuations of the formula $\neg\Phi$. Since Φ is bounded, only finitely many time-points need to be taken into account. However, the evaluation at a time-point is delayed by the monitoring algorithm until it reads the data of the relevant future time-points.

To efficiently determine at each time-point the violating elements of Φ, we evaluate the formula $\neg\Phi$ bottom-up and store intermediate results in finite relations. These are updated in each iteration and reused in later iterations. We require that $\neg\Phi$ can be rewritten to a formula so that the intermediate results are always finite relations. In particular, the use of negation and quantification is syntactically restricted. These restrictions are adapted from database query evaluation [1]. Before starting the monitoring process, MONPOLY checks whether the given formula has these properties.

Implementation. MONPOLY is written in the OCaml programming language. The code is mainly functional, making only sparse use of OCaml's imperative programming-language features and not using OCaml's object layer.

The code is structured in modules. For instance, there are modules for operations on MFOTL formulas, relations, and first-order structures. There are also modules for parsing formulas and log files. Finally, there is a module that implements the monitoring algorithm [7]. Since the algorithm manipulates relations extensively, the data structure used to represent relations has a huge impact on the monitor's efficiency. Currently, MONPOLY uses the data type for sets from OCaml's standard library, which is implemented using balanced binary trees.

Since the implementation is modular, MONPOLY can easily be modified and extended. For example, modifying MONPOLY so that it processes log files in another format is straightforward, as is using other data structures for representing and manipulating relations. The source code of MONPOLY is publicly available from the web page `http://projects.developer.nokia.com/MonPoly`.

3   Experimental Evaluation

We have evaluated MONPOLY's performance on several policies on synthetically generated data. For example, for the simple publishing policy (1), MONPOLY processes a log file with 25,000 entries in 0.4 seconds on a standard desktop computer. It uses 30 MBytes of memory. Monitoring the more complex policy where approvals must be signed by managers[1] takes MONPOLY 2.25 seconds, where 60 MBytes of memory are used. Other examples of our evaluation include MFOTL formalizations of transaction policies, the Chinese-wall policy, and

---

[1] The MFOTL formalization of this policy is $\Box\forall r.\forall a.\,publish(r,a) \rightarrow \blacklozenge_{\leq 7\,days} \exists m.\,\underline{manager}(m,a) \land approve(r,m)$. Here, $\underline{manager}(m,a)$ encodes that m is a manager of the accountant a, which might change over time. It abbreviates the formula $\neg manager_f(m,a) \mathsf{S}\, manager_s(m,a)$, where S denotes the temporal past operator $since$ and the predicates $manager_s$ and $manager_f$ represent system events that mark the start and the finish of the relation of m being a's manager.

separation-of-duty constraints, and are given in [6]. MONPOLY performs significantly better than our previous prototype implementation in Java, used in [6]. A reason for this improvement is that the fragment MONPOLY handles is slightly more restrictive but formulas in this fragment are evaluated more efficiently.

We have also used MONPOLY in a case study with industry: monitoring the usage of data within Nokia's data-collection campaign.[2] The campaign collects contextual information from cell phones of about 180 participants, including phone locations, call and SMS information, and the like. Given the data's high sensitivity, usage-control policies govern what actions may and must not be performed on the data. We formalized these policies in MFOTL, obtaining 14 formulas. We used MONPOLY to check them on different log files, each corresponding to roughly 24 hours of logged data. The largest logs contain around 85,000 time-points and one million system events. On such log files, the running times for the different policies on a standard desktop computer range from 10 seconds for simple access-control policies to 7 hours for complex policies employing nested temporal operators. The memory requirements are also modest: even for the complex policies, MONPOLY never used more than 500 MBytes of memory and these peaks occurred infrequently. Further details on the policies, the setup, MONPOLY's performance, and our findings in this case study are given in [5].

4   Related Tools

MONPOLY targets automated compliance checking in IT systems where actions are performed by distributed and heterogeneous system components. Monitoring tools for related applications are BeepBeep [10], Orchids [13], Monid [12], and LogScope [3]. BeepBeep monitors a web-client application for the conformance of its communication with the web service's interface specifications expressed in LTL-FO$^+$, a first-order extension of the linear-time temporal logic LTL. Orchids is a monitor for intrusion detection. It searches in an event stream for attack patterns, which are specified in a variant of future-time temporal logic and compiled into non-deterministic automata for fast pattern matching. Monid, similar to Orchids, is a tool for intrusion detection. It is based on the monitoring framework Eagle [2], where properties are specified by systems of parametrized equations with Boolean and temporal operators and a fixpoint semantics. LogScope can be seen as a restriction of RuleR [4]—a conditional rule-based system with an algorithm for runtime verification—tailored for log-file analysis. Properties in LogScope are given as conjunctions of data-parametrized temporal patterns and finite-state machines. These tools differ from MONPOLY in their specification languages and their underlying monitoring algorithms. For instance, LTL-FO$^+$ does not support temporal past operators but supports unbounded temporal future operators. Quantification in LTL-FO$^+$ is more restrictive than in the monitorable MFOTL fragment of MONPOLY, since quantified variables only range over data elements that appear in the system event that is currently processed. BeepBeep's monitoring algorithm for LTL-FO$^+$ is based on an extension of a tableaux construction for LTL.

---

[2] See http://research.nokia.com/page/11367 for details on the campaign.

Other runtime-verification approaches, implemented in tools like Temporal Rover [9], Lola [8], J-LO [14], and MOP [11], have primarily been developed and used for monitoring the execution of programs. Programs are instrumented so that relevant actions, like procedure calls and variable assignments, either directly trigger the inlined monitors or are forwarded to external monitors. Evaluating and comparing the performance of the different underlying monitoring algorithms experimentally remains as future work.

References

1. Abiteboul, S., Hull, R., Vianu, V.: Foundations of Databases: The Logical Level. Addison Wesley (1994)
2. Barringer, H., Goldberg, A., Havelund, K., Sen, K.: Rule-Based Runtime Verification. In: Steffen, B., Levi, G. (eds.) VMCAI 2004. LNCS, vol. 2937, pp. 44–57. Springer, Heidelberg (2004)
3. Barringer, H., Groce, A., Havelund, K., Smith, M.: Formal analysis of log files. J. Aero. Comput. Inform. Comm. 7, 365–390 (2010)
4. Barringer, H., Rydeheard, D.E., Havelund, K.: Rule systems for run-time monitoring: From Eagle to RuleR. J. Logic Comput. 20(3), 675–706 (2010)
5. Basin, D., Harvan, M., Klaedtke, F., Zălinescu, E.: Monitoring usage-control policies in distributed systems. In: Proc. of the 18th Int. Symp. on Temporal Representation and Reasoning, pp. 88–95. IEEE Computer Society (2011)
6. Basin, D., Klaedtke, F., Müller, S.: Monitoring security policies with metric first-order temporal logic. In: Proc. of the 15th ACM Symp. on Access Control Models and Technologies, pp. 23–33. ACM Press (2010)
7. Basin, D., Klaedtke, F., Müller, S., Pfitzmann, B.: Runtime monitoring of metric first-order temporal properties. In: Proc. of the 28th IARCS Annu. Conf. on Foundations of Software Technology and Theoretical Computer Science. Leibiz International Proceedings in Informatics (LIPIcs), vol. 2, pp. 49–60. Schloss Dagstuhl - Leibniz Center for Informatics (2008)
8. D'Angelo, B., Sankaranarayanan, S., Sánchez, C., Robinson, W., Finkbeiner, B., Sipma, H.B., Mehrotra, S., Manna, Z.: LOLA: Runtime monitoring of synchronous systems. In: Proc. of the 12th Int. Symp. on Temporal Representation and Reasoning, pp. 166–174. IEEE Computer Society (2005)
9. Drusinsky, D.: The Temporal Rover and the ATG Rover. In: Havelund, K., Penix, J., Visser, W. (eds.) SPIN 2000. LNCS, vol. 1885, pp. 323–330. Springer, Heidelberg (2000)
10. Hallé, S., Villemaire, R.: Browser-Based Enforcement of Interface Contracts in Web Applications with BeepBeep. In: Bouajjani, A., Maler, O. (eds.) CAV 2009. LNCS, vol. 5643, pp. 648–653. Springer, Heidelberg (2009)
11. Meredith, P.O., Jin, D., Griffith, D., Chen, F., Roşu, G.: An overview of the MOP runtime verification framework. Int. J. Softw. Tools Technol. Trans. (to appear)
12. Naldurg, P., Sen, K., Thati, P.: A Temporal Logic Based Framework for Intrusion Detection. In: de Frutos-Escrig, D., Núñez, M. (eds.) FORTE 2004. LNCS, vol. 3235, pp. 359–376. Springer, Heidelberg (2004)
13. Olivain, J., Goubault-Larrecq, J.: The ORCHIDS Intrusion Detection Tool. In: Etessami, K., Rajamani, S.K. (eds.) CAV 2005. LNCS, vol. 3576, pp. 286–290. Springer, Heidelberg (2005)
14. Stolz, V., Bodden, E.: Temporal assertions using AspectJ. In: Proc. of the 5th Workshop on Runtime Verification. ENTCS, vol. 144, pp. 109–124. Elsevier Science Inc. (2006)

MOPBox: A Library Approach to Runtime Verification
(Tool Demonstration)

Eric Bodden

Center for Advanced Security Research Darmstadt
Software Technology Group
Technische Universität Darmstadt, Germany
eric.bodden@cased.de

Abstract. In this work we propose *MOPBox*, a library-based approach to runtime verification. *MOPBox* is a Java library for defining and evaluating parametric runtime monitors. A user can define monitors through a simple set of API calls. Once a monitor is defined, it is ready to accept events. Events can originate from AspectJ aspects or from other sources, and they can be parametric, i.e., can contain variable bindings that bind abstract specification variables to concrete program values. When a monitor reaches an error state for a binding $\vec{v} = \vec{o}$, *MOPBox* notifies clients of a match for $\vec{v} = \vec{o}$ through a call-back interface. To map variable bindings to monitors, *MOPBox* uses re-implementations of efficient indexing algorithms that Chen et al. developed for JavaMOP.

We took care to keep *MOPBox* as generic as possible. States, transitions and variable bindings can be labeled not just with strings but with general Java Objects whose types are checked through Java Generics. This allows for simple integration into existing tools. For instance, we present ongoing work on integrating *MOPBox* with a Java debugger. In this work, transitions are labeled with breakpoints.

MOPBox is also a great tool for teaching: its implementations of monitor indexing algorithms are much easier to understand than the code generated by tools such as JavaMOP. Indexing algorithms use the Strategy Design Pattern, which makes them easily exchangeable. Hence, *MOPBox* is also the perfect tool to explore and test new algorithms for monitor indexing without bothering about the complex intricacies of code generation. In the future, we further plan to integrate *MOPBox* with the Clara framework for statically evaluating runtime monitors ahead of time.

1 Motivation and Description of *MOPBox*

In the past decade, researchers in Runtime Verification have developed a range of specialized tools for generating runtime monitors from formal specifications [1–5]. Typically, those tools support parametric monitor specifications, i.e, specifications that allow the monitoring of individual objects or even combinations of objects. Figure 1, for example shows a finite-state machine representing the

S. Khurshid and K. Sen (Eds.): RV 2011, LNCS 7186, pp. 365–369, 2012.
© Springer-Verlag Berlin Heidelberg 2012

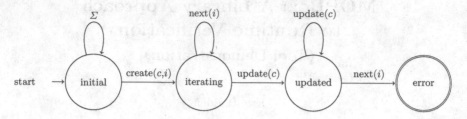

Fig. 1. Runtime monitor for FailSafeIter property [1]: Do not modify a collection while iterating over it

"FailSafeIter" property [1]: one should not use an iterator i for a collection any longer if c was updated after i had been created. In this case, there exists a single monitor instance (holding the state machine's internal state) for any combination of c and i occurring on the monitored program execution.

Research in Runtime Verification has made big leaps to making runtime monitoring of such parameterized properties efficient [3, 6–8] through the generation of property-specific monitoring code. However, efficiency should not be the only goal to pursue in runtime monitoring. While auto-generated monitoring code may be maximally efficient, it is generally hard to understand and debug. In addition, approaches based on code-generation often involve multiple, loosely integrated tools, hindering integration of those tools into other applications.

Another problem with those loosely integrated tool chains is that they hinder comparison of montoring approaches. In recent work, Purandare et al. perform an in-depth comparison with respect to the relative performance of several monitoring algorithms [9]. As the authors show, this performance can depend on the property to be monitored: different algorithms are ideal for different properties. Current tool chains cannot easily support multiple algorithms as they are not integrated.

2 Defining Monitor Templates

In this work we hence propose *MOPBox*, a library-based approach to runtime verification. *MOPBox* is a Java library for defining and evaluating parametric runtime monitors such as the one shown in Figure 1. With *MOPBox*, a user can define templates for runtime monitors through a simple set of API calls.[1] Figure 2 shows how a user would define a monitor template for the FailSafeIter property mentioned earlier.

First, in line 2, the user defines that she wishes to implement a template based on finite-state machines, with String labels on transitions and variable bindings that map from `Var` instances to any kinds of Objects. The range of template variables `Var` is defined as an enum in line 4.

---

[1] We use the phrase "monitor template" to denote a property that *MOPBox* should monitor. During the execution of the program under test, each template will generate a set of monitors, one monitor for each variable binding.

```
1  public class FailSafeIterMonitorTemplate
2     extends AbstractFSMMonitorTemplate<String,Var,Object> {
3
4  public enum Var{ C, I }
5
6  protected void fillAlphabet(IAlphabet<String,Var> a) {
7     a.makeNewSymbol("create", C, I);
8     a.makeNewSymbol("update", C);
9     a.makeNewSymbol("iter", I);
10 }
11
12 protected State<String> setupStatesAndTransitions() {
13    State<String> initial = makeState(false);
14    State<String> iterating = makeState(false);
15    State<String> updated = makeState(false);
16    State<String> error = makeState(true);
17
18    initial.addTransition(getSymbolByLabel("create"), iterating);
19    initial.addTransition(getSymbolByLabel("update"), initial);
20    initial.addTransition(getSymbolByLabel("iter"), initial);
21    iterating.addTransition(getSymbolByLabel("iter"), iterating);
22    iterating.addTransition(getSymbolByLabel("update"), updated);
23    updated.addTransition(getSymbolByLabel("update"), updated);
24    updated.addTransition(getSymbolByLabel("iter"), error);
25    return initial;
26 }
27
28 protected IIndexingStrategy<String,Var,Object> createIndexingStrategy() {
29    return new StrategyB();
30 }
31
32
33 protected void matchCompleted(IVariableBinding<Var, Object> binding) {
34    System.err.println("MATCH for binding: "+binding);
35 }
36
37 }
```

Fig. 2. Monitor template for FailSafeIter property in *MOPBox*

In lines 6–9, the user then lists the alphabet to be used, i.e., the different kinds of events that the monitors of this template should prepare to process. At this point the user also binds event names such as **create** to template variables C and I. In the example, event labels are Strings because the user chose type String as type parameter in line 2. One could have chosen other types of labels. In a current piece of work we are integrating *MOPBox* with the Java debugger of the Eclipse IDE [10]. In this setting, events are labeled with breakpoints that are triggered at debug time [11].

In lines 13–16, the user calls the factory method **makeState** to create the states that will make up the monitor template's state machine. An error state is created using **makeState(true)**. In lines 18–24, finally, the user defines the state machine's transition relation. At the end of the method, by convention, the user returns the machine's initial state.

```
1  after(Collection  c)  returning(Iterator  i):
2      call(* Iterable+.iterator()) && target(c) {
3      IVariableBinding<Var, Object> binding
4        = new VariableBinding<Var, Object>();
5      binding.put(Var.C,c);
6      binding.put(Var.I,i);
7      template.processEvent(
8          "create",
9          binding
10     );
11 }
```

Fig. 3. AspectJ advice dispatching "create" events to the monitor template

In lines 28–30, the user selects an indexing strategy. An indexing strategy implements an indexing algorithm that dispatches parameterized events to monitors for the appropriate parameter instances. In this example, the user opted for our implementation of Chen et al.'s *Algorithm B* [7]. *MOPBox* uses the Strategy Pattern [12] to make indexing strategies easily exchangeable. This also facilitates rapid prototyping and testing of new indexing algorithms. For instance, users can instantiate multiple monitor templates that use different indexing strategies but are otherwise identical. If for the same events one template finds a match and the other one does not, this indicates a bug in one of the indexing strategies. *MOPBox* holds no static state. To reset a monitor, one hence simply needs to re-instantiate a template's indexing strategy.

Last but not least, in lines 33–35, the user defines the call-back method `matchCompleted`. *MOPBox* will call this method automatically whenever one of the monitors of this template completes a match. *MOPBox* passes the matching variable binding into the method as a parameter.

3   Sending Events to Monitor Templates

In Figure 3 we show how users can use AspectJ [13] to send concrete program events to a monitor template. The AspectJ advice intercepts calls to `Collection.iterator()` and notifies the monitor template, passing in a variable binding mapping the template variables C and I to concrete program values. Users do not necessarily have to use aspects to generate events. In a current piece of work we are integrating *MOPBox* with the Java debugger of the Eclipse IDE [10]. In that case, events are triggered directly by the debugger's application interface.

References

1. Allan, C., Avgustinov, P., Christensen, A.S., Hendren, L., Kuzins, S., Lhoták, O., de Moor, O., Sereni, D., Sittampalam, G., Tibble, J.: Adding Trace Matching with Free Variables to AspectJ. In: OOPSLA, pp. 345–364 (October 2005)

2. Bodden, E.: J-LO - A tool for runtime-checking temporal assertions. Master's thesis, RWTH Aachen University (November 2005)
3. Chen, F., Roşu, G.: MOP: an efficient and generic runtime verification framework. In: OOPSLA, pp. 569–588 (October 2007)
4. Maoz, S., Harel, D.: From multi-modal scenarios to code: compiling LSCs into AspectJ. In: Symposium on the Foundations of Software Engineering (FSE), pp. 219–230 (November 2006)
5. Krüger, I.H., Lee, G., Meisinger, M.: Automating software architecture exploration with M2Aspects. In: Workshop on Scenarios and State Machines: Models, Algorithms, and Tools (SCESM), pp. 51–58 (May 2006)
6. Avgustinov, P., Tibble, J., de Moor, O.: Making trace monitors feasible. In: OOPSLA, pp. 589–608 (October 2007)
7. Chen, F., Roşu, G.: Parametric Trace Slicing and Monitoring. In: Kowalewski, S., Philippou, A. (eds.) TACAS 2009. LNCS, vol. 5505, pp. 246–261. Springer, Heidelberg (2009)
8. Chen, F., Meredith, P., Jin, D., Roşu, G.: Efficient formalism-independent monitoring of parametric properties. In: ASE, pp. 383–394 (2009)
9. Purandare, R., Dwyer, M., Elbaum, S.: Monitoring Finite State Properties: Algorithmic Approaches and Their Relative Strengths. In: Khurshid, S., Sen, K. (eds.) RV 2011. LNCS, vol. 7186, pp. 381–395. Springer, Heidelberg (2012)
10. Eclipse IDE, http://eclipse.org/
11. Bodden, E.: Stateful breakpoints: A practical approach to defining parameterized runtime monitors. In: ESEC/FSE 2011: Joint Meeting of the European Software Engineering Conference and the ACM SIGSOFT Symposium on the Foundations of Software Engineering. New Ideas Track (September 2011) (to appear)
12. Gamma, E., Helm, R., Johnson, R.E., Vlissides, J.M.: Design Patterns: Abstraction and Reuse of Object-Oriented Design. In: Nierstrasz, O.M. (ed.) ECOOP 1993. LNCS, vol. 707, pp. 406–431. Springer, Heidelberg (1993)
13. AspectJ team: The AspectJ home page (2003), http://eclipse.org/aspectj/

Elarva: A Monitoring Tool for Erlang

Christian Colombo, Adrian Francalanza, and Rudolph Gatt

Department of Computer Science, University of Malta, Malta

Abstract. The LARVA monitoring tool has been successfully applied to a number of industrial Java systems, providing extra assurance of behaviour correctness. Given the increased interest in concurrent programming, we propose ELARVA, an adaptation of LARVA for monitoring programs written in Erlang, an established industry-strength concurrent language. Object-oriented LARVA constructs have been translated to process-oriented setting, and the synchronous LARVA monitoring semantics was altered to an asynchronous interpretation. We argue how this loosely-coupled runtime verification architecture still permits monitors to actuate recovery actions.

1 Introduction

Ensuring correctness in highly concurrent systems, through either testing or model checking, is problematic because it is difficult to test for all possible behaviour interleavings. A case in point is code written in Erlang [1], an established industry-strength functional concurrent language used mainly in the Telecoms industry. Ensuring correctness in this language is made even harder by the fact that: (i) Erlang is not statically type-checked, preventing developers from filtering out certain errors at compile time; and (ii) Erlang supports hot-code swapping *i.e.*, modules can be replaced on-the-fly, increasing the set of possible outcomes of a system execution.

Runtime Verification (RV) is a promising approach towards ensuring Erlang software correctness as it provides a disciplined methodology for conducting the runtime checks necessary in the absence of static guarantees. Importantly, the approach does not suffer from coverage and state explosion issues associated with standard verification techniques for concurrency.

LARVA is a runtime monitoring tool targeting the correctness of Java code [2] enabling one to: (i) specify system properties with recovery actions (in case of violation) in terms of automata-based specifications, (ii) compile the properties into Java monitors, and (iii) instrument the monitors at byte-code level using techniques from Aspect-Oriented Programming (AOP) [5]. Through aspects, synthesised monitors are then automatically updated with events from the execution of the monitored system, triggering corrective actions where necessary, providing extra reassurance as to the correctness of the monitored software behaviour.

LARVA supports modular property specification in a number of ways. For instance (i) each object can be verified by a separate monitor through a mechanism of monitor parametrisation, and (ii) properties can be decomposed into sub-properties that can communicate with one another through channels. Erlang's actor-based concurrency model [4], which circumvents any shared memory through the use of message passing, is consistent with such a modular approach, making LARVA a sensible starting point for a monitoring framework for Erlang.

S. Khurshid and K. Sen (Eds.): RV 2011, LNCS 7186, pp. 370–374, 2012.

Porting LARVA to Erlang is however non-trivial, because: (i) Erlang does not have AOP support, the mechanism used by LARVA for monitor instrumentation; and (ii) Erlang is process-oriented whereas Java is object-oriented. In the rest of this proposal, we present ELARVA, an adaptation of LARVA to Erlang, giving an overview of how we tackled these issues and outline how we have evaluated our tool.

2 Solution Overview

In the absence of any AOP support, ELARVA employs Erlang's tracing facility for instrumentation; this makes monitoring asynchronous, which alters the nature of recovery actions. Moreover, adapting monitor parameterising constructs such as foreach to processes accentuated a shortcoming in LARVA's broadcast interpretation of channel communication, the extensive use of which made inter-monitor communication unwieldy; in ELARVA, channel communication was thus given a point-to-point interpretation.

2.1 Eliciting Events Asynchronously

Erlang's tracing mechanism enables us to hook on to Erlang's VM and receive the relevant events as messages to a *singleton* tracer process [1]. Monitors are set up as processes executing in parallel with the monitored system, where the tracer acts as a demultiplexer, reading the trace received and sending parts of it to the relevant monitors in non-blocking fashion, as shown in Fig. 1 (left). This setup has a number of advantages: (i) the system and the monitor can be running on separate machines, reducing the monitoring cost to that of tracing (ii) as opposed to LARVA, we can monitor a live system via ELARVA without having to stop the system and trace-compile it (iii) no errors are introduced in the monitored system as a result of instrumentation.

However, the non-blocking nature of Erlang message passing makes ELARVA's trace-based monitoring *asynchronous*, possibly detecting violations late. In general, this complicates a monitor's assessment of which sub-systems where effected by the violation. However, in the case of Erlang, adverse effects emanating from a violation can be confined since (i) processes do not share memories (ii) code is typically written in fail-fast fashion *i.e.*, processes fail as soon as anything abnormal is encountered and (iii) process dependencies can be explicitly delineated through mechanisms such as process linking [1], which propagates the failure to linked processes. Erlang process failure detection then allows the monitor localise the affected sub-system and take appropriate action. In fact, Erlang programs successfully achieve fault tolerance using these same mechanisms, through code patterns such as the Supervisor behaviour [1].

2.2 Parametrised Properties and Channel Communication

In ELARVA, the foreach construct was adapted to be parameterised by processes (as opposed to objects), so that a separate monitor could be replicated for every process spawned. Modularly decomposing and replicating monitors in this way simplifies specifications since each monitor can focus on one process instance only, communicating with other monitors whenever necessary, as opposed to having one monolithic monitor monitoring multiple processes.

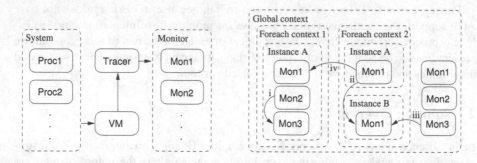

Fig. 1. Monitoring architecture in ELARVA *(left)*, Possible communication configurations *(right)*

This specification approach is also in line with Erlang code practices, which advocate for the structuring of programs into as many small shortlived processes as possible.[1] However, it quickly became apparent that the existing LARVA communication mechanism, based on broadcasts, created bottlenecks in settings with extensive use of monitor decomposition *i.e.*, smaller communicating sub-monitors that are replicated on a per-process basis. As depicted in Fig. 1 (right), this was rectified in ELARVA by allowing monitors to select the destination of their communication from the following: (i) across monitors of the same instance, (ii) across monitors of different instances, (iii) from global to `foreach` context, and (iv) across `foreach` contexts.

3   Case Study

We consider a hospital management system where patients can place requests for medical reports and medical reports are issued once all the doctors concerned give their approval; note that patient requests are handled concurrently. Each patient and each doctor are modelled as a process and interact with a "main office" central process we refer to as the "hub" for short, see Fig. 2 (left).

Despite its simplicity, a number of correctness properties can be identified over this system such as: (i) A patient receives a report only if a request has been placed earlier, (ii) A patient never receives the medical report of another patient, (iii) A report received by a patient must be approved by at least two doctors overseeing that patient.

In what follows we give an intuition of how we monitor the third property outlined for this hospital system. A monitor is defined *foreach* patient process and *foreach* doctor process, depicted by dotted boxes in Fig. 2 (right). The following are the steps involved in a medical report request/response, lead by the labelled solid edges in Fig. 2 (right): (i) the patient, Pat1, requests a report, and the patient monitor, MP1 detects it (through tracing, denoted by a *dashed edge*), (ii/iii) the hub forwards the report request to the doctors, Doc1 and Doc2 (no monitor activity), (iv/v) the doctors reply to the request by either approving or rejecting the report and the respective doctor monitors, MD1 and MD2, detect this (denoted by the respective dashed edge), (vi) the patient receives

---

[1] Often referred to as concurrency-oriented programming, this allows the virtual machine to better apportion computation amongst the multiple processing units on a multicore machine [1].

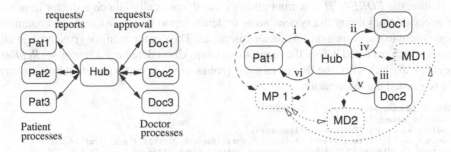

Fig. 2. The hospital management system setup *(left)*, with monitors *(right)*

the report and the patient monitor detects it (see respective dashed edge). At this point, the patient monitor communicates with the doctor monitors (denoted by the respective *dotted edges*) to ensure that the report received was indeed authorised by the respective doctors.[2] If no two approving doctors are found then the monitor can conclude that the property was violated and an action is taken, possibly restarting the patient with the unauthorised report.

The monitors depicted in Fig. 2 can be setup through the following larva scripts specifying monitor automata, where transitions (backslash-separated triples consisting of an event detection, a condition, and an action to be executed if the condition is satisfied) take the property from one state to the next. Using the following event definitions:

```
EVENTS { RecRep = RECEIVE {backend_response,{Pat,Id,Diagnosis}}
         Ack    = CHANNEL {doc_response,{Pat,Id,Res}}
         AskAck = CHANNEL {mon_comm,{Doc,Id,Time}}
         RepRes = SEND {doc_response,{Doc,Res,Pat,Id}} }
```

For each patient process we need to detect report receipt, communicate with doctor monitors to confirm the approval of the report, receive an acknowledgement from the doctor monitors (indicating approval (yes), rejection (no) or indifference (ok)), and checks whether a violation has occurred. The *FOREACH* construct below automatically applies the monitoring logic to each patient joining the hospital system: upon the receipt of a report (*RecRep* event), the patient monitor sends a channel communication to all doctors, indicating the identifier and the timestamp of the report involved; the patient monitor then listens for *Ack* events and decides whether a violation has occurred.

```
FOREACH {patient,newPatient,[_]} { TRANSITIONS {
  start-> wait [RecRep\\cnt=numDocs,cntYes=0,{channel,{foreach,doctor,{'AskAck',{_,Id,Time}}}}]
  wait -> wait [Ack\Res=="ok" and cnt>1\cnt--]
  wait -> wait [Ack\Res=="yes" and cntYes<1\cntYes++]
  wait -> ok   [Ack\Res=="yes" and cntYes>0\] } }
  wait -> violation [Ack\Res=="no" or (Res=="ok" and cnt==1)\] } }
```

---

[2] Since monitoring is asynchronous, detection for either (iv/v) may not have happened by the time the doctor monitors receive the patient monitor communications *i.e.*, a race condition. Hence when a patient monitor detects the received patient report, it communicates with the relevant doctor monitors to ensure that the report has been approved by at least two of the doctors. Before the doctor monitors reply to the patient monitors, they are forced to make the necessary trace detections, thus reaching a synchronisation point with the patient monitor.

Below, the *FOREACH* construct allows us to dynamically launch a doctor monitor for every doctor joining the system, so as to detect report response events and communicate them to the corresponding patient monitors. The doctor monitor goes through all events which occurred before the report timestamp. Upon detecting a response (*RepRes* event) or the lack of it, the doctor monitor replies to the specific patient monitor (*Pat*) that requested the information.

```
FOREACH {doctor,newDoctor,[_]} { TRANSITIONS {
  idle -> detect [AskAck\\]
  detect -> detect [Event\eventTime<Time\]
  detect -> idle [Event\eventTime>Time\{channel,{foreach,patient,{'Ack',{Pat,Id,"ok"}}}}]
  detect -> idle [RepRes\\{channel,{foreach,patient,{'Ack',{Pat,Id,Res}}}}] } }
```

4   Evaluation

ELARVA was compared to Exago [3], an offline property-based Erlang monitoring tool. Both were successfully used to specify correctness properties of the hospital management system (introduced in the previous section). However, Exago necessitated the inclusion of substantial Erlang code-chunks; this blurred the distinction between code and specification logic and introduced the possibility of inserting further errors through the code chunks. By contrast, ELARVA was able to specify the properties using the tool logic (called DATES), the translation of which was automated by the monitor compiler. Another disadvantage of Exago was that it is an offline tool, which exclude the possibilities of applying reparatory actions in case of violations.

5   Conclusion

Through ELARVA, we have extended the LARVA tool and provided a minimally intrusive runtime monitoring framework to monitor expressive properties on Erlang code, whereby the limited intrusiveness makes it more palatable to potential adopters from the Erlang community. We aim to improve ELARVA by (i) investigating means of eliciting system events in a decentralised fashion, unlike the present centralised tracing mechanism relying on the Erlang VM and (ii) supporting distribution, so as to enable monitoring across machines.

References

1. Armstrong, J.: Programming Erlang. The Pragmatic Bookshelf (2007)
2. Colombo, C., Pace, G.J., Schneider, G.: Larva — Safer Monitoring of Real-Time Java Programs (tool paper). In: SEFM, pp. 33–37. IEEE (November 2009)
3. Erdödi, A.: Exago: Property monitoring via log file analysis. Presented at the Erlang User Group Meeting, London (2010)
4. Hewitt, C., Bishop, P., Steiger, R.: A universal modular actor formalism for artificial intelligence. In: IJCAI, pp. 235–245. Morgan Kaufmann (1973)
5. Kiczales, G., Lamping, J., Mendhekar, A., Maeda, C., Lopes, C.V., Loingtier, J.-M., Irwin, J.: Aspect-Oriented Programming. In: Aksit, M., Auletta, V. (eds.) ECOOP 1997. LNCS, vol. 1241, pp. 220–242. Springer, Heidelberg (1997)

DA-BMC: A Tool Chain Combining Dynamic Analysis and Bounded Model Checking*

Jan Fiedor, Vendula Hrubá, Bohuslav Křena, and Tomáš Vojnar

FIT, Brno University of Technology, Czech Republic

Abstract. This paper presents the DA-BMC tool chain that allows one to combine dynamic analysis and bounded model checking for finding synchronisation errors in concurrent Java programs. The idea is to use suitable dynamic analyses to identify executions of a program being analysed that are suspected to contain synchronisation errors. Some points in such executions are recorded, and then the executions are reproduced in a model checker, using its capabilities to navigate among the recorded points. Subsequently, bounded model checking in a vicinity of the replayed execution is used to confirm whether there are some real errors in the program and/or to debug the problematic execution of the program.

1 Introduction

Despite the constantly growing pressure on quality of software applications, many software errors still appear in the field. One class of errors which can be found in software applications more and more frequently are concurrency-related errors, which is a consequence of the growing use of multi-core processors. Such errors are hard to find by testing since they may be very unlikely to appear. One way to increase chances to detect such an error is to use various *dynamic analyses* (such as Eraser [6] for detection of data races) that try to extrapolate the witnessed behaviour and give a warning about a possible error even if such an error is not really witnessed in any testing run. A disadvantage of such analyses is that they often produce false alarms. To avoid false alarms, one can use *model checking* based on a systematic search of the state space of the given program [1], but this approach is very expensive. In this paper, we describe a tool chain denoted as *DA-BMC*[1] that tries to combine advantages of both dynamic analysis and (bounded) model checking.

In our tool chain, implementing the approach proposed in [3], we use the infrastructure offered by the *Contest* tool [2] to implement suitable dynamic analyses over Java programs and to record selected points of the executions of the programs that are suspected to contain errors. We then use the *Java PathFinder (JPF)* model checker [5] to replay the partially recorded executions, using JPF's capabilities of state space generation to heuristically navigate among the recorded points. In order to allow the navigation, the JPF's state space search strategy, including its use of partial order reduction to reduce the searched state space, is suitably modified. Bounded model checking is

* This work was supported by the Czech Science Foundation (project P103/10/0306), the Czech Ministry of Education (projects COST OC10009 and MSM 0021630528), and the BUT FIT project FIT-S-11-1.

[1] http://www.fit.vutbr.cz/research/groups/verifit/tools/da-bmc

S. Khurshid and K. Sen (Eds.): RV 2011, LNCS 7186, pp. 375–380, 2012.
© Springer-Verlag Berlin Heidelberg 2012

then performed in the vicinity of the replayed executions, trying to confirm that there is really some error in the program and/or to debug the recorded suspicious behaviour.

We illustrate capabilities of DA-BMC on several case studies, showing that it really allows one to benefit from advantages of both dynamic analysis and model checking.

2 Recording Suspicious Executions

The first step when using DA-BMC is to use a suitable *dynamic analysis* to identify executions suspected to contain an error and to record some information about them—recording the entire executions would typically be too costly. In DA-BMC, this phase is implemented on top of the *Contest tool* [2]. Contest provides a listener architecture (implemented via Java byte-code instrumentation) on top of which it is easy to implement various dynamic analyses. We further refer to two such analyses, namely, Eraser+ and AtomRace intended for detection of data races (and, in the second case, also atomicity violations), which have been implemented as Contest plugins in [4]. Further analyses can, of course, be added. Contest also provides a noise injection mechanism which increases the probability of manifestation of concurrency-related errors.

In order to record executions, we have implemented another specialised listener on top of Contest. We record information about an execution in the form of a *trace* which is a sequence of *monitored events* that contains partial information about some of the events that happen during the execution. In particular, Contest allows us to monitor the following events: *thread-related* events (thread creation, thread termination), *memory-access-related* events (before integer read, after integer read, before float write, after float write, etc.), *synchronisation-related* events (after monitor enter, before monitor exit, join, wait, notify, etc.), and some *control-related* events (basic block entry, method enter, and method exit). The user can choose only some of such events to be monitored. As shown in our case studies, one should mainly consider synchronisation-related and memory-access-related events, which help the most when dealing with the inherent non-determinism of concurrent executions.

Each monitored event contains information about the source-code location from which it was generated (class and method name, line and instruction number) and the thread which generated it. The recorded trace also contains information produced by the applied dynamic analysis which labels some of the monitored events as suspicious from the point of view of causing an error.

3 Replaying Recorded Traces

The second step when using DA-BMC is to reproduce suspicious executions recorded as traces of monitored events in a model checker. More precisely, there is no guarantee that the same execution as the one from which the given trace was recorded will be reproduced. The tool will simply try to generate some execution whose underlying trace corresponds with the recorded trace. It is also possible to let the model checker generate more executions with the same trace.

In DA-BMC, we, in particular, use the *Java PathFinder (JPF)* model checker [5]. JPF provides several state space search strategies, but also allows one to add new user-specific search strategies. Moreover, it provides a listener mechanism which is useful for performing various analyses of the searched state space and/or for guiding the search strategies to a specific part of the state space. JPF uses several state space reduction techniques, including partial order reduction (POR), which out of several transitions that lead from a certain state may explore only some [1].

A recorded trace is replayed by navigating JPF through the state space of a program such that the monitored events encountered on the search path correspond with the ones in the recorded trace. The states being explored during the search are stored in a priority queue. The priority of the inserted states depends on the chosen search strategy (DFS and BFS are supported). In each step, the next parent state to be processed is obtained from the queue. After that, all relevant children of the parent state are generated. Here, we should note that, in JPF, a transition between a parent and child states represents, in fact, a sequence of events happening in a running program. This sequence is chosen by the POR to represent all equivalent paths between the two states. Into the priority queue, we only save the child states that may appear on a path corresponding to the recorded trace. In other words, each program event encountered within the JPF's transition between the parent and child states must either be an event which is not monitored (and hence ignored), or an event which corresponds with the one stored in the recorded trace at an appropriate position. This correspondence is checked during the generation of a transition in JPF.

Sometimes, it is also necessary to influence the POR used by JPF. That happens when the POR decides to consider another permutation of the events than the one actually present in the trace. Then, the POR is forced to use the needed permutation as follows. If the generation of the sequence of events that the POR wants to compose into a single transition encounters some monitored event, and this event differs from the one expected in the recorded trace, then we force JPF to finish the generation of the sequence of events to be put under a single transition and to create a new state. The navigation algorithm then searches the transitions enabled in this state that correspond with the recorded trace (if there is none, the search backtracks).

Since the replaying is driven by a sequence of monitored events generated from the Contest's instrumentation of the given program, we run the instrumented byte-code in JPF. We, however, make JPF skip all the code that is a part of Contest in order not to increase the size of the state space being searched. Moreover, Contest not only adds some instructions into the code, but also replaces some original byte-code instructions. This applies, e.g., for the instructions wait, notify, join, etc. In this case, when such an instruction is detected in JPF, we dynamically replace it with the original instruction.

As the JPF's implementation of sleep() ignores interruption of sleeping threads, we provide a modified implementation of the interrupt() and sleep() methods which correctly generate an exception if a thread is interrupted by another thread when sleeping. For that to work correctly, the possibility of branching of the execution after sleep() must be enabled in JPF.

Still, it might not be possible to replay a trace if the program depends on input or random data or if it uses some specific dynamic data structures like hash tables where, e.g., objects might be iterated in a different order in each run of the program. In these cases, it is necessary to modify the source code of the analysed program, e.g., by adding JPF data choice generators to eliminate these problems.

4 Bounded Model Checking

As we have already said above, the trace recorded from a suspicious execution does not identify the execution from which it was generated in a unique way. Moreover, even the original suspicious execution based on which the applied dynamic analysis generated a warning about the possibility of some error needs not contain an actual occurrence of the error (even if the error is real). To cope with such situations, apart from possibly exploring several paths through the state space corresponding with the recorded trace, we use bounded model checking that starts from the states from which an event that is marked as suspicious is enabled, or from some of its predecessors. The latter is motivated by the fact that once a suspicious event is reached, it may already be too late for a real error to manifest.

To be able to use bounded model checking to see whether an error really appears in the program, it is expected that the user supplies a JPF listener capable of identifying occurrences of the error (in our experiments, which concentrate on data races, we, e.g., use a slight modification of the `PreciseRaceDetector` listener available in JPF). The listeners looking for occurrences of errors may be activated either at the very beginning of replaying of a trace, or they may be activated at the beginning of each application of bounded model checking. The user is allowed to control both the depth of the bounded model checking as well as the number of backward steps to be taken from a suspicious event before starting bounded model checking.

5 Experiments

To demonstrate capabilities of DA-BMC, we consider four case studies. The first two, *BankAccount* and *Airlines*, are simple programs (with 2 or 3 classes, respectively) in which a data race over a single shared variable can happen. The *DiningPhilosophers* case study is a simple program (3 classes) implementing the problem of dining philosophers with a possibility of a deadlock. Finally, our last case study, *Crawler*, is a part of an older version of an IBM production software (containing 19 classes) with a data race manifesting more rarely and further in the execution. All the tests were performed on a machine with 2 Dual-Core AMD Opteron processors at 2.8GHz.

First, we measured the slowdown of program executions when recording various types of events. When recording all the possible types of events mentioned above, the slowdown was about 30-40 %. When recording only thread and memory-access-related events, the slowdown was just about 20-30 % but the number of corresponding paths found by JPF increased by about 50 %. Note, however, that the slowdown depends a lot on the structure of a program.

Next, we performed a series of tests in which we measured how often a real error is identified when replaying a trace and performing bounded model checking (BMC) in its vicinity. We let JPF to always backtrack 3 states from the state before a suspicious event and to use the maximum BMC depth of 10. The results are shown in Table 1. We distinguish whether 1 or up to 5 paths corresponding to the recorded trace were explored, using either DFS or BFS. For each of these settings and each case study, the left part of Table 1 gives the percentage of recorded traces based on which a real error

Table 1. Finding real errors in traces produced by Eraser

No. of traces	Error discovery ratio (traces found / BMC runs)				Time/memory consumption (sec/MB)			
	DFS		BFS		DFS		BFS	
	1	5	1	5	1	5	1	5
Bank	46%(1/1)	49%(2/2)	46%(1/1)	46%(2/2)	2/517	4/633	3/522	5/659
Airlines	100%(1/1)	100%(1/1)	100%(1/1)	100%(1/1)	1/482	1/482	1/482	1/482
DinPhil	100%(1/1)	100%(1/1)	100%(1/1)	100%(1/1)	11/417	20/411	20/414	22/413
Crawler	7%(0.8/15)	7%(1.8/34)	2%(0.5/49)	2%(1.2/50)	122/1312	268/1479	311/2857	321/3020

Table 2. Efficiency of finding errors using DFS in traces of Crawler produced by AtomRace

Traces searched

No. of backtracked states / Max depth of BMC					
	3/10	5/15	10/30	15/45	20/60
1	66%	71%	78%	84%	90%
5	71%	73%	80%	85%	90%

	Max depth of bounded model checking					
States	30	40	50	60	70	80
10	78%(0)	78%(1)	78%(3)	-	-	-
20	-	90%(0)	-	90%(2)	90%(2)	90%(2)
30	-	-	92%(2)	-	94%(0)	-
40	-	-	-	-	-	89%(5)

was found. Further, in brackets, it is shown how many corresponding paths were on average found by JPF for a single trace, and how many times BMC was on average applied when analysing a single trace. The right part of Table 1 then gives the corresponding time and memory consumption. Clearly, BFS has higher time and memory requirements than DFS (mainly because it performs significantly more runs of BMC). It is also less successful in finding an error if the error manifests later in the execution (like in Crawler). It can also be seen that the number of corresponding paths searched has a little contribution to the overall success of finding a real error.

The low percentage of real errors found in traces of Crawler is mostly due to the number of false alarms produced by Eraser that were eliminated by DA-BMC, which nicely illustrates one of the main advantages of using DA-BMC. Further, note that classical model checking as offered by JPF did not find any error in this case since it ran of our deadline of 8 hours (DFS) or ran out of the 24GB of memory available to JPF (BFS). To analyse how successful DA-BMC is in finding real errors in traces recorded in Crawler and how the success ratio depends on the various settings of DA-BMC, we have then done experiments with traces recorded using the AtomRace analysis, which does not produce any false alarms. The results can be seen in Table 2. Its left part shows how the percentage of real errors found depends on the number of explored paths corresponding to the recorded trace, the number of states backtracked from the state before a suspicious event, and the maximum BMC depth. The right part analyses in more detail how the percentage depends on the number of backtracked states and the maximum BMC depth (a single path corresponding to a recorded trace is analysed). The numbers in brackets express the percentage of replays which reached a 10 minute timeout. We can see that while increasing the number of searched corresponding paths has some influence on the error detection, it is evident that the BMC settings have a much greater impact. Moreover, the number of backtracked states increases the chances to find an error much more than the increased maximum depth of BMC.

6   Conclusion

We have presented DA-BMC—a tool chain combining dynamic analysis and bounded model checking for finding errors in concurrent Java programs (and also for debugging them). We have demonstrated on several case studies that DA-BMC allows one to combine the lower price of dynamic analysis with the higher precision of model checking.

References

1. Baier, C., Katoen, J.-P.: Principles of Model Checking. MIT Press (2008)
2. Edelstein, O., Farchi, E., Goldin, E., Nir, Y., Ratsaby, G., Ur, S.: Framework for Testing Multi-threaded Java Programs. Concurrency and Computation: Pract. and Exp. 15(3-5) (2003)
3. Hrubá, V., Křena, B., Vojnar, T.: Self-healing Assurance Based on Bounded Model Checking. In: Moreno-Díaz, R., Pichler, F., Quesada-Arencibia, A. (eds.) EUROCAST 2009. LNCS, vol. 5717, pp. 295–303. Springer, Heidelberg (2009)
4. Křena, B., Letko, Z., Nir-Buchbinder, Y., Tzoref-Brill, R., Ur, S., Vojnar, T.: A Concurrency Testing Tool and Its Plug-Ins for Dynamic Analysis and Runtime Healing. In: Bensalem, S., Peled, D.A. (eds.) RV 2009. LNCS, vol. 5779, pp. 101–114. Springer, Heidelberg (2009)
5. Visser, W., Havelund, K., Brat, G., Park, S., Lerda, F.: Model Checking Programs. Automated Software Engineering Journal 10(2) (2003)
6. Savage, S., Burrows, M., Nelson, G., Sobalvarro, P., Anderson, T.: Eraser: A Dynamic Data Race Detector for Multi-threaded Programs. In: Proc. of SOSP 1997. ACM Press (1997)

Monitoring Finite State Properties: Algorithmic Approaches and Their Relative Strengths

Rahul Purandare, Matthew B. Dwyer, and Sebastian Elbaum

Department of Computer Science and Engineering,
University of Nebraska - Lincoln, Lincoln NE 68588, USA
{rpuranda,dwyer,elbaum}@cse.unl.edu

Abstract. Monitoring complex applications to detect violations from specified properties is a promising field that has seen the development of many novel techniques and tools in the last decade. In spite of this effort, limiting, understanding, and predicting the cost of monitoring has been a challenge. Existing techniques primarily target the overhead caused by the large number of monitor instances to be maintained and the large number of events generated by the program that are related to the property. However, other factors, in particular, the algorithm used to process the sequence of events can significantly influence runtime overhead. In this work, we describe three basic algorithmic approaches to finite state monitoring and distill some of their relative strengths by conducting preliminary studies. The results of the studies reveal non-trivial differences in runtime overhead when using different monitoring algorithms that can inform future work.

1 Introduction

Over the past decade, researchers have developed a number of finite state monitoring techniques and implemented those techniques in tools that can be used to analyze large complex applications [2, 3, 5, 7–9, 12, 13]. These tools typically model sequencing properties as finite state automata (FSA) and check whether a program satisfies them during runtime. When monitoring programs, the property FSA must be *bound* to data values. For example, monitoring a property that expresses the legal sequencing of calls on a Java class requires that the value of the receiver object be used to correlate calls – a call on one instance of the class is generally independent of calls on other instances of the class. For each collection of objects that is related to a property an instance of a *monitor* is created and all subsequent calls on those objects generate *events* that are routed to track the state of the monitor, based on the FSA, and detect property violations.

In spite of the progress made in the field of runtime monitoring, there exist programs for which monitoring with respect to certain properties incurs significant runtime overhead which hinders the application of monitoring in practice [14]. The overhead of monitoring is strongly dependent on both the number of monitors that are created and the number of events generated by the program execution. These quantities can vary significantly with the program and property that are monitored [14, 16].

S. Khurshid and K. Sen (Eds.): RV 2011, LNCS 7186, pp. 381–395, 2012.

Holding program and property constant reveals that the choice of monitoring algorithm can influence monitoring overhead. Monitoring pmd for the property FailSafeIter using the algorithm in Tracematches [1] yields an overhead of 175%, which is essentially equivalent to the overhead incurred when using Java-MOP [8]. Switching the property to hasNext, for the same program, results in a significant reduction in overhead using the Tracematches algorithm, to 52%, whereas the overhead using JavaMOP rises to 191% [14]. If we now switch the program to bloat, while keeping the property hasNext, the story changes. Tracematches incurs an overhead of 2452% compared to an overhead of 1112% for JavaMOP [14]. The relative advantage of monitoring algorithms, with respect to overhead, can vary significantly with the program execution and property.

Generating a complete characterization of the cost of runtime monitoring algorithms is extremely difficult since the details of programs, properties, algorithm implementation decisions, and platform details can interact in subtle but important ways. In this paper, we take a more modest approach. Inspired by the recent work in data race detection [11], we seek to hold platform and implementation details constant while exploring the relative strengths of the basic algorithmic approaches to monitoring finite-state properties.

We explore two well-studied algorithmic approaches and one new approach. *Object-based* monitoring, as implemented by JavaMOP, maintains sets of monitors associated with class instances related to the property in question. *State-based* monitoring, as implemented by Tracematches, maintains sets of monitors associated with each state of the property FSA. *Symbol-based* monitoring, which is an extension of our adaptive online monitoring [10], maintains a set of monitors relevant to each symbol of the property FSA.

The main contributions of this paper are four-fold. First, we introduce a new algorithmic approach to monitoring finite-state properties (Section 2.3). Second, we provide a simplified presentation of algorithms that have been used to implement state-of-art monitoring tools, which allows comparison of the essential attributes that govern their performance. Third, we present the results of a preliminary study performed that highlights the comparative strengths of finite-state monitoring algorithms (Section 3). This study uses custom-built implementations of the algorithms that minimize differences in implementation details, such as indexing data structures, to promote comparability across algorithms (Section 3.1). Fourth, we analyze factors related to the monitored program and property and the algorithms themselves that appear to explain the relative effectiveness of monitoring algorithms (Section 3.3). We begin with a detailed presentation of algorithms for monitoring finite-state properties.

2   Monitoring Approaches

A finite-state property can be encoded as an FSA, $\phi = (S, \Sigma, \delta, s_0, A)$ where: S is a set of states, Σ is the alphabet of symbols, $s_0 \in S$ is the initial state, $A \subseteq S$ are the accepting states and $\delta : (S \times \Sigma) \rightarrow S$ is the state transition function. Let O denote the set of objects created in the program that are related to property ϕ

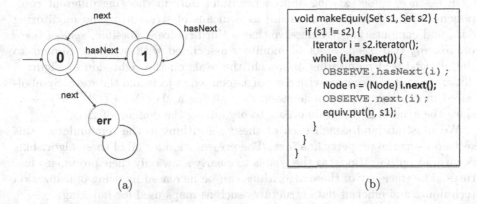

```
void makeEquiv(Set s1, Set s2) {
    if (s1 != s2) {
        Iterator i = s2.iterator();
        while (i.hasNext()) {
            OBSERVE.hasNext(i);
            Node n = (Node) i.next();
            OBSERVE.next(i);
            equiv.put(n, s1);
        }
    }
}
```

(a)   (b)

Fig. 1. (a) Property HasNext and (b) a fragment of code showing usage of the property

and 2^O the powerset of those objects. To simplify the following explanation, let us assume that the order of objects involved in an event does not matter. Thus, all approaches to runtime monitoring record a monitoring relation $M: 2^O \times S$.

Program statements that are related to ϕ are mapped, through instrumentation, to an event whose type is $2^O \times \Sigma$. For example, Figure 1(a) represents the iterator property HasNext, that specifies that a call to next() must be preceded by a call to hasNext(). When the instrumentation OBSERVE.hasNext(i) executes it generates an event $(\{i\}, hasNext)$ reflecting the fact that iterator i has had a hasNext() call performed on it.

The key functionality of runtime monitoring of finite-state properties involves processing the event to update the appropriate state components of the monitoring relation. In essence, monitoring implements a variant of δ that is enriched to include the relevant objects as a parameter, i.e., $\Delta: (2^O \times S \times \Sigma) \to S$. Algorithms for monitoring can be viewed as different strategies for implementing Δ — more specifically how computation over the domain of Δ is organized.

JavaMOP uses an *object-based monitoring* approach which defines a monitor as a set of related objects and a state of the FSA. The ovals on the right side of each subfigure in Figure 2 illustrate a set of monitors with a set of associated objects on the top, e.g., $\{i1\}$, and the state on the bottom, e.g., 0. Note that there may be more than one object associated with a monitor. Object-based monitoring can be understood as realizing a $\Delta_O: 2^O \to ((S \times \Sigma) \to S)$ which curries the 2^O parameter of Δ to reflect the fact that objects are the primary key to organizing the domain of Δ.

Tracematches uses a *state-based monitoring* approach which defines for each state of the property FSA a set of monitors each of which records a set of related objects. The rectangles on the lower parts of Figure 4 illustrate a set of monitors, depicted as ovals, each consisting of a set of objects, e.g., $\{i1\}$. State-based monitoring can be understood as realizing a $\Delta_S: S \to ((2^O \times \Sigma) \to S)$ since the state is the primary key to organizing the domain of Δ.

In essence, these existing approaches differ only in choosing different components of the domain of Δ to use as a means of structuring the monitoring data and computation. We observe that a third choice is possible, *symbol-based monitoring* that keeps a set of monitors associated with symbols. Similar to the object-based monitoring approach, the ovals on the right side of Figure 5 illustrate a set of monitors with a set of associated objects and the state. Symbol-based monitoring can be understood as realizing a $\Delta_\Sigma\colon \Sigma \to ((2^O \times S) \to S)$ since the symbol is the primary key to organizing the domain of Δ.

We illustrate and sketch each of these algorithms in the remainder of this section using the property HasNext. The presentation for all of these algorithms is without optimizations, as the goal is to clearly show only their prominent features. The efficiency of these algorithms can be increased by using optimization techniques and efficient data structures such as maps used for indexing.

Monitor Indexing. The state-of-art monitoring tools [3, 8] support monitor indexing for efficiently locating the set of monitors that need to be updated when a program event is generated; events include information on a set of related program objects and they are used to "lookup" the set of monitors. An indexing scheme groups objects that are related to a common symbol. A map that holds the related objects as keys, is then used to locate associated monitors. Current tools typically use multi-level maps where each map provides access to the next level by using exactly one object as a key. Monitors associated with the objects used to access them are located at the leaf nodes of such an *index-tree*. Alternatively, multi-key maps may be used where all the related objects together form a single key. An object-based monitoring tool such as JavaMOP includes support for all symbols for indexing. A state-based tool like Tracematches may permit at most a single index tree at every state that is formed by the intersection of the sets of objects associated with outgoing symbols with the variables that are guaranteed to be bound in that state. The reason for this difference is that a state-based tool may need to move monitors from one indexing structure to another depending on state transitions, and this monitor movement is expensive. The indexing options can be *enabled* or *disabled* in the tools. Since indexing is standard in object-based monitoring we include it in our presentation, but for the remaining algorithms we elide the details of indexing for clarity. In the study in Section 3, all of our algorithm implementations use an equivalent indexing scheme and implementation.

Matching Approach. The trace of events generated by a program can be matched against the FSA specification using two different approaches. In *complete* matching the trace is tested for membership in the language of the FSA. If the property FSA represents a legal behavior, then a violation can be detected before the program terminates, if a trace prefix cannot be extended to an accepting trace. On the other hand, if the property FSA represents an illegal behavior, then a violation can be detected, if a trace prefix can be extended to a matching trace. Alternatively, FSA properties can also be specified using *suffix* matching. These

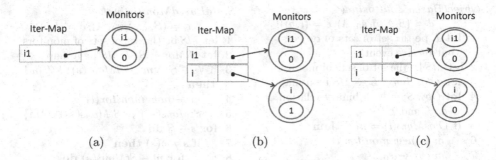

Fig. 2. Example of Object-based Monitoring: (a) Before the generation of a creation event ({i}, hasNext); (b) After the generation of a creation event ({i}, hasNext); (c) After the generation of event ({i}, next);

properties are supposed to hold beginning at any point in the program trace. The algorithms presented in this section focus on complete matching, but can support suffix matching with minor modifications [15].

2.1 Object-Based Monitoring

Figure 2 illustrates a generic object-based monitoring scheme for complete matching that is tool-independent. Figure 2(a) shows an example of the monitoring data structures before the execution of a hasNext() call. The call generates a monitoring *event* $e = (l, b)$, where l in this case is $\{i\}$, and b is the FSA symbol hasNext. The scheme provides a map, keyed by sets of related objects that have been involved in previous events. Property HasNext has only one type of object associated. In practice, there may be properties that have multiple objects associated and for efficiency reasons, multiple maps may be provided. The values corresponding to the keys are sets of monitors that are associated with the objects. In this case these sets will be singleton, because there can only be one monitor associated with any iterator object. The value sets have been shown by dots and the corresponding set members have been shown by the arrows originating from the dots.

Figure 2(b) shows the situation after the scheme handles the first hasNext event. Since no monitors are associated with the newly created object referenced by the iterator variable i, a new monitor is created and references to it are associated with the new key $\{i\}$.

Figure 2(c) shows how a subsequent next event, which is triggered by a call to i.next(), is handled. The monitor associated with i in the map is retrieved. For each such monitor, an FSA transition is simulated to update the state. In this example, the monitor associated with i was previously in state 1 so it is updated to $\delta(1, \text{next}) = 0$ based on the FSA in Figure 1(a).

An algorithm for object-based monitoring is sketched in the left part of Figure 3. Lines 5–7 handle the creation of new monitors which are initialized to the FSA start state. This is only performed if no map entries exist for the associated objects. Lines 8–10 add the new monitor to the sets of monitors that are

ObjectBasedMonitoring(
$$\phi = (S, \Sigma, \delta, s_0, A), e = (l, b))$$

1 **let** L be the set of sets of objects that receive events.

2 **let** MS be the set of sets of monitors.

3 **let** $ObjsMons : L \rightarrow MS$ be a map.

4 **let** $ObjsSym$ be a binary relation over L and Σ.

5 **if** $ObjsMons(l) = null$ **then**

6     $m \leftarrow new\ monitor(l)$

7     $m.cur \leftarrow s_0$

8   **for** $l' \subseteq l$ **do**

9   **if** $\exists \sigma \in \Sigma : (l', \sigma) \in ObjsSym$ **then**

10           $ObjsMons(l') \leftarrow ObjsMons(l') \cup \{m\}$

11 $ms \leftarrow ObjsMons(l)$

12 **for** $m \in ms$ **do**

13     $m.cur \leftarrow \delta(m.cur, b)$

14 **if** $m.cur = err$ **then**

15   **report error**

StateBasedMonitoring(
$$\phi = (S, \Sigma, \delta, s_0, A), e = (l, b))$$

1 **let** MS be the set of sets of monitors

2 **let** $StMons : S \rightarrow MS$ be a map

3 **if** $\forall s \in S : \forall m \in StMons(s) : l \not\subseteq m.l$ **then**

4     $m \leftarrow new\ monitor(l)$

5     $StMons(s_0) \leftarrow StMons(s_0) \cup \{m\}$

6 **for** $s \in S$ **do**

7   **if** $s \neq \delta(s)$ **then**

8   **for** $m \in StMons(s)$ **do**

9   **if** $l \subseteq m.l$ **then**

10              $StMons(s) \leftarrow StMons(s) - \{m\}$

11              $StMons(\delta(s)) \leftarrow StMons(\delta(s)) \cup \{m\}$

12   **if** $\delta(s) = err$ **then**

13   **report error**

Fig. 3. Object-based Monitoring (left) and State-based Monitoring (right)

associated with each subset of l that may witness a future event. Finally, lines 11–13 simulate FSA transitions for the states in every monitor associated with the objects involved in the event. If any of the monitors goes to the error state an error is reported as shown by lines 14–15.

2.2 State-Based Monitoring

Figure 4 illustrates a generic and tool-independent state-based monitoring scheme for complete matching for the same property and program fragment that was shown in the earlier example. Monitoring is performed over a single copy of the property FSA. A set of monitors are associated with each state and those monitors are moved between states based on the events encountered and δ.

Figure 4(a) shows the situation just before the execution of a call to `hasNext()`. The monitoring system searches for monitors associated with i by querying the sets associated with each FSA state. It fails to find any monitor, so it creates a new monitor, which consists of just the objects (in this case only the object referenced by i), and adds it to the set associated with state $\delta(0, \text{hasNext}) = 1$, where state 0 is the FSA start state. The result is shown in Figure 4(b). Lines 3–5 in the right part of Figure 3, which sketches a basic state-based monitoring algorithm, describe the monitor creation steps in detail.

Figure 4(c) shows how the subsequent `next` event is handled. The monitor sets for each state are searched, lines 6–9 in the algorithm, to find monitors involving i. This results in an instance $\{i\}$ at state 1 being found. The monitor

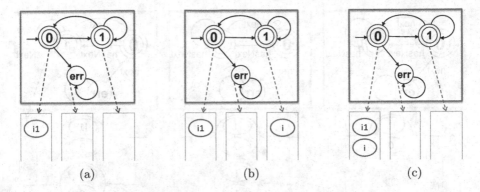

Fig. 4. Example of State-based Monitoring without Monitor Indexing: (a) Before the generation of a creation event ({i}, hasNext); (b) After the generation of a creation event ({i}, hasNext); (c) After the generation of event ({i}, next);

is then moved to the appropriate state depending on the encountered symbol as shown in lines 10–11. In the example, this causes the monitors to be removed from state 1's set and added to the set for $\delta(0, \text{next}) = 0$. Line 7 skips the move for self-loop[1] transitions. Lines 12–13 show that if the target state is the error state an error is reported.

2.3   Symbol-Based Monitoring

Monitors need to be tracked, that is, their states need to be updated, only for the symbols that change their states. In other words, a monitoring tool can exploit the property structure by skipping the symbols that result in self-loops. In this section, we present a symbol-based monitoring approach that would use symbol-specific monitor pools to organize monitors based on their states. We illustrate our approach with an example.

Figure 5 illustrates a symbol-based monitoring scheme that maintains a pool of monitors for every symbol, in this case hasNext and next. Figure 5(a) shows a snapshot of the monitoring data structures just before the execution of a hasNext() call. The monitor corresponding to object reference $i1$ is already present and since it is in state 0, both of the monitor pools are holding references to it. This is because neither of the symbols self-loop in this state. After observing symbol hasNext(), the monitor tool realizes that no monitor exists for this reference and the object reference has not been seen previously as indicated by the set $TrackedObjs$. Hence, as shown in Figure 5(b), a new monitor is created and is pushed to state $\delta(0, \text{hasNext}) = 1$. Since only the next symbol is active in this state, the new monitor is added only in the pool associated with the symbol next. Finally, after receiving the next call, the new monitor is pushed back to

---

[1] In this paper, we use the term self-loop to refer to the cycles of length 1 and the term loop to refer to the cycles of length greater than 1.

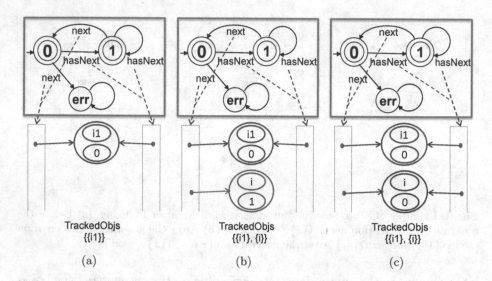

Fig. 5. Example of Symbol-based Monitoring without Monitor Indexing: (a) Before the generation of a creation event ({i}, hasNext); (b) After the generation of a creation event ({i}, hasNext); (c) After the generation of event ({i}, next);

state $\delta(1, \text{next}) = 0$ and as shown in Figure 5(c), it is added to back to both of the monitor pools as both of the symbols are active in state 0.

Lines 7–9 in Figure 6, which sketches a symbol-based monitoring algorithm, describe the monitor creation steps. The newly created monitor is then added to the pools associated with all non-self-looping symbols as described by lines 10–11. A set *TrackedObjs* is maintained to keep track of objects that have been monitored so far. This set is maintained because a monitor moved to a *trap* state, that is a state in which all symbols self-loop, may be removed from all the maps, in which case the monitoring tool may fail to infer whether the monitor was moved to a trap state or the objects involved in the event never had any associated monitor. The tool needs to create a new monitor for the latter case, but not for the former. Lines 12–14 describe updating this set for all relevant sets of objects related to the event. In the example, it is the singleton set $\{i\}$ as shown in Figure 5(b). Alternatively, the set may only keep track of objects that were moved to a trap state. A map *OutTrans* keeps a set of non-self-looping symbols for every state.

Lines 17–25 describe the steps in performing a transition on associated monitors corresponding to an observed symbol. As described by lines 19–20, an error is reported if any of the monitors moves to the error state. Lines 21–25 describe a loop that ensures that the monitor is added only to the pools corresponding to non-self-looping transitions and deleted from all other pools.

The adaptive online analysis [10] can be seen as a variant of symbol-based monitoring approach, that drops the symbol instrumentation dynamically when there are *no* monitors interested in the symbol. Compared to that approach,

$SymbolBasedMonitoring(\phi = (S, \Sigma, \delta, s_0, A), e = (l, b))$

1 **let** L be the set of sets of objects that receive events.
2 **let** $TrackedObjs$ be the set of related sets of tracked objects.
3 **let** MS be the set of sets of monitors.
4 **let** $OutTrans : S \rightarrow 2^\Sigma$ be a map.
5 **let** $AssocObjs : \Sigma \times L \rightarrow L$ be a map.
6 **let** $SymMons : \Sigma \rightarrow MS$ be a map.
7 **if** $(\forall m \in SymMons(b): l \not\subseteq m.l) \land (l \notin TrackedObjs)$ **then**
8      $m \leftarrow new\ monitor(l)$
9      $m.cur \leftarrow s_0$
10   **if** $b \in OutTrans(s_0)$ **then**
11         $SymMons(b) \leftarrow SymMons(b) \cup \{m\}$
12   **for** $l' \subseteq l$ **do**
13   **if** $\exists \sigma \in \Sigma : AssocObjs(\sigma, l) \neq \emptyset$
14             $TrackedObjs \leftarrow TrackedObjs \cup l'$
15 $ms \leftarrow SymMons(b)$
16 **for** $m \in ms$ **do**
17   **if** $l \subseteq m.l$ **then**
18         $m.cur \leftarrow \delta(m.cur, b)$
19   **if** $m.cur = err$ **then**
20   report error
21   **for** $\sigma \in \Sigma$ **do**
22   **if** $\sigma \in OutTrans(m.cur)$ **then**
23                 $SymMons(\sigma) \leftarrow SymMons(\sigma) \cup \{m\}$
24   **else**
25                 $SymMons(\sigma) \leftarrow SymMons(\sigma) - \{m\}$

Fig. 6. Algorithm for Symbol-based Monitoring

the approach presented in this section is more light-weight in that it does not need any additional infrastructure or dynamic instrumentation. Unlike stutter-equivalent loop transformation technique [16], this optimization comes with a non-zero but small cost for referencing. However, an update corresponding to *non-self-looping* transitions could be expensive depending on the number of associated monitors and symbols. Moreover, it may only optimize self-loops and not any arbitrary loops of length greater than one. However, it can optimize repeating symbols irrespective of their source in the program. In addition, it does not incur an extra cost of expensive static program analysis as it only needs to analyze the property structure.

3   Relative Strengths of Monitoring Algorithms

The approaches presented in Section 2 differ mainly in the way the monitors are organized, accessed and manipulated. Those differences provide the approaches their inherent strengths and weaknesses. In this section, we first present a preliminary study performed to understand those strengths and weaknesses. We then interpret the results with the help of the algorithms presented in Section 2.

Table 1. Finite-state properties. Self-loops over the trap state are not considered.

No.	Name	Regular Expression	#Obj	#St	#Sym	Loop	Self
1	FailSafeIter	$create\ next^*update^+next$	2	5	3	✗	✓
2	HasNext	$(hasNext^+next)^*hasNext$	1	3	2	✓	✓
3	Writer	$create(writeW|writeO)^*$ $(closeW|closeO)^+(writeW|writeO)$	2	5	3	✗	✓
4	SafeSyncCol	$(sync\ asyncCreateIter)|$ $(sync\ syncCreateIter\ accessIter)$	2	5	3	✗	✗

3.1   Evaluation

Artifacts. We selected 4 properties for monitoring, namely, FailSafeIter, Has-Next, Writer and SafeSyncCol as described in Table 1. The FailSafeIter property ensures that a collection is not updated while it is iterated. The Writer property checks that a Writer is not used after it or its OutputStream is closed. The SafeSyncCol property specifies that a non-synchronized iterator should not be created for a synchronized collection and if a synchronized iterator is created, it should not be accessed in an unsynchronized way. These properties have been used and described in previous work [6, 14, 16]. All of the selected properties except HasNext are multi-object properties that involve 2 types of objects. None of the properties except HasNext have loops of length greater than 1. All of the properties except SafeSyncCol have self-loops, however, even SafeSyncCol has a self-loop if we consider the trap state.

Also following the same previous work, we selected the bloat and pmd benchmarks from DaCapo version 2006-10 [4] since they were found to incur overhead of at least 5% for at least one of the selected properties[2]. In addition, we used JGraphT version 0.8.1, a Java open source graph manipulation library consisting of 172 classes, and monitored the load test supplied with the release for the selected properties, repeating a previous experimental setup [16].

Monitor Implementation. We used JavaMOP 2.1 to build an object-based monitor for each of the 4 properties. We developed the state-based and the symbol-based monitors for the properties by using the aspect generated by JavaMOP 2.1 as a baseline and then making minimal changes that were essential to encode the algorithmic differences. This allowed us to use the same pointcuts and supporting data structures. JavaMOP implements an efficient indexing scheme to provide faster access to monitors. Using the same map data structures used by JavaMOP, we provided indexing support to the state-based and symbol-based monitors, which ensured that no approach gets an undue advantage in monitor retrieval due to differences in the indexing data structures. To limit the number of monitors that are moved during state updates, Tracematches provides only

---

[2] Executions times recorded when overheads were smaller than 5% were highly inconsistent so we did not consider such artifacts.

Table 2. Variation in the percentage runtime overheads caused by different combinations of programs, properties and approaches. The figures shown in the bold are minimum overheads for that combination.

No.	Property	Benchmark	Object-based	State-based	Symbol-based
1	FailSafeIter	bloat	764.6	695.8	**508.3**
2	FailSafeIter	pmd	39.1	32.6	**30.4**
3	FailSafeIter	jgrapht	106.5	117.8	**80.4**
4	HasNext	bloat	**283.3**	922.9	708.3
5	HasNext	pmd	**10.9**	28.3	21.7
6	HasNext	jgrapht	**21.7**	100.0	100.0
7	Writer	bloat	6.3	6.3	**4.2**
8	Writer	pmd	6.5	**0**	**0**
9	Writer	jgrapht	-	-	-
10	SafeSyncCol	bloat	**939.6**	1179.4	981.3
11	SafeSyncCol	pmd	**39.1**	41.3	41.3
12	SafeSyncCol	jgrapht	**108.7**	110.9	110.9

partial indexing support. While efficient for uni-object properties, this leads to significant inefficiencies for multi-object properties. In our implementation of state-based and symbol-based monitoring, we provide full indexing support which makes them comparable to object-based monitoring. These decisions allow us to eliminate differences due to implementation decisions and focus our study on the core algorithmic differences between approaches.

Measurements. DaCapo provides a standard means of recording runtimes — the converge option which repeatedly runs the program until the variation in execution time is within ±3%. We ran each benchmarks at least 6 times for every property and algorithm, and report the mean of the execution times after convergence. When the runs did not converge, we report the mean of the times taken by the warmup runs. JGraphT does not use the DaCapo infrastructure so, we ran the program 6 times for every property and approach and report the mean of the execution times. We used used ajc 1.6.8 to weave all of the monitors into the programs and compiled using JVM 1.6.0. All programs were run on an Opteron 250 running CentOS 5.2 using the JVM 1.6.0 with 14 GB of heap available. All the data report is in terms of percentage overhead relative to execution of the program without monitoring.

3.2   Results

Table 2 shows the percentage overheads incurred by various benchmark and property combinations for all of the three monitoring approaches.

For the property FailSafeIter, the symbol-based monitoring approach incurs the lowest overhead independently of the program. We conjecture that this is due to the presence of self-loops in the property that are frequently executed.

Self-loops allow both symbol and state-based monitoring approaches very efficiently process events, as we discus below. Moreover, this property has no loops that transit multiple states. This ensures that every monitor performs only a small number of state transitions — bounded by the total number of states — which avoids significant degradation in performance of symbol and state-based monitoring due to state changes. The difference between state and symbol-based approaches is related to the fact that state-based must perform a lookup at every property state per event, whereas symbol-based needs to perform only two lookups per event, that include one in the associated symbol map and the other in the `TrackedObjs` set. The pair FailSafeIter and jgrapht breaks the overall trend in that state-based monitoring performs worse than object-based monitoring. A more detailed analysis reveals that for this program there is a single monitor associated with each Collection object which reduces the advantage of state-based due to self-loop processing to the point where object-based is cheaper.

For the property HasNext, we conjecture that state and symbol-based monitoring suffer due to the frequent change of monitor states which is a costly operation under these algorithms. Since object-based monitoring processes every event the same way, state change or not, it performs better. We note that HasNext does have a self-loop, yet it is only executed when the program performs consecutive calls to `hasNext()`, which is quite rare. This shows that property structure alone, e.g., whether it has a self-loop, is not sufficient for predicting an algorithm's performance. The pattern of program generated event traces and how they drive FSA transitions must be considered as well.

The property Writer is similar in structure to FailSafeIter but its events are less common so it incurs in much smaller overhead. Here again, symbol-based monitoring incurs the lowest overhead. One interesting aspect of this property are the disjunctions of symbols, e.g., $writeW|writeO$ at a state lead to the same state. Generally more symbols will lead to worse performance for a symbol-based algorithm. While our implementation forgoes any optimizations, it is easy to calculate equivalence classes of symbols with respect to δ and modify event generating instrumentation to use a single representative symbol for each class to further reduce overhead.

The property SafeSyncCol has neither loops nor self-loops. This means that the symbol-based and state-based approaches do not have an advantage over the object-based approach. The data shows that, as expected, object-based monitoring performs well since it is insensitive to the number of states and the number of symbols — factors that impact the cost of the other approaches.

3.3   Factors Impacting Overhead

For a given program and property, clearly the number of events and monitors will strongly influence overhead. Based on the results of our study, however, we hypothesize that additional factors can influence the relative advantages of different monitoring algorithms. Specifically we believe these factors to be important: i) the presence of property loops of length greater than 1, ii) the presence of property self-loops, iii) the number of monitors associated with related objects

Table 3. Factors impacting performance

Approach	Loops	Self-loops	#Mon	#St	#Sym
Object-based Monitoring	-	-	✗	-	-
State-based Monitoring	✗	✓	?	✗	-
Symbol-based Monitoring	✗	✓	?	-	✗

for multi-object properties, iv) the number of property automaton states, and v) the number of property symbols. The first three factors are related to the interaction of program execution and property structure, whereas the last two are purely related to property structure.

Table 3 summarizes how the factors may impact the monitoring performance for various approaches. In the table, - indicates that the factor has limited impact, ✓ indicates that the impact may be significant and favorable and ✗ indicates that the impact may be significant and unfavorable. ? indicates that the impact of this factor depends on other factors, as explained below.

We conjecture that state and symbol-based monitoring will perform poorly if the states are changed frequently which can only happen when loops exist in the property. For both of these approaches, a state change is an expensive operation which may either involve locating and moving monitors to another state as shown by lines 7–11 in Figure 3 for the state-based monitoring and by lines 16–25 in Figure 6 for the symbol-based monitoring. Both approaches can, however, efficiently handle self-loops since no map operation except a lookup is required. This is shown by the condition on line 7 in Figure 3 and line 15 in Figure 6 that retrieves a set of only those monitors that change their state for the observed symbol, when indexing is provided. In contrast, the object-based monitoring is less sensitive to loops or self-loops as all the events are handled uniformly irrespective of a state change.

Multi-object properties may associate more than one monitor with an object involved in an event. Handling such an event requires accessing all of those monitors and performing a transition on each one of them. This means that the work performed in handling an event would be proportional to the number of associated monitors for the object-based monitoring as shown by line 11 in Figure 3 that retrieves all the associated monitors and then performs a transition on each one of them as shown by lines 12–13. However, for the state-based monitoring and the symbol-based monitoring, this cost could be either low or high depending on whether the transitions are *self-looping* in which case all of them would be skipped or they change monitor states respectively.

The cost of monitor lookup in the case of state-based monitoring is proportional to the number of states as described in line 6 in Figure 3. Similarly, for the symbol-based monitoring approach, the cost of state transition requires removing monitors from current pools and adding to the pools depending on the non-self-looping symbols as described in lines 21–25 in Figure 6. In the worst

Table 4. Percentage runtime overheads when monitoring multiple properties

Properties	bloat			pmd			jgrapht		
	Obj	State	Sym	Obj	State	Sym	Obj	State	Sym
All	**2043.8**	2795.8	2177.3	73.9	95.7	**63.0**	187	267.4	**163**
FSI,W,SSC	1710.4	1931.3	**1306.3**	65.2	69.6	**47.8**	169.6	182.6	**104.3**
FSI,W	768.8	664.6	**491.7**	39.1	32.6	**23.9**	106.5	113	**82.7**

case, this number may reach the total number of symbols to be manipulated. Hence, the cost of handling an event may grow in proportion to the number of symbols in the case of the symbol-based monitoring.

Multiple Properties. It is evident from these results that some properties would be more favorable to some approaches if the properties possess certain attributes, including the presence of loops and self-loops that can be exercised by a program. To understand the overall impact of these factors on the performance of the approaches, we combined the properties in different ways and monitored the programs. The results are available in Table 4.

The first row corresponds to the case when we combined all four properties. Since this combination includes properties that are favorable to symbol-based and properties that are favorable to object-based monitoring, the lowest overhead approach depends on the program. Dropping HasNext leaves just one property on which object-based performed best. Row two reports the results on that combination with symbol-based achieving the lowest overhead on both programs. Row three result is no surprise, since it retains just the properties that were favorable to symbol-based monitoring.

4   Conclusion and Future Work

We have provided a uniform presentation of three algorithmic approaches to finite state runtime monitoring, including the symbol-based monitoring which has not been implemented yet by any state-of-art monitoring tools. Our analysis and preliminary study of these approaches revealed some of their relatives strengths and weaknesses in different program and properties contexts. Further studies are needed to provide more evidence on whether the relationships between properties and program attributes, and the relative strength and weaknesses of the approaches hold in general. Equipped with this information, we plan to explore whether additional static or dynamic program analyses might be used to predict when a specific monitoring approach or combination of approaches would yield the best performance.

Acknowledgments. This material is based in part upon work supported by Air Force Office of Scientific Research under Award #9550-10-1-0406, and #9550-09-1-0687. We would like to thank Eric Bodden and Pavel Avgustinov for providing clarification on some issues related to Tracematches.

References

1. Allan, C., Avgustinov, P., Christensen, A.S., Hendren, L., Kuzins, S., Lhoták, O., de Moor, O., Sereni, D., Sittampalam, G., Tibble, J.: Adding trace matching with free variables to AspectJ. In: Conference on Object-oriented Programming, Systems, Languages, and Applications, pp. 345–364 (2005)
2. Arnold, M., Vechev, M., Yahav, E.: QVM: an efficient runtime for detecting defects in deployed systems. In: Conference on Object-Oriented Programming Systems, Languages, and Applications, pp. 143–162 (2008)
3. Avgustinov, P., Tibble, J., de Moor, O.: Making trace monitors feasible. In: Conference on Object-Oriented Programming Systems, Languages, and Applications, pp. 589–608 (2007)
4. Blackburn, S.M., Garner, R., Hoffman, C., Khan, A.M., McKinley, K.S., Bentzur, R., Diwan, A., Feinberg, D., Frampton, D., Guyer, S.Z., Hirzel, M., Hosking, A., Jump, M., Lee, H., Moss, J.E.B., Phansalkar, A., Stefanović, D., VanDrunen, T., von Dincklage, D., Wiedermann, B.: The DaCapo benchmarks: Java benchmarking development and analysis. In: Conference on Object-Oriented Programming Systems, Languages, and Applications, pp. 169–190 (2006)
5. Bodden, E.: Efficient hybrid typestate analysis by determining continuation-equivalent states. In: International Conference on Software Engineering, pp. 5–14 (2010)
6. Bodden, E., Hendren, L., Lhoták, O.: A Staged Static Program Analysis to Improve the Performance of Runtime Monitoring. In: Bateni, M. (ed.) ECOOP 2007. LNCS, vol. 4609, pp. 525–549. Springer, Heidelberg (2007)
7. Chen, F., Roşu, G.: Java-MOP: A Monitoring Oriented Programming Environment for Java. In: Halbwachs, N., Zuck, L.D. (eds.) TACAS 2005. LNCS, vol. 3440, pp. 546–550. Springer, Heidelberg (2005)
8. Chen, F., Roşu, G.: Mop: an efficient and generic runtime verification framework. In: Conference on Object-Oriented Programming Systems, Languages, and Applications, pp. 569–588 (2007)
9. d'Amorim, M., Havelund, K.: Event-based runtime verification of Java programs. In: International Workshop on Dynamic Analysis, pp. 1–7 (2005)
10. Dwyer, M.B., Kinneer, A., Elbaum, S.: Adaptive online program analysis. In: International Conference on Software Engineering, pp. 220–229 (2007)
11. Flanagan, C., Freund, S.N.: FastTrack: efficient and precise dynamic race detection. In: Conference on Programming Language Design and Implementation, pp. 121–133 (2009)
12. Havelund, K., Roşu, G.: An overview of the runtime verification tool Java PathExplorer. Formal Methods in System Design 24(2), 189–215 (2004)
13. Kim, M., Viswanathan, M., Kannan, S., Lee, I., Sokolsky, O.V.: Java-MaC: A run-time assurance approach for Java programs. Formal Methods in System Design 24(2), 129–155 (2004)
14. Meredith, P., Jin, D., Chen, F., Roşu, G.: Efficient monitoring of parametric context-free patterns. Journal of Automated Software Engineering 17(2), 149–180 (2010)
15. Purandare, R.: Exploiting Program and Property Structure for Efficient Runtime Monitoring. PhD thesis, University of Nebraska-Lincoln (May 2011)
16. Purandare, R., Dwyer, M.B., Elbaum, S.: Monitor optimization via stutter-equivalent loop transformation. In: Conference on Object-Oriented Programming Systems, Languages, and Applications, pp. 270–285 (2010)

Unbounded Symbolic Execution
for Program Verification

Joxan Jaffar[1], Jorge A. Navas[1], and Andrew E. Santosa[2]

[1] National University of Singapore
{joxan,navas}@comp.nus.edu.sg
[2] University of Sydney, Australia
santosa@it.usyd.edu.au

Abstract. Symbolic execution with interpolation is emerging as an alternative to CEGAR for software verification. The performance of both methods relies critically on interpolation in order to obtain the most general abstraction of the current symbolic or abstract state which can be shown to remain error-free. CEGAR naturally handles unbounded loops because it is based on abstract interpretation. In contrast, symbolic execution requires a special extension for such loops.

In this paper, we present such an extension. Its main characteristic is that it performs *eager subsumption*, that is, it always attempts to perform abstraction in order to avoid exploring redundant symbolic states. It balances this primary desire for more abstraction with the secondary desire to maintain the *strongest loop invariant*, for earlier detection of infeasible paths, which entails less abstraction. Occasionally certain abstractions are not permitted because of the reachability of error states; this is the underlying mechanism which then causes *selective unrolling*, that is, the unrolling of a loop along relevant paths only.

1 Introduction

Symbolic execution [22] is a method for program reasoning that uses *symbolic values* as inputs instead of actual data, and it represents the values of program variables as symbolic expressions as functions of the input symbolic values. A *symbolic execution tree* depicts all executed paths during the symbolic execution. A *path condition* is maintained for each path and it is a formula over the symbolic inputs built by accumulating constraints which those inputs must satisfy in order for execution to follow that path. A path is *infeasible* if its path condition is unsatisfiable. Otherwise, the path is *feasible*.

Symbolic execution was first developed for program testing [22], but it has been subsequently used for bug finding [8] and verification condition generation [3,18], among others. Recently, symbolic execution has been used for software verification [21,24,15] as an alternative to existing model checking techniques based on *CounterExample-Guided Abstraction Refinement* (CEGAR) [9,2]. Essentially, the general technique followed by symbolic execution-like tools starts with the concrete model of the program and then, the model is checked for the desired property via *symbolic execution* by proving that all paths to certain error nodes are infeasible (i.e., error nodes are unreachable).

The first challenge for symbolic execution is the exponential number of symbolic paths. The approaches of [21,24,15] tackle successfully this fundamental problem by eliminating from the concrete model those facts which are *irrelevant* or *too-specific* for

S. Khurshid and K. Sen (Eds.): RV 2011, LNCS 7186, pp. 396–411, 2012.

(a)	(b)	(c)	(d)
ℓ_0 `x=0;`	ℓ_0 `lock=0;new=old+1;`	ℓ_0 `x=0;y=0;z=1;`	ℓ_0 `assume(y>=0);`
ℓ_1 `while(x < n) {`	ℓ_1 `while(new!=old) {`	ℓ_1 `while(*) {`	ℓ_1 `x=0;`
ℓ_2 `x++;`	ℓ_2 `lock=1;old=new;`	ℓ_2 `if(*)`	ℓ_2 `while(x < 10000) {`
ℓ_3 `}`	ℓ_3 `if(*){`	ℓ_3 `skip;`	ℓ_3 `y++;x++;`
ℓ_4 `if(x<0)`	ℓ_4 `lock=0;new++;}`	ℓ_4 `else`	ℓ_4 `}`
ℓ_{error} `error()`	ℓ_5 `}`	ℓ_5 `x++;,y++;`	ℓ_5 `if(y+x< 10000)`
ℓ_5	ℓ_6 `if(lock==0)`	ℓ_6 `foo();`	ℓ_{error} `error()`
	ℓ_{error} `error()`	ℓ_7 `x=x-y;`	ℓ_6
	ℓ_7	ℓ_8 `}`	
		ℓ_9 `if(z ` $\neq$ ` 1)`	
		ℓ_{error} `error()`	
		ℓ_{10}	

Fig. 1. Programs with Loops

proving the unreachability of the error nodes. This learning phase consists of computing *interpolants* in the same spirit of *nogood learning* in SAT solvers. Informally, an interpolant is a generalization of a set of states for splitting between "good" and "bad" states. The use of symbolic execution with interpolants is thus similar to CEGAR [16,23], but symbolic execution has some benefits [24]:

1. It does not explore *infeasible paths* avoiding the expensive refinement in CEGAR.
2. It avoids expensive *predicate image* computations of, for instance, the *Cartesian* [1,7] and *Boolean* [5] abstract domains.
3. It can recover from *too-specific* abstractions in opposition to monotonic refinement schemes often used in CEGAR.

The main remaining challenge for symbolic execution is due to unbounded loops which make the symbolic execution tree not just large, but *infinite*. This means that some *abstraction* must be performed on the symbolic states in order to obtain finiteness. Our previous work [21] assumed that loop invariants are inferred automatically by other means (e.g., abstract interpretation). The main disadvantage is the existence of false alarms. Another solution is proposed in [15] where abstraction refinement 'a la' CE-GAR is performed as a separate process for loops but lacking of the benefits of symbolic execution mentioned above. Finally, [24] proposes a naive *iterative deepening* method which unwinds loops iteratively performing finite symbolic execution until a fixed depth, while inferring the interpolants needed to keep the error nodes unreachable. Amongst these interpolants, only those which are loop invariant are kept and it is checked whether they still prove unreachability of error nodes. If yes, the program is safe. Otherwise, the depth is increased and the process is repeated. Although simple, this approach has the advantage of that it performs symbolic execution also within loops as [21] and without reporting false alarms.

Example 1 (Iterative Deepening). Consider the program in Fig. 1(a). To force termination, the iterative deepening method executes the program considering one iteration of the loop. Using interpolants, ℓ_4 is annotated with $x \geq 0$ by using weakest precondition. This interpolant preserves the infeasibility of the error path. Then, the remaining step is to check whether the interpolant is invariant. Since $x \geq 0$ is an inductive invariant interpolant, we can prove that the program is safe.

This program illustrates the essence of the iterative deepening approach which obtains generalization by interpolation and relies on the heuristics that a bounded proof may highlight how to make the unbounded proof. However, this approach has one major drawback: its naive iterative deepening cannot terminate in programs like the one in Fig. 1(b) due to the impossibility of discovering disjunctive invariant interpolants. We elaborate more on the reason below. Meanwhile, we mention that this example has been often used to highlight the strength of CEGAR [17] for handling unbounded loops. Further, its essential characteristic is present in real programs as we will show in Sec. 5.

In this paper, we propose a new method to enhance symbolic execution for handling unbounded loops but yet without losing the intrinsic benefits of symbolic execution. This method is based on three design principles: (1) *abstract loops* in order for symbolic execution to attempt to terminate, (2) *preserve* as much as possible the inherent benefits of symbolic execution (mainly, earlier detection of infeasible paths) by propagating the *strongest loop invariants*[1], whenever possible, and (3) *refine progressively* imprecise abstractions in order to avoid reporting false alarms.

The central idea is to unwind loops iteratively while computing *speculative loop invariants* which make the symbolic execution of the loop converge quickly. The algorithm attempts to minimize the loss of information (i.e., ability of detecting infeasible paths) by computing the *strongest* possible invariants and it checks whether error nodes are unreachable. If yes, the program is safe. Otherwise, a counterexample is produced and analyzed to test if it corresponds to a concrete counterexample in the original program. If yes, the program is reported as unsafe. Otherwise, these speculative invariants are too coarse to ensure the safety conditions and the algorithm introduces a refinement phase similar to CEGAR in which it computes those interpolants needed to ensure the unreachability of the error nodes, resulting in *selective* unrolling only at points where the invariant can no longer be produced due to the strengthening introduced by the interpolants.

Example 2 (Selective Unrolling and Path Invariants). Consider our key example in Fig. 1(b). We first explain why simple unrolling with iterative deepening does not work here. Essentially, there are two paths in the loop body, and the required safety property $lock \neq 0$ is not invariant along both paths. In fact, we require the disjunctive loop invariant $new \neq old \vee lock \neq 0$, and this entails far more than simple invariant discovery. Thus loop unrolling does not terminate with successive deepenings. In more detail, we execute first one iteration of the loop. Using interpolants, ℓ_1 is annotated with $new \neq old$. We test if the interpolant $new \neq old$ is inductive invariant. Since it is not we cannot keep it and we execute the program considering now two iterations of the loop. During the second iteration of the loop, both paths $\pi_1 \equiv \ell_1 \rightarrow \ell_2 \rightarrow \ell_3 \rightarrow \ell_5 \rightarrow \ell_1$ and $\pi_2 \equiv \ell_1 \rightarrow \ell_2 \rightarrow \ell_3 \rightarrow \ell_4 \rightarrow \ell_5 \rightarrow \ell_1$ must be unrolled. From π_1 the symbolic execution proves the unreachability of ℓ_{error} adding the interpolant $old = new \wedge lock \neq 0$. From π_2, simple unrolling with iterative deepening will add the interpolant $new \neq old$ after executing

---

[1] By *strongest* we mean assuming that only discovery methods based on enumeration and testing are available.

the second iteration of the loop. Since the interpolant is not inductive invariant yet after this second iteration, we cannot keep it and the unrolling process runs forever.

In our algorithm, we proceed as follows. We also execute the symbolic path $\ell_1 \to \ell_2 \to \ell_3 \to \ell_5 \to \ell_{1'}$[2]. We then examine the constraints at the entry of the loop ℓ_1 (i.e., called *loop header*) to discover which abstraction at ℓ_1 makes possible that the symbolic state at $\ell_{1'}$ can imply (be *subsumed* by) the state at ℓ_1. We use the notion of *path-based loop invariant*. A path-based loop invariant[3] is a formula whose truth value does not change after the symbolic execution of the path. Clearly, the constraints $lock = 0$ and $new = old + 1$ at ℓ_1 are no longer path-invariants after the execution of the path. We then decide to generalize at ℓ_1 the constraints $lock = 0$ and $new = old + 1$ to *true*. As a consequence, the constraints at $\ell_{1'}$ can imply now the constraints at ℓ_1. The objective here is to achieve the convergence of the loop by forcing subsumption between a node and its ancestor.

Next, we backtrack and we execute the path $\ell_3 \to \ell_4 \to \ell_{5'}$. The symbolic state at $\ell_{5'}$ is subsumed by the interpolant computed at ℓ_5 since $lock = 0 \wedge old = new + 1$ trivially implies *true*. After we have executed the loop, we execute the path $\ell_1 \to \ell_6 \to \ell_{error}$ which is now feasible due to the abstraction we performed at ℓ_1. We then trigger a counterexample-guided refinement phase 'a la' CEGAR. First, we check that the path $\ell_0 \to \ell_1 \to \ell_6 \to \ell_{error}$ is indeed spurious due to the abstraction at ℓ_1. Next, we strengthen the abstraction at ℓ_1 in order to make the error node unreachable. The interpolant $new = old + 1$ will be sufficient here. Finally, we ensure that the interpolant $new = old + 1$ cannot be generalized again at ℓ_1, and we restart the process again.

After we restart we will reach the node $\ell_{1'}$ again and we will try to weaken the symbolic state at ℓ_1 s.t. the state at $\ell_{1'}$ can be subsumed, as we did before. However, the situation has now changed since we cannot abstract the interpolant $new = old + 1$ added by the refinement, and hence, we decide to unroll $\ell_{1'}$ with the symbolic state $lock = 1 \wedge old = new$. We prove that the error node is not reachable from $\ell_{1'}$ and during backtracking annotate both $\ell_{1'}$ and ℓ_5 with the interpolant $\overline{\Psi} \equiv (old = new) \wedge (lock \neq 0)$. This strengthening avoids now that the path $\ell_3 \to \ell_4 \to \ell_{5'}$ can be subsumed since $lock = 0 \wedge new = old + 1$ does not imply $\overline{\Psi}$. We continue the path and encounter $\ell_{1''}$. It is easy to see that $\ell_{1''}$ cannot be subsumed by its sibling $\ell_{1'}$ since the symbolic state at $\ell_{1''}$ ($lock = 0 \wedge new = old + 1$) does not imply $\overline{\Psi}$ neither. However, we can still force $\ell_{1''}$ to be subsumed by its ancestor ℓ_1 by abstracting the state at ℓ_1 using the notion of path-invariant again. Note that the subsumption already holds and hence, we can halt exploring the path without further abstraction.

Therefore, we have seen that selective unrolling only at points where we cannot force subsumption (e.g., at $\ell_{1'}$) with an ancestor can help termination. The main advantage of selective unrolling is that it may achieve termination even if disjunctive invariants are needed for the proof. However, it also introduces some new challenges.

Example 3 (Lazy Subsumption versus Strongest Invariants). Consider the program in Fig. 1(c). Say we explore first the path $\ell_0 \to \ell_1 \to \ell_2 \to \ell_3 \to \ell_6 \to \ell_7 \to \ell_8 \to \ell_{1'}$. Assuming that foo() only changes its local variables, the symbolic state at $\ell_{1'}$ is $x = 0 \wedge y =$

---

[2] Note that $\ell_{1'}$ and ℓ_1 correspond to the same location where primed versions refer to different symbolic states in the symbolic execution tree.

[3] Should not be confused with the term "path invariants" used in [6].

$0 \wedge z = 1$ which already implies the symbolic state at ℓ_1. As usual, during backtracking we annotate the symbolic states with their corresponding interpolants. The next path explored is $\ell_2 \rightarrow \ell_4 \rightarrow \ell_5 \rightarrow \ell_{6'}$. In principle, the symbolic state at $\ell_{6'}$ with constraints $x = 1 \wedge y = 1 \wedge z = 1$ entails *true*, the interpolant at ℓ_6. We therefore can stop the exploration of the path at $\ell_{6'}$ avoiding exploring foo() again.

However, a key observation is that the constraints $x = 0$ and $y = 0$ are not path-invariant if we would only consider the path $\ell_1 \rightarrow \ell_2 \rightarrow \ell_4 \rightarrow \ell_5 \rightarrow \ell_{6'}$. We face then here an important dilemma. On one hand, one of our design principles is to compute the strongest possible loop invariants. However, note that the constraint $x = 0$ is in fact invariant if subsumption would not take place at $\ell_{6'}$ due to the execution of $x = x - y$ at ℓ_7. On the other hand, we may suffer the path explosion problem if we would not subsume other paths.

We adopt the solution of lazily subsuming other paths whenever possible while abstracting further the symbolic states of the loop headers even if we may lose the opportunity of computing the strongest loop invariants.

Coming back to the example, subsumption takes place at $\ell_{6'}$ but we must also abstract the symbolic state at ℓ_1 discarding the constraints $x = 0$ and $y = 0$ although we can still keep $z = 1$. In spite of this abstraction the transition $\ell_9 \rightarrow \ell_{error}$ is infeasible. However, as with the program in Fig. 1(b), we may have some interpolants that strengthen the path-based loop invariants in order to make the error nodes unreachable. For the sake of discussion, assume the condition at ℓ_9 is $x \neq 0$. Then, the path $\ell_1 \rightarrow \ell_9 \rightarrow \ell_{error}$ would be feasible since $z = 1 \wedge x \neq 0$ is satisfiable. We then check that the path $\ell_0 \rightarrow \ell_1 \rightarrow \ell_9 \rightarrow \ell_{error}$ is indeed spurious due to the abstraction at ℓ_1 and discover that the interpolant $x = 0$ suffices to make the error node unreachable. As a consequence of this refinement, after restart the subsumption at $\ell_{6'}$ now cannot take place since the constraint $x = 0$ is not allowed to be abstracted at ℓ_1. We therefore continue exploring the path $\ell_{6'} \rightarrow \ell_7 \rightarrow \ell_8 \rightarrow \ell_{1''}$. The symbolic state at $\ell_{1''}$ ($x = 0 \wedge y = 1 \wedge z = 1$) entails the one at ℓ_1 if we abstract the constraint $y = 1$ to true. As a result, the analysis of the loop can still terminate and the error can be proved unreachable.

Example 4 (Other Benefits of Propagating Invariants). It is well-studied that the discovery of loop invariants can speedup the convergence of loops [6]. The bounded program in Fig. 1(d) illustrates the potential benefits of propagating invariants by our symbolic execution-based approach wrt CEGAR.

CEGAR (e.g., [7,25]) discovers the predicates $(x = 0), (x = 1), \ldots, (x = 10000 - 1)$ and also $(y \geq 0), (y \geq 1), \ldots, (y \geq 10000)$, and hence full unwinding of the loop is needed. Say symbolic execution explores the path $\ell_0 \rightarrow \ell_1 \rightarrow \ell_2 \rightarrow \ell_3 \rightarrow \ell_4 \rightarrow \ell_{2'}$. It is straightforward to see that $y \geq 0$ is invariant. The next symbolic path is $\ell_2 \rightarrow \ell_5 \rightarrow \ell_{error}$ with the generalized constraint $y \geq 0$ at ℓ_2. As a result, the symbolic path is infeasible since the formula $y \geq 0 \wedge x \geq 10000 \wedge y + x < 10000$ is unsatisfiable, and hence, we are done without unwinding the loop.

2 Related Work

Similar to [16,23] our algorithm discovers invariant interpolants that prove the unreachability of error nodes. However, we differ from them because we abstract only at loops discovering loop invariants as strong as possible and hence, we still explore a significant smaller number of infeasible paths. Moreover, we avoid the expensive predicate image computations with predicate abstraction [17,2]. A recent paper [5] mitigates partially these problems by encoding large loop-free blocks into a Boolean formula relying on the capabilities of an SMT solver, although for loops the same issues still remain. Synergy/DASH/SMASH [14,4,13] use test-generation features to enhance the process of verification. The main advantage comes from the use of symbolic execution provided by DART [12] to make the refinement phase cheaper. The main disadvantage is that these methods cannot recover from too-specific refinements (see program diamond in [24]).

To the best of our knowledge, the works of [20,21] are the first in using symbolic execution with interpolation in pursuit of verifying a target property. However, [20] does not consider loops and [21] relies on abstract interpretation in order to compute loop invariants, and as a result, false alarms can be reported. Alternatively, the verification problem can be seen as a translation to a Boolean formula that can then be subjected to a SAT or SMT solver. It is a fact that symbolic execution with interpolation can be considered analogous to conflict clause learning in DPLL style SAT solvers. [15] adopts this approach by mapping the verification problem of loop-free programs into a solving SMT instance, and adding conflict clauses into the SAT solver whenever infeasible paths are detected. In presence of loops, [15] allows choosing between different methods. One is the use of abstract interpretation for discovering loop invariants that allow termination similar to [21]. Another alternative is the use of CEGAR but losing the ability of detecting eagerly infeasible paths within loops.

Our closest related work is McMillan [24]. This work can be dissected in two parts. For loop-free fragments, this work is in fact covered by the earlier works [20,21] and hence, equivalent to ours here. However, we differ in the way we handle unbounded loops. [24] follows the iterative deepening method explained in Sec. 1 and hence, may not converge for some realistic programs as we have shown. Finally, [24] computes summaries for functions and support recursive functions. Our implementation currently performs function inlining and does not cover recursive functions. We consider these extensions however to be an orthogonal issue which we can address elsewhere.

3   Background

Syntax. We restrict our presentation to a simple imperative programming language, where all basic operations are either assignments or assume operations, and the domain of all variables are integers. The set of all program variables is denoted by *Vars*. An *assignment* x := e corresponds to assign the evaluation of the expression e to the variable x. In the *assume* operator, assume(c), if the boolean expression c evaluates to *true*, then the program continues, otherwise it halts. The set of operations is denoted by *Ops*.

We model a program by a *transition system*. A transition system is a quadruple $\langle \Sigma, I, \longrightarrow, O \rangle$ where Σ is the set of states and $I \subseteq \Sigma$ is the set of initial states. $\longrightarrow \subseteq \Sigma \times \Sigma \times Ops$ is the transition relation that relates a state to its (possible) successors executing operations. This transition relation models the operations that are executed when control flows from one program location to another. We shall use $\ell \xrightarrow{\text{op}} \ell'$ to denote a transition relation from $\ell \in \Sigma$ to $\ell' \in \Sigma$ executing the operation op $\in Ops$. Finally, $O \subseteq \Sigma$ is the set of final states.

Symbolic Execution. A *symbolic state* σ is a triple $\langle \ell, s, \Pi \rangle$. The symbol $\ell \in \Sigma$ corresponds to the next program counter (with special program counters $\ell_{end} \in O$ to denote a final location and ℓ_{error} for an error location). The symbolic store s is a function from program variables to terms over input symbolic variables. Each program variable is initialized to a fresh input symbolic variable. The *evaluation* $[\![e]\!]_s$ of an arithmetic expression e in a store s is defined as usual: $[\![v]\!]_s = s(v)$, $[\![n]\!]_s = n$, $[\![e+e']\!]_s = [\![e]\!]_s + [\![e']\!]_s$, $[\![e-e']\!]_s = [\![e]\!]_s - [\![e']\!]_s$, etc. The evaluation of Boolean expression $[\![b]\!]_s$ can be defined analogously. Finally, Π is called *path condition* and it is a first-order formula over the symbolic inputs and it accumulates constraints which the inputs must satisfy in order for an execution to follow the particular corresponding path. The set of first-order formulas and symbolic states are denoted by *FO* and *SymState*, respectively. Given a transition system $\langle \Sigma, I, \longrightarrow, O \rangle$ and a state $\sigma \equiv \langle \ell, s, \Pi \rangle \in$ *SymState*, the symbolic execution of $\ell \xrightarrow{op} \ell'$ returns another symbolic state σ' defined as:

$$\sigma' \triangleq \begin{cases} \langle \ell', s, \Pi \wedge [\![c]\!]_s \rangle & \text{if op} \equiv \mathsf{assume}(c) \text{ and } \Pi \wedge [\![c]\!]_s \text{ is satisfiable} \\ \langle \ell', s[x \mapsto [\![e]\!]_s], \Pi \rangle & \text{if op} \equiv \mathsf{x := e} \end{cases} \quad (1)$$

Note that Eq. (1) queries a *theorem prover* for satisfiability checking on the path condition. We assume the theorem prover is sound but not complete. That is, the theorem prover must say a formula is unsatisfiable only if it is indeed so.

Overloading notation, given a symbolic state $\sigma \equiv \langle \ell, s, \Pi \rangle$ we define $[\![\cdot]\!]$: *SymState* $\rightarrow$ *FO* as the projection of the formula $(\bigwedge_{v \in Vars} [\![v]\!]_s) \wedge [\![\Pi]\!]_s$ onto the set of program variables *Vars*. The projection is performed by elimination of existentially quantified variables.

A *symbolic path* $\pi \equiv \sigma_0 \cdot \sigma_1 \cdot ... \cdot \sigma_n$ is a sequence of symbolic states such that $\forall i \bullet 1 \leq i \leq n$ the state σ_i is a *successor* of σ_{i-1}. A symbolic state $\sigma' \equiv \langle \ell', \cdot, \cdot \rangle$ is a successor of another $\sigma \equiv \langle \ell, \cdot, \cdot \rangle$ if there exists a transition relation $\ell \xrightarrow{op} \ell'$. A path $\pi \equiv \sigma_1 \cdot \sigma_2 \cdot ... \cdot \sigma_n$ is *feasible* if $\sigma_n \equiv \langle \ell, s, \Pi \rangle$ such that $[\![\Pi]\!]_s$ is satisfiable. If $\ell \in O$ and σ_n is feasible then σ_n is called *terminal* state. Otherwise, if $[\![\Pi]\!]_s$ is unsatisfiable the path is called *infeasible* and σ_n is called *infeasible* state. A state $\sigma \equiv \langle \ell, \cdot, \cdot \rangle$ is called *subsumed* if there exists another state $\sigma' \equiv \langle \ell, \cdot, \cdot \rangle$ such that $[\![\sigma]\!] \models [\![\sigma']\!]$. If there exists a feasible path $\pi \equiv \sigma_0 \cdot \sigma_1 \cdot ... \cdot \sigma_n$ then we say σ_k ($0 \leq k \leq n$) is *reachable* from σ_0 in k *steps*. We say σ'' is reachable from σ if it is reachable from σ in some number of steps. A *symbolic execution tree* characterizes the execution paths followed during the symbolic execution of a transition system by triggering Eq. (1). The nodes represent symbolic states and the arcs represent transitions between states. We say a symbolic execution tree is *complete* if it is finite and all its leaves are either terminal, infeasible or subsumed.

Bounded Program Verification via Symbolic Execution. We follow the approach of [21]. We will assume a program is annotated with assertions of the form if (!c) then error(), where c is the safety property. Then the verification process consists of constructing a complete symbolic execution tree and proving that error is unreachable from all symbolic paths in the tree. Otherwise, the program is unsafe. One of the challenges to build a complete tree is the exponential number of symbolic paths. An interpolation-based solution to this problem was first proposed in [21] which we also follow in this paper. Given an infeasible state $\sigma \equiv \langle \ell, s, \Pi \rangle$ we can generate a formula $\overline{\Psi}$ (called *interpolant*) which still preserves the infeasibility of the state but using a weaker (more general) formula than the original $[\![\sigma]\!]$. The main purpose of using $\overline{\Psi}$ rather than the original formula associated to the symbolic state σ is to increase the likelihood of subsumption.

Definition 1 (Interpolant). *Given two first-order logic formulas ϕ_1 and ϕ_2 such that $\phi_1 \wedge \phi_2$ is unsatisfiable a Craig interpolant [10] is another first-order logic formula $\overline{\Psi}$ such that (a) $\phi_1 \models \overline{\Psi}$, (b) $\overline{\Psi} \wedge \phi_2$ is unsatisfiable, and (c) all variables in $\overline{\Psi}$ are common variables to ϕ_1 and ϕ_2.*

The symbolic execution of a program can be augmented by annotating each symbolic state with its corresponding interpolant such that the interpolant represents the sufficient conditions to preserve the unreachability of the error nodes. Then, the notion of subsumption can be redefined as follows.

Definition 2 (Subsumption with Interpolants). *Given two symbolic states σ and σ' such that σ is annotated with the interpolant $\overline{\Psi}$, we say that σ' is subsumed by σ if $[\![\sigma']\!]$ implies $\overline{\Psi}$ (i.e., s.t. $[\![\sigma']\!] \models \overline{\Psi}$).*

4 Algorithm

A full description of our algorithm is given in Fig. 2 and Fig. 3. For clarity and making the reader familiar with our algorithm, we start by explaining only the parts corresponding to the bounded symbolic execution engine used in [21,24]. Having done this, we will explain how this basic algorithm can be augmented for supporting unbounded programs which is the main technical contribution of this paper.

The input of the algorithm is an initial symbolic state $\sigma_k \in SymState$, the transition system $\mathcal{P}$, an initial empty path π, and an empty *subsumption table* $\mathcal{M}$. We use the key k to refer unambiguously to the symbolic state σ in the symbolic execution tree. In order to perform subsumption tests our algorithm maintains the table $\mathcal{M}$ that stores entries of the form $\langle \ell, k \rangle : \overline{\Psi}$, where $\overline{\Psi}$ is the interpolant at program location ℓ associated with a symbolic state k in the symbolic execution tree. The interpolants are generated by a procedure Interp : $FO \times FO \rightarrow FO$ that takes two formulas and computes a Craig interpolant following Def. 1, Sec. 3. The output of the algorithm is the subsumption table if the program is safe. Otherwise, the algorithm aborts.

Bounded Verification via Symbolic Execution with Interpolation. The algorithm for bounded verification using symbolic execution with interpolants consists of building a complete symbolic execution tree while testing error nodes are not reachable.

The algorithm starts by testing if the path is infeasible at line 1. If yes, an interpolant is generated to avoid exploring again paths which have the same infeasibility reason. Next, if the error node is reachable (line 3) then the error must be real since for bounded programs no abstraction is done and hence, the program is reported as unsafe at line 7. The next case is when the end of a path (i.e, terminal node) has been encountered. The algorithm simply adds an entry in the *subsumption table* whose interpolant is *true* (line 9) since the symbolic path is feasible and hence, there is no false paths to preserve. Otherwise, a subsumption test at line 10 is done in order for the symbolic execution to attempt at halting the exploration of the path. For bounded programs, this test is

UnboundedSymExec($\sigma_k \equiv \langle \ell, s, \Pi \rangle, \mathcal{P}, \pi, \mathcal{M}$)

```
 1:   if  [[Π]]_s is unsat then                                              /* infeasible path */
 2:      return  M ∪ {⟨ℓ,k⟩ : INTERP([[σ_k]], false)}
 3:   else if  (ℓ = ℓ_error) then
 4:      if ∃ σ_h ≡ ⟨ℓ_h, ·, ·⟩ in π s.t. ℓ_h is a loop header and
              [[σ_h]] ∧ [[Π]]_s is unsat then                               /* spurious error */
 5:         return  REFINEANDRESTART(σ_h, σ_k, P, π, M)
 6:      else
 7:         printf("The program is unsafe") and abort()                      /* real error */
 8:   else if  (ℓ = ℓ_end) then                                             /* end of path */
 9:      return  M ∪ {⟨ℓ,k⟩ : true}
10:   else if  Ψ̄ := (SUBSUMED(σ_k, M) ) ≠ ⊥ then                          /* sibling-sibling subsumed */
11:      return  M ∪ {⟨ℓ,k⟩ : Ψ̄}
12:   else if  ∃ ⟨ℓ, ·, ·⟩ in π then                                       /* cyclic path */
13:      foreach σ_h in π s.t. σ_h ≡ ⟨ℓ, ·, ·⟩ do
14:         if (NONPATHINV(σ_h, σ_k, M) ≠ ⊥) then                          /* child-ancestor subsumed */
15:            return  M ∪ {⟨ℓ,k⟩ : true}
16:      endfor
17:      goto 19
18:   else
19:      Ψ̄ := true
20:      foreach transition relation ℓ --op--> ℓ' ∈ P do                    /* forward symbolic execution */
21:         σ'_{k'} ≜ { ⟨ℓ', s, Π ∧ [[c]]_s⟩        if op ≡ assume(c) and fresh k'
                       { ⟨ℓ', s[x ↦ [[e]]_s], Π⟩   if op ≡ x := e and fresh k'
22:         M := UNBOUNDEDSYMEXEC(σ'_{k'}, P, π · σ_k, M)
23:         Ψ̄ := Ψ̄ ∧ (∧_{⟨·,k'⟩:Ψ̄ ∈ M}  ŵp(op, Ψ̄))                     /* backward symbolic execution */
24:      endfor
25:      return  M \ {⟨ℓ,k⟩ : Ψ̄''} ∪ {⟨ℓ,k⟩ : Ψ̄ ∧ Ψ̄''}
```

Fig. 2. Algorithm for Unbounded Symbolic Execution with Interpolation

quite straightforward because it suffices to check whether the current symbolic state implies any interpolant computed previously for the same program location following Def. 2, Sec. 3. This is done at line 46, Fig. 3. If the test holds, it returns the interpolant associated with the subsuming node (line 50). Otherwise, it returns $\perp$ at line 51 to point out that the subsumption test failed.

In the remaining case, the symbolic execution moves forward one level in the symbolic execution tree. The foreach loop (lines 20-24) executes one symbolic step for each successor node [4] and it calls recursively to the main procedure UnboundedSymExec with each successor state (line 22). Once the recursive call returns the key remaining step is to compute an interpolant that generalizes the symbolic execution tree at the current node while preserving the unreachability of the error nodes. The procedure $\widehat{wp} : Ops \times FO \to FO$ computes ideally the *weakest precondition (wp)* [11] which is

---

[4] Note that the rule described in line 21 is slightly different from the one described in Sec. 3 because no satisfiability check is performed. Instead, this check is postponed and done by line 1.

NONPATHINV($\sigma_h \equiv \langle \ell, s, \cdot \rangle, \sigma_k, \mathcal{M}$)

26: let $\overline{\Psi}$ be s.t. $\langle \ell, h \rangle : \overline{\Psi} \in \mathcal{M}$. Otherwise, let $\overline{\Psi}$ be $true$
27: let $I \equiv c_1 \wedge \ldots \wedge c_n$ be $[\![\sigma_h]\!]$
28: $i := 1, NonInv := \emptyset$
29: repeat
30:      if $[\![\sigma_k]\!] \models I \models \overline{\Psi}$ then
31:          foreach $\sigma \equiv \langle \cdot, s, \cdot \rangle$ s.t. σ is k-reachable $(k > 0)$ from σ_h
32:              replace s with HAVOC(s, MODIFIES($NonInv$))
33:          endfor
34:          return
35:      else
36:          $I := I - c_i$ /* delete from I the constraint c_i */
37:          $NonInv := NonInv \cup \{c_i\}$
38:          $i := i + 1$
39: until $(i > n)$
40: return $\bot$

REFINEANDRESTART($\sigma_h \equiv \langle \ell, \cdot, \cdot \rangle, \sigma_k, \mathcal{P}, \pi, \mathcal{M}$)

41: let π be $\sigma_0 \cdots \sigma_{h-1} \cdot \sigma_h \cdots$
42: $\overline{\Psi} := $ INTERP($[\![\sigma_h]\!], [\![\sigma_k]\!]$)
43: $\mathcal{M} := \mathcal{M} \setminus \{\langle \ell', k' \rangle : \overline{\Psi}' \mid \langle \ell', k' \rangle : \overline{\Psi}', \sigma_{k'}$ is k-reachable $(k > 0)$ from $\sigma_h\}$
44: $\mathcal{M} := \mathcal{M} \setminus \{\langle \ell, h \rangle : \overline{\Psi}'\} \cup \{\langle \ell, h \rangle : \overline{\Psi} \wedge \overline{\Psi}'\}$
45: return UNBOUNDEDSYMEXEC($\sigma_h, \mathcal{P}, \sigma_0 \cdots \sigma_{h-1}, \mathcal{M}$)

SUBSUMED($\sigma_k \equiv \langle \ell, \cdot, \cdot \rangle, \mathcal{M}$)

46: if $\exists \langle \ell', k' \rangle : \overline{\Psi} \in \mathcal{M}$ s.t. $(\ell = \ell')$ and $([\![\sigma_k]\!] \models \overline{\Psi})$ then
47:      if k and k' have a common $loop\ header\ ancestor$ σ_h in the tree then
48:          if (NONPATHINV($\sigma_h, \sigma_k, \mathcal{M}$) $\neq \bot$) then return $\overline{\Psi}$
49:          else return $\bot$
50:      else return $\overline{\Psi}$
51: return $\bot$

Fig. 3. NONPATHINV, REFINEANDRESTART and SUBSUMED Procedures

the weakest formula on the initial state ensuring the execution of an operation in a final state, assuming it terminates. In practice, we approximate wp by making a linear number of calls to a theorem prover following the techniques described in [21]. The final interpolant $\overline{\Psi}$ added in the *subsumption table* is a first-order logic formula consisting of the *conjunction* of the result of $\widehat{wp}$ on each child's interpolant (line 23).

Unbounded Verification via Symbolic Execution with Interpolation. For handling unbounded loops we need to augment the basic algorithm described so far in several ways.

Loop abstractions. The main abstraction is done whenever a *cyclic path* is detected by forcing subsumption between the current node and any of its ancestors. The mechanism to force subsumption takes the constraints from the symbolic state associated with the *loop header* (i.e., entry point of the loop) and it abstracts any non-invariant constraint after the execution of that particular path. By doing this, we can ensure that the symbolic state of the current node implies the abstracted symbolic state of its ancestor. Here, we use the concept of *path-based loop invariant*. Using Floyd-Hoare notation, given a path π and a constraint c, we say c is path-based invariant along π if $\{c\}\ \pi\ \{c\}$. That is, whenever c holds of the symbolic state before the execution of *path*, then c will hold afterward.

Let us come back to the algorithm in Fig. 2. In line 12 we have detected a cyclic path. The foreach loop (lines 13-16) forces subsumption between the current symbolic state and any of its ancestors. The procedure NONPATHINV in Fig. 3 attempts the current state σ_k to imply some generalization of its ancestor state σ_h. This generalization is basically to discover a loop invariant at the symbolic context of the loop header. Clearly, this procedure has a huge impact in the symbolic execution since our ability of detecting infeasible paths depends on the precision of this generalization. This task is, in general, undecidable and even if the strongest invariants can be computed by enumeration of all possible combinations of candidates and testing them it is, in general, exponential.

The greedy method followed in NONPATHINV is quite simple but it works well in practice and it requires a linear number of calls to a theorem prover. The invariant is a subset of the constraints at the symbolic state σ_h, called I. Initially, I contains all the constraints in σ_h (line 27). At each iteration of the repeat loop (lines 29-39), we test if the symbolic state at σ_k entails I (line 30). If yes, we are done. Otherwise, we delete one constraint from I and repeat the process.

Notice that the invariance property is not closed under intersection since the intersection of two invariants may not be an invariant, in general. However, we construct loop invariants by testing path-by-path and discarding non-invariant constraints from the symbolic state of the loop header. This is equivalent to the computation of path-based loop invariants for each path within a loop and then intersect them at the loop header. This is correct because NONPATHINV keeps only invariants which are closed under intersection. This limitation, in principle, preclude us to compute the strongest invariants but based on our experience it is not a problem and it is vital for an efficient implementation.

Finally, once we have discovered the generalization of the symbolic state of the loop header in order for the test at line 30 to hold one remaining step is to propagate the abstraction to the rest of the symbolic execution tree. For clarity, we omit the full process because although trivial it is quite tedious. The basic idea is to propagate the generalization to all current and future reachable states in the symbolic execution tree from the header by abstracting their symbolic stores (lines 31-33). We define HAVOC($s, Vars$) as $\forall v \in Vars \bullet s[v \mapsto z]$, where z is a fresh variable, and MODIFIES($c_1 \ldots c_n$) which takes a sequence of constraints and it returns the set of variables that may be modified during its execution. As a result, NONPATHINV has also *side effects* since it may change other symbolic states in the tree.

Refine and Restart. Clearly, the use of abstractions can mitigate the termination problems of symbolic execution but it may introduce false alarms. We therefore add a new case at line 4 in our algorithm to test whether abstract counterexamples correspond to counterexamples in the concrete model of the program. Clearly, this case resembles the refinement phase in CEGAR. Whenever a counterexample is found, we test whether the original symbolic constraints along the path are indeed satisfiable using the solver. If yes, the error must be real. Otherwise, we inspect all loop headers in the counterexample and find out which one introduced an abstraction that cannot keep the error nodes unreachable. Once we have found the loop header, the procedure REFINEANDRESTART, described in Fig. 3, infers an interpolant that excludes that particular counterexample (line 42) and restarts the symbolic execution from that loop header at line 45. It is worth mentioning that although our algorithm can then perform expensive refinements as CEGAR, the refinements are confined only to loop headers as in opposition to CE-GAR where refinements may involve any program point. This is an important feature for performing more efficient refinements in our implementation.

Interestingly now, the interpolants added by REFINEANDRESTART can affect the abstractions done by procedure NONPATHINV explained so far. Let us come back to NONPATHINV. In principle, we can always find a path invariant *true* by deleting all constraints. However, note that the test at line 30 is restrained by ensuring that the candidate invariant must entail the interpolant associated with the loop header obtained possibly from a previous refinement. If this entailment does not hold, the procedure NONPATHINV fails. This is, in fact, our mechanism to unroll selectively those points where the invariant can no longer be produced due to the strengthening introduced by the interpolants.

Subsumption. The program of Fig. 1(c) in Sec. 1 illustrated that in presence of loops the subsumption test (SUBSUMED, Fig. 3) cannot be simply an entailment test. Whenever we attempt at subsuming a symbolic state within a loop, we need additionally to be aware of which constraints may not be path-invariant anymore and generalize the symbolic state of the nearest loop header accordingly. That is the reason of SUBSUMED calling NONPATHINV at line 48. If NONPATHINV fails (i.e., it could not generalize the state of the loop header) then subsumption cannot take place.

Moreover, the correctness of SUBSUMED assumes that whenever a loop header h is annotated with its interpolant $\overline{\Psi}$, the subsumption table $\mathcal{M}$ is updated in such way that all entries associated with program points within the loop with entry h must *conjoin* their interpolants with $\overline{\Psi}$. For clarity again, this update is omitted from the algorithm description but considered in our implementation.

We conclude this section showing how our algorithm executes the program in Fig 1(b), Sec. 1 and proves that it is safe.

Example 5 (Running example of Fig 1(b), Sec. 1.). The initial algorithm state is $\sigma_0 \equiv \langle \ell_0, [lock \mapsto S_{lock}, old \mapsto S_{old}, new \mapsto S_{new}], true \rangle$, $\pi \equiv nil$, and $\mathcal{M} \equiv \emptyset$.

First iteration. We first execute the successor of σ_0 obtaining $\sigma_1 \equiv \langle \ell_1, [lock \mapsto 0, old \mapsto S_{old}, new \mapsto S_{old} + 1], true \rangle$. Then, we continue augmenting the path by running the foreach loop (lines 20-24) and calling recursively to UNBOUNDEDSYMEXEC (line 22) until we find a cyclic path (line 12) $\ell_0 \rightarrow \ell_1 \rightarrow \ell_2 \rightarrow \ell_3 \rightarrow \ell_5 \rightarrow \ell_1$ with $\pi \equiv \sigma_0 \cdot \sigma_1 \cdot \sigma_2 \cdot \sigma_3 \cdot \sigma_5$, $\mathcal{M} \equiv \emptyset$, and $\sigma_{1'} \equiv \langle \ell_1, [lock \mapsto 1, old \mapsto S_{old} + 1, new \mapsto S_{old} + 1], S_{old} + 1 \neq S_{old} \rangle$. We call NONPATHINV($\sigma_1, \sigma_{1'}, \mathcal{M}$). The formulas $[\![\sigma_1]\!] \equiv lock = 0 \wedge new = old + 1$ and $[\![\sigma_{1'}]\!] \equiv lock = 1 \wedge old = new$ are obtained by projecting the symbolic states of σ_1 and $\sigma_{1'}$ onto the variables *lock*, *old* and *new*. The test at line 30 holds after deleting from I the constraints $lock = 0$ and $new = old + 1$, since these two constraints are not path-invariant. We backtrack up to σ_3 which after the loop abstraction has been propagated (lines 31-33) is $\langle \ell_3, [lock \mapsto 1, old \mapsto S_{new}, new \mapsto S_{new}], true \rangle$. We then execute $\ell_3 \rightarrow \ell_4 \rightarrow \ell_5$, obtaining the state $\sigma_{5'} \equiv \langle \ell_5, [lock \mapsto 0, old \mapsto S_{old}, new \mapsto S_{old} + 1], $ $true \rangle$ but $\mathcal{M}$ contains now two new entries $\{\langle \ell_1, 1' \rangle : true, \langle \ell_5, 5 \rangle : true\}$. As a result, SUBSUMED($\sigma_{5'}, \mathcal{M}$) (line 10) succeeds since the interpolant associated with ℓ_5 is $true$. In addition, since the symbolic states σ_5 and $\sigma_{5'}$ are within a loop whose header is denoted by σ_1 we call NONPATHINV($\sigma_1, \sigma_{5'}, \mathcal{M}$) which also succeeds without making further generalization.

We continue backtracking up to σ_1 with $\mathcal{M} \equiv \{\langle \ell_2, 2 \rangle : true, \langle \ell_3, 3 \rangle : true, \langle \ell_4, 4 \rangle : true, \langle \ell_5, 5 \rangle : true, \langle \ell_5, 5' \rangle : true, \langle \ell_1, 1' \rangle : true\}$. Recall that the symbolic state σ_1 was generalized, and hence, the state σ_6 is $\langle \ell_6, [lock \mapsto S_{lock}, new \mapsto S_{new}, old \mapsto S_{old}], $ $S_{new} = S_{old} \rangle$, by lines 31-33 (NONPATHINV) and symbolic execution of $\ell_1 \rightarrow \ell_6$. Then, we continue executing symbolically until we finally reach ℓ_{error} with $\sigma_{error} \equiv \langle \ell_{error}, [lock \mapsto S_{old}, new \mapsto S_{new}, old \mapsto S_{old}], S_{new} = S_{old} \wedge S_{lock} = 0 \rangle$. We check $[\![\sigma_1]\!] \equiv (lock = 0 \wedge new = old + 1) \wedge [\![\sigma_{error}]\!] \equiv (old = new \wedge lock = 0)$ is unsatisfiable (line 4). We then call REFINEANDRESTART($\sigma_1, \sigma_{error}, \sigma_0 \cdot \sigma_1 \cdot \sigma_6, \mathcal{M}$) (line 5). We compute the interpolant $new = old + 1$ that excludes the counterexample by calling INTERP($[\![\sigma_1]\!], [\![\sigma_{error}]\!]$) (line 42), delete all elements from $\mathcal{M}$ which were added by any state reachable from σ_1 (line 43), add a new element with the new interpolant (i.e., $\mathcal{M} \equiv \{\langle \ell_1, 1 \rangle : new = old + 1\}$) (line 44), and finally, we restart by calling UNBOUNDEDSYMEXEC (line 45).

Second iteration. After restart, we detect again the cyclic path $\ell_0 \rightarrow \ell_1 \rightarrow \ell_2 \rightarrow \ell_3 \rightarrow \ell_5 \rightarrow \ell_1$ with σ_1 and $\sigma_{1'}$ as before, and call NONPATHINV. The key difference is that $\mathcal{M} \equiv \{\langle \ell_1, 1 \rangle : new = old + 1\}$. Therefore, the test at line 30 (NONPATHINV) always fails and the procedure returns $\perp$ (line 40) without performing any generalization.

We then unroll the state $\sigma_{1'}$ by executing $\ell_1 \rightarrow \ell_2$ (second loop unroll) and obtaining the infeasible symbolic state $\sigma_{2'} \equiv \langle \ell_2, [lock \mapsto 1, old \mapsto S_{old} + 1, new \mapsto S_{old} + 1], S_{old} + 1 \neq S_{old} \wedge S_{old} + 1 \neq S_{old} + 1 \rangle$. We then backtrack and execute the path $\ell_1 \rightarrow \ell_6 \rightarrow \ell_{error}$. The state at ℓ_{error} is infeasible now. We backtrack again, adding in $\mathcal{M} \equiv \{\langle \ell_1, 1' \rangle : old = new \wedge lock \neq 0, \langle \ell_5, 5 \rangle : old = new \wedge lock \neq 0, \ldots\}$ (by weakest precondition of the two infeasible paths), until we execute the path $\ell_3 \rightarrow \ell_4 \rightarrow \ell_5$ again (from the first loop unroll). We call SUBSUMED as we did in the first iteration but now the symbolic state $\sigma_{5'}$ cannot be subsumed because the formula $[\![\sigma_{5'}]\!] \equiv lock = 0 \wedge new = old + 1$ does not entail the interpolant $\langle \ell_5, 5 \rangle \in \mathcal{M}$. We execute another transition reaching ℓ_1 and detect again a cyclic path with the state $\sigma_{1''} \equiv \langle \ell_1, [lock \mapsto 0, old \mapsto S_{old}, new \mapsto S_{old} + 1], S_{old} + 1 \neq S_{old} \rangle$. We call NONPATHINV($\sigma_1, \sigma_{1''}, \mathcal{M}$). The formulas associated with σ_1 and $\sigma_{1''}$ are $[\![\sigma_1]\!] \equiv lock = 0 \wedge new = old + 1$ and $[\![\sigma_{1''}]\!] \equiv lock = 0 \wedge new = old + 1$. Therefore, it is easy to see that NONPATHINV succeeds without any further abstraction and hence, we can obtain a complete symbolic execution tree without error nodes.

5   Results

We report the results of the evaluation of our prototype implementation called TRACER [5] on several real-world C programs, commonly used in the verification community and

---

[5] TRACER is built in CLP($\mathcal{R}$) [19], a Constraint Logic Programming (CLP) system that provides incremental constraint solving for real linear arithmetic and efficient projection based on the Fourier-Motzkim algorithm. TRACER is available along with some tests and benchmarks, at http://www.clip.dia.fi.upm.es/~jorge/tracer.

compared with the iterative deepening algorithm used in McMillan [24]. The first two programs are Linux device drivers: qpmouse and tlan. The next four programs are Microsoft Windows device drivers: kbfiltr, diskperf, floppy, and cdaudio. The program tcas is an implementation of a traffic collision avoidance system. The program is instrumented with ten safety conditions, of which five are violated. We omit the unsafe cases since there is no differences between TRACER and iterative deepening. Finally, ssh_clnt.1 and ssh_srvr.2 are a client and server implementation of the ssh protocol.

TRACER models the heap as an array. The CLP($\mathcal{R}$) solver has been augmented to decide linear arithmetic formulas over real variables with read/update arrays in order to check the satisfiability and entailment of formulas. Functions are inlined and external functions are modeled as having no side effects and returning an unknown value.

The results on Intel 2.33Ghz 3.2GB are summarized in Table 1. We present two sets of numbers. For ITERDEEP (Iterative Deepening) the number of nodes of the symbolic execution tree (S) and the total time in seconds (T), and for TRACER these two numbers and also the column R that shows the number of *restarts* performed by TRACER. A restart occurs when an abstraction for a loop discovered by TRACER is too coarse to prove the program is safe.

Based on the numbers shown in Table 1 we can conclude that the overhead of our approach pays off. The main overhead comes basically from the frequent use of the procedure NONPATHINV since this procedure is used whenever the algorithm attempts at subsuming a node. In spite of this, the overhead is quite reasonable. More importantly, the key difference is that our approach can terminate with the programs ssh_clnt.1 and ssh_srvr.2. However, an iterative deepening cannot terminate the proof after 2 hours or 2.5Gb of memory consumption. The reason is similar to the one present in the program of Fig. 1(b) in Sec. 1: disjunctive invariant interpolants are needed for the proof.

Table 1. *Iterative Deepening* vs TRACER

Program	LOC	ITERDEEP		TRACER		
		S	T(s)	S	T(s)	R
qpmouse	400	1033	1.5	1033	1.99	1
tlan	8069	4892	12.3	4892	13.5	0
kbfiltr	5931	1396	1.56	1396	2.59	0
diskperf	6984	5465	16.8	5465	18.46	0
floppy	8570	4965	8.33	4995	13.26	2
cdaudio	8921	13512	27.98	13814	34.48	3
tcas-1a	394	5386	6.59	5386	7.08	0
tcas-1b	394	5405	6.42	5405	6.89	0
tcas-2a	394	5386	6.36	5386	6.84	0
tcas-3b	394	5375	6.33	5375	6.87	0
tcas-5a	394	5386	6.38	5386	6.88	0
ssh_clnt.1	2521	∞	∞	47825	593	77
ssh_srvr.2	2516	∞	∞	44213	462	63

Finally, it is worth mentioning that in the current version of TRACER we have not implemented any heuristics in the refinement phase. It is well known that heuristics can have a huge impact in the convergence of the algorithm reducing the number of refinements.

6   Conclusions

We extended symbolic execution with interpolation to address unbounded loops in the context of program verification. The algorithm balances *eager subsumption* in order to prune symbolic paths with the desire of discovering the *strongest loop invariants*, in order to detect earlier infeasible paths. Occasionally certain abstractions are not permitted because of the reachability of error states; this is the underlying mechanism which then causes *selective unrolling*, that is, the unrolling of a loop along relevant paths only. Moreover, we implemented our algorithm in a prototype called TRACER and presented some experimental evaluation.

References

1. Ball, T., Cook, B., Levin, V., Rajamani, S.K.: SLAM and Static Driver Verifier: Technology Transfer of Formal Methods inside Microsoft. In: Boiten, E.A., Derrick, J., Smith, G.P. (eds.) IFM 2004. LNCS, vol. 2999, pp. 1–20. Springer, Heidelberg (2004)
2. Ball, T., Majumdar, R., Millstein, T., Rajamani, S.K.: Automatic Predicate Abstraction of C Programs. In: PLDI 2001, pp. 203–213 (2001)
3. Beckert, B., Hähnle, R., Schmitt, P.H. (eds.): Verification of Object-Oriented Software. The KeY Approach. LNCS (LNAI), vol. 4334, pp. 375–405. Springer, Heidelberg (2007)
4. Beckman, N.E., Nori, A.V., Rajamani, S.K., Simmons, R.J.: Proofs from Tests. In: ISSTA 2008, pp. 3–14 (2008)
5. Beyer, D., Cimatti, A., Griggio, A., Keremoglu, M.E., Sebastiani, R.: Software Model Checking via Large-Block Encoding. In: FMCAD 2009 (2009)
6. Beyer, D., Henzinger, T.A., Majumdar, R., Rybalchenko, A.: Path Invariants. In: PLDI 2007, pp. 300–309 (2007)
7. Beyer, D., Henzinger, T.A., Jhala, R., Majumdar, R.: The Software Model Checker BLAST. Int. J. STTT 9, 505–525 (2007)
8. Cadar, C., Ganesh, V., Pawlowski, P.M., Dill, D.L., Engler, D.R.: Exe: Automatically Generating Inputs of Death. In: CCS 2006, pp. 322–335 (2006)
9. Clarke, E., Grumberg, O., Jha, S., Lu, Y., Veith, H.: CounterrExample-Guided Abstraction Refinement. In: Emerson, E.A., Sistla, A.P. (eds.) CAV 2000. LNCS, vol. 1855, Springer, Heidelberg (2000)
10. Craig, W.: Three uses of Herbrand-Gentzen theorem in relating model theory and proof theory. Journal of Symbolic Computation 22 (1955)
11. Dijkstra, E.W.: A Discipline of Programming. Prentice-Hall (1976)
12. Godefroid, P., Klarlund, N., Sen, K.: DART: Directed Automated Random Testing. In: PLDI 2005, pp. 213–223 (2005)
13. Godefroid, P., Nori, A.V., Rajamani, S.K., Tetali, S.D.: Compositional must program analysis: unleashing the power of alternation. In: POPL 2010, pp. 43–56 (2010)
14. Gulavani, B.S., Henzinger, T.A., Kannan, Y., Nori, A.V., Rajamani, S.K.: Synergy: A New Algorithm for Property Checking. In: SIGSOFT 2006/FSE-14, pp. 117–127 (2006)
15. Harris, W.R., Sankaranarayanan, S., Ivančić, F., Gupta, A.: Program Analysis via Satisfiability Modulo Path Programs. In: POPL 2010, pp. 71–82 (2010)
16. Henzinger, T.A., Jhala, R., Majumdar, R., McMillan, K.L.: Abstractions from Proofs. In: POPL 2004, pp. 232–244 (2004)
17. Henzinger, T.A., Jhala, R., Majumdar, R., Sutre, G.: Lazy Abstraction. In: POPL 2002 (2002)
18. Jacobs, B., Piessens, F.: The Verifast Program Verifier (2008)
19. Jaffar, J., Michaylov, S., Stuckey, P.J., Yap, R.H.C.: The CLP($\mathcal{R}$) Language and System. ACM TOPLAS 14(3), 339–395 (1992)

20. Jaffar, J., Santosa, A.E., Voicu, R.: Efficient Memoization for Dynamic Programming with Ad-hoc Constraints. In: AAAI 2008, pp. 297–303 (2008)
21. Jaffar, J., Santosa, A.E., Voicu, R.: An Interpolation Method for CLP Traversal. In: Gent, I.P. (ed.) CP 2009. LNCS, vol. 5732, pp. 454–469. Springer, Heidelberg (2009)
22. King, J.C.: Symbolic Execution and Program Testing. Com. ACM, 385–394 (1976)
23. McMillan, K.L.: Lazy Abstraction with Interpolants. In: Ball, T., Jones, R.B. (eds.) CAV 2006. LNCS, vol. 4144, pp. 123–136. Springer, Heidelberg (2006)
24. McMillan, K.L.: Lazy Annotation for Program Testing and Verification. In: Touili, T., Cook, B., Jackson, P. (eds.) CAV 2010. LNCS, vol. 6174, pp. 104–118. Springer, Heidelberg (2010)
25. Podelski, A., Rybalchenko, A.: ARMC: The Logical Choice for Software Model Checking with Abstraction Refinement. In: Hanus, M. (ed.) PADL 2007. LNCS, vol. 4354, pp. 245–259. Springer, Heidelberg (2006)

Execution Trace Exploration
and Analysis Using Ontologies*

Newres Al Haider[1], Benoit Gaudin[2], and John Murphy[1]

[1] University College Dublin
[2] University of Limerick

Abstract. Dynamic analysis is the analysis of the properties of a running program. In order to perform dynamic analysis, information about the running program is often collected through execution traces. Exploring and analyzing these traces can be an issue due to their size and that knowledge of a human expert is often needed to derive the required conclusions. In this paper we provide a framework in which the semantics of execution traces, as well as that of dynamic analyses, are formally represented through ontologies. In this framework the exploration and analysis of the traces is enabled through semantic queries, and enhanced further through automated reasoning on the ontologies. We will also provide ontologies to represent traces and some basic dynamic analysis techniques, along with semantic queries that enable these techniques. Finally we will illustrate our approach through an example.

1 Introduction

This paper deals with program trace exploration and analysis and proposes an approach to represent, explore and analyse traces at a conceptual level, hence facilitating the way experts handle a raw set of traces. Program trace analysis, and more broadly *Dynamic Analysis* (DA) [7], has proven to be useful for tasks such as program comprehension or problem determination (see e.g. [13]). Although DA techniques aim to automate parts of the analysis, human intervention is often required. As traces are complex objects, human involvement is generally supported through various trace exploration and visualization tools [20]. These tools offer functionalities such as filtering and compaction, that make it possible to render traces more readable for analysis. Experts are then required in order to perform these trace simplifications and determine interesting properties, or concepts, about the analyzed trace.

In this paper, we propose and implement an approach that uses a knowledge base to store the various concepts related to traces and analyses, as well as their specific instances. Within this framework experts can explore and analyse traces, through semantic queries. Through the use of reasoners these interactions are further enhanced, by (partially) automating the derivation of the trace properties, in which the user of the

* The research leading to these results has received funding from the European Community's Seventh Framework Programme (FP7/2007-2013) under the grant agreement FP7- 258109. This work was also supported, in part, by Science Foundation Ireland grants 03/CE2/I303_1 and 10/CE/I1855 to Lero - the Irish Software Engineering Research Centre (www.lero.ie).

S. Khurshid and K. Sen (Eds.): RV 2011, LNCS 7186, pp. 412–426, 2012.
© Springer-Verlag Berlin Heidelberg 2012

framework is interested in. In order to implement such a framework, we need to be able to model the various concepts involved in the traces and analyses in a formal way. This model need to be capable of not only representing existing automated techniques, but automate and/or facilitate the manual reasoning of an expert. An ontology based model for traces and analysis is capable of providing these features.

Ontologies provide a way to formally and explicitly represent knowledge in a domain, in the form of concepts and relationships between them [17]. They therefore offer an adequate framework to define DA related concepts as well as their relationships and instances related to these concepts, i.e. traces. Ontologies have various benefits such as enabling the reuse of knowledge, and separating operational and domain knowledge [12]. They can also possess a sound mathematical background based on Description Logics (DL) [6]. These logic based formalisms that are decidable, which allows for effective computation of certain properties of the knowledge defined in these ontologies. They therefore offer automation for certain reasoning tasks [28, 18]. They also provide querying facilities that can rely on this type of automatic reasoning, hence providing an intelligent layer on top of basic ontology instances. To our knowledge, they have never been considered for Dynamic Analysis, except in [4].

In order to achieve an ontology based framework for trace exploration and analysis, several issues need to be solved and addressed in this paper. A common issue with program traces, that they can get very large for non-trivial applications. The resulting scalability issues effect not only the storage of traces in ontologies, but also the querying and the reasoning capabilities used to perform and/or enable dynamic analysis. There exist ways to mitigate the issues arising from the large amount of data, in the specific case of an ontological framework, as we will explore in the paper as well as provide our solutions for these problems.

The rest of this paper is structured as follows: Section 2 motivates our general approach of formally modelling trace and dynamic analysis knowledge through an example. Section 3 presents an introduction on ontologies. In Section 4 we explain how ontologies could be used to represent the (concepts) of traces and dynamic analysis as well as provide support for trace exploration and dynamic analysis. The various practical issues of dealing with trace and dynamic analysis knowledge will be described in Section 5, along with our proposed solutions to them. We will also provide ontologies for traces and dynamic analysis. We show how these ontologies can be used in conjunction with the querying system and reasoners on a non-trivial example in Section 6. Finally in Section 7 we discuss the benefits and limitations of this approach, and outline future works.

2   Motivating Example

The ultimate goal of this work is to provide an approach and a tool for automation of dynamic analysis tasks. This approach relies on defining dynamic analysis concepts that can be queried and reasoned about in order to automate a greater part of analyses. Existing dynamic analysis techniques have been designed and implemented, such as Frequency Spectrum Analysis [7], Semantic Views [21] and Trace Metrics [19]. These techniques allow for automatic analyses of traces, and result in concepts such as views, view comparisons, metrics, frequencies, frequency clusters etc. Our approach considers designing dynamic analyses techniques from existing ones, through a combination and variation of such concepts. These new techniques can be defined through some languages that help combine dynamic analyses concepts and allow for automatic computation of outputs for these techniques. This approach aims to ease the design and implementation of such analyses. Moreover, automation makes it possible for the designer to explore trace properties and interact with the trace set as it is currently possible with visualization tools such, as those described in [20].

In order to illustrate and motivate our approach, we consider a calculator application presented in Example 1.

Example 1. We consider a basic calculator with a graphical interface, presented in Figure 1.

Fig. 1. A basic calculator example

A trace corresponds to the set of all the methods associated to events triggered when clicking the buttons represented in Figure 1, i.e. $0, \ldots, 9, +, -, *, /, =$ and 'clear'. For instance, event '0' represents the call of the method activated when button '0' is pressed.

In this example, we assume that the exception related to the division by zero has not been handled by the programmer. In this case, a sequence such as

$$3, +, 5, =, -, 4 * 2, /, 0, =, \text{exception}$$

can be observed. Event 'exception' represents the occurrence of an exception corresponding to a division by zero that is observable at runtime.

Considering the calculator application presented in Example 1, the following traces, containing information about the buttons pressed by the user as well as the occurrence of exceptions can be observed:

$$3, +, 5, =, -, 4 * 2, /, 0, =, \text{exception} \tag{1}$$

$$1, +, 23, +, 4, -13, /, 5, \text{clear}, 1, +, 23, +, 4, -, 13, /, 4, = \tag{2}$$

$$42, *, 3, -, 4, *, 13, =, 43, /, 0, =, \text{exception}, \text{clear}, 43, /, 3, = \tag{3}$$

$$4567, -, 3, -, 334, -673, +, 5, /, 2, =, +, 4, =, *, 3, =, -, 234, = \qquad (4)$$

$$2, +, +, +, +, +, = \qquad (5)$$

We also consider concepts as presented in Figure 2. This figure actually represents two types of concepts. First concepts related to program errors and issues and also concepts related to trace analysis such as invariants, metrics, views, etc. It is also assumed that these concepts are related to each other. For instance, runtime exception are program faults and trace invariants are a type of invariants, but there can be many more. Therefore, some concepts can be sub-concepts of others and this type of relationship is represented by an edge between concepts of Figure 2.

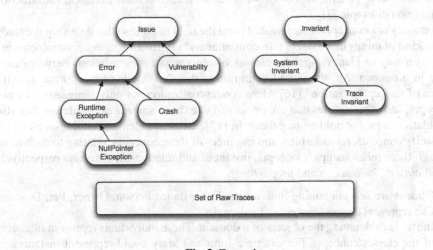

Fig. 2. Example

Our approach considers a system where such concepts are available and it is assumed that algorithm are implemented that automatically match these concepts to traces provided as inputs of the system. These concepts can be used to describe different and even more complex concepts, representing the output of some analysis. This description can be expressed through some logic language and allows for automatic computation of outputs for the described analyses.

Considering Example 1 again, one may have little knowledge about the system and dynamic analysis techniques but may be interested in high level concepts such as:

Invariants related to traces related to system issues.

It would then be desired that this concept is automatically related to the following parts of the known sequences:

$$/, 0, =, \text{exception} \qquad (6)$$

It would then make it clear that the issues reported by the traces (1) to (5) are all related to dividing by 0.

This paper describes our approach to achieve such an interactive system capable of (semi-) automatically performing some analyses on traces. In Section 3, we will introduce some background on ontologies. Due to their formal semantics and available reasoners and query systems we will show that ontologies indeed represent a very adequate framework for dealing with concepts and relationship between them.

3   Background

In this section we provide a reader with a brief introduction to representing knowledge with ontologies, as well as the various methods we employ to query and reason with such knowledge. We assume the reader already has some passing familiarity with dynamic analysis in general, otherwise we refer the reader to some excellent introduction available on this topic [7].

Ontology is a concept that originated from the field of philosophy, denoting the study of the kind of things that exist [5]. In computer and information science, ontologies are used as a way to identify specific classes of objects and their relations between each other in a domain. An often cited definition is that "an ontology is a formal specification of conceptualization" [16]. Here conceptualization not only represents objects, concepts, and other entities that are presumed to exist in some area of interest, but also the relationships that hold among them. In [17], the author defines ontologies as a way to specify concepts, relationships, and instances of these concepts, relating to each other through these relationships. Concepts, instances and relationships are also respectively called *classes*, *individuals* and *properties*.

- Classes are sets containing individuals. For instance Person, Owner, Pet, Dog and Cat represent classes/concepts of a domain.
- Individuals denoting the objects of a domain. These individuals represent instances of the classes/concepts. For example John and Mary could represent instances of the class Person, while Fido could represent an instance of both classes Pet and Dog.
- Properties that are binary relationships between individuals. The fact that John has a pet called Fido can be modelled with a property hasPet(John, Fido).

There exist various ways to extend this basic definition in order to more expressively represent knowledge. Classes can be organised hierarchically. For example the class Owner can be seen as a subclass of Person. Classes can also be further restricted through properties: the Owner class can be defined as a Person for which at least one hasPet property holds. Similarly extra meaning can be added to properties, by defining various characteristics for them such as transitivity, cardinality restrictions, symmetry and others.

The exact expressiveness of an ontology, as well as the ability to perform various reasoning task with it, depends on the specific semantics used. As explained in [9], there is a tradeoff between the expressiveness of a knowledge representation system and the ease of reasoning over the representation of that language. Ontologies often have formal semantics based on Description Logic (DL) ([6]). DLs are logic based formalisms with different decidable fragments, corresponding to different expressiveness, used to represent and to reason about knowledge.

The formal semantic of ontologies make it possible to reason about their contents. These reasoners can deduce facts related to the concepts and relationships as well as classify instances with respect to the concepts that characterize them. Ontologies can also be equipped with a querying system that allows to retrieve information contained in the ontology. More particularly, it is possible to formulate very expressive queries using the semantics defined in the ontologies to retrieve the required knowledge. This form of query is called a *semantic query*. A simple example of such query would be "Who are the persons that own pets?" that returns a set of instances which fulfills this query.

Ontology querying systems and reasoners are often combined in order to benefit from the deductive ability of the reasoner when querying. For instance, consider the case where the ontology has two classes where *DogOwner* is a subclass of *PetOwner*, as well as an individual, *Alfred* for whom it is explicitly given that he is a member of the class *DogOwner*. In this case a possible query would be to return the set of individuals that are members of the *PetOwner* class. Without a reasoner, the previous query would not include *Alfred* as a *DogOwner* as it not given explicitly. With a reasoner fact that he is indeed member of the class *DogOwner* can be inferred, and the query would return this information.

In practice, inference is performed by a reasoner before any query is submitted, in order to make sure such information can be retrieved. With some querying systems it is also possible to update the ontology directly after a query, giving the ability to perform reasoning on the set of newly deduced information.

The Web Ontology Language (OWL) [24] is the ontology language used to describe the various ontologies in this paper. This is a W3C standard [3] ontology language that is one of the most commonly used [10]. It allows for various amounts of expressivity through its sub-languages, called profiles in the latest specification of the language OWL2. OWL can also be seen as an extension of the information and graph specification language RDF [23], In RDF the underlying structure of any knowledge is a set of triples, in the form of a subject, predicate and object. This allows for any OWL ontology represented as a set of RDF triples. For example the fact that , *Alfred owns* the dog *Fido* can be represented as the triple (*Alfred,owns,Fido*), where *Alfred* is the subject, *owns*the predicate and *Fido* the object. Indeed many ontology representation frameworks, especially those we are interested in representing traces and dynamic analyses. store ontologies as triples. As every fact in an ontological knowledge base is a triple, we use it as a measure of the overall size of the ontology as well as a shorthand notation for statements such as the above mentioned (*Alfred,owns,Fido*) that might be part of an ontology.

4 Approach

This section gives an overview of our approach for combining ontologies and DA techniques at a conceptual level. Figure 3 illustrates our approach. It relies on both a trace and dynamic analyses ontology to represent concepts from both domains. First traces are collected from a software system and used as input to populate the *trace ontology*. This corresponds to mapping the trace elements to basic trace related concepts. For instance, the notion of the various event types, such as those created at method entry and exit. The trace ontology contains concepts that are used in the raw traces. Most traces contain concepts such as these events and various attributes to the events to denote the trace information. These attributes can range from the timestamp of the events, to the method that has been invoked, the object that has been used, and other such additional descriptions. Note that in addition to the raw trace information, concepts regarding the source code and the software, can also be considered. As it has been previously noted in [29] such knowledge can also be relevant to dynamic analysis.

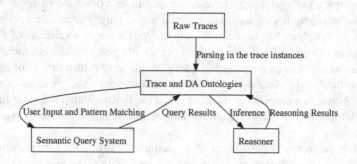

Fig. 3. Approach Overview

Once the (trace) ontology is populated with instance information there are two processes that can occur in conjunction with another:

Reasoners can be used to deduce facts through inference, given the knowledge already in the ontology. As it was explained in Section 3, it is possible to infer various statements through the reasoner. To give a more specific example to DA, we can define a trace as a *bad trace* concept, if one or more *issue* occurs it. In this case the concept that a trace is a *bad trace* can be derived through reasoning if its condition is satisfied. This is of course only one example, in practice many more complex concepts can be inferred.

Semantic querying (querying as a shorthand) would allow the user intending to explore the traces, to define specific criteria based on the semantics represented in the ontologies. This enables the user to create queries based concepts, properties and individuals that can be found in the trace. For example the user could retrieve the all the traces where the *frequency* of an event involving *method* . Queries allows us to easily combine various concepts as well. For example the concept of Frequency Clusters of Frequency Spectrum Analysis [7] could be combined with that of semantic views [21] in order to create a view based on such clusters.

Many results can often be derived through a combination of these approaches: a concept that is used for reasoning could be derived through queries and vice versa. This results in a robust framework for both trace exploration (where the queries would be supported through reasoning) as well as automated analysis (where the queries could help derive facts that would drive the inference).

5 Methodology

In this section we give an overview of the various issues in representing traces and dynamic analysis with ontologies, as well as performing such analysis. We will show what these issues are, how they can be tackled and we give an ontological representation of traces and some dynamic analyses.

A major issue with representing traces in general, but especially with ontologies, is the size of the traces. Consider a simple relationship *before*, denoting that one event is before the other. It seems quite natural to have this relationship in our ontology expressed. However if we are to represent the fact that each event is before another, this would require a creation for a lot of these facts, once per each event pair, which would lead to a very large representation of the trace as an ontology. An alternative way would be to define the *before* relationship as a transitive property and link only the consecutive elements of the trace explicitly. In this case however, the reasoner would deduce the facts that were not given explicitly, and would quickly end up in the aforementioned situation.. For example, given the that the trace consists of three events, *e1*, *e2* and *e3*, and it is explicitly given that *e1* is *before* *e2* and *e2* is *before* *e3* it will also be deduced that *e1* is *before* *e3*. This is a correct conclusion. but it means that after inference we would end up with a dataset that again contains the *before* relationship per pair of events. The cause of these problems is that when representing the traces, we need to represent a large number of individuals, and additional fact that grows in the size of the number of individuals, or even more, is costly to represent. Therefore we need to take care of the various elements represented per trace element or per pair of trace elements, and minimize them whenever possible.

There are a number solutions possible for this issue. One could for example, externalize certain aspects of the trace to a more compact storage format, or simply not represent every possibly information in the raw traces. This later can be done, for example, through the use of metrics to estimate the traces. The issue with these approaches is that they either lose knowledge that might be relevant for further analyses and/or make the semantics of the ontologies harder to overview and use. Indeed one of the strong assets of ontologies is being able to query directly about the semantics, and that these semantics can be defined in way that is in line with the experts view of the domain. By adding an extra layer of semantics to deal with the large size of the traces, we run the risk of weakening the usability of the ontologies by adding concepts and relationships unrelated to the events themselves.

We propose the following Trace ontology as seen in Figure 4 in which we provide an ontology with a reasonable balance between efficient representation of the traces and clarity of the semantics. In this ontology there exist *SingleEvent* events denoting atomic events and *MultiEvent* events, such as *WholeTraces*, that denote events that contain other events. The various event types are similar to those mentioned with existing analysis techniques [21] and the set of event categories can easily be extended to fit any type of event in the trace. The structure of a trace is preserved fully through *WholeTrace* concept which can have a relationship *contain* to a list of event signatures represented by a string. Those event signatures are unique for each unique event, and is one of the many attributes with which an event can be described. These attributes are referred to using properties, such as *hasMethodName*, *hasPackageName*, to denote the name of the method and respectively package involved in that event.

Note that the presented ontology is very generic and small, with only a few event types, and no concepts for multi-threading, but in practice such ontology is often already sufficient for many trace representations and can be expanded with more specific concepts as needed. Because of its genericness and lack of complexity, we also call this trace ontology the Low-level Trace ontology, or more simply the Low-level Ontology.

The ontology for the dynamic analysis techniques, part of which can be seen in Figure 5, is actually an extension of the Low-level ontology. It uses concepts and relationships defined from the Low-level trace ontology and adds to them concepts and relationships for the analysis of the trace. Although they are not a complete translation, the concepts in this ontology were taken from various trace- and dynamic analysis techniques such as Frequency Spectrum Analysis [7], Semantic Views [21] and Trace Metrics [19], as well as some general concepts deemed useful to derive from traces. There are five main categories of these analysis concepts in the ontology: comparison analyses where two or more traces are compared. metrics analysis which derive metrics such as frequencies about the traces, views which are selections of trace elements based on some criteria and patterns that can be encountered, Under these main categories there are many sub concepts that can be derived. It is also possible for a concept to belong to multiple superclasses, for example an invariant could be seen as a pattern analysis as well as a comparison. In addition there is also an extended set of properties as well: for example *refersMaximum* and *refersTotal* to denote a maximum frequency or a total value respectively.

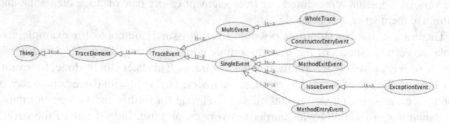

Fig. 4. The Concepts of the Low-level Trace Ontology

Storage of the ontologies can be an issue as even with the above trace ontology, large traces result in a large set of individuals. As mentioned in the Section 3 ontologies can be stored as a set of triples (in the case of OWL ontologies as a set of RDF triples). There exist frameworks that are capable of storing a large number of these types of triples efficiently. These, so called, *triple stores* equipped with a scalable repository system, allow for a storage solution to large RDF graphs, and as a consequence large OWL ontologies, which we require for our ontological representation of traces and dynamic analysis. An example of such a scalable triple store capable of storing ontologies would be Jena framework [11]using one of its persistency options or the OWLIM framework.

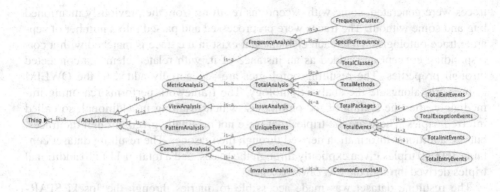

Fig. 5. Some Concepts of the Dynamic Analysis Ontology

Given that the ontologies are stored as triples, we can make use of the SPARQL query language [25] to query the ontologies. This is a query language for RDF triples, but as these triples can constitute an OWL ontology as well, we are able to query OWL ontologies. It allows to perform querying by specifying a graph pattern, which can be matched by using variables and other statements. Its latest version has features, such as aggregates, that are essential to perform certain kind of analyses, and SPARQL-Update language allows us to directly update the resulting dataset from the result of the queries. We make use of the Joseki SPARQL server [2], to make use of these recent features.

Reasoning on this dataset can also be an issue.due to the resulting size of the traces. Most description logic reasoners are in-memory reasoners that run into issues quickly even with moderately small traces. A possible solution is to split the dataset into segments which arc able to fii in memory and can be reasoned on. This however can interfere with certain analyses. Some frameworks, such as OWLIM [22] that we use in our example, have some recent implementations with a reasoner capable of handling large datasets.

6   Example

In this section, we illustrate the approach presented in this work through an example. We consider the traces of an open-source, Java, file synchronization application called DirSyncPro [15]. Analysis on these traces was performed using an implementation of the framework proposed in Section 5. In this section we show a few of these analyses.

DirSyncPro possesses a graphical interface that allows to create, save and open synchronization profiles/configurations. In this example, we illustrate our approach with the DirSyncPro functionality related to the opening of existing configuration files. In version 1.4b1, this feature exhibits a program warning, corresponding to the occurrence of a nullpointer exception.

The class files within the.jar file of the application were instrumented with the Javassist tool[1]. The bytecode was modified in a way that whenever an object was created, a method initialized, a method exited or an exception occurred a String was outputted indicating the type of the event, and the method signature. Using this setup 8 separate traces were generated, some with exceptions resulting from the previously mentioned bug and some without. The traces were preprocessed and parsed into a number of separate trace ontologies. Here each element that exist in the trace is matched with a corresponding concept and added as an instance of it, with related elements connected through properties. The resulting ontologies are sequentially added to the OWLIM framework, alongside the analysis ontology. The framework performs reasoning immediately after the adding of the ontologies. which resulting in additional, so called inferred triples. These are the triples that were not originally given through the traces, but are additional information derived through the reasoner. The resulting dataset contains 360060 triples given explicitly through the traces, and a total of 114540 additional triples derived through the OWLIM reasoner.

The resulting dataset was made accessible to queries through the Joseki SPAR-QLserver [2]. There were many different queries implemented, but due to space constraints we only show a select number of them to detail the possibilities of utilising semantic queries in our framework. In the following queries, the *lowlevel* and *danalysis* are shorthand for the URI of the trace and analysis ontologies. Similarly *rdf* and *list* denote the URI of the ontology for the basic rdf elements (such as the type-of relation) and the way to manipulate lists.

SELECT DISTINCT ?package
WHERE ?event lowlevel:refersPackageName ?package

The first, very simple, query retrieves the list of the packages that can be found in all the traces. It also shows off the general feature of these queries where a pattern of triples can be made, which may include variables, after which the matched data can be manipulated. Here we search for all the events that refer to a package name, with the package name as a variable, to get the list of all the packages as it can be seen in Figure 6.

package
"dirsyncpro.tools"
"dirsyncpro"
"dirsyncpro.gui"
"dirsyncpro.job"
"dirsyncpro.sync"
"dirsyncpro.message"
"dirsyncpro.schedule"
"dirsyncpro.gui.swing"
"dirsyncpro.gui.jobtree"
"dirsyncpro.gui.scheduletree"
"dirsyncpro.gui.filtertree"
"dirsyncpro.gui.verifier"
"dirsyncpro.gui.syncq"
"dirsyncpro.gui.messagetable"
"dirsyncpro.gui.scheduletable"
"dirsyncpro.xml"
"dirsyncpro.updater"

Fig. 6. The list of packages in all the traces

```
SELECT DISTINCT (count(?eventsignature) AS ?totalmethodentryevents)
?event lowlevel:refersSignature ?eventsignature.
?event rdf:type lowlevel:MethodEntryEvent .
```

The second query counts the number of *MethodEntryEvent* types in the dataset. This uses the aggregates feature of the query language to compute totals, which can be useful for subsequent analyses. In this case the result was 448 of such events.

```
SELECT DISTINCT ?tracesignature ?eventsignature ?index
?trace lowlevel:refersSignature ?tracesignature.
?trace lowlevel:contains ?list .
?list list:index (?index ?eventsignature).
?event lowlevel:refersSignature ?eventsignature.
?event rdf:type lowlevel:IssueEvent .
```

tracesignature	eventsignature	index
"DirSyncProTrace1"	"Exception_NullPointerException"	"1586" ^^<http://www.w3.org/2001/XMLSchema#integer>
"DirSyncProTrace3"	"Exception_NullPointerException"	"892" ^^<http://www.w3.org/2001/XMLSchema#integer>
"DirSyncProTrace4"	"Exception_NullPointerException"	"32" ^^<http://www.w3.org/2001/XMLSchema#integer>

Fig. 7. The list of issues in all the traces

The third query returns all the issues are found in the traces along with their trace-name and location, as shown in Figure 7. Note that none of the raw traces contain any concept of *issue* explicitly, these facts have been inferred through the reasoner, using the subclass relationship between exception and issue. If the same query was asked on a system without any reasoning, it would have returned zero results.

```
INSERT DATA
<http://example/frequencyanalysis1>rdf:type analysis:FrequencyCluster .
<http://example/frequencyanalysis1>analysis:refersMaximum 20 .
<http://example/frequencyanalysis1>analysis:refersMinimum 5 .
```

Finally the datasets themselves can also be directly updated through queries. The above query would create a frequency cluster in which the maximum of the cluster is 20 and the minimum is 5. Once this fact is inserted into an ontology it can be used in the same way as trace information is. For example it is possible to write a query to populate the cluster with only those events that have a total of occurrences within the range of this cluster.

Note that this is just a small glance of the abilities of the query language in conjunction with the reasoner. For a more complete overview of the used querying and reasoning implementations capabilities we refer the reader to the Joseki[2] and respectively the OWLIM specification [22].

7   Conclusion and Future Work

In this paper we have presented a system in which ontologies are used to as a knowledge model for traces as well as dynamic analysis, with which trace exploration and dynamic analyses can be performed easier and more automatically. Although the traces used in our test cases were reasonably modest, the storage, querying and reasoning frameworks on which it is built, most notably OWLIM, is capable of storing and working with millions of triples [8].

While the combination of dynamic analysis and ontologies is a relatively recent idea [4], there exist similar works in the field of static analysis and ontologies [27, 30]. One of the main issues of combining DA and ontologies is due to the problems of ontologies and reasoners when faced with large amounts of, ordered facts. Improving on the reasoning capabilities of ontological frameworks on such knowledge bases, would yield great improvements for our approach. There are some similar issues being dealt within the field of stream reasoning in ontologies [14], where reasoning is done on streams of ordered data. The main difference is that in our case, when dealing with existing traces, the set of ordered facts is finite and fully known beforehand.

The proposed framework is capable of handling actual programs with reasonably sized traces, but the amount of facts generated with this approach might not make it suitable for very large applications and/or extremely large traces. As previously mentioned there exist many factors involved in making the system scalable, such as the type of information represented, the reasoning used, etc. Although the current options suit the type of traces and applications similar to the example, a more through exploration of these is needed in the future.

There are various ways in which the presented framework could be improved. The trace and analysis ontologies can both be expanded to include more concepts relating to traces analyses. Furthermore the deriving of analyses through queries can be more integrated with the framework. Ideally we would even be able to access external tools from the query system as needed.

A strong feature of ontologies is that many different types of knowledge can be integrated. In the realm of dynamic analyses, we could have ontologies represent use cases, bugs reports, and test cases within this framework. There also exist substantial work in the field of static analysis and ontologies in using source code and documentation as a knowledge base [27, 30, 26]. By integrating these into the framework we could enable a better integration of dynamic and static analysis using ontologies.

One goal for our approach, and indeed for many others in dynamic analysis, is to limit, if not eliminate the need for costly and time consuming analysis by experts. In this context, using ontologies to represent traces and analysis can be seen as a form of program comprehension performed not only for and by human users but by some degree for the analysis software itself. By creating a more robust framework with which this can happen could will enable analyses currently done by an expert to partially or even fully performed by the analysis software.

References

[1] Javassist, http://www.javassist.org

[2] Joseki sparql server, http://www.joseki.org

[3] The world wide web consortium, w3c, http://www.w3.org

[4] Al Haider, N., Nixon, P., Gaudin, B.: An approach for modeling dynamic analysis using ontologies. In: WODA 2010: Proceedings of the Eighth International Workshop on Dynamic Analysis, pp. 1–6. ACM, New York (2010)

[5] Antoniou, G., Franconi, E., van Harmelen, F.: Introduction to Semantic Web Ontology Languages. In: Eisinger, N., Małuszyński, J. (eds.) Reasoning Web 2005. LNCS, vol. 3564, pp. 1–21. Springer, Heidelberg (2005)

[6] Baader, F.: The description logic handbook: theory, implementation, and applications. Cambridge Univ. Pr. (2003)

[7] Ball, T.: The Concept of Dynamic Analysis. SIGSOFT Softw. Eng. Notes 24(6), 216–234 (1999)

[8] Bizer, C., Schultz, A.: The berlin sparql benchmark. International Journal on Semantic Web and Information Systems-Special Issue on Scalability and Performance of Semantic Web Systems (2009)

[9] Brachman, R.J., Levesque, H.J.: The tractability of subsumption in frame-based description languages. In: Proc. of the 4th Nat. Conf. on Artificial Intelligence (AAAI 1984), pp. 34–37 (1984)

[10] Cardoso, J.: The semantic web vision: Where are we? IEEE Intelligent Systems 22(5), 84–88 (2007)

[11] Carroll, J.J., Dickinson, I., Dollin, C., Reynolds, D., Seaborne, A., Wilkinson, K.: Jena: implementing the semantic web recommendations. In: Proceedings of the 13th International World Wide Web Conference on Alternate Track Papers & Posters, pp. 74–83. ACM (2004)

[12] Chandrasekaran, B., Josephson, J.R., Benjamins, V.R.: What are ontologies, and why do we need them? IEEE Intelligent Systems 14(1), 20–26 (1999)

[13] Cornelissen, B., Zaidman, A., van Deursen, A., Moonen, L., Koschke, R.: A systematic survey of program comprehension through dynamic analysis. Technical Report TUD-SERG-2008-033, Delft University of Technology (2008)

[14] Della Valle, E., Ceri, S., van Harmelen, F., Fensel, D.: It's a streaming world! reasoning upon rapidly changing information. IEEE Intelligent Systems 24(6), 83–89 (2009)

[15] Dirsyncpro, http://www.dirsyncpro.org

[16] Gruber, T.R.: Toward principles for the design of ontologies used for knowledge sharing. Int. J. Hum.-Comput. Stud. 43(5-6), 907–928 (1995)

[17] Gruber, T.: Ontology, entry in the encyclopedia of database systems (2009)

[18] Haarslev, V., Möller, R.: Description of the racer system and its applications. In: Goble, C.A., McGuinness, D.L., Möller, R., Patel-Schneider, P.F. (eds.) Description Logics. CEUR Workshop Proceedings, vol. 49 (2001)

[19] Hamou-Lhadj, A., Lethbridge, T.C.: Measuring various properties of execution traces to help build better trace analysis tools. In: Proceedings of the 10th IEEE International Conference on Engineering of Complex Computer Systems, ICECCS 2005, pp. 559–568 (June 2005)

[20] Hamou-Lhadj, A., Lethbridge, T.C.: A survey of trace exploration tools and techniques. In: CASCON 2004: Proceedings of the 2004 Conference of the Centre for Advanced Studies on Collaborative Research, pp. 42–55. IBM Press (2004)

[21] Hoffman, K.J., Eugster, P., Jagannathan, S.: Semantics-aware trace analysis. SIGPLAN Not. 44(6), 453–464 (2009)

[22] Kiryakov, A., Ognyanov, D., Manov, D.: OWLIM – A Pragmatic Semantic Repository for OWL. In: Dean, M., Guo, Y., Jun, W., Kaschek, R., Krishnaswamy, S., Pan, Z., Sheng, Q.Z. (eds.) WISE 2005 Workshops. LNCS, vol. 3807, pp. 182–192. Springer, Heidelberg (2005)

[23] Klyne, G., Carroll, J.J., McBride, B.: Resource description framework (RDF): Concepts and abstract syntax. Changes (2004)

[24] Motik, B., Patel-Schneider, P.F., Parsia, B., Bock, C., Fokoue, A., Haase, P., Hoekstra, R., Horrocks, I., Ruttenberg, A., Sattler, U., et al.: OWL 2 web ontology language: Structural specification and functional-style syntax. W3C Working Draft, W3C (2008)

[25] Pérez, J., Arenas, M., Gutierrez, C.: Semantics and Complexity of SPARQL. In: Cruz, I., Decker, S., Allemang, D., Preist, C., Schwabe, D., Mika, P., Uschold, M., Aroyo, L.M. (eds.) ISWC 2006. LNCS, vol. 4273, pp. 30–43. Springer, Heidelberg (2006)

[26] Ratiu, D., Deissenboeck, F.: Programs are knowledge bases. In: 14th IEEE International Conference on Program Comprehension, ICPC 2006, pp. 79–83 (2006)

[27] Ratiu, D., Feilkas, M., Jürjens, J., Keynes, M., Britain, G.: Extracting domain ontologies from domain specific APIs. In: Proceedings of the 12th European Conference on Software Maintenance and Reengineering (CSMR 2008), vol. 26. IEEE CS (2008)

[28] Sirin, E., Parsia, B., Grau, B.C., Kalyanpur, A., Katz, Y.: Pellet: A practical owl-dl reasoner. Web Semantics: Science, Services and Agents on the World Wide Web 5(2), 51–53 (2007)

[29] Zeller, A., für Softwaretechnik, L.: Program analysis: A hierarchy. In: Proceedings of the ICSE Workshop on Dynamic Analysis (WODA 2003), pp. 6–9. Citeseer (2003)

[30] Zhang, Y.: An Ontology-based Program Comprehension Model. PhD thesis, Concordia University (2007)

Monitoring Realizability*

Rüdiger Ehlers and Bernd Finkbeiner

Reactive Systems Group
Saarland University
66123 Saarbrücken, Germany

Abstract. We present a new multi-valued monitoring approach for linear-time temporal logic that classifies trace prefixes not only according to the existence of correct and erroneous continuations, but also according to the strategic power of the system and its environment to avoid or enforce a violation of the specification. We classify the monitoring status into four levels: (1) the worst case is a *violation*, where no continuation satisfies the specification any more; (2) *unrealizable* means that the environment can force the system to violate the specification; (3) *realizable* means that the system can enforce that the specification is satisfied; (4) the best case, *fulfilled*, indicates that all possible continuations satisfy the specification. Because our approach recognizes situations where the system cannot avoid a violation even though there may still be continuations in which the specification is satisfied, our approach detects errors earlier, and it detects errors that are missed by less detailed classifications. We give an asymptotically optimal construction of multi-valued monitoring automata based on parity games.

1 Introduction

One of the guiding principles of runtime monitoring is that violations of the specification should be reported *as early as possible*, giving the user (or controller) time to act before the violation causes serious harm. The principle means that the monitor must reason about the future: we issue a warning as soon as we can *predict* that a violation is about to occur. The standard implementation of this idea is to consider a finite trace as *bad* if all its infinite extensions violate the specification. In other words, as long as there *exists* a future in which the specification is satisfied, we assume that this future will actually occur and do not issue a warning.

In this paper, we revisit this optimistic interpretation of the future. In reality, not all future actions are under the system's control. It is therefore possible to reach situations where the system can no longer *avoid* the violation, even though there exists some continuation in which the violation does not occur. Such situations are important early indicators of failure: we know for sure that

---

* This work was partly supported by the German Research Foundation (DFG) under the project SpAGAT (grant no. FI 936/2-1) in the priority programme "Reliably Secure Software Systems – RS3".

S. Khurshid and K. Sen (Eds.): RV 2011, LNCS 7186, pp. 427–441, 2012.

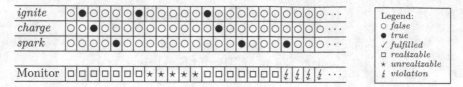

Fig. 1. Example execution and monitoring trace of a faulty ignition controller. The controller responds correctly to the first ignition request, by charging the coil and then emitting a spark. The specification is realizable (□), but not fulfilled (✓), because there exists a continuation that violates the specfication. After the second ignition request, the controller fails to charge the coil. The monitor therefore switches from *realizable* to *unrealizable* (⋆). At the third ignition request, the monitor switches back to *realizable* and stays, because the controller responds correctly, in *realizable* until the spontaneous third spark occurs. At this point, the monitor recognizes a *violation* (♮).

the system does not satisfy its specification, we just cannot guarantee that the violation will be visible on the execution we are about to see.

Consider a car ignition controller that needs to charge a coil before emitting a spark, and that is, to save energy, only allowed to start charging when an ignition request is issued. The controller has an input signal *ignite* and two output signals *charge* and *spark*, whose behavior could be specified in linear-time temporal logic as follows (abstracting from implementation details like the charging time and other activities of the ignition controller):

$$\psi = \neg spark \ \wedge \ \neg spark \, \mathcal{W} \, charge \ \wedge \Box(spark \to \bigcirc (\neg spark \, \mathcal{W} \, charge))$$
$$\wedge \ \neg charge \ \wedge \ \Box(\bigcirc charge \to ignite) \ \wedge \ \Box(ignite \to \bigcirc\Diamond spark)$$

Under what circumstances should we raise an alarm? Clearly, it is appropriate to issue a warning if *charge* is activated without an ignition request or if a spark is emitted without previously charging the coil. In both situations, the specification is definitely violated, because there is no possible continuation into the future that would satisfy the specification. However, a smart observer would be able to recognize problems earlier than that. Suppose an ignition request is given, but the system does not *immediately* charge the coil in the next step. It is easy to see that this is a mistake, because now the system can no longer prevent the conjunct □ (*ignite* → ○◇*spark*) from becoming false: if no more ignition requests come in, then the coil will never be charged, and, hence, the spark can never be emitted.

How can we recognize such mistakes? One way to characterize the situation is to observe that there exists an extension that violates the specification. This condition is easy to check, we simply monitor the negation of the specification as well. However, issuing a warning whenever there exists a violating extension would be overly pessimistic: Since, right from the start, there always exists a path that violates the specification, we would continuously warn that things "may" go wrong.

The exact right time for the warning is when there is an ignition request but the coil is not charged in the very next step. At this point, we not only know that there exists a continuation that violates the specification, we can actually identify the inputs a malicious environment would need to produce in order to *enforce* that the violation will occur. We say that in this situation the specification is *unrealizable*. While it is still too early to tell if the specification will really become violated (if a second ignition comes in and the system charges the coil at that time, things are fine), the system under observation must be faulty because there is no system that satisfies the specification for all possible future inputs.

In this paper, we give a precise analysis of the possible futures by distinguishing the different roles played by *outputs*, which are under the system's control, and *inputs*, which are chosen by the (potentially hostile) environment. This results in a finer classification of the monitoring situation with four different conditions, going from worst case to best case as follows:

1. *violation:* the specification is definitely violated, i.e., there is no more continuation that satisfies the specification;
2. *unrealizable:* the specification is not violated but unrealizable, i.e., the environment can force the system to violate the specification;
3. *realizable:* the specification is not fulfilled but realizable, i.e., there is a continuation in which the specification is violated, but the system can enforce that the specification is satisfied; and
4. *fulfilled:* the specification is definitely satisfied, i.e., there is no continuation that violates the specification.

Figure 1 shows an execution trace of a faulty ignition controller, which occasionally fails to charge the coil and at some point produces a spontaneous spark. The monitor starts out in condition *realizable*, and switches to *unrealizable* when there is an ignition request but the coil is not charged. This alert is serious: a bug has been detected. However, the monitor does not report a violation yet, and indeed, in the trace, the user reacts by requesting another ignition, and when, this time, the coil is charged, the monitor switches back to *realizable*. Only when, later, there is a spontaneous spark, the monitor raises the alarm: the specification is definitely violated at that point.

Semantically, our approach is a departure from the classic linear-time approach to runtime monitoring. Distinguishing inputs and outputs naturally leads to *games*, rather than sets of traces, as the underlying model of computation. Figure 2 shows the game between the ignition controller and its environment. The two players take turns. In the states owned by the system player the ignition controller chooses the outputs, in the states owned by the environment player, the environment chooses the inputs. The winning condition is expressed as a parity condition: if the highest number that appears infinitely often during a play of the game is even, then the system player wins, otherwise the environment player wins. From the initial state, the system player has a winning strategy: always stay in states A through F. If the system player deviates from this strategy by moving from state C to state G, then the environment player has a winning strategy: from state G, always move to state H, never back to C. If, however, the environment player does at some point move back to C, then

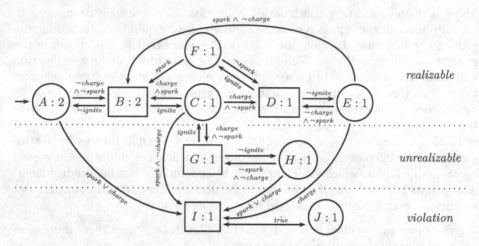

Fig. 2. Parity game between the ignition controller and its environment. Positions owned by the system player are shown as circles, positions owned by the environment as squares. The system player has a winning strategy from states A through F, the environment player has a winning strategy in all other states. From states I and J, the environment player wins no matter how the strategy is chosen. A runtime monitor tracing this game will report *realizable* in states A through F, *unrealizable* in states G and H, and *violation* in states I and J.

the system player has again a winning strategy. The game is definitely lost for the system player if the play reaches states I or J, indicating that the system player has issued a spark or charge out of turn. From these states, the game is won by the environment player, no matter which moves are chosen.

The runtime monitor traces the states in the game while processing the observations from the monitored system. In states A through F, the status is *realizable*, because the system player has a winning strategy, in states G and H, the status is *unrealizable*, because the environment player has a winning strategy, and in states I and J, the status is *violation*, because the environment player wins independently of the strategy. In the paper, we explain the construction of the game and the resulting monitor in more detail. We start by converting the specification to an equivalent deterministic parity automaton and its corresponding parity game. Solving the game partitions the automaton into sets of states corresponding to the four monitoring conditions. Based on this classification, we construct a finite-state machine that implements the monitor.

In the last technical section of the paper, Section 4, we add one more twist to the game-based analysis: in addition to recognizing whether one of the players has a winning strategy, we check if the violation or fulfillment of the specification can be enforced *in a finite number of steps*. This allows the user to estimate the urgency of the *unrealizable* monitoring status: if the number of steps is finite, then the system is in imminent danger; if not, we know that, while the system cannot avoid the violation without help from the environment, the system can at least *delay* the violation for an unbounded number of steps.

Related work. There has been a long debate in runtime verification about the best way to translate specifications, which refer to infinite computations, into monitors, which are limited to observing finite prefixes. Kupferman and Vardi coined the term *informative prefix* for prefixes that "tell the whole story" why a specification is violated [11]. The advantage of informative prefixes is that one can monitor the specification without analyzing the future. For example, one can translate the specification into a small equivalent alternating automaton and track the active states in disjunctive or conjunctive normal form [7]. However, informative prefixes are usually longer than necessary. For example, an informative prefix of the specification   *false* has length one, although one could deduce the violation of the formula without seeing any trace at all. In order to recognize violations earlier, one needs to quantify over the possible futures. A prefix is *bad* [11] if there is no infinite extension that satisfies the specification. In order to construct a monitor that recognizes the bad prefixes, one translates the formula into an equivalent nondeterministic Büchi automaton, eliminates all states with empty language, and then determinizes with a powerset construction into an automaton on finite words that recognizes the bad prefixes. d'Amorim and Roşu showed that the runtime overhead caused by monitoring can be reduced significantly by recognizing when the observed prefix can no longer be extended to a bad prefix and pruning such "Never-Violate" states from the monitor [3].

Our approach to check *realizability* in addition to satisfiability builds on algorithms for reactive synthesis. In synthesis, we check whether the specification is realizable, i.e., whether there exists an implementation for the given specification. Similar to our monitoring approach, one analyzes the game between the system and its environment and searches for a winning strategy for the system player [2]. The key difference between checking and monitoring realizability is, however, that in synthesis we only check for the existence of a strategy from the initial state, whereas in monitoring we make this judgment again and again, as we observe a growing prefix of a trace.

The monitoring work that is closest to our approach is *interface monitoring* as proposed by Pnueli et al. [16]. In this work, an interface monitor is compiled from a module implementation together with its interface specification. The analysis considers a game, where the nondeterminism of the module is seen as one player and the interface behavior as the other. It is assumed that the interface is trying to satisfy both its own specification and the global specification, and the module is trying to produce a violation. In contrast to this approach, we monitor the behavior of the system rather than its interface, because we are interested in execution faults where the behavior of the system deviates from its specification. In order to obtain monitors of reasonable size, we also avoid encoding the implementation of any part of the system into the monitor.

The approach of this paper can be seen as an extension of three-valued monitoring of linear-time temporal logic [1]. Taking the input/output interface of a system into account significantly increases the usefulness of multi-valued monitoring, because now even violations of liveness constraints that depend on input to the system can be detected.

2   Monitoring Reactive Systems

We are interested in monitoring *reactive systems*, which interact with their environment over a potentially infinite run. We start by recalling standard notions and constructions from runtime monitoring.

2.1   Preliminaries

Interfaces. The *interface* of a reactive system is defined as a tuple $\mathcal{I} = (\mathrm{AP}_I, \mathrm{AP}_O)$, where AP_I is a finite set of input signals to the system and AP_O is a finite set of output signals. Together, the two sets form the *atomic propositions* $\mathrm{AP} = \mathrm{AP}_I \uplus \mathrm{AP}_O$ of the system. During the execution of the system, it produces a (potentially infinite) word $w = w_0 w_1 \ldots$, where, in every step, the valuation of the input signals is read and the respective valuation of the output signals is produced, i.e., for every $i \in \mathbb{N}$, $w_i \in 2^{\mathrm{AP}_I} \times 2^{\mathrm{AP}_O}$. We call the words produced by the execution of a system also the *traces* of the system. Depending on whether it is assumed that in every step first the input or output is read, the system model corresponds to the one of Mealy or Moore machines [13], respectively. The techniques in this paper are equally applicable in both models, although we assume a Moore machine model in the following.

Execution trees. The behavior of a (deterministic) reactive system with interface $\mathcal{I} = (\mathrm{AP}_I, \mathrm{AP}_O)$ can be represented as an infinite tree $\langle T, \tau \rangle$, where $T \subseteq (2^{\mathrm{AP}_I})^*$ is the set of nodes of the tree, and $\tau : T \to 2^{\mathrm{AP}_O}$ is the labeling function of the tree, i.e., it decorates every node of the tree with an output. The meaning of an execution tree is as follows. If $t = t_0 \ldots t_n \in T$ is the input of the system read since the system went into service, then $\tau(t)$ is the output of the system in the $n+1$st clock cycle. We say that an infinite *path* $p = p_0 p_1 \ldots \in (2^{\mathrm{AP}_I})^\omega$ *induces* a word/trace $w = (p_0, \tau(\epsilon))(p_1, \tau(p_0))(p_2, \tau(p_0 p_1)) \ldots \in (2^{\mathrm{AP}_I} \times 2^{\mathrm{AP}_O})^\omega$ in the execution tree. An execution tree is called *full* if $T = (2^{\mathrm{AP}_I})^*$.

The idea behind execution trees is that the decision of the next output is based on the entire history of inputs received so far. A reactive system is assumed to have a full execution tree: because it has no control over the input, any input sequence can arise during its execution.

We say that an execution tree (or a reactive system represented by the tree) satisfies some word language $L \subseteq (2^{\mathrm{AP}_I} \times 2^{\mathrm{AP}_O})^\omega$ if every word that is induced by some path in the tree is contained in L.

Linear-time temporal logic (LTL). LTL [14] is a commonly used specification logic for reactive systems. LTL describes linear-time properties, i.e., sets of correct traces. Formulas in LTL are built from atomic propositions, Boolean operators and the temporal operators $\Box$ (globally), $\Diamond$ (finally), $\mathcal{U}$ (until) and $\mathcal{W}$ (weak until). Given an infinite trace $w = w_0 w_1 \ldots \in (2^{\mathrm{AP}})^\omega$ over some set of atomic propositions AP, we define the satisfaction of an LTL formula inductively over the structure of the LTL formula. Let ϕ_1 and ϕ_2 be LTL formulas and w^i denote the suffix of a word $w = w_0 w_1 \ldots$ starting from the ith element, i.e., $w^i = w_i w_{i+1} \ldots$. The semantics of LTL is defined as follows:

- $w \models p$ if and only if (iff) $p \in w_0$ for $p \in \mathrm{AP}$
- $w \models \neg\psi$ iff not $w \models \psi$
- $w \models (\phi_1 \vee \phi_2)$ iff $w \models \phi_1$ or $w \models \phi_2$
- $w \models (\phi_1 \wedge \phi_2)$ iff $w \models \phi_1$ and $w \models \phi_2$
- $w \models \bigcirc\phi_1$ iff $w^1 \models \phi_1$
- $w \models \Box\phi_1$ iff for all $i \in \mathbb{N}$, $w^i \models \phi_1$
- $w \models \Diamond\phi_1$ iff there exists some $i \in \mathbb{N}$ such that $w^i \models \phi_1$
- $w \models (\phi_1 \mathcal{U} \phi_2)$ iff there exists some $i \in \mathbb{N}$ such that for all $0 \le j < i$, $w^j \models \phi_1$ and $w^i \models \phi_2$
- $w \models (\phi_1 \mathcal{W} \phi_2)$ iff for every $i \in \mathbb{N}$ such that $w^0 \not\models \phi_2$, $w^1 \not\models \phi_2$, ..., $w^{i-1} \not\models \phi_2$ and $w^i \not\models \phi_2$, also for all $0 \le j < i$, $w^j \models \phi_1$.

The set of traces that satisfy an LTL formula is called its *language*. The *length* of an LTL formula is defined as the number of occurrences of operators and atomic propositions. We say that an execution tree (or a reactive system) satisfies an LTL formula ψ if it satisfies the language of the formula.

Runtime monitoring. As discussed under related work, there are multiple definitions of the LTL runtime monitoring problem. The "standard" problem defined in the following is based on three-valued monitoring [1]. We wish to observe the trace of the reactive system and raise an *alarm* whenever the trace prefix cannot be completed into an infinite trace that satisfies the specification, and to raise a *success* signal whenever the trace cannot be completed to one that does not satisfy the specification. Given an LTL formula ϕ over a set of atomic propositions AP, we can build a *monitor automaton* for ϕ, i.e., a finite state machine that observes the input and output of a system and where every state is labeled by *safe*, *unknown* or *bad*. During the run of the monitor, the state labels represent whether the prefix trace observed witnesses the violation or satisfaction of the formula by every continuation of the prefix trace. Formally, such a monitor is represented as a tuple $\mathcal{M} = (S, \Sigma, \delta, s_0, L)$, where S is the set of states, $\Sigma = 2^{\mathrm{AP}}$ is the input alphabet, $\delta : S \times \Sigma \to S$ is the transition function, $s_0 \in S$ the initial state and $L : S \to \{safe, unknown, bad\}$ is the labeling function. We also say that (S, Σ, δ, s_0) is the *transition structure* of $\mathcal{M}$. Given a finite word $w = w_0 w_1 \ldots w_n \in (2^{\mathrm{AP}})^n$, we say that w induces a (prefix) run $\pi = \pi_0 \ldots \pi_{n+1}$ in $\mathcal{M}$ such that $\pi_0 = s_0$ and for every $i \in \{0, \ldots, n\}$, we have $\pi_{i+1} = \delta(\pi_i, w_i)$. By abuse of notation, we write $\pi_{n+1} = \delta(s_0, w_0 \ldots w_n)$.

A finite-state machine $\mathcal{M} = (S, \Sigma, \delta, s_0, L)$ with $\Sigma = 2^{\mathrm{AP}}$ represents a monitor for an LTL formula ϕ over AP if the following conditions are satisfied: (1) for every $w \subset (2^{\mathrm{AP}})^*$, $L(\delta(s_0, w)) = bad$ if and only if for all $w' \in (2^{\mathrm{AP}})^\omega$, $ww' \not\models \phi$ (so the formula can no longer be satisfied); and (2) for every $w \in (2^{\mathrm{AP}})^*$, $L(\delta(s_0, w)) = good$ if and only if for all $w' \in (2^{\mathrm{AP}})^\omega$, $ww' \models \phi$ (so the formula will be satisfied whatever happens in the future). We call the set of prefix traces that lead to a good state in a monitor the *good prefixes*, and the prefix traces that lead to a bad state in a monitor its *bad prefixes*.

Constructing runtime monitors for LTL. There are standard constructions to translate LTL formulas to monitor automata. For reference, we quickly recall the construction described in [1]. We start by building nondeterministic automata for both the specification and its negation. In these automata, we prune states with empty language and then determinize with a powerset construction. The product of the resulting deterministic finite-word automaton represents a monitor with a doubly-exponential number of states in the length of the original specification. As shown by Kupferman and Vardi [11], there is a doubly-exponential lower bound and the construction is therefore essentially optimal[1].

2.2   Constructing Monitors from Deterministic Parity Automata

In preparation for our main construction in Section 3, which is based on parity games, we now present an alternative monitor construction via deterministic parity automata.

A *deterministic parity automaton* is a tuple $\mathcal{A} = (Q, \Sigma, \delta, q_0, c)$ with the set of states Q, the alphabet Σ, the transition function $\delta : Q \times \Sigma \to Q$, the initial state q_0 and the coloring function $c : Q \to \mathbb{N}$. Given an infinite word $w = w_0 w_1 \ldots$, w induces a run $\pi = \pi_0 \pi_1 \ldots$ over $\mathcal{A}$, where $\pi_0 = q_0$ and for every $i \in \mathbb{N}$, $\pi_{i+1} = \delta(\pi_i, w_i)$. Likewise, a finite word $w = w_0 w_1 \ldots w_n$ induces a finite run $\pi = \pi_0 \pi_1 \ldots \pi_{n+1}$ in $\mathcal{A}$ where $\pi_0 = q_0$ and for every $i \in \{0, \ldots, n\}$, we have $\pi_{i+1} = \delta(\pi_i, w_i)$. We say that an infinite word w is in the language of $\mathcal{A}$, denoted by $\mathcal{L}(\mathcal{A})$, if and only if for the run $\pi = \pi_0 \pi_1 \ldots$, the highest number occurring infinitely often in the sequence $c(\pi_0), c(\pi_1), c(\pi_2), \ldots$ is even. For the scope of this paper we require, without loss of generality, the transition function to be a complete function. We refer to (Q, Σ, δ, q_0) as the *transition structure* of $\mathcal{A}$.

Given an LTL formula ϕ over a set of atomic propositions AP, we can translate ϕ to a deterministic parity automaton $\mathcal{A}$ over the alphabet 2^{AP} such that for every infinite word $w \in (2^{\text{AP}})^\omega$, we have $w \models \phi$ if and only if $w \in \mathcal{L}(\mathcal{A})$. The automaton $\mathcal{A}$ has $2^{O(2^n n \log n)}$ states and $3(n+1)2^n$ colors [18].

In order to build a monitor for an LTL formula from its equivalent deterministic parity automaton, we need to identify the states with universal or empty language. Given an automaton $\mathcal{A} = (Q, \Sigma, \delta, q_0, c)$, for every $q \in Q$, we denote by $\mathcal{A}_q$ the automaton $(Q, \Sigma, \delta, q, c)$, i.e., the same automaton but with a different initial state. If for a $q \in Q$, $\mathcal{L}(\mathcal{A}_q) = \emptyset$, we say that q has an *empty language*, or if $\mathcal{L}(\mathcal{A}_q) = \Sigma^\omega$, we say that q has *universal language*. To identify the states with empty language, we check each of the automata $\mathcal{A}_q$ for $q \in Q$ for emptiness (see [5] for a suitable procedure). States with universal language are identified by doing the same on a version of the automaton where 1 is added to every color, which complements the language of each state. Based on the sets of states with the empty and universal language, we identify bad and good prefixes:

---

[1] Kupferman and Vardi prove a $2^{2^{\Omega(\sqrt{n})}}$ lower bound, while the construction from [1] leads to an automaton of size 2^{2^n}, where n denotes the length of the LTL formula. The difference is negligible, however, because we can carry out a precise finite-state machine minimization [8] after the construction of the monitor.

Lemma 1. *Let $\mathcal{A} = (Q, 2^{\mathrm{AP}}, \delta, q_0, c)$ be a deterministic parity automaton that is obtained by a translation from an LTL formula ψ over the set of atomic propositions* AP, $E \subseteq Q$ *be the set of the states of $\mathcal{A}$ that have an empty language, and* $U \subseteq Q$ *be the set of states of $\mathcal{A}$ that have a universal language.*

For every finite word $w \in (2^{\mathrm{AP}})^*$, w induces a run in $\mathcal{A}$ that ends in a state in E iff w is a bad prefix for ψ. Likewise, w induces a run in $\mathcal{A}$ that ends in a state in U iff w is a good prefix for ψ.

With this lemma, we can now transform the deterministic parity automaton into a monitor: we take the same set of states, label every state with an empty parity automaton language with *bad* and every state with a universal parity automaton language with *good*.

The monitor based on the parity automaton is slightly larger than the one described in the previous subsection ($2^{O(2^n n \log n)}$ states compared to 2^{2^n} states)[2]. The advantage of using the transition structure of the deterministic parity automaton is, however, that it allows us to recognize realizability, as we will see in the following section.

3   Monitoring Realizability

As discussed in the introduction, a monitor that only detects bad and good prefixes misses early indicators of failure, where the environment can enforce a violation of the specification. Such a violation of *realizability* means that the system under observation is incorrect, because there exists an input that will cause a violation of the specification, but the situation is less severe than the occurrence of a bad prefix, because the bad input might not actually occur during the current run of the system.

3.1   Parity Games

In a parity game, two players play for an infinite duration of time. The game consists of a set of states, which are connected by labeled edges. Every state is assigned to one of the two players, *Player 0* and *Player 1*. The game is played by moving a pebble along the edges of the game. Whenever the pebble is on a state that belongs to the some player, this player gets to choose the action. The pebble then moves according to the edge function to a state of the opposing player. Every state has a color. A play is won by Player 0 if the highest color visited infinitely often along the play is even.

Formally, a *parity game* is a tuple $\mathcal{G} = (V_0, V_1, \Sigma_0, \Sigma_1, E_0, E_1, v_{in}, c)$. $V = V_0 \uplus V_1$ are the states, where the states in V_0 belong to Player 0 and the states in V_1 belong to Player 1. Σ_0 and Σ_1 are the action sets, $E_0 : V_0 \times \Sigma_0 \to V_1$ and $E_1 : V_1 \times \Sigma_1 \to V_0$ are the edge functions of the two players. Additionally, $v_{in} \in V$ is the initial state and $c : V \to \mathbb{N}$ is the coloring function.

---

[2] We can apply precise finite-state machine minimization [8] after the construction to obtain a monitor of equal size.

A *decision sequence* in $\mathcal{G}$ is a sequence $\rho = \rho_0^0 \rho_0^1 \rho_1^0 \rho_1^1 \ldots$ such that for all $i \in \mathbb{N}$, $\rho_i^0 \in \Sigma_0$ and $\rho_i^1 \in \Sigma_1$. A decision sequence ρ induces an infinite *play* $\pi = \pi_0^0 \pi_0^1 \pi_1^0 \pi_1^1 \ldots$ if $\pi_0^0 = v_0$ and for all $i \in \mathbb{N}$, $p \in \{0, 1\}$, $E_p(\pi_i^p, \rho_i^p) = \pi_{i+p}^{1-p}$.

Given a play $\pi = \pi_0^0 \pi_0^1 \pi_1^0 \pi_1^1 \ldots$, we say that π is winning for Player 0 if $\max\{c(v) \mid v \in V_0, v \in \inf(\pi_0^0 \pi_1^0 \ldots)\}$ is even, where the function inf maps a sequence to the set of elements that appear infinitely often in the sequence. If a play is not winning for Player 0, it is winning for Player 1.

Given some parity game $\mathcal{G} = (V_0, V_1, \Sigma_0, \Sigma_1, E_0, E_1, v_0, \mathcal{F})$, a strategy for Player 0 is a function $f : (\Sigma_0 \times \Sigma_1)^* \to \Sigma_0$. Likewise, a strategy for Player 1 is a function $f : (\Sigma_0 \times \Sigma_1)^* \times \Sigma_0 \to \Sigma_1$. In both cases, a strategy maps prefix decision sequences to an action to be chosen next. A decision sequence $\rho = \rho_0^0 \rho_0^1 \rho_1^0 \rho_1^1 \ldots$ is said to be *in correspondence with* f if for every $i \in \mathbb{N}$, we have $\rho_n^p = f(\rho_0^0 \rho_0^1 \ldots \rho_{n+p-1}^{1-p})$. A strategy is *winning* for Player p if all plays in the game that are induced by some decision sequence that is in correspondence to f are winning for Player p.

Parity games are *determined*, which means that there exists a winning strategy for precisely one of the players. We call a state $v \in V$ winning for player p if the player has a winning strategy in the modified game where the initial state has been changed to v.

Parity games and reactive systems. Parity games are a common model for the interaction of a system with its environment. Player 0 represents the system, Player 1 the environment. Player 0's actions thus consist of the outputs, Player 1's actions of the inputs.

We can translate a given LTL formula into a parity game such that there is an execution tree that satisfies the formula along all its words if and only if there exists a winning strategy for Player 0 from the initial state. Given a winning strategy f, we can build a suitable execution tree $\langle T, \tau \rangle$ by taking the decisions of the system player as the tree labels: $T = (2^{\mathrm{AP}_I})^*$ and $\tau(t_0 \ldots t_n) = f((\tau(\epsilon), t_0)(\tau(t_0), t_0 t_1)(\tau(t_0 t_1), t_0 t_1 t_2) \ldots (\tau(t_0 \ldots t_{n-1}), t_0 \ldots t_n))$ for every $t_0 \ldots t_n \in T$.

Definition 1. *Given a deterministic parity automaton $\mathcal{A} = (Q, \Sigma, \delta, q_0, c)$ with $\Sigma = 2^{\mathrm{AP}_I} \times 2^{\mathrm{AP}_O}$, we build its induced parity game $\mathcal{G} = (Q, Q \times 2^{\mathrm{AP}_O}, 2^{\mathrm{AP}_O}, 2^{\mathrm{AP}_I}, E_0, E_1, q_0, c')$ with*

$$\forall v_0 \in Q, x_0 \in \Sigma_0, E_0(v_0, x_0) = (v_0, x_0);$$
$$\forall v_0 \in Q, x_0 \in \Sigma_0, x_1 \in \Sigma_1, E_1((v_0, x_0), x_1) = \delta(v_0, (x_1, x_0));$$
$$\forall v_0 \in Q, x_0 \in \Sigma_0, c'(v_0) = c(v_0) \text{ and } c'((v_0, x_0)) = 0.$$

Lemma 2. *Given a deterministic parity automaton $\mathcal{A} = (Q, \Sigma, \delta, q_0, c)$ with $\Sigma = 2^{\mathrm{AP}_I} \times 2^{\mathrm{AP}_O}$, there exists a winning strategy for the system player from the initial state of the game induced by $\mathcal{A}$ iff there exists an execution tree for the interface $(\mathrm{AP}_I, \mathrm{AP}_O)$ for which all induced words are in $\mathcal{L}(\mathcal{A})$.*

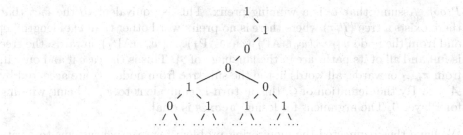

Fig. 3. Example bobble tree over $\mathrm{AP}_I = \{i\}$ and $\mathrm{AP}_O = \{o\}$. The tree branches according to 2^{AP_I}, where the left children correspond to $i = 0$ and the right children correspond to $i = 1$. The tree nodes are labelled by the value of o. The tree has the split word $\{i, o\}\{o\}\emptyset$ and describes the past behaviour of a reactive system with interface $\mathcal{I} = (\mathrm{AP}_I, \mathrm{AP}_O)$ after having read $\{i\}\emptyset\emptyset$ from its initial state. The tree branches according to all possible inputs from the split node onwards.

3.2 Recognizing Realizability

We now formalize the situations in which the monitor should report *realizable* and *unrealizable*. We call prefixes that lead to a realizable situation *winning* and prefixes that lead to an unrealizable situation *losing*, corresponding to the intuition that, in a realizable situation, Player 0 has a winning strategy, and in an unrealizable situation, all strategies of Player 0 lose. The formal definition is based on the concept of bobble trees, which are a special case of execution trees: Bobble trees combine the representation of the *past* of an execution, which is a prefix trace, with the representation of the *future*, which is a full tree.

A *bobble tree* $\langle T, \tau \rangle$ has a split node $\bar{t} = \bar{t}_0 \ldots \bar{t}_n \in T$ such that for every node $t \in T$ either t is a prefix of $\bar{t}$, or $\bar{t}$ is a prefix of t and furthermore $\bar{t}t' \in T$ for every $t' \in 2^{\mathrm{AP}_I}$. Thus, the tree has a single unique path to the split node $\bar{t}$ and is full only from that point onwards. We call the prefix word $w = (\tau(\epsilon), \bar{t}_0)(\tau(\bar{t}_0), \bar{t}_1) \ldots (\tau(\bar{t}_0 \ldots \bar{t}_{n-1}), \bar{t}_n)$ the *split word* of $\langle T, \tau \rangle$. Figure 3 shows an example of a bobble tree.

Definition 2. *Let* $\mathcal{I} = (\mathrm{AP}_I, \mathrm{AP}_O)$ *be an interface and* $L \subseteq (2^{\mathrm{AP}_I} \times 2^{\mathrm{AP}_O})^\omega$ *be a language. We say that some prefix word* $w = w_0 \ldots w_n \in (2^{\mathrm{AP}_I} \times 2^{\mathrm{AP}_O})^*$ *is a winning prefix (for* L*) if there exists some bobble tree with split word* w *that satisfies* L*. Likewise, we say that some prefix word* $w = w_0 \ldots w_n \in (2^{\mathrm{AP}_I} \times 2^{\mathrm{AP}_O})^*$ *is a losing prefix if all bobble trees with split word* w *do not satisfy* L*.*

It is easy to see that bad prefixes are special cases of losing prefixes, and dually, good prefixes are special cases of winning prefixes. The following theorem forms the basis of our approach for monitoring for winning and losing prefixes:

Theorem 1. *Let* $\mathcal{A} = (Q, \Sigma, \delta, q_0, c)$ *be a deterministic parity automaton with* $\Sigma = 2^{\mathrm{AP}_I} \times 2^{\mathrm{AP}_O}$ *and* $\mathcal{G}$ *be the corresponding parity game. For every prefix word* $w = w_0 \ldots w_n \in \Sigma^*$ *with its associated path* $\pi = \pi_0 \ldots \pi_{n+1}$ *in* $\mathcal{A}$*,* w *is a winning/losing prefix for* $\mathcal{L}(\mathcal{A})$ *iff* π_{n+1} *is a state in* $\mathcal{G}$ *that is winning/losing for Player 0, respectively.*

Proof. Assume that w is a winning prefix. This is equivalent to the fact that there exists a tree $\langle T, \tau \rangle$ where there is no prefix word other than w of length $|w|$ and from the node $w|_I = (w_0 \cap \mathrm{AP}_I)(w_1 \cap \mathrm{AP}_I) \dots (w_n \cap \mathrm{AP}_I)$ onwards, the tree is full and all of its paths are in the language of $\mathcal{A}$. This is the case if and only if, from π_{n+1} onwards, all words in the the sub-tree from node $w|_I$ are accepted by $\mathcal{A}_{\pi_{n+1}}$. By the definition of $\mathcal{G}$, this in turn is equivalent to π_{n+1} being winning for Player 0. The argument for losing prefixes is dual. $\square$

We have thus connected the monitoring problem for reactive systems to parity game solving. Since parity games are determined (i.e., every state is winning for precisely one of the two players), we directly obtain as a corollary:

Corollary 1. *Let $\mathcal{A} = (Q, \Sigma, \delta, q_0, c)$ be a deterministic parity automaton with $\Sigma = 2^{\mathrm{AP}_I} \times 2^{\mathrm{AP}_O}$. Every finite word $w \in \Sigma^*$ is either a winning or a losing prefix.*

A monitor can therefore only encounter the following four situations: *fulfilled* if the prefix is good, *realizable* if the prefix is winning but not good, *unrealizable* if the prefix is losing but not bad, and *violation* if the prefix is bad.

We construct the monitor by identifying which states in the deterministic parity automaton are winning for Player 0 in the respective game, and combine the information with the information about states in the automaton witnessing *good* and *bad* prefixes. The monitor has the same transition structure as the parity automaton. In terms of complexity, we obtain the following:

Theorem 2. *Let $\mathcal{I} = (\mathrm{AP}_I, \mathrm{AP}_O)$ be an interface and ψ be an LTL formula over $\mathrm{AP}_I \uplus \mathrm{AP}_O$. Building a finite-state machine that distinguishes between bad (and losing), losing, winning and good (and winning) prefixes is 2EXPTIME-complete.*

Proof. For the lower bound, we note that the 2EXPTIME-complete [15] problem of checking the realizability of LTL formulas is a special case: If we synthesize a monitor, we can easily check for the realizability of a specification by testing whether the initial state of the monitor machine is labeled by *good* or *winning*.

For the upper bound, we start by building an automaton $\mathcal{A}$ with $2^{O(2^n n \log n)}$ states and $3(n+1)2^n$ colors [18] that is equivalent to ψ, where n is the length of ψ. Dividing the set of states in the corresponding game into the winning ones and the losing ones can be done in time $2^{|\mathrm{AP}_I| + |\mathrm{AP}_O|} m^{O(d)}$ [9], where m is the number of states in the game (i.e., $m = (2^{|\mathrm{AP}_O|} + 1) \cdot 2^{O(2^n n \log n)}$) and d is the number of colors in the game (i.e., $d = 3(n+1)2^n$). Combined with the effort to identify the monitor states that represent good and bad prefixes, we obtain a doubly-exponential time bound for this procedure. $\square$

4   Finitary Winning and Losing Prefixes

We now add a further refinement to the classification of monitoring situations: we distinguish situations in which the system or environment can enforce fulfillment or violation, respectively, in *finite* time. The extended classification provides helpful information about the urgency of the problem behind the *unrealizable* status. Suppose, for example, that the monitor of a flight control system informs an airplane pilot that the environment of the control system can force a violation of the specification in finite time. Since a violation of the specification is imminent, the pilot might take drastic action in such a case, such as perform an emergency landing. If, on the other hand, the environment needs infinite time to enforce a violation, there is much more time for diagnosis and decision. It may well be a better idea to continue the flight and report the system malfunction (or incorrect specification) after the regular landing.

In this section, we define *finitary winning* and *finitary losing* prefixes and show how to adapt the monitor construction from the previous section to also detect these. Using this addition, our monitors for reactive systems now have six monitoring conditions, going from worst case to best case as follows:

1. *violation:* the prefix is bad;
2. *unrealizable with finite time:* the prefix is finitary losing but not bad;
3. *unrealizable with infinite time:* the prefix is losing but not finitary losing;
4. *realizable with infinite time:* the prefix is winning but not finitary winning;
5. *realizable with finite time:* the prefix is finitary winning but not good; and
6. *fulfilled:* the prefix is good.

We begin by formalizing the definition of finitary losing and winning prefixes.

Definition 3. *Let $\mathcal{A} = (Q, \Sigma, \delta, q_0, c)$ be a deterministic parity automaton with $\Sigma = 2^{AP_I} \times 2^{AP_O}$. We say that some prefix word $w = w_0 \ldots w_n \in (2^{AP_I} \times 2^{AP_O})^*$ is a finitary winning prefix if there exists some bobble tree $\langle T, \tau \rangle$ with split word w such that every infinite word in $\langle T, \tau \rangle$ has a good prefix word. Likewise, we say that some prefix word $w = w_0 \ldots w_n \in (2^{AP_I} \times 2^{AP_O})^*$ is a finitary losing prefix if for all bobble trees $\langle T, \tau \rangle$ with split word w, there exists an infinite word in $\langle T, \tau \rangle$ that has a bad prefix word.*

The following lemma characterizes the finitary winning and losing prefixes in terms of the parity game, which allows us to base the monitors for such prefixes on the framework described in the previous sections.

Lemma 3. *Let $\mathcal{A} = (Q, \Sigma, \delta, q_0, c)$ be a deterministic parity automaton with $\Sigma = 2^{AP_I} \times 2^{AP_O}$, $E \subseteq Q$ be the states of $\mathcal{A}$ that have an empty language, $U \subseteq Q$ be the set of states of $\mathcal{A}$ that have a universal language and $\mathcal{G}$ be the game corresponding to $\mathcal{A}$.*

- *For every prefix word $w = w_0 \ldots w_n \in \Sigma^*$, w is a finitary winning prefix iff for the corresponding prefix run $\pi = \pi_0 \ldots \pi_{n+1}$, Player 0 has a strategy from state π_{n+1} to eventually visit U.*
- *For every prefix word $w = w_0 \ldots w_n \in \Sigma^*$, w is a finitary losing prefix iff for the corresponding prefix run $\pi = \pi_0 \ldots \pi_{n+1}$, Player 1 has a strategy from state π_{n+1} to eventually visit E.*

As a consequence, we can again use the transition structure of the deterministic parity automaton for our monitor. The only addition to the previous monitor construction is that we need to identify the states in the game which allow Player 0 and Player 1 to force the play into one of the states whose corresponding state in the parity automaton has a universal or empty language, respectively. For this purpose, we apply a standard *attractor* [12] construction on the game graph. To compute the finitary winning states, we initialize the attractor with the states U whose language is universal and then repeatedly add states owned by Player 0 that have an outgoing edge into the attractor, and states owned by Player 1 where all outgoing edges lead into the attractor. The fixpoint of this construction contains exactly those states where Player 0 can force the game into U in a finite number of states. Analogously, we compute the finitary losing states with an attractor that is initialized with the states E whose language is empty, and where we repeatedly add states owned by Player 1 with an edge to the attractor and states owned by Player 0 where all edges lead to the attractor. The computation of the attractor sets takes linear time in the size of the game [12]. We obtain as a corollary:

Corollary 2. *Let $\mathcal{I} = (\mathrm{AP}_I, \mathrm{AP}_O)$ be an interface and ψ be an LTL formula over $\mathrm{AP}_I \uplus \mathrm{AP}_O$. Building a finite-state machine that distinguishes between bad, finitary losing, losing, winning, finitary winning, and good prefixes is 2EXPTIME-complete.*

5   Conclusion

We have presented a new multi-valued monitoring approach for linear-time temporal logic that classifies trace prefixes not only according to the correctness of the continuations, but also according to the strategic power available to the system and its environment in order to avoid or enforce a violation. The game-based approach has several advantages over the classic approaches: the game-based analysis detects errors earlier, it detects errors that are missed by purely trace-based approaches, and it can indicate the urgency with which a violation is to be expected.

Our constructions are optimal in the complexity-theoretic sense. A potential drawback of our approach is that we construct a deterministic automaton. Other monitoring techniques construct nondeterministic or universal automata, which are, in theory, exponentially more compact. The determinization is then often done symbolically, for example in hardware using individual flip-flops for the states of the nondeterministic or universal automaton (cf. [6]).

However, experiments with state-of-the-art LTL-to-automata translators have shown that nondeterministic automata are not necessarily smaller than deterministic automata. For many practical specifications, the deterministic automaton is in fact smaller than the nondeterministic automaton originally produced by the translator [10,4]. Constructing deterministic automata and applying an efficient symbolic encoder [17] may thus even lead to smaller, faster and more memory-efficient monitors.

References

1. Bauer, A., Leucker, M., Schallhart, C.: Runtime verification for LTL and TLTL. ACM Transactions on Software Engineering and Methodology 20(4) (2011)
2. Büchi, J., Landweber, L.: Solving sequential conditions by finite-state strategies. Trans. AMS (138) (1969)
3. D'Amorim, M., Roşu, G.: Efficient Monitoring of ω-Languages. In: Etessami, K., Rajamani, S.K. (eds.) CAV 2005. LNCS, vol. 3576, pp. 364–378. Springer, Heidelberg (2005)
4. Ehlers, R.: Minimising Deterministic Büchi Automata Precisely Using SAT Solving. In: Strichman, O., Szeider, S. (eds.) SAT 2010. LNCS, vol. 6175, pp. 326–332. Springer, Heidelberg (2010)
5. Ehlers, R.: Short Witnesses and Accepting Lassos in ω-Automata. In: Dediu, A.-H., Fernau, H., Martín-Vide, C. (eds.) LATA 2010. LNCS, vol. 6031, pp. 261–272. Springer, Heidelberg (2010)
6. Finkbeiner, B., Kuhtz, L.: Monitor Circuits for LTL with Bounded and Unbounded Future. In: Bensalem, S., Peled, D.A. (eds.) RV 2009. LNCS, vol. 5779, pp. 60–75. Springer, Heidelberg (2009)
7. Finkbeiner, B., Sipma, H.: Checking finite traces using alternating automata. Formal Methods in System Design 24(2), 101–127 (2004)
8. Hopcroft, J.E.: An n log n algorithm for minimizing the states in a finite automaton. In: Kohavi, Z. (ed.) The Theory of Machines and Computations, pp. 189–196. Academic Press (1971)
9. Jurdziński, M.: Small Progress Measures for Solving Parity Games. In: Reichel, H., Tison, S. (eds.) STACS 2000. LNCS, vol. 1770, pp. 290–301. Springer, Heidelberg (2000)
10. Klein, J., Baier, C.: Experiments with deterministic ω-automata for formulas of linear temporal logic. Theor. Comput. Sci. 363(2), 182–195 (2006)
11. Kupferman, O., Vardi, M.Y.: Model checking of safety properties. Formal Methods in System Design 19(3), 291–314 (2001)
12. Küsters, R.: 6 Memoryless Determinacy of Parity Games. In: Grädel, E., Thomas, W., Wilke, T. (eds.) Automata, Logics, and Infinite Games. LNCS, vol. 2500, pp. 95–106. Springer, Heidelberg (2002)
13. Müller, S.M., Paul, W.J.: Computer architecture: complexity and correctness. Springer, Heidelberg (2000)
14. Pnueli, A.: The temporal logic of programs. In: FOCS, pp. 46–57. IEEE (1977)
15. Pnueli, A., Rosner, R.: On the Synthesis of an Asynchronous Reactive Module. In: Ronchi Della Rocca, S., Ausiello, G., Dezani-Ciancaglini, M. (eds.) ICALP 1989. LNCS, vol. 372, pp. 652–671. Springer, Heidelberg (1989)
16. Pnueli, A., Zaks, A., Zuck, L.D.: Monitoring interfaces for faults. Electr. Notes Theor. Comput. Sci 144(4), 73–89 (2006)
17. Sentovich, E., Singh, K., Lavagno, L., Moon, C., Murgai, R., Saldanha, A., Savoj, H., Stephan, P., Brayton, R.K., Sangiovanni-Vincentelli, A.L.: SIS: A system for sequential circuit synthesis. Technical Report UCB/ERL M92/41, EECS Department, University of California, Berkeley (1992)
18. Y., M., Vardi, T.W.: Automata: from logics to algorithms. In: Flum, J., Grädel, E., Wilke, T. (eds.) Logic and Automata: History and Perspectives. Texts in Logic and Games, vol. (2), pp. 629–736. Amsterdam University Press (2007)

Runtime Verification of Traces under Recording Uncertainty*

Shaohui Wang, Anaheed Ayoub, Oleg Sokolsky, and Insup Lee

Department of Computer and Information Science
University of Pennsylvania
{shaohui,anaheed}@seas.upenn.edu, {sokolsky,lee}@cis.upenn.edu

Abstract. We present an on-line algorithm for the runtime checking of temporal properties, expressed as past-time Linear Temporal Logic (LTL) over the traces of observations recorded by a "black box"-like device. The recorder captures the observed values but not the precise time of their occurrences, and precise truth evaluation of a temporal logic formula cannot always be obtained. In order to handle this uncertainty, the checking algorithm is based on a three-valued semantics for past-time LTL defined in this paper. In addition to the algorithm, the paper presents results of an evaluation that aimed to study the effects of the recording uncertainty on different kinds of temporal logic properties.

1   Introduction

Data recorders are very important in the design of safety-critical systems. They allow system manufacturers and government regulators to collect data that help to diagnose the problem in case of a system failure. The best known example of a data recorder is the flight data recorder (FDR), also known as the "black box," that most aircraft are equipped with.

There is much interest in incorporating similar technology into medical devices. Adverse events—that is, cases where the patient was harmed during the application of the device—have to be reported to regulators. However, without data recording capability, analysis of adverse events becomes very difficult or even impossible. Thus, we are seeing the same kinds of adverse events repeated over and over again.

A preliminary design of a data recorder, called *life data recorder* (LDR) for medical devices has been proposed by Bill Spees, safety researcher at the U.S. Food and Drug Administration [18]. The LDR would collect updates of device state variables and relevant event occurrences and periodically transfer recorded snapshots to non-volatile storage. In doing so, the information about exact ordering of events within the recording period is lost. We can thus view a recorded trace as an abstraction of a concrete execution trace, so that the same abstract trace may arise from a number of concrete traces.

---

* Research is supported in part by the National Science Foundation grants CNS-0834524, CNS-0930647, and CNS-1035715.

S. Khurshid and K. Sen (Eds.): RV 2011, LNCS 7186, pp. 442–456, 2012.

In this paper, we are concerned with checking past-time LTL properties of system executions, that is, concrete traces. We assume, however, that all observations become available only after a snapshot is recorded. Thus we have only the abstract trace of the execution to work with. We therefore reinterpret LTL formulas in a way that reflects uncertainty in abstract traces. We introduce a three-valued semantics, under which a formula evaluates to true on an abstract trace Tr only if the same formula would evaluate to true on every concrete trace that is consistent with Tr. Dually, a formula is false on an abstract trace only if it is false on every consistent concrete trace. Otherwise, the outcome is uncertain.

We extend the algorithm of [10] to handle our three-valued semantics. The interesting aspect of the extension is that the algorithm operates on abstract traces; however, the formulas express properties of concrete traces, and there may be multiple concrete states between two abstract state. Thus, in each abstract state we need to reason about the segments of possible concrete traces since the previous abstract state, as well as refer to the truth values of subformulas calculated in the previous abstract state.

The paper is organized as follows. Section 2 defines abstract and concrete traces and describes the LDR recording scheme. Section 3 defines the three-valued semantics of past-time LTL over abstract traces and presents our runtime checking algorithm according to the semantics. Section 4 presents the evaluation of our checking algorithm on randomly generated traces. We conclude with an overview of related work in Section 5 and a discussion on possible future work in Section 6.

2   The Trace Model

In temporal logic based runtime verification, the primary task is to check a temporal logic formula on a given trace. A trace is usually regarded as a sequence of states, while the contents of states vary in different settings or domains. In this section, we describe the recording scheme of the LDR[18], and define two notions of traces, namely concrete traces and abstract traces.

2.1   LDR Recording Scheme

An LDR collects updates to a set of variables generated by a medical device and periodically records snapshots of their values in permanent memory. Three types of variables are recorded by the LDR: (a) process variables, (b) synchronized events, and (c) asynchronized events. The latter two together are called fast changers. At the time-out of every period, called a *frame*, a vector of 32-bit words is recorded to some non-volatile external storage. Recorded values are put to the vector slots according to a scheme specified by a *dictionary*, described as follows.

Process variables represent essential state information for the medical device, and are assumed not to change more than once during every frame. Each process variable is assigned one slot in the snapshot vector. It may be either empty, if the value did not change during the frame, or contain the new value for the process variable.

Synchronized events are fast changers that may occur multiple times within a frame. They are recorded according to the time of their occurrences relative to the beginning of the current frame. One frame is divided into a fixed number (S, throughout the paper) of *subframes* of equal intervals, for all synchronized events. We have $F = S \times I$, where F is the snapshot period (frame interval length), and I is the subframe interval length. Each synchronized event consumes S consecutive slots in the snapshot vector, starting from a designated base slot b. Assuming the beginning of the current frame is at time t, then an occurrence of a synchronized event at time t' ($t' < t + F$) is recorded to the slot numbered $b + \lfloor (t' - t)/I \rfloor$. Similar to process variables, we assume that there are no more than one occurrence per subframe for each synchronized event.

Asynchronized events are fast changers which exhibit bursty behavior: occasionally, they may change more than once per subframe, but the number of changes within a frame is bounded. Similar to synchronized events, a fixed number (A, throughout the paper) of consecutive slots are assigned to each asynchronized event. In one frame, at most A occurrences of an asynchronized event may happen. They are sequentially recorded one slot per occurrence, starting from the designated base slot b. No timing constraints with regards to subframes are imposed on asynchronized events. Only that they arrived in the order they are recorded in a frame is known.

Additional specifications of the LDR recording scheme in [18], such as encryption of data, external storages, etc., are tangential to our focus and omitted.

An example LDR recording. Fig. 1(a) shows an example segment of an LDR recording for a process variable x and a synchronized event y with at most four occurrences per frame ($S = 4$). The shaded cells in Column 0 represent the initial values for x and y. Each of the following columns is a snapshot vector for one frame in the recording session from the LDR. Frame 1 (shaded) is depicted in Fig. 1(b). The variable x (marked 'x') changes from 2 to 3, and y (marked 'o') changes from 4 to 3, to 2, and to 4, in the first, second, and third subframes, respectively. A dash entry in the snapshot vector means no events recorded.

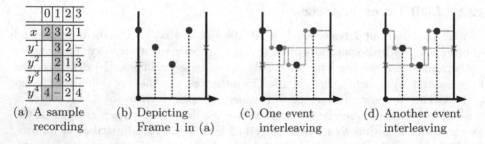

(a) A sample recording   (b) Depicting Frame 1 in (a)   (c) One event interleaving   (d) Another event interleaving

Fig. 1. Sample segment of an LDR recording

Recorded traces may exhibit uncertainties in capturing system executions. Fig. 1(c) shows one possible system event interleaving which produces the shaded recording in Fig. 1(a). The smaller dots represent the actual events which alter the values of the relative variables. In this case, the change of x occurs in between the first and the second changes of y. Fig. 1(d) shows another, where the change of x occurs in between the second and the third changes of y. It can be seen that in this example there are four possible different system event interleavings which produce the shaded recording in Column 1 in Fig. 1(a).

2.2   Concrete Traces and Abstract Traces

In this paper, we differentiate two notions of traces, the concrete and the abstract. Informally, a concrete trace is a sequence of concrete states, where each of them is a mapping of variables to their values. An abstract trace is a sequence of abstract states, where each of them is, in our setting, an LDR recorded vector. We assume that concrete and abstract traces are finite.

Definition 1 (Concrete State and Concrete Trace). *Assuming a set V of variables and a domain D for their values, a concrete state is a mapping $f : V \to D$ of variables to their values. A concrete trace $p = p_0 \ldots p_m$ of length m is a sequence of concrete states $p_0, \ldots, p_m$.*

Definition 2 (Abstract State and Abstract Trace). *An abstract trace Tr is the sequence of snapshot vectors recorded by an LDR. Each snapshot vector is an abstract state.*

Concrete traces are not observed directly, but are captured by recordings from the LDR component, i.e., abstract traces. For example in Fig. 1, the snapshot vector for Frame 1 represents four concrete traces for (x, y) below, with the second and third depicted in Fig. 1(c) and Fig. 1(d), respectively:

$$(2,4) \xrightarrow{x} (3,4) \xrightarrow{y} (3,3) \xrightarrow{y} (3,2) \xrightarrow{y} (3,4),$$
$$(2,4) \xrightarrow{y} (2,3) \xrightarrow{x} (3,3) \xrightarrow{y} (3,2) \xrightarrow{y} (3,4),$$
$$(2,4) \xrightarrow{y} (2,3) \xrightarrow{y} (2,2) \xrightarrow{x} (3,2) \xrightarrow{y} (3,4),$$
$$(2,4) \xrightarrow{y} (2,3) \xrightarrow{y} (2,2) \xrightarrow{y} (2,4) \xrightarrow{x} (3,4).$$

We particularly note that an abstract state in our setting is essentially an acyclic transition system and captures a set of concrete traces. We say that any concrete trace that an abstract state captures is consistent with the abstract state.

As can be seen from the above example, the end states for each concrete trace in a frame are the same. This is due to the fact that at the end of each frame, all of the variables have been changed to their respective last values.

We use $Tr(0 : n)$, or simply Tr, to represent the abstract trace of length n, $Tr(i)$ (a snapshot vector) to represent the ith abstract state of Tr, and $Tr(i)_e$ to denote the concrete state at the end of the ith abstract state $(1 \leq i \leq n)$. $Tr(i)_e$ is computed from $Tr(i)$ by simply scanning through the vector $Tr(i)$ and establishing the mapping from each variable to its last value in the vector $Tr(i)$. If nothing is recorded in $Tr(i)$ for a variable, its value from $Tr(i-1)_e$ is used. $Tr(0)$, which gives an initial value to every monitored variable, is a special case: it is, in effect, a concrete state, and fills exactly one slot in the vector for each variable.

We use $Path(Tr(i))$ to represent the set of concrete traces consistent with the abstract state $Tr(i)$, and the variable p^i to range over elements in $Path(Tr(i))$. When necessary, a concrete trace p^i of length m_i is written as $p^i = p_0^i \ldots p_{m_i}^i$. Note that for a given i, all concrete traces in $Path(Tr(i))$ are of the same length, which is equal to the number of variable changing events recorded in Frame i, so a single i is subscripted to m. The superscript i is often omitted when the context is clear. The following notations refer to the same concrete state for a given i: $Tr(i)_e$, $p_{m_i}^i$, and p_0^{i+1}.

Without loss of generality, we assume that all concrete traces for a given frame are not zero-length, since zero-length concrete traces result from abstract states where no changes to variable values occur, in which case the abstract state can be removed from our considerations.

For a span of n frames, the concrete traces are constructed by sequentially concatenating one concrete trace from each of the n frames. The concatenations at the boundaries of frames are consistent since the end values of variables in one frame are the same as their initial values in the next. We generalize the notation $Path(Tr(n))$ to $Path(Tr(0:n))$ to denote the set of concatenated concrete traces from abstract trace $Tr(0:n)$. We also generalize the concept of consistency between a concrete trace and an abstract trace naturally.

3   Syntax and Semantics of Past-Time LTL

In real time systems, we often need to specify system properties with past-time LTL formulas and monitor system variables to check if the formulas are satisfied. The semantics for past-time LTL formulas on a concrete trace is standard [13,15]. Also, to facilitate efficient runtime checking, it is convenient to define the semantics in a recursive fashion so that it is unnecessary to keep the history trace [10].

Checking past-time LTL properties on abstract traces, however, is different in that uncertainty arises when events are gathered in batch mode—a snapshot of a frame capturing a magnitude of events in the system—with their interleavings only partially known.

It is our main concern in this paper to both continue using the past-time LTL to describe system properties due to their succinctness and familiarity to the verification community, and handle the uncertainty in checking properties on the recorded abstract traces due to the unknown event interleavings.

Our approach is to keep the syntax for past-time LTL but introduce a new three-valued semantics based on standard semantics for concrete traces. A formula φ evaluates to true on an abstract trace Tr only if φ evaluates to true on all concrete traces consistent with Tr; φ evaluates to false on Tr only if it is false on every concrete trace consistent with Tr; otherwise it is undecided.

In this section, we first review the syntax of past-time LTL and its standard semantics and runtime checking algorithm, and then define the new semantics and extend the runtime checking algorithm to our three-valued semantics.

3.1 Syntax and Standard Semantics for Past-Time LTL

We assume all predicates on a set V of variables are the atomic formulas. We use the variable a to range over the set of atomic formulas, and $a(p_j)$ to represent the truth value of predicate a evaluated on concrete state p_j. The syntax rules for building formulas from atomic ones are as follows.

Definition 3 (Syntax for Formulas)

$$\varphi := true \mid false \mid a \mid \neg\varphi \mid \varphi \wedge \varphi \mid \varphi \vee \varphi \mid \odot\varphi \mid \diamondsuit\varphi \mid \boxdot\varphi \mid \varphi\, \mathcal{S}\, \varphi$$

For example, $(x = 14)\,\mathcal{S}\,(x \geq y)$ is a well formed formula. Intuitively, $\odot\,\phi$ reads "previously ϕ", meaning ϕ was true at the immediately previous state; $\diamondsuit\,\phi$ reads "once ϕ", meaning there was some time in the past when ϕ was true; $\boxdot\,\phi$ reads "always in the past ϕ", meaning that ϕ was always true in the past; and $\phi\,\mathcal{S}\,\psi$ reads "ϕ (weakly) since ψ", meaning that either ϕ was always true in the past, or ψ held somewhere in the past and since then ϕ has always been true. The formal definition of the semantics is as follows.

Definition 4 (Standard Semantics for Past-Time LTL[10,13,15]). *A concrete trace $p = p_0 \ldots p_m$ of length m satisfies a past-time LTL formula φ, written $p \models \varphi$, is inductively defined on the structure of φ as follows.*

$$
\begin{aligned}
&p \models true && \textit{is always true} \\
&p \models false && \textit{is always false} \\
&p \models a && \textit{iff} \quad a(p_m) \textit{ holds} \\
&p \models \neg\psi && \textit{iff} \quad p \not\models \psi \\
&p \models \phi \wedge \psi && \textit{iff} \quad p \models \phi \textit{ and } p \models \psi \\
&p \models \phi \vee \psi && \textit{iff} \quad p \models \phi \textit{ or } p \models \psi \\
&p \models \odot\phi && \textit{iff} \quad m > 0 \textit{ and } p_0 \ldots p_{m-1} \models \phi, \textit{ or } m = 0 \textit{ and } p_0 \models \phi \\
&p \models \diamondsuit\phi && \textit{iff} \quad p_0 \ldots p_j \models \phi \textit{ for some } 0 \leq j \leq m \\
&p \models \boxdot\phi && \textit{iff} \quad p_0 \ldots p_j \models \phi \textit{ for all } 0 \leq j \leq m \\
&p \models \phi\,\mathcal{S}\,\psi && \textit{iff} \quad \textit{either } p \models \boxdot\phi, \textit{ or } (p_0 \ldots p_j \models \psi \textit{ for some } 0 \leq j \leq m \\
& && \qquad\qquad \textit{and } p_0 \ldots p_k \models \phi \textit{ for all } j < k \leq m)
\end{aligned}
$$

The Runtime Checking Algorithm. The verification of a formula φ on a concrete trace p is based on the fact that the semantics in Definition 4 can be stated in a recursive fashion. For example, the semantics for the "since" operator $\mathcal{S}$ can be equivalently stated as

$$p \models \phi\,\mathcal{S}\,\psi \quad \textit{iff} \quad p \models \psi, \textit{ or } (p \models \phi \textit{ and } (m > 0 \textit{ implies } p_0 \ldots p_{m-1} \models \phi\,\mathcal{S}\,\psi)). \quad (1)$$

A runtime formula checker can cache the intermediate result of checking $\phi\,\mathcal{S}\,\psi$ on trace $p_0 \ldots p_{m-1}$ to use in the checking of $\phi\,\mathcal{S}\,\psi$ on trace p, according to the recursive semantics. In general, the checker iterates through all concrete states from p_0 through p_m. In each concrete state p_i, the checker keeps the satisfaction results of all subformulas of φ on the trace $p_0 \ldots p_{i-1}$ (which we call the *checker state*). The checker updates its state based on the values in p_i, as defined in [10].

We illustrate the algorithm with an example before we provide an extension in the next subsection, where we define three-valued semantics for past-time LTL. To check the truth value of $(x = 3)\,\mathcal{S}\,(x \geq y)$ in the trace for (x, y):

$$p = p_0 \ldots p_4 = (2,5) \to (3,5) \to (3,3) \to (3,4) \to (3,6),$$

we follow the procedure of evaluating the subformulas $\phi \equiv (x = 3)$, $\psi \equiv (x \geq y)$, and $\phi \mathcal{S} \psi$.

Step	$\models$	$\phi \equiv (x = 3)$	$\psi \equiv (x \geq y)$	$\phi \mathcal{S} \psi$
0.	p_0	F	F	F
1.	$p_0 p_1$	T	F	F
2.	$p_0 p_1 p_2$	T	T	T
3.	$p_0 p_1 p_2 p_3$	T	F	T
4.	$p_0 p_1 p_2 p_3 p_4$	T	F	T

Each line in the table is the checker state for use in its next line. In deciding that $p_0 p_1 p_2 p_3 \models \phi \mathcal{S} \psi$ is true, for example, the facts that $p_0 p_1 p_2 p_3 \models \phi$ is true (from the current state) and that $p_0 p_1 p_2 \models \phi \mathcal{S} \psi$ is true (from the checker state) are used against the alternative semantics for the "since" operator $\mathcal{S}$ defined in (1).

3.2   Three-Valued Semantics for Past-Time LTL

Inspired by [12], we define a new semantics for the past-time LTL formulas against abstract traces. A formula φ is true on an abstract trace Tr only if φ evaluates to true on all concrete traces consistent with Tr; φ evaluates to false on Tr only if it is false on every concrete trace consistent with Tr; otherwise it is undecided. We use the semantic notions $[\![Tr \models \varphi]\!] = \top$, $[\![Tr \models \varphi]\!] = \bot$, and $[\![Tr \models \varphi]\!] =?$ to indicate the three cases, respectively, where $\top$, $\bot$, and ? are truth values in three-valued logics to represent true, false, and unknown. The truth table for a commonly accepted variant of three-valued logics, namely the Kleene logic[11], is shown in Definition 5.

Definition 5 (Truth Table for Kleene Logic). *The following is the truth table for Kleene logic. (A and B are truth values.)*

A		$\top$			$\bot$			?	
B	$\top$	$\bot$	?	$\top$	$\bot$	?	$\top$	$\bot$	?
$A \vee_3 B$	$\top$	$\top$	$\top$	$\top$	$\bot$	?	$\top$	?	?
$A \wedge_3 B$	$\top$	$\bot$	?	$\bot$	$\bot$	$\bot$	?	$\bot$	?
$\neg_3 A$		$\bot$			$\top$			?	

We now consider the three-valued semantics for an abstract trace Tr of length n and a past-time LTL formula φ. We assume Tr and φ is fixed in the sequel.

We define the semantics in a recursive fashion, assuming the checking for the partial trace $Tr(0:i)$ is finished and the checking result of $[\![Tr(0:i) \models \psi]\!]$ for any (proper) subformula ψ of φ is available. We denote such information with a so called *subformula value mapping* $SV_i : \texttt{SubFormulas}(\varphi) \to \{\top, \bot, ?\}$ which, for a subformula ψ of φ, $SV_i(\psi) = [\![Tr(0:i) \models \psi]\!]$.

To establish the recursive semantic definition from $[\![Tr(0:i) \models \varphi]\!]$ to $[\![Tr(0:i+1) \models \varphi]\!]$, we use an auxiliary semantic function $\texttt{checkOne}$ which takes a subformula value mapping, a concrete trace, and a formula, and returns a result from $\{\top, \bot, ?\}$. The intended use of function $\texttt{checkOne}$ is that, when called with $\texttt{checkOne}(SV_i, p, \varphi)$, where SV_i is the subformula value mapping for φ on trace

$Tr(0 : i)$, and p is one concrete trace from $Path(Tr(i+1))$, the function returns whether φ is satisfied on all, none, or some (neither all nor none) concrete traces formed by concatenating any concrete trace in $Path(Tr(0 : i))$ with p.

Definition 6. *Given a subformula value mapping SV, a formula φ, and a concrete trace $p = p_0 \ldots p_m$, the function* $\texttt{checkOne}(SV, p, \varphi)$ *is defined inductively on the structure of φ, as follows.*

$$\texttt{checkOne}(SV, p, true) = \top$$
$$\texttt{checkOne}(SV, p, false) = \bot$$
$$\texttt{checkOne}(SV, p_0, \ldots p_m, a) = \begin{cases} \top, & \text{if } a(p_m) \text{ holds,} \\ \bot, & \text{if } a(p_m) \text{ does not hold,} \end{cases}$$
$$\texttt{checkOne}(SV, p, \neg\psi) = \neg_3\texttt{checkOne}(SV, p, \psi)$$
$$\texttt{checkOne}(SV, p, \phi \wedge \psi) = \texttt{checkOne}(SV, p, \phi) \wedge_3 \texttt{checkOne}(SV, p, \psi)$$
$$\texttt{checkOne}(SV, p, \phi \vee \psi) = \texttt{checkOne}(SV, p, \phi) \vee_3 \texttt{checkOne}(SV, p, \psi)$$
$$\texttt{checkOne}(SV, p_0 \ldots p_m, \odot \phi) = \begin{cases} SV(\odot \phi), & \text{if } m = 0, \\ SV(\phi), & \text{if } m = 1, \\ \texttt{checkOne}(SV, p_0 \ldots p_{m-1}, \phi), & \text{if } m > 1. \end{cases}$$

$$\texttt{checkOne}(SV, p_0 \ldots p_m, \Diamond \phi) = \begin{cases} \top, & \text{if } SV(\Diamond \phi) = \top, \text{ or } (m > 0 \text{ and} \\ & \quad (\texttt{checkOne}(SV, p_0 \ldots p_{m-1}, \Diamond \phi) = \top \\ & \quad \text{or } \texttt{checkOne}(SV, p_0 \ldots p_m, \phi) = \top)), \\ \bot, & \text{if } SV(\Diamond \phi) = \bot, \text{ and } (m > 0 \text{ implies} \\ & \quad (\texttt{checkOne}(SV, p_0 \ldots p_{m-1}, \Diamond \phi) = \bot \\ & \quad \text{and } \texttt{checkOne}(SV, p_0 \ldots p_m, \phi) = \bot)), \\ ?, & \text{otherwise.} \end{cases}$$

$$\texttt{checkOne}(SV, p_0 \ldots p_m, \Box \phi) = \begin{cases} \top, & \text{if } SV(\Box \phi) = \top, \text{ and } (m > 0 \text{ implies} \\ & \quad (\texttt{checkOne}(SV, p_0 \ldots p_{m-1}, \Box \phi) = \top \\ & \quad \text{and } \texttt{checkOne}(SV, p_0 \ldots p_m, \phi) = \top)), \\ \bot, & \text{if } SV(\Box \phi) = \bot, \text{ or } (m > 0 \text{ and} \\ & \quad (\texttt{checkOne}(SV, p_0 \ldots p_{m-1}, \Box \phi) = \bot \\ & \quad \text{or } \texttt{checkOne}(SV, p_0 \ldots p_m, \phi) = \bot)), \\ ?, & \text{otherwise.} \end{cases}$$

$$\texttt{checkOne}(SV, p_0 \ldots p_m, \phi \mathcal{S} \psi) = \begin{cases} SV(\phi \mathcal{S} \psi), & \text{if } m = 0, \\ \top, & \text{if } m > 0 \text{ and } (\texttt{checkOne}(SV, p_0 \ldots p_m, \psi) = \top \\ & \quad \text{or } (\texttt{checkOne}(SV, p_0 \ldots p_{m-1}, \phi \mathcal{S} \psi) = \top \\ & \quad \text{and } \texttt{checkOne}(SV, p_0 \ldots p_m, \phi) = \top)), \\ \bot, & \text{if } m > 0, \texttt{checkOne}(SV, p_0 \ldots p_m, \psi) = \bot \\ & \quad \text{and } (\texttt{checkOne}(SV, p_0 \ldots p_{m-1}, \phi \mathcal{S} \psi) = \bot \\ & \quad \text{or } \texttt{checkOne}(SV, p_0 \ldots p_m, \phi) = \bot), \\ ?, & \text{otherwise.} \end{cases}$$

It is worthwhile to note that the $\texttt{checkOne}$ function is recursive in terms of the length of the concrete trace p, and thus can be turned into an efficient algorithm using the idea from the runtime checking algorithm illustrated in Subsection 3.1.

Definition 7 (Three-Valued Semantics for Past-Time LTL). *An abstract trace Tr of length n satisfying a past-time LTL property φ, written $[\![Tr \models \varphi]\!]$, is inductively defined on the structure of φ, as follows.*

$$[\![Tr \models true]\!] = \top$$
$$[\![Tr \models false]\!] = \bot$$
$$[Tr(0 : n) \models a] = \begin{cases} \top, & \text{if } a(Tr(n)_e) \text{ holds,} \\ \bot, & \text{if } a(Tr(n)_e) \text{ does not hold,} \end{cases}$$

$$[\![Tr \models \neg\psi]\!] = \neg_3 [\![Tr \models \psi]\!]$$
$$[\![Tr \models \phi \wedge \psi]\!] = [\![Tr \models \phi]\!] \wedge_3 [\![Tr \models \psi]\!]$$
$$[\![Tr \models \phi \vee \psi]\!] = [\![Tr \models \phi]\!] \vee_3 [\![Tr \models \psi]\!]$$

if φ *is* $\odot \phi$, $\Diamond \phi$, *or* $\Box \phi$,

$$[\![Tr(0:n) \models \varphi]\!] = \begin{cases} \top, & \text{if } (n = 0 \text{ implies } Tr(0) \models \varphi) \text{ and } (n > 0 \text{ implies} \\ & \forall p \in Path(Tr(n)) : \texttt{checkOne}(SV_{n-1}, p, \varphi) = \top), \\ \bot, & \text{if } (n = 0 \text{ implies } Tr(0) \not\models \varphi) \text{ and } (n > 0 \text{ implies} \\ & \forall p \in Path(Tr(n)) : \texttt{checkOne}(SV_{n-1}, p, \varphi) = \bot), \\ ?, & \text{otherwise.} \end{cases}$$

$$[\![Tr(0:n) \models \phi \, S \, \psi]\!] = \begin{cases} \top, & \text{if } (n = 0 \text{ implies } Tr(0) \models \phi \vee \psi) \text{ and } (n > 0 \text{ implies} \\ & \forall p \in Path(Tr(n)) : \texttt{checkOne}(SV_{n-1}, p, \phi \, S \, \psi) = \top), \\ \bot, & \text{if } (n = 0 \text{ implies } Tr(0) \not\models \phi \, S \, \psi) \text{ and } (n > 0 \text{ implies} \\ & \forall p \in Path(Tr(n)) : \texttt{checkOne}(SV_{n-1}, p, \phi \, S \, \psi) = \bot), \\ ?, & \text{otherwise.} \end{cases}$$

The definition is also recursive in the length n of the abstract trace $Tr(0:n)$, since the satisfaction results of subformulas of φ on trace $Tr(0:n-1)$ are encapsulated in the subformula value mapping SV_{n-1}. Note that the recursion stops at $n = 0$, where $Tr(0)$ is a concrete state and $SV_0(\psi)$ for a subformula ψ of φ is defined to be $\top$ if $\psi(Tr(0))$ holds, and $\bot$ otherwise.

3.3 An Example

In this section we provide an example illustrating the runtime checking algorithm which translates the recursive definitions of our three-valued semantics into an iterative procedure, and in the next section we present the algorithm.

Consider the formula $\varphi \equiv \odot \odot \odot \Diamond (x = y)$ on the abstract trace Tr of length 3 shown in Fig. 2, where x and y are both process variables. The iterative steps are shown in Fig. 2(c), explained below.

Starting from the initial (concrete) state $(1, 2)$, all subformulas of φ are checked and the subformula value mapping SV_0 is updated. Then for Frame i ($i = 1, 2, 3$), each box labeled $\#j$ ($j = 1, 2$) is checked with a call to the auxiliary function $\texttt{checkOne}(SV_{i-1}, p^{\#j}, \varphi)$. Since $\texttt{checkOne}$ is recursively defined on the length of the concrete trace $p^{\#j}$, inside each box labeled $\#j$, the entries are computed column by column. For example, the $(4, 2)$ column of box $\#1$ in Frame 2 is the result of checking the initial segment $(4, 3) \rightarrow (4, 2)$ of concrete trace $p^{\#1} = (4, 3) \rightarrow (4, 2) \rightarrow (3, 2)$, which is an intermediate step in the call to $\texttt{checkOne}(SV_1, p^{\#1}, \varphi)$.

The values are computed according to Definition 6, except that recursive calls to $\texttt{checkOne}(SV, p_0 \ldots p_{m-1}, \_)$ from $\texttt{checkOne}(SV, p_0 \ldots p_m, \_)$, and the calls to $\texttt{checkOne}(SV, p_0 \ldots p_m, \psi)$ from $\texttt{checkOne}(SV, p_0 \ldots p_m, \varphi)$, where ψ is a subformula of φ, are replaced with table lookups.

After each box $\#j$ in Frame i is computed, for any subformula ψ of φ, $SV_i(\psi)$ is updated to $\top$ if all entries in the last columns of each box $\#j$ (shaded in Fig. 2(c)) and row ψ is $\top$; to $\bot$ if they are all $\bot$; and to $?$ otherwise. Checking for Frame $i + 1$ begins after the update of SV_i. When the algorithm finishes, $SV_3(\varphi)$ is the result of checking $\varphi \equiv \odot \odot \odot \Diamond (x = y)$ on the abstract trace Tr.

	0	1	2	3
x	1	4	3	–
y	2	3	2	3

(a) Abstract Trace

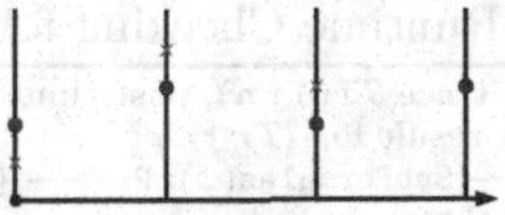

(b) Depicting the Abstract Trace

	Initial State		Frame 1					Frame 2					Frame 3	
	(1, 2)	SV_0	$p^{\#1}: \to(1,3)\to(4,3)$ $p^{\#2}: \to(4,2)\to(4,3)$				SV_1	$p^{\#1}: \to(4,2)\to(3,2)$ $p^{\#2}: \to(3,3)\to(3,2)$				SV_2	$p^{\#1}: \to(3,3)$	SV_3
			#1 (1,3)	#1 (4,3)	#2 (4,2)	#2 (4,3)		#1 (4,2)	#1 (3,2)	#2 (3,3)	#2 (3,2)		#1 (3,3)	
$x = y$	F	$\bot$	$\bot$	$\bot$	$\bot$	$\bot$	$\bot$	$\bot$	$\bot$	$\top$	$\bot$	$\bot$	$\top$	$\top$
$\Diamond(x = y)$	F	$\bot$	$\bot$	$\bot$	$\bot$	$\bot$	$\bot$	$\bot$	$\bot$	$\top$	$\top$	?	$\top$	$\top$
$\odot \Diamond(x = y)$	F	$\bot$	$\bot$	$\bot$	$\bot$	$\bot$	$\bot$	$\bot$	$\bot$	$\bot$	$\top$	?	?	?
$\odot \odot \Diamond(x = y)$	F	$\bot$	$\bot$	$\bot$	$\bot$	$\bot$	$\bot$	$\bot$	$\bot$	$\bot$	$\bot$	$\bot$	?	?
$\odot \odot \odot \Diamond(x = y)$	F	$\bot$	$\bot$	$\bot$	$\bot$	$\bot$	$\bot$	$\bot$	$\bot$	$\bot$	$\bot$	$\bot$	$\bot$	$\bot$

(c) Runtime Checking Algorithm Steps

Fig. 2. Example for Runtime Checking Algorithm

This example shows the "hybrid" nature of the `checkOne` calculation: some subformulas of φ are evaluated on the concrete states of p, while others are looked up in the checker state of the preceding abstract state.

3.4 Checking Past-Time LTL Formulas against Abstract Traces

In this subsection, we present the algorithm, shown in Algorithm 1, for checking the truth value of a given past-time LTL formula φ and a given abstract trace Tr of length n, based on our recursive semantics in Definition 7. It is an extended version of the runtime checking algorithm based on the recursive definition for past-time LTL formulas on concrete traces [10].

We use the notation `SubFormulas`(φ) for the list of subformulas of φ, and assume the *enumeration invariant* in the algorithm: for any formula ψ at position j in `SubFormulas`(φ), all subformulas of ψ are at positions smaller than j.

4 Experiments

We implemented, in Python, a prototype of the past-time LTL checker described in the preceding sections. To evaluate our implementation and gain insights into the utility of the three-valued semantics, we also built a test environment that generates random abstract traces for a given LDR configuration file, and random past-time LTL formulas from a set of formula templates. Having generated sets of abstract traces and formulas, we evaluated each formula on every trace. This section summarizes the obtained results.

The formula templates were taken from common LTL specifications from the Spec Patterns project at Kansas State University [17]. For each of our five chosen categories, five temporal templates are specified: globally, before, after, between/and, and after/until. We altered the formulas for the twenty-five chosen templates from future-time to past-time, by replacing the future-time operators

---

Algorithm 1. Runtime Checking for Past-time LTL on Abstract Traces

---

input : abstract trace $Tr(0:n)$, past-time LTL formula φ
output: checking result for $[\![Tr \models \varphi]\!]$
initialization: sf$\longleftarrow$SubFormulas(φ); Pre$\longleftarrow$ {} (empty mapping); Now$\longleftarrow$ {};
for $j = 1$ **to** $length($sf$)$ **do**
 if sf$[j]$ *is true* **then** Pre$[true]\longleftarrow \top$;
 if sf$[j]$ *is false* **then** Pre$[false]\longleftarrow \perp$;
 if sf$[j]$ *is atomic formula a* **then**
   if $a(Tr(0))$ *holds* **then** Pre$[a] \longleftarrow \top$ **else** Pre$[a] \longleftarrow \perp$;

 if sf$[j]$ *is* $\neg\psi$ **then** Pre$[\neg\psi] \longleftarrow \neg_3Pre[\psi]$;
 if sf$[j]$ *is* $\phi \vee \psi$ **then** Pre$[\phi \vee \psi] \longleftarrow$Pre$[\phi]\vee_3Pre[\phi]$;
 if sf$[j]$ *is* $\phi \wedge \psi$ **then** Pre$[\phi \wedge \psi] \longleftarrow$Pre$[\phi]\wedge_3Pre[\phi]$;
 if sf$[j]$ *is* $\odot\phi$, $\diamond\phi$, *or* $\boxdot\phi$ **then** Pre$[$sf$[j]] \longleftarrow$Pre$[\phi]$;
 if sf$[j]$ *is* $\phi\,\mathcal{S}\,\psi$ **then** Pre$[\phi\,\mathcal{S}\,\psi] \longleftarrow$Pre$[\psi]\vee_3Pre[\phi]$;

for $i = 1$ **to** n **do**
 for $j = 1$ **to** $length($sf$)$ **do**
  if sf$[j]$ *is true* **then** Now$[true]\longleftarrow \top$;
  if sf$[j]$ *is false* **then** Now$[false]\longleftarrow \perp$;
  if sf$[j]$ *is atomic formula a* **then**
    if $a(Tr(i)_e)$ *holds* **then** Now$[a] \longleftarrow \top$ **else** Now$[a] \longleftarrow \perp$;

  if sf$[j]$ *is* $\neg\psi$ **then** Now$[\neg\psi] \longleftarrow \neg_3Now[\psi]$;
  if sf$[j]$ *is* $\phi \vee \psi$ **then** Now$[\phi \vee \psi] \longleftarrow$Now$[\phi]\vee_3Now[\phi]$;
  if sf$[j]$ *is* $\phi \wedge \psi$ **then** Now$[\phi \wedge \psi] \longleftarrow$Now$[\phi]\wedge_3Now[\phi]$;
  if sf$[j]$ *is* $\odot\phi$, $\diamond\phi$, $\boxdot\phi$, *or* $\phi\,\mathcal{S}\,\psi$ **then**
    forall $p \in Path(Tr(i))$ **do**
     check$[p] \leftarrow$ checkOne$($Pre$, p, \varphi)$;
     result$[p] \leftarrow$ check$[p]($sf$[j])$;
    if *each element of* result *is* $\top$ **then** Now$[$sf$[j]] \longleftarrow \top$;
    else if *each element of* result *is* $\perp$ **then** Now$[$sf$[j]] \longleftarrow \perp$;
    else Now$[$sf$[j]] \longleftarrow$?;

 Pre$\longleftarrow$Now;
return Now$[\varphi]$;

$\Box$ (globally), $\diamond$ (eventually), $\bigcirc$ (next state), and $\mathcal{W}$ (weak until) with their past-time counterparts $\boxdot$, $\diamondsuit$, $\odot$, and $\mathcal{S}$, respectively. The strong until operator $\mathcal{U}$ was replaced with the strong since operator $\mathcal{S}_s$, and then transformed according to the equivalence $P\,\mathcal{S}_s\,Q \equiv (P\,\mathcal{S}\,Q) \wedge \diamondsuit Q$.

Table 1 lists all the specification templates used in our experiments. Note that the natural language description for each category has also been changed accordingly. For instance, the category "S precedes P" in future-time logic refers to traces where P cannot be true until an S happens $((\neg P)\,\mathcal{W}\,S)$. Its past-time counterpart $((\neg P)\,\mathcal{S}\,S)$ states that "S concluded P", i.e., if a P was observed, there must have later been an observation of S after which P was always false.

Twenty-five instances for each of the twenty-five formula templates were generated, with atomic symbols (P, Q, R, etc.) in the templates replaced with randomly generated atomic formulas, in our case predicates involving LDR recorded variables, e.g., $a + 42 \leq b$. Forty abstract traces all of length 20 were also randomly generated, according to the dictionary for a process variable a and two synchronous events b and c, with at most four recordings per frame ($S = 4$).

Therefore in our experiments, a total of 40(# traces) $\times$ 25(# templates) $\times$ 25(# instances / template) = 25,000 trace-formula combinations were tested. For each given abstract trace Tr and given formula instance φ, we collected the results for $[\![Tr(0) \models \varphi]\!]$, $[\![Tr(0:1) \models \varphi]\!]$, ..., $[\![Tr(0:20) \models \varphi]\!]$ as a sequence

Table 1. Past-time LTL Formula Templates

		1. globally	2. after R	3. before Q
A.	absence (P was false)	$\boxdot \neg P$	$\diamondsuit R \rightarrow (\neg P\, \mathcal{S}_s\, R)$	$\boxdot (Q \rightarrow \boxdot \neg P)$
B.	existence (P became true)	$\diamondsuit P$	$(\neg R)\, \mathcal{S}\, (P \wedge \neg R)$	$\boxdot (\neg Q) \vee \diamondsuit (Q \wedge \diamondsuit P)$
C.	universality (P was true)	$\boxdot P$	$\diamondsuit R \rightarrow (P\, \mathcal{S}_s\, R)$	$\boxdot (Q \rightarrow \boxdot P)$
D.	conclusion (S concluded P)	$(\neg P)\, \mathcal{S}\, S$	$\diamondsuit R \rightarrow ((\neg P)\, \mathcal{S}_s\, (S \vee R))$	$\boxdot (\neg Q) \vee (Q \wedge ((\neg P)\, \mathcal{S}\, S))$
E.	cause (S weakly caused P)	$\boxdot (P \rightarrow \diamondsuit S)$	$\diamondsuit R \rightarrow ((P \rightarrow ((\neg R)\, \mathcal{S}_s\, (S \wedge \neg R)))\, \mathcal{S}_s\, R)$	$\boxdot (Q \rightarrow \boxdot (P \rightarrow \diamondsuit S))$

		4. between R and Q	5. before Q since R
A.	absence (P was false)	$\boxdot ((Q \wedge \neg R \wedge \diamondsuit R) \rightarrow ((\neg P)\, \mathcal{S}_s\, R))$	$\boxdot ((Q \wedge \neg R) \rightarrow ((\neg P)\, \mathcal{S}\, R))$
B.	existence (P became true)	$\boxdot ((Q \wedge R) \rightarrow ((\neg R)\, \mathcal{S}\, (P \wedge \neg R)))$	$\boxdot ((Q \wedge R) \rightarrow ((\neg R)\, \mathcal{S}_s\, (P \wedge \neg R)))$
C.	universality (P was true)	$\boxdot ((Q \wedge \neg R \wedge \diamondsuit R) \rightarrow (P\, \mathcal{S}_s\, R))$	$\boxdot ((Q \wedge \neg R) \rightarrow (P\, \mathcal{S}\, R))$
D.	conclusion (S concluded P)	$\boxdot ((Q \wedge \neg R \wedge \diamondsuit R) \rightarrow ((\neg P)\, \mathcal{S}_s\, (S \vee R)))$	$\boxdot ((Q \wedge \neg R) \rightarrow ((\neg P)\, \mathcal{S}\, (S \vee R)))$
E.	cause (S weakly causesd P)	$\boxdot ((Q \wedge \neg R \wedge \diamondsuit R) \rightarrow$ $((P \rightarrow ((\neg R)\, \mathcal{S}_s\, (S \wedge \neg R)))\, \mathcal{S}_s\, R))$	$\boxdot ((Q \wedge \neg R) \rightarrow$ $((P \rightarrow ((\neg R)\, \mathcal{S}_s\, (S \wedge \neg R)))\, \mathcal{S}\, R))$

of 21 values from $\{\top, \bot, ?\}$, which we call a *result sequence* for Tr and φ. So a total of $25,000 \times 21$(length of a result sequence) $= 525,000$ values of $\top$, $\bot$, or $?$ were collected.

The experiments were run on a Windows XP desktop with 2.8GHz Intel Core Duo CPU and 2Gb memory and finished within 7 hours. Profiling shows that 97.7% of the running time was spent on executing the `checkOne` function, due to the exponential number of concrete traces corresponding to an abstract state. A few of our observations are discussed below.

Frequency of uncertain outcomes. We first evaluated how often the uncertain result (?) happens. Table 2 lists our two measurements: (a) how many of the trace-formula combinations give uncertain checking results (the number of result sequences whose the last value is ?), and (b) how many of all the 525,000 results are uncertain (the total number of ? in all result sequences).

We see from Table 2 that, the uncertain results do not occur as often as one may expect. To explain this observation, we note that most of the temporal operators are insensitive to the uncertainty, and also the scope of uncertainty is bounded within one abstract state.

Propagation of uncertainties. We then consider that, given a trace Tr and a formula φ, if an observation of an uncertain result happened at abstract state i, i.e., $[\![Tr(0 : i) \models \varphi]\!] = ?$, whether it will be the case that all following outcomes in the result sequence are uncertain, i.e, $[\![Tr(0 : j) \models \varphi]\!] = ?$, for all $i \leq j \leq n$.

We identified 7,129 out of all the 25,000 result sequences where ? occurred at least once somewhere in the sequence, 3,660 of which (51.34%) exhibit outcomes with trailing uncertain values (?) up to the end of the respective sequence. Above, we saw that uncertain values do not occur often. However, once occurred, they tend to persist. This is consistent with the intuition that an uncertain result in one abstract state pollutes the checker state and affects all subsequent states.

Table 2. Chance of Uncertainty in Three-Valued Logic

Measurement	Uncertain Results	Total Cases	Percentage
(a)	3903	25,000	15.61%
(b)	63359	525,000	12.07%

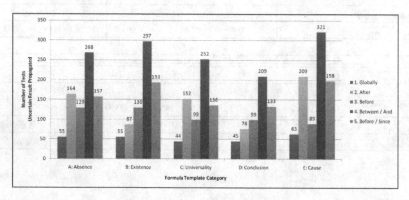

Fig. 3. Uncertainty Propagation

Fig. 3 plots which formula templates these 3,660 result sequences belong to. It is observed that templates in the "between/and" group are more likely to propagate uncertainty. This is partly due to the complex formula templates in the "between/and" group, which make the checker less likely to exit the uncertain state, compared to simpler templates in the "globally" group.

Impact of formula patterns. Another observation from the collected results is that, certain groups of formula templates exhibit patterned checking results.

The first group of formula templates includes $\{A.1, B.1, C.1\}$ in Table 1. The formula templates share the form that either $\diamond$ or $\boxdot$ quantifies over an atomic formula or its negation. The common patterns are either (a) all $\bot$ or all $\top$, or (b) a consecutive number of $\top$ (or $\bot$, respectively), followed by a consecutive number of ?, and then all $\bot$ (or $\top$, respectively).

This observation shows that, once a property with the $\boxdot$ operator has been falsified, it continues to be false; before this, it underwent being (probably trivially) true on *all* concrete traces, *some* concrete traces, and finally *none*. A dual result can be stated for the $\diamond$ operator.

A second group of templates involve the formulas where $\mathcal{S}$ is the main operator ($\{B.2, D.1\}$). The respective result sequences for formulas in this group show no obvious pattern, where the values $\top$, $\bot$, and ? almost randomly appear. This shows that randomly generated formulas with $\mathcal{S}$ as the main operator are more often determined locally in one abstract state.

5   Related Works

There are many runtime verification systems that formalize correctness properties in LTL, as seen for example in [12,4,8]. Different LTL variants have been defined based on semantics for finite traces [2,3,9]. The three-valued logic LTL_3 as an LTL logic with a semantics for finite traces has been used in [3]. The LDR traces in this paper are special cases of Mazurkiewicz traces[14] where the independence relation is defined by the LDR recording scheme. Alternative semantics of LTL formulas on Mazurkiewicz traces were studied (e.g., [5,7]) but were not based on a three-valued interpretation.

Compared to [3], this work used three-valued semantics for past-time LTL on traces with the LDR recording scheme, where the uncertainty in our case comes from unknown event interleavings; in [3], the uncertainty for LTL_3 was due to all possible unknown future suffixes of a finite trace. Although past-time LTL is not more expressive than LTL, it is exponentially more succinct and more convenient for specifying correctness properties for runtime verification over finite traces[9].

The technique of defining recursive semantics for checking temporal logic properties is standard to model checking [6] and runtime verification. [1,10], as well as the algorithm presented in this paper, are based on this technique.

[16,19] provide different approaches to randomly generating LTL formulas. We used templates from [17] in our experiments as the formula categorization helps study the relationship between satisfaction of formulas and their patterns.

6   Conclusion and Future Work

We considered a problem of runtime verification of past-time LTL properties over recorded traces, in which some information about the order of observations may be lost. We showed that a three-valued interpretation of the formulas is needed to reflect this uncertainty. We developed the appropriate semantics for past-time LTL and implemented the checking algorithm. Finally, we conducted an evaluation of checking several formula patterns over randomly generated traces and discussed the effects on uncertainty on checking outcomes.

We intend to extend this work in several directions. Extending the new semantics to the full LTL will require a non-trivial effort, and we also plan to tackle the effect of uncertainty on real-time properties. In the recorded traces, abstract states are timestamped when the state is recorded, but the time of actual observations is lost, resulting in additional uncertainty for the timed operators.

We believe that the implementation of the checker can be substantially improved by treating the set of concrete trace segments symbolically. A naive idea may be to simply run an LTL model checker on the transition system that represents the LDR trace model; however, we also need to construct the checker state in the previous abstract state for the right subformulas. Thus a more elaborate approach is needed.

Finally, we would like to consider a more precise semantic definition, so that a formula evaluates to $\top$ *if and only if* it is true on every concrete trace. The current semantics satisfies just the "only if" condition. Indeed, suppose we are checking the formula $\phi \vee \psi$, and ϕ holds exactly on those traces where ψ does not hold. Both ϕ and ψ evaluate to ?, but $\phi \vee \psi$ should evaluate to $\top$. One way to achieve this is to forego the Kleene logic and define the semantics of a formula directly in terms of the set of concrete paths on which the formula holds. Then, we can assign the truth value to each formula depending on whether this set is empty, or is equal to the set of all traces.

Acknowledgement. We would like to thank Klaus Havelund and Grigore Roşu for their insightful input and making their tools in [10] available. We also thank the anonymous reviewers for their comments to improve the paper.

References

1. Barringer, H., Goldberg, A., Havelund, K., Sen, K.: Program monitoring with LTL in EAGLE. In: Parallel and Distributed Processing Symposium (2004)
2. Bauer, A., Leucker, M., Schallhart, C.: Comparing LTL Semantics for Runtime Verification. Journal of Logic and Computation (JLC) 20, 651–674 (2010)
3. Bauer, A., Leucker, M., Schallhart, C.: Runtime verification for LTL and TLTL. ACM Transactions on Software Engineering and Methodology (2011)
4. Bodden, E.: J-LO—A tool for runtime-checking temporal assertions. Diploma thesis, RWTH Aachen University (November 2005)
5. Bollig, B., Leucker, M.: Deciding LTL over Mazurkiewicz traces. Data & Knowledge Engineering 44(2), 219–238 (2003)
6. Clarke, E., Grumberg, O., Peled, D.: Model Checking. MIT Press (1999)
7. Genest, B., Kuske, D., Muscholl, A., Peled, D.A.: Snapshot Verification. In: Halbwachs, N., Zuck, L.D. (eds.) TACAS 2005. LNCS, vol. 3440, pp. 510–525. Springer, Heidelberg (2005)
8. Havelund, K., Roşu, G.: Monitoring programs using rewriting. In: International Conference on Automated Software Engineering (2001)
9. Havelund, K., Roşu, G.: Synthesizing Monitors for Safety Properties. In: Katoen, J.-P., Stevens, P. (eds.) TACAS 2002. LNCS, vol. 2280, pp. 342–356. Springer, Heidelberg (2002)
10. Havelund, K., Roşu, G.: Efficient monitoring of safety properties. Int. J. Softw. Tools Technol. Transf. 6(2), 158–173 (2004)
11. Kleene, S.C.: Introduction to Metamathematics. D. Van Nostrand (1950)
12. Lee, I., Kannan, S., Kim, M., Sokolsky, O., Viswanathan, M.: Runtime assurance based on formal specifications. In: PDPTA 1999, pp. 279–287 (1999)
13. Manna, Z., Pnueli, A.: The temporal logic of reactive and concurrent systems: specification, vol. 1. Springer, Heidelberg (1992)
14. Mazurkiewicz, A.: Concurrent program schemes and their interpretations. Tech. rep., DAIMI Rep. PB 78, Aarhus University (1977)
15. Pnueli, A.: The temporal logic of programs. In: 18th Annual Symposium on Foundations of Computer Science, pp. 46–57. IEEE (1977)
16. Rozier, K., Vardi, M.: LTL Satisfiability Checking. In: Bošnački, D., Edelkamp, S. (eds.) SPIN 2007. LNCS, vol. 4595, pp. 149–167. Springer, Heidelberg (2007)
17. SAnToS Lab, Kansas State University: Property pattern mappings for LTL, http://patterns.projects.cis.ksu.edu/documentation/patterns/ltl.shtml
18. Spees, W.S.: Functional Requirement for LDR Component. Center for Devices and Radiological Health, FDA (2010)
19. Tauriainen, H., Heljanko, K.: Testing LTL formula translation into Büchi automata. STTT 4(1), 57–70 (2002)

Author Index